TECHNOLOGY COVERAGE

W9-AWI-662

Suggestions read the list on pages 33–35, and then examine the detailed suggestions and examples of applications that follow.

Researchers have found that most teachers do not incorporate current research findings into their classroom practices. One reason is because many research articles and textbooks provide only vague guidelines for classroom use and no concrete examples. But when new ideas are presented in a concrete and usable form, teachers are much more likely to try them out (Gersten & Brengelman, 1996). This is why *Psychology Applied to Teaching* places as much emphasis on concrete suggestions for teaching as on providing clear discussions of theory and research. But as useful as our suggestions might be, you cannot, as we mentioned earlier, use them as prescriptions. Every school building and every group of students is different. What worked well for one student or one class may fall flat with another. You have to learn how to adapt the suggestions in this book and any other books that you will read to the particular dynamics of each class. This is the essence of being a reflective teacher.

CASE IN PRINT

This feature presents a recent newspaper article that either 1) elaborates on an idea or technique described in the chapter, or 2) shows how an idea was applied by public school educators.

THE ROLE OF TECHNOLOGY IN LEARNING AND INSTRUCTION

As a teacher in the new millennium, you will undoubtedly want to be knowledgeable about the many ways technology can enhance your students' learning. We feel that it is important for prospective teachers to understand how technology can be integrated in the curriculum regardless of the content area or student age level. In fact, *Psychology Applied to Teaching* is th[...] cusses technology possibilities for [...] out the book, we will explore an a[...] simulations, tutorials, word process[...] tools, and point out how they can [...] All references to software and othe[...] be highlighted by a blue vertical ba[...]

Although technology is just c[...] nonetheless hope that this book pr[...] technology to foster students' inte[...] students with assistive devices, inc[...] push students to explore and art[...] classroom management, and help i[...]

As you examine some of the t[...] book, you should be thinking ab[...] learning environment of your clas[...] practice of basic facts or for studen[...] Web (a global system of interconn[...] puters to play games during free [...] with peers in other countries and [...] your role as a teacher changes wh[...] ties. Will you utilize technology t[...] environment, or will you select tec[...]

students a sense of confidence, personal responsibility, and control over their own learning (Collins, 1996).

Despite the differences in these two approaches to motivation, they are not mutually exclusive. Some of the most innovative and effective technological aids to learning combine both approaches. For example, the Jasper Challenge Series that we mentioned in Chapter 9 tries to engage intrinsic motivation by giving students control over and responsibility for how they collect, analyze, and use the data presented by the program and by embedding the task in a realistic context. Extrinsic rewards include class announcements of accomplishments, student demonstrations of problem-solving strategies, teacher praise for correct problem solutions, and feedback and encouragement from peers in other schools about one's problem solutions (Barron et al., 1995; Cognition and Technology Group at Vanderbilt, 1996). Other types of extrinsic rewards that can be used in conjunction with other technology-based approaches to learning include membership in multimedia clubs, special computer events and fairs for parents or the community, and certificates of recognition.

Technology can be used to support both extrinsic and intrinsic motivation

CAN TECHNOLOGY INCREASE MOTIVATION TO LEARN?

Now that we've established that computer-based technology can accommodate both extrinsic and intrinsic approaches to motivation, we can look at whether it does, in fact, increase students' motivation to learn.

Critics of computer-based learning argue that any observed increases in student motivation are likely to be short term and due largely to the novelty of the medium. But several studies have demonstrated that the use of computer-based instruction increases students' intrinsic motivation and performance. Diana Cordova and Mark Lepper (1996) found that rich fantasy contexts, personalization, and provision for student choice within children's software not only fosters intrinsic motivation and deeper engagement in learning but also boosts the amount that students learn, their perceived level of competence, and their levels of aspiration. In fact, in one four-month study, kindergarten children remained on-task about 90 percent of the time for the entire length of the study (Bergin, Ford, & Hess, 1993).

A decade-long evaluation of the Apple Classrooms of Tomorrow (ACOT) project by Judith Haymore Sandholtz, Cathy Ringstaff, and David Dwyer (1997) revealed that once the novelty factor has worn off, at least five factors affect student engagement with technology. First, motivation remains high when technology use is appropriate for the assignment and when teachers treat educational technology as one of many possible instructional tools. Second, technology must be integrated, or immersed, into the curriculum, not treated as a separate subject. Third, students are more engaged when using the computer as a tool than when the computer is mostly used as a drill-and-practice tutor. Fourth, teachers must adjust their use of technology to student ability levels; tasks that are too hard are likely to be frustrating, and tasks that are too simple are likely to be boring. Fifth, teachers must be willing to allow students more control over their own learning by using projects and interdisciplinary forms of learning.

USING MULTIMEDIA AND HYPERMEDIA TO INCREASE MOTIVATION

As indicated previously, the images, text, sound, video, and animation of multimedia and hypermedia can help gain student attention and make learning more relevant, thereby fostering a sense of learner control and intrinsic motivation (Becker & Dwyer, 1994).

Integrated technology coverage (in all chapters and SUGGESTIONS FOR TEACHING sections) addresses technological issues affecting the text's main themes and concepts.

Psychology Applied to Teaching

NINTH EDITION

Jack Snowman
Southern Illinois University

Robert Biehler

WITH
TECHNOLOGY CONTRIBUTOR
Curtis J. Bonk
Indiana University

Houghton Mifflin Company   Boston   New York

Senior Sponsoring Editor: Loretta Wolozin
Associate Editor: Lisa Mafrici
Senior Project Editor: Carol Newman
Senior Production/Design Coordinator: Sarah Ambrose
Senior Manufacturing Coordinator: Priscilla Bailey
Associate Marketing Manager: Jean Zielinski DeMayo

Cover design: Catherine Hawkes, Cat & Mouse

Cover image: Sonia Delauney, "Jeux d'infants," Sonia Delauney Archives,
Amsterdam.

Part opener credits: Part I, p. 23: Photodisc; Part II, p. 215: © Bill Bachmann/
All Stock/PNI; Part III, p. 369: © Tony Freedman/PhotoEdit/PNI; Part IV,
p. 435: © Bob Daemmrich/Stock Boston/PNI.

Printed in the U.S.A.

Library of Congress Catalog Card Number: 99-71936

ISBN: 0-395-96065-7

1 2 3 4 5 6 7 8 9-VH-03 02 01 00 99

Brief Contents

Contents

Part I   Student Characteristics   23

2 Stage Theories of Development   24

Part II Learning and Instruction 215

7 Behavioral and Social Learning Theories 216

8 Information-Processing Theory 250

Publisher's Foreword to the Ninth Edition: Continuity and Change

In 1971, Houghton Mifflin published *Psychology Applied to Teaching* by Robert Biehler. While other publishers turned down this complete, class-tested manuscript, an experienced editor at Houghton Mifflin acted on his hunch about its merits. Published first in both hardcover and paperback versions, the handbook-like paperback caught on like wildfire. Why? In 1971, educational psychology texts were imitations of introductory psychology—hardbound surveys of theory and research that largely ignored readers' needs for classroom applications. This book, with its emphasis on providing clear and useful examples of psychological principles, was the first to speak to its audience. This book was thus the leader as it shifted the course of introductory texts toward psychology applied to teaching.

Jack Snowman became coauthor of its Fourth Edition in 1982. His expertise in cognitive learning strategy, solid research background in learning and instruction, and his thoughtful analyses brought contemporary educational psychology perspectives to its content. Robert Biehler withdrew from teaching and from participation in its revision in successive editions. Today, *Psychology Applied to Teaching* retains its original hallmark qualities and benefits from Jack Snowman's dedication as its sole active author. We acknowledge his role and contribution by an appropriate shift in author sequence.

The Ninth Edition continues its leadership with emphases and new coverage most relevant to today's conditions, research, and applications in education. Original technology content is now integrated in each chapter, the result of collaboration between Jack Snowman and this edition's technology contributor, Curtis J. Bonk.

Also, much new content on diversity and inclusion is added in a set of chapters, starting with *Understanding Student Differences* (4). Significantly, this edition continues its coherent focus on what teaching and learning looks like in classrooms by adding a brand-new chapter, *Approaches to Instruction* (10). Change and continuity are the double-edged themes of its Ninth Edition. All of us involved in its development and production hope that it continues to work for its audience as an information source, as a set of practical ideas, and as a resource for on-the-job use in classrooms.

Preface

Although Robert Biehler has not been an active contributor to *Psychology Applied to Teaching* for several years, this edition contains many of the student-oriented features he pioneered over twenty-five years ago. The hallmark of *Psychology Applied to Teaching* is its usefulness to teachers. It is written for students enrolled in an introductory educational psychology course and is at once a basic source of information for prospective teachers and a resource for their future use as classroom teachers.

GOALS OF THE TEXT

This Ninth Edition of *Psychology Applied to Teaching* has been written to be used in three ways: 1) as a text that provides basic information, organized and presented so that it will be understood, remembered, and applied; 2) as a source of practical ideas about instructional techniques for student teachers and beginning teachers; and 3) as a means for teachers to improve their effectiveness as they gain experience in the classroom.

MAJOR FEATURES OF THE REVISION

Because of its central role in American society, education is a dynamic enterprise. Tens of thousands of people—including classroom teachers, school administrators, state education officials, politicians, and educational and psychological researchers—are constantly searching for and trying out new ideas to increase student learning and achievement. This is especially true of educational and psychological researchers. Since the last edition of this text, many new developments have occurred in social, emotional, and cognitive development (areas such as memory and problem solving); motivation; classroom assessment and management; multicultural education; inclusion of students with disabilities; and especially the use of computer-based technology to support student learning and achievement. The Ninth Edition of *Psychology Applied to Teaching* is extensively revised and updated, incorporating new developments in all its domains. Noteworthy themes of this revision include

- **Emphasis on technology** Each chapter contains at least one section, and sometimes several, on how technology can be used to address the main themes and concepts of that chapter. For example, the reader will find discussions of how such technology tools as multimedia, hypermedia, tutorial programs, simulation programs, telecommunications, and the World Wide Web can be used to foster cognitive development, address individual differences, promote greater multicultural understanding, make learning easier for students with disabilities, promote learning and problem solving for all students, increase motivation for learning, help teachers manage their classroom, and aid in assessment of students. In addition, most chapters provide addresses for World Wide Web sites that contain useful supplementary information and links to other relevant sites.

- **Increased emphasis on "Approaches to Instruction"** The new chapter on instructional approaches underscores this book's original contribution as the first educational psychology textbook to provide numerous specific examples and guidelines for applying psychological concepts and research findings to classroom teaching. That orientation has thus been amplified in this Ninth Edition with the inclusion of Chapter 10, "Approaches to Instruction," which links the writing of instructional objectives with five approaches to instruction that flow from different conceptions of learning.
- **New emphasis on diverse learners** With the increase of the range of student diversity teachers face in classrooms today, we have added more focused coverage of diverse learners. Material on diversity has been reorganized and consolidated in two extensively revised chapters: Chapter 4, "Understanding Student Differences," and Chapter 5, "Addressing Cultural and Socioeconomic Diversity."
- **Emphasis on real-life contexts** The Case in Print feature, which was introduced in the Eighth Edition, uses newspaper articles about actual classrooms that illustrate the relationship between chapter content and actual classroom practices. Because of this feature's popularity with both students and instructors, we have included more of them. They now appear in twelve of this edition's fifteen chapters.
- **Increased use of tables and graphics** To help students better understand and compare and contrast theories, concepts, and instructional approaches, additional tables and figures have been created.
- **Reflective teaching** The concept of reflective teaching, its importance, and the role that a personal journal can play in helping one become a more reflective teacher are introduced in Chapter 1. This theme is picked up again in Chapter 15 where students learn how to construct a personal journal and how useful this activity is to practicing teachers.

The major changes made to each chapter include the following:

CHAPTER 1: APPLYING PSYCHOLOGY TO TEACHING   The purpose of this chapter remains the same: to provide a framework that will help the reader understand the relevance of the subsequent fourteen chapters to the practice of teaching. We try to accomplish this purpose by describing what the field of educational psychology has to offer prospective teachers, pointing out the advantages and limitations of studying human behavior scientifically, describing the difference between the art and science of teaching, and noting how effective (meaning reflective) teachers combine the roles of teacher-as-artist and teacher-as-scientist. To highlight the teacher-as-artist concept, a new Case in Print was added to this chapter.

CHAPTER 2: STAGE THEORIES OF DEVELOPMENT   This chapter contains a new section on the importance of Erikson's Industry versus Inferiority stage to classroom teachers, a new section on using technology to promote cognitive development, and additional coverage of the Vygotskyian concept of scaffolding.

CHAPTER 3: AGE-LEVEL CHARACTERISTICS   This chapter contains updated material on Diana Baumrind's analysis of parenting styles, new material on the cognitive characteristics of primary grade, elementary grade, and middle school children, and updated statistics on substance abuse, depression, and suicide among adolescents. The technology section describes how technology can be used to promote literacy and interpersonal reasoning and reduce egocentrism. The discussions of cognitive styles and gender differences were moved to a new chapter (4) where they are discussed in more detail.

CHAPTER 4: UNDERSTANDING STUDENT DIFFERENCES   This is essentially a new chapter that is intended to give readers an understanding of some of the main ways in which students differ from one another. This chapter incorporates and expands on three topics that were covered in the previous edition: intelligence, cognitive styles, and gender differences. Emphasis is given to the recent work of Sternberg and Gardner in the area of intelligence, to the work of Sternberg on the nature of learning styles, and to recent research on gender differences in achievement and gender bias in the classroom. Technology sections accompany each of these three topics.

CHAPTER 5: ADDRESSING CULTURAL AND SOCIOECONOMIC DIVERSITY
This chapter contains new material on how well school textbooks address multicultural issues and on a successful bilingual education program called bilingual/immersion. The use of computer-based technology to increase multicultural awareness and improve the effectiveness of bilingual education is discussed in two separate sections.

CHAPTER 6: ACCOMMODATING STUDENT VARIABILITY   The research on ability grouping and inclusion has been updated. The discussion of learning disabilities has been expanded to include information on social skills and current thinking on the nature of attention deficit/hyperactivity disorder (ADHD). The discussion of the characteristics of gifted and talented students was revised to include current findings. The new technology section highlights the ways in which various technologies can assist both students with disabilities and gifted students to maximize their achievement.

CHAPTER 7: BEHAVIORAL AND SOCIAL LEARNING THEORIES   We have condensed the discussion of Skinner's work on programmed instruction and revised the discussion of the effects of computer-assisted instruction to clarify the difference between general effects and effects on students of different ages and ability levels. The technology section describes different types of computer programs and addresses the issue of program quality.

CHAPTER 8: INFORMATION-PROCESSING THEORY   We added new material that describes how Vygotsky's ideas relate to meaningful learning and metacognition and a new section on the role of visual imagery encoding. Research findings on the effects of self-questioning, note taking, and learning strategy training have been updated. The new technology section covers how technology can be used to represent knowledge, improve writing, reading, science and math achievement, and improve performance in art and music.

CHAPTER 9: CONSTRUCTIVIST LEARNING THEORY, PROBLEM SOLVING, AND TRANSFER   This chapter features a significantly expanded treatment of constructivism that is the basis for the subsequent sections on problem solving and transfer. The two main forms of constructivism—cognitive and social—are described and the strengths and weaknesses of constructivism are discussed. A new Case in Print provides a classroom illustration of the constructivist concept of situated learning.

The new technology section describes how various tools and programs can be used to foster meaningful learning and problem solving skills. The new chapter title highlights the three main topics of the chapter.

CHAPTER 10: APPROACHES TO INSTRUCTION   This is a new chapter whose intent is twofold: (1) to show how any approach to instruction must start with a specification of one's objectives and (2) to describe specific approaches to instruction that are consistent with behavioral, information processing, constructivist, humanistic, and social views of learning. Ways to supplement each approach with technology are also discussed. A new Case in Print illustrates how technology allows students to follow and participate in research projects around the globe.

CHAPTER 11: MOTIVATION   Since this chapter was extensively revised for the Eighth Edition, few changes were made for this edition. The main changes were moving the discussion of cooperative learning to Chapter 10 and including a new section on motivating students with technology.

CHAPTER 12: CLASSROOM MANAGEMENT   New to this chapter are discussions of how to use technology for classroom management and keeping at-risk students in school. An expanded section on school violence includes current data on the nature and frequency of school violence and descriptions of programs now being used in schools to reduce violence.

CHAPTER 13: ASSESSMENT OF CLASSROOM LEARNING   The discussion of performance assessment has been expanded by adding a figure that illustrates performance assessment, a new Case in Print that discusses how and why schools are using performance assessments, a section on scoring rubrics, and a figure that illustrates a scoring rubric. This chapter also has a new section that describes how technology can be used with various assessment methods.

CHAPTER 14: UNDERSTANDING AND USING STANDARDIZED TESTS   This chapter contains a new Case in Print that illustrates the use of performance measures in state-mandated assessments and a new section on how technology has affected the preparation for and administration of standardized tests.

CHAPTER 15: BECOMING A BETTER TEACHER BY BECOMING A REFLECTIVE TEACHER   This chapter continues the previous edition's emphasis on reflective teaching by describing how students can set up and use a reflective journal, by including a new section that cites both research and the experiences of veteran teachers on the effectiveness of keeping a Reflective Journal, by providing a new Case in Print that illustrates the value of reflective teaching, and by including a section on how technology can be used to help teachers record their reflections.

SPECIAL FEATURES OF THE TEXT

The following features, many of which were introduced in various earlier editions, have been selected, improved, and augmented to make this Ninth Edition more useful and effective than its predecessors.

KEY POINTS   At the beginning of each chapter, Key Points are listed under major headings. They also appear in the margins of pages opposite sections in which each point is discussed. The Key Points call attention to sections of the text that are considered to be of special significance to teachers and thus serve as instructional objectives.

SUGGESTIONS FOR TEACHING IN YOUR CLASSROOM   Most chapters include summaries of research findings and principles relating to a particular topic. These are followed by detailed descriptions of various ways in which the information and concepts might be applied in classrooms. Numerous examples of applications at different grade levels are supplied, and readers are urged to select and record applications that will fit their own particular personality, style, and teaching situation in a Reflective Journal. The Suggestions for Teaching are intended to be read while the book is used as a text and referred to by future teachers and in-service teachers after they have completed coursework. For ease in reference, these suggestions are surrounded by a colored border.

CASE IN PRINT   This feature uses recent news articles to demonstrate how a basic idea or technique in a chapter was applied by educators from the primary grades through high school and has proven to be extremely popular with users. Following each article are several open-ended questions designed to encourage the student to think more deeply about the issue in question. The purpose of the Case in Print feature is to illustrate to preservice teachers that the psychological theory and research that their instructors require them to learn does have real-world relevance. A Case in Print can be found in Chapters 1, 2, 4, 5, 6, 7, 8, 9, 10, 11, 12, 13, 14, and 15.

JOURNAL ENTRIES   This feature is intended to help students prepare and use a Reflective Journal when they teach. Readers are urged to use the journal entries, which appear in the margins, to prepare a personal set of guidelines for reference before and during the student teaching experience and during the first years of teaching. A guide for setting up and using a Reflective Journal is included in Chapter 15, "Becoming a Better Teacher by Becoming a Reflective Teacher."

RESOURCES FOR FURTHER INVESTIGATION   At the end of each chapter an annotated bibliography is presented, offering sources of information on the major topics covered in the chapter. Internet addresses for World Wide Web and gopher sites that provide additional useful information are also listed in this section. Please note the web sites were active at the time we prepared the text, but we, of course, are not responsible for their continued presence.

SUMMARY   A numbered set of summary statements appears after the Resources for Further Investigation. This feature is intended to help students review the main points of a chapter for upcoming examinations or class discussions.

KEY TERMS   Appearing after the Summary is a list of topics that are key aspects of the chapter. Understanding these topics is an essential part of understanding the chapter as a whole. To facilitate use of this feature, the page where each term is initially defined and discussed appears in parentheses.

DISCUSSION QUESTIONS   This feature appears after the Key Terms. Because understanding and retention of new information is enhanced when learners actively relate it to known ideas and experiences, the Discussion Questions ask the reader to reflect on how previous experiences (or possible future experiences) relate to the chapter material. These questions can serve as the focus for in-class discussion and out-of-class discussion.

GLOSSARY   A glossary of key terms and concepts is provided at the back of the book as an aid in reviewing for examinations or classroom discussion.

SPECIAL INDEXES OF PEDAGOGY   In addition to the detailed name and subject indexes at the end of the book, indexes to Suggestions for Teaching in Your Classroom, Applying Technology to Teaching, Resources for Further Investigation, and Case in Print are included inside the front and back covers.

INSTRUCTIONAL COMPONENTS THAT ACCOMPANY THE TEXT

STUDY GUIDE   The Study Guide for the Ninth Edition of *Psychology Applied to Teaching* was designed to help students formulate and carry out a strategy for mastering the Key Points. Students are provided general guidelines for analyzing their resources and learning materials, planning a learning strategy, carrying out the strategy, monitoring their progress, and modifying their strategy if they are dissatisfied with the results. As an integral part of the suggested tactics for learning, original concept maps are supplied for each major section of each chapter. These concept maps are schematic representations of how major topics, subtopics, and Key Points of a chapter relate to each other. Also included in the Study Guide are exercises designed to help students enhance memory and understanding of Key Point material, and two sets of review questions (multiple-choice and short-answer) to support student efforts at self-monitoring. Feedback is provided following the multiple-choice questions, explaining to students why each choice is either correct or wrong and referring students to specific pages in the text for verification and additional information.

INSTRUCTOR'S RESOURCE MANUAL   This teaching aid provides for each chapter a detailed lecture outline with supplementary teaching suggestions, a specification of new material to aid users of the Ninth Edition of *Psychology Applied to Teaching* in making the transition to the current edition, coverage of Key Points, supplementary discussion topics, student activities, extra references, listings of films, videotapes, software and Internet resources, and "Approaches to Teaching Educational Psychology," a compendium of teaching tactics from professors across the country.

TEST BANK   The thoroughly revised Test Bank includes test items consisting of multiple-choice items in alternate forms, short-answer questions, and essay questions. Consistent with this text's longstanding emphasis on mastery, each multiple-choice and short-answer question reflects a Key Point and either the Knowledge, Comprehension, Application, or Analysis level of Bloom's taxonomy. Feedback booklets allow instructors to point out misconceptions in students' reasoning.

TEST GENERATOR   This component is an interactive computerized version of the Test Bank.

TRANSPARENCIES   An extensive set of colorful transparencies consisting of figures, charts, and instructional aids in the text, is available upon adoption of the text.

DEDICATED WEB SITE: PSYCHOLOGY APPLIED TO TEACHING INSITE   Helping today's instructors and students learn how to use technology meaningfully is a primary strength of new content in this text. As a corollary, a dedicated, interactive web site for this text is now in the **Teacher Education Station**, Houghton Mifflin's Education web site. With **Psychology Applied to Teaching's INSITE**, you can access information and engage in activities in its distinct segments : *a) information b) experiences c) constructions*. You can also *share knowledge and experience* through discussion forums and contributed strategies and stories from other instructors and students. Flexible search option menus help tailor this site to particular instructor and student needs. To get an overview of what's in the site and how to use it, go to **http://www.hmco.com/college/Education** and click on **Psychology Applied to Teaching INSITE**.

TEACHER EDUCATION STATION WEB SITE   The Teacher Education Station web site (go to **http://www.hmco.com/college**, then click on Education) provides additional pedagogic support and resources for beginning and experienced professionals in education, including the unique **Project-Based Learning Space**. This page links to five extended problem-based projects and provides background theory about project-based learning.

VIDEOS   Videos are available to course adopters.

ACKNOWLEDGMENTS

While the content of a textbook is mostly the product of an author's knowledge, judgment, and communication skill, the suggestions of others play a significant role in shaping its final form. A number of reviewers made constructive suggestions and provided thoughtful reactions at various stages in the development of this manuscript. Thanks go out to the following individuals for their help:

Julius Gregg Adams, State University of New York College, Fredonia

Richard A. Couch, Clarion University

Malcolm L. Van Blerkom, University of Pittsburgh at Johnstown

Andrew D. Katayama, Southern Illinois University, Edwardsville

Dov Liberman, University of Houston

Verna Lynn McDonald, National University and CSU, San Marcos

Molly Nicaise, Santa Barbara City College

Daniel W. Stuempfig, California State University, Chico

I would also like to acknowledge the invaluable contributions and encouragement of the following members of the Houghton Mifflin editorial staff who helped make this text more accurate, readable, useful, and attractive than I could have made it myself: Merryl Maleska Wilbur, Carol Newman, Lisa Mafrici, Sarah Ambrose, Sara Hill, and Connie Gardner.

J.S.

Psychology
Applied to
Teaching

Applying Psychology to Teaching

As you begin to read this book, you may be asking yourself, "What will this book tell me about teaching that I don't already know?" The answer to that question depends on several factors, including your previous experiences with teaching and the number of psychology courses you have taken. Since you have been actively engaged in the process of formal education for a number of years, you already know a great deal about learning and teaching. You have had abundant opportunities to observe and react to more than one hundred teachers. You have probably read several hundred texts, finished all kinds of assignments, used a variety of software programs, and taken hundreds of examinations. Undoubtedly, you have also established strong likes and dislikes for certain subjects and approaches to teaching.

Yet despite your familiarity with education from the student's point of view, you have probably had limited experience with education from the teacher's point of view. Therefore, a major purpose of this book is to help you take the first steps in what will be a long journey to becoming an expert teacher.

Throughout this book we will describe many different psychological theories, concepts, and principles and illustrate how you might apply

KEY POINTS

These key points will help you learn the important information in this chapter. To help you study, they also appear in the margins of the pages, next to the text where they are discussed.

What Is Educational Psychology?

- Educational psychologists study how students learn in classrooms

How Will Learning About Educational Psychology Help You Be a Better Teacher?

- Teaching is complex work because it requires a wide range of knowledge and skills
- Research in educational psychology offers many useful ideas for improving classroom instruction
- Teachers who have had professional training are generally more effective

The Nature and Values of Science

- Unsystematic observation may lead to false conclusions
- Grade retention policies are influenced by unsystematic observation
- Scientific methods: sampling, control, objectivity, publication, replication

Complicating Factors in the Study of Behavior and Thought Processes

- Research focuses on a few aspects of a problem
- Constructivism: individuals differ in what they perceive and how they form ideas
- Differences of opinion due to selection and interpretation of data
- Accumulated knowledge leads researchers to revise original ideas

Good Teaching Is Partly an Art and Partly a Science

- Teaching as an art: emotions, values, flexibility
- Research provides a scientific basis for "artistic" teaching
- Good teachers combine "artistic" and "scientific" characteristics

Reflective Teaching: A Process to Help You Grow from Novice to Expert

- Reflective teachers think about what they do and why
- Reflective teachers have particular attitudes and abilities

them to teaching. The branch of psychology that specializes in understanding how different factors affect the classroom behavior of both teachers and students is **educational psychology.** In the next few sections we will briefly describe the nature of this field of study and highlight the different ways that you can use this book to become a more effective teacher. ■

What Is Educational Psychology?

Most educational psychologists, us included, would define their field as a scientific discipline that is concerned with understanding and improving how students acquire a variety of capabilities through formal instruction in classroom settings. According to David Berliner (1992a), for example, educational psychology should "study what people think and do as they teach and learn in a particular environment where education and training are intended to take place." This description of educational psychology suggests that to become the most effective teacher possible, you will need to understand such aspects of the learner as physical, social, emotional, and cognitive development; cultural, social, emotional, and intellectual differences; learning and problem-solving processes; self-esteem; motivation; testing; and measurement.

Educational psychologists study how students learn in classrooms

The importance of these topics to classroom learning has been recently underscored by the American Psychological Association (APA). In November 1997 the APA's Board of Educational Affairs proposed that efforts to improve education be based on a set of fourteen learner-centered psychological principles. These principles, which were derived from decades of research and practice, highlight the importance of learning processes, motivation, development, social processes, individual differences, and instructional practices in classroom learning. These are the same topics and principles that have long been emphasized by *Psychology Applied to Teaching.* A description of and rationale for each principle can be found on the following APA website: **http://www.apa.org/ed/lcp.html**.

We recognize that you may have some doubts right now both about your ability to master all of this material and the necessity to do so. To help you learn as much of this material as possible, we have incorporated into each chapter a number of helpful features that are described on pages 19–21. But first let's examine why the learning you will do in educational psychology is a worthwhile goal.

How Will Learning About Educational Psychology Help You Be a Better Teacher?

There's no question that knowledge about psychological concepts and their application to educational settings has the potential to help you be a better teacher. Whether that potential is ever fulfilled depends on how willing you are to maintain an open mind and a positive attitude. We say this because many prospective and practicing teachers have anything but a positive attitude when it comes to using psychological knowledge in the classroom. One teacher, for example, notes that "educational psychology and research are relatively useless because they rarely examine learning in authentic classroom contexts" (Burch, 1993). As you read

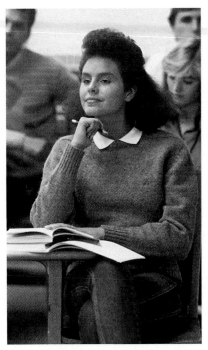

This book has been written so that you can use it as a student in a course in educational psychology, as a student teacher coping with all the new experiences of an "apprentice," and as a first-year teacher interested in perfecting instructional skills.

Teaching is complex work because it requires a wide range of knowledge and skills

through the next few paragraphs, as well as the subsequent chapters, you will see that criticisms like this are easily rebutted. We will offer a three-pronged argument to explain how educational psychology can help you be a better teacher, whether you plan to teach in an elementary school, a middle school, or a high school.

TEACHING IS A COMPLEX ENTERPRISE

The first part of our argument is that teaching is not the simple, straightforward enterprise some people imagine it to be; in fact, it ranks in the top quartile on complexity for all occupations (Rowan, 1994). There are many reasons for this complexity. In increasing ways, teachers have daily responsibility for diverse populations of students with varied and sometimes contradictory needs. But perhaps most fundamentally, the complexity of teaching derives from its decision-making nature. Teachers are constantly making decisions—before and after instruction as well as on the spot. To be informed and effective, these decisions should be based on a deep reservoir of knowledge and a wide range of skills.

The view that teaching is a complex activity that requires in-depth knowledge in a number of areas has been recognized by a group called the National Board for Professional Teaching Standards. This is an independent, nonprofit organization of educators, administrators, and political and business leaders whose mission is to establish clear and measurable standards for what accomplished teachers should know and be able to do and to identify those teachers through a voluntary system of certification. The board's standards are based on the following five propositions.

1. Teachers are committed to students and their learning.
2. Teachers know the subjects they teach and how to teach those subjects to students.
3. Teachers are responsible for managing and monitoring student learning.
4. Teachers think systematically about their practice and learn from experience.
5. Teachers are members of learning communities. (National Board for Professional Teaching Standards, 1994)

In general, the standards require teachers to be knowledgeable about learning and development, individual differences, motivation, self-concept, assessment, classroom management, and various approaches to instruction, all of which are covered in this textbook. Although the complexity inherent in teaching makes it a difficult profession to master, making progress toward that goal is also one of teaching's greatest rewards.

To help you prepare to take on these challenges and become an effective teacher, educational psychology offers not so much specific prescriptions about how to handle particular problems but, rather, general principles that you can use in a flexible manner. Fortunately, the research literature contains a wealth of these ideas.

RESEARCH THAT INFORMS TEACHERS

Contrary to the opinion ventured by the anonymous teacher quoted previously, the research literature contains numerous studies that were conducted under realistic classroom conditions and that offer useful ideas for improving one's instruction. There is consistent, classroom-based support for the following instructional practices

(Cruickshank, 1990; Porter & Brophy, 1988). The number in parentheses after each entry refers to the chapter in which we discuss that particular practice:

1. Using more advanced students to tutor less advanced students (5, 6)
2. Giving positive reinforcement to students whose performance meets or exceeds the teacher's objectives and giving corrective feedback to students whose performance falls short of the teacher's objectives (7, 10)
3. Communicating to students what is expected of them and why (10, 13)
4. Requiring students to respond to higher-order questions (8, 13)
5. Providing students with cues about the nature of upcoming tasks by giving them introductory information and telling them what constitutes satisfactory performance (7, 10, 13)
6. Teaching students how to monitor and improve their own learning efforts and offering them structured opportunities to practice independent learning activities (8, 10)
7. Knowing the misconceptions that students bring to the classroom that will likely interfere with their learning of a particular subject matter (9)
8. Creating learning situations in which students are expected to organize information in new ways and formulate problems for themselves (9)
9. Accepting responsibility for student outcomes rather than seeing students as solely responsible for what they learn and how they behave (11, 13)
10. Showing students how to work in small cooperative learning groups (10)

Research in educational psychology offers many useful ideas for improving classroom instruction

COURSEWORK AND COMPETENCE

The third part of our argument that educational psychology can help you be a better teacher concerns the courses you are currently taking, particularly this educational psychology course. Many researchers have asked the question "How do the courses teachers take as students relate to how capable they perceive themselves to be as teachers?" One means that researchers have used to determine the answer has been to ask beginning teachers to rate how prepared they feel to handle a variety of classroom tasks.

Yona Leyser, Laura Frankiewicz, and Rebecca Vaughn (1992) found that about half of the first-year teachers they surveyed said that their teacher-education classes had provided them with their first exposure to the instructional techniques they were now using in their own classrooms. In addition, most beginning teachers surveyed believed they were adequately or well prepared to deal with such tasks as understanding early adolescent development, assessing student achievement, understanding and responding to individual differences in ability, and promoting the social growth of students. Areas in which many felt uncomfortable included motivating students to learn, working with culturally diverse students, teaching exceptional students, managing the classroom, and teaching students how to use computers (e.g., Houston & Williamson, 1992–1993; Leyser, Frankiewicz, & Vaughn, 1992; Queen & Gretes, 1982; Scales, 1993). This textbook will address all of these issues, with special emphasis on most of those about which teachers reported discomfort. Our belief is that this course and this book will be one important means for helping you feel prepared to enter your first classroom.

Another way to gauge the value of teacher-education coursework is to look at the relationship between the courses teachers took as students and how effective they are as teachers. Patrick Ferguson and Sid Womack (1993) found that for students majoring in secondary education, the grades they received in their education courses were a better predictor of their subsequent effectiveness as teachers than either their grade-point average in their major (such as history, biology, math, English) or their specific knowledge (as measured by the specialty score on the National Teacher Examination).

Finally, there are the cases of individuals who make dramatic improvements in teaching effectiveness as a result of specific courses in a teacher education program. Linda Valli (1993) describes one individual who stopped working on his bachelor's degree in mathematics to teach full time at a parochial high school. After one year of teaching in which he described his classes as "basically out of control," he quit teaching, returned to college, and completed a teacher-education program in high school mathematics. Recalling the contributions of his educational psychology course, he judged his next teaching job as much more successful than his first.

Teachers who have had professional training are generally more effective

The Nature and Values of Science

For the most part, this book summarizes information produced by people who were trained as psychologists. In addition, the observations of individuals not classified as psychologists will sometimes be mentioned. Indeed, people with many different kinds of backgrounds have taken an interest in education, and their ideas will occasionally be noted at appropriate places in the chapters that follow. The primary purpose of this book, however, is to offer suggestions on how psychology (the scientific study of behavior and mental processes) might be applied to teaching. This text is based on the premise that information reported by scientists can be especially useful for those who plan to teach. Some of the reasons for this conviction become apparent when the characteristics of science are examined.

The values of science become clear when one understands some of the limitations of casual observation—and of unsystematic applications of such observations to behavior—and sees how the scientist tries to correct these weaknesses.

LIMITATIONS OF UNSYSTEMATIC OBSERVATION

Unsystematic observation may lead to false conclusions

Those who make unsystematic observations of human behavior may be easily misled into drawing false conclusions. For instance, they may treat the first plausible explanation that comes to mind as the only possible explanation. Or they may mistakenly apply a generalization about a single episode to superficially similar situations. In the process, they may fail to realize that an individual's reactions in a given situation are due primarily to unrecognized idiosyncratic factors that may never occur again or that the behavior of one person under certain circumstances may not resemble that of other persons in the same circumstances. In short, unsystematic observers are especially prone to noting only evidence that fits their expectations and ignoring evidence that does not. Ignorance of what others have discovered may cause such individuals to start at the same point when confronted with a problem—and to make the same mistakes others have made as they struggled to find solutions.

A clear example of the limitations of unsystematic observation is the practice of retaining children for a second year in a given grade because of poor achievement. Grade retention has long been used as a way of dealing with individual differences in learning rate, emotional development, and socialization skills. Retention rates between kindergarten and eighth grade in the United States are estimated to be as high as 20 percent (Roderick, 1995). In some school districts the retention rate for a given grade level is reported to be as high as 50 percent (Schultz, 1989).

The widespread use of retention in the United States and Europe continues even though most research clearly shows that retained students are 40 to 50 percent more likely to drop out of school than nonretained students and that low-achieving children who are promoted learn more the following year, have a stronger self-concept, and are better adjusted emotionally than similar children who are retained, even when the retention occurs as early as kindergarten (Haberman & Dill, 1993; Holmes, 1989; Mantzicopoulos & Morrison, 1992; Meisels & Liaw, 1993; Reynolds, 1992; Roderick, 1995). Grade retention continues to be recommended by some parents, schools, administrators, and teachers for the very reasons just cited—common sense suggests that repeating a grade should be beneficial to a student, and people tend to overgeneralize from the exceptional case in which the outcome was positive (Haberman & Dill, 1993; Roderick, 1995; Tomchin & Impara, 1992). The best way to minimize, if not avoid, the use of retention is to provide developmentally, cognitively, and culturally appropriate forms of instruction (Darling-Hammond & Falk, 1997). The major goal of this text is to help you become the kind of teacher who knows how to provide such instruction.

| Grade retention policies are influenced by unsystematic observation

STRENGTHS OF SCIENTIFIC OBSERVATION

Those who study behavior and mental processes scientifically are more likely to acquire trustworthy information than a casual observer is, and they are likely to apply what they learn more effectively because they follow the scientific procedures of sampling, control, objectivity, publication, and replication. In most cases a representative sample of subjects is studied so that individual idiosyncrasies are canceled out. An effort is made to note all plausible hypotheses to explain a given type of behavior, and each hypothesis is tested under controlled conditions. If all factors but one can be held constant in an experiment, the researcher may be able to trace the impact of a given condition by comparing the behaviors of those who have been exposed to it and those who have not.

| Scientific methods: sampling, control, objectivity, publication, replication

Observers make special efforts to be objective and to guard against being misled by predetermined ideas, wishful thinking, or selected evidence. Observations are made in a carefully prescribed, systematic manner, which makes it possible for observers to compare reactions.

Complete reports of experiments—including descriptions of subjects, methods, results, and conclusions—are published in professional journals. This dissemination allows other experimenters to replicate a study to discover if they obtain the same results. The existence of reports of thousands of experiments makes it possible to discover what others have done. This knowledge can then serve as a starting point for one's own speculations.

Complicating Factors in the Study of Behavior and Thought Processes

Although the use of scientific methods makes it possible to overcome many of the limitations of unscientific observation, the application of knowledge acquired in a scientific manner is subject to several complicating factors.

THE LIMITED FOCUS OF RESEARCH

Behavior is complex, changes with age, and has many causes. A student may perform poorly on a history exam, for example, for one or more of the following reasons: poorly developed study skills, inattentiveness in class, low interest in the subject, a poorly written text, low motivation to achieve high grades, vaguely worded exam questions, and/or difficulty with a particular type of exam question (compare-and-contrast essays, for example).

Research focuses on a few aspects of a problem

To understand how these factors affect performance on school-related tasks, research psychologists study at most only a few of them at a time under conditions that may not be entirely realistic. For example, a researcher who is interested in the effect of simulation software versus drill or tutorial software programs on conceptual understanding may recruit subjects who are equivalent in terms of social class, prior knowledge of the topic of the reading passage, and age; randomly assign them to one of two experimental groups; give them either a simulation program or a drill program to use; and then examine each group's responses to several types of comprehension items. As a consequence, most research studies provide specific information about a particular aspect of behavior. More comprehensive knowledge, however, is acquired by the combining and interrelating of separate studies that have looked at different aspects of a common problem.

INDIVIDUAL DIFFERENCES IN PERCEPTION AND THINKING

As we mentioned in the preceding section, researchers equate subjects in an experiment on one or more major characteristics (such as age, ability, gender, or prior knowledge) in order to draw unambiguous conclusions about the effect of a particular variable or procedure on a particular outcome. This scientific tactic does not always produce clear-cut results, however, because of unforeseen differences between individuals. Such differences are largely a result of the fact that ideas are not given from one person to another like so many packages but rather are actively *constructed* by each person (Brooks, 1990; Schifter, 1996; Wheatley, 1991). Many factors affect the form that an idea takes or whether it comes into existence at all. Some of these factors (which we will discuss at various points in the text) include age, gender, race, ethnic background, prior knowledge, problem-solving skills, and motivation. Because different factors come into play for different people and the same factors affect people differently, two people can read the same passage yet construct entirely different interpretations of its meaning. This concept (known as *constructivism*) is so fundamental to human behavior and to learning that we will return to it again and again in this text.

Constructivism: individuals differ in what they perceive and how they form ideas

SELECTION AND INTERPRETATION OF DATA

The amount of scientific information available on behavior and mental processes is so extensive that no individual could examine or interpret all of it. Accordingly, researchers learn to be highly selective in their reading. In addition, conclusions about the meaning of scientific results vary from one researcher to another. As you read this book, you will discover that there are differences of opinion among psychologists regarding certain aspects of development, motivation, and intelligence. Opposing views may be based on equally scientific evidence, but the way in which the evidence is selected and interpreted will vary. Just because a topic is studied scientifically does not necessarily mean that opinions about interpretations of the data will be unanimous.

Differences of opinion due to selection and interpretation of data

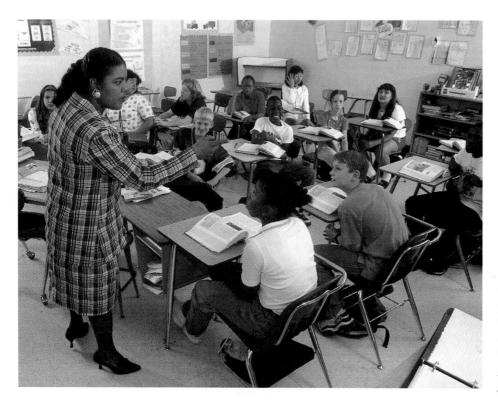

The constructivist view of learning holds that individual differences in such factors as age, gender, race, and ethnic background lead to differences in what people perceive and how they form ideas.

NEW FINDINGS MEAN REVISED IDEAS

Scientific information is not only voluminous and subject to different interpretations; it is also constantly being revised. A series of experiments may lead to the development of a new concept or pedagogical technique that is highly successful when it is first tried out. Subsequent studies, however, may reveal that the original research was incomplete, or repeated applications of a technique may show that it is less effective once the novelty has worn off. But frequent shifts of emphasis in education also reflect the basic nature of science. A quality of science that sets it apart from other intellectual processes is that the discoveries by one generation of scientists set the stage for more complete and far-reaching discoveries by the next. More researchers are studying aspects of psychology and education now than at any previous time in history. And thousands of reports of scientific research are published every month.

Accumulated knowledge leads researchers to revise original ideas

As our knowledge accumulates, it is inevitable that interpretations of how children learn and how we should teach will continue to change. We know more about development, learning, and teaching today than ever before, but because of the nature of some of the factors just discussed—and the complexity of human behavior—our answers are tentative and incomplete.

You should be aware, of course, that fads occur in education (just as they occur in other fields). Occasionally, national and/or international events cause changes in our political and social climate. These changes often result in pressures on education to "do something." And when large numbers of educators embrace a new practice without waiting for or paying attention to research findings, fads develop (see Slavin, 1989, for an example). One of our objectives in writing this text is to demonstrate the importance of basing your practices on principles that have some research support and, thereby, help you avoid contributing to fads.

In the last few pages we have asked you to consider some of the values of science, the strengths of scientific observation, and a few of the factors that complicate the scientific study of behavior and lead to frequent changes of emphasis in teaching techniques. These considerations help explain why this book stresses how psychology might be applied to teaching; they also support the position that information reported by scientists can be especially valuable for those who plan to teach. At the same time, our intention has been to acquaint you with a few of the limitations and sometimes unsettling byproducts of science.

The science of psychology has much to offer educators, but a scientific approach to teaching does have its limits. Because teaching is a dynamic *decision-making process*, you will be greatly aided by a systematic, objective framework for making your decisions; research on teaching and learning can give you that framework. But for the reasons just cited, research cannot give you a prescription or a set of rules that specify how you should handle every situation. Often you will have to make on-the-spot, subjective decisions about how to present a lesson, explain a concept, handle mass boredom, or reprimand a student. This contrast between an objective, systematic approach to planning instruction and the need to make immediate (yet appropriate) applications and modifications of those plans calls attention to a question that has been debated for years: Is teaching primarily an art or a science—or a combination of both?

Good Teaching Is Partly an Art and Partly a Science

Some educators have argued that teaching is an art that cannot be practiced—or even studied—in an objective or scientific manner (Dawe, 1984; Flinders, 1989; Hansgen, 1991; Highet, 1957; Rubin, 1985). For example, Gilbert Highet, a distinguished critic and professor of literature, argues in *The Art of Teaching* that successful teaching must be considered an art because it involves two things that cannot be objectively and systematically manipulated: emotions and values. In Highet's view:

> Teaching is not like inducing a chemical reaction: it is much more like painting a picture or making a piece of music, . . . like planting a garden or writing a friendly letter. You must throw your heart into it, you must realize that it cannot all be done by formulas, or you will spoil your work, and your pupils, and yourself. (1957, p. viii)

Examples of the emotions and values referred to by Highet include believing that teaching is one of society's most valuable and rewarding activities, that teaching must be done as well as possible every day, that it is important to get students excited about learning, and that there is no such thing as an unteachable student. The Case in Print on page 13 illustrates a first-year teacher who obviously subscribes to these beliefs.

When Highet states that teaching cannot all be done by formulas, he is urging teachers to be flexible. Flexibility, which can be thought of as a "feel" for doing the right thing at the right time, can take many forms. First, it means being able to choose from among all the techniques and information at your disposal to formulate effective lesson plans that take the diverse needs and interests of all your students into consideration. It means knowing, for example, when to present a formal lesson and when to let students discover things for themselves, when to be demanding and

Part of the art of teaching is knowing when to introduce an unusual assignment or activity that captures students' interest.

when to make few demands, when and to whom to give direct help and when and to whom to give indirect help.

Second, flexibility entails the communication of emotions and interest in a variety of ways. David Flinders (1989) describes a teacher who, when talking to students, would lean or step in their direction and maintain eye contact. At various times she would raise her eyebrows, nod her head, smile, and bring the index finger of her right hand to her lips, indicating serious consideration of the student's comments.

Third, flexibility includes the ability to improvise. When a lesson plan falls flat, the flexible teacher immediately thinks of an alternative presentation that recaptures the students' interest. Expert teachers actually plan improvisation into their lessons. Instead of writing out what they intend to do in great detail, expert teachers formulate general mental plans and wait to see how the students react before filling in such details as pacing, timing, and number of examples (Livingston & Borko, 1989; Westerman, 1991). Obviously, this type of high-wire act requires a great deal of experience and confidence.

Fourth, flexibility involves the willingness and resourcefulness to work around impediments. Teaching does not always occur under ideal circumstances, and teachers must sometimes cope with inadequate facilities, insufficient materials, interruptions, and other difficulties. Thus, **teaching as an art** involves emotions, values, and flexibility. Because these characteristics are intangible, they can be

| Teaching as an art: emotions, values, flexibility

Teaching Can Be a Rewarding Experience

Gilbert Highet, a distinguished critic and professor of literature, argues in The Art of Teaching *that successful teaching must be considered an art because it involves two things that cannot be objectively and systematically manipulated: emotions and values. . . . Examples of the emotions and values referred to by Highet include believing that teaching is one of society's most valuable and rewarding activities, that teaching must be done as well as possible every day, that it is important to get students excited about learning, and that there is no such thing as an unteachable student. (p. 11)*

SPECIAL YOUNG TEACHER WINS A $1,500 APPLE

CAROLYN BOWER
St. Louis Post-Dispatch, 9/7/96

Lisa Shipley will try almost anything to get her students' attention.

Macaroni for punctuation. Mr. Potato Head for a lesson in poetry personification. Popcorn for bribes.

"I always look at a lesson and say, 'Would that make me sleep?'" said Shipley, 24. "If it would, I would not do that to children."

Shipley, now in her second year as a seventh-grade teacher at A.B. Green Middle School in the Maplewood-Richmond Heights School District, is one of 51 teachers across the country selected recently to receive the Sallie Mae First Class Teacher Award.

The award, sponsored by the Student Loan Marketing Association, carries a $1,500 prize and an all-expense-paid trip to Washington Sept. 20. The award, in its 12th year, recognizes first-year teachers who have shown outstanding performance. In Illinois, the award will go to Sarah Drake, a history teacher at Naperville High School in Naperville, near Chicago.

The principal at A.B. Green, Arline Kalishman, recommended Shipley for the award. "This girl is such a winner," said Kalishman, whose school has won a national blue ribbon for excellence.

Kalishman gave these examples:

• Before Shipley's first teaching day a year ago, she compiled five notebooks, one for every seventh-grade teacher, to use in teaching novels. The books contained questions about novels, background information and suggested activities.

• Shipley helped train students for oratorical contests. Some students took first place.

• She sponsored the yearbook and got businesses to donate 10 cameras to students and to process their film for free.

• She oversaw the production of two plays.

• Shipley had her students decorate potatoes to teach the idea of inanimate objects taking on human characteristics.

• She had students redesign Frosty the Snowman in a simulated ad campaign to learn descriptive writing, persuasive writing and propaganda techniques.

• She compiled her own textbooks, such as an 80-page collection of poetry and a 50-page collection of short stories. The books discuss topics such as point of view, character and narrator.

Shipley gets some ideas from the Internet; others are her own creations. Raw test scores show Shipley's students performed as well or better than students in previous years, Kalishman said.

Shipley, who grew up in south St. Louis County, said she picked A.B. Green over 14 other job offers and $12,000 more pay in a wealthier district because "they needed me here." She likes to work with students from less-affluent homes, who appreciate what she does. She liked the freedom school officials offer to take risks with her 120 students.

Katie Mallon, 12, said, "She tries to make learning more fun."

Shipley said she was delighted but surprised to get the award.

"I don't feel I'm doing anything outstanding," she said. "I give the best I can every day so the kids will give their best. It's something everyone should do."

Questions and Activities

1. Lisa Shipley, the first-year teacher in this story, is obviously internally motivated, creative, and not shy about taking initiative. Do you think these are characteristics that people are born with or that develop with experience? If you think such characteristics are at least partly learnable, and if you think you might be lacking in one or more of these areas, what can you do to improve your levels of motivation, creativity, and leadership?

2. Good teachers spend a considerable amount of time preparing for class so that, as Lisa Shipley pointed out, students are not bored or turned off. In this chapter and in Chapter 15 we describe how to create a Reflective Journal as a way to help you plan, revise, and refine your instruction. If you would like to be as dynamic and effective as the teacher in this story, resolve to begin a Reflective Journal this semester and to add to it in the coming years.

3. This story illustrates that good teachers are internally motivated and committed to all aspects of their role. One way to start down the road to being this kind of teacher is to make a list of the special knowledge and talents you possess and to then think about the various school-related activities in which you could participate that would allow you to use those capabilities.

very difficult, if not impossible, to teach. Teachers must find these qualities within themselves.

The argument for **teaching as a science** is equally persuasive. Scholars such as Paul Woodring (1957), Nathaniel Gage (1984), David Berliner (1986), and Lee Shulman (1986) agree that the science of teaching, as such, does not currently exist. But they contend that it is possible and desirable to have a scientific basis for the art of teaching. By drawing on established research findings, both prospective and practicing teachers can be taught many of the prerequisites that make "artistic" teaching possible. Also, as Robert Slavin (1989) persuasively argues, working from a scientific basis helps teachers avoid the pitfall of subscribing to the latest fad. This argument, of course, rests on the existence of a usable body of research findings, which educational psychologists believe does exist. As evidence, you might consult "Toward a Knowledge Base for School Learning" (Wang, Haertel, & Walberg, 1993) and "Productive Thinking and Instruction: Assessing the Knowledge Base" (Walberg, 1990). The authors of both articles identify dozens of research-validated instructional practices that have been shown to improve achievement. For example, twenty-four of twenty-five studies found that giving teachers more instructional time—that is, giving students more time to learn—leads to higher achievement. (This finding is often used to support proposals for a longer school year.)

Research provides a scientific basis for "artistic" teaching

Other studies have demonstrated the benefits of alerting students to important material through the use of objectives and pretests, getting students involved in a task through the use of questions and homework, and providing corrective feedback and reinforcement with written comments, verbal explanations, and praise. Another example of usable research is analysis of the characteristics of expert teachers. One reason some teachers are experts is that they can quickly and accurately recall relevant knowledge from two large areas: subject-matter knowledge and knowledge of classroom organization and management (Berliner, 1986; Sternberg & Horvath, 1995). From the research being done in this area, we are learning how expert teachers acquire this knowledge, recall it, and use it appropriately.

Look back at the heading of this section. Notice that it reads "Good Teaching Is Partly an Art and Partly a Science," not "Teaching as an Art Versus Teaching as a Science." Our choice of wording indicates our belief that good teaching is a skillful blend of artistic and scientific elements. The teacher who attempts to base every action on scientific evidence is likely to come across as rigid and mechani-

Good teachers combine "artistic" and "scientific" characteristics

cal—perhaps even indecisive (when the scientific evidence is lacking or unclear). The teacher who ignores scientific knowledge about teaching and learning and makes arbitrary decisions runs the risk of using methods and principles of teaching that are ineffective.

Reflective Teaching: A Process to Help You Grow from Novice to Expert

Reflective teachers think about what they do and why

This blending of artistic and scientific elements can be seen in recent discussions of what is called **reflective teaching** (see, for example, Eby, 1994; Hatton & Smith, 1995; Ross, Bondy, & Kyle, 1993; and Schon, 1987). Reflective teachers are constantly engaged in thoughtful observation and analysis of their actions in the classroom before, during, and after interactions with their students.

Prior to instruction, reflective teachers may think about such things as the types of knowledge and skills students in a democratic society at the start of a new millennium need to learn, the kind of classroom atmosphere and teaching techniques that are most likely to produce this learning, and the kinds of assessments that will provide clear evidence that these goals are being accomplished (a topic that we discuss at some length in Chapters 13 and 14). Jere Brophy and Janet Alleman (1991) illustrate the importance of thinking about long-range goals by pointing out how the choice of goals affects content coverage and how content coverage affects teachers' choice of classroom activities. If, for example, one goal is for students to acquire problem-solving skills, students would likely be engaged in activities that call for inquiring, reasoning, and decision making. Debates, simulations, and laboratory experiments are just three examples of activities that might be used to meet such a goal. If, however, the goal is for students to memorize facts and information, students will likely be given activities that call for isolated memorization and recall. Worksheets and drill-and-practice exercises are typically used to meet this type of goal. The point here is that effective teachers are reflective—they think about these issues as a basis for drawing up lesson plans.

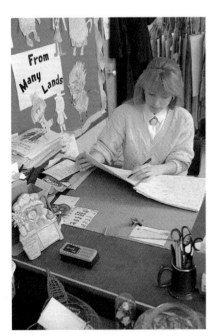

Reflective teachers set aside time to think about what they do in class, why they do it, and how their methods affect student performance.

As they interact with students, reflective teachers are highly aware of how students are responding to what they are doing and are prepared to make minor but significant changes to keep a lesson moving toward its predetermined goal. Consider an elementary school classroom in which some students are having difficulty understanding the relationship between the orbits of the planets around the sun and their position in the night sky. The teacher knows there is a problem because some students have a puzzled expression on their faces, while others cannot describe this phenomenon in their own words. Realizing that some students think in more concrete terms than others (a topic we will discuss in Chapter 2), the teacher decides to push the desks to the sides of the room and have the students simulate the planets by walking through their orbits. Notice how—all in the moment—this teacher engaged in thoughtful observation, spontaneous analysis, and flexible, resourceful problem solving.

For events that cannot be handled on the spot, some period of after-school time should be set aside for reflection. This is the time to assess how well a particular lesson met its objective, to wonder why some students rarely participate in class discussions, to ponder the pros and cons of grouping students by ability, and to formulate plans for dealing with these concerns.

To become a reflective teacher, you will need to acquire several attitudes and abilities. Three of the most important attitudes are an introspective orientation, an open-minded but questioning attitude about educational theories and practices, and the willingness to take responsibility for your decisions and actions. These attitudes need to be combined with the ability to view situations from others' perspectives (students, parents, principal, other teachers), the ability to find information that allows an alternative explanation of classroom events and that produces more effective instructional methods, and the ability to use compelling evidence in support of a decision (Eby, 1994; Ross, Bondy, & Kyle, 1993). We hasten to add that, although reflection is by nature largely a solitary activity, you should discuss your concerns with colleagues, students, and parents to get different perspectives on the nature of a problem and possible alternative courses of action.

| **Reflective teachers have particular attitudes and abilities** |

As you can probably see from this brief discussion, the reflection process is likely to work well when teachers have command of a wide range of knowledge about the nature of students, the learning process, and the instructional process. By mastering much of the content of this text, you will be that much more prepared than your less knowledgeable peers to make productive use of the time you devote to reflection.

Another factor that has been shown to contribute to teacher reflectivity is journal writing. Keeping a written journal forces you to express with some clarity your thoughts and beliefs about the causes of classroom events, how you feel about them, and what you might do about them (Bolin, 1990; Han, 1995). Thus, one potentially helpful way you might begin developing this reflective capacity is to follow our suggestion for compiling a Reflective Journal. In Chapter 15 we describe how you might set this journal up.

Uses of This Book

This book has been written so that it can be used in three ways. First, it is a text for a course in educational psychology intended to help you master an organized sampling of scientific knowledge about development, learning, objectives, motivation, evaluation, and classroom management. Second, it is a source of practical ideas and suggestions for use during your time as a student teacher and during your first years of teaching. Third, it is a resource to help you reflect on and analyze your own teaching when used in conjunction with the compilation of a Reflective Journal.

USING THIS BOOK TO ACQUIRE SCIENTIFIC INFORMATION

A substantial amount of scientific knowledge is of potential value to teachers. This book offers a selection of information from this pool of knowledge, organized so that you can learn and remember what you read as easily and effectively as possible. Chances are that your instructor will present lectures, organize discussions, provide videotapes and software programs, and perhaps arrange field trips that will tie in with what is discussed in assigned chapters of this text. Depending on the purposes and organization of the educational psychology course you are taking, this book may also serve as the basis for examinations and/or other types of evaluation.

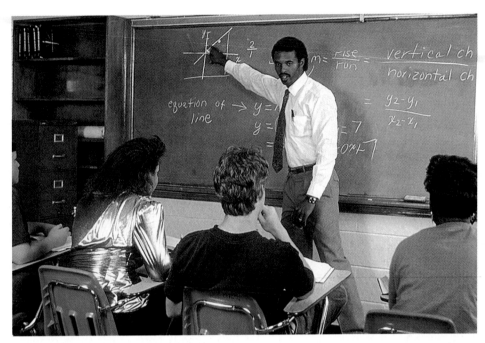

This book contains much scientific information and several features, such as suggestions for teaching, uses of technology, and suggestions for constructing a Reflective Journal, that will help you become an effective teacher during the early and later stages of your career.

The first way you can use this book, then, is to become well acquainted with an organized body of scientific information in the field of educational psychology. Since this book presently functions as the text for a course, you may be asked to learn some sections well enough to be able to answer test questions. Tests do, after all, act as incentives that motivate students to read with care, and they provide information about how well students understand what they have read. It is particularly desirable for you to read this book carefully during this quarter or semester so that you will become well acquainted with the second way of using the book.

USING THIS BOOK AS A SOURCE OF PRACTICAL IDEAS

The second way this book can be used is as a source of practical ideas on how to teach, especially in the diverse, demanding, and often technologically sophisticated classrooms of today. In addition to acquiring knowledge and learning principles that will serve as a general, all-purpose background for teaching, you should think of specific ways in which you might apply what you learn. Sooner or later you will engage in student teaching. You may be student-teaching at the same time you are taking educational psychology. But it is more likely that you will student-teach after you finish this book and that you will take one or more additional courses in methods of teaching. Your performance as a student teacher will probably be one of the most important factors considered when you apply for a teaching position. Furthermore, once you secure a job, your performance in the classroom will determine whether you will be offered a contract for a second year. Therefore, you will be eager to function as a prepared, confident, resourceful student teacher and first-year teacher. This book has been designed to help you get ready for your first teaching experiences and to enable you to find solutions to problems as they arise.

USING THIS BOOK TO BECOME A REFLECTIVE TEACHER

As you gain experience in the classroom, you should begin to observe your own teaching and reflect daily on what you feel is working and what is not. Because you cannot anticipate all the problems you will encounter in any classroom, you will need to continually make adjustments and engage in a process of trial and error. To make this process as constructive as possible, you should systematically analyze strengths and weaknesses in your teaching. The third way you can use this book (especially in conjunction with the compilation of your own Reflective Journal), then, is to analyze specific facets of your instructional techniques and plan how to correct errors and perfect successes.

Special Features of This Book

Several distinctive features of this book are intended to be used in rather specialized ways. These features include Key Points, Suggestions for Teaching in Your Classroom, one or more sections of every chapter that are devoted to discussing applications of technology to teaching, Resources for Further Investigation, and Journal Entries. In addition, your compilation of a separate component to accompany this book—the Reflective Journal—is recommended. This journal makes use of the text's Journal Entries and the Suggestions for Teaching.

KEY POINTS

At the beginning of each chapter, you will find a list of *Key Points*. The Key Points also appear within each chapter, printed in small type in the margins. These points have been selected to help you learn and remember sections of each chapter that are of special significance to teachers. (These sections may be stressed on exams, but they were originally selected not because they can serve as the basis for test items but because they are important.) If you tried to learn everything in this book, you would be working against yourself because some of the information you might memorize would interfere with the acquisition of other information. To reduce forgetting due to such interference, you are asked to concentrate on only a few sections in each chapter. To grasp the nature of the Key Points, turn to pages 24–25, which list points stressed under the major headings of Chapter 2. Then flip through the chapter to see how the appearance of the Key Points in the margins calls attention to significant sections of the text.

SUGGESTIONS FOR TEACHING IN YOUR CLASSROOM

In most of the chapters of this book, you will find summaries of research that serve as the basis for related principles or conclusions. These sets of principles or conclusions, in turn, are the foundation for *Suggestions for Teaching in Your Classroom*. Each suggestion is usually followed by a list of examples illustrating how it might be applied. In most cases examples are provided for both elementary and secondary grades since there usually are differences in the way a principle might be applied in dealing with younger and with older students. To permit you to find information relating to particular aspects of teaching, an index to the Suggestions for Teaching in Your Classroom is printed inside the front cover. To discover the nature of the

Suggestions read the list on pages 33–35, and then examine the detailed suggestions and examples of applications that follow.

Researchers have found that most teachers do not incorporate current research findings into their classroom practices. One reason is because many research articles and textbooks provide only vague guidelines for classroom use and no concrete examples. But when new ideas are presented in a concrete and usable form, teachers are much more likely to try them out (Gersten & Brengelman, 1996). This is why *Psychology Applied to Teaching* places as much emphasis on concrete suggestions for teaching as on providing clear discussions of theory and research. But as useful as our suggestions might be, you cannot, as we mentioned earlier, use them as prescriptions. Every school building and every group of students is different. What worked well for one student or one class may fall flat with another. You have to learn how to adapt the suggestions in this book and any other books that you will read to the particular dynamics of each class. This is the essence of being a reflective teacher.

CASE IN PRINT

This feature presents a recent newspaper article that either 1) elaborates on an idea or technique described in the chapter, or 2) shows how an idea was applied by public school educators.

THE ROLE OF TECHNOLOGY IN LEARNING AND INSTRUCTION

As a teacher in the new millennium, you will undoubtedly want to be knowledgeable about the many ways technology can enhance your students' learning. We feel that it is important for prospective teachers to understand how technology can be integrated in the curriculum regardless of the content area or student age level. In fact, *Psychology Applied to Teaching* is the first educational psychology textbook that discusses technology possibilities for teaching and learning in every chapter. Throughout the book, we will explore an assortment of educational technologies, including simulations, tutorials, word processors, hypermedia, multimedia, and on-line learning tools, and point out how they can have a significant impact on classroom learning. All references to software and other forms of computer technology in this book will be highlighted by a blue vertical bar, such as the one appearing here.

Although technology is just one spoke in the wheel of effective teaching, we nonetheless hope that this book provides you with greater awareness of how to use technology to foster students' intellectual development, provide special education students with assistive devices, increase time on task, augment or enhance learning, push students to explore and articulate ideas, motivate students, foster efficient classroom management, and help in the assessment of student work.

As you examine some of the technology resources and ideas mentioned in this book, you should be thinking about the ways in which they might enhance the learning environment of your classroom. Will you employ technology for drill and practice of basic facts or for students to locate and explore ideas on the **World Wide Web** (a global system of interconnected computers)? Will your students use computers to play games during free time, or will they be exchanging scientific data with peers in other countries and locales? You should also be thinking about how your role as a teacher changes when you choose different technologies and activities. Will you utilize technology to gain greater control of your classroom learning environment, or will you select technologies that allow your students more choices and personal responsibility for their own learning? Stated another way, will you be a manager or a facilitator of student learning?

We believe that the answers you give to the preceding questions regarding technology in the classroom will depend on each particular learning situation as well as on your overall learning goals. Hopefully, as you read the various chapters of this book, you will better appreciate the fact that there are many unique options and opportunities presented by educational technology that previous generations of teachers never had a chance to consider.

RESOURCES FOR FURTHER INVESTIGATION

In the chapters that follow, you will find suggestions that cover many facets of teaching. You are likely to conclude, however, that some information on particular aspects of teaching is not complete enough. Despite the book's attempt to provide at least partial solutions to the most common difficulties faced by teachers, you are bound, sooner or later, to become aware of problems that are not discussed in these pages. You may want additional data on some aspects of teaching, either while you are taking this course or after you are experienced enough to have time for a detailed look at some facet of education, psychology, or instruction. To allow for instances where you will need additional information, an annotated bibliography is provided at the end of each chapter. *Resources for Further Investigation* lists articles, books, and on-line (Internet) sources you might consult.

Two important points should be mentioned regarding Internet sources of information. First, all the databases and resources listed or described throughout this book have been checked for accuracy as of its publication date. The world of on-line information, however, is in constant flux—databases are updated, moved, renamed, or deleted from the Internet network every day. If you're unable to find one of the resources mentioned, we recommend that you consult your school's computer support person or your colleagues (since the most current information is often passed by word of mouth).

This brings up the second important point about on-line information: it is no more reliable (and in some cases is definitely less reliable) than what you may find in print. In particular, "newsgroups" and "discussion groups" are notorious for participants' distribution of incorrect, incomplete, or misleading advice or information. Our recommendation to you is to treat on-line information as you would print: try to stay with publishers or databases that are maintained by reputable sources, such as education or psychology departments of universities, major educational associations, the U.S. government, and so forth. Double-check the information you gather on-line—don't assume that because it appears on a computer that it is accurate! And remember that participating in a newsgroup discussion is most useful for generating new ideas or potential directions that you can pursue further on your own or with a group of classmates.

JOURNAL ENTRIES

Within the margins of each chapter, you will find numerous instances of the phrase *Journal Entries*. These marginal headings are related to the material just opposite in the text. They are intended to serve as suggested wordings for the headings of pages in a Reflective Journal that we strongly encourage you to keep. In Chapter 15, we describe the beneficial effects of reflection and journal writing on teaching, and we describe how you can use the Journal Entries to organize your first Reflective Journal.

Since you may need to concentrate on learning Key Points to demonstrate under-standing on exams during the course you are now taking, you may not have time to prepare the journal this quarter or semester. But after you have read this book as a text, you should go through it a second time for the purpose of developing a custom-designed journal.

RESOURCES FOR FURTHER INVESTIGATION

■ The Art and Science of Teaching

Louis J. Rubin examines teaching as art and teaching as the-ater in *Artistry in Teaching* (1985). Borrowing from the writ-ings of ancient Greek philosophers and the early twentieth-century philosopher John Dewey, James Garrison describes teaching as a creative calling that involves such factors as emotions, intuition, values, and practical wisdom in *Dewey and Eros: Wisdom and Desire in the Art of Teaching* (1997). In Chapter 1 of *Researching the Art of Teaching: Ethnography for Educational Use* (1996), Peter Woods summarizes the various arguments that have been made for teaching as an art, as a science, and as an activity that combines both art and science. Using a letter format, Vito Perrone covers such topics as de-ciding what to teach, engaging students, valuing differences, empowering teachers, and refining the craft of teaching in *A Letter to Teachers: Reflections on Schooling and the Art of Teach-ing* (1991).

To learn about the scientific knowledge base that under-lies teaching, you might want to look at *Putting Research to Work in Your School* (1993), by David Berliner and Ursula Casanova. In each of six sections (teaching, instructional strategies, learning, motivation, school and society, and test-ing), they point out how a research study has shed some light on a such relevant issues as how to make cross-age tutoring work, teaching memory skills to students, motivating stu-dents through project-based learning, and how standardized tests affect teachers.

Several handbooks provide excellent analyses of research on various aspects of teaching. Part 2 of the *Handbook of Research on Teaching* (3d ed., 1986), edited by Merlin Witt-rock, contains articles on teachers' thought processes, stu-dents' thought processes, teacher behavior and student achievement, and teaching functions. Part V of the *Handbook of Research on Teacher Education* (2d ed., 1996), edited by John Sikula, discusses the problems of beginning teachers, among other topics. Part IV of the *Handbook of Educational Psychology* (1996), edited by David C. Berliner and Robert C. Calfee, contains seven articles that deal with such issues as learning to teach, the beliefs and knowledge base of teachers, and teaching and learning in a classroom context. Section I, Part A of the *Handbook of Education and Human Develop-ment* (1996), edited by David R. Olson and Nancy Torrance, deals with the psychological foundations of teaching.

■ Reflective Teaching

Several books explain what it means to be a reflective teacher and describe the benefits that this approach to teach-ing can produce. The briefest of these books at 78 pages is Kenneth M. Zeichner's *Reflective Teaching: An Introduction*. Christopher M. Clark adds an interesting dimension to re-flective teaching in his book *Thoughtful Teaching* (1995). In addition to the common conception of a reflective teacher as one who solves problems and makes decisions, Clark's reflec-tive teacher is also considerate of the feelings and viewpoints of students and colleagues. Two other books on reflective teaching are *Reflective Teaching for Student Empowerment* (1993), by Dorene D. Ross, Elizabeth Bondy, and Diane W. Kyle, and *Reflective Planning, Teaching, and Evaluation* (1994), by Judith W. Eby.

SUMMARY

1. Educational psychology is a scientific discipline that at-tempts to understand and improve how students learn from instruction in classroom settings.

2. Learning about the research findings and principles of educational psychology can help you be a better teacher because (a) teaching is complex work that requires a wide range of knowledge and skills, (b) the research lit-erature contains numerous useful ideas for improving your instruction, and (c) teachers who have had profes-sional training are often more effective than those who have not had such training.

3. Unsystematic observations of students may lead teach-ers to draw false conclusions because of limited cases, unrecognized or unusual factors, and a tendency to ig-nore contrary evidence.

4. Even though scientific evidence does not support the practice of grade retention, it remains popular among teachers and parents because of unsystematic observa-tions about its effectiveness.

5. Scientifically gathered evidence is more trustworthy than casual observation because it involves sampling, control, objectivity, publication, and replication.

6. The scientific study of education is complicated by the limited focus of research, individual differences in perception and thinking, the inability of researchers to keep up with all published research, different interpretations of findings, and the ongoing accumulation of new knowledge.

7. Research on teaching and learning gives you a systematic, objective basis for making instructional decisions, but it cannot tell you how to handle every classroom situation. Many classroom decisions must be made on the spot. This contrast represents the science and the art of teaching.

8. Those who argue that teaching is an art point to communication of emotions, to values, and to flexibility as qualities that good teachers must possess but that are not easily taught.

9. Certain scholars contend that there is a scientific basis for teaching that can be taught and that draws on established research findings.

10. Good teachers strike a balance between the art and the science of teaching.

11. Reflective teachers constantly think about such issues as the worthwhileness of the goals they are trying to achieve, the types of teaching methods they use and how effective those methods are, and the extent to which their methods and goals are supported by scientific evidence.

KEY TERMS

educational psychology *(4)*   teaching as a science *(14)*   World Wide Web *(19)*
teaching as an art *(12)*   reflective teaching *(15)*

DISCUSSION QUESTIONS

1. Imagine that you are a second-grade teacher at the end of the school year. You have just finished telling your principal about a student who performed so poorly during the year that you question whether the student is adequately prepared for third grade. The principal suggests that the child repeat second grade next year. Given what you know about the research on retention, how would you respond to the principal's suggestion?

2. Think of or identify a popular instructional practice. Would you classify that practice as a fad or as the outgrowth of accumulated scientific knowledge? Why? How can you tell the difference between the two?

3. The effective teacher as artist displays enthusiasm and a sense of worthwhileness about content and teaching methods. At some point, however, you may be asked to teach a grade level or a subject for which you have little enthusiasm, or you may grow bored teaching the same grade level or subject in the same way year after year. How will you fulfill the role of teacher-artist if faced with these conditions?

4. The point was made in this chapter that good teachers strike a balance between the art and the science of teaching. How do they do so? Are they born with the right type of personality? Are they the products of good teacher-education programs? Or is some combination of these elements at work? If you believe that both factors play a role, which do you feel is more important?

5. The effective reflective teacher sets aside regular blocks of time to think about teaching activities and to make new plans. Most teachers complain about having insufficient time to reflect and plan. What would you do to make more time available?

Part I

Student Characteristics

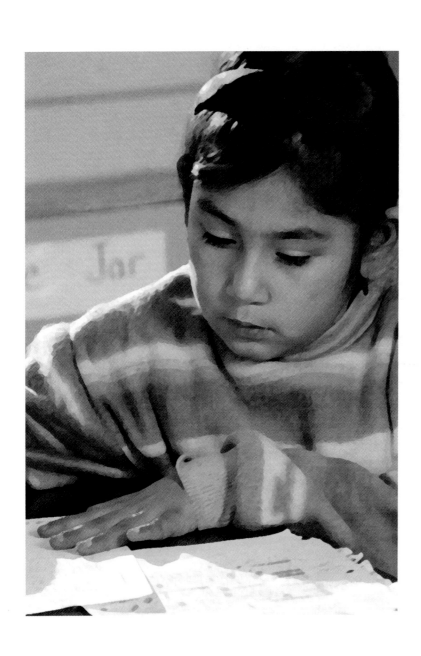

2 Stage Theories of Development

In Chapter 1 we pointed out that individuals vary in how they perceive and think about the world around them. This commonplace observation implies that you need to be aware of the major ways in which students differ from one another in order to design potentially effective lessons. What may work well for one part of your class may not work quite so well for another part. The lesson that was a huge success with last year's class may be a disaster with this year's group if you fail to take into account critical differences between the two classes. The five chapters that make up Part 1 will introduce you to how students may differ from one another in psychosocial development, cognitive development, age, mental ability, thinking style, achievement, ethnic background, and social class and discuss how those differences affect classroom learning.

Human development is a difficult topic to discuss because, in addition to analyzing many different forms of behavior, one must trace the way each type of behavior changes as a child matures. Authors of books on development have adopted different strategies for coping with this problem. Some have described theories that outline stages in the emergence of particular forms of behavior. Others have summarized significant types of behavior at successive age levels. Still others have examined specific types of behavior, noting age changes for every topic. Each approach has advantages and disadvantages.

Theories call attention to the overall sequence, continuity, and interrelatedness of aspects of development, but they typically account for only limited facets of behavior. Texts organized in terms of age levels make the reader aware of varied aspects of children's behavior at a given age but sometimes tend to obscure how particular types of behavior emerge and change. And although texts organized according to types of behavior do not have the limitation of the age-level approach, they may make it difficult for the reader to grasp the overall pattern of behavior at a particular stage of development.

In an effort to profit from the advantages and to minimize the disadvantages of each approach, Chapters 2 and 3 present discussions of development that combine all three. Chapter 2 focuses principally on Erik Erikson's psychosocial stages and Jean Piaget's cognitive stages, including a comparison of Piaget's views of cognitive development with those of Lev Vygotsky. This chapter also describes Piaget's ideas about moral development, Lawrence Kohlberg's extension of Piaget's work, and Carol Gilligan's criticism and modification of Kohlberg's theory. Chapter 3 describes age-level characteristics of students at five levels—preschool, primary school, elementary school, middle school, and high school. Discussion at each age level focuses on four types of behavior—physical, social, emotional, and cognitive. The information in these chapters will help you adapt teaching techniques to the students who are in the age range that you expect to teach. The first two chapters in this part describe patterns of behavior exhibited by typical children and adolescents.

The following three chapters are devoted to individual differences and how to deal with them. Chapter 4 discusses the nature of variability and how students vary with respect to gender, mental ability, and cognitive style. Chapter 5 describes the characteristics of students from different ethnic and social-class backgrounds. And Chapter 6 describes types of students who vary from their classmates to such an extent that they may require special kinds of education. ■

- Concrete operational stage: child is capable of mentally reversing actions but generalizes only from concrete experiences
- Formal operational stage: child is able to deal with abstractions, form hypotheses, engage in mental manipulations
- Adolescent egocentrism: one's thoughts and actions are assumed to be as central to others as to oneself
- Piaget's theory underestimates children's abilities
- Most adolescents are not formal operational thinkers
- Sequence of stages uniform across cultures but rate of development varies

Piaget and Vygotsky: The Role of Social Interaction and Instruction in Cognitive Development

- Piaget: cognitive development more strongly influenced by peers than by adults
- Instruction can accelerate development of schemes that have begun to form
- Vygotsky: cognitive development more strongly influenced by those more intellectually advanced
- Vygotsky: help students learn how to use psychological tools
- Vygotsky: cognitive development due to instruction in zone of proximal development

Using Technology to Promote Cognitive Development

- Computer-based simulations promote exploration and visual representations of abstract ideas, and correct misconceptions
- Computer programs can act as expert collaborative partners

Piaget, Kohlberg, and Gilligan: Moral Development

- Morality of constraint (moral realism): sacred rules, no exceptions, no allowance for intentions, consequences determine guilt
- Morality of cooperation (moral relativism): rules are flexible, intent important in determining guilt
- Preconventional morality: avoid punishment, receive benefits in return
- Conventional morality: impress others, respect authority
- Postconventional morality: mutual agreements, consistent principles
- Moral education programs may produce modest acceleration in moral development
- Males and females may use different approaches to resolve real-life moral dilemmas
- Moral knowledge does not always result in moral behavior

Erikson: Psychosocial Development

Of all the developmental theories that we could have chosen to discuss, why did we choose to open this chapter with Erik Erikson's theory of psychosocial development? There are several reasons for this choice. First, Erikson described psychological growth from infancy through old age. Thus, one can draw out instructional implications for every level of education from preschool through adult education. Second, Erikson's theory portrays people as playing an active role in their own psychological development through their attempts to understand, organize, and integrate their everyday experiences. Third, this theory highlights the important role played by cultural goals, aspirations, expectations, requirements, and opportunities in personal growth (a theme we will discuss in Chapter 4) (Newman & Newman, 1991).

Erikson's theory encompasses the life span, highlights the role of the person and culture in development

Although Erikson studied with Sigmund Freud, he concluded that Freud's tendency to stay in Vienna and interact with only a small and very select group of individuals had prevented the founder of psychoanalysis from fully appreciating how social and cultural factors (for example, values, attitudes, beliefs, and customs) influence behavior, perception, and thinking. Erikson decided to formulate a theory of development based on psychoanalytic principles but taking into account such influences.

BASIC PRINCIPLES OF ERIKSON'S THEORY

EPIGENETIC PRINCIPLE   Erikson based his description of personality development on the **epigenetic principle**, which states that in fetal development certain organs of the body appear at certain specified times and eventually "combine" to form a child. Erikson hypothesized that just as the parts of the body develop in interrelated ways in a human fetus, so the personality of an individual forms as the ego progresses through a series of interrelated stages. All these ego stages exist in some form from the very beginning, but each has a critical period of development.

Personality development based on epigenetic principle

PSYCHOSOCIAL CRISIS   In Erikson's view, personality development occurs as one successfully resolves a series of turning points, or psychosocial crises. Although the word *crisis* typically refers to an extraordinary event that threatens our well-being, Erikson had a more benign meaning in mind. Crises occur when people feel compelled to adjust to the normal guidelines and expectations that society has for them but are not altogether certain that they are prepared to fully carry out these demands. For example, Western societies expect children of elementary and middle school age (roughly six to twelve years) to develop a basic sense of industry, mostly through success in school, rather than one of inferiority. Adolescents are expected to come to terms with such questions as "Who am I?" and "Where am I going?" Young adults are expected to establish a relationship with another person rather than live physically and emotionally apart from others (Newman & Newman, 1991).

Personality grows out of successful resolution of psychosocial crises

Although Erikson described these crises in terms of desirable qualities and dangers, he did not mean to imply by this scheme that only positive qualities should emerge and that any manifestation of potentially dangerous traits is undesirable. He emphasized that people are best able to adapt to their world when they possess both the positive and negative qualities of a particular stage, provided the positive quality is significantly stronger than the negative quality. Try to imagine, for example, the personality of an individual who was never mistrustful (stage 1) or who never felt guilt (stage 3). Only when the negative quality outweighs the positive for any given stage or when the outcome for most stages is negative do difficulties in development and adjustment arise (Newman & Newman, 1991).

As you read through the following brief descriptions, keep in mind that a positive resolution of the issue for each stage depends on how well the issue of the previous stage was resolved. An adolescent who at the end of the industry versus inferiority stage strongly doubts her own capabilities and devalues the quality of her work, for example, may have trouble making the occupational commitments required for identity development (Marcia, 1991).

STAGES OF PSYCHOSOCIAL DEVELOPMENT[1]

The following designations, age ranges, and essential characteristics of the stages of personality development are proposed by Erikson in *Childhood and Society* (1963).

TRUST VERSUS MISTRUST (BIRTH TO ONE YEAR)   The basic psychosocial attitude to be learned by infants is that they can trust their world. Trust is fostered by "consistency, continuity, and sameness of experience" in the satisfaction by the parents of the infant's basic needs, which will permit children to think of their world as safe and dependable. Conversely, if care is inadequate, inconsistent, or negative, children will approach the world with fear and suspicion.

2 to 3 years: autonomy vs. shame and doubt

AUTONOMY VERSUS SHAME AND DOUBT (TWO TO THREE YEARS; PRESCHOOL)   Just when children have learned to trust (or mistrust) their parents, they must exert a degree of independence. If toddlers are permitted and encouraged to do what they are capable of doing at their own pace and in their own way—but with judicious supervision by parents and teachers—they will develop a sense of autonomy. But if parents and teachers are impatient and do too many things for young children or shame young children for unacceptable behavior, feelings of self-doubt will develop.

INITIATIVE VERSUS GUILT (FOUR TO FIVE YEARS; PRESCHOOL TO KINDERGARTEN)   The ability to participate in many physical activities and to use language sets the stage for initiative, which "adds to autonomy the quality of undertaking, planning, and 'attacking' a task for the sake of being active and on the move." If four- and five-year-olds are given freedom to explore and experiment, and if parents and teachers take time to answer questions, tendencies toward initiative will be encouraged. Conversely, if children of this age are restricted and made to feel that their activities and questions have no point or are a nuisance, they will feel guilty about acting on their own.

4 to 5 years: initiative vs. guilt

INDUSTRY VERSUS INFERIORITY (SIX TO ELEVEN YEARS; ELEMENTARY TO MIDDLE SCHOOL)   A child entering school is at a point in development when behavior is dominated by intellectual curiosity and performance. "He now learns to win recognition by producing things. . . . He develops a sense of industry." If the child is encouraged to make and do things well, helped to persevere, allowed to finish tasks, and praised for trying, industry results. If the child's efforts are unsuccessful or

6 to 11 years: industry vs. inferiority

---

[1] All quotations in "Stages of Psychosocial Development" are drawn from Chapter 7 of *Childhood and Society*.

if they are derided or treated as bothersome, a feeling of inferiority results. Children who feel inferior may never learn to enjoy intellectual work and take pride in doing at least one kind of thing really well. At worst, they may believe they will never excel at anything.

Identity Versus Role Confusion (Twelve to Eighteen Years; Middle Through High School)   The goal at this stage is development of those roles and skills that will prepare adolescents to eventually take a meaningful place in adult society. The danger at this stage is **role confusion**: having no clear conception of appropriate types of behavior that others will react to favorably. If adolescents succeed (as reflected by the reactions of others) in integrating roles in different situations to the point of experiencing continuity in their perception of self, identity develops. If they are unable to establish a sense of stability in various aspects of their lives, role confusion results.

Intimacy Versus Isolation (Young Adulthood)   To experience satisfying development at this stage, the young adult needs to establish close and committed intimate relationships and partnerships with other people. The hallmark of intimacy is the "ethical strength to abide by such commitments, even though they may call for significant sacrifices and compromises." Failure to do so will lead to a sense of aloneness.

Generativity Versus Stagnation (Middle Age)   "Generativity . . . is primarily the concern of establishing and guiding the next generation." Erikson's use of the term *generativity* is purposely broad. It refers, of course, to having children and raising them. In addition, it refers to the productive and creative efforts in which adults take part (for example, teaching) that have a positive effect on younger generations. Those unable or unwilling to "establish" and "guide" the next generation become victims of stagnation and self-absorption.

Integrity Versus Despair (Old Age)   Integrity is "the acceptance of one's one and only life cycle as something that had to be and that, by necessity, permitted of no substitutions. . . . Despair expresses the feeling that the time is now short, too short for the attempt to start another life and to try out alternate roads to integrity."

   Of Erikson's eight stages, the two you should pay particular attention to are industry versus inferiority and identity versus role confusion because they are the primary psychosocial issues that students must resolve during their elementary, middle school, and high school years. If you are committed to helping students learn as much as possible, then you need to have a basic understanding of these two stages so that your lesson plans and instructional approaches help students achieve a strong sense of industry and identity. The next two sections will briefly describe the major factors that contribute to students' sense of industry and of who they are and what they might become.

Helping Students Develop a Sense of Industry

Between kindergarten and sixth grade, most children are eager to demonstrate that they can learn new skills and successfully accomplish assigned tasks. One factor that has long been known to have a detrimental effect on one's sense of industry is competition for a limited number of rewards. If you have ever taken a class where the teacher graded exams or projects "on a curve," you are familiar with the most com-

12 to 18 years: identity vs. role confusion

Role confusion: uncertainty as to what behaviors others will react to favorably mon form that such competition takes in schools. What the teacher does is compare each student's score with the score of every other student in that class. The few students who achieve the highest scores receive the top grade, regardless of the actual level of their scores. Then a predetermined number of B's, C's, D's, and F's are awarded. Because the resulting distribution of grades looks something like the outline of a bell, it is often referred to as a "bell-shaped curve" (which explains the origin of the term "grading on the curve").

There are at least two reasons why this practice may damage a student's sense of industry. First, it limits the top rewards to a relatively small number of students regardless of each student's actual level of performance. If the quality of instruction is good and students learn most of what has been assigned, the range of scores will be relatively small. Consider the impact to your sense of industry if you respond correctly to 85 percent of the questions on an exam but earn only a grade of C. The same problem exists when, for whatever reasons, all students perform poorly. How much pride can you have in a grade of A or B when you know it is based on a low success rate? The senior author still remembers a college chemistry class where the top grade on an exam went to a student who answered only 48 percent of the questions correctly. Second, this practice guarantees that some students have to receive failing grades regardless, again, of their actual level of performance. Students who are forced into this unhealthy type of competition (there are acceptable forms of competition, which we describe in Chapter 10) may develop a sense of inadequacy and inferiority that will hamper them for the rest of their school career.

| Students' sense of industry hampered by unhealthy competition for grades

The solution to this problem is to base grades on realistic and attainable standards that are worked out ahead of time and communicated to the students. We describe in Chapter 14 how to do this. In Chapter 10 we describe several instructional approaches that will likely have a beneficial impact on students' sense of industry because they all promote learning and a sense of accomplishment. In general, they involve establishing a classroom atmosphere in which students feel accepted for who they are and understand that the teacher is as interested in their success as they are. These goals are accomplished by providing clear expectations as to what students should be able to do after a unit of instruction, designing lessons that are logical and meaningful, and using teaching methods that support effective learning processes.

HELPING STUDENTS FORMULATE AN IDENTITY

The most complex of Erikson's stages is identity versus role confusion; he has written more extensively about this stage than any other. Because this stage is often misunderstood, let's use Erikson's own words to describe the concept of **identity**: "An optimal sense of identity . . . is experienced merely as a sense of psychosocial well-being. Its most obvious concomitants are a feeling of being at home in one's body, a sense of 'knowing where one is going' and an inner assuredness of anticipated recognition from those who count" (1968, p. 165). As you may know either from your own experience or the experiences of others, the process of identity formation is not always smooth, nor does it always follow the same path. But by being aware of the problems and uncertainties that adolescents may experience as they try to develop a sense of who they are, you can help them positively resolve this major developmental milestone.

| Identity: accepting one's body, having goals, getting recognition

| Psychosocial moratorium delays commitment

TAKING A PSYCHOSOCIAL MORATORIUM For those individuals who are unprepared to make a career choice, Erikson suggested the possibility of a **psychosocial**

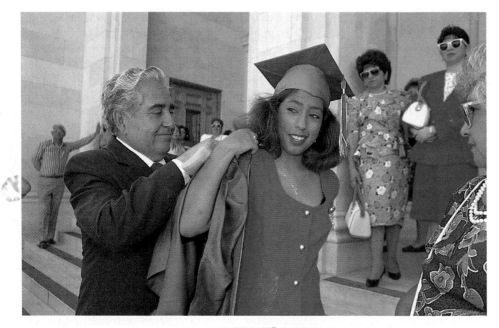

Identity, as Erikson defines it, involves acceptance of one's body, knowing where one is going, and recognition from those who count. A high school graduate who is pleased with his or her appearance, who has already decided on a college major, and who is admired by parents, relatives, and friends is likely to experience a sense of psychosocial well-being.

moratorium. This is a period marked by a delay of commitment. Such a postponement occurred in Erikson's own life: after leaving high school, Erikson spent several years wandering around Europe without making any firm decision about the sort of job he would seek. Under ideal circumstances, a psychosocial moratorium should be a period of adventure and exploration, having a positive, or at least neutral, impact on the individual and society.

ESTABLISHING A NEGATIVE IDENTITY   In some cases, however, the young person may engage in defiant or destructive behavior. A young person who is unable to overcome role confusion—or to postpone choices leading to identity formation by engaging in a positive psychosocial moratorium—may attempt to resolve inner conflict by choosing what Erikson refers to as a **negative identity.**

> The loss of a sense of identity is often expressed in a scornful and snobbish hostility toward the roles offered as proper and desirable in one's family or immediate community. Any aspect of the required role, or all of it—be it masculinity or femininity, nationality or class membership—can become the main focus of the young person's acid disdain. (1968, pp. 172–173)

For example, an adolescent boy whose parents have constantly stressed how important it is to do well in school may deliberately flunk out or quit school. Erikson explains such choices by suggesting that the young person finds it easier to "derive a sense of identity out of total identification with that which he is least supposed to be than to struggle for a feeling of reality in acceptable roles which are unattainable with his inner means" (1968, p. 176). If the young person who chooses a negative identity plays the role only long enough to gain greater self-insight, the experience may be positive. In some cases, however, the negative identity may be "confirmed" by the treatment the adolescent receives from those in authority. If such an individual is contemptuously referred to as a "failure," "delinquent," "punk," "loser," or "slacker" and treated with excessive punishment by parents, teachers, or law enforcement agencies, for example, the "young person may well put his energy into becoming exactly what the careless and fearful community expects him to be—and make a total job of it" (1968, p. 196).

ADOLESCENT IDENTITY STATUSES   Erikson's observations on identity formation have been usefully extended by James Marcia's notion of **identity statuses** (1966, 1980, 1991). Identity statuses, of which there are four, are styles or processes "for handling the psychosocial task of establishing a sense of identity" (Waterman & Archer, 1990, p. 35). Marcia (1980) developed this idea as a way to scientifically test the validity of Erikson's notions about identity.

Marcia established the four identity statuses after he had conducted semistructured interviews with a selected sample of male youths. The interviewees were asked their thoughts about a career, their personal value system, their sexual attitudes, and their religious beliefs. Marcia proposed that the criteria for the attainment of a mature identity are based on two variables: crisis and commitment. "Crisis refers to times during adolescence when the individual seems to be actively involved in choosing among alternative occupations and beliefs. Commitment refers to the degree of personal investment the individual expresses in an occupation or belief" (1967, p. 119). After analyzing interview records with these two criteria in mind, Marcia established four identity statuses that vary in their degree of crisis and commitment: identity diffusion, foreclosure, moratorium, and identity achievement. The moratorium and identity achievement statuses are generally thought to be more developmentally mature than the foreclosure and identity diffusion statuses because those individuals exhibiting the former have either evaluated alternatives and made a commitment or are actively involved in obtaining and evaluating information in preparation for a commitment (Archer, 1982).

As you read the brief descriptions of each identity type in Table 2.1, keep a few points in mind. First, the more mature identity statuses are slow to evolve. Among sixth graders only about 11 percent are likely to show any evidence of either an identity achievement or a moratorium status. By twelfth grade, only about 20 percent will have attained either status (Archer, 1982). Second, an identity status is not a once-and-for-all accomplishment. If an ego-shattering event (loss of a job, divorce) later occurs, individuals who have reached identity achievement, for example, may find themselves uncertain about old values and behavior patterns and once again in crisis. But for most individuals, a new view of oneself is eventually created. This cycling between certainty and doubt as to who one is and where one fits in society may well occur in each of the last three of Erikson's stages (Stephen, Fraser, & Marcia, 1992). Third, because identity is an amalgam of commitments from a number of different domains, only a small percentage (about 20 percent) of adolescents will experience a triumphant sense of having "put it all together." To cite just one example, an adolescent is more likely to have made a firm occupational choice but to be indecisive about gender role or religious values (Waterman, 1988).

Although the foreclosure status is the historical norm for Western societies, things can and do change. For example, individuals in moratorium were more numerous during the 1960s and 1970s than during the 1980s (Scarr, Weinberg, & Levine, 1986; Waterman, 1988). Also, recent evidence indicates that African-American adolescents are now more likely to be either in a moratorium status, in an identity achievement status, or in transition between these two statuses than in the foreclosure status of earlier generations (Watson & Protinsky, 1991). Gender differences are most apparent in the areas of political ideology, family/career priorities, and sexuality. With respect to political beliefs, males are more likely to exhibit

> Adolescents exhibit a particular process, called an identity status, for establishing an identity

Table 2.1	James Marcia's Identity Statuses			
Identity Status	**Crisis**	**Commitment**	**Characteristics**	
Diffusion	Not yet experienced. Little serious thought given to occupation, gender roles, values.	Weak. Ideas about occupation, gender roles, values are easily changed as a result of positive and negative feedback.	Not self-directed, disorganized, impulsive, low self-esteem, alienated from parents, avoids getting involved in schoolwork and interpersonal relationships.	**Individuals in identity diffusion avoid thinking about jobs, roles, values**
Foreclosure	Not experienced. May never suffer doubts about identity issues.	Strong. Has accepted and endorsed the values of the parents.	Close-minded, authoritarian, low in anxiety, has difficulty solving problems under stress, feels superior to peers, more dependent on parents for affection and approval than other statuses.	**Individuals in foreclosure unquestioningly endorse parents' goals and values**
Moratorium	Partially experienced. Has given some thought to identity-related questions.	Weak. Has not achieved satisfactory answers.	Anxious, dissatisfied with school, changes major often, daydreams, engages in intense but short-lived relationships, may temporarily reject parental values.	**Individuals in moratorium uncertain about identity**
Achievement	Fully experienced. Has considered and explored alternative positions regarding occupation, gender roles, values.	Strong. Has made self-chosen commitments to at least some aspects of identity.	Reflective decision-maker, high self-esteem, works effectively under stress, likely to form close interpersonal relationships. Usually the last identity status to emerge.	**Individuals who have reached identity achievement status have made their own commitments**

SOURCES: Bilsker & Marcia (1991); Blustein & Palladino (1991); Frank, Pirsch, & Wright (1990); Vondracek, Schulenberg, Skorikov, Gillespie, and Walheim (1995)

a foreclosure process and females a diffusion process. With respect to family/career priorities and sexuality, males are likely to be foreclosed or diffuse, whereas females are likely to express an identity achievement or a moratorium status (Archer, 1991).

A relevant question to ask about Marcia's identity statuses, particularly if you plan to teach in a foreign country or to instruct students with different cultural backgrounds, is whether these identity statuses occur only in the United States. The answer appears to be no. Researchers in such diverse countries as Korea, India, Nigeria, Japan, Denmark, and Holland report finding the same patterns (Scarr, Weinberg, & Levine, 1986).

CRITICISMS OF ERIKSON'S THEORY

Erikson's theory has been described as somewhat vague and difficult to test. As a result, researchers are not sure how best to measure such complex qualities as initiative and integrity or which kinds of experiences should be studied to discover how people cope with and successfully resolve psychosocial conflicts (Ochse & Plug, 1986; Sigelman & Shaffer, 1991).

Although Erikson occasionally carried out research investigations, most of his conclusions are based on personal and subjective interpretations that have been only partly substantiated by controlled investigations of the type that are valued by American psychologists. As a result, there have been only limited checks on Erikson's tendency to generalize from limited experiences. Some of his observations on identity, for example, reflect his own indecision about occupational choice.

Some critics argue that Erikson's stages reflect the personality development of males more accurately than that of females. According to Carol Gilligan (1982, 1988), for example, Erikson's theory is a more accurate description of male psychosocial development than of female psychosocial development. In particular, she feels that the process and timing of identity formation are different for each gender. Marcia (as cited in Scarr, Weinberg, & Levine, 1986) contends that beginning in about fourth grade (the industry versus inferiority stage), girls are as concerned with the nature of interpersonal relationships as they are with achievement, whereas boys focus mainly on achievement. And during adolescence, many young women seem to work through the crises of identity *and* intimacy simultaneously, whereas most young men follow the sequence described by Erikson—identity versus role confusion, then intimacy versus isolation (Gilligan, 1982; Ochse & Plug, 1986; Scarr, Weinberg, & Levine, 1986).

A final criticism is that Erikson's early stages, those covering ages two through eleven, seem to stress the same basic qualities. Autonomy, initiative, and industry all emphasize the desirability of permitting and encouraging children to do things on their own. Doubt, guilt, and inferiority all focus on the need for parents and teachers to provide sympathetic support.

If you keep these reservations in mind, however, you are likely to discover that Erikson's observations (as well as the identity statuses described by Marcia) will clarify important aspects of development. Suggestions for Teaching that take advantage of Erikson's observations follow. (These suggestions might also serve as the nucleus of a section in your Reflective Journal. Possible Journal Entries are indicated in the margins.)

SUGGESTIONS FOR TEACHING IN YOUR CLASSROOM

Applying Erikson's Theory of Psychosocial Development

1 **Keep in mind that certain types of behaviors and relationships may be of special significance at different age levels.**

Journal Entry
Ways to Apply Erikson's Theory (Preschool and Kindergarten)

2 **With younger preschool children, allow plenty of opportunities for free play and experimentation to encourage the development of autonomy, but provide guidance to reduce the possibility that children will experience doubt. Also avoid shaming children for unacceptable behavior.**

3 With older preschool children, encourage activities that permit the use of initiative and provide a sense of accomplishment. Avoid making children feel guilty about well-motivated but inconvenient (to you) questions or actions.

4 During the elementary and middle school years, help children experience a sense of industry by presenting tasks that they can complete successfully.

Journal Entry
Ways to Apply
Erikson's Theory
(Elementary
Grades)

Arrange such tasks so that students will know they have been successful. Play down comparisons and encourage cooperation and self-competition to limit feelings of inferiority. Also try to help jealous children gain satisfaction from their own behavior. (Specific ways to accomplish these goals will be described in several later chapters.)

5 At the secondary school level, keep in mind the significance of each student's search for a sense of identity.

The components of identity stressed by Erikson are acceptance of one's appearance, recognition from those who count, and knowledge about where one is going. Role confusion is most frequently caused by failure to formulate clear ideas about gender roles and by indecision about occupational choice.

Journal Entry
Ways to Apply
Erikson's Theory
(Secondary
Grades)

The American school system, particularly at the high school level, has been described as a place where individual differences are either ignored or discouraged and where negative feedback greatly outweighs positive feedback (e.g., Boyer, 1983; Csikszentmihalyi & Larson, 1984; Friedenberg, 1963; Murphy, 1987). When John Murphy (1987), a professor of education at Brooklyn College, asked his students to recall positive learning experiences from high school, few were able to do so. But as "someone who counts" to your students, you can contribute to their sense of positive identity by recognizing them as individuals and praising them for their accomplishments. If you become aware that particular students lack recognition from peers because of abrasive qualities or ineptness, and if you have the time and opportunity, you might also attempt to encourage social skills.

An excellent book to consult for this purpose is *Skill-Streaming the Adolescent: A Structured Learning Approach to Teaching Prosocial Skills* (Goldstein, Sprafkin, Gershaw, & Nein, 1980). This volume describes fifty specific skills that fall into five general categories: social skills, skills for dealing with feelings, skill alternatives to aggression, skills for dealing with stress, and planning skills. Each skill is taught by a four-step method:

Modeling (imitating those who use social skills effectively)

Role playing (gaining practice in social skills in simulated situations)

Performance feedback (improving techniques by noting their effectiveness or ineffectiveness)

Transfer of training (applying a technique that was learned in role-playing situations to everyday interactions with others)

Since the techniques are planned and structured, you will probably obtain the best results by following the procedures outlined in the book. But don't be afraid to experiment or make spontaneous changes.

You might be able to reduce identity problems resulting from indecisiveness about gender roles by having class discussions (for example, in social science courses) centering on changes in attitudes regarding masculinity, femininity, and family responsibilities. Following the suggestions of Jeanne Block (1973), you can encourage boys to become more sensitive to the needs of others and girls to be more achievement oriented. This approach to sex-role development that *combines* traditional "masculine" and feminine" behaviors is called psychological androgyny.

Another forum for such discussion is an on-line bulletin board or group in a computer-based classroom. On-line writing can be conducive to explorations of sensitive issues because it provides a slightly slower, more thoughtful pace and also allows male and female students an equal voice, even those who feel shy about speaking out loud in class. An on-line discussion, when carefully moderated by an experienced teacher, can both model and explore the territory of psychological androgyny.

Working with your school counselor, you may in some cases be able to help students make decisions about occupational choice by providing them with information (gleaned from classroom performance and standardized test results) about intellectual capabilities, personality traits, interests, and values (Lambert & Mounce, 1987). Or you may be able to help students decide whether to apply for admission to a college instead of entering the job market just after graduation. There are many ways to enable students to work toward short-term goals, particularly in your classroom. These will be described in detail in Chapters 10 and 11, which deal with approaches to instruction and motivation.

6 **Remember, the aimlessness of some students may be evidence that they are engaging in a psychosocial moratorium. If possible, encourage such individuals to focus on short-term goals while they continue to search for long-term goals.**

7 **Try to be patient if you suspect that disruptive behavior on the part of a student may be due to the acting out of a negative identity.**

When you must control negative behavior to preserve a satisfactory learning environment for other students, try to do it in such a way that the troublemaker is not confirmed as a troublemaker. One way is to make clear that you do not hold a grudge and that you have confidence in the student's ability to make positive contributions in class. (If possible, arrange opportunities for troublemakers to carry out assignments that will be positive and constructive.)

8 **Remain aware that adolescents may exhibit characteristics of different identity status types.**

Some may drift aimlessly; others may be distressed because they realize they lack goals and values. A few high school students may have arrived at self-chosen commitments; others may have accepted the goals and values of their parents.

If you become aware that certain students seem depressed or bothered because they are unable to develop a satisfactory set of personal values, consult your school psychologist or counselor. In addition, you might use the techniques just summarized to help these students experience at least a degree of identity achievement. Perhaps the main value of the identity status concept is that it calls attention to individual differences in the formation of identity. Because students in the foreclosure status will pose few, if any, classroom problems, you must keep in mind that foreclosure is not necessarily desirable for the individual student. Those experiencing identity diffusion or moratorium may be so bothered by role confusion that they are unwilling to carry out even simple assignments—unless you supply support and incentives.

Helping Young Children Develop

With younger preschool children, allow plenty of opportunities for free play and experimentation to encourage the development of autonomy, but provide guidance to reduce the possibility that children will experience doubt. Also avoid shaming children for unacceptable behavior.

With older preschool children, encourage activities that permit the use of initiative and provide a sense of accomplishment. Avoid making children feel guilty about well-motivated but inconvenient (to you) questions or actions. (p. 34)

PRESCHOOL TEACHERS MAP OUT STRATEGIES TO STEER CLEAR OF POWER STRUGGLES

BARBARA F. MELTZ
Boston Globe 12/10/98

Have you ever wished you could hide inside a cubby at your child's preschool and spy for a morning, just to make sure teachers aren't casting spells on the kids? What else, after all, could explain why teachers are able to bring children back into the fold calmly and quietly, without loss of self-esteem or a power struggle, while at home we back ourselves into corners, raise our voices, and say things we regret?

The truth is, preschool teachers do work a kind of magic. First, they create an environment that is totally child-centered: Everything a 3- or 4-year-old can reach is not only safe for her to use but intended to bring her enjoyment. Secondly, they focus entirely on the children: With no dinner to cook or laundry to fold, teachers have no distractions. Unfortunately, even if we could create the same environment at home right down to the red rug for circle time, even if we could free ourselves of other responsibilities, it wouldn't be enough.

"What teachers have that parents tend not to have is a repertoire of strategies to head off power struggles," says early childhood educator Ellen Galinsky. Power struggles are anathema to preschool teachers and should be to us, too. "As soon as you dig your heels in about how something has to happen, you take away what's most important to a preschool-age child: the ability to be autonomous, powerful, and strong, to do things himself," says Galinsky. She is president of Families and Work Institute in Manhattan and co-author of "The Preschool Years" (Ballantine Books).

It's not that parents don't have coping mechanisms; the problem is we often inadvertently feed into a power struggle.

To ensure success, she says, strategies need to be developmentally appropriate, tailored to the 3- and 4-year-old.

Gerry Pedrini, director of the Sunshine Nursery School in Arlington, says, "You'll never see a good preschool teacher issuing loud commands or scolding, because that doesn't make a child feel good, and feeling good is what leads to autonomy." You'll also rarely see a timeout chair in a quality setting, it's shaming.

So what should we do?

We asked directors of some of the area's leading preschools to share their strategies:

Offer Choices

This sounds simple but it backfires for parents if we let it drift into negotiation, says Pedrini. Negotiation gives a preschooler too much room to move around in, and too much power. "It creates anxiety," she says.

Offer a preschooler no more than three options; anything more is overwhelming. When choices are contained, a child accepts the boundaries and makes a selection. If he begins to negotiate—"How 'bout the cookie *before* dinner?"—stay on track: "That isn't one of the choices." Calmly repeat what they are.

Early childhood educator Janet Zeller, director of the Tufts University Educational Day Care Center, says choices work well because they empower a child and defuse the issue at the same time. "When you tell him, 'You can take the bath before we read a story or after,' he's in control of something desirable, the story, but not about what he doesn't want to do, which is the bath," she says. "It allows him to save face."

Say What You Want <u>Not</u>, What You Don't Want

Sentences that begin, "If you don't," tend to get us in trouble because what follows is typically a threat, says early childhood educator Judith T. Wagner: "'If you don't pick up your toys, then you can't watch the video.'"

It's as if a preschooler has a button set to automatically respond negatively to that kind of language. "Reacting against it is one of the ways they separate," says Wagner, who is professor of education and child development at Whittier College in California and director of Broadoaks Children's School there.

Substitute "when" for "if"—"When you pick up your toys, you can watch the video." That detoxifies your request by putting power in her hands, making it more likely she'll comply.

Always Tell Why

The typical preschooler responds to logic if it's genuine, offered with respect and offered before he is out of control. Keep your reasons simple, accurate, and age appropriate. "Parents have a tendency to go overboard with this," says Zeller. Here are examples she says a preschooler can understand: "You need to take this medicine so you won't have a fever and feel sick." "The reason I'm asking you not to pick your nose is because it will make it bleed." "It's not OK to swear because grown-ups will tell kids not to play with you."

Offer Praise

If you ask a 3-year-old to pick up the blocks and he puts only two in the bin, a parent is likely to focus on what didn't happen and react angrily: "You didn't pick up the blocks!" Before you know it, you're into a power struggle. But something good did happen: "You put two blocks in the bin. Good job!" By focusing on that—"Let me help you finish cleaning up"—you head off a battle and help define your expectations.

"Look for moments of goodness, even microscopic ones," says Chris Giguere, director of Lexington Playcare Center, a preschool in Lexington. Praise provides clarification for preschoolers, who aren't always clear about what we expect of them or what makes them good. Be as specific as possible.

Slow Down

Pedrini thinks a big reason we end up in power struggles is because we're always in a hurry. "Preschoolers move at a slower pace than grown-ups," she says. She tells parents to build in extra time so children can function at a pace that meets their needs. When you try to speed a transition, don't just issue a warning—"We have to go in five minutes"—but provide a definition: "You have time to read one more book."

Enlist Her Help in Problem Solving

This also empowers a preschooler, but it can easily backfire, says Kathy Roberts, director of the Dandelion School in Cambridge. Don't ask, "How can we solve this problem," until you state the problem clearly: "Your brother wants to build towers and it seems like you want to knock over towers."

Timing is critical. "Problem-solving doesn't work if the situation is too far gone," says Roberts. If you catch it early—you see a child about to knock over a block tower and you can engage him in some other activity before he does—then you can say, "Let me know when you aren't going to knock over Josh's tower." That tells him what he was doing wasn't good without shaming or humiliating him. It also puts control in his hands: "When I'm ready, I can play there again. It's up to me."

A less tricky way to problem-solve is after things have calmed down: "I wonder what we could do next time Josh wants to build and you don't." This won't work if you're angry, cautions Roberts. "Then it sounds like punishment."

Use Natural Consequences

This is another frequently talked about strategy that typically doesn't work with preschoolers unless the consequence is connected to the behavior in an obvious and immediate way. Sending a 4-year-old to her room or depriving her of TV later that day because she's teasing her 2-year-old sister won't make sense to her, says Roberts. But she will get the message if you tell her that you and Molly are going to a different room so Molly can play without being frustrated by her big sister. Then tell her, "If you want to join us, let us know when you're ready to play in a cooperative way." That tells her her behavior is a matter of choice and she has control of it.

Distract Him

Most parents know how to distract a child by engaging him in some other activity but few of us think about using humor as a distraction. When you see a power struggle looming because he won't put on his snowsuit, try to put it on yourself. Your mock cries of, "This doesn't fit me!" will tickle his funny bone and likely defuse the situation.

Planning Ahead

In the spirit of "an ounce of prevention . . . ," Ucci tells parents to anticipate a child's needs and reactions. If six cousins are visiting on Christmas, how will your preschooler cope with sharing? Talk about it—"I wonder how you'll feel if your cousins want to play with your teddy bears?"—and problem-solve: "You don't have to share all your toys; we could put the bears in the closet . . ."

Adding these strategies to your repertoire will reduce power struggles but may not eliminate them. When one erupts, Chris Giguere's advice is to end it as fast as possible. "It's your choice to let it escalate or not. You're the adult," she says.

Her favorite strategy for getting out of a power struggle in a way that no one loses face is something she calls "hand over hand:" "We step behind a child, take his hand under ours and do whatever needs to be done together, like pick up a book. 'We need to put the book away. Let's do it together.' Although a child may be unhappy, even crying, hand over hand is fast. It puts the incident behind you quickly," she says.

"Then it's up to the adult to be able to move on."

Questions and Activities

1. The stages of Erikson's theory that pertain to the preschool years are autonomy versus shame and doubt and initiative versus guilt. How do the preschool teachers in this article promote in young children a sense of autonomy and initiative and minimize or eliminate instances of shame, doubt, and guilt?

2. Successful preschool teachers create a child-centered environment in that all activities and materials support the child's psychosocial and cognitive development. How might this notion of child-centered instruction be applied to students from the primary grades through high school? You might want to take a look at the 14 learner-centered principles that were proposed by the American Psychological Association and that were mentioned in Chapter 1 before you formulate an answer. A description of each principle can be found at the following web site: **http://www.apa.org/ed/lcp.html**

3. Arrange to spend several hours at a preschool, spread over several days. Note how often the teachers use the techniques mentioned in this article (e.g., offer choices, say what you want, not what you don't want, slow down, use natural consequences). Which of the techniques used seem to be most effective? Which are least effective?

Piaget: Cognitive Development

BASIC PRINCIPLES OF PIAGET'S THEORY

Jean Piaget's conception of intellectual development reflects his basic interest in biology and knowledge. He postulated that human beings inherit two basic tendencies: **organization** (the tendency to systematize and combine processes into coherent general systems) and **adaptation** (the tendency to adjust to the environment). For Piaget, these tendencies govern both physiological and mental functioning. Just as the biological process of digestion transforms food into a form that the body can use, so intellectual processes transform experiences into a form that the child can use in dealing with new situations. And just as biological processes must be kept in a state of balance (through homeostasis), intellectual processes seek a balance through the process of **equilibration** (a form of self-regulation that all individuals use to bring coherence and stability to their conception of the world).

ORGANIZATION   As we just stated, *organization* refers to the tendency of all individuals to systematize or combine processes into coherent (logically interrelated) systems. When we think of tulips and roses as subcategories of the more general category *flowers*, instead of as two unrelated categories, we are using organization to aid our thinking process. This organizational capacity makes thinking processes efficient and powerful and allows for a better "fit," or adaptation, of the individual to the environment.

| Organization: tendency to systematize processes

SCHEMES   These are organized patterns of behavior or thought that children formulate as they interact with their environment, parents, teachers, and age-mates. **Schemes** can be behavioral (throwing a ball) or cognitive (realizing that there are many different kinds of balls). Whenever a child encounters a new experience that does not easily fit into an existing scheme, adaptation is necessary.

| Scheme: organized pattern of behavior or thought

ADAPTATION   This is the process of creating a good fit or match between one's conception of reality (one's schemes) and the real-life experiences one encounters. Adaptation, as described by Piaget, is accomplished by two subprocesses: **assimila-**

Activities that encourage children to create new ideas or schemes through experimentation, questioning, discussion, and discovery often produce meaningful learning because of the inherent drive toward equilibration.

Adaptation: tendency to adjust to environment

Assimilation: new experience is fitted into existing scheme

Accommodation: scheme is created or revised to fit new experience

tion and **accommodation**. A child may adapt either by interpreting an experience so that it fits an existing scheme (assimilation) or by changing an existing scheme to incorporate the experience (accommodation). Imagine a six-year-old who goes to an aquarium for the first time and calls the minnows "little fish" and the whales "big fish." In both cases the child is assimilating—attempting to fit a new experience into an existing scheme (in this case, the conception that all creatures that live in the water are fish). When her parents point out that, even though whales live in the water, they are mammals, not fish, the six-year-old begins to accommodate—to modify her existing scheme to fit the new experience she has encountered. Gradually (accommodations are made slowly, over repeated experiences), a new scheme forms that contains nonfish creatures that live in the water.

RELATIONSHIPS AMONG ORGANIZATION, ADAPTATION, AND SCHEMES   To give you a basic understanding of Piaget's ideas, we have talked about them as distinct elements. But the concepts of organization, adaptation, and schemes are all related. In their drive to be organized, individuals try to have a place for everything (accommodation) so they can put everything in its place (assimilation). The product of organization and adaptation is the creation of new schemes that allow individuals to organize at a higher level and to adapt more effectively.

EQUILIBRATION, DISEQUILIBRIUM, AND LEARNING   Piaget believed that people are driven to organize their knowledge in order to achieve the best possible adaptation to their environment. He calls this process *equilibration*. But what motivates people's drive toward equilibration? It is a state of *disequilibrium*, or a perceived discrepancy between an existing scheme and something new. In other words, when people encounter something that is inconsistent with or contradicts what they already know or believe, this experience produces a disequilibrium that they are driven to eliminate (assuming they are sufficiently interested in the new experience to begin with). A student may wonder why, for example, tomatoes and cucumbers are referred

Equilibration: tendency to organize schemes to allow better understanding of experiences

to as fruits in a science text since she has always referred to them as vegetables and has distinguished fruits from vegetables on the basis of sweetness. This discrepancy may cause the student to read the text carefully or to ask the teacher for further explanation. Gradually, the student reorganizes her thinking about the classification of fruits and vegetables in terms of edible plant roots, stems, leaves, and ovaries so that it is more consistent with the expert view. These processes are two sides of the learning coin: for equilibration to occur, disequilibrium must already have occurred. Disequilibrium can occur spontaneously within an individual through maturation and experience, or it can be stimulated by someone else (such as a teacher).

CONSTRUCTING KNOWLEDGE   Meaningful learning, then, occurs when people *create* new ideas, or knowledge (rules and hypotheses that explain things), from existing information (for example, facts, concepts, and procedures). To solve a problem, we have to search our memory for information that can be used to fashion a solution. Using information can mean experimenting, questioning, reflecting, discovering, inventing, and discussing. This process of creating knowledge to solve a problem and eliminate a disequilibrium is referred to by Piagetian psychologists and educators as **constructivism** (Blais, 1988; Brooks, 1990; Wheatley, 1991). It is a powerful notion that will reappear in a later chapter (Chapter 10) and in other forms. (The Discussion Questions at the end of each chapter are intended to stimulate constructivist thinking, as is the manner in which we encourage you to set up and use your journal for reflective thinking and teaching.)

STAGES OF COGNITIVE DEVELOPMENT

Organization and adaptation are what Piaget called *invariant functions*. This means that these thought processes function the same way for infants, children, adolescents, and adults. Schemes, however, are not invariant. They undergo systematic change at particular points in time. As a result, there are real differences between the ways younger children and older children think and between the ways children and adults think. The schemes of infants and toddlers, for example, are sensory and motor in nature. They are often referred to as *habits* or *reflexes*. In early childhood, schemes gradually become more mental in nature; during this period they are called *concepts* or *categories*. Finally, by late adolescence or early adulthood, schemes are very complex and result in what we call *strategic* or *planful* behavior.

On the basis of his studies, Piaget concluded that schemes evolve through four stages. Although these stages reflect a generally continuous pattern of cognitive development, children do not suddenly "jump" from one stage to the next. Their cognitive development follows a definite sequence, but they may occasionally use a more advanced kind of thinking or revert to a more primitive form. The *rate* at which a particular child proceeds through these stages varies, but Piaget believed the *sequence* is the same in all children.

Piaget's four stages are described in the following sections. To help you grasp the sequence of these stages, Table 2.2 briefly outlines the range of ages to which they generally apply and their distinguishing characteristics.

SENSORIMOTOR STAGE (INFANTS AND TODDLERS)   Up to the age of two, children acquire understanding primarily through sensory impressions and motor activities. Therefore, Piaget called this the *sensorimotor stage*. Because infants are unable to move around much on their own during the first months of postnatal existence, they develop schemes primarily by exploring their own bodies and senses.

Sensorimotor stage: schemes reflect sensory and motor experiences

Table 2.2	Piaget's Stages of Cognitive Development	
Stage	**Age Range**	**Characteristics**
Sensorimotor	Birth to two years	Develops schemes primarily through sense and motor activities. Recognizes permanence of objects not seen.
Preoperational	Two to seven years	Gradually acquires ability to conserve and decenter but not capable of operations and unable to mentally reverse actions.
Concrete operational	Seven to eleven years	Capable of operations but solves problems by generalizing from concrete experiences. Not able to manipulate conditions mentally unless they have been experienced.
Formal	Eleven years	Able to deal with abstractions, form hypotheses, solve problems systematically, engage in mental manipulations.

After toddlers learn to walk and manipulate things, however, they get into everything and build up a sizable repertoire of schemes involving external objects and situations.

An important cognitive development milestone, *object permanence*, occurs between the fourth and eighth months of this stage. Prior to this point, the phrase "out of sight, out of mind" is literally true. Infants treat objects that leave their field of vision as if they no longer exist. When they drop an object from their hands or when an object at which they are looking is covered, for example, they do not search for it. During the same period, however, intentional search behaviors become increasingly apparent.

Most children under two are able to use schemes they have mastered to engage in mental as well as physical trial-and-error behavior. By age two, toddlers' schemes have become more mental in nature. You can see this in the way toddlers imitate the behavior of others. They imitate people they have not previously observed, they imitate the behavior of animals, and, most important, they imitate even when the model is no longer present (this is called *deferred imitation*). These types of imitative behaviors show toddlers' increasing ability to think in terms of symbols.

PREOPERATIONAL STAGE (PRESCHOOL AND PRIMARY GRADES) The thinking of preschool and primary grade children (roughly two to seven years old) centers on mastery of symbols (such as words), which permits them to benefit much more from past experiences. Piaget believed that many symbols are derived from mental imitation and involve both visual images and bodily sensations (notice how the schemes of this stage incorporate and build on the schemes of the previous stage). Even though the thinking at this stage is much more sophisticated than that of one- and two-year-olds, preschool children are limited in their ability to use their new symbol-oriented schemes. From an adult perspective, their thinking and behavior are illogical.

Preoperational stage: child forms many new schemes but does not think logically

When Piaget used the term *operation*, he meant an action carried out through logical thinking. *Preoperational*, then, means prelogical. The main impediments to logical thinking that preschoolers have to overcome are *perceptual centration, irreversibility*, and *egocentrism*. You can see these impediments at work most clearly when children attempt to solve **conservation** problems, problems that test their ability to recognize that certain properties stay the same despite a change in appearance or position.

One of the best known conservation problems is conservation of continuous quantity. A child is taken to a quiet place by an experimenter, who then pours water (or juice or beans or whatever) into identical short glasses until the child agrees that each contains an equal amount. Then the water is poured from one of these glasses into a tall, thin glass. At that point the child is asked, "Is there more water in this glass (the experimenter points to the tall glass) or this one?" Immediately after the child answers, the experimenter asks, "Why do you think so?" If the child's response is evasive or vague, the experimenter continues to probe until the underlying thought processes become clear.

In carrying out this experiment (and many others similar to it) with children of different ages, Piaget discovered that children below the age of six or so maintain that there is more water in the tall, thin glass than in the short, squat glass. Even though they agree at the beginning of the experiment that the water in the two identical glasses is equal, young children stoutly insist that after the water has been poured the taller glass contains more. When asked, "Why do you think so?" many preschool children immediately and confidently reply, "Because it's taller." Children over the age of six or so, by contrast, are more likely to reply, "Well, it *looks* as if there's more water in this one because it's taller, but they're really the same."

One reason preoperational stage children have difficulty solving conservation problems (as well as other problems that require logical thinking) is **perceptual centration**. This is the very strong tendency to focus attention on only one characteristic of an object or aspect of a problem or event at a time. The young child focuses only on the height of the water in the two containers and ignores the differences in width and volume. Another way to put this is to say that the child has not yet mastered **decentration**—the ability to think of more than one quality at a time—and is therefore not inclined to contemplate alternatives.

The second impediment to logical thinking is **irreversibility**. This means that young children cannot mentally pour the water from the tall, thin glass back into the short, squat one (thereby proving to themselves that the glasses contain the same amount of water). For the same reason, these youngsters do not understand the logic behind simple mathematical reversals ($4 + 5 = 9$; $9 - 5 = 4$).

The third major impediment is **egocentrism**. When applied to preschool children, *egocentric* does not mean selfish or conceited. It means that youngsters find it difficult, if not impossible, to take another person's point of view. In their conversations and in experimental situations in which they are asked to describe how something would look if viewed by someone else, preschool children reveal that they often have difficulty seeing things from another person's perspective (Piaget & Inhelder, 1956). They seem to assume that others see things the same way they see them. As a result, attempts to explain the logic behind conservation are usually met with quizzical looks and the insistence (some would mistakenly call it stubbornness) that the tall, thin glass contains more water.

> **Perceptual centration, irreversibility, egocentrism: barriers to logical thought**

> **Egocentrism: assumption that others see things the same way**

CONCRETE OPERATIONAL STAGE (ELEMENTARY TO EARLY MIDDLE SCHOOL)

Through formal instruction, informal experiences, social contact, and maturation, children over the age of seven gradually become less influenced by perceptual centration, irreversibility, and egocentrism (DeVries, 1997). Schemes are developing that allow a greater understanding of such logic-based tasks as conservation (matter is neither created nor destroyed but simply changes shape or form or position), class inclusion (the construction of hierarchical relationships among related classes of items), and seriation (the arrangement of items in a particular order).

But operational thinking is limited to objects that are actually present or that children have experienced concretely and directly. For this reason, Piaget described the stage from approximately seven to eleven years as that of *concrete operations.* The nature of the concrete operational stage can be illustrated by the child's mastery of different kinds of conservation.

By the age of seven most children are able to correctly explain that water poured from a short, squat glass into a tall, thin glass is still the same amount of water. Being able to solve the water-pouring problem, however, does not guarantee that a seven-year-old will be able to solve a similar problem involving two balls of clay. A child who has just explained why a tall glass of water contains the same amount as a short one may inconsistently maintain a few moments later that rolling one of two equally sized balls of clay into an elongated shape causes the rolled one to become bigger.

Children in the primary and early elementary grades tend to react to each situation in terms of concrete experiences. The tendency to solve problems by generalizing from one situation to a similar situation does not occur with any degree of consistency until the end of the elementary school years.

Nevertheless, children in the concrete operational stage are often more capable of learning advanced concepts than most people realize. Kathleen Metz (1995) argues that Piaget's theory has been improperly interpreted as suggesting that formal science education should be delayed until children have started to demonstrate the capacity for formal operational reasoning. She provides evidence in support of the view that such abstract concepts as *theory, evidence,* and *hypothesis* begin to emerge during the elementary school years and are sufficiently understood by children that they should be included in science education programs.

Since most elementary grade students are in the concrete operational stage of development, science educators have concluded that children cannot think in hypothetical-deductive terms (e.g., "What if . . . ." "If I do such and such, then such and such should occur") but are limited to hands-on activities and to such descriptive forms of reasoning as observation, assigning objects to categories (class inclusion) and arranging objects in serial order (seriation). Metz cites evidence that preschool children begin to think in terms of simple categories and that most sixth graders can distinguish between theory and evidence. She also argues that Piaget's work with elementary school children indicates that although their thinking is based on concrete objects, they can construct from these experiences simple forms of such abstract concepts as time, speed, and probability. Consequently, she believes that elementary grade children can understand and carry out, in a simplified form, such advanced elements of scientific inquiry as posing questions, gathering and interpreting data, and revising one's theory on the basis of the data.

Although some Piagetian scholars (e.g., Kuhn, 1997) agree with Metz that children have the potential to design and carry out scientific inquiries, they caution that most children will be unable to truly understand the nature of scientific inquiry (such as changing one's beliefs in the light of contradictory evidence, drawing only conclusions that are supported by existing evidence, recalling and accurately summarizing the evidence that support one's conclusions, using the same methods and

Concrete operational stage: child is capable of mentally reversing actions but generalizes only from concrete experiences

Children who are within Piaget's preoperational stage of cognitive development have difficulty solving tasks that require logical reasoning because they focus on one aspect of a task at a time (perceptual centration), cannot reverse a sequence of steps in order to find the starting point of a problem (irreversibility), and cannot think of different ways of defining and solving problems (egocentrism).

logic from one inquiry to another) and use this understanding to regulate their subsequent behavior because of cognitive deficiencies that will not be overcome for several years. If, for example, you told a student at the concrete operational stage to assume that a feather could break a piece of glass and then asked him whether the deduction "If one hits the glass with a feather, then the glass will break" is true or false, he would likely respond that it is false because in his experience feathers do not break glass (Overton & Byrnes, 1991).

FORMAL OPERATIONAL STAGE (MIDDLE SCHOOL, HIGH SCHOOL, AND BEYOND)

When children *do* reach the point of being able to generalize and to engage in mental trial and error by thinking up hypotheses and testing them in their heads, Piaget said they have reached the stage of *formal operations.* The term *formal* reflects the ability to respond to the *form* of a problem rather than its content and to *form* hypotheses. For example, the formal operational thinker can read the analogies "5 is to 15 as 1 is to 3" and "Penny is to dollar as year is to century" and realize that, despite the different content, the form of the two problems is identical (both analogies are based on ratios). In the same way, the formal thinker can understand and use complex language forms: proverbs ("Strike while the iron is hot"), metaphor ("Procrastination is the thief of time"), sarcasm, and satire.

> **Formal operational stage:** child is able to deal with abstractions, form hypotheses, engage in mental manipulations

We can see the nature of formal operational thinking and how it differs from concrete operational thinking by looking at a simplified version of Piaget's rod-bending experiment. Adolescents are given a basin filled with water, a set of metal rods of varying lengths, and a set of weights. The rods are attached to the edge of the basin and the weights to the ends of the rods. The subject's task is to figure out how much weight is required to bend a rod just enough to touch the water. Let's say that our hypothetical subject picks out the longest rod in the set (which is 9 inches long), attaches it to the edge of the basin, and puts just enough weight on the end of it to get it to touch the water. This observation is then recorded. Successively shorter rods are selected, and the same procedure is carried out. At some point the subject comes to the 4-inch rod. This rod does not touch the water even when all of the weights have been attached to it. There are, however, three more rods, all of which are shorter than the last one tested.

This is where the formal and concrete operators part company. The formal operational thinker reasons that, if all of the available weights are not sufficient to bend the 4-inch rod enough to touch the water, the same will be true of the remaining rods. In essence, the rest of the experiment is done mentally and symbolically. The concrete operational thinker, however, continues trying out each rod and recording each observation independent of the others. Although both subjects reach the same conclusion, the formal operator does so through a more powerful and efficient process.

But remember that new schemes develop gradually. Even though adolescents can sometimes deal with mental abstractions representing concrete objects, most twelve-year-olds solve problems haphazardly, using trial and error. It is not until the end of the high school years that adolescents are likely to attack a problem by forming hypotheses, mentally sorting out solutions, and systematically testing the most promising leads.

Some interpreters of Piaget (for example, Ginsburg & Opper, 1988) note that a significant aspect of formal thought is that it causes the adolescent to concentrate more on possibilities than on realities. This is the ability that Erikson and others (for example, Kalbaugh & Haviland, 1991) suggest is instrumental in the emergence of the identity crisis. At the point when older adolescents can become aware of all the factors that have to be considered in choosing a career and can imagine what it might be like to be employed, some may feel so threatened and confused that they postpone the final choice. Yet the same capability can also help resolve the identity crisis because adolescents can reason about possibilities in a logical manner. An adolescent girl, for example, may consider working as a pediatrician, teacher, or child psychologist in an underprivileged environment because she has always enjoyed and sought out activities that allowed her to interact with children and has also been concerned with the effects of deprivation on development.

Although mastery of formal thought equips the older adolescent with impressive intellectual skills, it may also lead to a tendency for the burgeoning formal thinker to become preoccupied with abstract and theoretical matters. Herbert Ginsburg and Sylvia Opper interpret some of Piaget's observations on this point in the following way:

> In the intellectual sphere, the adolescent has a tendency to become involved in abstract and theoretical matters, constructing elaborate political theories or inventing complex philosophical doctrines. The adolescent may develop plans for the complete reorganization of society or indulge in metaphysical speculation. After discovering capabilities for abstract thought, he then proceeds to exercise them without restraint. Indeed, in the process of exploring these new abilities the adolescent sometimes loses touch with reality and feels that he can accomplish everything by thought alone. In the emotional sphere the adolescent now becomes capable of directing emotions at abstract ideals and not just toward people. Whereas earlier the adolescent could love his mother or hate a peer, now he can love freedom or hate exploitation. The adolescent has developed a new mode of life: the possible and the ideal captivate both mind and feeling. (1988, pp. 202–203)

David Elkind (1968) suggests that unrestrained theorizing about ideals without complete understanding of realities tends to make the young adolescent a militant rebel with little patience for parents or other adults who fail to find quick solutions to personal, social, and other problems. Only when the older adolescent begins to grasp the complexities of interpersonal relationships and of social and economic problems does more tempered understanding appear.

Elkind also suggests that the egocentrism of early childhood reappears in a different form as **adolescent egocentrism.** This occurs when high school students turn their new powers of thought on themselves and become introspective. The strong tendency to analyze self is projected on others. This helps explain why adolescents are so self-conscious: they assume their thoughts and actions are as central to others as to themselves. The major difference between the egocentrism of childhood and that of adolescence is summed up in Elkind's observation: "The child is egocentric in the sense that he is unable to take another person's point of view. The adolescent, on the other hand, takes the other person's point of view to an extreme degree" (1968, p. 153).

Elkind believes that adolescent egocentrism also explains why the peer group becomes such a potent force in high school. He observes:

> Adolescent egocentrism . . . accounts, in part, for the power of the peer group during this period. The adolescent is so concerned with the reactions of others toward him, particularly his peers, that he is willing to do many things which are opposed to all of his previous training and to his own best interests. At the same time, this egocentric impression that he is always on stage may help to account for the many and varied adolescent attention-getting maneuvers. (1968, p. 154)

Adolescent egocentrism: one's thoughts and actions are assumed to be as central to others as to oneself

Toward the end of adolescence, this form of exploitative egocentrism gradually declines. The young person comes to realize that other people are much more concerned with themselves and their problems than they are with him and his problems.

CRITICISMS OF PIAGET'S THEORY

UNDERESTIMATING CHILDREN'S CAPABILITIES   Among the thousands of articles that have been published in response to Piaget's findings are many that offer critiques of his work. Some psychologists argue that Piaget underestimated children's abilities not only because he imposed stringent criteria for inferring the presence of particular cognitive abilities, but also because the tasks he used were often complex and far removed from children's real-life experiences. The term *preoperational*, for instance, stresses what is absent rather than what is present. Within the last decade researchers have focused more on what preoperational children *can* do. The results (summarized by Bryant, 1984; Gelman & Baillargeon, 1983) suggest that preschoolers' cognitive abilities are more advanced in some areas than Piaget's work suggests.

| Piaget's theory underestimates children's abilities

OVERESTIMATING ADOLESCENTS' CAPABILITIES   Other evidence suggests that Piaget may have overestimated the formal thinking capabilities of adolescents. Research summarized by Constance Kamii (1984) revealed that only 20 to 25 percent of college freshmen were able to consistently use formal operational reasoning. Herman Epstein (1980) found that among a group of ninth graders, 32 percent were just beginning the concrete operational stage, 43 percent were well within the concrete operational stage, 15 percent were just entering the formal operational stage, and only 9 percent were mature formal operators. In addition, Norman Sprinthall and Richard Sprinthall (1987) reported that only 33 percent of a group of high school seniors could apply formal operational reasoning to scientific problem solving. Formal reasoning seems to be the exception, not the rule, throughout adolescence.

| Most adolescents are not formal operational thinkers

VAGUE EXPLANATIONS FOR COGNITIVE GROWTH   Piaget's theory has also been criticized for its vagueness in specifying the factors that are responsible for cognitive growth. Why, for example, do children give up conserving responses in favor of nonconserving responses at a particular age? On the basis of recent research, Robert Siegler (1994) believes that variability in children's thinking plays an influential role. For example, it is not uncommon to hear children use on successive occasions different forms of a given verb, as in "I ate it," "I eated it," and "I ated it." Similar variability has been found in the use of memory strategies (five-year-old and eight-year-old children do not always rehearse information they want to remember), addition rules, time-telling rules, and block-building tasks. Siegler's explanation is that variability gives the child a range of plausible options about how to deal with a particular problem. The child then tries them out in an attempt to see which one produces the best adaptation. Note the use of the qualifying word *plausible*. Most children do not try out any and all possible solutions to a problem. Instead, they stick to possibilities that are consistent with a problem's underlying principles.

CULTURAL DIFFERENCES   Questions have also been raised as to whether children from different cultures develop intellectually in the manner described by Piaget. The answer at this point is both yes and no. The sequence of stages appears to be universal, but the rate of development may vary from one culture to another (Dasen & Heron, 1981; Hughes & Noppe, 1991; Leadbeater, 1991; Rogoff & Chavajay, 1995).

| Sequence of stages uniform across cultures but rate of development varies

The average Eskimo child acquires the spatial concept of horizontalness faster than the average West African child. But many West African children (around the age of twelve or thirteen) understand conservation of quantity, weight, and volume sooner than Eskimo children do (Dasen & Heron, 1981). Although children in Western, industrialized societies (like ours) usually are not given baby-sitting responsibilities until they are at least ten years old because their high level of egocentrism prevents them from considering the needs of the other child, Mayan children in Mexican villages as young as five play this role because their culture stresses the development of cooperative behavior (Sameroff & McDonough, 1994).

Research conducted during the 1970s found that individuals living in non-Western cultures who had little formal education did not engage in formal operational thinking. Although these same people used concrete operational schemes when tested with the kinds of tasks used by Piaget, they usually did so at a later age than the Swiss children Piaget originally studied. This result was attributed to their lack of schooling, which left them unfamiliar with the language and conventions of formal testing. (Because school tasks emphasize logical forms of thinking, schooled individuals become proficient at such cognitive processes as organizing information into taxonomic categories, creating alternative ways of organizing information to satisfy different cognitive goals, understanding how two-dimensional drawings indicate the third dimension of depth, and formulating methods to deliberately memorize isolated bits of information.) But when concrete operational tasks were conducted with materials that were part of these people's everyday lives (such as asking children from Zambia to reproduce a pattern with strips of wire rather than with paper and pencil), they performed as well as Western children who drew the patterns on paper (Rogoff & Chavajay, 1995).

Now that you are familiar with Piaget's theory of cognitive development, you can formulate specific classroom applications. You might use the Suggestions for Teaching for the grade level you expect to teach as the basis for a section in your journal.

SUGGESTIONS FOR TEACHING IN YOUR CLASSROOM

Applying Piaget's Theory of Cognitive Development

General Guidelines

1 Focus on what children at each stage can do and avoid what they cannot meaningfully understand.

This implication must be interpreted carefully, as recent research has shown that children at the preoperational and concrete operational levels can do more than Piaget believes. In general, however, it is safe to say that since preoperational stage children (preschoolers, kindergartners, most first and some second graders) can use language and other symbols to stand for objects, they should be given many opportunities to describe and explain things through the use of artwork, body movement, role play, musical performance, and speech. Although the concepts of conservation, seriation, class inclusion, time, space, and number can be introduced, attempts at mastering them should probably be postponed until children are in the concrete operational stage.

Concrete operational stage children (grades 3–6) can be given opportunities to master such mental processes as ordering, seriating, classifying, reversing, multiplying, dividing, subtracting, and adding by manipulating concrete objects or symbols. Exercises that involve theorizing, hypothesizing, or generalizing about abstract ideas should be avoided.

Formal operational stage children (grades 7 through high school) can be given activities that require hypothetical-deductive reasoning, reflective thinking, analysis, synthesis, and evaluation.

2 **Because individuals differ in their rates of intellectual growth, gear instructional materials and activities to each student's developmental level.**

3 **Because intellectual growth occurs when individuals attempt to eliminate a disequilibrium, instructional lessons and materials that introduce new concepts should provoke interest and curiosity and be moderately challenging in order to maximize assimilation and accommodation.**

4 **Although information (facts, concepts, procedures) can be efficiently transmitted from teacher to student through direct instruction, knowledge (rules and hypotheses) is best created by each student through the mental and physical manipulation of information.**

Accordingly, lesson plans should also include opportunities for activity, manipulation, exploration, discussion, and application of information. Small-group science projects are one example of how this goal can be implemented.

5 **Since students' schemes at any given time are an outgrowth of earlier schemes, point out to them how new ideas relate to old ideas and allow students a better understanding of something. Memorization of information for its own sake should be avoided.**

6 **Begin lessons with concrete objects or ideas and gradually shift explanations to a more abstract and general level.**

Preschool, Elementary, and Middle School Grades[2]

1 **Become thoroughly familiar with Piaget's theory so that you will be aware of how your students organize and synthesize ideas. You may gain extra insight if you analyze your own thinking, since you are likely to discover that in some situations you operate at a concrete, rather than an abstract, level.**

Journal Entry
Ways to Apply Piaget's Theory (Preschool, Elementary, and Middle School Grades)

2 **If possible, assess the level and the type of thinking of each child in your class. Ask individual children to perform some of Piaget's experiments and spend most of your time listening to each child explain her reactions.**

---

[2] These guidelines are adapted from Bryant (1984); Bybee and Sund (1982); Elkind (1989); Ginsburg and Opper (1988); and Wadsworth (1989).

3 **Remember that learning through activity and direct experience is essential. Provide plenty of materials and opportunities for children to learn on their own.**

4 **Arrange situations to permit social interaction, so that children can learn from one another.**

Hearing others explain their views is a natural way for students to learn that not everyone sees things the same way. The placement of a few advanced thinkers with less mature thinkers is more likely to facilitate this process than is homogeneous grouping.

5 **Plan learning experiences to take into account the level of thinking attained by an individual or group.**

Encourage children to classify things on the basis of a single attribute before you expose them to problems that involve relationships among two or more attributes. Ask many questions, and give your students many opportunities to explain their interpretations of experiences so that you can remain aware of their level of thinking.

6 **Keep in mind the possibility that students may be influenced by egocentric speech and thought.**

Allow for the possibility that each child may assume that everyone else has the same conception of a word that he has. If confusion becomes apparent or if a child becomes impatient about failure to communicate, request an explanation in different terms. Or ask several children to explain their conception of an object or a situation.

Middle School and Secondary Grades[3]

Journal Entry
Ways to Apply Piaget's Theory (Middle School and Secondary Grades)

1 **Become well acquainted with the nature of concrete operational thinking and formal thought so that you can recognize when your students are resorting to either type or to a combination of the two.**

2 **To become aware of the type of thinking used by individual students, ask them to explain how they arrived at solutions to problems. Do this either as part of your classroom curriculum or in response to experimental situations similar to those devised by Piaget.**

3 **Teach students how to solve problems more systematically. (Suggestions for doing this will be provided in Chapters 8 and 9.)**

4 **Keep in mind that some high school students may be more interested in possibilities than in realities.**

If class discussions become unrealistically theoretical and hypothetical, call attention to facts and practical difficulties. If students are contemptuous of unsuccessful

---

[3] Many of these suggestions are derived from points made in Chapter 7 of *Young Children's Thinking* (Almy, Chittenden, & Miller, 1966).

attempts by adults to solve school, local, national, and international problems, point out the complexity of many situations involving conflicts of interest, perhaps by summarizing arguments from both sides.

5 **Allow for the possibility that younger adolescents may go through a period of egocentrism that will cause them to act as if they are always on stage and to be extremely concerned about the reactions of peers.**

Piaget and Vygotsky: The Role of Social Interaction and Instruction in Cognitive Development

From the time Piaget's work first became known to large numbers of American psychologists in the early 1960s until the 1980s, it was the dominant explanation of cognitive development. Not that Piaget didn't have his critics. As the last section made clear, many psychologists challenged one aspect or another of his work. But there were no competing explanations of cognitive development. Beginning in the early 1980s, however, the ideas of a Russian psychologist by the name of Lev Vygotsky began to appear in the psychological literature with increasing frequency. A contemporary of Piaget who died prematurely from tuberculosis in 1934, Vygotsky had very different views about the major forces that shape learning and thinking, particularly about the role of social interaction and formal instruction.

PIAGET'S VIEWS

Piaget believed that cognitive development is caused by two general factors: heredity and environmental experience. Heredity establishes the basic nature of physical structures (such as the brain), the development of physical structures, the existence of reflexes (sucking, grasping, crying), and the tendency to organize experiences and adapt to the environment (through assimilation, accommodation, and equilibration). Experience refers to the variety of interactions we have with the world. These interactions can be classified in three ways: physical experiences, mental experiences, and social experiences. Picking up a bunch of rocks and estimating their size and weight are physical experiences. Arranging the rocks in sequence from smallest to largest or lightest to heaviest is a mental experience. (Piaget used the term *logico-mathematical knowledge* because this type of knowledge is created from schemes based on logic and mathematics.) Watching other people behave, listening to other people's ideas, and discussing ideas with others are examples of social experience. Physical, mental, and social experiences occur spontaneously in the course of everyday living as well as formally as a part of classroom instruction.

Of these two general factors, Piaget believed that heredity is more influential than the various environmental experiences in determining the basic course and rate of cognitive development because heredity directly affects such fundamental processes as maturational growth, organization, and accommodation. Environmental experiences, particularly social interactions with adults and peers, have an indirect effect on cognitive development—they supply the stimulus for further development (Crain, 1992).

THE ROLE OF SOCIAL INTERACTION   When it comes to social experiences, Piaget clearly believed that peer interactions do more to spur cognitive development than do interactions with adults. The reason is that children are more likely to discuss, analyze, and debate the merits of another child's view of some issue (such as who should have which toy or what the rules of a game should be) than they are to take serious issue with an adult. The balance of power between children and adults is simply too unequal. Not only are most children quickly taught that adults know more and use superior reasoning, but also the adult always gets to have the last word: argue too long and it's off to bed with no dessert. But when children interact with one another, the outcome is more dependent on how well each child uses her wits.

Piaget: cognitive development more strongly influenced by peers than by adults

It is the need to understand the ideas of a peer or playmate in order to formulate responses to those ideas that leads to less egocentrism and the development of new, more complex mental schemes. Put another way, a strongly felt sense of cognitive conflict automatically impels the child to strive for a higher level of equilibrium. Formal instruction by an adult expert simply does not have the same impact regardless of how well designed it might be. That is why parents and teachers are often surprised to find children agreeing on some issue after having rejected an adult's explanation of the very same thing. Thus, educational programs that are patterned after Piaget's ideas usually provide many opportunities for children to interact socially and to discover through these interactions basic ideas about how the world works (Crain, 1992; Rogoff, 1990; Tudge & Winterhoff, 1993).

As proof of the feasibility of this approach, William Damon and Erin Phelps (1991) describe a study they conducted in which fourth graders who worked collaboratively were more successful than similar students who did not work collaboratively at solving mathematical, spatial reasoning, and balance scale problems. As the authors put it, this "is a process that strongly facilitates intellectual growth, because it forces subjects to bring to consciousness the ideas that they are just beginning to grasp intuitively" (p. 182).

THE ROLE OF INSTRUCTION   Even though Piaget believed that formal instruction by expert adults will not significantly stimulate cognitive development, not all American psychologists have been willing to accept this conclusion at face value. Over the past twenty years, dozens of experiments have been conducted to determine whether it is possible to teach preoperational stage children to understand and use concrete operational schemes or to teach students in the concrete operational stage to grasp formal operational reasoning.

The main conclusion of psychologists who have analyzed and evaluated this body of research is, unfortunately, one of uncertainty (see, for example, Case, 1975; Good & Brophy, 1995; Nagy & Griffiths, 1982; Sprinthall, Sprinthall, & Oja, 1994). Because of shortcomings in the way some studies were carried out and disagreements about what constitutes evidence of true concrete operational thinking or formal operational thinking, a decisive answer to this question is simply not available. Nevertheless, something of value can be gleaned from the research on cognitive acceleration. Two recent analyses of this literature (Sigelman & Shaffer, 1991; Sprinthall, Sprinthall, & Oja, 1994) conclude that children who are in the process of developing the schemes that will govern the next stage of cognitive functioning can, with good-quality instruction, be helped to refine those schemes a bit faster than would normally be the case. For example, teachers can teach the principle of conservation by using simple explanations and concrete materials and by allowing children to manipulate the materials. This means that teachers should nurture the process of cognitive growth at any particular stage by presenting lessons in a form that is consistent with but slightly more advanced than the students' existing schemes. The objective here is to help students assimilate and accommodate new and different experiences as efficiently as possible.

Instruction can accelerate development of schemes that have begun to form

VYGOTSKY'S VIEWS

Whereas Piaget saw cognitive development arising from attempts to overcome cognitive conflict through the internal and genetically determined processes of assimilation, accommodation, and equilibration, Vygotsky believed that such development is largely due to social processes, particularly interactions with others who are more skilled and competent in what he called the technologies, or psychological tools, of a culture (Rogoff, 1990; Tudge & Winterhoff, 1993).

THE ROLE OF SOCIAL INTERACTION   As cultures develop, people create such psychological tools as speech, writing, and numbering to help them master their environment. Early explorers, for example, created maps to help them represent where they had been, communicate that knowledge to others, and plan future trips. Children are first introduced to a culture's major psychological tools through social

Jean Piaget believes that children's schemes develop more quickly when children interact with one another than when they interact with adults. But Lev Vygotsky believes that children learn more from the instructional interactions they have with those who are more intellectually advanced, particularly if the instruction is designed to fall within the child's zone of proximal development.

interactions with their parents and later through more formal interactions with classroom teachers.

Vygotsky: cognitive development more strongly influenced by those more intellectually advanced

Unlike Piaget, Vygotsky believed that children gain significantly from the knowledge and conceptual tools handed down to them by those who are more intellectually advanced, be they peers, older children, or adults. Consider, for example, a simple concept like grandmother. In the absence of formal instruction, a primary grade child's concept of grandmother is likely to be very narrow in scope because it is based on personal experience ("My grandmother is seventy years old, has gray hair, wears glasses, and makes the best apple pie"). But when children are helped to understand the basic nature of the concept with such instructional tools as family tree diagrams, they understand the notion of grandmother (and other types of relatives) on a broader and more general basis. They can then use this concept to compare family structures with friends and, later on, do genealogical research. This example also reveals Vygotsky's basic view of instruction. Its basic purpose is not simply to add one piece of knowledge to another like pennies in a piggy bank, but to stimulate and guide cognitive development (Crain, 1992; Rogoff, 1990).

THE ROLE OF INSTRUCTION   Vygotsky drew a distinction between the type of information that preschool children learn and the type of information that children learn (or should learn) when they attend school. During early childhood children acquire what Vygotsky called **spontaneous concepts**. That is, they learn various facts and concepts and rules (such as how to speak one's native language and how to classify objects in one's environment), but they do so for the most part as a byproduct of such other activities as engaging in play and communicating with parents and playmates. This kind of knowledge is unsystematic, unconscious, and directed at the child's everyday concrete experiences. Hence Vygotsky's use of the term *spontaneous*.

Schooling, however, should be directed to the learning of what Vygotsky called **scientific concepts**. Scientific concepts are the psychological tools mentioned earlier that allow us to consciously and systematically manipulate our environment. Common examples of such tools are language, formulas, memory techniques, concepts, rules, symbols, and signs. Vygotsky believed that the proper development of a child's mind depended on learning how to use these psychological tools, and this would occur only if classroom instruction was properly designed. This meant providing students with explicit and clear verbal definitions as a first step.

Contemporary Russian psychologists have extended Vygotsky's notions of spontaneous and scientific concepts. They use the term **empirical learning** to refer to the way in which young children acquire spontaneous concepts. The hallmark of empirical learning is that the most observable characteristics of objects and events are noticed and used as a basis for forming general concepts. The main limitation of this approach is that salient characteristics are not necessarily critical or defining characteristics, and it is the latter that form the basis of correct concept formation. For example, in the absence of formal instruction, children come to believe that any utterance that has two or more words is a sentence, that whales are fish, and that bamboo is not a type of grass.

Vygotsky: help students learn how to use psychological tools

Theoretical learning, on the other hand, uses psychological tools to learn scientific concepts. As these general tools are used repeatedly with a variety of problems, they are gradually internalized and generalized to a wide variety of settings and problem types. Good-quality instruction, in this view, is aimed at helping children move from the very practical empirical learning to the more general theoretical learning and from using psychological tools overtly with the aid of an adult to using these tools by themselves mentally (Karpov & Bransford, 1995).

Here's an example that compares the efficacy of the empirical and theoretical approaches: Two groups of six-year-old children were taught how to write the twenty-two letters of the Russian alphabet. Group 1 was taught using the empirical approach. The teacher gave the students a model of each letter, showed them how to write each one, and also gave a verbal explanation of how to write each letter. The students then copied each letter under the teacher's supervision. When they produced an acceptable copy of a letter, the next one was given. Group 2 was taught using the theoretical approach. First, students were taught to analyze the shape of each letter so they could identify where the direction of the contour of each line changed. Then they were to place dots in those locations outlining the change in contour. Finally, they were to reproduce the pattern of dots on another part of the page and connect the dots with a pencil.

The speed with which the children in each group learned to accurately produce the letters of the alphabet differed by quite a large margin. The average student in the empirical group needed about 170 trials to learn the first letter and about 20 trials to write the last letter. The number of trials taken to learn all twenty-two letters was about 1,230. The average student in the theoretical group required only about 14 trials to learn how to correctly write the first letter, and from the eighth letter on needed only one trial per letter. The number of trials needed to learn all twenty-two letters for the second group was about 60. Furthermore, these students were able to use the general method they were taught to help them learn to write the letters of the Latin and Arab alphabets (Karpov & Bransford, 1995).

The discussion of empirical and theoretical learning illustrates Vygotsky's belief that well-designed instruction is like a magnet. If it is aimed slightly ahead of what children know and can do at the present time, it will pull them along, helping them master things they cannot learn on their own. We can illustrate this idea by paraphrasing an experiment described by Vygotsky (1986). He gave two eight-year-olds of average ability problems that were a bit too difficult for them to solve on their own. (Although Vygotsky did not specify what types of problems they were, imagine that they were math problems.) He then tried to help the children solve the problems by giving them leading questions and hints. With this aid he found that one child was able to solve problems designed for twelve-year-olds, whereas the other child could reach only a nine-year-old level.

Vygotsky referred to the difference between what a child can do on his own versus what can be accomplished with some assistance as the zone of proximal development (ZPD). The size of the first eight-year-old's zone is 4, whereas the second child has a zone of 1. According to Vygotsky, students with wider zones are likely to experience greater cognitive development when instruction is pitched just above the lower limit of their ZPD than will students with narrower zones because the former are in a better position to capitalize on the instruction.

Helping students answer difficult questions or solve problems by giving them hints or asking leading questions is an example of a technique called scaffolding. Just as a building that is under construction is supported by external scaffolding until it is strong enough to stand on its own, Vygotsky recommended that teachers similarly support learning in its early phases. The purpose of scaffolding is to help students acquire knowledge and skills they would not have learned on their own. As the student demonstrates mastery over the content in question, the learning aids are faded and removed. Scaffolding techniques that are likely to help students traverse their ZPD include prompts, suggestions, checklists, modeling, rewards, feedback, cognitive structuring (using such devices as theories, categories, labels, and rules for helping students organize and understand ideas), and questioning (Gallimore & Tharp, 1990;

Vygotsky: cognitive development due to instruction in zone of proximal development

Ratner, 1991). As students approach the upper limit of their ZPD, their behavior becomes smoother, more internalized, and more automatized. Any assistance offered at this level is likely to be perceived as disruptive and irritating.

Vygotsky's notion of producing cognitive development by embedding instruction within a student's zone of proximal development is an attractive one and has many implications for instruction. In Chapter 8, for example, we will describe how this notion was used to improve the reading comprehension skills of low-achieving seventh graders. Whether it can be used to greatly accelerate students' passage through Piaget's stages remains to be seen.

Using Technology to Promote Cognitive Development

As we mentioned earlier, Piaget and Vygotsky believed that people use physical, mental, and social experiences to construct personal conceptions (schemes) of what the world is like. Although there are numerous opportunities throughout the course of each day to watch what other people do, to try out ideas, and to interact with others, we are normally limited to the physical and social stimuli that make up our immediate environment because of such factors as distance, time, and cost. Technology, however, greatly reduces these limitations and thus has the potential to expand the range of our experiences. For instance, there are electronic tools for **computer conferencing** (also known as *Web-based conferencing* or *on-line discussion forums*), **videoconferencing**, group brainstorming, expert feedback, **real-time chatting**, peer debating, and polling student opinions (Fetterman, 1996; Harasim, Hiltz, Teles, & Turoff, 1995). Computer conferencing occurs when individuals at different locations log onto a computer site, voice their view on a particular subject, and/or respond to the views of others. Videoconferencing involves a real-time visual communication with one or more individuals in other locations. Real-time chatting is similar to videoconferencing except that the conversations occur on a computer network and are written. With all these new instructional tools, technology is bringing new learning forums and opportunities into our schools. But how do these technological advances relate to theories of cognitive development?

TECHNOLOGY APPLIED TO PIAGET

There are at least two main ways in which technology can be used in schools to support Piaget's original ideas about the cognitive development of young children: (1) as a simulation tool, or microworld, for displaying knowledge and repairing misconceptions and errors in thinking, and (2) as a source for same-age peers to debate issues, thereby fostering cognitive conflict and disequilibrium.

Computers provide many routes to knowledge and can help restructure common student misconceptions (for example, that the seasons are caused by the closeness of the earth to the sun or that electrical current is equal in all parts of a circuit). One way technology can overcome such misconceptions is to create explorable **microworlds**, or simulated learning environments, that allow students to get a sense of how things work in the real world (Nickerson, 1995). One such microworld, the Geometric Supposer, provides students with an electronic drawing board to test mathematical hypotheses while constructing, measuring, and investigating figures such as triangles, quadrilaterals, and circles (Lampert, 1995, Schwartz, 1995). Microworlds foster cognitive development by encouraging student exploration, student control, and visual representation of abstract ideas.

A **microcomputer-based laboratory (MBL)** can also be used to build on existing knowledge and correct misconceptions. In an MBL, one or more sensors are attached to a microcomputer to generate graphs of physical reactions. The following anecdote illustrates how helpful an MBL can be. When seventh- and eighth-grade students were asked to draw a graph depicting how fast a bicyclist travels uphill, downhill, and on flat stretches, their products represented the hills and valleys rather than the bicyclist's speed. That is, they drew an ascending line to represent the bicyclist's speed going uphill without realizing that such a line represented the downhill portion of the journey since it indicated increasing speed. In effect, they drew pictures that represented the exact opposite of what they were asked to represent. The students' graph-interpretation skills were significantly improved by having them work with an MBL. As the student applied a source of energy to one of the sensors—heating up and allowing to cool down a beaker of water, for example—a corresponding graphic representation was instantly created on the computer's screen (Kozma, 1991).

MBL sensors and probes have been developed since the late 1970s for such variables as temperature, heat, force, brain waves, heart rate, voltage, and humidity to help clarify confusing laws of nature (Ruopp, Gal, Drayton, & Pfister, 1993). In a review of twenty MBL studies, Mary Nakhleh (1994) found that MBL applications show promise in altering or restructuring students' faulty understandings of key science concepts. Evidently, MBLs foster important cognitive changes by representing information in multiple ways and graphing information quickly enough for connections between symbolic representations and the real world to be made.

A second way to put Piaget's ideas into practice is to use technology to promote cognitive conflict. Remember that, according to Piaget, cognitive development is contingent on students confronting others who have contradictory thoughts and claims,

> **Computer-based simulations promote exploration and visual representations of abstract ideas, and correct misconceptions**

Computer-based technology can be used to promote cognitive development in ways that are consistent with both Piaget's and Vygotsky's views.

thereby creating internal tension and conflict. When students notice a discrepancy or a contradiction from what they believe, they are motivated to find more information and move back to a state of equilibrium. One way to accomplish this goal is to have students debate with peers over a computer network. Curt Bonk and Jack Cummings (1998), for example, discuss how World Wide Web–based debates can be used to get students to reflect on the different positions people take on controversial issues. Students are also encouraged to consult the original source material used by their opponents. Such a technique, they argue, enhances the quality of student rebuttals and reaction papers. The advantage of a computer network, as we pointed out earlier, is that the peers one debates can be students in the class down the hall, students in another school district, students in another state, or even students in another country. This kind of easy access to others greatly increases the probability that students will encounter people who hold truly divergent views on issues.

TECHNOLOGY APPLIED TO VYGOTSKY

As with Piaget, there are at least two ways to link educational technology with the ideas of Vygotsky: (1) using the computer as an expert peer or collaborative partner to support skills and strategies that can be internalized by the learner, and (2) using the computer as a tool to link learners to more knowledgeable peers and experts, who establish a master-novice apprenticeship and scaffold the student's learning.

Computer programs can act as expert collaborative partners

Vygotsky believed that children gain significantly from the knowledge and conceptual tools handed down to them by those who are more intellectually advanced, be they peers, older children, or adults. Roy Pea (1985) and Gavriel Salomon (1988) were among the first to suggest that the computer might play the same role as more capable tutors with such tasks as writing an essay or reading a book. Basically, the computer is programmed to provide prompts and expert guidance during reading and writing tasks. These supports, or scaffolds, are gradually faded as students become more competent at regulating their own behavior. According to some researchers (Bereiter & Scardamalia, 1987), such support is vital in writing, since young children often lack the cognitive resources and skills to move beyond simple knowledge telling in their compositions. Salomon, who helped develop both the Reading Partner and Writing Partner software tools, found that they improved children's reading comprehension, essay writing, effort, and awareness of useful self-questioning strategies (Salomon, Globerson, & Guterman, 1989; Zellermayer, Salomon, Globerson, & Givon). Other studies, however, have not always reported such positive results (Bonk & Reynolds, 1992; Daiute, 1985; Reynolds & Bonk, 1996).

The second technology-based technique that has been derived from Vygotsky's view of cognitive development is the **cognitive apprenticeship** (Bonk & Cunningham, 1998; Brown, Collins, & Duguid, 1989). Like the traditional master-apprentice relationship in the skilled crafts and trades, a mentor works closely with a learner to develop the learner's cognitive skills. Also like the traditional apprenticeship, mentors provide students with real-life tasks that are to be performed under realistic conditions. The learner moves from newcomer to expert by first observing the mentor and then participating in some tasks. Gradually, there is a shift in responsibility for solving the task from the expert or teacher to the student as the student moves from the fringes of the community to a more central role within it. As that happens, new skills are tested and hopefully internalized.

When this master-apprentice relationship occurs on a computer network, it is called a **teleapprenticeship** (Levin, Kim, & Riel, 1990; Teles, 1993). The education and technology literature is filled with examples of teleapprenticeships in

K-12 education (Schrum & Berenfeld, 1997). For instance, international weather projects such as the Kids as Global Scientists (KGS) project (Songer, 1998), the Collaborative Visualization (CoVis) project (Edelson, Pea, & Gomez, 1996; Pea, 1993), and the Global Learning and Observations to Benefit the Environment (GLOBE) program (Singletary & Jordan, 1996) all involve students in genuine scientific data collection and reporting. The collaborative relationships that students establish with peers and mentors creates in students a strong sense of participation in what is called a community of practice.

Richard Ruopp et al. (1993) documented how an electronic community of physics teachers, in a project called Labnet, was able to use microcomputer-based laboratories (MBLs) to get students to share and compare their experimental findings across sites, while simultaneously providing a vehicle for teacher pooling of talents and discussion of lesson plans. Such a project is a prime example of two-tiered scaffolding (Gaffney & Anderson, 1991), wherein consultants and experts scaffolded teachers, who in turn scaffolded students. With the rise in telecommunications and collaborative technologies for the Internet, the possibilities for working on-line with specialists, practitioners, or content experts is bound to increase.

Piaget, Kohlberg, and Gilligan: Moral Development

PIAGET'S ANALYSIS OF THE MORAL JUDGMENT OF THE CHILD

Because he was intrigued by *all* aspects of children's thinking, Piaget became interested in moral development. He began his study of morality by observing how children played marbles. (He first took the trouble to learn the game himself, so that he would be able to understand the subtleties of the conception.) Piaget discovered that interpretations of rules followed by participants in marble games changed with age.

AGE CHANGES IN INTERPRETATION OF RULES   Four- to seven-year-olds just learning the game seemed to view rules as interesting examples of the social behavior of older children. They did not understand the rules but tried to go along with them. Seven- to ten-year-olds regarded rules as sacred pronouncements handed down by older children or adults. At about the age of eleven or twelve, children began to see rules as agreements reached by mutual consent. Piaget concluded that younger children see rules as absolute and external.

Even though children ranging from the age of four to about ten do not question rules, they may frequently break them because they do not understand rules completely. After the age of eleven or so, children become increasingly capable of grasping why rules are necessary. At that point, Piaget concluded, they tend to lose interest in adult-imposed regulations and take delight in formulating their own variations of rules to fit a particular situation. Piaget illustrated this point by describing how a group of ten- and eleven-year-old boys prepared for a snowball fight (1965, p. 50). They divided themselves into teams, elected officers, decided on rules to govern the distances from which the snowballs could be thrown, and agreed on a system of punishments for those who violated the rules. Even though they spent a substantial amount of playtime engaging in such preliminary discussions, they seemed to thoroughly enjoy their newly discovered ability to make up rules to supplant those that had previously been imposed on them by their elders.

MORAL REALISM VERSUS MORAL RELATIVISM   The way children of different ages responded to rules so intrigued Piaget that he decided to use the interview method to obtain more systematic information about moral development. He made up pairs of stories and asked children of different ages to discuss them. Here is a typical pair of stories:

> A: There was a little boy called Julian. His father had gone out and Julian thought it would be fun to play with father's ink-pot. First he played with the pen, and then he made a little blot on the table cloth.

> B: A little boy who was called Augustus once noticed that his father's ink-pot was empty. One day that his father was away he thought of filling the ink-pot so as to help his father, and so that he should find it full when he came home. But while he was opening the ink-bottle he made a big blot on the table cloth. (1965, p. 122)

After reading these stories, Piaget asked, "Are these children equally guilty? Which of the two is naughtiest, and why?" As was the case with interpretations of rules, Piaget found that younger children reacted to these stories differently from older children. The younger children maintained that Augustus was more guilty than Julian because he had made a bigger inkblot on the tablecloth. They took no account of the fact that Julian was misbehaving and that Augustus was trying to help his father. Older children, however, were more likely to base their judgment of guilt on the intent of each child.

Piaget referred to the moral thinking of children up to the age of ten or so as the **morality of constraint,** but he also calls it *moral realism.* (Remember our definition of *decentration* in the earlier discussion of Piaget's theory. How do you think the young child's lack of decentration might affect her moral reasoning?) The thinking of children of eleven or older Piaget called the **morality of cooperation.** He also occasionally uses the term *moral relativism.* Piaget concluded that the two basic types of moral reasoning differ in several ways. We summarize these differences in Table 2.3.

Morality of constraint (moral realism): sacred rules, no exceptions, no allowance for intentions, consequences determine guilt

Morality of cooperation (moral relativism): rules are flexible, intent important in determining guilt

KOHLBERG'S DESCRIPTION OF MORAL DEVELOPMENT

Just as James Marcia has elaborated Erikson's concept of identity formation, Lawrence Kohlberg has elaborated Piaget's ideas on moral thinking. Kohlberg believes that (1) moral reasoning proceeds through fixed stages, and (2) moral development can be accelerated through instruction.

KOHLBERG'S USE OF MORAL DILEMMAS   As a graduate student at the University of Chicago in the 1950s, Lawrence Kohlberg became fascinated by Piaget's studies of moral development. He decided to expand on Piaget's original research by making up stories involving moral dilemmas that would be more appropriate for older children. Here is the story that is most often mentioned in discussions of his work:

> In Europe a woman was near death from cancer. One drug might save her, a form of radium that a druggist in the same town had recently discovered. The druggist was charging $2,000, ten times what the drug cost him to make. The sick woman's husband, Heinz, went to everyone he knew to borrow the money, but he could only get together about half of what it cost.

Table 2.3	Morality of Constraint versus Morality of Cooperation
Morality of Constraint (Typical of Six-year-olds)	**Morality of Cooperation (Typical of Twelve-year-olds)**
Holds single, absolute moral perspective (behavior is right or wrong)	Is aware of different viewpoints regarding rules
Believes rules are unchangeable	Believes rules are flexible
Determines extent of guilt by amount of damage	Considers the wrongdoers' intentions when evaluating guilt
Defines moral wrongness in terms of what is forbidden or punished	Defines moral wrongness in terms of violation of spirit of cooperation
(Notice that these first four differences call attention to the tendency for children below the age of ten or so to think of rules as sacred pronouncements handed down by external authority.)	
Believes punishment should stress atonement and does not need to "fit the crime"	Believes punishment should involve either restitution or suffering the same fate as one's victim
Believes peer aggression should be punished by an external authority	Believes peer aggression should be punished by retaliatory behavior on the part of the victim*
Believes children should obey rules because they are established by those in authority	Believes children should obey rules because of mutual concerns for rights of others
(Notice how these last three differences call attention to the tendency for children above the age of ten or so to see rules as mutual agreements among equals.)	

*Beyond the age of twelve, adolescents increasingly affirm that reciprocal reactions, or "getting back," should be a response to good behavior, not bad.

SOURCES: Freely adapted from interpretations of Piaget (1932) by Kohlberg (1969) and Lickona (1976).

He told the druggist that his wife was dying and asked him to sell it cheaper or let him pay later, but the druggist said "No." The husband got desperate and broke into the man's store to steal the drug for his wife. Should the husband have done that? Why? (1969, p. 376)

KOHLBERG'S SIX STAGES OF MORAL REASONING   After analyzing the responses of ten- to sixteen-year-olds to this and similar moral dilemmas, Kohlberg (1963) eventually developed a description of six stages of moral reasoning. Be forewarned, however, that Kohlberg has revised some of his original stage designations and that descriptions of the stages have been modified since he first proposed them. In different discussions of his stages, therefore, you may encounter varying descriptions. The outline presented in Table 2.4 is a composite summary of the sequence of moral development as it has been described by Kohlberg, but you should expect to find differences if you read other accounts of his theory.

The scoring system Kohlberg developed to evaluate a given response to a moral dilemma is extremely complex. Furthermore, the responses of subjects are lengthy and may feature arguments about a particular decision. To help you understand a bit more about each Kohlberg stage, simplified examples of responses to a dilemma

Table 2.4	Kohlberg's Stages of Moral Reasoning

LEVEL 1: PRECONVENTIONAL MORALITY. (Typical of children up to the age of nine. Called *preconventional* because young children do not really understand the conventions or rules of a society.)

Stage 1 Punishment-obedience orientation. The physical consequences of an action determine goodness or badness. Those in authority have superior power and should be obeyed. Punishment should be avoided by staying out of trouble.

Stage 2 Instrumental relativist orientation. An action is judged to be right if it is instrumental in satisfying one's own needs or involves an even exchange. Obeying rules should bring some sort of benefit in return.

LEVEL 2: CONVENTIONAL MORALITY. (Typical of nine- to twenty-year-olds. Called *conventional* since most nine- to twenty-year-olds conform to the conventions of society because they *are* the rules of a society.)

Stage 3 Good boy–nice girl orientation. The right action is one that would be carried out by someone whose behavior is likely to please or impress others.

Stage 4 Law-and-order orientation. To maintain the social order, fixed rules must be established and obeyed. It is essential to respect authority.

LEVEL 3: POSTCONVENTIONAL MORALITY. (Usually reached only after the age of twenty and only by a small proportion of adults. Called *postconventional* because the moral principles that underlie the conventions of a society are understood.)

Stage 5 Social contract orientation. Rules needed to maintain the social order should be based not on blind obedience to authority but on mutual agreement. At the same time, the rights of the individual should be protected.

Stage 6 Universal ethical principle orientation. Moral decisions should be made in terms of self-chosen ethical principles. Once principles are chosen, they should be applied in consistent ways.*

* In an article published in 1978, several years after Kohlberg had originally described the six stages, he described the last stage as an essentially theoretical ideal that is rarely encountered in real life.

SOURCE: Based on descriptions in Kohlberg (1969, 1976, 1978).

such as that faced by Heinz are noted. For maximum clarity, only brief typical responses to the question "Why shouldn't you steal from a store?" are mentioned.

Preconventional morality: avoid punishment, receive benefits in return

Stage 1: punishment-obedience orientation. "You might get caught." (The physical consequences of an action determine goodness or badness.)

Stage 2: instrumental relativist orientation. "You shouldn't steal something from a store, and the store owner shouldn't steal things that belong to you." (Obedience to laws should involve an even exchange.)

Conventional morality: impress others, respect authority

Stage 3: good boy–nice girl orientation. "Your parents will be proud of you if you are honest." (The right action is one that will impress others.)

Stage 4: law-and-order orientation. "It's against the law, and if we don't obey laws, our whole society might fall apart." (To maintain the social order, fixed rules must be obeyed.)

Postconventional morality: mutual agreements, consistent principles

Stage 5: social contract orientation. "Under certain circumstances laws may have to be disregarded—if a person's life depends on breaking a law, for instance." (Rules should involve mutual agreements; the rights of the individual should be protected.)

Stage 6: universal ethical principle orientation. "You need to weigh all the factors and then try to make the most appropriate decision in a given situation. Sometimes it would be morally wrong *not* to steal." (Moral decisions should be based on consistent applications of self-chosen ethical principles.)

CRITICISMS AND EVALUATIONS OF KOHLBERG'S THEORY   Is Kohlberg's contention that moral reasoning proceeds through a fixed universal sequence of stages accurate? Based on analysis of research on moral development, Martin Hoffman (1980) feels that although Kohlberg's sequence of stages may not be true of every individual in every culture, it may provide a useful general description of how moral reasoning develops in American society. Carol Gilligan (1979), whose position we will discuss in detail later on, has proposed two somewhat different sequences that reflect differences in male and female socialization.

What about Kohlberg's view that moral development can be accelerated through direct instruction? Is this another "mission impossible," as some critics contend? Research on this question has produced some limited but moderately positive results. Most of these studies have used a teaching method known as *direct discussion* or *dilemma discussion*. After reading a set of moral dilemmas (like the one about Heinz and the cancer drug) and identifying those issues that could help resolve the dilemma, students, under the teacher's guidance, discuss the different ways each of them chose to resolve the dilemma. This process can involve challenging one another's thinking, reexamining assumptions, building lines of argument, and responding to counterarguments.

Alan Lockwood (1978), after summarizing the findings of almost a dozen studies on acceleration of moral reasoning, concludes that the strongest effects (about half a stage increase in reasoning) occurred among individuals whose reasoning reflected stages 2 and 3. The effect of the instruction varied considerably from one subject to another. Some individuals showed substantial increases in reasoning; others showed no change. A more recent and comprehensive review of research on this topic by Andre Schlaefli, James Rest, and Stephen Thoma (1985) revealed similar conclusions. The authors found that moral education programs produced modest positive effects. They also found that the strongest effects were obtained with adult subjects.

Paul Vitz (1990) criticizes the use of moral dilemmas on the grounds that they are too far removed from the kinds of everyday social interactions in which children and adolescents engage. He prefers instead the use of narrative stories, be they fictional or real accounts of others, because they portray such basic moral values as honesty, compassion, fairness, and hard work in an understandable context.

Moral education programs may produce modest acceleration in moral development

EDUCATIONAL IMPLICATIONS OF KOHLBERG'S THEORY   Carol Harding and Kenneth Snyder (1991) believe that teachers can make productive use of contemporary films to illustrate moral dilemmas mainly because film is an attractive medium to students, and several types of moral dilemmas are often portrayed in the space of about two hours. To highlight the dilemma of the rights of the individual versus the rights of others in a community, Harding and Snyder recommend the films *Platoon* and *Wall Street*. The former is a story about the Vietnam War and contains scenes of American soldiers burning villages and abusing villagers who are suspected of having ties to or of being the enemy. In response to such scenes, students can be asked such questions as, "Should the enemy in war be granted certain rights, or is personal survival more important?" *Wall Street* is a story about a corporate raider who uses borrowed money to take control of public companies and then sells off the assets (thereby eliminating people's jobs) to enrich himself.

The Tom Snyder educational software company offers a series of computer-based programs titled Decisions, Decisions, in which students identify and discuss moral dilemmas such as protecting the environment or using drugs. Students discuss each situation and choose a response within the program as a group. Each response is stored by the program and in turn affects the development and outcome of the following situations to illustrate that events do not occur in isolation and that all decisions have consequences.

If films or computer programs are not available but you occasionally wish to engage your students in a discussion of moral dilemmas, the daily newspaper is an excellent source of material. Biology teachers, for example, can point to stories of the conflicts produced by machines that keep comatose patients alive or by medical practices based on genetic engineering. Other science teachers might bring in articles that describe the moral dilemma produced by the debate over nuclear power versus fossil fuel. Civics or government teachers could use news items that reflect the dilemma that arises when freedom of speech conflicts with the need to curtail racism.

GILLIGAN'S VIEW OF IDENTITY AND MORAL DEVELOPMENT

Carol Gilligan (1982, 1988) argues that Erikson's view of identity development and Kohlberg's view of moral development more accurately describe what occurs with adolescent males than with adolescent females. In her view, Erikson's and Kohlberg's ideas emphasize separation from parental authority and societal conventions. Instead of remaining loyal to adult authority, individuals as they mature shift their loyalty to abstract principles (for example, self-reliance, independence, justice, and fairness). This process of detachment allows adolescents to assume a more equal status with adults. It's almost as if adolescents are saying, "You have your life, and I have mine; you don't intrude on mine, and I won't intrude on yours."

But, Gilligan argues, many adolescent females have a different primary concern. They care less about separation and independence and more about remaining loyal to others through expressions of caring, understanding, and sharing of experiences.

Carol Gilligan believes that Erikson's theory of identity development and Kohlberg's theory of moral development do not accurately describe the course of identity formation and moral reasoning in females. She believes that adolescent females place a higher value on caring, understanding, and sharing of experiences than they do on independence, self-reliance, and justice.

Detachment for these female adolescents is a moral problem rather than a sought-after developmental milestone. The problem for them is how to become autonomous while also being caring and connected.

Given this view, Gilligan feels that adolescent females are more likely to resolve Erikson's identity versus role confusion and intimacy versus isolation crises concurrently rather than consecutively. The results of at least one study (Ochse & Plug, 1986) support this view. With respect to Kohlberg's theory, Gilligan argues that because females are socialized to value more highly the qualities of understanding, helping, and cooperation with others than that of preserving individual rights, and because this latter orientation is reflected most strongly in Kohlberg's two conventional stages, females are more likely to be judged to be at a lower level of moral development than males.

Stephen Thoma (1986) offers a partial answer to Gilligan's criticism. After reviewing more than fifty studies on gender differences in moral development, he draws three conclusions. First, the effect of gender on scores from the Defining Issues Test (the DIT is a device that uses responses to moral dilemmas to determine level of moral reasoning) was very small. Less than one-half of 1 percent of the differences in DIT scores was due to gender differences. Second, females almost always scored higher. This slight superiority for females appeared in every age group studied (middle school, high school, college, adults). Third, differences in DIT scores were strongly associated with differences in age and level of education. That is, individuals who were older and who had graduated from college were more likely to score at the postconventional level than those who were younger and who had less education. Thoma's findings suggest that females are just as likely as males to use justice and fairness concepts in their reasoning about *hypothetical* moral dilemmas.

But there is one aspect of Gilligan's criticism that cannot be answered by Thoma's analysis of existing research. She argues that when females are faced with their own real-life moral dilemmas (abortion, civil rights, environmental pollution) rather than hypothetical ones, they are more likely to favor a caring/helping/cooperation orientation than a justice/fairness/individual rights orientation. Perhaps the best approach that educators can take when they involve students in discussions of moral issues is to emphasize the utility of *both* orientations.

| **Males and females may use different approaches to resolve real-life moral dilemmas** |

DOES MORAL THINKING LEAD TO MORAL BEHAVIOR?

Hugh Hartshorne and Mark May (1929, 1930a, 1930b) observed thousands of children at different age levels reacting in situations that revealed their actual moral behavior. Hartshorne and May also asked the children to respond to questions about hypothetical situations to reveal how much they understood about right and wrong behavior. Elementary school children, for example, were allowed to correct their own papers or record their own scores on measures of athletic skill without being aware that accurate measures were being made independently by adult observers. The children were also asked what they *thought* was the right thing to do in similar situations.

A comparison of the two sets of data made it possible to determine, among other things, whether children practiced what they preached. What Hartshorne and May discovered, however, was that many children who were able to describe right kinds of behavior in hypothetical situations indulged in wrong behavior in real-life situations. Children reacted in specific, rather than consistent, ways to situations that called for moral judgment. Even a child who was rated as among the most honest in

| **Moral knowledge does not always result in moral behavior** |

a group would behave in a dishonest way under certain circumstances. A boy who was an excellent student but an indifferent athlete, for example, would not cheat when asked to correct his own paper, but he *would* inflate scores on sports skills.

Another significant, and dismaying, discovery made by Hartshorne and May was that children who went to Sunday school or who belonged to such organizations as the Boy Scouts or Girl Scouts were just as dishonest as children who were not exposed to the kind of moral instruction provided by such organizations. Hartshorne and May concluded that one explanation for the ineffectiveness of moral instruction in the 1920s was that too much stress was placed on having children memorize values such as the Ten Commandments or the Boy Scout oath and law. The two researchers suggested that it would be more effective to invite children to discuss real-life moral situations as they occurred. Instead of children chanting "Honesty is the best policy," for example, Hartshorne and May urged teachers to call attention to the positive consequences of honest acts. If a student in a school reported that she had found money belonging to someone else, the teacher might praise the child and ask everyone in the class to think about how relieved the person who had lost the money would be to get it back.

The necessity for teachers and parents to follow Hartshorne and May's suggestion of becoming directly involved in the moral education of children in both word and deed was made clear in three publications. In *The Moral Child*, William Damon argues that "children acquire moral values by actively participating in adult-child and child-child relationships that support, enhance, and guide their natural moral inclinations" (1988, p. 118). A critical aspect of these relationships is that parents, teachers, and other adults must explain the reasons for requiring children to exhibit certain moral behaviors. Fred Schab (1991) surveyed more than twelve hundred high school students in 1969 and 1989 on cheating in school and other aspects of dishonesty. Over that twenty-year period, he found that fear of failure was the most common reason for cheating and that it occurred most often in math and science classes. School was judged the worst place by these students to teach the value of honesty. Finally, Cecilia Wainryb and Elliott Turiel (1993) found that what is considered to be correct or moral behavior is determined in part by people's beliefs about the validity of relevant information. For example, in response to a scenario in which a father spanked his son for misbehaving, some people believed that the father's behavior was right because they believed that corporal punishment facilitates learning. Those who judged the father's behavior to be wrong either believed that children do not learn when spanked or were not sure about the nature of the relationship between corporal punishment and learning. Moreover, most of the participants said they would change their judgment of the father's action if they could be convinced that their original belief about the relationship between corporal punishment and learning desired behaviors was false.

Piaget's description of cognitive development and Kohlberg's description of moral reasoning development help explain some of Hartshorne and May's conclusions. Elementary school children are in the concrete operational stage. They think in terms of actual experiences and treat situations that look different in different ways. Because many of these youngsters are also at Kohlberg's third stage (good boy–nice girl), their moral behavior is influenced by their eagerness to please or impress others. Thus, the inability of elementary school children to comprehend and apply general principles in varied situations and their desire to do what they think will please or impress authority figures may partly explain the ineffectiveness of moral instruction that stresses the memorization of abstract principles.

SUGGESTIONS FOR TEACHING IN YOUR CLASSROOM

Encouraging Moral Development

1 Recognize that younger children will respond to moral conflicts differently from older children.

Journal Entry
Ways to En-
courage Moral
Development

2 Try to take the perspective of students and stimulate their perspective-taking abilities.

3 Develop an awareness of moral issues by discussing a variety of real and hypothetical moral dilemmas and by using daily opportunities in the classroom to heighten moral awareness. (Moral education should be an integral part of the curriculum; it should not take place during a "moral education period.")

4 Create a classroom atmosphere that will enhance open discussion. (For example, arrange face-to-face groupings, be an accepting model, foster listening and communication skills, and encourage student-to-student interaction.)

Specific suggestions for supervising classroom discussions offered by Richard Hersh, Diana Paolitto, and Joseph Reimer (1979) include the following:

Highlight the moral issue to be discussed. (Describe a specific real or hypothetical moral dilemma.)

Ask "why?" questions. (After asking students what they would do if they were faced with the moral dilemma under discussion, ask them to explain why they would act that way.)

Complicate the circumstances. (After students have responded to the original dilemma, mention a factor that might complicate matters—for example, the involvement of a best friend in the dilemma.)

Use personal and naturalistic examples. (Invite students to put themselves in the position of individuals who are confronted by moral dilemmas described in newspapers or depicted on television.)

Before you use any techniques of moral education in your classes, it would be wise to check with your principal. In some communities parents have insisted that they, not teachers, should take the responsibility for moral instruction.

RESOURCES FOR FURTHER INVESTIGATION

■ Erikson's Description of Development

Erik Erikson's books are of considerable significance for their speculations about development and education. In the first six chapters of *Childhood and Society* (2d ed., 1963), he describes how studying Native Americans and observing patients in treatment led him to develop the Eight Ages of Man (described in Chapter 7 of the book). In the final chapters of this book, Erikson uses his conception of development to analyze the lives of Hitler and Maxim Gorky. *Identity: Youth and Crisis* (1968) features a revised description of the eight stages of development, with emphasis on identity and role confusion. Erikson comments on many aspects of his work in an interview with Richard Evans, published under the title *Dialogue with Erik Erikson* (1967). And James Marcia reviews research on identity statuses in "Identity in Adolescence," in *Handbook of Adolescent Psychology* (1980), edited by Joseph Adelson.

■ Piaget's Theory of Cognitive Development

Jean Piaget has probably exerted more influence on theoretical discussions of development and on educational practices than any other contemporary psychologist. Of his own books, you might wish to consult *The Language and Thought of the Child* (1952a), *The Origins of Intelligence in Children* (1952b), and *The Psychology of the Child* (1969), the last of which was written in collaboration with Barbel Inhelder. Howard Gruber and Jacques Vonèche have edited *The Essential Piaget: An Interpretive Reference and Guide* (1977), which Piaget describes in the foreword as "the best and most complete of all anthologies of my work." An inexpensive paperback that provides a biography of Piaget and an analysis of his work is *Piaget's Theory of Intellectual Development* (3d ed., 1988), by Herbert Ginsburg and Sylvia Opper. Other books about Piaget are *Piaget for Teachers* (1970), by Hans Furth; *Piaget's Theory of Cognitive and Affective Development* (4th ed., 1989), by Barry Wadsworth; *Theories of Developmental Psychology* (3d ed., 1993), by Patricia Miller; and *Piaget's Theory: Prospects and Possibilities* (1992), edited by Harry Beilin and Peter Pufall.

An on-line source of information and relevant publications for Piaget is the Jean Piaget Society database, located at **http://www.wimsey.com/~chrisl/JPS/JPS. html**. It contains electronic journals and conference information and is dedicated to "the presentation and discussion of scholarly work on issues related to human knowledge and its development."

■ Vygotsky's Theory of Cognitive Development

Comprehensive descriptions and analyses of Lev Vygotsky's ideas about cognitive development can be found in *Vygotsky and Education: Instructional Implications and Applications of Sociohistorical Psychology* (1990), edited by Luis Moll; *Vygotsky's Sociohistorical Psychology and Its Contemporary Application* (1991), by Carl Ratner; and *Lev Vygotsky: Revolutionary Scientist* (1993), by Fred Newman and Lois Holzman. The proceedings of an annual conference on Vygotsky and his work can be found on-line at **http://www.glasnet.ru/~vega/vygodsky/ index.html**. The proceedings include a number of original papers, including one by Vygotsky's daughter.

■ Piaget's Description of Moral Development

Piaget describes his observations on moral development in *The Moral Judgment of the Child* (1965). Thomas Lickona summarizes research investigations stimulated by Piaget's conclusions in "Research on Piaget's Theory of Moral Development," in *Moral Development and Behavior: Theory, Research, and Social Issues* (1976), an excellent compilation of articles on all aspects of morality, which he edited.

■ Kohlberg's Stages of Moral Development

If you would like to read Kohlberg's own account of the stages of moral development, examine "Moral Stages and Moralization: The Cognitive-Developmental Approach," in *Moral Development and Behavior: Theory, Research, and Social Issues* (1976), edited by Thomas Lickona. Kohlberg discusses changes in his theory in "Revisions in the Theory and Practice of Moral Development," in *New Directions for Child Development: Moral Development* (1978), edited by William Damon. Techniques for encouraging moral development by taking account of Kohlberg's stages are described in *Promoting Moral Growth: From Piaget to Kohlberg* (1979), by Richard Hersh, Diana Paolitto, and Joseph Reimer. A discussion of current research on moral development can be found in *Approaches to Moral Development: New Research and Emerging Themes* (1993), edited by Andrew Garrod.

■ Gilligan's Analysis of Adolescent Development

If you would like to know more about the basis of Carol Gilligan's critique of Erikson's and Kohlberg's theories and her arguments for a broader view of adolescent development, start with her widely cited book *In a Different Voice: Psychological Theory and Women's Development* (1982). Briefer and more recent analyses of this issue are "Adolescent Development Reconsidered," a chapter in *Adolescent Social Behavior and Health* (1987), edited by Charles Irwin Jr.; and "Exit Voice Dilemmas in Adolescent Development," a chapter in *Mapping the Moral Domain: A Contribution of Women's Thinking to Psychological Theory and Education* (1988), edited by Carol Gilligan, Janie Ward, Jill Taylor, and Betty Bardige.

SUMMARY

1. Erikson's theory of psychosocial development is notable because it covers the life span, describes people as playing an active role in their own psychological development as opposed to passively responding to external forces, and emphasizes the role played by cultural norms and goals.

2. Erikson's theory is based on the epigenetic principle of biology. Just as certain parts of the fetus are formed at certain times and combine to produce a biologically whole individual at birth, certain aspects of personality develop at certain times and combine to form a psychologically whole individual.

3. Erikson's theory describes eight stages, from birth through old age. The stages that deal with the personality development of school-age children are initiative versus guilt (four to five years), industry versus inferiority (six to eleven years), and identity versus role confusion (twelve to eighteen years).

4. Forcing students to compete with one another for grades is likely to have a negative effect on their sense of industry.

5. Individuals with a strong sense of identity are comfortable with their physical selves, have a sense of purpose and direction, and know they will be recognized by others.

6. When faced with making an occupational choice, some adolescents declare a psychosocial moratorium; others establish a negative identity.

7. Erikson's observations about identity were extended by Marcia, who described four identity statuses: diffusion, foreclosure, moratorium, and identity achievement.

8. Erikson's theory has been criticized for its heavy reliance on personal experience, for its inaccuracies in terms of female personality development, and for its failure to specify how individuals move from stage to stage.

9. Piaget believed that individuals inherit two basic intellectual tendencies: organization (the tendency to combine mental processes into more general systems) and adaptation (the tendency to adjust to the environment).

10. Adaptation occurs through the processes of assimilation (fitting an experience into an existing scheme) and accommodation (changing a scheme or creating a new one to incorporate a new experience).

11. A scheme is a mental framework that guides our thoughts and actions.

12. Equilibration is the process of trying to organize a system of schemes that allows us to adapt to current environmental conditions. Equilibration is produced by a state of disequilibrium.

13. Piaget concluded on the basis of his studies that schemes evolve through four stages: sensorimotor (birth to two years), preoperational (two to seven years), concrete operational (seven to eleven years), and formal operational (twelve to eighteen years).

14. During the sensorimotor stage, the infant and toddler use senses and motor skills to explore and understand the environment.

15. In the preoperational stage, the child masters symbol systems but cannot manipulate symbols logically.

16. In the concrete operational stage, the child is capable of logical thinking, but only with ideas with which he has had firsthand experience.

17. During the formal operational stage, the individual is capable of hypothetical reasoning, dealing with abstractions, and engaging in mental manipulations.

18. Systematic instruction may have modest positive effects on the rate of cognitive development as long as the schemes that will govern the next stage have already begun to develop.

19. Piaget's theory has been criticized for underestimating children's abilities, for overestimating the capability of adolescents to engage in formal operational thinking, for vague explanations of how individuals move from stage to stage, and for not addressing cultural differences.

20. Piaget identified two types of moral reasoning in children: morality of constraint (rules are inflexible and external) and morality of cooperation (rules are flexible and internal).

21. Vygotsky believed that cognitive development is aided by explicitly teaching students how to use cognitive tools to acquire basic concepts and by teaching within a student's zone of proximal development.

22. Computer-based technology can be used to support Piaget's view of cognitive development through programs that help students explore and construct knowledge, formulate concrete representations of abstract ideas, and understand the ideas of others.

23. Computer-based technology can be used to support Vygotsky's view of cognitive development through programs that play the role of an expert tutor who provides a high degree of support and structure that is gradually withdrawn (scaffolding) and through computer links

that allow students to participate in actual scientific studies.

24. Kohlberg defined six stages in the development of moral reasoning: punishment-obedience, instrumental relativist, good boy–nice girl, law and order, social contract, and universal ethical principle.

25. Structured discussions based on moral dilemmas may have some positive effects on the rate of development of moral reasoning.

26. Gilligan maintains that Erikson's theory of identity development and Kohlberg's theory of moral development more accurately describe male development than female development.

27. Studies show that children's moral behavior varies in different circumstances.

Key Terms

epigenetic principle *(26)*
role confusion *(28)*
identity *(29)*
psychosocial moratorium *(29)*
negative identity *(30)*
identity statuses *(31)*
psychological androgyny *(35)*
organization *(38)*
adaptation *(38)*
equilibration *(38)*
schemes *(38)*
assimilation *(38)*
accommodation *(39)*

constructivism *(40)*
conservation *(42)*
perceptual centration *(42)*
decentration *(42)*
irreversibility *(42)*
egocentrism *(42)*
adolescent egocentrism *(45)*
spontaneous concepts *(53)*
scientific concepts *(53)*
empirical learning *(53)*
theoretical learning *(53)*
zone of proximal development (ZPD)
   (54)

scaffolding *(54)*
computer conferencing *(55)*
videoconferencing *(55)*
real-time chatting *(55)*
microworlds *(55)*
microcomputer-based laboratory (MBL)
   (56)
cognitive apprenticeship *(57)*
teleapprenticeship *(57)*
morality of constraint *(59)*
morality of cooperation *(59)*

Discussion Questions

1. According to Erikson, the way in which personality develops among six- to eleven-year-old children depends on their attaining a sense of industry and avoiding a sense of inferiority. Suppose you were an elementary school teacher. What kinds of things would you do to help your students feel more capable and productive? What kinds of things would you avoid doing?

2. Between the ages of twelve and eighteen, personality development revolves around establishing an identity and avoiding role confusion. American high schools are often criticized for not helping adolescents resolve this conflict. Do you agree? Why? What do you think could be done to improve matters?

3. From Piaget's point of view, why is it wrong to think of children as "small adults"?

4. In response to reports that American schoolchildren do not score as well as many European and Asian schoolchildren on standardized achievement tests, some critics of American education argue that we should begin formal schooling earlier than age five and that it should focus on mastery of basic reading and computation skills. How would Piaget respond to this proposal?

5. How would you respond to a parent (or colleague) who argued that students have better things to do in class than discuss ways of resolving moral dilemmas?

3

Age-Level Characteristics

The theories described in Chapter 2 call attention to stages of psychosocial, cognitive, and moral development. Although these types of behavior are important, they represent only a small part of the behavior repertoire of a child or adolescent. To describe the many aspects of development that are of potential significance to teachers, we must analyze types of behavior that are not directly related to the theories already discussed or to those (learning and information processing) that will be discussed in Part 2. This chapter will present such an overview of types of behavior at different age and grade levels that are not directly related to any particular theory. In selecting

KEY POINTS

These key points will help you learn the important information in this chapter. To help you study, they also appear in the margins of pages, next to the text where they are discussed.

Preschool and Kindergarten

- Large-muscle control better established than small-muscle control and eye-hand coordination
- Play patterns vary as a function of social class, gender, and age
- Gender differences in toy preferences and play activities noticeable by kindergarten
- Young children stick to own language rules

Primary Grades

- Primary grade children have difficulty focusing on small print
- Accident rate peaks in third grade because of confidence in physical skills
- Rigid interpretation of rules in primary grades
- To encourage industry, use praise, avoid criticism

Elementary Grades

- Boys slightly better at sports-related motor skills; girls better at flexibility, balance, rhythmic motor skills
- Peer group norms for behavior begin to replace adult norms
- Self-concept becomes more generalized and stable; is based primarily on comparisons with peers
- Delinquents have few friends, are easily distracted, are not interested in schoolwork, lack basic skills
- Elementary grade students reason logically but concretely

Middle School

- Girls' growth spurt occurs earlier, and so they look older than boys of same age
- After growth spurt, boys have greater strength and endurance
- Early-maturing boys likely to draw favorable responses
- Late-maturing boys may seek attention
- Late-maturing girls likely to be popular and carefree
- Average age of puberty: girls, eleven; boys, fourteen
- Discussion of controversial issues may be difficult because of strong desire to conform to peer norms
- Teenagers experience different degrees of emotional turmoil
- Environment of middle schools does not meet needs of adolescents, leading to lower levels of learning
- Self-efficacy beliefs for academic and social tasks become strong influences on behavior

High School

- Sexual activity among male, female teens due to different factors
- Adolescents likely to be confused about appropriateness of premarital sex
- Parents influence values, plans; peers influence immediate status
- Girls more likely than boys to experience anxiety about friendships
- Depression most common among females, teens from poor families
- Depression may be caused by negative cognitive set, learned helplessness, sense of loss
- Depression and unstable family situation place adolescents at risk for suicide
- Political thinking becomes more abstract, less authoritarian, more knowledgeable

points for emphasis, we used one basic criterion: Does this information about development have potential significance for teachers?

To organize the points to be discussed, we have divided the developmental span into five levels, corresponding to common grade groupings in schools: preschool and kindergarten (three, four, and five years), primary grades (1, 2, and 3; six, seven, and eight years), elementary grades (4 and 5; nine and ten years), middle school grades (6, 7, and 8; eleven, twelve, and thirteen years), and high school grades (9, 10, 11, and 12; fourteen, fifteen, sixteen, and seventeen years). Because the way grades are grouped varies, you may find yourself teaching in a school system where the arrangement described in this chapter is not followed. In that case simply refer to the appropriate age-level designations and, if necessary, concentrate on two levels rather than one.

You should also read the rest of the chapter with care. Even though you presently anticipate that you will teach a particular grade level, you may at some point teach younger or older students. You may also gain awareness of continuities of development and come to realize how some aspects of the behavior of older children were influenced by earlier experiences. Indeed, even though a particular type of behavior is discussed at a level where it is considered to be of special significance, that behavior may be important at any age level.

Various types of behavior at each of the five levels are discussed under these headings: physical, social, emotional, and cognitive characteristics. Following each characteristic are implications for teachers. To help you establish a general conception of what children are like at each level, brief summaries of the types of behavior stressed by the theorists discussed in the preceding chapter are listed in a table near the beginning of each section (Tables 3.1, 3.2, 3.3, 3.4, and 3.7). ■

Preschool and Kindergarten (Three, Four, and Five Years)

PHYSICAL CHARACTERISTICS: PRESCHOOL AND KINDERGARTEN

Journal Entry
Active Games

1. *Preschool children are extremely active. They have good control of their bodies and enjoy activity for its own sake.* Provide plenty of opportunities for the children to run, climb, and jump. Arrange these activities, as much as possible, so that they are under your control. If you follow a policy of complete freedom, you may discover that thirty improvising three- to five-year-olds can be a frightening thing. In your Reflective Journal you might note some specific games and activities that you could use to achieve semicontrolled play.

Journal Entry
Riot-Stopping Signals and Activities

2. *Because of an inclination toward bursts of activity, kindergartners need frequent rest periods. They themselves often don't recognize the need to slow down.* Schedule quiet activities after strenuous ones. Have rest time. Realize that excitement may build up to a riot level if the attention of "catalytic agents" and their followers is not diverted. In your journal you might list some signals for calling a halt to a melee (for example, playing the opening chords of Beethoven's Fifth Symphony on the piano) or for diverting wild action into more or less controlled activity (marching around the room to a brisk rendition of "Stars and Stripes Forever").

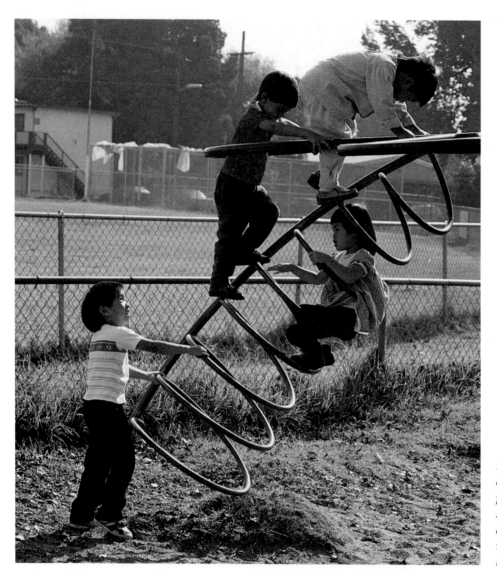

Preschool and kindergarten children are very active and possess good gross motor skills. As a result, they enjoy activities that involve climbing, running, throwing, and kicking.

3. *Preschoolers' large muscles are more developed than those that control fingers and hands. Therefore, preschoolers may be quite clumsy at, or physically incapable of, such skills as tying shoes and buttoning coats.* Avoid too many small-motor activities, such as pasting paper chains. Provide big brushes, crayons, and tools. In your journal you might note other activities or items of king-sized equipment that would be appropriate for the children's level of muscular development.

Journal Entry
Allowing for Large-Muscle Control

4. *Young children find it difficult to focus their eyes on small objects. Therefore, their eye-hand coordination may be imperfect.* If possible, minimize the necessity for the children to look at small things. (Incomplete eye development is the reason for large print in children's books.) This is also important to keep in mind if you are planning to use computers or software programs—highly graphic programs requiring a simple "point and click" response are most appropriate for very young students.

Large-muscle control better established than small-muscle control and eye-hand coordination

Table 3.1	Applying Stage Theories of Development to the Preschool and Kindergarten Years

Stage of psychosocial development: initiative vs. guilt. Children need opportunities for free play and experimentation as well as experiences that give them a sense of accomplishment.

Stage of cognitive development: preoperational thought. Children gradually acquire the ability to conserve and center but are not capable of operations and are unable to mentally reverse operations.

Stage of moral development: morality of constraint, preconventional. Rules are viewed as unchangeable edicts handed down by those in authority. Punishment-obedience orientation focuses on physical consequences rather than on intentions.

General factors to keep in mind: Children are having their first experiences with school routine and interactions with more than a few peers and are preparing for initial academic experiences in group settings. They need to learn to follow directions and get along with others.

5. *Although children's bodies are flexible and resilient, the bones that protect the brain are still soft.* Be extremely wary of blows to the head in games or fights between children. If you notice an activity involving such a blow, intervene immediately; warn the class that this is dangerous and explain why.

6. *Although boys are bigger, girls are ahead of boys in practically all other areas of development, especially in fine motor skills, so don't be surprised if boys are clumsier at manipulating small objects.* It may be desirable to avoid boy-girl comparisons or competition involving such skills.

SOCIAL CHARACTERISTICS: PRESCHOOL AND KINDERGARTEN

1. *Most children have one or two best friends, but these friendships may change rapidly. Preschoolers tend to be quite flexible socially; they are usually willing and able to play with most of the other children in the class. Favorite friends tend to be of the same gender, but many friendships between boys and girls develop.* Young children are quite adept at figuring out which social and linguistic skills elicit responses from playmates. Typical gambits include inviting a peer to engage in rough-and-tumble play, offering an object to a playmate, offering to exchange objects with a playmate, sticking to the topic of a conversation, moving close to the person to whom one is speaking, and asking a question or giving a command (Guralnick, 1986). You might make it a habit to notice whether some children seem to lack the ability or confidence to join others. In some cases a child may prefer to be an observer. But if you sense that a child really wants to get to know others, you might provide some assistance.

Journal Entry
How Much Control
Is Necessary?

2. *Play groups tend to be small and not too highly organized; hence they change rapidly.* You should not be concerned if children flit constantly from one activity to another. Such behavior is normal for this age group, although it may sometimes drive you wild. You might think about how much control you will want to exert over your students, particularly during free-play periods. At what point is insistence on silence and sedentary activities justifiable? Should you insist that students stick with self-selected activities for a given period of time?

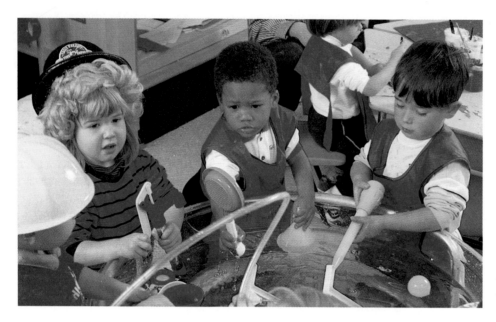

Young children engage in a variety of types of play. These play patterns may vary as a function of social class and gender.

3. *Younger children exhibit different types of play behavior.* Mildred Parten (1932) observed the free play of children in a preschool and noted the types of social behavior they engaged in. Eventually, she was able to write quite precise descriptions of six types of **play behavior**:

> *Unoccupied behavior.* Children do not really play at all. They either stand around and look at others for a time or engage in aimless activities.
>
> *Solitary play.* Children play alone with toys that are different from those used by other children within speaking distance of them. They make no attempt to interact with others.
>
> *Onlooker behavior.* Children spend most of their time watching others. They may kibitz and make comments about the play of others, but they do not attempt to join in.
>
> *Parallel play.* Children play *beside* but not really with other children. They use the same toys in close proximity to others but in an independent way.
>
> *Associative play.* Children engage in rather disorganized play with other children. There is no assignment of activities or roles; individual children play in their own ways.
>
> *Cooperative play.* Children engage in an organized form of play in which leadership and other roles are assigned. The members of the group may cooperate in creating some project, dramatize some situation, or engage in some sort of coordinated enterprise.

4. *Play patterns may vary as a function of social class and gender.* Kenneth Rubin, Terence Maioni, and Margaret Hornung (1976) observed and classified the free play of preschoolers according to their level of social and cognitive participation. The four levels of social participation they observed (solitary, parallel, associative, and cooperative) were taken from the work of Parten. The four

levels of cognitive participation they observed were taken from the work of Sara Smilansky (1968) (who based them on Piaget's work) and are as follows:

Functional play. Making simple, repetitive muscle movements with or without objects.

Constructive play. Manipulating objects to construct or create something.

Dramatic play. Using an imaginary situation.

Games with rules. Using prearranged rules to play a game.

The Parten and Rubin et al. studies found that children of lower socioeconomic status engaged in more parallel and functional play than their middle-class peers, whereas middle-class children displayed more associative, cooperative, and constructive play. Girls engaged in more solitary- and parallel-constructive play and in less dramatic play than did the boys. Boys engaged in more solitary-functional and associative-dramatic play than did girls.

These studies call attention to the variety of play activities common to preschool children. This knowledge may help you determine if a child *prefers* solitary play or plays alone because of shyness or lack of skills for joining in associative or cooperative play.

5. *Quarrels are frequent, but they tend to be of short duration and are quickly forgotten.* When thirty children are thrown together for the first time in a restricted environment with a limited number of objects to be shared, disputes over property rights and similar matters are inevitable. Do not be surprised if you find that the majority of quarrels and aggressive acts involve two or more boys. Research has shown that males are more likely than females to behave aggressively. The gender difference in aggression is greatest among preschoolers and least noticeable among college students (Hyde, 1986). Whenever possible, let the children settle these differences on their own; intervene only if a quarrel gets out of hand. If you do have to intervene, you might try one of two tactics: suggest that one or both children engage in another equally attractive activity, or impose a turn-taking rule. (Other methods of classroom control will be discussed in Chapter 12.)

6. *Awareness of gender roles and gender typing is evident.* By the time children enter kindergarten, most of them have developed awareness of gender differences and of masculine and feminine roles (Wynn & Fletcher, 1987). This awareness of **gender roles** shows up very clearly in the toys and activities that boys and girls prefer. Boys are more likely than girls to play outdoors, to engage in rough-and-tumble play, and to behave aggressively. Boys play with toy vehicles and construction toys, and they engage in action games (such as football). Girls prefer art activities, doll play, and dancing (Carter, 1987). Gender role differences are often reinforced by the way parents behave. Boys are encouraged to be active and independent, whereas girls are encouraged to be more docile and dependent. Peers may further reinforce these tendencies. A boy or girl may notice that other children are more willing to play when he or she selects a gender-appropriate toy.

Therefore, if you teach preschool children, you may have to guard against a tendency to respond too soon when little girls ask for help. If they *need* assistance, of course you should supply it; but if preschool girls can carry out tasks on their own, you should urge them to do so. You might also remind yourself

Play patterns vary as a function of social class, gender, and age

Gender differences in toy preferences and play activities noticeable by kindergarten

Journal Entry
Encouraging Girls to Achieve, Boys to Be Sensitive

that girls need to be encouraged to become more achievement oriented and boys to become more sensitive to the needs of others.

EMOTIONAL CHARACTERISTICS: PRESCHOOL AND KINDERGARTEN

1. *Kindergarten children tend to express their emotions freely and openly. Anger outbursts are frequent.* It is probably desirable to let children at this age level express their feelings openly, at least within broad limits, so that they can recognize and face their emotions. In *Between Parent and Child* (1965) and *Teacher and Child* (1972), Haim Ginott offers some specific suggestions on how a parent or teacher can help children develop awareness of their feelings. His books may help you work out your own philosophy and techniques for dealing with emotional outbursts.

Suppose, for example, that a boy who was wildly waving his hand to be called on during share-and-tell time later knocks down a block tower made by a girl who monopolized sharing time with a spellbinding story of a kitten rescued by firefighters. When you go over to break up the incipient fight, the boy angrily pushes you away. In such a situation Ginott suggests you take the boy to a quiet corner and engage in a dialogue such as this:

You: It looks as if you are unhappy about something, Pete.

Boy: Yes, I am.

You: Are you angry about something that happened this morning?

Boy: Yes.

You: Tell me about it.

Boy: I wanted to tell the class about something at sharing time, and Mary talked for three hours, and you wouldn't let me say anything.

You: And that made you mad at Mary and at me?

Boy: Yes.

You: Well, I can understand why you are disappointed and angry. But Mary had an exciting story to tell, and we didn't have time for anyone else to tell what they had to say. You can be the very first one to share something tomorrow morning. Now how about doing an easel painting? You always do such interesting paintings.

Ginott suggests that when children are encouraged to analyze their own behavior, they are more likely to become aware of the causes of their feelings. This awareness, in turn, may help them learn to accept and control their feelings and find more acceptable means of expressing them. But because these children are likely to be in Piaget's preoperational stage of intellectual development, bear in mind that this approach may not be successful with all of them. The egocentric orientation of four- to five-year-olds makes it difficult for them to reflect on the thoughts of self or others. Anger outbursts are more likely to occur when children are tired, hungry, and/or exposed to too much adult interference. If you take such conditions into account and try to alleviate them (by providing a nap or a snack, for example), temper tantrums may be minimized.

Journal Entry
Helping Students
Understand Anger

2. *Jealousy among classmates is likely to be fairly common at this age since kindergarten children have much affection for the teacher and actively seek approval. When there are thirty individuals competing for the affection and attention*

Journal Entry
Ways to Avoid
Playing Favorites

of just one, some jealousy is inevitable. Try to spread your attention around as equitably as possible, and when you praise particular children, do it in a private or casual way. If one child is given lavish public recognition, it is only natural for the other children to feel resentful. Think back to how you felt about teachers' pets during your own school years. If you have observed or can think of other techniques for minimizing jealousy, jot them down in your journal.

COGNITIVE CHARACTERISTICS: PRESCHOOL AND KINDERGARTEN

Journal Entry
Handling Sharing

1. *Kindergartners are quite skillful with language. Most of them like to talk, especially in front of a group.* Providing a sharing time gives children a natural opportunity for talking, but many will need help in becoming good listeners. Some sort of rotation scheme is usually necessary to divide talking opportunities between the gabby and the silent extremes. You might provide activities or experiences for less confident children to talk about, such as a field trip, a book, or a film. In your journal you might note some comments to use if students start to share the wrong thing (such as a vivid account of a fight between their parents) or if they try to one-up classmates (for example, "Your cat may have had five kittens, but *our* cat had a *hundred* kittens"). For titillating topics, for instance, you might say, "There are some things that are private, and it's better not to talk about them to others."

Young children stick to own language rules

2. *Preschoolers may stick to their own rules in using language.* One of the most intriguing aspects of **early language development** is the extent to which children stick to their own rules. This tendency is so strong that Roger Brown (1973) concludes that efforts by parents and teachers to speed up acquisition of correct speech may not always be successful. Evidence to back up this conclusion is provided in an ingenious study by Jean Berko (1958). Berko found that when four-year-olds were shown pictures and told, for example, "Here is a goose, and here are two geese" and were then asked to complete the sentence "There are two _____," most said, "Gooses."

Given this strong tendency of children to use their own rules of grammar, you should probably limit any attempts at grammar instruction to modeling the correct forms. The possibility of getting youngsters to use adult forms of grammar is outweighed by the risk of inhibiting their spontaneous use of language. Direct and systematic instruction in grammar should be delayed until second or third grade.

3. *Competence is encouraged by interaction, interest, opportunities, urging, limits, admiration, and signs of affection.* Studies of young children rated as highly competent (Ainsworth & Wittig, 1972; White & Watts, 1973) show that to encourage preschoolers to make the most of their abilities adults should:

Interact with the child often and in a variety of ways.

Show interest in what the child does and says.

Provide opportunities for the child to investigate and experience many things.

Permit and encourage the child to do many things.

Urge the child to try to achieve mature and skilled types of behavior.

Journal Entry
Encouraging Competence

Establish firm and consistent limits regarding unacceptable forms of behavior, explain the reasons for these as soon as the child is able to understand, listen to complaints if the child feels the restrictions are too confining and give additional reasons if the limits are still to be maintained as originally stated.

Show that the child's achievements are admired and appreciated.

Communicate love in a warm and sincere way.

Diana Baumrind's (1971, 1991) analysis of authoritative, authoritarian, permissive, and rejecting-neglecting child-rearing approaches shows why such techniques contribute to competence in children. Baumrind found that parents of competent children are **authoritative parents**. They have confidence in their abilities as parents and therefore provide a model of competence for their children to imitate. When they establish limits and explain reasons for restrictions, they encourage their children to set standards for themselves and to think about *why* certain procedures should be followed. And because these parents are warm and affectionate, their positive responses are valued by their children as rewards for mature behavior. The children of authoritative parents tend to be self-motivated. They stand up for what they believe, yet are able to work productively with others.

Authoritarian parents, by contrast, make demands and wield power, but their failure to take into account the child's point of view and their lack of warmth lead to resentment and insecurity on the part of the child. Children of authoritarian parents may do as they are told, but they are likely to do so out of compliance or fear, not out of a desire to earn love or approval. They also tend to be other-directed rather than inner-directed.

Permissive parents, as defined by Baumrind, are disorganized, inconsistent, and lack confidence, and their children are likely to imitate such behavior. Permissive parents make few demands of their children, allow them to make many of their own decisions, do not require them to exhibit mature behavior, and tend to avoid confrontations with their children. As a result, such children are markedly less assertive and intellectually skilled than are children from authoritative homes.

Rejecting-neglecting parents do not make demands on their children, nor do they respond to their emotional needs. They do not structure the home environment, are not supportive of their children's goals and activities, and may actively reject or neglect their child-rearing responsibilities. Children of rejecting-neglecting parents are the least socially and intellectually competent of the four types.

You might refer to these observations not only when you plan how to encourage competence but also when you think about the kind of classroom atmosphere you hope to establish.

Primary Grades (1, 2, and 3; Six, Seven, and Eight Years)

PHYSICAL CHARACTERISTICS: PRIMARY GRADES

1. *Primary grade children are still extremely active. Because they are frequently required to participate in sedentary pursuits, energy is often released in the form of nervous habits—for example, pencil chewing, fingernail biting, and general*

fidgeting. You will have to decide what noise and activity level should prevail during work periods. A few teachers insist on absolute quiet, but such a rule can make children work so hard at remaining quiet that they cannot devote much effort to their lessons. The majority of teachers allow a certain amount of moving about and talking. Whatever you decide, be on the alert for the point of diminishing returns—whether from too much or too little restriction.

To minimize fidgeting, avoid situations in which your students must stay glued to their desks for long periods. Have frequent breaks and try to work activity (such as bringing papers to your desk) into the lessons themselves.

Journal Entry
Building Activity
into Classwork

2. *Children at these grade levels still need rest periods; they become fatigued easily as a result of physical and mental exertion.* Schedule quiet activities after strenuous ones (story time after recess, for example) and relaxing activities after periods of mental concentration (art after spelling or math).

3. *Large-muscle control is still superior to fine coordination. Many children, especially boys, have difficulty manipulating a pencil.* Try not to schedule too much writing at one time. If drill periods are too long, skill may deteriorate and children may develop a negative attitude toward writing or toward school in general.

4. *Many primary grade students may have difficulty focusing on small print or objects. Quite a few children may be farsighted because of the shallow shape of the eye.* Try not to require too much reading at one stretch. Be on the alert for signs of eye fatigue (rubbing the eyes or blinking). When you are preparing class handouts, be sure to print in large letters or use a primary grade typewriter. Until the lens of the eye can be easily focused, young children have trouble looking back and forth from near to far objects.

Primary grade children have difficulty focusing on small print

Another vision problem encountered by preschool and primary grade children is amblyopia, or "lazy eye." In normal vision the muscles of the two eyes work together to fuse their two images into one. If the eye muscles are not coordinated, however, children may experience double vision. In their efforts to cope with this problem, children may try to eliminate one image by closing one eye, tilting their heads, or blinking or rubbing their eyes. You should watch for

Table 3.2	Applying Stage Theories of Development to the Primary Grade Years

Stage of psychosocial development: industry vs. inferiority. Students need to experience a sense of industry through successful completion of tasks. Try to minimize and correct failures to prevent development of feelings of inferiority.

Stage of cognitive development: transition from preoperational to concrete operational stage. Students gradually acquire the ability to solve problems by generalizing from concrete experiences.

Stage of moral development: morality of constraint, preconventional. Rules are viewed as edicts handed down by authority. Focus is on physical consequences, meaning that obeying rules should bring benefit in return.

General factors to keep in mind: Students are having first experiences with school learning, are eager to learn how to read and write, and are likely to be upset by lack of progress. Initial attitudes toward schooling are being established. Initial roles in a group are being formed, roles that may establish a lasting pattern (for example, leader, follower, loner, athlete, or underachiever).

signs of amblyopia and let the parents know if you detect one or more signs of lazy eye in any of your students.

Although many children at this age have had extensive exposure to computer games and video games at home or outside of school, and therefore have begun to develop greater eye-hand coordination with images on-screen, it's still appropriate to select software programs that incorporate easy-to-see graphics and easy-to-click buttons to avoid frustration.

5. *At this age children tend to be extreme in their physical activities. They have excellent control of their bodies and develop considerable confidence in their skills. As a result, they often underestimate the danger involved in their more daring exploits. The accident rate is at a peak in the third grade.* You might check on school procedures for handling injuries, but also try to prevent reckless play. During recess, for example, encourage class participation in "wild" but essentially safe games (such as relay races involving stunts) to help the children get devil-may-care tendencies out of their systems. In your journal you might list other games to use for this purpose.

> **Accident rate peaks in third grade because of confidence in physical skills**
>
> **Journal Entry**
> Safe but Strenuous Games

6. *Bone growth is not yet complete. Therefore, bones and ligaments can't stand heavy pressure.* If you notice students indulging in strenuous tests of strength (punching each other on the arm until one person can't retaliate, for example), you might suggest that they switch to competition involving coordinated *skills*. During team games, rotate players in especially tiring positions (for example, the pitcher in baseball).

SOCIAL CHARACTERISTICS: PRIMARY GRADES

The characteristics noted here are typical of both primary and elementary grade students and underlie the elementary-level characteristics described in the next section.

1. *Children become somewhat more selective in their choice of friends and are likely to have a more or less permanent best friend.* Friendships are typically same-sex relationships marked by mutual understanding, loyalty, cooperation, and sharing. Competition between friends should be discouraged as it can become intense and increase their dissatisfaction with each other. Although friends disagree with each other more often than with nonfriends, their conflicts are shorter, less heated, and less likely to lead to a dissolving of the friendship (Hartup, 1989).

You might use a device called a sociogram to identify friendships, cliques, and children who are social isolates and then give tentative assistance to children who have difficulty in attracting friends. Also, be on the alert for feuds, which can develop beyond good-natured quarreling and teasing. For detailed information on how to construct and use sociograms, consult *Sociometry in the Classroom*, by Norman Gronlund (1959), or "Sociometrics: Peer-Referenced Measures and the Assessment of Social Competence," by Scott McConnell and Samuel Odom (1986).

> **Journal Entry**
> Using Sociometric Techniques

2. *Children during this age span often like organized games in small groups, but they may be overly concerned with rules or get carried away by team spirit.* Keep in mind that, according to Piaget, children at this age practice the morality of constraint: they find it difficult to understand how and why rules should be adjusted to special situations. When you divide a class into teams, you may be amazed at the amount of rivalry that develops (and the noise level generated). One way to reduce both the rivalry and the noise is to promote the idea that games should

> **Journal Entry**
> Enjoyable Team Games
>
> **Rigid interpretation of rules in primary grades**

be fun. Another technique is to rotate team membership frequently. If you know any especially good—but not excessively competitive—team games, note them in your journal. You might also consult *Cooperative Learning: Theory, Research, and Practice* (2d ed., 1995), by Robert Slavin, for descriptions of several team learning games that emphasize cooperation.

Journal Entry
Handling Feuds
and Fights

3. *Quarrels are still frequent. Words are used more often than physical aggression, but many boys (in particular) may indulge in punching, wrestling, and shoving.* Occasional fights are to be expected, but if certain children, especially the same pair, seem to be involved in one long battle, you should probably try to effect a truce. But give children a chance to work out their own solutions to disagreements as social conflict is effective in spurring cognitive growth (Smith, Johnson, & Johnson, 1981; Tudge & Rogoff, 1989).

EMOTIONAL CHARACTERISTICS: PRIMARY GRADES

1. *Primary grade students are sensitive to criticism and ridicule and may have difficulty adjusting to failure.* Young children need frequent praise and recognition. Because they tend to admire or even worship their teachers, they may be crushed by criticism. Provide positive reinforcement as frequently as possible and reserve your negative reactions for nonacademic misbehavior. Scrupulously avoid sarcasm and ridicule. Remember that this is the stage of industry versus inferiority; if you make a child feel inferior, you may prevent the development of industry.

To encourage industry, use praise, avoid criticism

Journal Entry
Spreading Around
Responsibilities

2. *Most primary grade children are eager to please the teacher.* They like to help, enjoy responsibility, and want to do well in their schoolwork. The time-honored technique for satisfying the urge to help is to assign jobs (eraser cleaner, wastebasket emptier, paper distributor, and the like) on a rotating basis. In your journal you might note other techniques—for example, were there any particular responsibilities you enjoyed as a student?

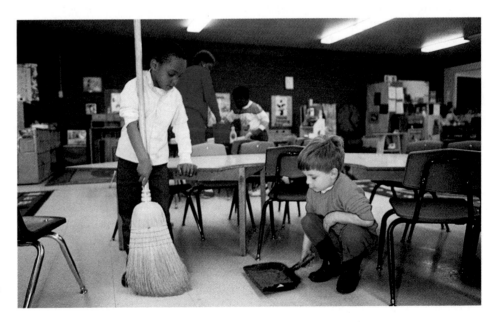

Most elementary school students eagerly strive to obtain "helping" jobs around the classroom. Accordingly, you may wish to arrange a rotating schedule for such jobs.

3. *Children of this age are becoming sensitive to the feelings of others.* Unfortunately, this permits them to hurt others deeply by attacking a sensitive spot without realizing how devastating their attack really is. It sometimes happens that teasing a particular child who has reacted to a gibe becomes a group pastime. Be on the alert for such situations. If you are able to make a private and personal appeal to the ringleaders, you may be able to prevent an escalation of the teasing, which may make a tremendous difference in the way the victim feels about school.

COGNITIVE CHARACTERISTICS: PRIMARY GRADES

1. *Assign primary grade children relatively short tasks and switch periodically from cognitively demanding activities to less demanding activities.* Researchers have known for some time that because of continuing neurological development and limited experience with formal learning tasks, primary grade children do not learn as efficiently as older children. What has only recently been demonstrated is that providing youngsters with periodic breaks, such as recess, increases their ability to attend to and perform well on subsequent classroom tasks. The nature of the recess activity does not seem to be important. It can be physical activity in a schoolyard or playing games in class. The explanation for this effect can be found in a principle that is almost as old as psychology itself—distributed practice. As we discuss in Chapter 8, learning large amounts of complex material occurs most efficiently when it is taken in relatively small chunks and is interspersed with different kinds of tasks. The less desirable alternative, which is massed practice, is to try to master the same amount of material in one relatively long session (Pellegrini & Bjorklund, 1997).

Journal Entry
Assigning Short
and Varied Tasks

2. *Children of this age like to talk and have much more facility in speech than in writing.* Primary grade children are eager to recite, regardless of whether they know the right answer. The high school teacher may have difficulty stimulating voluntary class participation, but not the primary grade teacher. The problem here is more likely to be one of controlling participation so that children speak up only when called on. Frequent reminders to take turns and to be good listeners are often necessary. And even if you are successful in this area, you may feel a bit unsettled to find that a student, after wildly waving a hand or pumping an arm to be recognized, supplies a hopelessly wrong answer. You may want to develop some phrases that gently and/or humorously indicate that an answer is erroneous or irrelevant. If you come up with some good ones, jot them down in your journal.

Journal Entry
Ways to Handle
Wrong Answers

3. *Because of the literal interpretation of rules associated with this stage of development, primary grade children may tend to be tattletales.* Sometimes telling the teacher that someone has broken a school or class rule is due to a child's level of moral development, sometimes it is due to jealousy or malice, and sometimes it is simply a way to get attention or curry favor. If a child calls your attention to the misbehavior of others and you respond by saying, "Don't be a tattletale," the child may be hurt and confused. If you thank the child too enthusiastically and then proceed to punish the culprit, you may encourage most members of the class to begin to inform on each other. Perhaps the best policy is to tell an informant that you already are aware of the errant behavior and that you intend to do something about it. Then you might follow up by talking to the offending parties.

Elementary Grades (4 and 5; Nine and Ten Years)

PHYSICAL CHARACTERISTICS: ELEMENTARY GRADES

1. *Both boys and girls become leaner and stronger.* In general, there is a decrease in the growth of fatty tissue and an increase in bone and muscle development, although this process occurs more rapidly in boys. In a year's time the average child of this age will grow about 2 inches and gain about 5 pounds. As a result, they have a lean and gangly look. Beginning at about age nine and lasting until about age fourteen, girls are slightly heavier and taller than boys. Because secondary sex characteristics have not yet appeared, boys and girls can be mistaken for one another. This is particularly likely to happen when girls have close-cropped hair, boys have very long hair, and both genders wear gender-neutral clothing (Hetherington & Parke, 1993; LeFrançois, 1995; Mitchell, 1990).

2. *Obesity can become a problem for some children of this age group.* Because nine- and ten-year-olds have more control over their eating habits than younger children do, there is a greater tendency for them to overeat, particularly junk food (foods high in calories and fat but low in nutritional value). When this eating pattern is coupled with a relatively low level of physical activity (mainly because of television watching) and a genetic predisposition toward obesity, children become mildly to severely overweight. Not only do overweight children put themselves at risk for cardiovascular problems later in life, but they also become targets for ridicule and ostracism in the present from peers (Hetherington & Parke, 1993; Mitchell, 1990).

Journal Entry
Minimizing Gender Differences in Motor Skill Performance

3. *Although small in magnitude, gender differences in motor skill performance are apparent.* Boys tend to outperform girls on tasks that involve kicking, throwing, catching, running, broad jumping, and batting. Girls surpass boys on tasks that require muscular flexibility, balance, and rhythmic movements. These

Table 3.3	Applying Stage Theories of Development to the Elementary Grade Years

Stage of psychosocial development: industry vs. inferiority. Keep students constructively busy; try to play down comparisons between best and worse learners.

Stage of cognitive development: concrete operational. Except for the most intellectually advanced students, most will need to generalize from concrete experiences.

Stage of moral development: morality of constraint; transition from preconventional to conventional. A shift to viewing rules as mutual agreements is occurring, but "official" rules are obeyed out of respect for authority or out of a desire to impress others.

General factors to keep in mind: Initial enthusiasm for learning may fade as the novelty wears off and as the process of perfecting skills becomes more difficult. Differences in knowledge and skills of fastest and slowest learners become more noticeable. "Automatic" respect for teachers tends to diminish. Peer group influences become strong.

differences may be due in part to gender role stereotyping. That is, because of socialization differences, girls are more likely to play hopscotch and jump rope, whereas boys are more likely to play baseball and basketball.

Boys slightly better at sports-related motor skills; girls better at flexibility, balance, rhythmic motor skills

One benefit of attaining mastery over large and small muscles is a relatively orderly classroom. Fourth and fifth graders can sit quietly for extended periods and concentrate on whatever intellectual task is at hand (Hetherington & Parke, 1993; Mitchell, 1990). Another benefit is that children enjoy arts and crafts and musical activities.

4. *This is a period of relative calm and predictability in physical development.* Growth in height and weight tends to be consistent and moderate, hormonal imbalances are absent; disease occurs less frequently than at any other period; and bodily coordination is relatively stable (Hetherington & Parke, 1993; Mitchell, 1990).

SOCIAL CHARACTERISTICS: ELEMENTARY GRADES

1. *The peer group becomes powerful and begins to replace adults as the major source of behavior standards and recognition of achievement.* During the early school years, parents and teachers set standards of conduct, and most children try to live up to them. But by the later elementary grades, children are more interested in getting along with one another without adult supervision. Consequently, children come to realize that the rules for behavior within the peer group are not quite the same as the rules for behavior within the family or the classroom.

Peer group norms for behavior begin to replace adult norms

This newfound freedom can have a down side. Because children of this age typically want to be accepted by their peers, have a relatively naive view of right and wrong, and do not have enough self-assurance to oppose group norms, they may engage in behaviors (shoplifting, fighting, prejudice against outsiders) that they would not exhibit at home or in the classroom (Mitchell, 1990).

Journal Entry
Moderating the Power of Peer Group Norms

2. *Friendships become more selective and gender based.* Elementary grade children become even more discriminating than primary grade children in the selection of friends and playmates as they associate mainly with peers of the same age and gender. Although children of this age will rarely refuse to interact with members of the opposite sex when directed to do so by parents and teachers, they will avoid each other's company when left to their own devices. Most children choose a best friend who is usually of the same gender. These relationships, based usually on common ideas, outlooks, and impressions of the world, may last through adolescence (Mitchell, 1990).

EMOTIONAL CHARACTERISTICS: ELEMENTARY GRADES

1. *During this period, children develop a global and moderately stable self-image.* Susan Harter (1988, 1990) and William Damon (1988) have made extensive studies of how children formulate their **self-image**. According to both researchers, the overall picture upper elementary grade children have of themselves, a mental self-portrait, so to speak, is made up of two components: a description of their physical, social, emotional, and cognitive attributes (normally referred to as **self-concept**) and the evaluative judgments they make about those attributes (normally referred to as **self-esteem**). They may, for example,

describe themselves as being taller but clumsier than most others or as having a lot of friends because of superior social skills.

There are several important facts to keep in mind about the formulation of a child's self-portrait. First, it is more generalized than is the case for primary grade children because it is based on information gained over time, tasks, and settings. A child may think of herself as socially adept not just because she is popular at school but because she has always been well liked and gets along well with adults as well as peers in a variety of situations. It is this generalized quality that helps make self-portraits relatively stable. Second, as the previous paragraph implies, comparison with others is the fundamental basis of a self-portrait during the elementary grades. This orientation is due in part to the fact that children are not as egocentric as they were a few years earlier and are developing the capability to think in terms of multiple categories. It is also due to the fact that competition and individualism are highly prized values in many Western cultures. Consequently, children will naturally compare themselves to one another ("I'm taller than my friend") as well as to broad-based norms ("I'm tall for my age") in an effort to determine who they are. But, as William Damon and Daniel Hart (1988) point out, comparison is a less important basis for building a self-image in cultures where competition and individualism are downplayed.

Third, the self is described for the first time in terms of emotions (pride, shame, worry, anger, happiness) and how well they can be controlled. Fourth, a child's sense of self is influenced both by the information and attitudes that are communicated by such significant others as parents, teachers, and friends and by how competent the child feels in areas where success is important. The implications of this fact will be discussed in many of the remaining chapters of the text.

Since major developmental changes usually do not occur during the elementary grades, a child's self-image will remain fairly stable for a few years if there are no major changes in the child's home or social environment. But, as you will see in the latter part of this chapter, the developmental changes that typically occur during the middle school and high school grades often produce dramatic changes in the sense of self.

2. *Disruptive family relationships, social rejection, and school failure may lead to delinquent behavior.* Gerald Patterson, Barbara DeBarsyshe, and Elizabeth Ramsey (1989) marshal a wide array of evidence to support their belief that delinquent behavior is the result of a causal chain of events that originates in childhood with dysfunctional parent-child relationships. In their view, poor parent-child relationships lead to behavior problems, which lead to peer rejection and academic failure, which lead to identification with a deviant peer group, which results in delinquent behavior. Parents of such children administer harsh and inconsistent punishment, provide little positive reinforcement, and do little monitoring and supervising of each child's activities.

Because these children have not learned to follow adult rules and regulations but have learned how to satisfy their needs through coercive behavior, they are rejected by their peers, are easily distracted when doing schoolwork, show little interest in the subjects they study, and do not master many of the basic academic skills necessary for subsequent achievement. Attempts at short-circuiting this chain of events stand a greater chance of success if they begin early and are multifaceted. In addition to counseling and parent training, mastery of basic academic skills is important.

Self-concept becomes more generalized and stable; is based primarily on comparisons with peers

Journal Entry
Ways to Improve Students' Self-Concept

Delinquents have few friends, are easily distracted, are not interested in schoolwork, lack basic skills

COGNITIVE CHARACTERISTICS: ELEMENTARY GRADES

1. *The elementary grade child can think logically, although such thinking is constrained and inconsistent.* In terms of Piaget's stages, upper elementary grade children are concrete operational stage thinkers. Most will have attained enough mastery of logical schemes that they can understand and solve tasks that involve such processes as class inclusion (understanding the superordinate-subordinate relationships that make up hierarchies), seriation, conservation, and symbolic representation (reading maps, for example), provided that the content of the task refers to real, tangible ideas that the child has either experienced or can imagine. But general and abstract ideas often escape the elementary-age child. For example, sarcasm, metaphor, and allegory are usually lost on concrete stage thinkers. A similar fate usually befalls the idea that knowledge is often the product of inferential reasoning and may therefore be rejected as untrue if flaws in the reasoning can be shown. Concrete thinkers either accept or reject what authority figures tell them on the basis of rather arbitrary criteria.

The knowledge base of fourth- and fifth-grade children contains many misconceptions, and they may behave illogically. To prove a point or win a debate with a classmate or playmate, the upper elementary child may reel off a string of facts, some of which reflect authoritative sources, some of which are exaggerations, and some of which are invented on the spot. A ten-year-old may believe, for example, that people can live for several months without eating and that vacant houses are haunted. As John Mitchell (1990) humorously put it, "Many kids possess a gift for compressing the largest number of words into the smallest amount of thought." (p. 213)

| **Elementary grade students reason logically but concretely**

2. *On tasks that call for simple memory skills, elementary grade children often perform about as well as adolescents or adults. But on tasks that require more complex memory skills, their performance is more limited.* When tasks call for recognizing previously learned information, such as vocabulary words or facts about a person or event, or for rehearsing several items for immediate use, elementary grade children can perform about as well as older students. Relatively simple memory processes like recognition or rote repetition approach their maximum levels by this point in cognitive development. But the same is not true for tasks that require such advanced memory processes as elaboration and organization. When asked to sort a set of pictures into categories, for example, elementary grade children create fewer and more idiosyncratic categories (which are generally less effective for later recall of the items in the category) than do older children or adults. Similarly, less than half of a group of ten-year-olds in one study devised a way to help them remember to take a batch of cupcakes out of an oven after thirty minutes had elapsed whereas 75 percent of a group of fourteen-year-olds did (Kail, 1990).

Middle School (Grades 6, 7, and 8; Eleven, Twelve, and Thirteen Years)

In this section we use the term *adolescent* for the first time. Although it may strike you as odd to think of eleven- and twelve-year-olds as adolescents, developmental

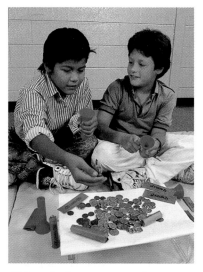

Although elementary grade children understand the logical basis for tasks such as classification, seriation, and conservation, they can solve such tasks only if they are based on concrete objects and ideas.

psychologists typically apply this term to individuals as young as ten years of age. The reason they do is because the onset of puberty is taken as the primary characteristic that defines the passage from middle childhood to adolescence (Allen, Splittgerber, & Manning, 1993; Balk, 1995). Although a variety of terms are used to denote the initial period of change that marks the adolescent years (ages ten to fourteen), we use two of the more popular: *early adolescent* and *emerging adolescent*.

PHYSICAL CHARACTERISTICS: MIDDLE SCHOOL

1. *Physical growth tends to be both rapid and uneven.* During the middle school years, the average child will grow 2 to 4 inches per year and gain 8 to 10 pounds per year. But some parts of the body, particularly the hands and feet, grow faster than others. Consequently, middle school children tend to look gangly and clumsy (Ames & Miller, 1994). Because girls mature more rapidly than boys, their **growth spurt** begins at about age ten and a half, reaches a peak at about age twelve, and is generally complete by age fourteen (Dusek, 1991).

The result of this timing difference in the growth spurt is that many middle school girls look considerably older than boys of the same age. After the growth spurt, however, the muscles in the average boy's body are larger, as are the heart and lungs. Furthermore, the body of the mature male has a greater capacity than that of the female for carrying oxygen in the blood and for neutralizing the chemical products of muscular exercise, such as lactic acid. Thus, the average male has greater strength and endurance than the average female (Tanner, 1972).

If you notice that students are upset about sudden growth (or lack of it), you might try to help them accept the situation by explaining that things will eventually even out. To reduce the unhappiness that arises from conflicts between physical attributes and gender roles, you might try to persuade students that being male or female should not in itself determine what a person does.

> **Girls' growth spurt occurs earlier, and so they look older than boys of same age**

> **After growth spurt, boys have greater strength and endurance**

> **Journal Entry**
> Helping Students Adjust to the Growth Spurt

Table 3.4	**Applying Stage Theories of Development to Middle School Years**

Stage of psychosocial development: transition from industry vs. inferiority to identity vs. role confusion. Growing independence leads to initial thoughts about identity. There is greater concern about appearance and gender roles than about occupational choice.

Stage of cognitive development: beginning of formal operational thought for some. There is increasing ability to engage in mental manipulations and test hypotheses.

Stage of moral development: transition to morality of cooperation, conventional level. There is increasing willingness to think of rules as flexible mutual agreements; "official" rules are still likely to be obeyed out of respect for authority or out of a desire to impress others.

General factors to keep in mind: Growth spurt and puberty influence many aspects of behavior. An abrupt switch occurs (for sixth graders) from being the oldest, biggest, most sophisticated students in elementary school to being the youngest, smallest, least knowledgeable students in middle school. Acceptance by peers is extremely important. Students who do poor schoolwork begin to feel bitter, resentful, and restless. Awareness grows of a need to make personal value decisions regarding dress, premarital sex, and code of ethics.

After reviewing research on early and later maturation, Norman Livson and Harvey Peskin (1980) conclude that differences in physical maturation are likely to produce specific differences in later behavior (see Table 3.5). The **early-maturing boy** is likely to draw favorable responses from adults (because of his adult appearance), which promotes confidence and poise (thus contributing to leadership and popularity with peers). The **late-maturing boy**, by contrast, may feel inferior and attempt to compensate for his physical and social frustration by engaging in bossy and attention-getting behavior. The very success of the early-maturing boy in high school, however, may cause him to develop an inflexible conception of himself, leading to problems when he must deal with new or negative situations later in life. The need for the late-maturing boy to cope with difficult adjustment situations in high school may equip him to adapt to adversity and change later in life.

	Early-maturing boys likely to draw favorable responses
	Late-maturing boys may seek attention

Livson and Peskin observe that the late-maturing boy is psychologically and socially out of step with peers, and the same applies to the **early-maturing girl**. The **late-maturing girl**, whose growth is less abrupt and whose size and appearance are likely to reflect the petiteness featured in stereotyped views of femininity, shares many of the characteristics (poise, popularity, leadership

Late-maturing girls likely to be popular and carefree

Table 3.5	The Impact of Early and Late Maturation	
Maturational Stage	**Characteristics as Adolescents**	**Characteristics as Adults**
Early-maturing boys	Self-confident, high in self-esteem, likely to be chosen as leaders (but leadership tendencies more likely in low-SES boys than in middle-class boys)	Self-confident, responsible, cooperative, sociable. But also rigid, moralistic, humorless, and conforming
Late-maturing boys	Energetic, bouncy, given to attention-getting behavior, not popular, lower aspirations for educational achievement	Impulsive and assertive. But also insightful, perceptive, creatively playful, able to cope with new situations
Early-maturing girls	Not popular or likely to be leaders, indifferent in social situations, lacking in poise (but middle-class girls more confident than those from low-SES groups), more likely to date, smoke, and drink earlier	Self-possessed, self-directed, able to cope, likely to score high in ratings of psychological health
Late-maturing girls	Confident, outgoing, assured, popular, likely to be chosen as leaders	Likely to experience difficulty adapting to stress, likely to score low in ratings of overall psychological health

SOURCES: Clausen (1975); Hetherington & Parke (1993); Jones (1957, 1965); Livson & Peskin (1980); Mussen & Jones (1957); Peterson & Taylor (1980).

tendencies) of the early-maturing boy. The advantages enjoyed by the late-maturing girl are not permanent, however. Livson and Peskin report that "the stress-ridden early-maturing girl in adulthood has become clearly a more coping, self-possessed, and self-directed person than the late-maturing female in the cognitive and social as well as emotional sectors. . . . It is the late-maturing female, carefree and unchallenged in adolescence, who faces adversity maladroitly in adulthood" (1980, p. 72).

Journal Entry
Helping Early and
Late Maturers
Cope

If late-maturing boys in your classes appear driven to seek attention or inclined to brood about their immaturity, you might try to give them extra opportunities to gain status and self-confidence by succeeding in schoolwork or other nonathletic activities. If you notice that early-maturing girls seem insecure, you might try to bolster their self-esteem by giving them extra attention and by recognizing their achievements.

2. *Pubertal development is evident in practically all girls and in many boys.* From ages eleven through thirteen, most girls develop sparse pubic and underarm hair and exhibit breast enlargement. In boys the testes and scrotum begin to grow and lightly pigmented pubic hair appears (Hetherington & Parke, 1993).

Average age of puberty:
girls, eleven; boys, fourteen

3. *Concern and curiosity about sex are almost universal, especially among girls.* The average age of puberty for girls in the United States is eleven years (Dusek, 1991); the range is from eight to eighteen years. For boys the average age of puberty is fourteen years; the range is from ten to eighteen years. Since sexual maturation involves drastic biological and psychological adjustments, children are concerned and curious. It seems obvious that accurate, unemotional answers to questions about sex are desirable. However, for your own protection you should find out about the sex education policy at your school. Many school districts have formal programs approved by community representatives and led by designated educators. Informal spur-of-the-moment class discussions may create more problems than they solve.

SOCIAL CHARACTERISTICS: MIDDLE SCHOOL

1. *The development of interpersonal reasoning leads to greater understanding of the feelings of others.* Robert L. Selman (1980) has studied the development of **interpersonal reasoning** in children. Interpersonal reasoning is the ability to understand the relationship between motives and behavior among a group of people. The results of Selman's research are summarized in Table 3.6. The stages outlined there reveal that during the elementary school years children gradually grasp the fact that a person's overt actions or words do not always reflect inner feelings. They also come to comprehend that a person's reaction to a distressing situation can have many facets. Toward the end of the elementary school years—and increasingly during adolescence—children become capable of taking a somewhat detached and analytical view of their own behavior as well as the behavior of others.

Not surprisingly, a child's interpersonal sensitivity and maturity seem to have an impact on relationships with others. Selman (1980) compared the responses of seven- to twelve-year-old boys who were attending schools for children with learning and interpersonal problems with the responses of a matched group of boys attending regular schools. The boys attending special schools were below average for their age in understanding the feelings of others.

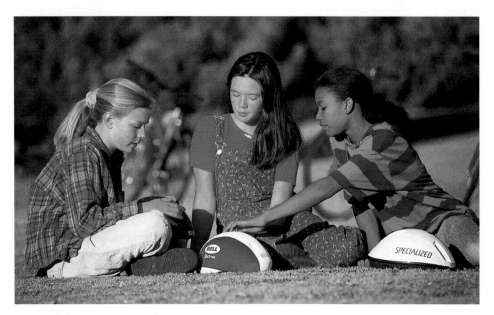

During the middle school years, children acquire greater sensitivity to the beliefs and feelings of others.

Selman believes that teachers and therapists might be able to aid children who are not as advanced in role-taking skills as their age-mates by helping them become more sensitive to the feelings of others. If an eight-year-old boy is still functioning at the egocentric level, for example, he may fail to properly interpret the behavior of classmates and become a social isolate. Selman describes how one such boy was encouraged to think continually about the reasons behind his social actions and those of others and acquired sufficient social sensitivity to learn to get along with others.

Discussion techniques Selman recommends can be introduced in a natural, rather than a formal, way. If you see a boy react with physical or verbal abuse when jostled by a playmate, for example, you might say, "You know, people don't always intentionally bump into others. Unless you are absolutely sure that someone has hurt you on purpose, it can be a lot pleasanter for all concerned if you don't make a big deal out of it."

Journal Entry
Ways to Promote Social Sensitivity

2. *The desire to conform reaches a peak during the middle school years.* Early adolescents find it reassuring to dress and behave like others, and they are likely to alter their own opinions to coincide with those of a group. When you encourage student participation in class discussions, you may need to be alert to the tendency for students at these grade levels to be reluctant to voice minority opinions. If you want them to think about controversial issues, it may be preferable to invite them to write their opinions anonymously rather than voice them in front of the rest of the class.

Discussion of controversial issues may be difficult because of strong desire to conform to peer norms

EMOTIONAL CHARACTERISTICS: MIDDLE SCHOOL

1. *Some early adolescents go through a period of "storm and stress."* Starting with G. Stanley Hall, who wrote a pioneering two-volume text on adolescence in 1904, some theorists have described adolescence as a period of turmoil. Feelings of confusion, anxiety, and depression; extreme mood swings; and low levels of self-confidence are felt to be typical of this age group. Some of the

Table 3.6	Stages of Interpersonal Reasoning Described by Selman

Stage 0: egocentric level (about ages 4 to 6). Children do not recognize that other persons may interpret the same social event or course of action differently from the way they do. They do not reflect on the thoughts of self and others. They can label the overtly expressed feelings of others but do not comprehend cause-and-effect relations of social actions.

Stage 1: social information role taking (about ages 6 to 8). Children are able in limited ways to differentiate between their own interpretations of social interactions and the interpretation of others. But they cannot simultaneously think of their own view and those of others.

Stage 2: self-reflective role taking (about ages 8 to 10). Interpersonal relations are interpreted in specific situations whereby each person understands the expectations of the other in that particular context. Children are not yet able to view the two perspectives at once, however.

Stage 3: multiple role taking (about ages 10 to 12). Children become capable of taking a third-person view, which permits them to understand the expectations of themselves and of others in a variety of situations as if they were spectators.

Stage 4: social and conventional system taking (about ages 12 to 15+). Each individual involved in a relationship with another understands many of the subtleties of the interactions involved. In addition, a societal perspective begins to develop. That is, actions are judged by how they might influence *all* individuals, not just those who are immediately concerned.

SOURCE: Adapted from discussions in Selman (1980).

reasons cited for this turbulence are rapid changes in height, weight, and body proportions; increases in hormone production; the task of identity formation; increased academic responsibilities; and the development of formal operational reasoning (Jackson & Bosma, 1990; Peterson, 1988; Susman, 1991).

Since the 1970s, however, a number of psychologists have questioned whether turmoil is universal during the emerging adolescent (and later) years (for example, see Hill, 1987; Jackson & Bosma, 1990; Peterson, 1988). In one study (Offer & Offer, 1975) 79 percent of a group of middle-class adolescent boys were classified as falling into one of three categories: *continuous growth*, *surgent growth*, and *tumultuous growth*. Boys in the continuous growth group (23 percent of the sample) were easily able to cope with the various physiological, social, emotional, and cognitive changes they experienced. Boys in the surgent growth group (35 percent) alternated between difficult and easy periods, although in general they were reasonably well adjusted. Only 21 percent, those in the tumultuous growth group, exhibited the type of chronic turmoil that marked early accounts of adolescent emotional development. (The remaining 21 percent could not be classified, although they were closest to the first two groups.)

Although the Offer and Offer study was limited to adolescent males, gender differences in psychological adjustment have been documented. Boys who exhibit problems during adolescence are more likely to have had similar problems in childhood, whereas girls are more likely to initially exhibit problems in adolescence. Achievement situations are more likely to produce anxiety responses in boys, whereas girls are more likely to become anxious in interpersonal

Teenagers experience different degrees of emotional turmoil

situations. Finally, girls are more likely than boys to increasingly exhibit signs of depression (Peterson, 1988).

2. *As a result of the continued influence of egocentric thought, middle school students are typically self-conscious and self-centered.* Because emerging adolescents are acutely aware of the physical and emotional changes that are taking place within them, they assume that everyone else is just as interested in, and is constantly evaluating, their appearance, feelings, and behavior. Consequently, they are deeply concerned about such things as what type of clothing to wear for special occasions, with whom they should and should not be seen in public (they should never be seen with their parents at the mall, for example), and how they greet and talk with various people. Not surprisingly, what interests middle school students a great deal either does not interest or annoys adults.

Another manifestation of adolescent egocentrism is the assumption that adults do not, indeed cannot, understand the thoughts and feelings of early adolescence. It's as if the early adolescent believes she is experiencing things no one else has ever experienced before. Hence, a teen or preteen will likely say to a parent, "You just don't know what it feels like to be in love" (Wiles & Bondi, 1993).

COGNITIVE CHARACTERISTICS: MIDDLE SCHOOL

1. *Because of the psychological demands of early adolescence, middle school students need a classroom environment that is open, supportive, and intellectually stimulating.* Early adolescence is an unsettling time for students because of changes in their physical development, social roles, cognitive development, and sexuality. Another source of stress is coping with the transition from the elementary grades to a middle school or junior high. Partly because of these personal and environmental stresses, the self-concept, academic motivation, and achievement levels of adolescents decline, sometimes drastically. Are schools at

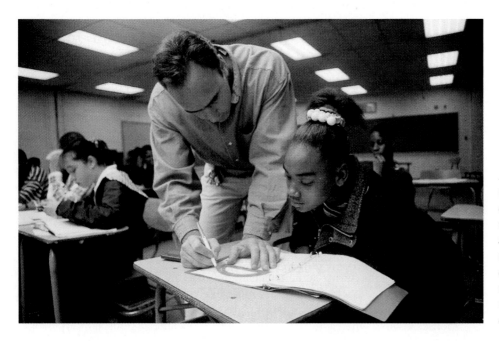

Early adolescents are faced with several developmental challenges. Consequently, middle school teachers should make a special effort to establish a supportive classroom atmosphere in which students can meet their social, emotional, and cognitive needs.

all to blame for these problems? Perhaps they are. Jacquelynne Eccles and her associates (1993) provide persuasive evidence that these negative changes are due in part, perhaps in large part, to the fact that the typical school environment does not meet the needs of developing adolescents.

Their argument is based on an analysis of the psychological needs of early adolescence and the kinds of changes that take place in classroom organization, instruction, and climate as one moves from the last of the elementary grades to the first of the middle school or junior high grades (usually seventh grade). Early adolescent development is characterized by an increased need for autonomy, a focus on oneself (resulting in an acute self-consciousness), the importance of peer acceptance, concerns about identity, and the capacity for abstract thought. The typical junior high/middle school environment, however, is largely incompatible with the needs of the typical adolescent. For one thing, instead of providing students with opportunities to make decisions about such things as classroom rules, seating arrangements, homework assignments, and time spent on various tasks, teachers impose most of the requirements and limit the choices students can make about what, where, and how to do things. Second, students perceive their relationships with their teachers as being less friendly, supportive, and caring in comparison to the teachers they had in sixth grade. Third, competition and social comparisons among students are increased as a result of such practices as whole-class instruction, ability grouping, normative grading (see Chapter 14 for a discussion of this practice), and public evaluations of one's work. Small-group instruction is infrequent, and individualized instruction almost never occurs. Fourth, middle school/junior high teachers rate themselves as being less effective with students, particularly in mathematics, than do sixth-grade teachers. This attitude seems to affect the students, for by the end of their first year in middle school they rate themselves less capable in math, have lower expectations for success in math, and see it as being a more difficult subject to master than they did in sixth grade. Finally, many classroom tasks involve low-level seatwork, verbatim recall of information, and little opportunity for discussion or group work. In one study of eleven junior high school science classes, the most frequent activity was copying information from the board or textbook onto worksheets.

2. Self-efficacy becomes an important influence on intellectual and social behavior. As we mentioned in point 1 of social characteristics, middle school children become capable of analyzing both their own view of an interpersonal interaction and that of the other person. This newfound analytic ability is also turned inward, resulting in evaluations of one's intellectual and social capabilities. Albert Bandura (1986), a learning theorist whom we will discuss in Chapter 7, coined the term **self-efficacy** to refer to how capable people believe they are at dealing with one type of task or another. Thus, a student may have a very strong sense of self-efficacy for math ("I know I can solve most any algebraic equation"), a moderate degree of self-efficacy for certain athletic activities ("I think I play baseball and basketball about as well as most kids my age"), and a low sense of self-efficacy for interpersonal relationships ("I'm just no good at making friends").

These self-evaluative beliefs influence what activities students choose and for how long they will persist at a given task, particularly when progress becomes difficult. Students with a moderate to strong sense of self-efficacy will persist at a task long enough to obtain the success or corrective feedback that

Environment of middle schools does not meet needs of adolescents, leading to lower levels of learning

Self-efficacy beliefs for academic and social tasks become strong influences on behavior

leads to expectations of future success. Students with a low sense of self-efficacy, however, tend to abandon tasks at the first sign of difficulty, thereby establishing a pattern of failure, low expectations of future success, and task avoidance. Since self-efficacy beliefs grow out of personal performance, observation of other people doing the same thing, and verbal persuasion, you can help students develop strong feelings of self-efficacy by following the suggestions we will make in Chapters 7, 8, and 10 about modeling and imitation, learning strategies, and effective forms of instruction, respectively.

High School (Grades 9, 10, 11, and 12; Fourteen, Fifteen, Sixteen, and Seventeen Years)

PHYSICAL CHARACTERISTICS: HIGH SCHOOL

1. *Most students reach physical maturity, and virtually all attain puberty.* Although almost all girls reach their ultimate height, some boys may continue to grow even after graduation. Tremendous variation exists in height and weight and in rate of maturation. As noted earlier, late-maturing boys seem to have considerable difficulty adjusting to their slower rate of growth. There is still concern about appearance, although it may not be as strong as during the middle school years. Glandular changes leading to acne may be a source of worry and self-consciousness to some students. The most significant glandular change accompanying puberty is arousal of the sex drive.

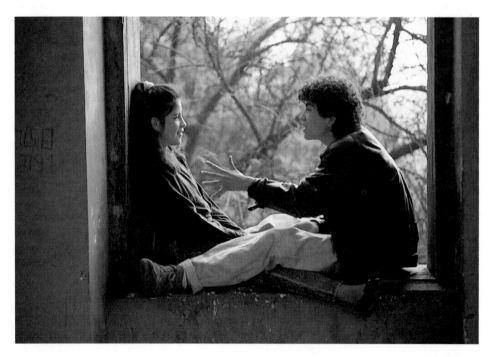

Many adolescents may experience confusion about sexual relationships. They are expected to be interested in sex, but at the same time attitudes towards sex are often imbued with strong moral overtones.

Table 3.7	Applying Stage Theories of Development to the High School Years

Stage of psychosocial development: identity vs. role confusion. Concerns arise about gender roles and occupational choice. Different identity statuses become apparent.

Stage of cognitive development: formal thought for many students. There is increasing ability to engage in mental manipulations, understand abstractions, and test hypotheses.

Stage of moral development: morality of cooperation, conventional level. There is increasing willingness to think of rules as mutual agreements and to allow for intentions and extenuating circumstances.

General factors to keep in mind: achievement of sexual maturity has a profound effect on many aspects of behavior. Peer group and reactions of friends are extremely important. There is concern about what will happen after graduation, particularly for students who do not intend to continue their education. Awareness grows of the significance of academic ability and importance of grades for certain career patterns. There is a need to make personal value decisions regarding use of drugs, premarital sex, and code of ethics.

2. *Many adolescents become sexually active but experience confusion regarding sexual relationships.* Recent surveys reveal that 78 percent of males and 63 percent of females have engaged in sexual intercourse at least once by age nineteen. The percentages for African-American, Hispanic-American, and white males are 92 percent, 78 percent, and 75 percent, respectively. For African-American, Hispanic-American, and white females, the percentages are 77 percent, 59 percent, and 61 percent, respectively (Irwin & Millstein, 1991).

For a group of eleven hundred adolescents, J. Richard Udrey (1990) found that initiation of sexual intercourse in white males was strongly related to hormone production and was only weakly related to the discouraging or encouraging efforts of parents, schools, friends, and the media. It was not unusual for adolescent males to experience a tenfold increase in testosterone levels over a period of six months. The initiation of sexual intercourse among white females, however, was more strongly associated with such social factors as grades in school and whether friends had engaged in sexual intercourse than with increases in hormone levels. For African-American females, the factors that best predicted onset of sexual intercourse were pubertal development and sexual intentions. The factors associated with initial sexual intercourse in African-American males could not be determined as most of them reported having had at least one sexual intercourse experience prior to the initial interview.

Sexual activity among male, female teens due to different factors

In a discussion of the development of sexuality in adolescence, Patricia Miller and William Simon (1980) point out that puberty, a biological event, causes adolescents to function as "self-motivated sexual actors," which is a social event. Miller and Simon comment that in technological societies "young people are defined as sexually mature while simultaneously being defined as socially and psychologically immature" (1980, p. 383). The result is that adolescents are pulled first one way and then another regarding sexual relationships.

Adolescents likely to be confused about appropriateness of premarital sex

These findings illustrate the pressing need for sex education during the high school years. In particular, adolescents need to understand the distinction between sex and mature love. A major characteristic of mature love is that "the well-being of the other person is just a little bit more important than the well-being of the self" (Gordon & Gilgun, 1987, p. 180).

3. *Increased sexual activity among adolescents has led to high rates of births outside of marriage and to sexually transmitted diseases.* Recent surveys indicate that about 65 percent of all adolescent mothers (about 307,000 as of 1991) are unmarried and that the rate at which babies are born to unmarried adolescent females has quadrupled since 1960. Younger white females and African-American females are most likely to be unmarried at the birth of their child (Coates & van Widenfeldt, 1991). Some factors that predict adolescent pregnancy include being a member of a particular race, having a mother who was pregnant as an adolescent, coming from a low-income family, coming from a one-parent family, and having low self-esteem (Coates & van Widenfeldt, 1991; Stiffman, Earls, Robins, Jung, & Kulbok, 1987). One factor contributing to the high rate of teenage pregnancies and births is the relatively low level of contraceptive use. Less than 50 percent of all adolescents regularly use some form of contraception (Conger, 1991).

The relatively high levels of sexual activity and low levels of regular contraception among adolescents are particularly worrisome as they put adolescents at risk for contracting **sexually transmitted diseases (STDs)**. According to some experts, STDs among adolescents in the United States have reached epidemic proportions. One estimate is that as many as 2.5 million teens are infected each year with an STD (Wiles & Bondi, 1993). The highest rates of STDs are found among younger adolescent females (fifteen years or younger) and inner-city minority youths. More than 60 percent of the STD cases reported annually occur among individuals under the age of twenty-five. And about 25 percent of the cases occur among individuals between the ages of fifteen and nineteen (Boyer & Hein, 1991).

The worst of the STDs is, of course, acquired immune deficiency syndrome (AIDS) because there is no known cure. Although the number of AIDS cases among adolescents is currently low, it will rise in the future, potentially becoming a major problem. The percentage of adolescents who test positive for human immunodeficiency virus (HIV, the viral cause of AIDS) ranges from about 2 percent to 6 percent (Rotheram-Borus & Koopman, 1991). Because HIV has a long incubation period, AIDS symptoms may not show up for several years. Consequently, the proportion of today's teens who will be diagnosed with AIDS in their twenties will be more than the 2 percent to 6 percent figure just cited.

SOCIAL CHARACTERISTICS: HIGH SCHOOL

1. *Parents are likely to influence long-range plans; peers are likely to influence immediate status.* A number of studies have attempted to compare the beliefs, attitudes, and values of parents and those of their children and also to compare the extent to which parent-peer and peer-peer opinions agree and conflict. Studies of values (reviewed by Feather, 1980), of political thinking (reviewed by Gallatin, 1980), of moral development (reviewed by Hoffman, 1980), and of occupational choice (reviewed by Rogers, 1972) lead to the conclusion that high school students are probably influenced in these areas of their lives more by parents than by peers. But a visit to any high school will reveal that in terms of dress, hairstyles, interests, social relationships, and the like, the influence of peers is extremely potent.

Not surprisingly, most conflicts between parents and their adolescent children are about such peer-influenced issues as personal appearance, friends, dating, hours, and eating habits (Hill, 1987). The hypothesis that parents and peers

Parents influence values, plans; peers influence immediate status

influence different aspects of adolescent behavior has been developed by Clay Brittain (1967), who suggests that parents have a greater impact on decisions that have implications for the future (such as choice of a career), whereas peers influence decisions that involve current status and identity needs (such as choice of friends). The influence of parents appears to be greatest when there are mutual affection and respect between parent and child (Baumrind, 1991; Hill, 1987).

2. *Girls seem to experience greater anxiety about friendships than boys do.* Factors that cause girls to become concerned about the reactions of others were summarized in the preceding chapter. Adolescent girls tend to seek intimacy in friendships (Coleman, 1980). Boys, in contrast, often stress skills and interests when they form friendships, and their tendencies to be competitive and self-reliant may work against the formation of close relationships with male companions. Because adolescent girls often wish to form an intimate relationship with another girl, they are more likely than boys to experience anxiety, jealousy, and conflicts regarding friendships with same-sex peers. You should not be surprised, therefore, if secondary school girls are much more preoccupied with positive and negative aspects of friendships than boys are.

Girls more likely than boys to experience anxiety about friendships

3. *Many high school students are employed after school.* Part-time employment among adolescents who attend school has increased in recent years and is more prevalent in the United States than in other industrialized countries. Between 1953 and 1983 the percentage of sixteen- and seventeen-year-old boys who attended school and worked part time grew from 29 to 36 percent. The increase for girls was even more dramatic—a doubling from 18 to 36 percent. By 1987 the combined part-time employment figure for both sexes was 41 percent. According to self-report data, about 60 percent of high school sophomores and 75 percent of seniors engage in part-time employment to some degree. Sophomore boys who work average about fifteen hours a week; senior boys average about twenty-one hours a week. Sophomore and senior girls average about eleven and eighteen hours, respectively.

The pros and cons of after-school employment have been vigorously debated. On the positive side, it is thought to enhance self-discipline, a sense of responsibility, self-confidence, and attitudes toward work. On the negative side, part-time employment leaves less time for homework, participation in extracurricular activities, and development of friendships; it may also lead to increased stress, lower grades, and lower career aspirations (Mortimer, 1991).

EMOTIONAL CHARACTERISTICS: HIGH SCHOOL

1. *Many psychiatric disorders either appear or become prominent during adolescence. Included among these are eating disorders, substance abuse, schizophrenia, depression, and suicide.* Eating disorders are much more common in females than in males. *Anorexia nervosa* is an eating disorder characterized by a preoccupation with body weight and food, behavior directed toward losing weight, peculiar patterns of handling food, weight loss, intense fear of gaining weight, and a distorted perception of one's body. This disorder occurs predominantly in females (about 94 percent of the cases) and usually appears between the ages of fourteen and seventeen (Halmi, 1987).

Bulimia nervosa is a disorder in which binge eating (uncontrolled, rapid eating of large quantities of food over a short period of time), followed by self-induced vomiting, is the predominant behavior. Binges are typically followed

Many high school students, girls in particular, experience periods of depression, loneliness, and anxiety. Because severe depression often precedes a suicide attempt, teachers should refer students they believe to be depressed to the school counselor.

by feelings of guilt, depression, self-disgust, and fasting. Bulimia is a disorder that also appears predominantly in adolescent females (Halmi, 1987).

Adolescents who engage in *substance abuse* (tobacco, alcohol, and controlled substances such as marijuana and cocaine) not only jeopardize their physical and emotional health but increase their risk of doing poorly in school or of dropping out of school. Surveys of ten- through eighteen-year-olds report that:

• Twelve percent smoked a half pack or more of cigarettes a day.

• Fifteen percent had five or more drinks in a row, three or more times in the past two weeks.

• Five percent smoked marijuana twenty or more times within the past month.

• Three percent used cocaine three or more times within the past month. (Kazdin, 1993)

Although *schizophrenia* (a thinking disorder characterized by illogical and unrealistic thinking, delusions, and hallucinations) is relatively rare among adolescents, it is the most frequently occurring psychotic disorder, and the number of cases diagnosed between the ages of twelve and eighteen is steadily increasing. In about half of the cases, behavioral abnormalities such as odd, unpredictable behavior; social isolation; and rejection by peers were first noticeable in childhood (Conger, 1991; Rutter, 1990).

2. *The most common type of emotional disorder during adolescence is depression.* Estimates of **depression** among high school youths range from 7 to 28 percent depending on the level of depression being examined and the criteria being used to measure it. The most common forms of depression, from least to

most serious, are *depressed mood, depressive syndrome, and clinical depression.* The most common form of depression among adolescents is depressed mood. This state is primarily characterized by feelings of sadness or unhappiness, although emotions such as anxiety, fear, guilt, anger, and contempt are frequently present as well. According to parents' reports, 10 to 20 percent of boys and 15 to 20 percent of girls were in a depressed mood in the past six months. But if you ask adolescents themselves, the percentages are higher. About 20 to 35 percent of boys and 25 to 40 percent of girls report having been in a depressed mood (Peterson, Compas, Brooks-Gunn, Stemmler, Ey, & Grant, 1993). Individuals from low-income families are typically the most depressed. Depression in adolescents often precedes substance abuse (Petti & Larson, 1987). Prior to puberty, twice as many boys as girls exhibit depressive syndromes; after puberty the ratio is just the opposite (Cicchetti & Toth, 1998; Rutter, 1990). Females may exhibit greater tendencies than males to feel depressed, but this does not mean that such reactions occur only in high school girls. Extreme feelings of depression are the most common reason that teenagers of both sexes are referred to psychiatric clinics.

Depression most common
among females, teens from
poor families

Common symptoms of depression include feelings of worthlessness, crying spells, and suicidal thoughts, threats, and attempts. Additional symptoms are moodiness, social isolation, fatigue, hypochondriasis, and difficulty in concentrating (Cicchetti & Toth, 1998; Peterson et al., 1993). High school students who experience such symptoms typically try to ward off their depression through restless activity or flight to or from others. They may also engage in problem behavior or delinquent acts carried out in ways that make it clear they are appealing for help. (A depressed fifteen-year-old boy may carry out an act of vandalism, for instance, at a time when a school authority or police officer is sure to observe the incident.)

Aaron Beck (1972) suggests that depression consists of a *cognitive set* made up of negative views of oneself, the world, and the future. Martin Seligman (1975) proposes that depression is caused by *learned helplessness,* which leads to feelings of having no control over one's life. Irving Weiner (1975) emphasizes that depression typically involves a *sense of loss* that may have many causes. Depression may stem from the abrupt end of a personal relationship through death, separation, or broken friendship. An individual may undergo a sharp drop in self-esteem as a result of failure or guilt. Or a person may experience a loss of bodily integrity following illness, incapacitation, or disfigurement.

Depression may be caused by
negative cognitive set, learned
helplessness, sense of loss

Although many techniques exist for changing a negative self-concept to a positive view of self, one effective approach to minimizing depression is to help as many of your students as possible to experience success as they learn. Techniques to accomplish that goal will be discussed in the next seven chapters of this book.

Journal Entry
Helping Students
Overcome
Depression

3. *If depression becomes severe, suicide may be contemplated.* Suicide is a major cause of death among adolescents. Among fifteen- to nineteen-year-olds it accounts for 11.3 deaths per 100,000. Only motor vehicle accidents and homicides claim more victims. (Homicide occurs at the rate of 11.7 per 100,000 adolescents.) And the trend has been an increasing one. Between 1960 and 1988, adolescent suicide rose by more than 200 percent while the suicide rate for the general population increased by 17 percent (Garland & Zigler, 1993).

Two or three times as many females as males *attempt suicide,* almost always by taking an overdose of drugs. But four times as many young males as females *complete suicide*, usually with a gun. Prior to age twelve, *completed suicides* are rare (0.006 cases per 100,000). Between the ages of twelve and sixteen, however, there is a hundredfold increase and then an additional tenfold increase between the ages of sixteen and nineteen (7.6 cases per 100,000) (Petti & Larson, 1987; Rutter, 1990).

Although the suicide rate for Native Americans is higher than for any other ethnic group, there is considerable variation across tribes. The rate for Navahos is close to the national average (12 per 100,000), while the rate among some Apache tribes is as high as 43 per 100,000 (Garland & Zigler, 1993).

The single most important signal of a youth at risk for suicide is depression. Along with the common symptoms noted earlier under point 2, signs of depression include poor appetite, weight loss, changes in sleeping patterns, difficulty in concentrating, academic problems, and poor self-concept. These symptoms take on added significance when accompanied by a family history of suicide or parents who commit abuse or use drugs and alcohol excessively. The factors that usually trigger a suicide include a shameful or humiliating experience, such as perceived failure at school or rejection by a romantic partner or parent (Garland & Zigler, 1993; Strother, 1986).

Depression and unstable family situation place adolescents at risk for suicide

If you notice that a student in one of your classes seems extremely depressed, take the trouble to ask if there is anything you can do to provide support. Your interest and sympathy may prevent a suicide attempt. Also, be aware that recent prevention efforts include school-based programs. These programs, which are run by a mental health professional and/or an educator, are typically directed to high school students, their parents, and their teachers. They usually include a review of suicide statistics, a list of warning signs, a list of community mental health resources and how to contact them, and a discussion of how one refers a student or peer to counseling. Unfortunately, there is as yet too little research to know how effective such programs are in reducing the adolescent suicide rate (Garland & Zigler, 1993).

COGNITIVE CHARACTERISTICS: HIGH SCHOOL

1. *High school students become increasingly capable of engaging in formal thought, but they may not use this capability.* High school students are more likely than younger students to grasp relationships, mentally plan a course of action before proceeding, and test hypotheses systematically. Without supervision and guidance, however, they may not use such capabilities consistently. Accordingly, you might take advantage of opportunities to show students at these grade levels how they can function as formal thinkers. Call attention to relationships and to ways that previously acquired knowledge can be applied to new situations. Provide specific instruction in techniques of problem solving. (Ways you might do this will be discussed in Chapter 9.) Although your advice may be ignored by some students, others will probably take it more seriously. Despite the constant attempts of adolescents to appear totally self-sufficient and independent, they still view parents and teachers as knowledgeable authority figures when it comes to school achievement (Amiram, Bar-Tal, Alona, & Peleg, 1990).

2. *Between the ages of twelve and sixteen, political thinking becomes more abstract, liberal, and knowledgeable.* Joseph Adelson (1972, 1986) used an interview approach to obtain information about the development of political

thought during the adolescent years. At the start of the interviews, the subjects were requested to imagine that one thousand people had ventured to an island in the Pacific for the purpose of establishing a new society. The respondents were then asked to explain how these people might establish a political order; devise a legal system; establish a balance among rights, responsibilities, personal liberty, and the common good; and deal with other problems of public policy.

The analysis of the interview responses showed no significant gender differences in the understanding of political concepts and no significant differences attributable to intelligence and social class, although brighter students were better able to deal with abstract ideas and upper-class students were less likely to be authoritarian. The most striking and consistent finding was the degree to which the political thinking of the adolescent changed in the years between twelve and sixteen. Adelson concluded that the most significant changes were (1) an increase in the ability to deal with such abstractions as freedom of speech, equal justice under law, and the concept of community; (2) a decline in authoritarian views; (3) an increase in the ability to imagine the consequences of current actions; and (4) an increase in political knowledge.

Political thinking becomes more abstract, less authoritarian, more knowledgeable

Increased ability to deal with abstractions is a function of the shift from concrete to formal operational thought. When thirteen-year-olds were asked, "What is the purpose of laws?" a typical answer was "So people don't steal or kill" (Adelson, 1972, p. 108). A fifteen- or sixteen-year-old, by contrast, was more likely to say, "To ensure safety and enforce the government" (p. 108).

When considering punishment for crimes, younger children (Piaget's moral realists) hold the conviction that laws are immutable and that punishment should be stern. But by fourteen and fifteen, the adolescents interviewed by Adelson were more likely to consider circumstances and individual rights and to recommend rehabilitation rather than punishment.

If you will be teaching courses in social studies, you may find this information useful in lesson planning. It may also help you understand why students may respond to discussions of political or other abstract matters in different ways.

Selecting Technologies for Different Age Levels

As this chapter and the preceding one indicate, your teaching approaches will be influenced by the developmental level of your students. Your incorporation of educational technology will be no different. For kindergarten and primary grade teachers, tools to enhance student literacy are likely to be a priority. Elementary, middle school, and high school teachers will be more interested in tools that promote thinking, problem solving, and communication.

TECHNOLOGY AND LITERACY

Technology and literacy have always been intertwined. In most societies, spoken language resulted in the development of various media (stone, wood, and paper, for example) with which to record, store, and transmit ideas. As written information became more widely available and as societies became more technological, the need for increasing numbers of literate people grew. With the availability of word processors today, ideas can be swiftly recorded, rearranged, modified, and copied. Writing technologies have emerged during the past decade to help young children prewrite and rewrite their text, publish their stories, write reactions to stories they have read, and store data banks of words being learned (Rowland & Scott, 1992). In addition, voice synthesis or feedback allows students to hear how their stories sound, thereby building their phonemic awareness and assisting in the transition from listening and speaking to reading and writing (Balajthy, 1988; Lehrer, Levin, DeHart, & Comeaux, 1987). There are also numerous software tools to help children learn such vital reading skills as differentiating phonics sounds and letter blends, sounding out words, and recognizing rhyming patterns.

One of the more controversial early literacy tools, IBM's Writing to Read program, has been used with kindergarten and first grade students since 1983. In Writing to Read (WTR), students rotate among five workstations, where they work on phonics skills, electronically type their stories, listen to tape-recorded stories, write stories using pen and paper, and practice making letter sounds and words. At the heart of this program is a speech synthesizer that helps students learn forty-two phoneme, or letter-sound, combinations presented in ten instructional cycles (Labbo, Murray, & Phillips, 1995-1996). To extend these efforts, IBM has also developed Writing to Write (WTW), a literature-based approach for second, third, and fourth graders that includes both partner and individual activities such as paired editing, cooperative learning groups, and journal writing (Keeler, 1996).

Evaluations of WTR claim that the program promotes an environment that is rich in student conversation and successful writing (Casey & Martin, 1994). Some studies have also determined that it produces higher levels of reading and writing and more positive student attitudes than traditional classes (Casey & Martin, 1994; Gredler, 1997).

Despite these positive reports, WTR does have its limits. Research shows that the positive results found during kindergarten are not always maintained in first grade (Gredler, 1997), and the system is costly (Slavin, 1990). WTR classrooms have also been described as inflexible, fragmented, discouraging of student creativity, allowing few choices, too focused on discrete activities and time requirements, and lacking links back to regular classroom activities (Huenecke, 1992a, 1992b).

Another computer program for developing literacy skills of young children, Bubble Dialogue, provides an environment resembling a cartoon strip in which young students can create a dialogue between characters (Jones & Selby, 1997). Bubble Dialogue supports dialogue and role play between pairs of students by using "thought" and "speech" bubbles to foster student expression of ideas and interaction. Students work on their writing skills by inserting text into the empty comic strip balloons. The theoretical basis of this tool is Vygotsky's belief, mentioned in the last chapter, that language development needs to take place first in the social world so as to provide a meaningful basis for internalizing the rules of language use. Research by Charoula Angeli and Donald Cunningham (1998) indicates that Bubble Dialogue promotes student articulation of ideas, development of thought processes and word meanings, and acquisition of sentence structure awareness.

Since there is a natural distancing effect in Bubble Dialogue (characters do the talking and thinking rather than the child), this tool is useful for exploring controversial topics and sensitive issues (Eakin, 1997). For instance, it can be used as a therapeutic tool for adopted or foster children as well as those suffering from abuse (Jones & Selby, 1997).

Using Technology to Reduce Egocentrism

As we pointed out in Chapter 2, primary to elementary grade children are limited by egocentrism in their ability to think logically. Egocentrism, as you may recall, is the inability to understand the world from any perspective but your own. According to Jean Piaget, who first proposed the concept, the main factor that contributes to the decline of egocentrism is exposure to different points of view through social interaction. Since these interactions do not have to be face-to-face, it is quite possible that sharing experiences and points of view through a computer network or bulletin board may produce the same result.

Judi Harris (1997) notes that World Wide Web networking activities can be structured to foster six different types of interpersonal exchanges: (1) "keypals," who are students from two or more locations matched as e-mail pals; (2) global classrooms, wherein two or more classrooms anywhere in the world can study a common topic together; (3) electronic "appearances" by famous people or electronic commemorations of important historical events; (4) **electronic mentoring,** wherein subject-matter experts use e-mail or the Web to help learners understand a concept or complete a task; (5) question-and-answer services such as "Ask-A-Geologist"; and (6) impersonation projects in which participants communicate as someone else, often a famous historical figure.

Effect of Technology on Cognitive and Interpersonal Reasoning

One type of program that allows students to interact electronically with experts and explorers around the world is **adventure learning**. For instance, students from various schools might get together for virtual field trips to places like the Statue of Liberty for insights on immigration policies or the Civil War battlefield at Gettysburg for demonstrations of military tactics (Siegel & Kirkley, 1998). They also might communicate electronically with explorers traversing the Arctic tundra or the Amazon rain forest. While on virtual field trips, students are electronically transported to the actual site to view historical reenactments, listen to experts, ask questions, and electronically correspond with peers across the nation.

Electronic conferencing allows students to assume roles. For instance, middle school and high school students who assume the role of famous historical characters on sensitive environmental issues exhibit higher levels of dialogue and interpersonal reasoning than would be expected by Selman's (1980) developmental scheme (Bonk & Sugar, 1998).

Although these preliminary examples show how role play and peer collaboration might encourage student interpersonal reasoning, they also illustrate how online learning communities will open new windows to global education in the twenty-first century and, hopefully, empower students to examine and appreciate the complexity of real-world events as they occur.

RESOURCES FOR FURTHER INVESTIGATION

■ How Children Develop

Helen Bee describes how children develop physically, socially, emotionally, and cognitively in *The Developing Child* (8th ed., 1997). Robert V. Kail does the same in *Children and Their Development* (1998).

■ Children's Play Behavior

In *Children, Play, and Development* (1991), Fergus Hughes discusses the history of play in the Western world; different theories of play; cultural differences in play behaviors; patterns of play among toddlers, preschoolers, school-age children, and adolescents; gender differences in play; and the play behaviors of children with disabilities. Sandra Heidemann and Deborah Hewitt (1992), in *Pathways to Play*, describe the play categories of Mildred Parten and the proper conditions for children's play (such as time, space, and props), give a checklist for observing play behaviors, and explain how to use the results of the checklist for teaching children different play skills.

■ Cognitive Development

Henry Wellman and Susan Gelman (1992) describe what three- to five-year-olds understand about the workings of their own mind and those of others in "Cognitive Development: Foundational Theories of Core Domains," which is in volume 43 of the *Annual Review of Psychology*. Discussions of the biological, social, and school factors that influence cognitive development can be found in *Directors of Development: Influences on the Development of Children's Thinking* (1991), edited by Lynn Okagaki and Robert Sternberg.

■ Teaching the Middle School Grades

Transforming Middle Level Education (1992), edited by Judith L. Irvin, contains twenty chapters that discuss various aspects of middle school education. Chapters that might be of particular interest are "A Portrait of Diversity: The Middle Level Student" (Chapter 2), by Joel Milgram; "Young Adolescents' Perceptions of School" (Chapter 3), by Linda R. Kramer; "Appropriate Grouping Practices for Middle Level Students" (Chapter 14), by Robert Spear; and "Developmentally Appropriate Instruction: The Heart of the Middle School" (Chapter 16), by Judith Irvin. In *Changing Middle Schools: How to Make Schools Work for Young Adolescents* (1994), Nancy Ames and Edward Miller describe the experiences of four urban Indiana middle schools that were part of a restructuring program called the Middle Grades Improvement Program.

Characteristics of Adolescence

For a good overall treatment of the major developmental changes that occur during adolescence—biological, cognitive, moral reasoning, self-concept and self-esteem, identity, gender role socialization, sexuality, vocational choice—consult the second edition of *Adolescent Development and Behavior* (1991), by Jerome Dusek.

Advanced treatments of biological development during adolescence can be found in *Handbook of Adolescent Psychology* (1987), edited by Vincent van Hasselt and Michel Hersen. In particular, consult Chapter 3, "Biological Theoretical Models of Adolescent Development," and Chapter 7, "Pubertal Processes: Their Relevance for Developmental Research."

Useful, though advanced, information about the emotional aspects of adolescence can be gleaned from several chapters of *Handbook of Adolescent Psychology* (1987), just mentioned. Chapter 9 covers adolescent sexuality, Chapter 16 discusses depression and suicide, and Chapter 17 discusses the causes and nature of substance abuse.

In *Adolescent Stress* (1991), edited by Mary Ellen Colten and Susan Gore, fourteen authors discuss such sources of adolescent stress as negative emotions, conflicts with parents, drug use, pregnancy, and abuse at home and how adolescents try to cope with them. Robert D. Ketterlinus and Michael E. Lamb (1994), in *Adolescent Problem Behaviors: Issues and Research*, describe how such factors as sexual behavior, delinquency, risk taking, and childhood victimization give rise to troublesome behaviors among adolescents.

SUMMARY

1. Preschool and kindergarten children are quite active and enjoy physical activity. But incomplete muscle and motor development limits what they can accomplish on tasks that require fine motor skills, eye-hand coordination, and visual focusing.

2. The social behavior of preschool and kindergarten children is marked by rapidly changing friendships and play groups, a variety of types of play, short quarrels, and a growing awareness of gender roles.

3. Kindergartners openly display their emotions. Anger and jealousy are common.

4. Kindergartners like to talk and are reasonably skilled at using language. Preschoolers tend to apply their own rules of grammar. An authoritative approach by parents is more likely to produce competent preschoolers than is an authoritarian, or permissive, or rejecting-neglecting approach.

5. Primary grade children exhibit many of the same physical characteristics as preschool and kindergarten children (high activity level, incomplete muscle and motor development, frequent periods of fatigue). Most accidents occur among third graders because they overestimate their physical skills and underestimate the dangers in their activities.

6. Friendships are typically same sex and are made on a more selective basis by primary grade children. Quarrels among peers typically involve verbal arguments, although boys may engage in punching, wrestling, and shoving.

7. Primary grade students are becoming more emotionally sensitive. As a result, they are more easily hurt by criticism, respond strongly to praise, and are more likely to hurt another child's feelings during a quarrel.

8. Primary grade students like to speak up in class. They learn best when tasks are relatively short and when less cognitively demanding tasks occasionally follow more cognitively demanding tasks.

9. Elementary grade boys and girls become leaner and stronger and tend to have a gangly look. But some run the risk of becoming overweight because of poor eating habits and lack of exercise. Boys usually outperform girls on such sports-related motor skills as kicking, throwing, catching, running, and jumping, whereas girls often surpass boys on such play-related motor skills as flexibility, balance, and rhythm.

10. The peer group becomes a strong influence on the norms that govern the behavior of elementary grade children.

11. Friendships in the elementary grades become even more selective and gender based than they were in the primary grades.

12. A child's self-image (self-concept plus self-esteem) becomes more stable and generalized during the elementary grades. As a result of the decline of egocentric thought and the competitive nature of American society, self-image is based primarily on comparisons with peers.

13. Delinquency occurs more frequently among elementary grade children than at earlier ages and is associated with dysfunctional parent-child relationships and academic failure.

14. The thinking of elementary grade children, although more logical, can be wildly inconsistent and is constrained by the limitations of Piaget's concrete operational stage.

15. Although most children grow rapidly during the middle school years, girls grow more quickly and begin puberty earlier than boys. Early versus late maturation in boys and girls may affect subsequent personality development.

16. The social behavior of middle school children is increasingly influenced by peer group norms and the develop-

ment of interpersonal reasoning. Children are now capable of understanding why they behave as they do toward others and vice versa.

17. Because the peer group is the primary source for rules of acceptable behavior, conformity and concern about what peers think reach a peak during the middle school years.

18. Although anxiety, worry, and concern about self-esteem, physical appearance, academic success, and acceptance by peers are prominent emotions among many adolescents, some cope with these emotions better than others.

19. The climate of many middle school classrooms does not meet the social, emotional, and intellectual needs of early adolescents.

20. Self-efficacy beliefs, or how competent one feels at carrying out a particular task, begin to stabilize during the middle school years and influence the willingness of students to take on and persist at various academic and social tasks.

21. Physical development during the high school years is marked by physical maturity for most students and by puberty for virtually all. Sexual activity increases.

22. The long-range goals, beliefs, and values of adolescents are likely to be influenced by parents, whereas immediate status is likely to be influenced by peers. Many teens have part-time, after-school employment.

23. Eating disorders, substance abuse, schizophrenia, depression, and suicide are prominent emotional disorders among adolescents. Depression is the most common emotional disorder during adolescence. Depression coupled with an unstable family situation places adolescents at risk for suicide.

24. Cognitively, high school students become increasingly capable of formal operational thought, although they may function at the concrete operational level a good deal of the time. The influence of formal operational reasoning can be seen in political thinking, which becomes more abstract and knowledgeable.

25. Technologies that aid student learning and development are available for every age level, ranging from beginning reading and writing programs for primary and elementary grade children to complex simulations, problem solving and telecommunication programs for high school students.

KEY TERMS

play behavior *(74)*
gender roles *(75)*
early language development *(77)*
authoritative parents *(78)*
authoritarian parents *(78)*
permissive parents *(78)*
rejecting-neglecting parents *(78)*
self-image *(84)*

self-concept *(84)*
self-esteem *(84)*
growth spurt *(87)*
early-maturing boy *(88)*
late-maturing boy *(88)*
early-maturing girl *(88)*
late-maturing girl *(88)*
interpersonal reasoning *(89)*

self-efficacy *(93)*
sexually transmitted diseases
   (STDs) *(96)*
depression *(98)*
electronic mentoring *(103)*
adventure learning *(103)*

DISCUSSION QUESTIONS

1. Given the physical, social, emotional, and cognitive characteristics of preschool and kindergarten children, what type of classroom atmosphere and instructional tactics would you use to foster learning and enjoyment of school?

2. The primary and elementary years correspond to Erikson's stage of industry versus inferiority. The implication of this stage is that educators should do whatever is necessary to encourage a sense of industry and competence in each student. On a scale of 1 to 10, where 1 is the low end of the scale, how well do you think schools accomplish this goal? If your rating was lower than 10, what is it that schools do (or not do) that prevented you from assigning a perfect rating?

3. During the middle school years, the peer group becomes the general source for rules of behavior. Why? What advantages and disadvantages are associated with a situation in which the peer group establishes the norms for behavior?

4. Given the high rates of illegitimate births and sexually transmitted diseases among high school students, you could persuasively argue that adolescents should receive more sex education than they do. What are the advantages and disadvantages of providing this education in the school instead of in the home?

Understanding Student Differences

4

Sit back for a few minutes and think about some of your friends and classmates over the past twelve years. Make a list of their physical characteristics (height, weight, visual acuity, athletic skill, for example), social characteristics (outgoing, reserved, cooperative, sensitive to the needs of others, assertive), emotional characteristics (self-assured, optimistic, pessimistic, egotistical), and intellectual characteristics (methodical, creative, impulsive, good with numbers, terrible at organizing ideas). Now analyze your descriptions in terms of similarities and differences. In all likelihood, they point to many ways in which your friends and classmates have been alike, but to even more ways in which they have differed from one another. Indeed, although human beings share many important characteristics, they also differ from one another in significant ways (and we tend to notice the differences more readily than the similarities).

Now imagine yourself a few years from now, when your job as a teacher is to help every student learn as much as possible despite all the ways and the extent to which students differ from one another. By fourth grade, for example, the range

KEY POINTS

These key points will help you learn the important information in this chapter. To help you study, they also appear in the margins of pages, next to the text where they are discussed.

The Nature and Measurement of Intelligence

- Intelligence test scores most closely related to school success
- Intelligence tests not good predictors of job success, marital happiness, life happiness
- IQ scores can change with experience, training
- Intelligence involves more than what intelligence tests measure
- Triarchic theory: part of intelligence is ability to achieve personal goals
- Multiple intelligences theory: intelligence composed of 7 distinct forms of intelligence
- Individuals with a high level of a particular intelligence may use it in different ways
- Factors other than high levels of a particular intelligence influence interests, college major, career choice
- Triarchic theory suggests that instruction and assessment should be matched to students' ability patterns
- Various technology tools may strengthen different intelligences

Learning Styles

- Learning styles are preferences for dealing with intellectual tasks in a particular way
- Impulsive students prefer quick action; reflective students prefer to collect and analyze information before acting
- Field-independent students prefer their own structure; field-dependent students prefer to work within existing structure
- Legislative style prefers to create and plan; executive style prefers to follow explicit rules; judicial style prefers to evaluate and judge
- Teachers should use various instructional methods to engage all styles of learning at one time or another
- Teachers should use various test formats to accurately measure what students with various styles have learned

Gender Differences and Gender Bias

- Girls score higher on tasks that require retrieval of verbal information from long-term memory; boys score higher on tasks that require transforming mental representations, math and science knowledge
- Differences in math and science achievement most apparent at the high school level
- Gender bias: responding differently to male and female students without having sound educational reasons for doing so
- Gender bias can affect course selection, career choice, and class participation of male and female students
- Loss of voice: students suppress true beliefs about various topics in the presence of parents, teachers, and classmates of opposite sex
- Females have less access to, interest in, and time on computers than do males

of achievement in some classes is greater than four grade levels. Some children's reading or math skills may be at the second-grade level, while other children may be functioning at the fifth-grade level. By sixth grade, about one-third of all children will be working one grade level or more below the average student in class (Biemiller, 1993). The variability among any group of students is one reason why teaching is both interesting and challenging.

Richard Snow, who has written extensively about individual differences in education and how to deal with them, has summarized this challenge as follows:

> Individual differences among students present a pervasive and profound problem to educators. At the outset of instruction in any topic, students of any age and in any culture will differ from one another in various intellectual and psychomotor abilities and skills, in both general and specialized prior knowledge, in interests and motives, and in personal styles of thought and work during learning. These differences, in turn, appear directly related to differences in the students' learning progress. (1986, p. 1029)

The significance of these observations on variability is that although it usually will be essential for you to plan lessons, assignments, and teaching techniques by taking into account *typical* characteristics, you will also have to expect and make allowances for differences among students. Over the next two chapters we examine four broad characteristics that distinguish one group of students from another and that you should have some understanding of because of their demonstrated effect on learning. In this chapter we focus on differences in mental ability (usually referred to as *intelligence*), learning styles, and gender. In Chapter 5 we explore two related characteristics that are becoming more important every year: cultural and socioeconomic background. Teachers and researchers have demonstrated a strong interest in all five characteristics in recent years, and much has been written about them. ■

The Nature and Measurement of Intelligence

THE ORIGIN OF INTELLIGENCE TESTING

The form and content of contemporary intelligence tests owe much to the pioneering work of French psychologist Alfred Binet. In 1904, Binet was appointed to a commission of experts charged by the minister of public instruction for the Paris school system with figuring out an accurate and objective way of distinguishing between children who could profit from normal classroom instruction and those who required special education. Since the point of this project was to predict degree of future academic success, Binet created a set of questions and tasks that reflected the same cognitive processes as those demanded by everyday classroom activities. Thus, Binet's first scale measured such processes as memory, attention, comprehension, discrimination, and reasoning.

In 1916, Lewis Terman of Stanford University published an extensive revision of Binet's test. This revision, which came to be known as the Stanford-Binet, proved to be extremely popular. One reason for its popularity was that Terman, following the 1912 suggestion of a German psychologist named William Stern, expressed a child's level of performance as a global figure called an intelligence quotient. Stern's original formula divided a child's mental age, which was determined by performance on the test, by the child's chronological age and multiplied the resulting figure by 100 to eliminate fractional values (Seagoe, 1975).

Intelligence test scores most closely related to school success

Intelligence tests not good predictors of job success, marital happiness, life happiness

We have provided this abbreviated history lesson to illustrate two important points. First, the form and function of contemporary intelligence tests have been directly influenced by the task Binet was given nearly a hundred years ago. Intelligence test items are still selected on the basis of their relationship to school success. Thus, predictions about job success, marital bliss, happiness in life, or anything else made on the basis of an IQ score are attempts to make the test do something for which it was not designed. As some psychologists have pointed out, this type of test might better have been called a test of scholastic aptitude or school ability rather than a test of intelligence. The second point concerns Stern and Terman's use of the IQ as a quantitative summary of a child's performance. Binet, worried that educators would use a summary score as an excuse to ignore or get rid of uninterested or troublesome students, never endorsed this application. His intent was "to identify in order to help and improve, not to label in order to limit" (Gould, 1981, p. 152). Later in this section we will see that Binet's concern was well placed. First, however, we will turn to a more detailed consideration of what intelligence tests do and do not measure.

WHAT TRADITIONAL INTELLIGENCE TESTS MEASURE

In 1904 British psychologist Charles Spearman noticed that children given a battery of intellectual tests (such as the memory, reasoning, and comprehension tests used by Binet and Terman) showed a strong tendency to rank consistently from test to test: children who scored high (or average or below average) on memory tests tended to score high (or average or below average) on reasoning and comprehension tests. Our use of the words *tendency* and *tended* indicates, of course, that the rankings were not identical. Some children scored well on some tests but performed more poorly on others. Spearman explained this pattern by saying that intelligence is made up of two types of factors: a general factor (abbreviated as *g*) that affected performance on all intellectual tests and a set of specific factors (abbreviated as *s*) that affected performance only on specific intellectual tests. Spearman ascribed to the *g* factor the tendency for score rankings to remain constant over tests. That the rankings varied somewhat from test to test, he said, resulted from individual differences in specific factors. Not surprisingly, Spearman's explanation is called the two-factor theory of intelligence.

When you examine such contemporary intelligence tests as the Stanford-Binet, the Wechsler Intelligence Scale for Children–III, or the Wechsler Adult Intelligence Scale–Revised (1981), you will notice that the items in the various subtests differ greatly from one another. They may involve performing mental arithmetic, explaining the meanings of words, describing how two things are alike, indicating what part is missing from a pictured object, reproducing a pictured geometric design with blocks, or tracing a path through a maze. These varied items are included because, despite their apparent differences, they relate strongly to one another and to performance in the classroom. In other words, intelligence tests still reflect Binet's original goal and Spearman's two-factor theory. In practice, the examiner can combine the scores from each subtest into a global index (the IQ score), offer a prediction about the tested individual's degree of academic success for the next year or so, and make some judgments about specific strengths and weaknesses.

LIMITATIONS OF INTELLIGENCE TESTS

So where does all this leave us in terms of trying to decide what traditional intelligence tests do and do not measure? Four points seem to be in order.

Individually administered intelligence tests (such as the one shown here) are usually given to determine eligibility for a special class because they were designed to predict, and are moderately good predictors of, academic performance.

1. The appraisal of intelligence is limited by the fact that it cannot be measured directly. Our efforts are confined to measuring the overt manifestations (responses to test items) of what is ultimately based on brain function and experience.

2. The intelligence we test is a sample of intellectual capabilities that relate to classroom achievement better than they relate to anything else. That is why, as stated earlier, many psychologists prefer the terms *test of scholastic aptitude* or *test of school ability*.

3. Since current research demonstrates that the cognitive abilities measured by intelligence tests can be improved with systematic instruction (Sternberg, 1998), intelligence test scores should not be viewed as absolute measures of ability. Many people—parents, especially—fail to grasp this fact. An IQ score is not a once-and-for-all judgment of how bright a child is. It is merely an estimate of how successful a child is in handling certain kinds of problems at a particular time on a particular test *as compared with other children of the same age.*

4. Since IQ tests are designed to predict academic success, anything that enhances classroom performance (such as a wider range of factual information or more effective learning skills) will likely have a positive effect on intelligence test performance. In other words, IQ scores are not necessarily permanent. Research on the stability of IQ scores shows that, although they do not change significantly for most people, they can change dramatically for given individuals, and changes are most likely to occur among individuals who were first tested as preschoolers (Brody, 1992). This last point is often used to support early intervention programs like Head Start and Follow-Through.

IQ scores can change with experience, training

Because traditional theories of intelligence and their associated IQ tests view intelligence as being composed of a relatively small set of cognitive skills that relate best to academic success, and because the results of such tests are used primarily to place students in special programs, contemporary theorists have proposed broader conceptions of intelligence that have more useful implications for classroom instruction.

CONTEMPORARY VIEWS OF INTELLIGENCE

DAVID WECHSLER'S GLOBAL CAPACITY VIEW   As David Wechsler (1975) persuasively points out, *intelligence is not simply the sum of one's tested abilities.* Wechsler defines **intelligence** as the global capacity of the individual to act purposefully, to think rationally, and to deal effectively with the environment. Given this definition, which is endorsed by many psychologists, an IQ score reflects just one facet of a person's global capacity—the ability to act purposefully, rationally, and effectively on academic tasks in a *classroom* environment. However, people display intelligent behavior in other settings (at work, home, and play, for example), and other characteristics contribute to intelligent behavior (such as persistence, realistic goal setting, the productive use of corrective feedback, creativity, and moral and aesthetic values). A true assessment of intelligence would take into account behavior related to these other settings and characteristics.

Intelligence involves more than what intelligence tests measure

That such an assessment would be highly subjective and take a great deal of time is one reason current intelligence tests assess only a small sample of cognitive abilities. But if recent formulations of intelligence by psychologists Robert Sternberg (1985) and Howard Gardner (1983) become widely accepted, future intelligence tests may be broader in scope than those in use today. Even before such tests are devised, these theories serve a useful purpose by reminding us that intelligence is multifaceted and can be expressed in many ways.

ROBERT STERNBERG'S TRIARCHIC THEORY Like David Wechsler, Robert Sternberg (1985, 1996a) believes that most of the research evidence supports the view that intelligence has many facets, or dimensions, and that traditional mental ability tests measure just a few of these facets. Sternberg's **triarchic theory of intelligence** has, as its name suggests, three main parts: practical ability, creative ability, and analytical ability (see Figure 4.1). Sternberg's work is a break with tradition in two respects. First, it includes an aspect of intelligence that has been—and still is—largely overlooked: how people use practical intelligence to adapt to their environment. Second, Sternberg believes that each of these abilities can be improved through instruction and that students learn best when all three are called into play.

In describing the nature of practical intelligence, Sternberg argues that part of what makes an individual intelligent is the ability to achieve personal goals (for example, graduating from high school or college with honors, working for a particular company in a particular capacity, or having a successful marriage). One way to accomplish personal goals is to understand and adapt to the values that govern behavior in a particular setting. For example, if most teachers in a particular school (or executives in a particular company) place a high value on conformity and cooperation, the person who persistently challenges authority, suggests new ideas without being asked, or operates without consulting others will, in all likelihood, receive fewer rewards than those who are more willing to conform and cooperate. According to Sternberg's theory, this person would be less intelligent.

Where a mismatch exists and the individual cannot adapt to the values of the majority, the intelligent person explores ways to make the values of others more

Triarchic theory: part of intelligence is ability to achieve personal goals

Figure 4.1 The Three Components of Sternberg's Triarchic Theory

SOURCE: Adapted from Sternberg (1985); Sternberg, Ferrari, Clinkenbeard, & Grigorenko (1996).

consistent with his own values and skills. An enterprising student may try to convince her teacher, for example, that short-answer questions are better measures of achievement than essay questions or that effort and classroom participation should count just as much toward a grade as test scores. Finally, where all attempts at adapting or attempting to change the views of others fail, the intelligent person seeks out a setting where his behaviors are more consistent with those of others. For instance, many gifted and talented students will seek out private alternative schools where their particular abilities are more highly prized.

Sternberg's basic point is that intelligence should be viewed as a broad characteristic of people that is evidenced not only by how well they answer a particular set of test questions but also by how well they function in different settings. The individual with average test scores who knows how to get people to do what she wants is, in this view, at least as intelligent as the person who scores at the 99th percentile of a science test.

In an evaluation of the triarchic model (Sternberg, Ferrari, Clinkenbeard, & Grigorenko, 1996), 225 high school students who were considered by their school to be gifted were administered the Sternberg Triarchic Abilities Test and, on the basis of their scores, admitted to a special program called the Yale Summer Psychology Program. Five groups of students were identified: high in analytical ability, high in creative ability, high in practical ability, high in all three abilities, and low in all three abilities (those who scored below the mean of this group). These students then took a one-month summer course in college-level psychology that called for the use of memory, analysis, creativity, and practical abilities in the morning, but then split into groups that emphasized only one of those four abilities in the afternoon. Students in the analytical section, for example, analyzed the validity of theories, compared the relative merits of theories, and criticized experiments. Students in the creative section focused on generating new theories and experiments. Students in the practical section mostly worked on applying psychological concepts to everyday life. A memory-oriented condition was included as a traditional form of instruction against which the other three could be compared because many classrooms emphasize memorization of factual information.

Students' abilities to recall factual information, analyze concepts and theories, create new ideas, and apply psychological principles to everyday life were measured through homework assignments, a midterm and final examination (multiple-choice and essay items), and an independent project. The multiple-choice questions primarily measured recall. The homework assignments, essay questions, and course project were used to measure analytical, creative, and practical abilities. For example, the essay questions from the midterm asked students to discuss the advantages and disadvantages of having armed guards at school (analysis), describe what their ideal school would be like (creativity), and describe some problem they have been facing in their life and then give a practical solution (practicality).

There were two very interesting findings. First, students who were taught and tested in a way that matched their abilities performed significantly better than students who were mismatched. Second, most of the high-analytic students were white and from middle- to upper-middle-class homes, whereas most of the high-creative and high-practical groups were more racially, ethnically, and socioeconomically diverse.

A similar study (Sternberg, Torff, & Grigorenko, 1998) was done with third graders and eighth graders. Students in the experimental group received instruction that emphasized memory of facts as well as the triarchic skills of analytical, creative, and practical thinking. A second group of students received only analytical thinking instruction, while a third group received only memory-based instruction. Both age groups were tested with multiple-choice questions that measured recall of facts and open-ended questions that measured analytical, creative, and practical thinking skills. For example, the creative assessment for the third graders asked them to imagine a place where no one followed the rules at school or in the community and then write a story about a visit to this town. The practical assessment for the eighth graders asked them to describe how they would use psychological theory (which they had studied) to help someone quit smoking. On average, third-grade and eighth-grade students who received triarchically based instruction outscored the other two groups on all four measures.

HOWARD GARDNER'S MULTIPLE INTELLIGENCES THEORY   Howard Gardner's (1983) conception of intelligence, like Sternberg's, is broader than traditional conceptions. It is different from Sternberg's, however, in that it describes at least seven separate types of intelligence. Accordingly, Gardner's work is referred to as the **theory of multiple intelligences** (often referred to as MI theory). The intelligences described by Gardner are logical-mathematical, linguistic, musical, spatial, bodily-kinesthetic, interpersonal (understanding of others), and intrapersonal (understanding of self). Table 4.1 describes each of these intelligences and provides examples of the kind of person who best represents each one. Gardner is considering

Multiple intelligences theory: intelligence composed of 7 distinct forms of intelligence

Table 4.1	Gardner's Seven Intelligences	
Intelligence	**Core Components**	**End-States**
Logical-mathematical	Sensitivity to, and capacity to discern, logical or numerical patterns; ability to handle long chains of reasoning.	Scientist Mathematician
Linguistic	Sensitivity to the sounds, rhythms, and meanings of words; sensitivity to the different functions of language.	Poet Journalist
Musical	Abilities to produce and appreciate rhythm, pitch, and timbre; appreciation of the forms of musical expressiveness.	Violinist Composer
Spatial	Capacities to perceive the visual-spatial world accurately and to perform transformations on one's initial perceptions.	Sculptor Navigator
Bodily-Kinesthetic	Abilities to control one's body movements and to handle objects skillfully.	Dancer Athlete
Interpersonal	Capacities to discern and respond appropriately to the moods, temperaments, motivations, and desires of other people.	Therapist Salesman
Intrapersonal	Access to one's own feelings and the ability to discriminate among them and draw upon them to guide behavior; knowledge of one's own strengths, weaknesses, desires, and intelligences.	Person with detailed, accurate self-knowledge

SOURCE: Gardner & Hatch (1989).

Contemporary theories typically view intelligence as being composed of several types of capabilities. Howard Gardner's theory of multiple intelligences, for example, describes seven different ways of expressing intelligent behavior.

adding an eighth intelligence, to be called naturalist intelligence. This is the ability to notice the characteristics that distinguish one plant, mineral, or animal from another and to create useful classification schemes called taxonomies. Perhaps the greatest naturalist of all time was Charles Darwin (Checkley, 1997).

Since these intelligences are presumed to be independent of one another, an individual would likely exhibit different levels of skill in each of these domains. One student, for example, may show evidence of becoming an outstanding trial lawyer, novelist, or journalist because his linguistic intelligence produces a facility for vividly describing, explaining, or persuading. Another student may be able to manipulate aspects of sound (such as pitch, rhythm, and timbre) to produce musical experiences that people find highly pleasing. And the student who is adept at understanding her own and others' feelings and how those feelings relate to behavior would be exhibiting high intrapersonal and interpersonal intelligence. Like Sternberg's work, Gardner's theory cautions us against focusing on the results of IQ tests to the exclusion of other worthwhile behaviors.

Gardner's MI theory has become extremely popular among educators. As usually happens with such ideas, they are often misinterpreted. Many people, for example, believe that if one has a strength in a particular intelligence, one will excel on all tasks within that domain. Not so. A student with a high level of linguistic intelligence may be quite good at writing insightful essays on various topics but be unable to produce a good poem. Another student may excel at the kind of direct, fact-oriented style of writing that characterizes good newspaper reporting but be limited in her ability to write a long, highly analytical essay. Instead of focusing on how much intelligence students have, we need to attend to the different ways in which students make the most of their intelligences. For example, Thomas Hatch (1997), an associate of Gardner, describes how three children, all of whom were judged to have a high level of interpersonal intelligence, used that ability in different ways. One child was very adept at organizing the classroom activities of his classmates. The second was able to resolve conflicts among his classmates far better than anybody else in that class. The third child shunned leadership and was sometimes excluded from group activities, but excelled at forming friendships among his peers. He was so good at this that he was able to make friends with one of the least popular students in class.

A related misconception is to think that ability is destiny. Just because a child exhibits a high level of linguistic intelligence does not mean she will inevitably

Individuals with a high level of a particular intelligence may use it in different ways

Factors other than high levels
of a particular intelligence
influence interests, college
major, career choice

choose to major in English or journalism in college or seek a job as a writer. Not only do intelligences change over time in how they are used, but decisions about a college major and career are influenced by many other factors. The student who wrote such interesting stories as a child may grow up to be a college professor who excels at writing journal articles and textbooks (Hatch, 1997).

Finally, it is a misconception is that every child should be taught every subject in seven different ways in order to develop all of the intelligences. MI theory does not indicate or even suggest that such a step is necessary in order for learning to occur. In fact, it may be counterproductive if students are turned off by lessons that appear forced and contrived. And as a practical matter, there simply isn't enough time in the day to teach every lesson seven ways (Gardner, 1995; Hatch, 1997).

Gardner and his colleagues are now in the process of trying to validate the theory of multiple intelligences. In one program, called Arts PROPEL, junior and senior high school students in the Pittsburgh public schools were assessed for growth in the areas of music, creative writing, and the visual arts. In a second project, all students in an Indianapolis elementary school (called the Key School) were exposed to special classes and enrichment activities designed to enhance the various intelligences. A third effort, called Project Spectrum, is aimed at preschool and kindergarten children. Spectrum classrooms are equipped with a variety of materials that invite children to use one or another intelligence. For example, household objects that can be taken apart and reassembled afford children the opportunity to exercise spatial intelligence. Unlike traditional intelligence testing, where students respond to fairly brief written or spoken questions that are taken out of their naturally occurring context (where else would someone ask you to put together a puzzle in a limited amount of time?), Gardner and his associates measure intelligence by observing and evaluating what students do as they work through a variety of everyday tasks and projects. A preliminary assessment of Project Spectrum children provided partial support for Gardner's theory (Blythe & Gardner, 1990; Gardner & Hatch, 1989).

USING THE NEW VIEWS OF INTELLIGENCE TO GUIDE INSTRUCTION

The various theories of intelligence that were formulated during the first half of the twentieth century are of limited value to educators because they don't allow teachers to match instructional approaches and learning assessments to abilities. For example, since traditional intelligence tests, like the Stanford-Binet or the Wechsler

Intelligence Scale for Children–III, are designed to rank students according to how they score rather than to assess how they think, their basic educational use is to determine eligibility for programs for the gifted and talented, learning disabled, and mentally retarded (the subject of Chapter 6). What sets the views of Sternberg and Gardner apart is their belief in a broad view of intelligence that can inform instructional practice and improve student performance. As we have shown, the preliminary evidence suggests that these beliefs have merit. What follows are a few illustrations of how you can use their ideas in your classroom.

STERNBERG'S TRIARCHIC THEORY   Based on his triarchic theory, Sternberg proposes a teaching and assessment model that can be used to match forms of instruction and forms of assessment to different patterns of ability (Sternberg, 1996b, 1997a; Sternberg, Ferrari, Clinkenbeard, & Grigorenko, 1996). In this fashion, learning is maximized, since how one is taught and tested is consistent with one's dominant abilities. That doesn't mean *all* instruction and assessment should be made to match a student's dominant ability. Some attempts need to be made to strengthen abilities that are relatively weak.

> Triarchic theory suggests that instruction and assessment should be matched to students' ability patterns

Sternberg suggests that for any grade level and for any subject, teaching and testing can be designed to emphasize four general abilities:

1. Memory ability: recalling the who, what, where, when, and how of factual information. (As we pointed out earlier, although not an explicit part of Sternberg's theory, some memorization of factual information is necessary in any classroom.)
2. Analytical ability: analyzing, comparing, evaluating, and judging.
3. Creative ability: creating, inventing, imagining, and designing.
4. Practical ability: putting an idea into practice.

Instruction should involve all four abilities so it can take into account individual differences. At some point, each student has an opportunity to excel because the task and related test matches the student's ability. Table 4.2 shows how language arts, mathematics, social studies, and science can be taught so as to emphasize memory, analysis, creativity, and practicality.

GARDNER'S MULTIPLE INTELLIGENCES THEORY   Gardner's general recommendation for applying MI theory in the classroom is essentially the same as Sternberg's. He believes that teachers should use MI theory as a framework for devising alternative ways to teach subject matter. Some children learn a subject best when it is presented in a particular format or when it emphasizes a particular type of ability whereas other children learn well when the subject is taught under different conditions (Checkley, 1997).

MI theory should lead to increased transfer of learning. Because MI theory helps students mentally represent ideas in multiple ways, they are likely to develop a better understanding of the topic and be able to use that knowledge in the future in out-of-school settings.

Because MI theory stresses different ways of learning and expressing one's understanding, it fits well with the current emphasis on performance assessment (described in Chapters 13 and 14). For example, instead of using just multiple-choice questions to measure linguistic competence, teachers can ask students to play the role of newspaper editor and write an editorial in response to a current issue.

As we mentioned earlier, it is a mistake to think that every lesson has to be designed to involve all seven intelligences. But with a little thought, many lessons can

Table 4.2	Teaching Different Subjects from a Triarchic Perspective			
	Memory	**Analysis**	**Creativity**	**Practicality**
Language Arts	Remember the name of Tom Sawyer's aunt.	Compare the personality of Tom Sawyer to that of Huckleberry Finn.	Write a very short story with Tom Sawyer as a character.	Describe how you could use Tom Sawyer's power of persuasion.
Mathematics	Remember the mathematical formula Distance = Rate × Time.	Solve a mathematical word problem using the $D = R \times T$ formula.	Create your own mathematical word problem using the $D = R \times T$ formula.	Show how to use the $D = R \times T$ formula to estimate driving time from one city to another.
Social Studies	Remember a list of factors that led up to the U.S. Civil War.	Compare, contrast, and evaluate the arguments of those who supported slavery versus those who opposed it.	Write a page of a journal from the viewpoint of either a Confederate or a Union soldier.	Discuss the applicability of the lessons of the Civil War to countries today, like Yugoslavia.
Science	Name the main types of bacteria.	Analyze the means the immune system uses to fight bacterial infections.	Suggest ways to cope with the increasing immunity bacteria are showing to antibiotic drugs.	Suggest three steps that individuals might take to reduce the chances of bacterial infection.

SOURCE: Adapted from Sternberg (1997a).

be designed to include two or three. For example, a high school algebra teacher combined kinesthetic and logical-mathematical abilities to teach a lesson on graphing. Instead of using in-class paper-and-pencil exercises, this teacher took the students outside to the school's courtyard. Using the large cement pavement squares as a grid and the grooves between the squares as X and Y coordinates, she had the students stand at various junctures and plot their own location. In a visual arts class in a middle school, students studied the portraits produced by great artists and then, using various media, produced and displayed their own creations (spatial intelligence). Finally, as part of a primary grade lesson on studying birds and their nesting habits, students designed and built birdhouses and then noted whether or not the birds used them, thereby using spatial, bodily-kinesthetic, and logical-mathematical abilities. (Campbell, 1997).

USING TECHNOLOGY TO DEVELOP INTELLIGENCE

Since contemporary theories view intelligence as being made up of modifiable cognitive skills, you shouldn't be overly surprised that there are technology implications for the development of intelligence. In fact, Robert Sternberg (1997c), author of the triarchic theory, recently stated, "Technology can enable people to better develop their intelligence—no question about it" (p. 13). How can technology play this role? Consider the following possibilities.

Multimedia (a communication format integrating several types of media such as text, graphics, animation, sound, images, and video) and **hypertext** (a system of linking text in a nonlinear way, thereby enabling users to jump from one section of text to another section of the same document or to other documents, often through highlighted words) are two forms of technology that can have a positive impact on the analytical and creative abilities that make up most of Sternberg's theory of intelligence. **Hypermedia**, such as a computerized encyclopedia, is a marriage of multimedia and hypertext in which the learner can explore facts, concepts, or knowledge domains and immediately traverse to interesting links or appealing presentation formats.

For instance, a fourth-grade child interested in President John F. Kennedy could read information about his life, peruse a bibliography list, view photographs of the president with foreign dignitaries, hear selected pieces from his famous inaugural address and perhaps even watch some original video footage of the address, read related articles, explore a knowledge tree relating Kennedy to other political leaders, and connect to information about his family as well as his political adversaries. Since hypermedia encourages the rapid movement from one information resource to another (Grabe & Grabe, 1998), users can also view historical timelines and discover key events in history that occurred at the same time as Kennedy's presidency.

According to Hilary McLellan (1996), technology holds great promise in addressing the multiple intelligences theory promoted by Gardner. For instance, electronic role play and Web-based conferencing might promote students' interpersonal intelligence (McLellan, 1996). Intrapersonal intelligence might be aided by computer prompts, style checkers, and journal aids. Programs that make it easy to do concept mapping, flow charting, and three-dimensional imaging are closely tied to visual-spatial intelligence (Anderson-Inman, Knox-Quinn, & Horney, 1996). Idea generation and prewriting software tools, like IdeaFisher and INVENT, can assist verbal intelligence (Kellogg, 1989). Computer programming with tools like LOGO might help students' problem solving and logical-mathematical intelligence (Linn, 1985). There are also **CD-ROM**—compact discs that contain very large amounts of information that can be displayed on a computer screen—and other technologies addressing musical intelligence that help students see the musical scores as the music is played as well as video replay software that breaks down dance steps and tennis swings, thereby addressing bodily-kinesthetic skills. Clearly, there are technology tools for all the aspects of intelligence described by Sternberg and Gardner.

> **Various technology tools may strengthen different intelligences**

Whether one conceives of intelligence as being composed mainly of a general factor, of three related components, or of seven separate intelligences, psychologists agree that intelligence is an *ability*. Abilities are typically thought of as competencies or capabilities for performing intellectual tasks that are value directional. That is, it is better to have more of an ability than less of it. In recent years, psychologists have theorized about *how* students use their abilities. This characteristic is referred to as a *learning style*. Unlike abilities, styles are value neutral. All styles are adaptive under the right circumstances. In the next section, we will examine several styles of learning.

Learning Styles

When an individual shows a consistent preference over time and subject matter for perceiving, thinking about, and organizing information in a particular way, the term **learning style** is typically used to refer to that pattern of behavior. Some students, for example, prefer to think about the nature of a task, collect relevant information, and formulate a detailed plan before taking any action, while others prefer to run with the first idea they have and see where it leads. Some students prefer to work

> **Learning styles are preferences for dealing with intellectual tasks in a particular way**

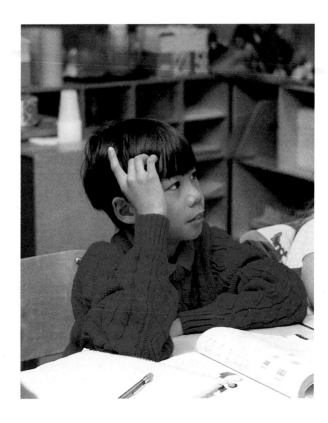

During the elementary years it becomes very apparent that students approach tasks in different ways. This preference for doing things in a particular way is often referred to as a cognitive style. Some students, for example, are impulsive thinkers who tend to react quickly when asked a question; other students are reflective thinkers who prefer to mull over things before answering.

on several aspects of a task simultaneously, while others prefer to work on one aspect at a time in a logical sequence.

Notice that styles are referred to as *preferences*. They are not fixed modes of behavior that we are locked into. When the situation warrants, we can, at least temporarily, adopt different styles, although some people are better than others at switching styles.

In the psychological literature on styles, a distinction is drawn between cognitive styles and learning styles. Because learning style is considered to be the more inclusive concept and because the implications for instruction are the same, we will use the term *learning style* throughout this section.

REFLECTIVITY AND IMPULSIVITY

One of the first learning style dimensions to be investigated was reflectivity/impulsivity. During the early 1960s, Jerome Kagan (1964a, 1964b) found that some students seem to be characteristically **impulsive**, whereas others are characteristically **reflective**. Impulsive students are said to have a fast conceptual tempo. When faced with a task for which there is no ready solution or a question for which the answer is uncertain, the impulsive student responds more quickly than students who are more reflective. In problem-solving situations, the impulsive student collects less information, does so less systematically, and gives less thought to various solutions than do more reflective students. Reflective students, in contrast, prefer to spend more time collecting information (which means searching one's memory as well as external sources) and analyzing its relevance to the solution before offering a response (Morgan, 1997).

Impulsive students prefer quick action; reflective students prefer to collect and analyze information before acting

Kagan discovered that when tests of reading and of inductive reasoning were administered in the first and second grades, impulsive students made more errors than reflective students. He also found that impulsiveness is a general trait; it appears early in a person's life and is consistently revealed in a great variety of situations.

FIELD-DEPENDENCE AND FIELD-INDEPENDENCE

Another very popular learning style dimension, known as field-dependence/field-independence, was proposed by Herbert Witkin (Witkin, Moore, Goodenough, & Cox, 1977) and refers to the extent to which a person's perception and thinking about a particular piece of information is influenced by the surrounding context. For example, when some individuals are shown a set of simple geometric figures and asked to locate each one (by outlining it with a pencil) within a larger and more complex display of intersecting lines, those with a **field-dependent style** take significantly longer to respond and identify fewer of them than individuals with a **field-independent style**. The former are labeled field-dependent because their perception is strongly influenced by the prevailing field. The latter are called field-independent because they are more successful in isolating target information despite the fact that it is embedded within a larger and more complex context.

> Field-independent students prefer their own structure; field-dependent students prefer to work within existing structure

Since field-dependence/field-independence is a style, and styles are assumed to generalize across tasks and situations, it is not surprising that its effects can also be seen when students deal with academic tasks and with other people. For example, the notes that field-dependent students take are more likely to reflect the structure and sequence of ideas as presented by the teacher or textbook author, whereas the notes of field-independent students are more likely to reflect their own ideas about structure and sequence. The significance of this difference in approach is clearly seen with materials and tasks that are poorly structured. Field-independent students usually perform better in these situations because of their willingness to create a more meaningful structure. In social situations, field-dependent people, in comparison to field-independent people, spend more time looking directly at the faces of others, are more aware of prevailing attitudes, values, and behaviors, prefer to be in the company of other people, and are generally thought of as more tactful, considerate, socially outgoing, and affectionate than field-independent individuals.

MENTAL SELF-GOVERNMENT STYLES

Robert Sternberg (1994), whose ideas on intelligence we discussed earlier in this chapter, has proposed an interesting learning style theory that is roughly modeled on the different functions and forms of civil government. Sternberg's **styles of mental self-government theory** describes thirteen styles that fall into one of five categories (functions, forms, levels, scope, and leaning) and are modeled after the structure of civil government. There are legislative, executive, and judicial functions; monarchic, hierarchic, oligarchic, and anarchic forms; global and local levels; internal and external scopes; and liberal and conservative leanings. Most individuals have a preference for one style within each category. In Table 4.3 we briefly describe the main characteristics of each style and suggest an instructional activity that is consistent with that style.

> Legislative style prefers to create and plan; executive style prefers to follow explicit rules; judicial style prefers to evaluate and judge

If you're wondering how to identify these styles, Sternberg offers a simple solution. Teachers can simply note the type of instruction that various students prefer and the test types on which they perform best.

Table 4.3	Matching Instructional Activities to Sternberg's Mental Self-Government Styles	
Styles	**Characteristics**	**Instructional Activities**
Legislative	Prefers to formulate rules and plans, imagine possibilities, and create ideas and products.	Require students to design science projects, write stories, imagine how historical figures might have done things differently, organize work groups.
Executive	Prefers to follow rules and guidelines.	Present well-organized lectures, require students to prepare book reports, work out answers to problems.
Judicial	Prefers to compare things and make evaluations about quality, worth, effectiveness.	Require students to compare literary characters, critique an article, evaluate effectiveness of a program.
Monarchic	Prefers to work on one task at a time or to use a particular approach to tasks.	Assign one project, reading assignment, or homework assignment at a time. Allow ample time to complete all aspects of the assignment before assigning another.
Hierarchic	Prefers to have several tasks to work on, deciding which one to do first, second, and so on, and for how long.	Assign several tasks that vary in length, difficulty, and point value and are due at various times over several weeks.
Oligarchic	Prefers to have several tasks to work on, all of which are treated equally.	Assign several tasks that are equivalent in length, difficulty, and point value.
Anarchic	Prefers an unstructured, random approach to learning that is devoid of rules, procedures, or guidelines.	Assign tasks and problems that require nonconventional thinking and methods, self-directed form of study.
Global	Prefers to have an overall view of a task before beginning work.	Require students to scan a reading assignment to identify major topics, create an outline before writing, formulate a plan before beginning a complex task.
Local	Prefers to identify and work on the details of a particular part of a task before moving to another part.	Present a detailed outline or overview of a lecture or project. Require students to identify and interrelate particular details of each part of a reading assignment.
Internal	Prefers to work alone.	Require seatwork, projects, and assignments that do not depend on others for completion.
External	Prefers to work with others.	Assign group projects or reports, encourage study groups, create discussion groups.
Liberal	Prefers to work out own solution to problems.	Assign projects for which students must work out solution procedures. For example, identify and report on proposed legislation that concerns the environment.
Conservative	Prefers to do things according to established procedures.	Assign homework or projects that specify the steps, procedures, or rules for accomplishing the task.

SOURCE: Adapted from Sternberg (1994).

USING AWARENESS OF LEARNING STYLES TO GUIDE INSTRUCTION

Teachers should use various instructional methods to engage all styles of learning at one time or another

Because the typical classroom contains two dozen or more students who, collectively, exhibit several styles, teachers must be flexible and learn to use a variety of teaching and assessment methods so that at some point every student's style is addressed (recall our discussion of the teacher-as-artist in Chapter 1). An impulsive boy, for example, may disrupt a class discussion by blurting out the first thing that pops into his head, thereby upstaging the reflective types, who are still in the process of formulating more searching answers. To minimize this possibility, you may want to have an informal rotation scheme for recitation or sometimes require that everyone sit and think about a question for two or three minutes before answering. To give the impulsive style its place in the sun, you might schedule speed drills or question-and-answer sessions covering previously learned basic material. To motivate students with a legislative style, have them describe what might have happened if a famous historical figure had acted differently than he or she did. For example, how might World War II have ended if President Harry Truman decided *not* to drop the atomic bomb on Japan? To motivate students with a judicial style, have them compare and contrast the literary characters Tom Sawyer (from the Mark Twain novel of the same name) and Holden Caulfield (from the J. D. Salinger novel *Catcher in the Rye*).

When you design your classroom assessments, keep in mind that multiple-choice tests, for example, match up nicely with the executive and conservative styles, while students with a legislative style are more likely to perform better on projects and performances. Try to use a variety of assessment methods both on each test and across all the tests given during a term. You may also want to consider letting students choose the type of assessment they prefer. Another reason for using various teaching techniques and testing formats is that it may stimulate students to expand their own repertoire of learning styles (Sternberg, 1994). You might want to peruse Table 4.3 again to review which methods of instruction are most likely to fit which styles.

Teachers should use various test formats to accurately measure what students with various styles have learned

Using Technology to Accommodate Learning Styles

Just as technology can be used to strengthen different forms of intelligence, so can it target different learning styles. Certainly, simulations and **virtual reality** (computer-generated environments that mimic real-life situations) tools have the potential to make key concepts and principles more concrete, and multimedia technology can help students who prefer either text communication, interactive visual displays, or auditory cues.

W. Patrick Dickson (1985) points out how visualizing mathetical equations and statistics allows visual learners to better understand the material and lets all learners move between different ways of representing information. By immediately presenting visual summaries of physical events, the microcomputer-based laboratory mentioned in Chapter 2 is a prime example of how technology might take advantage of multiple modalities. No longer are students left simply with masses of data; they can now see it displayed visually or hear it. When this occurs, students are freer to process information in a way that is consistent with their learning style.

In a series of three studies, Roy Clariana (1997) found that computer-assisted learning environments shifted both early adolescent and adult learners toward preferring more active and concrete learning experiences.

Gender Differences and Gender Bias

At the beginning of this chapter, we asked you to think about the ways in which friends and classmates over the past twelve or so years may have differed from one another. In all likelihood, you thought about how those people differed cognitively, socially, and emotionally. And with good reason. As we have seen so far in this chapter and in Chapters 2 and 3, students' academic performance is strongly influenced by their cognitive, social, and emotional characteristics. But there is another major characteristic you may have ignored: a student's gender. Although it may not be obvious, there are noticeable differences in the achievement patterns of males and females and in how they are taught. As Myra Sadker and David Sadker (1994) point out, "Sitting in the same classroom, reading the same textbook, listening to the same teacher, boys and girls receive very different educations" (p. 1). Just how different is the subject of the next few sections.

GENDER DIFFERENCES IN COGNITION AND ACHIEVEMENT

Although gender differences in cognitive functioning have decreased in some areas, they are large in other areas and have remained so for quite a few years. For example, girls achieve higher average scores on tasks that require quick access to verbal information in long-term memory. Examples of such tasks are synonym generation, associative memory, spelling, and mathematical calculation. Girls also excel in the learning of foreign languages, reading comprehension, writing, fine motor tasks, perceptual speed (finding a target letter in a large display of words), and speech articulation. Boys, on the other hand, achieve higher average scores on tasks that measure the ability to transform mental representations in memory (for example, rotating mental images of objects in space), aiming (for example, throwing balls or darts at a target), general knowledge, geography knowledge, math and science knowledge, mechanical reasoning, scientific reasoning, and verbal analogies. Some of these differences, by the way, are not limited to American students. In a recent study of mathematical and science knowledge, boys significantly outperformed girls in science in 75 percent of the forty-one countries that participated. In math they outscored girls in 15 percent of the participating countries. In no country did the girls outscore the boys (Halpern, 1997; Hedges & Nowell, 1995).

Some gender differences are either first noticeable or reach a peak at certain grade levels. For example, there are no gender differences in mathematical problem-solving ability among elementary and middle school students, but there are small to moderate differences favoring male high school students. At the high school level, boys score slightly higher in all math areas except algebra. On tests of science knowledge, high school boys outscore girls by the widest margin in the areas of physics, chemistry, earth science, and space science (Wellesley College Center for Research on Women, 1992).

Why do these differences exist? No one knows for sure although hormonal differences, differences in brain structure, and socialization differences are all thought to play a role. Despite increased awareness of how society reinforces gender-role stereotyping and measures taken to ensure greater gender equity, girls and boys continue to receive from a variety of sources different messages and incentives about what is considered to be appropriate behavior. One source of influence that is being intensively studied is the peer group. During the middle childhood years (roughly ages six through nine) boys and girls are often under more pressure from their peers to exhibit gender-typed behaviors, in order to maintain the group's identity, than they are from their parents. But these observations do not answer the question of causation. Are gender differences the result of social pressures to participate in some activities and not others, or are socialization patterns the result of biological differences, or do both factors play a role? We simply don't know yet.

Although you should be aware of gender differences in cognitive functioning and should take steps to try to reduce them, you should also keep the following points in mind. First, there are many tasks for which differences do not exist. Second, some differences do not appear until later in development. For example, boys and girls have

Girls score higher on tasks that require retrieval of verbal information from long-term memory; boys score higher on tasks that require transforming mental representations, math and science knowledge

Differences in math and science achievement most apparent at the high school level similar scores on tests of mathematical problem solving until adolescence, when boys begin to pull ahead. Third, what is true in general is not true of all individuals. Some boys score higher than most girls on tests of language use, and some girls score higher than most boys on tests of scientific reasoning. Finally, as Robert Sternberg and Howard Gardner have argued, virtually all cognitive skills can be improved to some degree with the aid of well-designed instruction (Halpern, 1997).

GENDER BIAS

If you asked your class a question and some students answered without waiting to be called on, how do you think you would react? Do you think you would react differently to male students than to female students? Don't be so sure that you would not. Studies have found that teachers are more willing to listen to and accept the spontaneous answers of male students than female students. Female students are often reminded that they are to raise their hand and be recognized by the teacher before answering. Boys also receive more extensive feedback than do girls, but are punished more severely than girls for the same infraction. These consistent differences in response to male and female students when there is no sound educational reason for doing so are the essence of **gender bias**.

> **Gender bias: responding differently to male and female students without having sound educational reasons for doing so**

Why do teachers react so differently to males and females? Probably because they are operating from traditional gender-role stereotypes—they expect boys to be more impulsive and unruly and girls to be more orderly and obedient (Matthews, Binkley, Crisp, & Gregg, 1998; Wellesley College Center for Research on Women, 1992).

Exposure to gender bias apparently begins early in a child's school life. Most preschool programs stress the importance of following directions and rules (impulse control) and contain many activities that facilitate small-muscle development and language skills. Since girls are typically better than boys in these areas *before* they go to preschool, the typical preschool experience does not help girls acquire new academically related skills and attitudes. For example, preschool-age girls are usually not as competent as boys at large-motor activities (such as jumping, climbing, throwing, digging) or investigatory activities (such as turning over rocks or pieces of wood to see what's under them). Lest you think that climbing, digging, and investigating one's environment are trivial behaviors, bear in mind that they are critical to the work of scientists who do field research (for example, botanists, geologists, anthropologists, oceanographers), occupations in which women are significantly underrepresented. Perhaps the designers of preschool curricula should make a greater effort to include these more male-oriented activities (Wellesley College Center for Research on Women, 1992).

Other students can be the source of gender bias as easily as the teacher can be. The authors of one study (Matthews, et al., 1998) observed a fifth-grade classroom for four months and made the following observations:

1. The class was divided into six small groups to work on ideas for a drug prevention program. Five of the groups chose a boy to deliver their report.

2. On another occasion the students again worked in groups to create a machine that would produce both sounds and action. After each group demonstrated its machine they called on other students to provide a name for it. Boys were called on 31 times while girls were called on 13 times.

3. After a science lab, a girl complained that the boys said that the way in which the girls were weighing items and comparing the weights was wrong.

Another girl remarked that the boys didn't want the girls to touch any of the equipment. Upon hearing this, one of the boys said that he thought the girls might drop or damage something.

4. Boys were more likely than girls to name a boy as the best student in mathematics and science, while the girls usually named a girl as the best in English.

5. Boys usually named another boy as the one who contributed most to class discussions, while girls named both boys and girls.

How Gender Bias Affects Students

Gender bias affects students in at least three ways: the courses they choose to take, the careers they consider, and the extent to which they participate in class activities and discussions.

COURSE SELECTION   High school students of both genders take about the same number and type of math courses, with one exception. About 7.6 percent of all boys take calculus, whereas only 4.7 percent of all girls enroll for this subject. Although girls take close to the same number of science courses as do boys, the type of courses each gender is most likely to take differs. Girls are more likely to take courses in the biological sciences whereas boys are more likely to take physics and advanced chemistry (Wellesley College Center for Research on Women, 1992).

CAREER CHOICE   As you may be aware because of numerous stories in the media, relatively few girls choose careers in science or mathematics. Among high school seniors from Rhode Island, 64 percent of the males who had taken physics and calculus were planning to major in science or engineering in college compared to only 18.6 percent of the females who had taken the same courses (Wellesley College Center for Research on Women, 1992).

Several factors are thought to influence the choice males and female students make to pursue a career in science or engineering. One is familiarity and interest in the tools of science. One study found that 51 percent of third-grade boys had used a microscope and 49 percent of eleventh-grade boys had used an electricity meter. The corresponding percentages for females were 37 percent and 17 percent, respectively (Wellesley College Center for Research on Women, 1992). In another study of middle school science classes that emphasized hands-on experiences by instructors who were committed to increasing girls' active participation, gender differences were noted. Boys spent more time than girls manipulating the equipment, thereby forcing girls to participate in more passive ways (Jovanovic & King, 1998). A second factor is perceived self-efficacy (how confident one feels in being able to meet the demands of a task). Although third-grade boys and girls are equally confident about their math abilities, by eleventh grade only 48 percent of girls are confident about their math skills as compared to 60 percent of the boys. Lack of confidence in math and science ability even appears among girls who have done well in previous courses. A third factor is encouragement from parents and teachers. Girls who major in science in college cite the encouragement of teachers as an important factor in their decision (Wellesley College Center for Research on Women, 1992). The Case in Print on pages 126–127 describes how one Massachusetts school is trying to interest more girls in math and science and related careers.

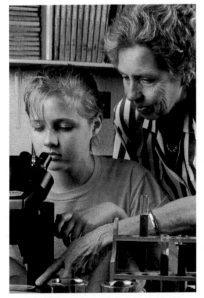

Because of gender bias in the classroom, relatively few girls take physics or chemistry courses or aspire to careers in science or engineering.

Correcting Gender Bias

Gender bias affects students in at least three ways: the courses they choose to take, the careers they consider, and the extent to which they participate in class activities and discussions. . . . High school students of both genders take about the same number and type of math courses, with one exception. About 7.6% of all boys take calculus whereas only 4.7% of all girls enroll for this subject. Although girls take close to the same number of science courses as do boys, the type of courses each gender is most likely to take differs. Girls are more likely to take courses in the biological sciences whereas boys are more likely to take physics and advanced chemistry. (p. 125)

WHY CAN'T SUSIE DO CALCULUS?

MICKEY BACA
Merrimack Valley Sunday
(Ipswich, MA) 8/7/94

Twelve-year-old Laura Young struggles to grip a small coated wire with a pair of wire snippers, as 13-year-old Juliana Cejka looks on.

The students are making telegraphs, using an electromagnet, a small battery and a washer suspended on an elastic: a typical science class exercise for middle school kids.

There is a difference in this classroom, however. There are no boys wielding the hammers and wire strippers.

This experimental two-week summer math and science program at the Nock Middle School in Newburyport is for girls only in hopes of making a dent in what most agree is a social failing in education. Somehow when girls reach middle school and early high school age, they begin falling behind in math and science.

By the time they reach high school and college, girls take a decided path away from the calculus, physics, biology and chemistry courses and instead select humanities and language courses.

In turn, researchers say, they are self-selecting themselves out of important and high-paying jobs in science and technology.

A growing body of research over the last decade suggests numerous reasons for the trend, from the different learning styles of girls and boys and social stereotyping of their abilities to teacher biases that channel more attention to boys.

Marcia O'Neil, an eighth grade language arts teacher at the Nock Middle School who has been following gender issues in education, proposed this ground-breaking summer program. . . . "If there were boys, I don't think the girls would be doing these projects. They'd be standing back and watching. A girl wouldn't have the hammer . . ."

In fact, a study of science classrooms cited by the American Association of University Women found that 79 percent of student-assisted science demonstrations were carried out by boys.

Researchers have also found that, even when girls do well in math and science, they don't receive the encouragement they need in order to pursue scientific careers. . . .

Carol Sund of The Network, a nonprofit education research firm in Andover . . . says girls lower their sights in general when they hit adolescence: "If you talk to a girl who is 10, she can do anything. She has all these hopes and dreams. If you talk to her at 13, she has much lower expectations."

What's more, Sund notes, studies that date back to the 1970s show that teachers channel more attention to males, calling on them more often, expecting more from them in math and science.

"Again, it's the boys being taught and the girls watching the boys being taught. It's the cheerleader/football player syndrome," Sund says. "We've trained girls to think that they are invisible in the classroom."

Girls do have a different learning style than boys, Sund acknowledges, tending to do better in a cooperative setting rather than the competitive environment most classrooms foster.

Schools have been slow to change teaching styles to accommodate female learning styles, according to Sund, and even to attempt to give girls the same amount of attention as that received by boys. Teacher behavior is difficult to change, she says, and some teachers don't agree that is should be changed.

Sund still gets teachers in training sessions that say girls and boys were made differently, and girls should remain quiet and supportive, she says. . . .

O'Neil herself remembers having trouble with math growing up. "My view of myself as a math student was compromised by attitudes."

If the girls across the room studying probability are suffering from "math anxiety," they aren't showing it. They're too busy calculating the odds of rolling certain number combinations on dice and betting pieces of candy on the outcome.

. . . Besides getting hands-on experience with math, science and computers, the girls in the Stars program are getting to hear first hand from women who work in fields involving math and science.

Today's luncheon speaker is Ann Gothro, an engineer working on the Boston Harbor tunnel project. . . .

One of the most important things you can get, Gothro advises the students, is hands-on experience.

Gothro didn't shy away from math and science when she was in middle and high school. In fact, she had quite the opposite problem, she tell the girls.

"I always took math and science in high school mainly because my dad (an engineer) decided I should. I remember being a little upset because my brothers always got to take cooking classes," she says. . . .

Superintendent Paul Dulac says combating gender biases in the city's classrooms really boils down to teacher strategies.

For example, he says, boys are more aggressive in the classroom and tend to pose more discipline problems. That could be why teachers tend to call on boys more, to keep them more engaged and out of trouble.

If that's the case, the superintendent says, teachers need to be trained in other ways to engage boys without neglecting the girls. . . .

"The bottom line is that we need to pay more attention to both male and female development to make sure both are developing their potential in math and science," says [middle school principal Doug] Lay, adding that "I think it's an issue that's more relevant to young women right now."

Education can't continue to "deliver one menu to students and expect them to be successful," Lay says.

Questions and Activities

1. This article describes several environmental influences on learning and classroom behavior and at least one innate factor. Go through the article to list these various influences and factors. Describe how they might interact with one another to affect your students' learning differently depending on their gender. Does this jibe with your own experience as a student? Why or why not?

2. The overall message of this article and of the experimental program is that girls can do and can enjoy math and science if certain environmental factors are rearranged. What lessons can you draw from this in terms of the assumptions you make about your students and the goals you should set for them? How does the final quote in the article—from Principal Lay—speak to this issue, and how does it specifically address the teacher's role in helping diverse individuals reach their potential?

3. Write a dialogue that might occur between Carol Sund and one of the teachers who say that "girls and boys were made differently and that girls should remain quiet and supportive." Which position is more reflective of the theories in this chapter? Think of ways you might call on knowledge you glean from this chapter to support that position.

4. Why might the years between ten and thirteen bring "lower expectations" for a girl? Combine new information you may have learned from this chapter with your own experiential knowledge. Reflect as you do so on ways in which you, as a future teacher, might be able to help reverse the direction of girls' lowered expectations.

CLASS PARTICIPATION   As we pointed out earlier, many children tend to adopt the gender role that society portrays as the most appropriate and acceptable. Through the influence of parenting practices, advertising, peer norms, textbooks, and teaching practices, girls are reinforced for being polite, helpful, obedient, nonassertive, quiet, and aware of and responsive to the needs of others. Boys are reinforced for being assertive, independent, aggressive, competitive, intellectually curious, and achievement-oriented. When females look at the world around them

Gender bias can affect course selection, career choice, and class participation of male and female students

they see relatively few women in positions of power and influence, relatively few women interviewed by the media for their opinion or expertise on various issues, and boys either ignoring or not taking seriously the suggestions and opinions offered by girls. The result, according to Carol Gilligan and others, is that adolescent girls learn to suppress their true personality and beliefs. Instead of saying what they really think about a topic, they either say that they have no opinion or they say what they think others want to hear. Gilligan refers to this behavior as **"loss of voice"** (Harter, Waters, & Whitesell, 1997).

Loss of voice: students suppress true beliefs about various topics in the presence of parents, teachers, and classmates of opposite sex

To measure the extent of loss of voice in different contexts, Susan Harter, Patricia Waters, and Nancy Whitesell gave questionnaires to several hundred students of both genders in grades 6 through 12. The questionnaire items asked students to rate how honestly they voiced their ideas when they were in the presence of teachers, male classmates, female classmates, parents, and close friends. Their main findings were:

1. Males and females are most likely to speak their mind when they are with close friends and classmates of the same gender but are less likely to do so when they are in the presence of members of the opposite gender, parents, and teachers.

2. Loss of voice did not increase between grades 6 and 12.

3. Equal numbers of males and females reported suppressing their true thoughts in certain circumstances.

4. Girls who strongly identified with the stereotypical female gender role were more likely than androgynous females (those who exhibit behaviors that are characteristic of both gender roles) to suppress their true thoughts when interacting with their teachers and male classmates. This difference between feminine and androgynous females disappeared with close friends and parents.

5. Androgynous males and females who said they were frequently encouraged and supported by teachers for expressing their views were most likely to speak their mind in classroom and other settings.

These findings have major implications for the way in which teachers address female students, particularly those who have adopted a strong feminine gender role, and for the use of constructivist approaches to teaching (mentioned in Chapters 1 and 2). Because constructivism relies heavily on free and open discussion to produce its effects, teachers need to carefully monitor the verbal exchanges that occur among students and to intervene when necessary to ensure that all students feel that their opinions are getting a fair and respectful hearing.

WORKING TOWARD GENDER EQUITY IN THE CLASSROOM

Although much of the literature on gender bias highlights the classroom obstacles that make it difficult for girls to take full advantage of their talents, gender equity is about producing an educational experience that will be equally meaningful for students of both genders. Susan McGee Bailey (1996), who has written extensively about gender issues in education, suggests the following three techniques to benefit both genders.

1. Use work arrangements and reward systems that will encourage all students to value a thorough understanding of a subject or task and that empha-

size group success as well as individual accomplishment. In Chapter 10 we will describe how a technique called cooperative learning does just this.

2.   Emphasize materials that highlight the accomplishments and characteristics of women (such as Indira Gandhi, Margaret Thatcher, and Madeline Albright) and women's groups.

3.   Talk about the practical, everyday applications of math and science. Although girls seem more interested in science when they understand how such knowledge transfers to everyday life, so do many boys. Nobody suffers when the curriculum is made more meaningful and relevant.

Charles Rop (1998) describes how Anna Kasov, a veteran high school teacher, teaches introductory chemistry. In high school and college Kasov found science to be a male-dominated profession that did not go out of its way to make women students feel comfortable or accepted. Consequently, her goal as a teacher is to combat the message that chemistry is not women's work and that interesting women are not scientists by creating a supportive atmosphere in her classroom. To accomplish her goal, Kasov (a) models how scientists think (formulate hypotheses about chemical processes, conduct experiments, use that evidence to support your hypotheses) and encourages students to do the same, (b) requires that students treat each others' ideas with respect, and (c) attends to how frequently girls and boys contribute to class discussions and to the nature of the contributions.

As Kasov and others have pointed out, science becomes more interesting for all students, but for girls in particular, when they understand its relevance. The following quote from Kasov about her own college experience is instructive:

> One of the things that I vividly remember is sitting in this lecture going through these biochemical cycles. I wondered where this happens—in the cell, in the nucleus, in the mitochondria? The guy didn't even bother to tell us. We were counting ATPs somewhere and I thought, "This is so stupid. I have no idea what this has to do with anything." (p. 60)

Consequently, she recommends giving girls opportunities to manipulate technology, deemphasizing competition in favor of collaborative problem solving, showing how the products of chemical research affect the everyday lives of people, and integrating chemical concepts with other subjects, such as history, literature, and the arts.

GENDER DIFFERENCES AND TECHNOLOGY: OVERCOMING THE GAP

During the 1980s and 1990s, numerous studies reported a gender gap with respect to computer technology. Among the more consistent findings are that, compared to males, females have less computer access at home, lower computer self-confidence and competence, less interest in and liking of computers, and less time using computers in school. Furthermore, girls take fewer computer classes in high school, exhibit higher anxiety related to computer technology, attend fewer computer camps, and receive differential parental expectations (Comber, Colley, Hargreaves, & Dorn, 1997; Corston & Colman, 1996; Kay, 1989; Krendl & Broihier, 1992; Shashaani,1994; Sutton, 1991). Two factors, parent encouragement to take computer courses and home ownership by parents, are typically the strongest predictors of these gender differences (Rocheleau, 1995; Shashaani, 1994).

Females have less access to, interest in, and time on computers than do males

Given the gender differences cited earlier, it is not surprising that males and females prefer different types of computer programs. Research consistently finds that boys prefer adventure software, video games, and computer programming, while girls often choose word processing packages, databases, and telecommunication tools (Lieberman, 1985).

Significant gender differences have also been found in student preferences for such computer-based environments as the Internet, CD-ROMs, Web-based conferencing, video conferencing, and teleconferencing. Female students favor more traditional methods of instruction and have less favorable perceptions of computer-based technology than do male students (Proost, Elen, & Lowyck, 1997). Such gender differences certainly strip away a tremendous number of learning opportunities for the female population. As Joella Gipson (1997) notes, these women will be less prepared to contribute to and profit from our increasingly technological society.

Although this computer technology gap often does not appear until the teenage years (Martin, Heller, & Mahmoud, 1992), gender differences do appear at lower grade levels. A recent study revealed that boys as young as first grade are often more aggressive and rude to girls in criticizing their computing choices and products, thereby shaking young girls' confidence (Nicholson, Gelpi, Young, & Sulzby, 1998). Not surprisingly, females perform better when using computers with females nearby than with a male audience (Corston & Colman, 1996).

What can be done to reduce the gender gap? Several things. First, since the research literature indicates that early positive experiences with computers are central to later success, teachers' attitudes and actions must demonstrate that the computer is equally important to both genders. Second, as computer technology expands in schools, teachers and administrators should try to embed it in reading, writing, history, and literature curricula, not just in math and science. Third, girls need more role models of female computer users both in their schools and in the workplace (Sanders, 1985). Fourth, parents may need training in raising their mathematical and technological expectations of their female children as well as advice on the role of computer technology in the home. Fifth, some scholars recommend computer camps, programs, and classes just for girls to interest them in science and technology careers (Gipson, 1997). Sixth, since males tend to dominate open computer workstations during free choice time (Kock, 1994), teachers might increase access time or require turn-taking practices on the computer (Nicholson et al., 1998). Finally, schools and teachers need to establish policies on software, thereby avoiding purchase of the more violent and insulting or demeaning products. They might choose to select new software games with female main characters and computer tools that appeal to girls.

In the next section we offer several Suggestions for Teaching that will help you better respond to differences in intelligence, learning styles, and gender.

SUGGESTIONS FOR TEACHING IN YOUR CLASSROOM

Addressing Student Differences

1 Design lessons and test items that call for memory, analytical, creative, and practical abilities.

2 Design lessons that emphasize different intelligences.

3 Recognize that different styles of learning call for different methods of instruction.

4 Help students become aware of the existence of gender bias.

5 Encourage girls to consider pursuing a career in science.

6 Recognize that you will not be able to address the various abilities and cognitive styles of all of your students all of the time.

1 **Design lessons and test items that call for memory, analytical, creative, and practical abilities.**

Robert Sternberg (1997a) has pointed out that many teachers tend to emphasize memory and analytical abilities, which is fine for students who are good either at memorizing facts or at breaking things down into their component parts and explaining how the parts relate to each other. But students whose abilities are in the creative and/or practical areas may appear to be less capable than they really are. You can get a better idea of each student's strengths and weaknesses and how well students have learned the subject matter you just taught by using a variety of instructional cues and test items.

To emphasize students' memory abilities when you teach and test, use prompts such as:

"Who said . . . ?"

"Summarize the ideas of . . ."

"Who did . . . ?"

"When did . . . ?"

"How did . . . ?"

"Describe . . ."

To emphasize students' analytical abilities when you teach and test, use prompts like:

"Why in your judgment . . . ?"

"Explain why . . ."

"Explain what caused . . ."

"Critique . . ."

To emphasize creative abilities, use prompts like:

"Imagine . . ."

"Design . . ."

"Suppose that . . ."

"What would happen if . . . ?"

To emphasize practical thinking, ask students to:

"Show how you can use . . ."

"Implement . . ."

"Demonstrate how in the real world . . ."

2 Design lessons that emphasize different intelligences.

As Howard Gardner and others point out, most of the tasks that we ask students to master reflect the linguistic and/or logical-mathematical forms of intelligence. But there are five other ways that students can come to know things and demonstrate what they have learned. Potentially, lesson plans for any subject can be designed that incorporate each of Gardner's seven intelligences. Here are a few examples suggested by Thomas Armstrong (1994) and David Lazear (1992).

Journal Entry
Encouraging the Development of Multiple Intelligences

Elementary Grades: Punctuation Marks

Bodily-kinesthetic: students use their bodies to mimic the shape of various punctuation marks.

Musical: students make up different sounds and/or songs for each punctuation mark.

Interpersonal: in small groups of four to six, students teach and test one another on proper punctuation usage.

Middle School Grades: American History

Linguistic: students debate the pros and cons of key historical decisions (such as Abraham Lincoln's decision to use military force to prevent the Confederate states from seceding from the Union, the Supreme Court decision in *Plessy v. Ferguson* that allowed separate facilities for African Americans and whites, or President Harry Truman's decision to drop the atomic bomb on Japan).

Musical: students learn about and sing some of the songs that were popular at a particular point in the country's history.

Spatial: students draw murals that tell the story of a historical period.

High School Grades: Boyle's Law (Physics)

Logical-mathematical: students solve problems that require the use of Boyle's law (for a fixed mass and temperature of gas, the pressure is inversely proportional to the volume, or $P \times V = K$).

Bodily-kinesthetic: students breathe air into their mouths, move it to one side of their mouths (so that one cheek is puffed out), indicate whether the pressure goes up or down, distribute it to both sides of their mouths, and indicate again whether the pressure goes up or down.

Intrapersonal: students describe times in their lives when they felt they were either under a lot of psychological pressure or little pressure and whether they felt as if they had either a lot of or a little psychological space.

3 Recognize that different styles of learning call for different methods of instruction.

Robert Sternberg's work on styles of mental self-government calls for the same approach to instruction and testing as does his work on intellectual abilities: use a variety of instructional methods and testing formats. Not only will you have a more accurate picture of what students know, but you will be helping them learn how to shift styles to adapt to changing conditions. For example, students with a judicial style have a preference for Why questions (for example, Why did the United States go to war with Iraq

Journal Entry
Allowing for Differences in Cognitive Style

after Iraq invaded Kuwait?) whereas students with a legislative style have a preference for Suppose or What If questions (for example, If you were President George Bush, would you have gone to war with Iraq?). Table 4.3 indicates which of Sternberg's learning styles are most compatible with paticular methods of instruction.

4 Help students become aware of the existence of gender bias.

Journal Entry
Taking Steps to
Eliminate Gender
Bias

The following techniques have all been used by teachers to demonstrate that males often receive preferential treatment in our society in somewhat subtle ways (Bailey, 1996; Rop, 1998; Rutledge, 1997).

Have students count how often in the space of a month male and female athletes are mentioned in the sports section of the local paper and have the students create a graph depicting the difference.

Have students survey similar-aged friends and classmates about the size of their allowance and report the results by gender.

Have students review several textbooks and record how often men and women are mentioned.

Have students keep a record of who participates in class discussions, how often they speak, for how long, and how they respond to comments made by male versus female classmates.

5 Encourage girls to consider pursuing a career in science.

Journal Entry
Encouraging Girls
to Excel in Math
and Science

Anna Kasov, the high school chemistry teacher we mentioned earlier, offers the following suggestions to teachers interested in encouraging adolescent girls to consider a career in science.

Either invite female scientists to class to talk about science as a career or arrange for an electronic exchange through e-mail.

Have students read articles written by female scientists, contact the authors with questions about the articles, and make a report to the class.

Contact recent female graduates who are majoring in science and ask them to talk to the class about their experiences.

6 Recognize that you will not be able to address the various abilities and cognitive styles of all of your students all of the time.

Although this chapter has described three major ways in which students differ from one another and explained why it is important to gear instruction to these differences, we do not want you to get the impression that you should strive to accommodate the unique needs of each student every minute of the day. When you have twenty-five or more students in a class, such a goal is nearly impossible. But that doesn't mean you should make no attempt to get to know and work with students as individuals either. You might, for example, mimic the practice of one teacher who assigned one day a month to each student. For that day, the student "owned" the teacher's free time. The child decided how she wished to use the teacher during that time, although the teacher felt free to raise questions and issues. All the students looked forward to their day, and the teacher had an opportunity to learn about the unique characteristics of each student (Sarason, 1993).

RESOURCES FOR FURTHER INVESTIGATION

■ The New Views of Intelligence

Frames of Mind: The Theory of Multiple Intelligences (1983) is Howard Gardner's initial description of his theory. Part I covers earlier views of intelligence, Gardner's critique of those views, and why he proposed a different kind of theory. Part II describes each of the seven intelligences as well as Gardner's assessment of his theory's strengths and weaknesses. Part III describes how various forms of schooling support the various intelligences. In *The Unschooled Mind: How Children Think and How Schools Should Teach* (1991), Gardner elaborates on how traditional forms of instruction and assessment limit what students learn and how schools that are modeled on his theory can help students improve the quality of their learning.

Robert Sternberg describes the origin and nature of his triarchic theory in *Beyond IQ: A Triarchic Theory of Human Intelligence* (1985). In *Teaching for Thinking* (1996), Sternberg and Louise Spear-Swerling use Sternberg's triarchic theory to illustrate the nature of good thinking, how various teaching techniques can be used to promote good thinking, and how teachers can evaluate the thinking of their students.

■ Learning Styles and Classroom Instruction

Rita and Kenneth Dunn describe and illustrate in the following two books dozens of teaching techniques designed to be compatible with a variety of learning styles: *Teaching Elementary Students Through Their Individual Learning Styles* (1992) and *Teaching Secondary Students Through Their Individual Learning Styles* (1993). In *Thinking Styles* (1997b), Robert J. Sternberg provides a very readable and detailed description of his theory of mental self-government styles, the factors that affect their development, and how teachers can use this knowledge to improve the classroom performance of students. The first chapter contains an interesting account of how Sternberg did poorly in his first psychology course and temporarily abandoned psychology as a college major because of a mismatch between his thinking style and that of his instructor.

■ The Impact of Gender Bias on Students

For any prospective or practicing teacher interested in learning how to reduce personal gender bias, as well as the gender bias of others, *Building Gender Fairness in Schools* (1988), by Beverly Stitt, is a useful resource. This book is made up of two parts. Part 1 contains a collection of six readings on various aspects of gender bias (for example, "Sexism in Education," "How Fair Is Your Language?" and "Confronting Sex Bias in Instructional Materials"). Part 2 contains a sequenced set of eleven instructional units, each of which presents a competency to be mastered by the preservice or in-service teacher. The competencies become increasingly complex and difficult. Unit 1, for example, attempts to develop an awareness of the effects of gender bias. The goal of Unit 5 is to identify gender-fair curriculum materials. And the goal of Unit 11 is to conduct applied research to develop policies and programs to achieve gender fairness.

Katherine Blick Hoyenga and Kermit Hoyenga (1993) discuss stereotypes and gender typing in Chapter 11 of *Gender-Related Differences: Origins and Outcomes*.

Myra and David Sadker describe the myriad ways in which schools—from the primary grades through college—discriminate mainly against girls, but also boys, thereby decreasing their motivation, self-esteem, and achievement in *Failing at Fairness: How America's Schools Cheat Girls* (1994). This book is more interesting than the usual treatise on this subject because of the many first-person anecdotes contained in its ten chapters.

SUMMARY

1. The extent to which students differ from one another can be substantial, even in the primary grades. By fourth grade, the range of achievement can vary by four or more grade levels.

2. The first practical test of intelligence was devised by Alfred Binet to identify students who would be best served in a special education program.

3. Because they were designed to predict academic success, intelligence tests predict that outcome better than they predict other outcomes, such as job success, marital happiness, or life satisfaction.

4. Traditional intelligence tests seem to measure a general intellectual factor and a factor specific to the particular test being taken.

5. Traditional intelligence tests measure a relatively small sample of cognitive skills that best relate to classroom achievement and can change over time as additional knowledge and skills are acquired.

6. Intelligence, broadly defined, is the global capacity of the individual to act purposefully, think rationally, and deal effectively with the environment.

7. Sternberg's triarchic theory of intelligence is composed of analytical, creative, and practical abilities. The practical component, which is the ability to adapt to one's environment in order to achieve personal goals, has been ignored by traditional theories.

8. Research has shown that students learn more when learning tasks require them to use their analytical, creative, and practical abilities.

9. Gardner's multiple intelligences theory holds that each person has seven distinct intelligences, some of which are more well developed than others. Gardner is considering adding naturalist intelligence as an eighth type.

10. Several misconceptions exist about Gardner's multiple intelligences theory. Individuals who have a high level of a particular intelligence should not be expected to excel on all tasks or to choose a career that calls for that intelligence. Because of other factors, students may use their skills in different ways. Also, it is not necessary, and may be counterproductive, to try to teach every subject in seven different ways.

11. Sternberg's triarchic theory implies that instruction and testing should be designed to involve memory, analytical, creative, and practical abilities.

12. To accommodate the different profiles of intelligences that exist in a typical classroom, Gardner recommends that teachers use MI theory as a framework for devising alternative ways of teaching subject matter.

13. Technology tools, such as hypermedia, Web-based conferencing, concept mapping, and CD-ROMs, can strengthen the different aspects of intelligence described by both Sternberg and Gardner.

14. A learning style is a consistent preference students have for perceiving, thinking about, and organizing information.

15. When faced with a question or a problem for which the answer is uncertain, students with an impulsive learning style spend less time than classmates with a reflective style collecting and analyzing information before making a response.

16. Students with a field-dependent learning style prefer to work in situations where the procedures are clear and well defined because they take their cue for acceptable behavior from the context in which they work. Students with a field-independent style prefer to work in situations where they can impose their own structure and procedures on a task.

17. Sternberg has proposed a theory of mental self-government that is modeled after the structure and functions of civil government and contains thirteen learning styles.

18. Girls tend to outscore boys on tests that require rapid retrieval of information from long-term memory, reading comprehension, writing, and foreign language proficiency whereas boys tend to outscore girls on tests that call for the transformation of mental representations, math and science knowledge, and scientific reasoning.

19. Many gender differences in cognitive functioning either reach a peak or first become noticeable at the high school level.

20. Gender bias is the consistent differential response (both positive and negative) to male and female students when there is no sound educational reason for doing so.

21. The likely source of gender bias, which is communicated by both teachers and students, is a belief in traditional gender-role stereotypes.

22. The persistent exposure of students to gender bias is thought to play a role, particularly for females, in the courses that students select in high school, the career choices they make, and the extent to which they participate in class discussions.

23. Both adolescent males and females have a tendency to not express their true beliefs and opinions when in the company of teachers, parents, and members of the opposite sex. This phenomenon is called "loss of voice."

24. As with science and mathematics, a gender gap exists with respect to computer technology. Compared to boys, girls have less access to, confidence in, interest about, and time on computers. Suggestions for reducing this gap include early positive experiences with computers; computer applications for subjects girls prefer, such as reading, writing, history, and literature; and access to female role models who use technology.

KEY TERMS

intelligence *(110)*
triarchic theory of intelligence *(111)*
theory of multiple intelligences *(113)*
multimedia *(117)*
hypertext *(117)*
hypermedia *(118)*

CD-ROM *(118)*
learning style *(118)*
impulsive *(119)*
reflective *(119)*
field-dependent style *(120)*
field-independent style *(120)*

styles of mental self-government
  theory *(120)*
virtual reality *(122)*
gender bias *(124)*
loss of voice *(128)*

DISCUSSION QUESTIONS

1. Imagine that you are sitting in the faculty lounge listening to a colleague describe one of her students. Your colleague points out that this student has a C+ average and received an IQ score of 92 (low average) on a recently administered test. She concludes that since the student is working up to his ability level, he should not be encouraged to set higher goals because that would only lead to frustration. Your colleague then asks for your opinion. How do you respond?

2. The theories of Robert Sternberg and Howard Gardner indicate that people can be intelligent in ways other than the traditional analytical, linguistic, and logical-mathematical forms that dominate school curricula, instruction, and assessment. Assuming they are correct, why have schools been so reluctant to explicitly and systematically address other abilities, such as musical, spatial, interpersonal, and practical abilities?

3. Analyze yourself in terms of the learning styles discussed in this chapter. Do you think you are more re-flective than impulsive? More field-dependent than field-independent? More legislative, executive, or judicial? Try to recall classroom situations that made you comfortable because they seemed to fit your style(s) and classroom situations where you were uncomfortable because of a mismatch between your style and that of the instructor. Now imagine the twenty-five or so students who will one day be in your classroom. Should you even try to design your lessons and assessments so they match the styles of most students at least some of the time? If so, how will you do that?

4. In this chapter we noted that both male and female students can be the target of gender bias and that such bias influences the course selection, achievement levels, and career choices of students. Can you recall any instances of gender bias from teachers or friends? If so, do you think it had any effect on your choice of career? Is it possible that you will one day act in a gender-biased way toward your own students?

Addressing Cultural and Socioeconomic Diversity

5

In the introduction to Chapter 2 we pointed out that if your instructional plans are to be effective, they have to take into account what your students are like. (The term *entering behavior* is typically used to refer to the characteristics students bring with them to class.) In Chapters 2 and 3 we described students in terms of their age-related differences in psychosocial, cognitive, and moral development, and we discussed how students typically are similar to and different from one another in terms of physical, social, and cognitive characteristics. In this chapter we will turn to two other important ways in which students differ—cultural background and language.

Culture is a term that describes how a group of people perceives the world; formulates beliefs;

KEY POINTS

These key points will help you learn the important information in this chapter. To help you study, they also appear in the margins of the pages, next to the text where they are discussed.

The Rise of Multiculturalism

- Cultural pluralism assumes every culture has own logic, no culture inherently better, all people somewhat culture-bound
- U.S. becoming more culturally diverse because of changes in immigration, birthrates

Taking Account of Your Students' Cultural Differences

- Culture: how a group of people perceives, believes, thinks, behaves
- Ethnocentrism: belief that one's own culture is superior to other cultures

- Ethnic group members differ in verbal and nonverbal communication patterns
- Ethnic group members may hold different values
- Ethnic group members may favor different learning arrangements and processes
- Many ethnic families of color earn less than white families
- Low-SES children more proficient with everyday language than with language of classroom
- Educationally disadvantaged children often have low motivation to achieve
- Low-SES males often place a low value on academic achievement
- Pygmalion effect: impact of teacher expectations leads to self-fulfilling prophecy
- Limited effect of teacher expectancy on IQ scores

- Strong effect of teacher expectancy on achievement, participation
- Teacher expectancies influenced by gender, attractiveness, achievement, social class, ethnic background

Multicultural Education Programs

- Multicultural programs aim to promote respect for diversity, reduction of ethnocentrism and stereotypes, improved learning
- Multicultural education can be approached in different ways
- Multicultural lessons organized around key concepts
- Peer tutoring improves achievement, interpersonal relationships, attitudes toward subjects
- Cooperative learning: students work together in small groups
- Cooperative learning fosters better understanding among ethnically diverse students

- Mastery learning: all students can master the curriculum
- Minority children score lower on tests, drop out of school sooner
- Minority dropout rate due to alienation, differences in values, poverty
- Multicultural understanding can be promoted by electronically linking students from different cultural backgrounds

Bilingual Education

- Two main approaches to bilingual education: transition, maintenance
- Transition programs focus on rapid shift to English proficiency
- Maintenance programs focus on maintaining native-language competence
- Bilingual education programs produce moderate learning gains

137

evaluates objects, ideas, and experiences; and behaves. It can be thought of as a blueprint that guides the ways in which individuals within a group do such important things as communicate with others (both verbally and nonverbally), handle time and space, express emotions, and approach work and play. The concept of culture typically includes ethnic group but can also encompass religious beliefs and socioeconomic status (Gollnick & Chinn, 1994).

Different groups of people will, of course, vary in their beliefs, attitudes, values, and behavior patterns because of differences in cultural norms. (By *norms* we mean the perceptions, beliefs, and behaviors that characterize most members of a group.) People who were raised with mainstream American values, for example, find acceptable the practice of adults gently patting children on the head but find unacceptable the practice of two boys holding hands. Most Vietnamese, in contrast, disapprove of the former but not the latter (Sadker & Sadker, 1991).

To provide the appropriate classroom and school conditions that will help your students from different cultural backgrounds master a common curriculum, you must come to understand and take into account your students' differing cultural backgrounds. For example, a culturally aware teacher will emphasize the way in which American society has been enriched by the contributions of many different ethnic groups (and place special emphasis on those ethnic groups to which the students belong) and will not schedule a major exam or field trip for a day when certain students are likely to be out of school in observance of a religious holiday.

The approach to teaching and learning that we will describe in this chapter, one that seeks to foster an understanding of and mutual respect for the values, beliefs, and practices of different cultural groups, is typically referred to as **multicultural education.** Because culturally diverse children often come to school with different language backgrounds, another related issue is bilingual education, described at the end of this chapter.   ∎

The Rise of Multiculturalism

FROM MELTING POT TO CULTURAL PLURALISM

More than most other countries, the United States is made up of numerous ethnic groups with widely diverse histories, cultural backgrounds, and values. In addition to the hundreds of thousands of African Americans who were brought to the United States as slaves, the United States was peopled by many waves of immigrants, mostly from Europe but also from Asia and Latin America. Throughout the eighteenth and nineteenth centuries, the United States needed large numbers of people to settle its western frontier, build its railroads, harvest its natural resources, and work in its growing factories. As Table 5.1 indicates, between 1820 and 1920 approximately 33 million people immigrated to the United States.

Throughout this period the basic view of American society toward immigrants was that they should divest themselves of their old customs, views, allegiances, and rivalries as soon as possible and adopt English as their primary language along with mainstream American ideals, values, and customs. This assimilation of diverse ethnic groups into one national mainstream was known as the **melting pot,** a term and viewpoint popularized in a 1909 play by Israel Zangwill called *The Melting Pot.* The main institution responsible for bringing about this assimilation was the public school (Levine & Havighurst, 1992).

Table 5.1	Immigrants to the United States		
Immigration Totals by Decade			
Years	Number	Years	Number
1820–1830	151,824	1911–1920	5,735,811
1831–1840	599,125	1921–1930	4,107,209
1841–1850	1,713,251	1931–1940	528,431
1851–1860	2,598,214	1941–1950	1,035,039
1861–1870	2,314,824	1951–1960	2,515,479
1871–1880	2,812,191	1961–1970	3,321,677
1881–1890	5,246,613	1971–1980	4,493,314
1891–1900	3,687,546	1981–1990	7,338,062
1901–1910	8,795,386	1991–1996	6,146,213
		Total	63,140,209

SOURCE: U.S. Department of Justice (1996).

The notion of America as a great melting pot was generally accepted until the social unrest of the late 1960s and early 1970s. As an outgrowth of urban riots and the civil rights movement, minority ethnic groups argued not only for bilingual education programs in public schools but also for ethnic studies. It might be said that many American citizens realized that they did not wish to fit the white Anglo-Saxon Protestant mold of a "traditional American" and began to express a desire to be Americans who have different characteristics. Michael Novak (1971) refers to this movement as the "rise of the unmeltable ethnics." Since the early 1970s factors such as discrimination, the desire to maintain culturally specific ideas and practices, and continued immigration from different parts of the world have served to maintain, if not accelerate, this trend toward cultural diversity (or **cultural pluralism,** to use the preferred term). Three basic principles on which cultural pluralism rests are (1) every culture has its own internal coherence, integrity, and logic; (2) no culture is inherently better or worse than another; and (3) all persons are to some extent culture-bound (Janzen, 1994).

Cultural pluralism assumes every culture has own logic, no culture inherently better, all people somewhat culture-bound

THE CHANGING FACE OF THE UNITED STATES

Given recent changes in birthrates and immigration patterns and population projections for the next thirty to fifty years, one could argue that the decline of the melting pot philosophy and the rise of cultural pluralism and multicultural education will only accelerate in the years ahead. Consider, for example, the following statistics.

Between 1981 and 1986, 89 percent of legal immigrants to the United States came from non-European countries. Most of these immigrants came from Asia (principally the Philippine Islands, Korea, and China) and the Americas (principally Mexico and Cuba) and settled in the major cities of California, New York, Texas, and Florida. In the ten-year period from 1981 to 1990, about 7.3 million legal immigrants arrived in the United States. This is the second-highest ten-year total since the all-time immigration record of 1901–1910. Adding to the change produced by immigration itself is the fact that immigrant mothers have a higher birthrate than native-born mothers. Native-born women in 1986 averaged 67.5 births per 1,000, while foreign-born women averaged 98.9 per 1,000 (Banks, 1994b; Bennett, 1995; Kellogg, 1988).

Between 1988 and 2020 the number of white non-Hispanic-American children from birth through age seventeen is expected to decline by 27 percent from 44.5 million to 32.3 million (or from 70 percent of the school-age population to 49 percent). The number of Hispanic-American children is expected to almost triple, increasing from 6.8 million (11 percent of the school-aged population) to 18.6 million (28 percent of the school-age population). The population of African-American youths under age eighteen is expected to grow from 9.6 million to 10.5 million, an increase of 9 percent. By 2020 African-American youths should account for approximately 16 percent of the school-age population (see Figure 5.1). And by the year 2020 the number of Asian-American and other minority school-age children is expected to almost double, increasing by about 2.3 million children (Natriello, McDill, & Pallas, 1990). As these figures make clear, the United States is rapidly on its way to becoming an even more ethnically diverse nation than ever before.

| **U.S. becoming more culturally diverse because of changes in immigration, birthrates**

Taking Account of Your Students' Cultural Differences

As we pointed out in the opening paragraphs of this chapter, culture refers to the way in which a group of people perceives, thinks about, and interacts with the world. It is a way of giving meaning to experiences. As Donna Gollnick and Philip Chinn put it, "Culture gives us a certain lifestyle that is peculiarly our own. It be-

Figure 5.1 Projected Change in Percentage of Children under Eighteen from Three Ethnic Groups Between 1988 and 2020

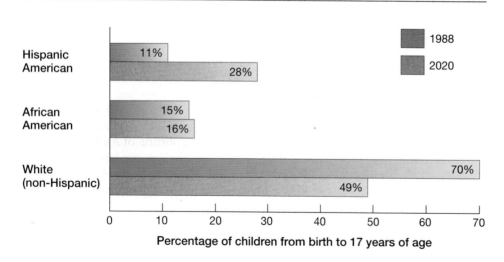

SOURCE: Adapted from Natriello, McDill & Pallas (1990).

Culture: how a group of people perceives, believes, thinks, behaves

comes so peculiar to us that someone from a different culture can easily identify us as Americans" (1994, p. 5). Two significant factors that most readily distinguish one culture from another are ethnicity and social class.

Because of the demographic changes we discussed earlier, familiarity with the similarities and differences of students from different ethnic groups and social classes is a necessity. But for you and your students to benefit from your knowledge of cultural diversity, you must view it in the proper perspective. The perspective we encourage you to adopt has three aspects. First, you should recognize that differences are not necessarily deficits. Students who subscribe to different value systems and who exhibit different communication patterns, time orientations, learning modes, motives, and aspirations should not be viewed as incapable students. Looking on ethnic and social-class differences as deficits usually stems from an attitude called *ethnocentrism*. This is the tendency of people to think of their own culture as superior to the culture of other groups. You may be able to moderate your ethnocentric tendencies and motivate your students to learn by consciously using instructional tactics that are congruent with the different cultural backgrounds of your students.

Ethnocentrism: belief that one's own culture is superior to other cultures

Second, recognize that the groups we and others describe with a general label are frequently made up of subgroups with somewhat different characteristics, and these subgroups may use a different label to refer to themselves. Navahos, for example, differ from the Hopi in physical appearance, dress, and hairstyle. Among Native American families who have only recently moved away from the reservation, the native tribal language may be the dominant language spoken at home (Soldier, 1997). Individuals who are called *Hispanic* often refer to themselves as either *Chicano, Latino, Mexicano, of Mexican descent,* or *of Spanish descent* (Losey, 1995).

Third, note that, although our descriptions of various ethnic groups may accurately portray some general tendencies of a large group of people, they may apply only partly or not at all to given individuals. One must always be careful in applying general knowledge to particular cases. The Mexican-American high school student who vehemently opposes abortion, for example, may do so more because of his Roman Catholic faith than because of cultural values concerning family relationships (Chinn & Plata, 1987–1988).

THE EFFECT OF ETHNICITY ON LEARNING

An **ethnic group** is a collection of people who identify with one another on the basis of one or more of the following characteristics: country from which one's ancestors came, race, religion, language, values, political interests, economic interests, and behavior patterns (Banks, 1994b; Gollnick & Chinn, 1994). Viewed separately, the ethnic groups in the United States, particularly those of color, are numerical minorities; collectively, however, they constitute a significant portion of American society (Banks, 1994b). Most Americans identify with some ethnic group (Irish Americans, German Americans, Italian Americans, African Americans, Chinese Americans, and Hispanic Americans, to name but a few). As a teacher you need to know how your students' ethnicity can affect student-teacher relationships.

Christine Bennett (1995) identifies five aspects of ethnicity that are potential sources of student-student and student-teacher misunderstanding: verbal communication, nonverbal communication, time orientation, social values, and learning modes and processes.

Students from different ethnic groups sometimes exhibit learning modality preferences. Native American, Mexican-American, and rural white students, for example, may favor a listening/speaking preference.

VERBAL COMMUNICATION PATTERNS   Problems with verbal communication can occur in a number of ways. Verbal exchanges in the classroom typically take the following form: the teacher elicits a comment from a student either by making a request or by asking a question, the student responds, and the teacher makes some sort of evaluative comment. But the conversations that occur between many Mexican-American parents and their children often lack the evaluative component. As a result, Mexican-American students may either be unsure of what to do with corrective feedback or may misinterpret its intent (Losey, 1995). An easy solution, and one that will benefit all of your students, is to explain the purpose of corrective feedback. Second, classroom discussions may not go as planned if teachers have students who do not understand or find confining the mainstream convention of "You take a turn and then somebody else takes a turn." Finally, because of differences in cultural experiences, some students may be very reluctant to speak or perform in public, whereas others may prefer exchanges that resemble a free-for-all shouting match. Some Native American children, for example, prefer to work on ideas and skills in private. A public performance is given only after an acceptable degree of mastery is attained (Bennett, 1995; Vasquez, 1990). This last practice is not as unique to Native American culture as it might seem at first glance. Music lessons and practices are typically done in private, and public performances are not given until a piece or program is mastered.

NONVERBAL COMMUNICATION   A form of nonverbal communication that is highly valued by mainstream American culture is direct eye contact. Most people are taught to look directly at the person to whom they are speaking, as this behavior signifies honesty on the part of the speaker and interest on the part of the listener. Among certain Native American, Hispanic, and Asian cultures, however, averting one's eyes is a sign of deference to and respect for the other person, whereas looking

| Ethnic group members differ in verbal and nonverbal communication patterns

at someone directly while being corrected is a sign of defiance. Thus, an Asian-, a Hispanic-, or a Native American student who looks down or away when being questioned or corrected about something is not necessarily trying to hide guilt or ignorance or to communicate lack of interest (Bennett, 1995; Howe, 1994).

TIME ORIENTATION   Mainstream American culture is very time oriented. People who know how to organize their time and work efficiently are praised and rewarded. We teach our children to value such statements as "Time is money" and "Never put off until tomorrow what you can do today." Nowhere is this time orientation more evident than in our schools. Classes begin and end at a specified time regardless of whether one is interested in starting a project, pursuing a discussion, or finishing an experiment. But for students whose ethnic cultures are not so time-bound (Hispanic Americans and Native Americans, for example), such a rigid approach to learning may be upsetting. Indeed, it may also be upsetting to some students who reflect the mainstream culture (Bennett, 1995).

SOCIAL VALUES   Two values that lie at the heart of mainstream American society are competition ("Competition brings out the best in people") and rugged individualism ("People's accomplishments should reflect their own efforts"). Since schools tend to reflect mainstream beliefs, many classroom activities are competitive and done on one's own for one's personal benefit. Mexican-American students, however, are more likely to have been taught to value cooperative relationships and family loyalty. These students may thus prefer group projects; they may also respond more positively to praise that emphasizes family pride rather than individual glory (Bennett, 1995; Vasquez, 1990).

> **Ethnic group members may hold different values**

INSTRUCTIONAL FORMATS AND LEARNING PROCESSES   Finally, ethnic groups may differ in terms of the instructional formats and learning processes they prefer. According to research summarized by Christine Sleeter and Carl Grant (1994), most elementary teachers use a teacher-centered, large-group approach to instruction in which all students work from the same text, workbook, and worksheets. At the high school and middle school levels, the typical classroom arrangement is rows of chairs facing the front of the room and a teacher who governs exchanges with students by talking, asking questions, and listening to answers. This approach to teaching may be somewhat incompatible with the learning conditions favored by students from other cultural backgrounds. African-American students, for example, seem to favor cooperative arrangements, content about people, discussion, and hands-on learning. One educational consequence of teaching students with these preferences might be the instruction of math concepts through descriptions of or active engagement in problems that involve buying, trading, or borrowing (Sleeter & Grant, 1994).

> **Ethnic group members may favor different learning arrangements and processes**

Some researchers have found that many Native Americans prefer visual imagery and drawing rather than verbal propositions as a way to mentally represent knowledge and deductively oriented rather than inductively oriented lessons. That is, they perform better when lessons begin with an overview and proceed to an examination of the parts, as opposed to an approach that stresses the details first and then draws general conclusions. Because Navajo students are taught by their culture to treat serious learning as private, they may not fully participate in such traditionally Western activities as tests, debates, and contests (Bennett, 1995; Guild, 1994; Soldier, 1997).

Evidence that the cultural background of students influences the learning process they use comes from the work of Nola Purdie and John Hattie (1996). They sought to determine if there is any truth to the common perception that Japanese students tend to be literal learners who emphasize memorizing at the expense of their own views and interpretations. People who believe this description attribute it to the emphasis in Japanese culture on subordination of individual viewpoints to the group's perceptions and goals.

Purdie and Hattie found that the Japanese students they interviewed chose memorizing as their most preferred learning process while a similar group of Australian students gave it a very low preference rating (eighteenth out of twenty-four options). A group of Japanese students who had been living in Australia for almost three years at the time of the study were in between these two extremes.

These findings suggest that although cultural background does influence choice of learning activity, the effects of culture seem to diminish as one becomes more accustomed to and comfortable with the values and practices of another culture.

THE EFFECT OF SOCIAL CLASS ON LEARNING

The social class from which a student comes also plays an influential role in a student's behavior. **Social class** is an indicator of an individual's or a family's relative standing in society. It is determined by such factors as annual income, occupation, amount of education, place of residence, types of organizations to which family members belong, manner of dress, and material possessions. The first three factors are used by the federal government to determine the closely related concept of **socioeconomic status (SES)**. The influence of social class is such that the members of working-class Hispanic-American and Irish-American families may have more in common than the members of an upper-middle-class Hispanic-American family and those of a working-class Hispanic-American family (Gollnick & Chinn, 1994).

Because of the severe and long-lasting historic pattern of discrimination experienced by ethnic groups of color in the United States, many members of these groups have fewer years of education, a less prestigious occupation, and a lower income than the average white person. Significantly, more African-American, Hispanic-American, and Native American adolescents drop out of high school than do whites, thereby shortening their years of education. And because they have less education, people of color are more likely to be unemployed or working in such low-paying occupations as office clerk, private house cleaner, and manual laborer.

In 1994, 22 percent of American children lived in families with incomes below the poverty level. Almost half of those children lived in families whose incomes were at least 50 percent below the official poverty threshold. Although most of these children are white (meaning of European ancestry), Figure 5.2 shows that the poverty rates among African-American, Native American, and certain Hispanic-American children are usually two to three times higher than that for white children (McLoyd, 1998).

Many ethnic families of color earn less than white families

Many low-SES students are what might be called educationally disadvantaged or educationally at-risk (Natriello, McDill, & Pallas, 1990) because they are continually exposed to various adverse factors that inhibit physical, social, emotional, and intellectual development. Before you read about some of these factors in the following paragraphs, we caution you to keep in mind that these differences appear to

Figure 5.2 Percentage of Families Within Ethnic Groups Living below Poverty Level in 1995

SOURCE: U.S. Bureau of the Census (1996).

* Percentages for Native Americans are from 1989 and are the most currently available.

be largely due to environmental causes. On tests of cognitive development between low-SES children and those from more advantaged homes, significant score differences do not appear until after two years of age (Sanders-Phillips, 1989).

1. Many low-SES Americans do not receive satisfactory health care. For example, African-American women have a high level of such pregnancy complications as toxemia, hemorrhage, hypertension, heart disease, infection, and diabetes. In addition, inadequate diets during pregnancy are common (Sanders-Phillips, 1989). As a consequence, there is a greater incidence of premature births, birth defects, and infant mortality among low-SES children as compared to middle-class children (as consistently revealed by National Institutes of Health statistics). Since poor children do not receive medical or dental care regularly, accurate statistics on general health are difficult to compile. It seems reasonable to assume, however, that the same inadequate nutrition and health care that leads to elevated infant mortality rates probably also leads to higher rates of illness in later years. In other words, low-SES children probably continue to suffer from untreated illnesses at a rate that may be at least twice that of middle-class children (Sanders-Phillips, 1989).

2. Educationally disadvantaged students are more likely than middle-class students to grow up in one-parent families (the father usually being the missing parent). Although some studies have shown that the presence of only one parent may be a major factor contributing to low achievement, other studies have failed to confirm this finding (Levine & Havighurst, 1992).

3. Both low-SES and middle-SES children are adept at the language of ordinary conversation. Such interchanges are grammatically simple, utilize stereotyped expressions, do not communicate ideas or emotions precisely, and make heavy use of gesture and inflection to transmit meaning. This form of language is sometimes referred to as "public" or "restricted" language. However, low-SES children are much less proficient than middle-class children in the use of the "formal" or "elaborated" language of the classroom. Elaborated language is more precise in conveying meaning; it is also a more effective tool for organizing experiences because it includes the bases for associations among ideas (Levine & Havighurst, 1992).

Low-SES children more proficient with everyday language than with language of classroom

4. Educationally disadvantaged children typically have not been exposed to a wide variety of experiences. The parents of middle-class children in the United States frequently function as teachers, although *tutors* would be a more appropriate word, since instruction is often given to one child at a time. Every time they talk to their children, answer questions, take them on trips, and buy books or educational toys, parents provide knowledge and experiences that accumulate to make school learning familiar and easy. A child who does not receive such continual tutoring in the home is clearly at a disadvantage when placed in competitive academic situations (Levine & Havighurst, 1992). Furthermore, there has been increasing concern about the development of a "technological underclass" of children whose families cannot afford to provide access to computers and on-line services at home.

5. Many low-SES students may not be strongly motivated to do well in school because of lower levels of a characteristic called *need for achievement*. A need for achievement (which is discussed more fully in Chapter 11) is a drive to accomplish tasks and is thought to be one of the main reasons why people vary in their willingness to invest time and energy in the achievement of a goal. Recent research suggests that low-SES African-American students score lower than comparable groups of white students on tests of need for achievement, but this racial difference is considerably smaller among middle-class samples. (Cooper & Dorr, 1995).

Educationally disadvantaged children often have low motivation to achieve

6. Many low-SES students, particularly African-American males, do not place a high value on academic achievement. Sandra Graham (1997) found that African-American middle school female students admired, respected, and wanted to be like their female classmates who got good grades and followed school rules, indicating that these girls valued effort and achievement. But the responses of the boys were quite different. They were least likely to nominate their high-achieving classmates as individuals whom they admired, respected, and wanted to emulate. This gender difference appears to be valid; Graham has replicated it in two other samples of African-American adolescents. Graham notes that data from other studies indicate that African-American males recognize the importance of working hard and fulfilling one's potential. But for reasons that are not yet understood, many of them adopt an indifferent attitude toward high levels of school achievement.

Low-SES males often place a low value on academic achievement

7. Many educationally disadvantaged students experience role confusion and have poor self-esteem (Pollard, 1993). As Erik Erikson has stressed, two key components of identity are being accepted by those who count and knowing where one is going. An educationally disadvantaged adolescent who has no definite career plans after leaving school (with or without a diploma) is more

likely to experience role confusion than a sense of identity achievement. If such an adolescent is unable to find a job (a common occurrence, given that the unemployment rate for minority-group youths is typically several times greater than the average rate for that age group), low self-esteem may contribute to the formation of a negative identity.

A clear and chilling example of the last three characteristics is offered by Marc Elrich (1994), a sixth-grade teacher in a Maryland school district just outside of Washington, D.C. His class of twenty-nine students was composed almost entirely of African-American and Hispanic-American low-SES youths who saw no value in education and who exhibited low self-esteem and low expectations. To prompt a discussion of self-esteem, he showed them a film based on a Langston Hughes story about an African-American youth who attempts to steal the purse of an elderly African-American woman. He fails, and the woman takes him into her home, where she tries to change his attitudes and behavior. The message of the film is that with love we all learn that we have it within ourselves to be better people. When Elrich asked for reactions to the film, this exchange occurred:

Student: As soon as you see a black boy, you know he's gonna do something bad.

Teacher: Just because he's black, he's bad?

Student: Everybody knows that black people are bad. That's the way we are. (p. 12)

When Elrich asked who else agreed with that assessment, twenty-four students raised their hands. Further discussion revealed that most of the students agreed with the following statements:

- Blacks are poor and stay poor because they're dumber than whites (and Asians).
- Black people don't like to work hard.
- Black men make women pregnant and leave.
- Black boys expect to die young and unnaturally.
- White people are smart and have money.
- Asians are smart and have money.
- Asians don't like blacks or Hispanics.
- Hispanics are more like blacks than whites. They can't be white so they try to be black.
- Hispanics are poor and don't try hard because, like blacks, they know it doesn't matter. They will be like blacks because when you're poor, you have to be bad to survive. (p. 13)

According to Elrich, his students' view of the world was that

hard work does not equal success in their world; instead, it means that parents are gone and children take care of children, they told us. The people who have the material goods that reflect the good life get their money through guns and drugs. Wimps die young and live in fear. Tough guys die young but are proud. Bosses are white and workers are black, and black people don't do important things, except in school books. In their world, few aspire to be doctors, scientists, or lawyers. (1994, p. 14)

During the course of the year, Elrich prompted discussions of slavery, racism, and class. In an attempt to help his students understand that the effects of bigotry and racism are not necessarily permanent, he pointed out that two hundred years ago life for most whites was harsh and not terribly free, especially in Europe, and that ideas about race and class were taught and promoted in the interest of a few—primarily very wealthy and privileged—white men. But over time and with persistent effort, many of these barriers to personal advancement were either eliminated or drastically reduced. Therefore, his students could influence what they became if they worked at doing so.

THE EFFECT OF ETHNICITY AND SOCIAL CLASS ON TEACHERS' EXPECTATIONS

So far we have described how students' ethnic and social-class backgrounds influence their approach to and success with various learning tasks. Now we would like to tell you how those and other characteristics often affect (consciously and unconsciously) the expectations that teachers have for student performance and how those expectations affect the quantity and quality of work that students exhibit. This phenomenon has been extensively studied since 1968 and is known variously as the *Pygmalion effect*, the *self-fulfilling prophecy*, and the **teacher expectancy effect**. By becoming aware of the major factors that influence teachers' perceptions of and actions toward students, you may be able to reduce subjectivity to a minimum, particularly with students whose cultural backgrounds are very different from your own.

The teacher expectancy effect basically works as follows: (1) on the basis of such characteristics as race, SES, ethnic background, dress, speech pattern, and test scores, teachers form expectancies about how various students will perform in class; (2) those expectancies are subtly communicated to the students in a variety of ways; and (3) students come to behave in a way that is consistent with what the teacher expects.

This phenomenon was first proposed by Robert Rosenthal and Lenore Jacobson in their 1968 book, *Pygmalion in the Classroom*. They described an experiment in which first- through sixth-grade teachers were led to believe that certain children had untapped potential and were "likely to show unusual intellectual gains in the year ahead" because of their scores on a new kind of ability test. In fact, the test was composed of standard items and the designated students were chosen at random. Nevertheless, Rosenthal and Jacobson reported that the students who were labeled potential achievers showed significant gains in intelligence quotient (IQ) and that the reason for these gains was that their teachers expected more of them. The authors referred to this phenomenon as the Pygmalion effect because they felt that teacher expectations had influenced the students to become intelligent in the same way that the expectations of the mythical Greek sculptor Pygmalion caused a statue he had carved to come to life.

| Pygmalion effect: impact of teacher expectations leads to self-fulfilling prophecy

RESEARCH ON THE EFFECTS OF TEACHERS' EXPECTANCIES   Given the obvious implications of teacher expectancy effects for shaping student behavior, researchers wasted no time investigating its validity and limits. Despite the dramatic results reported by Rosenthal and Jacobson, subsequent research showed that the effect of teacher expectancy on IQ scores was essentially limited to first- and second-grade students, was moderate in strength at those grade levels, and occurred only when it was induced within the first two weeks of the school year (Raudenbush, 1984). Apparently, once teachers have had an opportunity to observe and interact with their own students, they view these experiences as more credible and informative than the results of a mental ability test.

| Limited effect of teacher expectancy on IQ scores

But research that has investigated the effect of teacher expectancy on class-room *achievement* and *participation* has generally found sizable positive *and* negative effects (for example, Braun, 1976; Brophy, 1983; Cooper, 1979; Rosenthal, 1985). In addition, it appears that teacher expectations are more likely to maintain already existing tendencies than to drastically alter well-established behaviors. For example, primary grade teachers react differently to students in the fast-track reading group than to students in the slow-track group. When working with the more proficient readers, teachers tend to smile, lean toward the students, and establish eye contact more often. Criticism tends to be given in friendlier, gentler tones. The oral reading errors of proficient readers are often overlooked. When corrections are given, they are made at the end of the sentence or other meaningful unit rather than in the middle of such units. And comprehension questions are asked more often than factual questions as a means of monitoring students' attention to the reading selection.

In contrast, less proficient readers are corrected more often and in places that interrupt meaningful processing of the text, are given less time to decode difficult words or to correct themselves, and are asked low-level factual questions as a way of checking on their attention. Teachers' body posture is often characterized by frowning, pursing the lips, shaking the head, pointing a finger, and sitting erect. In sum, through a variety of subtle ways, teachers communicate to students that they expect them to perform well or poorly and then create a situation that is consistent with the expectation. As a result, initial differences between good and poor readers either remain or widen over the course of the school career (Wuthrick, 1990).

FACTORS THAT HELP CREATE EXPECTANCIES   In addition to documenting the existence of teacher expectancy effects and the conditions under which they occur, researchers have sought to identify the factors that might create high or low teacher expectations. Here is a list of some important factors taken from analyses by Carl Braun (1976), Gloria Ladson-Billings (1994), Vonnie McLoyd (1998), and Sonia Nieto (1996):

Attractive children are often perceived by teachers to be brighter, more capable, and more social than unattractive children.

Teachers tend to approve of girls' behavior more frequently than they approve of boys' behavior.

Female teachers tend to perceive the behavior of girls as closer to the behavior of "ideal students" than do male teachers.

Middle-class students are expected to receive higher grades than low-SES students, even when their IQ scores and achievement test scores are similar.

Teachers tend to perceive children from poor homes as less mature, less capable of following directions, and less capable of working independently than children from more advantaged homes.

Teachers are more influenced by negative information about students (for example, low test scores) than they are by neutral or positive information.

Teachers appear to spend more time and to interact more frequently with high achievers than with low achievers.

High-achieving students receive more praise than low-achieving ones.

It is important to bear in mind that these factors (plus others such as ethnic background, knowledge of siblings, and impressions of parents) usually operate *in*

Marginal notes:

Strong effect of teacher expectancy on achievement, participation

Teacher expectancies influenced by gender, attractiveness, achievement, social class, ethnic background *concert* to produce an expectancy. A teacher may be influenced not just by a single test score but also by appearance, grades assigned by other teachers, and so forth.

Multicultural Education Programs

The concept of multicultural education has been around for some time. Many of the elements that constitute contemporary programs were devised sixty to seventy years ago as part of a then-current emphasis on international education (Gollnick & Chinn, 1994). In the next section we will give you some idea of what it might be like to teach today from a multicultural perspective by describing the basic goals, assumptions, and characteristics of modern programs.

ASSUMPTIONS AND GOALS

The various arguments in favor of multicultural education that are made by its proponents (for example, Banks, 1994a, 1994c; Bennett, 1995; Garcia, 1994; Gollnick & Chinn, 1994; Ogbu, 1992; Singer, 1994) stem from several assumptions. These assumptions and the goals that flow from them appear in Table 5.2.

BASIC APPROACHES AND CONCEPTS

APPROACHES   James Banks (1994a, 1994c), a noted authority on multicultural education, describes four approaches to multicultural education. Most multicultural programs, particularly those in the primary grades, adopt what he calls the *contributions approach*. Here, ethnic historical figures whose values and behaviors are consistent with American mainstream culture (for example, Booker T. Washington, Sacajawea) are studied, whereas individuals who have challenged the dominant view (such as W. E. B. DuBois, Geronimo) are ignored. A second approach, which incorporates the first, is called the *additive approach*. Here, an instructional unit

In order for children to understand and appreciate different cultural values and experiences, those values and experiences have to be integrated into the curriculum and rewarded by the teacher.

Table 5.2	Common Assumptions and Goals of Multicultural Education Programs

Assumptions of Multicultural Education	Goals of Multicultural Education
U.S. culture is formed by the contributions of different cultural groups.	Promote self-acceptance and respect for other cultures by studying the impact ethnic groups have had on American society.
Individuals must have self-esteem and group esteem to productively work with people from other cultures.	Reduce ethnocentrism and increase positive relationships among members of different ethnic groups by understanding the viewpoints and products of these groups.
Learning about the achievements of one's cultural group will raise self- and group esteem.	Promote understanding of the origins and inaccuracy of ethnic stereotypes (e.g., African Americans are violent, Jews are stingy, Asian Americans excel at math and science, Hispanic Americans are hot-tempered).
American society benefits from positive interactions between members of different cultural groups.	Give all students a sense of being valued and accepted by expressing positive attitudes, by using appropriate instructional methods, and by formulating fair disciplinary policies and practices.
Academic performance is enhanced when teachers incorporate various cultural values and experiences into instructional lessons.	Help students master basic reading, writing, and computation skills by embedding them in a personally meaningful (i.e., ethnically related) context.

Multicultural programs aim to promote respect for diversity, reduction of ethnocentrism and stereotypes, improved learning

composed of concepts, themes, points of view, and individual accomplishments is simply added to the curriculum. The perspective from which they are viewed, however, tends to be that of the mainstream.

Multicultural education can be approached in different ways

A third approach produces what Banks calls the *transformation approach*. Here, the assumption is that there is no one valid way of understanding people, events, concepts, and themes. Rather, there are multiple views, each of which has something of value to offer. For example, the view of the early pioneers who settled the American West could be summed up by such phrases as "How the West Was Won" and "The Westward Movement." But the Native American tribes who had lived there for thousands of years may well have referred to the same event as "How the West Was Taken" or "The Westward Plague." You may recognize that the transformation approach is based on the principle of constructivism (discussed in Chapters 1 and 2). Because this approach requires the concrete operational schemes described in Chapter 2, it is typically introduced at the middle school level. Finally, there is the *social action approach*. It incorporates all of the components of the previous approaches and adds the requirement that students make decisions and take actions concerning a concept, issue, or problem being studied.

CONCEPTS Regardless of which approach you use, Banks (1994a) suggests that multicultural units and lessons be organized around a set of key concepts that

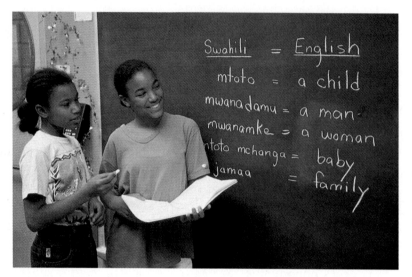

Advocates of multicultural education believe that ethnic minority students learn more effectively when some of their learning materials and assignments contain ethnically related content.

incorporate a range of facts, generalizations, and subject-matter disciplines. These concepts can be used to analyze a particular ethnic group or to compare and contrast groups. The following set of key concepts and associated questions illustrates what Banks has in mind.

Multicultural lessons organized around key concepts

Identity: To what extent is the group aware of its ethnic identity, and how does the group express that identity?

Culture: What ethnic elements (for example, values, customs, perspectives) are present in the group's culture today? How is the group's culture reflected in its music, literature, and art?

Immigration: From what country or countries did this group originate? When and in what numbers did this group immigrate to the United States?

Ethnic community: To what extent are members of the group concentrated within particular geographic regions?

Racism and discrimination: In what ways has this group been subjected to racism and discrimination?

Communication: To what extent and why do members of the group encounter problems when communicating with other ethnic groups?

Self-concept: How have the group's societal experiences affected the self-concepts of its members?

Power: What is the group's social, political, and economic status? To what extent does the group exercise power within the community? Within the larger society?

Acculturation: To what extent has the group influenced and been influenced by the mainstream society?

CHARACTERISTICS OF EFFECTIVE MULTICULTURAL TEACHERS

Although Banks's ideas about how to structure multicultural education programs are well conceived, they require the efforts of effective teachers for their potential benefits to be realized. Eugene García (1994), on the basis of his own research and that of others, identifies several characteristics that contribute to the success some teachers have in teaching students from culturally diverse backgrounds. Briefly stated, the effective multicultural teacher:

1. Provides students with clear objectives.
2. Continuously communicates high expectations to the student.
3. Monitors student progress and provides immediate feedback.
4. Has several years' experience in teaching culturally diverse students.
5. Can clearly explain why she uses specific instructional techniques (like the ones described in the next section).
6. Strives to embed instruction in a meaningful context. For example, a topic from one subject, such as controlling crop damaging insects with insecticide, could be extended to other subjects (examining the effects of insecticide on human health, graphing crop yields sprayed with various types and amounts of insecticides).
7. Provides opportunities for active learning through small-group work and hands-on activities. One teacher, for example, created writing workshops in which students wrote, revised, edited, and published their products for others to read.
8. Exhibits a high level of dedication. Effective multicultural teachers are among the first to arrive at school and among the last to leave, work weekends, buy supplies with their own money, and are constantly looking for opportunities to improve their instructional practices. If these characteristics sound familiar, it's because we discussed them in Chapter 1 as part of what makes teaching an art.
9. Enhances students' self-esteem by having classroom materials and practices reflect students' cultural and linguistic backgrounds.
10. Has a strong affinity for the students. Effective multicultural teachers describe their culturally diverse students in such terms as "I love these children like my own" and "We are a family here."

INSTRUCTIONAL GOALS, METHODS, AND MATERIALS

Teachers whose classes have a high percentage of children from ethnic minority and low-SES backgrounds often assume that they need to emphasize mastery of basic skills (such as computation, spelling, grammar, and word decoding) because minority and low-SES students are often deficient in those skills. Although this approach does improve children's performance on tests of basic skills, some educators argue that it does so at the expense of learning higher-level skills and that it is possible for students from poverty backgrounds to acquire both basic and higher-level skills. The following section summarizes the results of one study that investigated this issue.

BASIC SKILLS VERSUS CONCEPTUAL UNDERSTANDING   Michael Knapp, Patrick Shields, and Brenda Turnbull (1995) studied the teaching practices of almost 140 first- through sixth-grade classrooms in fifteen elementary schools that served large numbers of children from low-SES families to determine if the assumption that low-SES children can acquire both basic and higher-level skills is true. Over a two-year period these authors studied classrooms where the learning of basic skills was paramount as well as classrooms that emphasized higher-level and more meaningful outcomes. Teachers in the first group made extensive use of drill and practice, tasks that were limited in their demands, and tasks that could be completed quickly. Teachers in the second group used classroom discussions to let students work out the reasons behind mathematical procedures or to explore alternative solutions to math problems, required students to read longer passages and gave them opportunities to discuss what they had read, taught them reading comprehension strategies, and gave them more extended writing assignments.

Knapp and his colleagues found that children whose instruction emphasized conceptual understanding and problem solving performed better on mathematics, reading comprehension, and writing test items that measured advanced skills than their counterparts whose instruction focused on mastery of basic skills. And their performance on basic skill items was either no worse and sometimes better than that of students whose teachers emphasized the learning of basic skills.

The three instructional tactics that are recommended most often by proponents of multicultural education are peer tutoring, cooperative learning, and mastery learning. Although each of these techniques can be used with any group of students and for most any purpose, they are so well suited to the goals of multicultural education that the phrase "culturally responsive teaching" has been used to describe them (Wlodkowski & Ginsberg, 1995).

PEER TUTORING   As its name implies, **peer tutoring** involves the teaching of one student by another. The students may be similar in age or separated by one or more years. (The latter arrangement is usually referred to as cross-age tutoring.) The theoretical basis of peer tutoring comes from Jean Piaget's notions about cognitive development. Recall from our discussion of Piaget in Chapter 2 that cognitive growth depends on the presence of a disequilibrating stimulus that the learner is motivated to eliminate. When children with different cognitive schemes (because of differences in age, knowledge, or cultural background) are forced to interact with each other, cognitive conflict results. Growth occurs when children try to resolve this conflict (through assimilation and accommodation) by comparing and contrasting each other's views. The presumed benefits of peer tutoring include improved communication skills, an increased awareness of the perspectives of others, an increased ability to analyze ideas and provide feedback to others, higher levels of achievement, and a more positive attitude toward the subject being studied (Foot, Shute, & Morgan, 1990). This technique—as well as the one we will discuss next, cooperative learning—is effective for many different students, but especially for Hispanic-American and Native American children, whose cultural backgrounds place a high value on cooperation and mentoring (Sadker & Sadker, 1991).

Strong support for peer tutoring has been provided by subsequent studies involving a variety of students and yielding many different outcomes. In particular, peer tutoring has been shown to increase the arithmetic skills of low-achieving elementary school students from low-SES backgrounds (Fantuzzo, Polite, & Grayson, 1990); the self-esteem and achievement of students with learning disabilities (Beirne-Smith, 1991; Byrd, 1990); and the arithmetic accuracy, self-concept, attitude toward mathematics, and social interactions between tutor and tutee of students with behavioral disorders (Franca, Kerr, Reitz, & Lambert, 1990). Two conditions seem to account for the success of peer tutoring. One is the presence of an explicit set of guidelines that informs the tutor and tutee of their respective roles and responsibilities. The other is the holding of the tutor accountable for the performance of the tutee (Fantuzzo, Riggio, Connelly, & Dimeff, 1989).

Peer tutoring improves achievement, interpersonal relationships, attitudes toward subjects

COOPERATIVE LEARNING   Closely related to peer tutoring is cooperative learning. The general idea behind **cooperative learning** is that by working in small, heterogeneous groups (of four or five students total) and by helping one another master the various aspects of a particular task, students will be more motivated to learn, will learn more than if they had to work independently, and will forge stronger interpersonal relationships than they would by working alone.

| Cooperative learning: students work together in small groups

There are several forms of cooperative learning, one of which is Student Team Learning. Student Team Learning techniques are built on the concepts of team reward, individual accountability, and equal opportunities for success. *Team reward* means that teams are not in competition with one another for limited rewards. All of the teams, some of them, or none of them may earn whatever rewards are made available depending on how well the team's performance matches a predetermined standard. *Individual accountability* means that each member of the team must perform at a certain level (on a quiz, for example) for the team's effort to be judged successful. It is not permissible for one team member's above-average performance to compensate for another team member's below-average performance. Finally, *equal opportunities for success* allow students of all ability levels to contribute to their team's success by improving on their own past performances (Slavin, 1995).

Robert Slavin (1995), a leading exponent of cooperative learning, reports that cooperative learning produced significantly higher levels of achievement than did noncooperative arrangements in sixty-three of ninety-nine studies (64 percent). The results for the Student Team Learning programs have been the most consistently positive. Of particular relevance to this chapter are the findings that students who cooperate in learning are more apt to list as friends peers from different ethnic groups and are better able to take the perspective of a classmate than are students who do not work in cooperative groups.

| Cooperative learning fosters better understanding among ethnically diverse students

Although cooperative learning is a generally effective instructional tactic, it is likely to be particularly useful with Hispanic-American and Native American students. Children from both cultures often come from extended families that emphasize cooperation and sharing. Thus, these students may be more prepared than

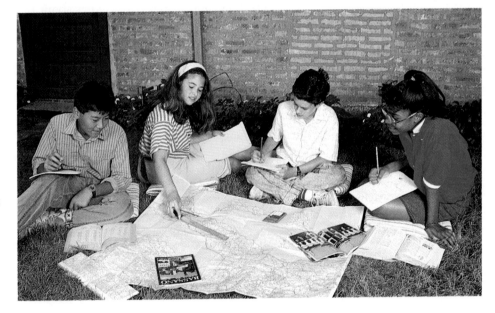

Students from different cultural backgrounds who learn in small cooperative groups are more likely to make friends with one another than are culturally different students who do not interact with one another.

other individuals to work productively as part of a group by carrying out their own responsibilities as well as helping others do the same (Sadker & Sadker, 1991; Soldier, 1989). We will have more to say about cooperative learning and its effects on motivation in Chapter 11.

MASTERY LEARNING   The third instructional tactic, **mastery learning**, is an approach to teaching and learning that assumes most students can master the curriculum if certain conditions are established. These conditions are that students (a) have sufficient aptitude to learn a particular task, (b) have sufficient ability to understand instruction, (c) are willing to persevere until they attain a certain level of mastery, (d) are allowed whatever time is necessary to attain mastery, and (e) are provided with good-quality instruction.

Mastery learning: all students can master the curriculum

Mastery learning proponents assume that all of these conditions can be created if they are not already present. Aptitude, for example, is seen as being partly determined by how well prerequisite knowledge and skills have been learned. And perseverance can be strengthened by the deft use of creative teaching methods and various forms of reward for successful performance. The basic mastery learning approach is to clearly specify what is to be learned, organize the content into a sequence of relatively short units, use a variety of instructional methods and materials, allow students to progress through the material at their own rate, monitor student progress in order to identify budding problems and provide corrective feedback, and allow students to relearn and retest on each unit until mastery is attained (Block, Efthim, & Burns, 1989). We will describe mastery learning in more detail in Chapter 14.

Like the research on peer tutoring and cooperative learning, the research on mastery learning has generally been positive. On the basis of a comprehensive review of this literature, Chen-Lin Kulik, James Kulik, and Robert Bangert-Drowns (1990) conclude that mastery learning programs produce moderately strong effects on achievement. The average student in a mastery learning class scored at the 70th percentile on a classroom examination, whereas the average student in a conventional class scored at the 50th percentile. The positive effect of mastery learning was slightly more pronounced for lower-ability students. As compared to students in conventional classes, those in mastery classes had more positive feelings about the subjects they studied and the way in which they were taught.

TEXTBOOKS   Let's assume that you have decided to incorporate a multicultural orientation into your classroom lessons. Can you count on the history or social studies textbook that has been chosen by your school district to provide adequate coverage of this topic? Probably not. Jesus Garcia (1993) examined how various ethnic groups have been portrayed in elementary and high school social studies and history textbooks over the past fifty years. Although contemporary textbooks provide broader coverage of various ethnic groups than did earlier textbooks, Garcia concludes that their coverage is still superficial. Discussions of African Americans, for example, include such topics as slavery, Reconstruction, the civil rights movement, black organizations, free blacks in Colonial America, and the development of black churches. But none of these topics is discussed in great depth. The same conclusion was drawn about the treatments of Irish, Italian, Jewish, and Polish Americans.

The implication for teachers who believe that their classroom should have a strong multicultural emphasis is that their school's textbook should probably be viewed as just a starting point. The teacher who is committed to providing students a strong multicultural experience will have to seek out high quality supplementary materials. Our Resources for Further Investigation at the end of the chapter is a good place to start.

A RATIONALE FOR MULTICULTURAL EDUCATION

Some people seem to believe that multicultural education programs represent a rejection of basic American values and that this opposition to traditional values is the only rationale behind such programs. We feel this belief is mistaken on both counts. We see multicultural programs as being consistent with basic American values (such as tolerance of differences and equality of opportunity) and consider them to be justified in several ways.

One argument in favor of multicultural programs is that they foster teaching practices that are effective in general as well as for members of a particular group. For example, expressing an interest in a student through occasional touching and smiling and allowing the child to tutor a younger student are practices likely to benefit most students, not just those of Hispanic-American origin.

A second argument in favor of multicultural education is that all students may profit from understanding different cultural values. For example, the respect for elders that characterizes Native American and Asian-American cultures is likely to become increasingly desirable as the percentage of elderly Americans increases over the years. Similarly, learning the Native American value of living in harmony with nature may come to be essential as we run out of natural resources and attempt to alleviate environmental pollution (Triandis, 1986).

A third argument in support of multicultural education programs is that the United States is becoming an increasingly multicultural society (because of the immigration and birthrate trends mentioned earlier) and students thus need to understand and know how to work with people of cultures different from their own. (See Case in Print, pages 158–159, for a discussion of how prevalent behavior based on stereotypes still is and how it can be confronted.)

A fourth argument for multicultural education programs is that they expose students to the idea that "truth" is very much in the eye of the beholder. From a European perspective, Christopher Columbus did indeed discover a new world. But from the perspective of the Arawak Indians who were native to the Caribbean, Columbus invaded territories that they had occupied for thousands of years. Similarly, one can describe the history of the United States as one in which continual progress toward democratic ideals has been made or as one in which progress has been interrupted by conflict, struggle, violence, and exclusion (Banks, 1993).

And last but not least, multicultural programs can encourage student motivation and learning. These programs demonstrate respect for a child's culture and teach about the contributions that the student's group has made to American society. Proponents argue that these features both personalize education and make it more meaningful. Conversely, when children perceive disrespect for their cultural background, the result can be disastrous. Consider the following comment by a Mexican-American student who realizes for the first time that his teachers viewed him as both different and inferior:

> One recreation period, when we were playing our usual game of soccer, I took time out to search for a rest room. I spotted a building on the north side of the playground and ran for it. As I was about to enter, a teacher blew her whistle very loudly, freezing me on the spot. She approached me and demanded to know where I was going, who I was, and what I was doing on

Confronting Multicultural Misunderstanding

A third argument in support of multicultural education programs is that the United States is becoming an increasingly multicultural society . . . and students thus need to understand and know how to work with people of cultures different from their own. (p. 157)

STUDENTS EMBRACE CHANCE TO TALK OUT FRUSTRATIONS

PHILIP DINE

St. Louis Post-Dispatch 5/21/95

A lanky 15-year-old with a quick smile, Phuc Chau does not look like a youngster ready to fight. But after five years of school in St. Louis, fighting ranks high among skills he's learned—and now hopes to unlearn.

"Kids don't like us, don't like us Asians. White kids, black kids. I don't like kids calling me names, so I fight," he says, that smile never straying far from his lips.

Phuc, an eighth-grader at International Studies Middle School, says insults hurled at him or his 15 Vietnamese school buddies "make me very angry."

At least once a month, he says, two or three students approach him with hostile intentions.

They make fun of the way I talk or play with my friends," he says. "They call me 'Ching,' or they say 'Chung, chung, chung, bung, bung, bung.'" Things weren't too bad when he started in third grade at Hamilton Elementary, probably because the children were small, he says. But by sixth grade he found himself engaging in fisticuffs. In recent years, it seems, his temper has flashed as frequently at his smile. But that will stop, he abruptly lets on, fixing his black eyes on his listener. No more fighting, no more trouble.

"I know how to think," he confides. "I got to worry about my education."

And what brought this on?

A girlfriend, "kind of smart," who's given him a new perspective.

Phuc is one of a dozen youngsters gathered this particular day at an informal discussion group called "safehaven," held Friday afternoons in the basement of St. Pius V Church in south St. Louis. Ron Klutho, who teaches foreign students in area schools and started the sessions three years ago, worried that some kept their struggles bottled up when the school day ended.

Many left lands of devastating poverty or smoldering ethnic hatred. Yet what stands out are their descriptions of the chaos and wildness they find in American society and in the schools that have served as agents for assimilation for generations of immigrants.

Several praise their teachers but wonder about their schoolmates.

The Da Silva brothers, Claudio, 18, of Roosevelt High School, and Joao, 15, of Soldan High, grab chairs and want to talk.

Five years ago the brothers emigrated here from Angola with their parents, brother and three sisters after stops in Namibia and Botswana. Their father, a former educator fluent in six languages, works in a factory making cleaning products.

This country, the brothers assert, is full of opportunity. But they can't understand the way young people act, clowning around when the teacher is talking or taunting foreign students for supposedly getting government handouts.

Joao says that jabs about whether he lived in a hut or ever wrestled a lion stem from insecurity and ignorance. So he ignores them.

He has an engaging smile, is confident yet unassuming, and his rapid, nearly accentless English is spiced with "Hey oh" and "Check this out." It's easy to picture him in his drama class. Yet, he says, most of his friends are foreign classmates, who accept him more readily than do Americans.

"Vietnamese kids do good in school, in math for instance," Joao says. "Sometimes American kids become jealous. They say, 'Hey, you cheated.' They try to excuse themselves, instead of facing the fact that, hey, they don't study."

Another African student in the city's schools, a fourth-grader named John, joins the conversation.

The United States "is a good country," he says. "They have everything you need to live. Back home, school doesn't have so much. But they don't make fun of you. Everybody learns."

"Here, white people make fun of black people, black people make fun of white people. You get mad, say something out loud, you get in trouble."

The Da Silva brothers nod. Not a day goes by without the brothers thinking of the people dying back home from war and poverty—and hoping for the time their education will be finished so they can go back and make a difference.

That makes it all the harder, they say, to understand why people who have choices fight so much.

"This could be a great place," Claudio says.

Questions and Activities

1. In this article there are both indications of hope and indications of hopelessness in terms of young people's attitudes toward different races and cultures and how it might be possible to change these attitudes. Identify two positive and two negative aspects. Consider how your role as a teacher might come into play vis-à-vis these aspects. How might your role be different if you were an elementary school teacher, a middle school teacher, or a high school teacher?

2. Imagine that you had some of these students—both the foreign students and the American students they describe—in your class. Do you think the instructional tactics you have learned about in this chapter could be used to try to alter the non-minority students' negative behavior and attitudes as well as offer effective instruction to the minority students? Which ones might be most effective and why? Can you think of other tactics or methods that you would like to try?

3. As a future teacher, what important lesson do you draw from the fact that a "safehaven" environment for airing feelings that get "bottled up" has proved helpful for these students? Name some specific ways in which you might put this knowledge to use inside and outside your classroom.

4. In a related article, the reporter states that until a recent and ongoing influx of immigrants and refugees, St. Louis was a "decidedly monoglot area." In other words, the population was fairly homogeneous, and students were not exposed to different cultural groups. Although this certainly does not excuse negative and stereotyping behavior, it might help explain it. If you become a teacher in a homogeneous and non-culturally diverse district, how might you work toward building tolerance and dispelling cultural ignorance? Describe several ways in which you could put to use the tactics and approaches in this chapter to increase multicultural awareness in such a situation.

that side of the playground. I was dumbfounded and afraid to respond, so she took me by the ear and escorted me back across the playground to the south side. Her parting remark was a stern admonition not to cross the line and to stay with all the other Mexicans.

At that very moment I stopped, turned, and looked at the school as if for the first time. I saw a white line painted across the playground. On one side were the white children playing; on my side were the Mexicans. Then I looked at the building, which was divided in half. The office was in the center, with two wings spreading north and south—one wing for whites and the other for Mexicans. I was overwhelmed with emotions that I could not understand. I was hurt, disappointed, and frustrated. But more than anything else, I was profoundly angry. (Mendoza, 1994, p. 294)

Statistical evidence of the need for multicultural programs can be seen in the disappointing academic performance of a significant number of minority-group students. Compared to white high school sophomores and seniors, African-American, Hispanic-American, and Native American students score lower on standardized tests of vocabulary, reading, writing, mathematics, and science (Levine & Havighurst, 1992). These differences appear early. Recent results from the National Assessment of Educational Progress reveal that the reading and writing skills of African-American and Hispanic-American children are substantially below those of white children as early as third grade (Pallas, Natriello, & McDill, 1989).

Given these achievement differences, it should come as no surprise that there are parallel differences in school dropout rates. Whereas 8.9 percent of whites drop out of school before graduation, 13.6 percent of African Americans, 35.3 percent of Hispanic Americans, and 44.5 percent of Native Americans do so (Bennett, 1995). Investigations into the reasons why minority students leave school prematurely have found that individual factors, school environment factors, social-class factors, and economic factors may all play a role. Compared to white students who stay in school, minority dropouts have lower levels of motivation, lower self-esteem, and weaker academic skills; they are also more impulsive. In addition, dropouts nearly always report a sense of alienation from school because of low teacher expectations, expressions of racial or ethnic group prejudice from teachers and students, and unfair discrimination. Students required to repeat grades (recall our discussion of this topic in Chapter 1) are among the most likely to drop out of school.

> **Minority children score lower on tests, drop out of school sooner**

Differences in social-class values can also contribute to low levels of achievement and a subsequent early exit from school. Two middle-class values, order and discipline, fit nicely with the expectations and activities of schools. In contrast, values typically held by low-SES groups—such as avoiding trouble with authorities, developing physical prowess, and establishing independence from external control—are not likely to be as productive in achieving school success (Tidwell, 1989).

> **Minority dropout rate due to alienation, differences in values, poverty**

Finally, minority students who do poorly in school and leave early typically come from the poorest households. In 1995 the poverty rate for white children was 6.4 percent, whereas 27 percent of Hispanic-American children and 26.4 percent of African-American children were living in poverty (U.S. Bureau of the Census, 1996). Multicultural theorists believe that the inclusion of ethnically related content and activities in the curriculum will make classroom assignments more meaningful and will help minority students master basic reading, writing, computational, and reasoning skills (Banks, 1994a; Vasquez, 1990).

BRIDGING THE CULTURAL AND SES GAP WITH TECHNOLOGY

As we stated earlier, a basic purpose of multicultural education is to give students the opportunity to learn about the characteristics of people from different cultures and to try to understand how those individuals view the world. For schools that draw from an ethnically, racially, and socioeconomically diverse population, acquiring firsthand experience about the history, beliefs, and practices of different cultures is not likely to be a major problem. But schools that draw from more homogeneous populations are likely to be limited to such resources as books, magazines, and videotapes. This limitation on multicultural education may be surmounted soon, however, by the ability of technology to—in a very real sense—bring the world to the student.

Martha Irwin, Peggy Moore, and Judy Stevenson (1994) describe one multimedia project intended to enhance students' multicultural literacy. Their hypertext program, Multicultural Links, is a rich resource for discovering maps of various countries, text and graphic information about people and their countries, annotated information on various multicultural books, mini-biographies about prominent people in various countries, and a multicultural calendar of events in history, holidays, and other items of worldwide interest. Such a wealth of images, historical data, maps, literature, and events from cultures around the world (for example, various national anthems) should help students appreciate and better communicate with people from different cultures. Irwin et al. (1994) have also developed hypertext tools to allow students to construct their own knowledge of these cultures and rep-

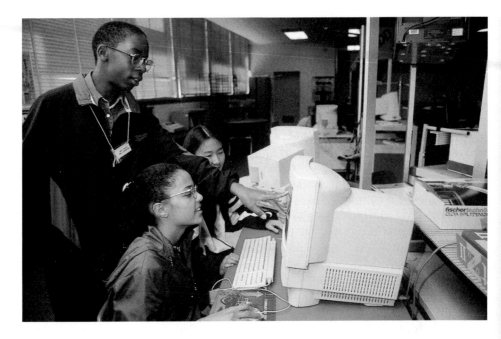

Computer-based technology helps students learn more about other cultures and social classes by providing access to various reference sources and individuals from almost anywhere in the world.

resent their knowledge of key facts and concepts on interconnected cognitive maps. Future steps include the ability to create video and audio documentaries of resource people from various cultures that learners can view and compare.

Technological innovations like hypermedia linkages, responding to ideas on an electronic bulletin board, or sharing ideas via videoconferencing with one's peers across time zones and geographic distance can help teachers and students see new points of view and attain a greater respect for diversity (Kontos & Mizell, 1997). Kerry Freedman and Meihui Liu (1996) found that despite clear differences in attitudes and communication patterns, telecommunication projects among nonnative Asian-American students, Native American students on a reservation, and white rural students encouraged more questioning and interaction than occurred in face-to-face settings. A similar project in Connecticut attempted to increase respect and tolerance for other cultures through videoconferences between an urban and suburban school. Discussions of lifestyle, local stores, city services, hand gun problems, and explorations of the concept of diversity were eye-opening for these students.

Multicultural understanding can be promoted by electronically linking students from different cultural backgrounds

Another noteworthy program is the AT&T Learning Network (Riel, 1990, 1993), which has recently evolved into the International Education and Resource Network (I*EARN) (Riel, 1996). In this program, learning circles, or small electronic communities of six to nine classes from across the world, are matched by theme or interest (for example, societal problems, journalism, history, etc.). Learning circles were established for several reasons, one of which was to raise awareness of different perspectives on global issues. Each learning circle works through six phases: getting ready, introductions, planning circle projects, exchanging student work, organizing circle publications, and closing the circle (Riel, 1993).

These types of electronic networking tools open up unique possibilities for cross-class or cross-cultural collaboration and mentoring (Riel, 1996). Imagine if one of the learning circle partners for your students was located in the former West Germany when the Berlin Wall was coming down or in Israel when Scud missiles were thundering in from Iraq. What if you received daily eyewitness reports from such locations right in your classroom, as one teacher's high school classes in Seattle did (Golub, 1994)? What an incredible opportunity for your students to gain access to new information, analyze and evaluate it, and communicate their own insights and ideas.

Earlier in this chapter we indicated that many students from low-SES homes are considered to be at-risk for educational failure because of adverse conditions surrounding their physical, social, emotional, and cognitive development. Creative technology products may be able to reduce the numbers of at-risk students who perform at low levels or drop out of school altogether. One multimedia environment, MOST (Multimedia Environments That Organize and Support Learning Through Technology), was designed to engage at-risk middle school and high school students in authentic tasks that develop their literacy skills (Bransford et al., 1996; Cognition and Technology Group at Vanderbilt, 1994). Students create interesting multimedia products that teach their parents, teachers, peers, and others about important life concepts and issues such as drug abuse, AIDS, and driving safety, all while working on their literacy skills. Technological supports, or scaffolds, are embedded in MOST environments to foster student reading comprehension, listening, communication, and information generation skills. Besides engaging students in a meaningful learning context, MOST environments attempt to build on student strengths and connect to out-of-school experiences.

MOST environments have three common components. First, they involve a videodisc and animated tutor which helps students in word recognition and decoding as well as text passage comprehension. Brief video clips are linked to readings to provide video anchors that enrich student passage comprehension. Word fluency is fostered through a speaker-dependent voice recognition system which students train to identify their voice. To build up a library of voice patterns, a human tutor, wearing a bow tie and glasses, asks students to repeat a set of words from a 400-word master list. Through this voice recognition system, students can interact with the program and speak with the tutor. Second, students can use the Multimedia Producer to create their own multimedia productions by using this shell to enter text, digital sound, or video by controlling a videodisc player. When done, student work can be put on display, thereby allowing students who are developmentally behind their peers to make noteworthy classroom contributions. Third, the use of two-way videoconferencing brings students into contact with content area specialists, designers, other schools, and the surrounding community.

Now that you are familiar with the nature and goals of multicultural education programs and some of the instructional tools that are available to you, the following Suggestions for Teaching should help you get started.

SUGGESTIONS FOR TEACHING IN YOUR CLASSROOM

Promoting Multicultural Understanding and Classroom Achievement

1 Use every possible means for motivating educationally disadvantaged students to do well in school.

2 Use a variety of instructional techniques to help educationally disadvantaged students master both basic and higher-order knowledge and skills.

3 Be alert to the potential dangers of labeling. Concentrate on individuals while guarding against the impact of stereotyping.

    a. Remember that in addition to being a skilled teacher, you are also a human being who may at times react subjectively to students.

    b. Take systematic steps to ensure that you treat all students equitably, regardless of their backgrounds.

    c. Use information about students' backgrounds to help them become more effective students.

4 Help make students aware of the contributions that specific ethnic groups have made to the development of the United States and the world.

5 Assign projects and activities that allow students to demonstrate culture-specific knowledge and skills and that encourage students to learn from and about each other's cultures.

6 Encourage students to identify with representatives of their ethnic group who have achieved success.

7 At the secondary level, involve students in activities that explore cultural differences in perceptions, beliefs, and values.

8 Make every effort to contact and work with the parents of ethnic minority students.

1 Use every possible means for motivating educationally disadvantaged students to do well in school.

Perhaps the major reason many educationally disadvantaged students do poorly in school is not lack of ability but lack of interest in learning. As the account of Marc Elrich (1994), the sixth-grade teacher whose experiences we summarized earlier, makes clear, a number of circumstances may conspire to prevent such students from acquiring a desire to do well in school: lack of encouragement from parents, the absence of role models in the form of parents and siblings who have benefited from schooling, a level of aspiration set low to avoid possible failure, and lack of success leading to a low need for achievement.

Support for this argument comes from a recent study of factors that contributed to African-American seventh, eighth, and ninth graders staying in school (Connell, Halpern-Felsher, Clifford, Crichlow, & Usinger, 1995). These researchers found that support from parents at home and from teachers at school contributed to feelings of academic competence, autonomy (schoolwork is related to important personal goals and/or is intrinsically interesting), and relatedness to others at school. Students with high levels of competence, autonomy, and relatedness were more likely to be successful in school and to stay in school than were students with low levels of these characteristics.

2 Use a variety of instructional techniques to help educationally disadvantaged students master both basic and higher-order knowledge and skills.

Research from the 1970s (for example, Brophy & Evertson, 1976) found that the classroom and standardized test performance of educationally disadvantaged students improves when teachers

Journal Entry
Using Productive Techniques of Teaching

- Eliminate distractions and maximize the amount of time students actually spend working on a task.
- Determine what and how quickly subject matter is learned.
- Establish high expectations and a classroom climate that supports achievement.
- Break tasks down into small, easy-to-manage pieces and arrange the pieces in a logical sequence.
- Have students work on specific exercises in small groups.

- Ask direct questions that have direct answers.
- Provide frequent opportunities for practice and review.
- Provide timely corrective feedback.

Designing classroom instruction along these guidelines has both benefits and costs. The benefits are that students spend more time on-task, success tends to be more consistent, and more students reach a higher level of mastery of content knowledge and skills. The main cost is the lack of transfer that usually occurs when knowledge and skills are learned as isolated segments in a nonmeaningful context. A second cost is that students have few opportunities to interact with one another (the benefits of which were mentioned in Chapter 2 and will be further described in Chapters 10 and 11).

If teachers combine the eight guidelines just mentioned with current learning theory and research (see, for example, Knapp & Shields, 1990; Knapp, Shields, & Turnbull, 1995; Means & Knapp, 1991; Natriello, McDill, & Pallas, 1990, as well as Chapters 9 and 10 of this book), they may be able to raise the basic skill level of educationally disadvantaged students *and* improve their ability to transfer what they have learned to meaningful and realistic contexts. To accomplish this goal, a teacher should also

- Provide opportunities for students to apply ideas and skills to real-life or realistic situations in order to make the lesson more meaningful. For example, students might, after collecting and analyzing information, write letters to the mayor and/or city council requesting more streetlights for increased safety at night or improvements to basketball courts and baseball fields.

- Allow students the opportunity to discuss among themselves the meaning of ideas and their potential applications. In making a request of a government official, students should be encouraged to discuss which arguments are likely to be most effective and how they would respond should the official turn their proposal down.

- Embed basic skills instruction within the context of complex and realistic tasks. Letter-writing campaigns, for example, can be used to practice such basic English skills as vocabulary acquisition, spelling, punctuation, and grammar. Science projects can be used to practice a variety of mathematics skills.

- Point out how classroom tasks relate to students' out-of-school experiences. One example is to draw attention to the basic similarities between poetry and rap, a form of song common to many African-American students.

- Model for and explain to students the various thinking processes that are activated and used when one engages in a complex task. As you will see when you read Chapter 8, effective learners approach tasks strategically, which is to say they analyze the task, formulate a plan for dealing with it, use a variety of specific learning skills, and monitor their progress. These are fundamental learning processes that are almost never made explicit to students.

- Gradually ease students into the process of dealing with complex and realistic tasks. There is no question that the approach described in these bulleted points carries with it more risk for failure than was the case for the structured, small-scale approach of the 1970s. But much of this risk can be minimized by *scaffolding*, which we described in Chapter 2. As you may recall, in scaffolding the teacher initially provides a considerable amount of support through explanations, demonstrations, and prompts of various types. As students demonstrate their ability to carry out more of a task independently, the scaffolding is withdrawn.

3 **Be alert to the potential dangers of labeling. Concentrate on individuals while guarding against the impact of stereotyping.**

Myrna Gantner (1997), an eighth-grade teacher in an inner-city middle school near the Mexican border, learned the following lessons about treating her Hispanic students as individuals:

- Treat Hispanic students the same as you would treat any student. When teachers believe that inner-city Hispanic students are less capable than other students, they tend to give them less time and attention. Students quickly notice these differences and may respond with lower-quality work and more disruptive behavior.

- Don't prejudge students. If you believe that most Hispanic children use drugs, belong to gangs, or have limited academic ability, students will eventually become aware of your prejudice and act accordingly. Gantner's students said they were most appreciative of teachers who were interested in them as individuals, had high expectations for them, and showed them how to achieve their goals.

- Don't ridicule or make fun of students' limited English proficiency. The best way to acquire proficiency in a second language is to use it frequently. Students will be less inclined to do so if they think teachers and other students will laugh at their mistakes.

a. **Remember that in addition to being a skilled teacher, you are also a human being who may at times react subjectively to students.**

Journal Entry
Ways to Minimize
Subjectivity

Try to control the influence of such factors as name, ethnic background, gender, physical characteristics, knowledge of siblings or parents, grades, and test scores. If you think you can be honest with yourself, you might attempt to describe your prejudices so that you will be in a position to guard against them. (Do you tend to be annoyed when you read descriptions of the exploits of members of a particular religious or ethnic group, for example?) Try to think of a student independently of her siblings and parents.

b. **Take systematic steps to ensure that you treat all students equitably, regardless of their backgrounds.**

One way to be fair and consistent in the way you interact with students is to keep a Question and Recitation Record. By periodically referring to this record, you will know whether you are calling on all students about the same number of times. Strive to be consistently positive and enthusiastic when asking questions or responding to answers. Don't hesitate or introduce vocal inflections when calling on less capable students. Such public signs of hesitation or lack of confidence may be communicated to the student and contribute to a negative expectancy effect. Refer to Table 11.2, page 396, to make your praise effective.

Another technique you might use is a Positive Reinforcement Record in an effort to say favorable things about the work of all students. If after keeping such a record for two weeks, you discover that you have not said a single positive thing to one or more individuals, make it a point to praise them at least as regularly as you do others.

c. Use information about students' backgrounds to help them become more effective students.

If you become aware of students' previous low grades or are presented with low test scores, give individuals identified as poor learners the benefit of the doubt. Use the information to try to help low-scoring students improve their classroom performance and keep in mind that many factors (such as anxiety, differences in cultural values about the importance of tests, and misunderstanding of instructions) may artificially lower test scores.

4 Help make students aware of the contributions that specific ethnic groups have made to the development of the United States and the world.

The first principle suggested by Nicholas Appleton (1983) for implementing a multicultural education program is that each student should examine his own ethnic background before examining the backgrounds of others. Appleton's rationale is that racism in the United States has had a negative impact on the self-concepts of ethnic minority children. Since self-concept is related to achievement, it is important to help students develop positive attitudes about their ethnic heritage. One suggestion for accomplishing this goal is to invite family members of students (and other local residents) of different ethnic backgrounds to the classroom. Ask them to describe the values subscribed to by members of their group and explain how those values have contributed to life in the United States and to the world in general.

Journal Entry
Ways to Promote Awareness of Contributions of Ethnic Minorities

5 Assign projects and activities that allow students to demonstrate culture-specific knowledge and skills and that encourage students to learn from and about one another's cultures.

You might encourage students from similar ethnic and religious backgrounds to get together at designated periods and prepare presentations for the rest of the class. Ask them to illustrate and explain the art, music, beliefs, and ceremonies of their particular group. On special holidays honored by different groups, the entire class can take part in the celebration, perhaps including the preparation of appropriate decorations and food.

Another opportunity for cultural interaction is provided by the global Internet. For example, a database maintained by St. Olaf College in Minneapolis, Minnesota, is dedicated to matching students with intercultural pen pals. Such exchanges among students can promote shared cultural knowledge and understanding, especially in schools whose populations are relatively homogeneous. The Intercultural Pen Pal server is located at **http://www. stolaf.edu/network/iecc.**

6 Encourage students to identify with representatives of their ethnic group who have achieved success.

Erikson has called attention to the role confusion experienced by many minority-group Americans. He has also concluded that one of the most important factors leading to a sense of identity is occupational choice. You might help minority-group students avoid role confusion and develop a sense of identity by acquainting them with the accomplishments of eminent and successful people who share their ethnic background. Models might practice in the professions, business, education, or the arts. Identifying with prominent people can help youngsters develop a sense of their group's identity as successful Americans. Once that identity is achieved, individuals can freely cherish the language and culture of their heritage without risking role confusion.

7 At the secondary level, involve students in activities that explore cultural differences in perceptions, beliefs, and values.

A well-conceived multicultural education program cannot, and should not, avoid or minimize the issue of cultural conflict. There are at least two reasons for helping students examine this issue. One is that conflict has been a constant and salient aspect of relationships among cultural groups. Another is that cultural conflicts often produce changes that benefit all members of a society (a prime example being the civil rights boycotts, marches, and demonstrations of the 1960s).

Cultural conflicts arise from differences in perceptions, beliefs, and values. American culture, for example, places great value on self-reliance. Americans generally respect and praise individuals who, through their own initiative, persistence, and ingenuity, achieve substantial personal goals; and they tend to look down on individuals who are dependent on others for their welfare. Consequently, American parents who are financially dependent on their children, even though the children may be prosperous enough to support them, would probably feel ashamed enough to hide the fact. The same situation in China would likely elicit a different reaction because of different values about self-reliance and family responsibilities. Chinese parents who are unable to provide for themselves in their old age but have children successful enough to support them might well brag about it to others (Appleton, 1983).

Journal Entry
Ways to Help
Students Explore
Conflicts Between
Cultures

One technique for exploring cultural conflict is to have students search through newspapers and news magazines for articles that describe clashes. Ask them to identify the source of the conflict and how it might be positively resolved. Another technique is to involve students in games that simulate group conflict. Class members can, for example, play the role of city council members who represent the interests of diverse ethnic groups and who have been ordered by the federal government to integrate their school system (Appleton, 1983). Both the use of simulations and the discussion of newspaper articles will probably work best at the high school level because adolescents are better able than younger students to understand the abstract concepts involved in these activities.

8 Make every effort to contact and work with the parents of ethnic minority students.

Linda Holman (1997) is the principal of an elementary school in El Paso, Texas. In her school 43 percent of the 700 students have limited English proficiency and are recent immigrants to the United States. To help students and their parents make a successful transition to a new country and school system, Holman makes the following suggestions.

- During the first week of the school year, hold parent-teacher-child conferences. Be willing to hold these meetings in the parents' home and during the evening hours if necessary.
- Recruit bilingual parent volunteers to help teachers and staff members talk with parents and students.

- In discussing classroom tasks and student performance with parents, avoid technical terminology and acronyms. Not only does this result in fewer misunderstandings, but it lessens the sense of inferiority that some parents feel.
- Encourage parents to work with their children in their native language in order to build a strong foundation for second-language learning.

Lee Little Soldier (1997) makes the same recommendation about meeting with parents to teachers who have Native American students. He states that parents may at first be intimidated by the atmosphere of the school. Offering to work with them in the comfort of their home indicates the school's interest in the family as well as the child.

Bilingual Education

As we mentioned earlier, almost 750,000 legal immigrants a year for the ten-year period from 1981 through 1990 arrived in the United States. Not surprisingly, many of the school-age children of these families have either limited or no English proficiency. To address this need, the federal government provides financial support for the establishment of bilingual education programs. Because language is viewed as an important part of a group's culture, many school districts integrate bilingual education with multicultural education. In this section we will examine the nature and effectiveness of bilingual education programs.

Before we consider different approaches to bilingual education, there are three general points we would like you to keep in mind. First, bilingual programs have become an emotionally charged and politicized topic (see, for example, Rothstein, 1998). Educators, parents, and legislators have strong opinions regarding what time and resources should be devoted to helping students master native-language skills and whether such programs should include cultural awareness goals. Some individuals favor moving students into all-English classes as quickly as possible (in June 1998, Californians voted to eliminate their state's bilingual education program and to provide a one-year immersion program instead); others believe that students should have a firm grasp of their native language *and* English before attempting to make the transition to regular classes. Although research on this issue is helpful because it informs us about what *is*, such research cannot tell us what we *should do* about what we know. Second, some language-minority students may suffer from problems that bilingual education alone cannot solve. If (as noted earlier) parents do not model the types of behaviors valued by schools or encourage their children to exhibit such behaviors, learning difficulties often result. Finally, no one approach to bilingual education is likely to be equally effective for all language-minority students. What works well for some low-SES Puerto Rican children may not work well for middle-class Cuban children and vice versa.

GOALS AND APPROACHES

Most bilingual education programs have a common long-term goal but differ in their approach to that goal. The goal is to help minority-language students acquire as efficiently as possible the English skills they will need to succeed in school and

Two main approaches to bilingual education: transition, maintenance

society. The approaches to that goal usually fall into one of two categories: *transition* or *maintenance*.

Programs that have a transition approach teach students wholly (in the case of non-English-proficient students) or partly (in the case of limited-English-proficient students) in their native language so as not to retard their academic progress, but only until they can function adequately in English. At that point they are placed in regular classes, where all of the instruction is in English. To make the transition time as brief as possible, some programs add an ESL (English as a second language) component. Supporters of this approach point out that much of what occurs in classrooms takes the form of verbal directions, descriptions, and explanations; question-and-answer sessions; and references to abstract ideas. The ability to speak a common language allows individuals to feel part of a larger group. Most current programs are transitional in nature, possibly because this was the goal espoused by such early legislation as the Bilingual Education Act of 1968 (Bowman, 1989; Hakuta & Garcia, 1989).

Transition programs focus on rapid shift to English proficiency

Programs that have a maintenance approach try to maintain or improve the students' native-language skills prior to instruction in English. Supporters of maintenance programs point to the results of psychological and linguistic studies that suggest that a strong native-language foundation supports the subsequent learning of both English and subject-matter knowledge. In addition, many proponents of multicultural education favor a maintenance approach because they see language as an important part of a group's cultural heritage (Hakuta & Garcia, 1989; Hakuta & Gould, 1987).

Maintenance programs focus on maintaining native-language competence

Some bilingual education scholars (for example, Thomas & Collier, 1997–1998) are critical of both transitional and maintenance bilingual education programs because they are remedial in nature, and students who participate in such programs tend to be perceived as inferior in some respect. They favor a third approach that is gaining in popularity. Commonly referred to as **bilingual/immersion**, *dual language*, or *two-way bilingual*, this approach is viewed more positively since

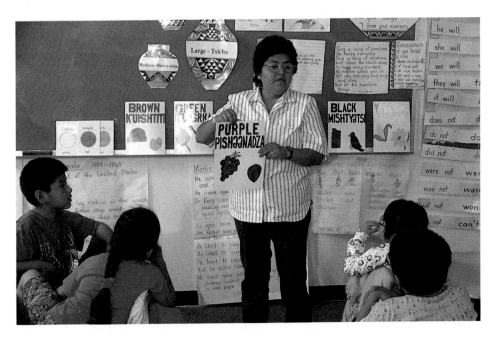

Some bilingual education programs emphasize using the student's native language competence to help the student learn English as quickly as possible. Other programs emphasize the maintenance or improvement of both the student's native language and English.

all students participate for the purpose of academic enrichment. Bilingual/immersion programs are used in over two hundred schools in the United States. Although most of these programs are English/Spanish, other programs include Korean, French, Cantonese, Navajo, Japanese, Arabic, Portuguese, Russian, and Mandarin Chinese as the minority language. Bilingual/immersion programs combine two features from other bilingual programs: maintenance of the minority language and immersion of language majority students (English) in the minority language. The essence of dual language programs is that subject matter instruction is provided in *two* languages to *all* students.

Canada and Miami, Florida, have two of the oldest and largest bilingual/immersion programs. Canada, as you may know, has always had a large French-speaking population, mostly in the Province of Québec. Because many parents wanted their children to be proficient in both English and French, Canadian schools in the 1960s began a K-12 program. In kindergarten and first grade, 90 percent of the instruction is in French and the remaining 10 percent is in English. From grade 2 through grade 5 the proportion gradually shifts to 50/50. By grade 6 most students can work equally well on any subject matter in either language.

The impetus for a bilingual/immersion program in the Miami area was the large number of individuals who emigrated from Cuba. As with all bilingual/immersion programs, students whose primary language is Spanish *and* students whose primary language is English participate in the program together. Unlike the Canadian model, which has a strong immersion component in the early grades (80 to 90 percent of the instruction is in French), teachers in Miami's program teach in Spanish for half the day and in English for the other half of the day at all grade levels.

Bilingual/immersion education programs typically include the following features:

- At least six years of bilingual instruction
- High-quality instruction in both languages
- Separation of the two languages for instruction (for example, by time of day, day of the week, or even by week)
- Use of the minority language for teaching and classroom discussion at least 50 percent of the time.
- A roughly balanced percentage of students for whom each language is primary
- Use of peer tutoring

RESEARCH FINDINGS

In comparison to immersion (English-only) programs, how successful have bilingual education programs been in helping non-English-speaking students learn English and other subjects? After analyzing twenty-three studies, Anne Willig (1985) concludes that participation in bilingual education programs produced small to moderate gains on tests of reading, language skills, mathematics, and total achievement when measured by tests in English. When measured by tests administered in the student's native language, however, participation in bilingual education led to significantly better performance on tests of listening comprehension, reading, writing, total language, mathematics, social studies, and attitudes toward school and self.

ESL programs appear to have a generally positive effect on a variety of reading comprehension skills. After reviewing sixty-seven studies, Jill Fitzgerald (1995) concludes that ESL students recognized cognate vocabulary (related words) fairly well (there was a wide range of proficiency for this outcome), demonstrated the ability

Bilingual education programs produce moderate learning gains

to monitor their comprehension, and used prior knowledge to help them understand and remember what they read.

Students who participate in bilingual/immersion programs score at or above grade level on subject matter tests and score higher on reading and mathematics tests than limited-English-proficient students who are taught only in English. Perhaps because of this reason, the bilingual/immersion program in New York City was so popular that students who wanted to participate had to be selected by lottery (Genesee & Cloud, 1998; Thomas & Collier, 1997–1998).

TECHNOLOGY AND BILINGUAL EDUCATION

Multimedia, hypermedia, and other technologies are enhancing opportunities for bilingual students and limited-English proficient (LEP) students to learn mathematics (Kinard & Bitter, 1997) as well as the English language (Heath, 1996). With some technology tools, students can hear the pronunciation of a word, see how it is used in context, see a picture of the word if appropriate, explore links to definitions and related words, discover the origin of the word, and construct personal glossaries (Liu, 1994). Using CD-ROM technology, there are now "books on disk" for young children and second language learners that allow them to see the story (for example, *The Tale of Peter Rabbit*) as it is being read. Not only do students see the words highlighted as they are pronounced, but in some of these packages they can click on an object and the word for it is simultaneously pronounced and displayed on the screen. Importantly, students control the pace, style, and amount of interaction and repetition (Fabris, 1992–1993).

RESOURCES FOR FURTHER INVESTIGATION

■ Multicultural Education: Theory and Practice

James Banks offers a brief (seven chapters, 121 pages) introduction to multicultural education in *An Introduction to Multicultural Education* (1994a). A more detailed discussion can be found in his *Teaching Strategies for Ethnic Studies* (6th ed., 1997). Part 1 discusses goals for multicultural programs, key concepts, and planning a multicultural curriculum. Parts 2 through 5 provide background information about ten ethnic groups and strategies for teaching about each group. Part 6 provides an example of a multicultural unit and an evaluation strategy. The book concludes with such useful appendices as a list of videotapes and films on U.S. ethnic groups, a bibliography of books about women of color, and a chronology of key events concerning ethnic groups in U.S. history.

Another practical book is *Comprehensive Multicultural Education: Theory and Practice* (3d ed., 1995), by Christine Bennett. Part 1 of this book (Chapters 1 to 3) presents the case for multicultural education. Part 2 (Chapters 4 to 6) describes culturally based individual differences that affect teaching and learning. Part 3 (Chapters 7 and 8) presents a model for multicultural education, guidelines for instruction, and a set of twenty-two illustrative lessons. The lessons include statements of goals and objectives, a description of the instructional sequence, a list of needed materials, and a means for evaluating how well the objectives were met.

Cultural Diversity in Schools: From Rhetoric to Practice (1994), edited by Robert DeVillars, Christian Faltis, and James Cummins, contains chapters on the use of cooperative learning in culturally diverse classrooms, the promotion of positive cross-cultural attitudes, the management of behavior in the culturally diverse classroom, and the use of computer technology in culturally diverse and bilingual classrooms.

A large number of multicultural resources are available on the Internet. Several good starting points include:

Multicultural Internet Sites:
  http://www.qualcomm.com/users/gnash/mcult.html

Intercultural Pen Pals:
  http://www.stolaf.edu/network/iecc

The TIME Project (Telecommunications in Multicultural Education):
  http://www.cgrg.ohio-state.edu/~scott/timaeusl.html

■ Ethnic Minority Groups

American Indian Leaders: Studies in Diversity (1980), edited by R. David Edmunds, contains chapters on twelve Native American leaders from the mid-1700s to the present. For information on how to obtain books, films, and reports about African Americans, Asian Americans, Hispanic Americans, and Native Americans, consult *Guide to Multicultural Resources* (1989), edited by Charles Taylor. *Sourcebook of Hispanic Culture in the United States* (1982), edited by David Foster, contains several chapters on the history, anthropology, sociology, literature, and art of Hispanic-American groups living in the United States. Angela Carrasquillo provides a comprehensive discussion of Hispanic-American children and youths in the United States in *Hispanic Children and Youth in the United States: A Resource Guide* (1991). Chapter 12 contains the names and addresses as well as brief descriptions of fifteen Hispanic-American advocacy groups. For information about various aspects of development among African-American adolescents, see *Black Adolescence: Current Issues and Annotated Bibliography* (1990), by the Consortium for Research on Black Adolescence.

An Internet search using the names of particular cultural groups or names of individuals may be the best way to find specific resources on-line.

■ Bilingual Education

Judith Lessow-Hurley offers a brief (69 pages), readable overview and introduction to bilingual education in *A Commonsense Guide to Bilingual Education* (1991). Appendix A contains the addresses of two national evaluation assistance centers that provide technical assistance to state and local education agencies concerning methods of assessing the needs of limited-English-proficiency students. Appendix B contains the addresses of sixteen multifunctional resource centers that provide technical assistance to educational personnel in bilingual programs.

The political issues that often surround bilingual education as well as various programmatic and instructional issues are discussed in *Bilingual Education: Politics, Practice, and Research* (1993), edited by Beatriz Arias and Ursula Casanova.

Teaching English as a Second Language: A Resource Guide (1994), by Angela Carrasquillo, contains eleven chapters that discuss such topics as language acquisition, individual differences in language learning, different types of ESL programs, and characteristics of ESL programs at different grade levels. Chapter 12 includes addresses for organizations that provide various publications and services to individuals involved in ESL programs.

An excellent on-line directory is maintained at the University of Texas, Austin. Its address is **http://www.edb.utexas. edu/coe/depts/CI/bilingue/resources.html**.

Kathryn Lindholm and Halford Fairchild describe the evaluation of a bilingual/immersion program in a southern California school district in Chapter 8 of *Bilingual Education: Issues and Strategies* (1990, edited by Amado Padilla, Halford Fairchild, and Concepción Valadez).

SUMMARY

1. Culture refers to the perceptions, emotions, beliefs, ideas, experiences, and behavior patterns that a group of people has in common.

2. Beginning in the 1960s the notion of the United States as a cultural melting pot became less popular, and the concept of cultural diversity, or cultural pluralism, increased in popularity. As the latter became more widely accepted, calls were made for the establishment of multicultural education programs in American public schools.

3. The concept of cultural pluralism assumes that every culture is internally consistent and logical, that no culture is inherently inferior or superior to another, and that all people are somewhat culture-bound.

4. Because of immigration patterns and high birthrates in some ethnic groups, the United States is becoming an increasingly diverse country.

5. Two important factors that distinguish one culture from another are ethnicity and social class.

6. People of the same ethnic group typically share many of the following characteristics: ancestral country of origin, race, religion, values, political interests, economic interests, and behavior patterns.

7. Ethnic differences in communication patterns and preferences, time orientation, values, and thinking styles can lead to misunderstandings among students and between students and teachers.

8. Social class indicates an individual's or a family's relative position in society in terms of such factors as income, occupation, level of education, place of residence, and material possessions.

9. Educationally disadvantaged students often receive irregular health care, experience child-care practices that do not effectively prepare them for school, are not exposed to a wide variety of experiences, are not motivated to do well in school, and have low career aspirations.

10. The teacher expectancy effect, also known as the self-fulfilling prophecy or the Pygmalion effect, occurs when teachers communicate a particular expectation about how a student will perform and the student's behavior changes so as to be consistent with that expectation.

11. Although the effect of teacher expectancy on IQ scores originally reported by Rosenthal and Jacobson has never been fully replicated, research has demonstrated that teacher expectancy strongly affects classroom achievement and participation in both positive and negative ways.

12. Factors that seem to play a strong role in producing a teacher expectancy effect include a student's gender,

compliance, achievement, attractiveness, social class, and ethnic background.

13. Multicultural education programs assume that minority students will learn more and have a stronger self-concept if teachers understand, accept, and reward the thinking and behavior patterns characteristic of the students' culture.

14. Effective multicultural teachers use such proven instructional techniques as providing clear objectives, communicating high expectations, monitoring progress, providing immediate feedback, and making lessons meaningful. In addition, they have experience in teaching culturally diverse classes, exhibit a high level of dedication, and have a strong affinity for their students.

15. Peer tutoring, cooperative learning, and mastery learning are three generally effective instructional tactics that are particularly well suited to multicultural education programs.

16. Calls for multicultural education were stimulated by changing immigration and birthrate patterns, low levels of school achievement by many ethnic minority children, and students' need to work productively with members of other cultures.

17. For students who live in culturally homogeneous communities, an increased understanding of the characteristics of students from different cultural backgrounds and the problems they face can be gained by using such technological tools as videoconferencing and electronic networks.

18. Most bilingual education programs reflect either a transition goal or a maintenance goal. Transition programs teach students in their native language only until they speak and understand English well enough to be placed in a regular classroom. Maintenance programs try to maintain or improve students' native-language skills prior to instruction in English.

19. Bilingual immersion programs, in which subject matter instruction is provided in both the minority and majority languages to all students, are growing in popularity.

KEY TERMS

culture *(137)*
multicultural education *(138)*
melting pot *(138)*
cultural pluralism *(139)*

ethnic group *(141)*
social class *(144)*
socioeconomic status (SES) *(144)*
teacher expectancy effect *(148)*

peer tutoring *(154)*
cooperative learning *(155)*
mastery learning *(156)*
bilingual/immersion *(169)*

DISCUSSION QUESTIONS

1. Culture refers to the way in which a group of people views the world; formulates beliefs; evaluates objects, ideas, and experiences; and behaves. Ethnocentrism often causes people to view the cultural beliefs and practices of others as deficits. How can you use the concept of constructivism (mentioned in Chapters 1, 2, and 9) to help students overcome any ethnocentrism they may have and understand the beliefs and practices of other cultures?

2. The school dropout rate for African-American, Hispanic-American, and Native American students is two to three times the rate for white students. A likely contributing factor is the sense of alienation from school that grows out of low teacher expectations, expressions of racial or ethnic group prejudice, and discrimination.

What steps might you take to reduce or eliminate this sense of alienation in students?

3. How have your experiences with members of ethnic or racial minority groups been similar to or different from what you have heard and read about those groups?

4. On pages 150–151 we briefly describe four approaches to multicultural education: contributions, additive, transformation, and social action. What advantages and disadvantages do you see for each approach? Which approach would you use? Why?

5. On pages 151–152 we describe a set of key concepts proposed by James Banks around which multicultural lessons and units can be organized. Why are these concepts so important that Banks labels them *key* concepts?

6 Accommodating Student Variability

Prior to the turn of the century, few educators had to deal with the challenge of teaching extremely diverse groups of students. Most communities were fairly small, and students in a given school tended to come from similar ethnic and economic backgrounds. Because poorer families often viewed a child's labor as more important than a complete, formal education, and many states had not yet enacted compulsory attendance laws, many low-socioeconomic status (SES) children did not attend school regularly or at all. In 1900, for example, only 8.5 percent of

KEY POINTS

These key points will help you learn the important information in this chapter. To help you study, they also appear in the margins of pages, next to the text where they are discussed.

Ability Grouping

■ Ability grouping assumes intelligence is inherited, reflected by IQ, unchangeable, and instruction will be superior

■ No research support for between-class ability grouping

■ Joplin Plan and within-class ability grouping for math and science produce moderate increases in learning

■ Between-class ability grouping negatively influences teaching goals and methods

■ Joplin Plan and within-class ability grouping may allow for better-quality instruction

The Individuals with Disabilities Education Act (PL 101–476)

■ Before placement, student must be given complete, valid, and appropriate evaluation

■ IEP must include objectives, services to be provided, criteria for determining achievement

■ Students with disabilities must be educated in least restrictive environment

■ Mainstreaming: policy of placing students with disabilities in regular classes

■ Inclusion policy aims to keep students with disabilities in regular classroom for entire day

■ Procedural safeguards intended to protect rights of student

■ Students who are learning disabled, speech impaired, mentally retarded, or emotionally disturbed most likely to be served under PL 101–476

■ Multidisciplinary assessment team determines if student needs special services

■ Classroom teacher, parents, several specialists prepare IEP

Students with Mental Retardation

■ Students with mild retardation may frustrate easily, lack confidence and self-esteem

■ Students with mild retardation tend to oversimplify, have difficulty generalizing

■ Give students with mild retardation specific assignments that can be completed quickly

Students with Learning Disabilities

■ Learning disabilities: disorders in basic processes that lead to learning problems not due to other causes

■ Students with learning disabilities have problems with perception, attention, memory, metacognition

■ Help students with learning disabilities to reduce distractions, attend to important information

Students with Emotional Disturbance

■ Emotional disturbance: poor relationships, inappropriate behavior, depression, fears

■ Term *behavior disorder* focuses on behavior that needs to be changed, objective assessment

■ Students with behavior disorders tend to be either aggressive or withdrawn

■ Foster interpersonal contact among withdrawn students

■ Use techniques to forestall aggressive or antisocial behavior

Gifted and Talented Students

■ Gifted and talented students show high performance in one or more areas

■ Minorities underrepresented in gifted classes because of overreliance on test scores

■ Gifted and talented students differ from their nongifted peers intellectually and emotionally

■ Separate classes for gifted and talented students aid achievement but may lower academic self-concept of some students

Using Technology to Assist Exceptional Students

■ Federal legislation has led to the development of various assistive technologies eligible students attended high school (Boyer, 1983), and these students were almost entirely from the upper and middle classes (Gutek, 1992). In addition, children with mental, emotional, or physical disabilities were either sent to special schools, educated at home, or not educated at all. In comparison with today's schools, then, earlier student populations were considerably less diverse. This chapter explains why schools became more diverse and how educators have attempted to meet the needs of increasingly diverse classrooms. ■

Historical Developments

THE GROWTH OF PUBLIC EDUCATION AND AGE-GRADED CLASSROOMS

By 1920 public education in the United States was no longer a small-scale and optional enterprise, largely because of three developments. First, by 1918 all states had passed compulsory attendance laws. Second, child labor laws had been enacted by many states, as well as by Congress in 1916, to eliminate the hiring of children and adolescents in mines and factories. Third, large numbers of immigrant children arrived in the United States from 1901 through 1920. During those years, 14.5 million individuals, mostly from eastern and southern Europe, arrived on U.S. shores (Morris, 1961). The result was a vast increase in the number and diversity of children attending elementary and high school.

Educators initially dealt with this growth in student variability by forming age-graded classrooms. Introduced in the Quincy, Massachusetts, schools in the mid-1800s, these classrooms grouped all students of a particular age together each year to master a certain portion of the school's curriculum (Gutek, 1992). The main assumptions behind this approach were that teachers could be more effective in helping students learn and that students would have more positive attitudes toward themselves and school when classrooms were more *homogeneous* than *heterogeneous* (Oakes, 1985; Peltier, 1991). Regardless of whether these assumptions were well founded (an issue we will address shortly), they were (and still are) so widely held by educators that two additional approaches to creating even more homogeneous groups were eventually implemented—ability grouping and special class placement.

ABILITY-GROUPED CLASSROOMS

Ability grouping involved the use of standardized mental ability or achievement tests to create groups of students who were considered very similar to each other in learning ability. In elementary and middle schools, students typically were (and frequently still are) placed in low-, average-, or high-ability groups. At the high school level, students were placed into different tracks that were geared toward such different post-high school goals as college, secretarial work, or vocational school.

Ability grouping was another means for school authorities to deal with the large influx of immigrant students. Since many of these children were not fluent in English and had had limited amounts of education in their native countries, they scored much lower on standardized tests when compared to American test norms. In addition, many of these children came from poor homes and were in poor health. At the time their assignment to a low-ability group seemed both the logical and appropriate thing to do (Wheelock, 1994).

In the first major part of this chapter, we will look at current applications of ability grouping, which nowadays takes several forms and is still used to reduce the normal range of variability in cognitive ability and achievement found in the typical classroom.

SPECIAL EDUCATION

For more or less normal children, age grading and ability testing were seen as workable approaches to creating more homogeneous classes. But compulsory attendance laws also brought to school many children with mild to severe mental and physical disabilities. These students were deemed incapable of profiting from any type of normal classroom instruction and so were assigned to special schools. Unfortunately, and as Alfred Binet feared, the labeling of a student as mentally retarded or physically disabled often resulted in a vastly inferior education. Early in this century, special schools served as convenient dumping grounds for all kinds of children who could not adapt to the regular classroom (Ysseldyke & Algozzine, 1995).

In the latter two-thirds of this chapter, we will detail the varied types and degrees of special class placement for children whose intellectual, social, emotional, or physical development falls outside (above as well as below) the range of normal variation. In discussing this approach, we pay particular attention to Public Law (PL) 101-476, which was enacted to counter past excesses of special class placement and to encourage the placement of children with disabilities in regular classes to the greatest extent possible.

Ability Grouping

Ability grouping is a widespread practice (for example, Oakes, Quartz, Gong, Guiton, & Lipton, 1993; Wheelock, 1994). Nearly 60 percent of all elementary schools use some form of between-class ability grouping. In the middle grades some form of ability grouping exists in 82 percent of schools, and approximately 80 percent of all high schools place students into tracks on the basis of standardized test scores. In this section we will describe the most common ways in which teachers group students by ability, examine the assumptions that provide the rationale for this practice, summarize research findings on the effectiveness of ability grouping, and look at alternative courses of action.

TYPES OF ABILITY GROUPS

Four approaches to ability grouping are popular among educators today: *between-class ability grouping, regrouping,* the *Joplin Plan,* and *within-class grouping.* Given their widespread use, you may be able to recall a few classes in which one or another of these techniques was used. If not, you will no doubt encounter at least one of them during your first year of teaching.

BETWEEN-CLASS ABILITY GROUPING   The goal of **between-class ability grouping** is that each class be made up of students who are homogeneous in standardized intelligence or achievement test scores. Three levels of classes are usually

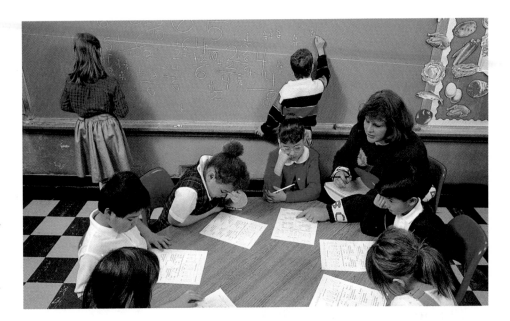

In ability grouping, students are selected and placed in homogeneous groups with other students who are considered to have very similar learning abilities.

formed—high, average, and low. Students in one ability group typically have little or no contact with students in others during the school day. Although each group covers the same subjects, a higher group does so in greater depth and breadth than lower groups. At the high school level, this approach is often called *tracking*. Groups are usually referred to as college preparatory, business/secretarial, vocational/technical, and general.

REGROUPING   The groups formed under a **regrouping** plan are more flexible in assignments and are narrower in scope than between-class groups. Students of the same age, ability, and grade but from different classrooms come together for instruction in a specific subject, usually reading or mathematics. If a student begins to significantly outperform the other members of the group, a change of group assignment is easier since it involves just that particular subject. Regrouping has two major disadvantages, however. First, it requires a certain degree of planning and cooperation among the teachers involved. They must agree, for example, to schedule reading and arithmetic during the same periods. Second, many teachers are uncomfortable working with children whom they see only once a day for an hour or so.

JOPLIN PLAN   The **Joplin Plan** is a variation of regrouping. The main difference is that regroupings take place *across* grade levels. For example, all third, fourth, and fifth graders whose grade equivalent scores in reading are 4.6 (fourth grade, sixth month) would come together for reading instruction. The same would be done for mathematics. The Joplin Plan has the same advantages and disadvantages as simple regrouping.

WITHIN-CLASS ABILITY GROUPING   The most popular form of ability grouping, occurring in almost all elementary school classes, **within-class ability grouping** involves the division of a single class of students into two or three groups for reading and math instruction. Like regrouping and the Joplin Plan, within-class ability grouping has the advantages of being flexible in terms of group assignments and being restricted to one or two subjects. In addition, it eliminates the need for cooperative scheduling. One disadvantage of this approach is that the teacher needs to be skilled at keeping the other students in the class productively occupied while working with a particular group.

ASSUMPTIONS UNDERLYING ABILITY GROUPING

When ability grouping was initiated earlier in this century, much less was known about the various factors that affect classroom learning. Consequently, educators simply assumed certain things to be true. One of those assumptions was that intelligence, which affects the capacity to learn, was a fixed trait and that little could be done to change the learning capacity of individuals. A second assumption was that intelligence was adequately reflected by an intelligence quotient (IQ) score. A third assumption was that all students would learn best when grouped with those of similar ability (Marsh & Raywid, 1994; Oakes & Lipton, 1992). Although these assumptions are still believed to be true by many educators, the research evidence summarized here and elsewhere in this book casts doubt on their validity.

> **Ability grouping assumes intelligence is inherited, reflected by IQ, unchangeable, and instruction will be superior**

EVALUATIONS OF ABILITY GROUPING

Because ability grouping has been practiced in one form or another for several decades and occurs in virtually all school districts, its effects have been intensively studied (for example, Brewer, Rees, & Argys, 1995; Hoffer, 1992; Kulik & Kulik, 1991; Lou, Abrami, Spence, Poulsen, Chambers, & d'Apollonia, 1996; Marsh & Raywid, 1994; Raudenbush, Rowan, & Cheong, 1993; Slavin, 1990a). The main findings of these analyses are as follows:

1. There is little to no support for between-class ability grouping. Students assigned to low-ability classes generally performed worse than comparable students in heterogeneous classes. Students assigned to average-ability classes performed at about the same level as their nongrouped peers. High-ability students sometimes performed slightly better in homogeneous classes than in heterogeneous classes.

> **No research support for between-class ability grouping**

2. Regrouping for reading or mathematics can be effective if the instructional pace and level of the text match the student's actual achievement level rather than the student's nominal grade level. In other words, a fifth grader who scores at the fourth-grade level on a reading test should be reading out of a fourth-grade reading book.

3. The Joplin Plan yields moderately positive effects compared with instruction in heterogeneous classes.

4. Within-class ability grouping in mathematics and science in grades 1 through 12 produced modestly positive results (about eight percentile ranks) compared with whole-class instruction and an even smaller positive effect (about four percentile ranks) when compared with mixed-ability groups. Average-achieving students benefit most from being placed in homogeneous-ability groups, while low-achieving students benefit most from being placed in mixed-ability groups. Because within-class ability grouping for reading is an almost universal practice at every grade level, researchers have not had the opportunity to compare its effectiveness with whole-class reading instruction. Nevertheless, it would be reasonable to expect pretty much the same results for reading as were found for mathematics and science.

> **Joplin Plan and within-class ability grouping for math and science produce moderate increases in learning**

5. Students in homogeneously grouped classes scored the same as students in heterogeneously grouped classes on measures of self-esteem.

6. Students in high-ability classes had more positive attitudes about school and higher educational aspirations than did students in low-ability classrooms.

7. Between-class ability grouping affected the quality of instruction received by students.

   a. The best teachers were often assigned to teach the highest tracks, whereas the least experienced or weakest teachers were assigned to teach the lowest tracks.

   b. Teachers of high-ability classes stressed critical thinking, self-direction, creativity, and active participation, whereas teachers of low-ability classes stressed working quietly, following rules, and getting along with classmates. This effect was particularly noticeable in math and science.

   c. Teachers of low-ability groups covered less material and simpler material than did teachers of high-ability groups.

   d. Teachers of low-ability students expected and demanded less of them than did teachers of high-ability students.

Between-class ability grouping negatively influences teaching goals and methods

To Group or Not to Group?

The findings just summarized suggest three courses of action. The first course is to discontinue the use of full-day, between-class ability groups. Despite the fact that almost 60 percent of the nation's elementary schools, 82 percent of its middle schools, and 80 percent of its high schools continue to use this form of ability grouping, students do not learn more or feel more positively about themselves and school. This is a case in which even widely held beliefs must be modified or eliminated when the weight of evidence goes against them.

The second course of action is to use only those forms of ability grouping that produce positive results: within-class grouping and the Joplin Plan, especially for reading and mathematics. We don't know at present why these forms of ability grouping work. It is *assumed* that the increase in class homogeneity allows for more appropriate and potent forms of instruction (for example, greater flexibility in moving students into and out of a particular group, greater availability of high-achieving role models, and greater effort by the teacher to bring lower-achieving groups up to the level of higher-achieving groups). If this assumption is correct, within-class ability grouping and the Joplin Plan must be carried out in such a way that homogeneous groups are guaranteed to result. The best way to achieve similarity in cognitive ability among students is to group them on the basis of past classroom performance, standardized achievement test scores, or both. The least desirable (but most frequently used) approach is to base the assignments solely on IQ scores.

Joplin Plan and within-class ability grouping may allow for better-quality instruction

The third course of action is to dispense with all forms of ability grouping and use a variety of organizational and instructional techniques that will allow the teacher to cope with a heterogeneous class or to use these same techniques in conjunction with the Joplin Plan or within-class grouping. For instance, you might use with all students instructional techniques that are associated with high achievement. These would include making clear presentations, displaying a high level of enthusiasm, reinforcing students for correct responses, providing sufficient time for students to formulate answers to questions, prompting correct responses, providing detailed feedback about the accuracy of responses, requiring a high level of work and effort, and organizing students into small, heterogeneous learning groups (a technique known as cooperative learning, which we mentioned in the previous chapter and will discuss in detail in Chapter 10). Other ideas include optional honors activities, pullout (meaning programs that occur outside the classroom) challenge classes that are available to all students, study skills classes for low-achieving students, and small-group projects (Oakes & Wells, 1998).

The Individuals with Disabilities Education Act (PL 101-476)

Many of the criticisms and arguments marshaled against ability grouping have come to be applied as well to special classes for students with disabilities. In addition, the elimination of racially segregated schools by the U.S. Supreme Court in the case of *Brown v. Board of Education* (1954) established a precedent for providing students with disabilities an equal opportunity for a free and appropriate education (Ornstein & Levine, 1993). As a result, influential members of Congress were persuaded in the early 1970s that it was time for the federal government to take steps to correct the perceived inequities and deficiencies in our educational system. The result was a landmark piece of legislation called Public Law 94-142, the Education for All Handicapped Children Act. PL 94-142 has been revised and expanded twice since it was signed into law in November 1975—initially in 1986 as the Handicapped Children's Protection Act (PL 99-457) and most recently in October 1990 as the Individuals with Disabilities Education Act (IDEA, PL 101-476). Since all of the features that were written into PL 94-142 and PL 99-457 were carried over into PL 101-476, we will use that name and public law number in the description and discussion that follow.

✓ MAJOR PROVISIONS OF PL 101-476

A FREE AND APPROPRIATE PUBLIC EDUCATION   The basic purpose of PL 101-476 is to ensure that all individuals from birth through age twenty-one who have an identifiable disability, regardless of how severe, receive at public expense supervised special education and related services that meet their unique educational needs. These services can be delivered in a classroom, at home, in a hospital, or in a specialized institution and may include physical education and vocational education as well as instruction in the typical academic subjects (Office of the Federal Register, 1994).

 PREPLACEMENT EVALUATION   Before a child with a disability can be placed in a program that provides special education services, "a full and individual evaluation of the child's educational needs" must be conducted. Such an evaluation must conform to the following rules:

Before placement, student must be given complete, valid, and appropriate evaluation

1. Tests must be administered in the child's native language.
2. A test must be valid for the specific purpose for which it is used.
3. Tests must be administered by trained individuals according to the instructions provided by the test publisher.

4. Tests administered to students who have impaired sensory, manual, or speaking skills must reflect aptitude or achievement rather than the impairment.

5. No single procedure (such as an IQ test) can be the sole basis for determining an appropriate educational program. Data should be collected from such non-test sources as observations by other professionals (such as the classroom teacher), medical records, and parental interviews.

6. Evaluations must be made by a multidisciplinary team that contains at least one teacher or other specialist with knowledge in the area of the suspected disability.

7. The child must be assessed in all areas related to the suspected disability (Office of the Federal Register, 1994).

When you deal with students whose first language is not English, it is important to realize that standardized tests are designed to reflect cultural experiences common to the United States and that English words and phrases may not mean quite the same thing when translated. Therefore, these tests may not be measuring what they were developed to measure. In other words, they may not be valid. The results of such assessments should therefore be interpreted very cautiously (Nuttall, 1987; Wilen & Sweeting, 1986).

INDIVIDUALIZED EDUCATION PROGRAM   Every child who is identified as having a disability and who receives special education services must have an **individualized education program (IEP)** prepared. The IEP is a written statement that describes the educational program that has been designed to meet the child's unique needs. The IEP must include the following elements:

1. A statement of the child's present levels of educational performance

2. A statement of annual goals, including short-term instructional objectives

IEP must include objectives, services to be provided, criteria for determining achievement

3. A statement of the specific special education and related services to be provided to the child and the extent to which the child will be able to participate in regular educational programs

4. The projected dates for initiation of services and the anticipated duration of the services

5. Appropriate objective criteria and evaluation procedures and schedules for determining, on at least an annual basis, whether short-term objectives are being achieved (Office of the Federal Register, 1994)

The IEP is to be planned by a multidisciplinary team composed of the student's classroom teacher in collaboration with a person qualified in special education, one or both of the student's parents, the student (when appropriate), and other individuals at the discretion of the parents or school. (An example of an IEP is depicted on page 189.)

LEAST RESTRICTIVE ENVIRONMENT   According to the 1994 *Code of Federal Regulations* that governs the implementation of PL 101-476, educational services must be provided to children with disabilities in the **least restrictive environment** that their disability will allow. A school district must identify a continuum of increasingly restrictive placements (instruction in regular classes, special classes, home instruction, instruction in hospitals and institutions) and, on the basis of the multidisciplinary team's evaluation, select the least restrictive setting that will best meet

Students with disabilities must be educated in least restrictive environment the student's special educational needs. This provision is often referred to as **main-streaming** since the goal of the law is to have as many children with disabilities as possible, regardless of the severity of the disability, enter the mainstream of education by attending regular classes with nondisabled students.

> **Mainstreaming: policy of placing students with disabilities in regular classes**

Although PL 101-476 clearly allows for *more restrictive* placements than those of the regular classroom "when the nature or severity of the disability is such that education in regular classes with the use of supplementary aids and services cannot be achieved satisfactorily" (Office of the Federal Register, 1994, p. 54), there has been a movement in recent years to eliminate this option. Known as **inclusion** or **full inclusion**, this extension of the mainstreaming provision has become one of the most controversial outgrowths of PL 101-476 (as the Case in Print illustrates). As most proponents use the term, *inclusion* means keeping special education students in regular classrooms and bringing support services to the children rather than the other way around. <u>*Full inclusion*</u>, however, refers to the practice of eliminating all pullout programs *and* special education teachers and of providing regular classroom teachers with training in teaching special needs students so that they can teach these students in the regular classroom (Rogers, 1993; Smelter, Rasch, & Yudewitz, 1994; Staub & Peck, 1994–1995).

> **Inclusion policy aims to keep students with disabilities in regular classroom for entire day**

The proponents of inclusion and full inclusion often raise three arguments to support their position. First, research suggests that special needs students who are segregated from regular students perform more poorly academically and socially than comparable students who are mainstreamed (McLeskey & Waldron, 1996). Second, given the substantial body of evidence demonstrating the propensity of children to observe and imitate more competent children (see, for example, Schunk, 1987), it can be assumed that students with disabilities will learn more by interacting with nondisabled students than by attending homogeneous classes. Third, the Supreme Court in *Brown v. Board of Education* declared the doctrine of "separate but equal" to be unconstitutional. Therefore, pullout programs are a violation of the civil rights of children with special needs because these programs segregate them from

The least restrictive environment provision of the Individuals with Disabilities Education Act (PL 101-476) has led to mainstreaming—the policy that children with disabilities should attend regular classes to the maximum extent possible.

Inclusion—"Dumping" Students or Helping Them Reach Their Potential?

*Although PL 101-476 clearly allows for more restrictive placements than those of the regular classroom "when the nature or severity of the disability is such that education in regular classes with the use of supplementary aids and services cannot be achieved satisfactorily" (Office of the Federal Register, 1994, p. 54), there has been a movement in recent years to eliminate this option. Known as **inclusion** or **full inclusion**, this extension of the mainstreaming provision has become one of the most controversial outgrowths of PL 101-476. (p. 182)*

TEACHING THE DISABLED: HOW FAR MUST SCHOOLS GO?

KILEY ARMSTRONG, AP

St. Louis Post-Dispatch 4/26/94

It was a touching moment—Anastasia Somoza, looking up from her wheelchair at the White House to plead that her more severely disabled twin, Alba, be allowed to attend regular school.

President Bill Clinton's eyes filled up with tears. And her wish, expressed at a town meeting last year, was soon granted.

But this fairy tale and its 10-year-old heroines have not yet found a happy ending. Alba's parents claim she was "dumped" into the regular classroom without the help she needs to succeed.

Her mother, Mary Somoza, promotes a concept called "inclusion": allowing children, whatever the nature of their handicap, to spend their entire day in a regular classroom, with special services brought to them.

The family contends that the city's Board of Education has violated Alba's rights. Somoza attorney Salem Katsh says the law requires "every effort" to include disabled children in regular classrooms, with whatever help they might need.

Katsh said the Somozas are "asking for compensatory services: special tutoring, special training for communications, an outside consultant to monitor the board's compliance with relief. We are asking for a motorized wheelchair . . . to prevent fatigue."

"For too long, these children were shunted aside," agreed Larry Becker, attorney for the city Board of Education. But he argues that inclusion is "a theory, not a legal mandate." Federal law says handicapped children should be educated in "the least restrictive environment"—and "least restrictive," Becker says, should not mean "regular classroom."

The Board of Education is holding on the case; no ruling is expected until May, at the earliest.

In the meantime, the Somozas claim that the schools continue to fail their daughter, as they have failed her since she was 5 years old.

The girls are great-granddaughters of Nicaraguan dictator Anastasio Somoza, who was assassinated in 1956. One of his sons, Anastasio, the girls' great-uncle, was overthrown by the Sandinistas in 1979.

Anastasia and Alba have cerebral palsy. Anastasia, who has a milder form of the disease, speaks clearly—at times eloquently—and has attended regular classes from the start.

Alba, a quadriplegic, cannot speak but communicates with nods, moans, and glances toward symbols on her "communication board." Experts say both sisters have above-average IQs.

Luanna Meyer, a special education teacher from Syracuse University who testified for the family, said that Alba "understands virtually everything said to her in English and Spanish."

"She laughs at a joke, frowns or nods her head appropriately," said Meyer. Despite her physical limitations, Alba "is a very bright little girl. . . . With today's technology, she could become a rocket scientist."

Mary Somoza said Alba functioned at a normal grade level after preschool. But "when she started public school, year after year she regressed."

She was placed in a special education class with one teacher and 15 students who ranged from the learning disabled to the emotionally disturbed to those with speech or physical impairments.

Her individualized education plan, said Mary Somoza, was poorly coordinated and "inadequately written." During the years she was "in segregated classrooms, she didn't receive any education," Katsh contends.

Last June, four months after Anastasia's chat with the president, the school system decided to allow Alba into a regular fourth-grade class at Public School 234 in Manhattan.

The family says the school system merely responded to the publicity with "window dressing"—"dumping" Alba into the classroom.

Does she like her new class? Alba answered yes "with a smiling face," said Anastasia, who often acts as her sister's interpreter.

"Socially, of course, she's better off," said Mary Somoza. But "academically, it's the same."

Mary Somoza estimates that, despite her intelligence, Alba is doing schoolwork at only the first- or second-grade level. Said Meyer: "There seems to have been a judgment that she wasn't able to learn certain things, such as literacy."

Not surprisingly, the Board of Education's lawyer disagrees with any suggestion that the schools are at fault.

"We don't think it's dumping when you plan for the child's enrollment, plan for a special teacher, for integrated therapy in the classroom, for communication devices and a communication specialist," Becker said.

He said a special education teacher works with both Alba and her classroom teacher. The curriculum has been adapted for Alba. An aide helps her with health needs. And an occupational therapist, physical therapist and communication specialist are at her service.

Becker said the board is fulfilling its legal requirements toward Alba.

But not enough, says Alba's mother.

Questions and Activities

1. Consider the points made in this chapter by the proponents and the opponents of inclusion, and apply them to this particular situation. List the specific pros and cons for Alba and for her classmates of her being educated in the regular classroom. You might extend your analysis into a debate between both sides in this article. You could use as a takeoff point for one position the attorney's statement that the "least restrictive environment should not always mean 'regular classroom'"; and for the other position, the special education teacher's observation that in the right environment Alba "could become a rocket scientist."

2. Alba's mother makes the comment in this article that "socially, of course [Alba's] better off" than she was in the segregated special education classroom. What does this comment imply to you about how inclusion works on a personal and a social basis? Can you think of some personal benefits that might emerge from inclusion for the other students as well as for the students with special needs?

3. Imagine that you are Alba's regular fourth-grade classroom teacher. You have twenty-five other students in your class. What is the greatest challenge you might face in terms of Alba's education? How might you best balance Alba's needs and those of your other students? Try to devise some solutions to these challenges, and reconsider and augment these when you have finished studying this chapter.

4. According to research results reported earlier in this chapter, ability grouping affects the quality of instruction students receive, including the fact that "teachers of low-ability students expected and demanded less of them than did teachers of high-ability students." How might this finding relate to the fact that Alba regressed when she was in the segregated special education classroom? Does it form a strong argument in your own mind of inclusion? If not, why not? What important lessons can you draw from this finding about your own expectations of your students, whether they be special education or regular education students?

their nondisabled peers in programs that are assumed to be separate but equal (Smelter, Rasch, & Yudewitz, 1994; Staub & Peck, 1994–1995). The opponents of inclusion often cite cases of students who fail to learn basic skills, of students whose disabilities interrupt the normal flow of instruction, or of teachers who are ill prepared to adequately assist the various special needs students who are placed in their classes (for example, Baines, Baines, & Masterson, 1994; Idstein, 1993; Kauffman, Lloyd, Baker, & Reidel, 1995; McLeskey & Waldron, 1996).

The evidence that bears on the inclusion issue is a combination of anecdotes (reports about individual cases) and experiments that compare inclusive versus noninclusive practices for special-needs students. It seems to indicate, at least for now, that inclusion works well for some students but produces modest or no benefits for others. On the basis of this evidence (for example, Baker, Wang, & Walberg, 1994–1995; Raison, Hanson, Hall, & Reynolds, 1995; Staub & Peck, 1994–1995; Stevens & Slavin, 1995; Zigmond et al., 1995), three conclusions seem warranted. One is that inclusion may not be an appropriate course of action for every child with a disability. Two, inclusion will likely work best where the presence of a disabled student stimulates the teacher to improve the general quality of classroom instruction (see, for example, the February 1996 issue of *Educational Leadership*, and Choate, 1997). Finally, for students who are mainstreamed, IEPs should be written so as to better reflect what a given student probably can and cannot accomplish.

Procedural safeguards intended to protect rights of student

PROCEDURAL SAFEGUARDS   The basic purpose of the various procedural safeguards that were written into PL 101-476 is to make sure that parents are fully informed about the actions a school district intends to take to classify their child as having a disability, to protect the legal rights of parents and their child, and to provide a way to resolve disputes about any aspect of the process. Among other rights, parents have the right to inspect their child's education records; obtain an independent assessment of their child; obtain written prior notice of identification, assessment, and placement procedures; request a due process hearing; appeal the results of a due process hearing; or file a lawsuit in state or federal court. A due process hearing is a fact-finding procedure that is intended to resolve disagreements between the school district and the parents of a child with a disability. Such hearings are usually composed of a hearing officer, the parents of the disabled child, school district personnel (such as the classroom teacher, the principal, and the school psychologist), and attorneys for the parents and the school district.

WHAT PL 101-476 MEANS TO REGULAR CLASSROOM TEACHERS

By the time you begin your teaching career, the original legislation governing the delivery of educational services to the disabled, PL 94-142, will have been in effect for more than twenty years. Each state was required to have established laws and policies for implementing the various provisions by 1978. Thus, the trial-and-error process that inevitably follows a radical departure from previous routine will have taken place by the time you enter a classroom. The first guiding principle to follow, therefore, is *"Find out what the local ground rules are."* You will probably be told during orientation meetings about the ways PL 101-476 is being put into effect in your state and local school district. But if such a presentation is not given or is incomplete, it would be wise to ask about guidelines you should follow. Your second guiding principle, then, should be *"When in doubt, ask."* With these two caveats in mind, consider some questions you may be asking yourself about the impact of PL 101-476 as you approach your first teaching job.

WHAT KINDS OF DISABLING CONDITIONS ARE INCLUDED UNDER PL 101-476?   According to the U.S. Department of Education (1998), during the 1996–1997 academic year, 5.78 million children and youths from birth through age twenty-one (about 7 percent of the total number of individuals in this age group) received special education services under PL 101-476. Most of these children (4.81 million) were between the ages of six and seventeen.

PL 101-476 recognizes thirteen categories of students with disabilities. Many states use the same categories. Others use fewer, more inclusive classification schemes. The thirteen categories described in the legislation are listed as follows in alphabetical order, with brief definitions of each type:

Autism. Significant difficulty in verbal and nonverbal communication and social interaction that adversely affects educational performance.

Deaf-blindness. Impairments of both hearing and vision, the combination of which causes severe communication, developmental, and educational problems. The combination of these impairments is such that a child's educational and physical needs cannot be adequately met by programs designed only for deaf children or blind children.

Deafness. Hearing impairment so severe that, even with hearing aids, a child has problems processing speech.

Hearing impairment. Permanent or fluctuating difficulty in understanding speech that adversely affects educational performance and is not included under the definition of deafness.

Mental retardation. Significant subaverage general intellectual functioning accompanied by deficits in adaptive behavior (how well a person functions in social environments).

Multiple disabilities. Two or more impairments (such as mental retardation-blindness and mental retardation-orthopedic, but not deaf-blindness) that cause such severe educational problems that a child's needs cannot be adequately met by programs designed solely for one of the impairments.

Orthopedic impairments. Impairment in a child's ability to use arms, legs, hands, or feet that significantly affects that child's educational performance.

Other health impairments. Conditions such as asthma, hemophilia, sickle cell anemia, epilepsy, heart disease, and diabetes that so limit the strength, vitality, or alertness of a child that educational performance is significantly affected.

Serious emotional disturbance. Personal and social problems exhibited in an extreme degree over a period of time that adversely affect a child's ability to learn and get along with others.

Specific learning disability. A disorder in one or more of the basic psychological processes involved in understanding or using language that leads to learning problems not traceable to physical disabilities, mental retardation, emotional disturbance, or cultural/economic disadvantage.

Speech or language impairment. A communication disorder such as stuttering, impaired articulation, or a language or voice impairment that adversely affects educational performance.

Traumatic brain injury. A brain injury due to an accident that causes cognitive or psychosocial impairments that adversely affect a child's educational performance.

Visual impairment including blindness. A visual impairment so severe that, even with corrective lenses, a child's educational performance is adversely affected.

The percentages of each type of student who received special educational services during the 1996–1997 school year are indicated in Table 6.1. As you can see,

Table 6.1	Students Receiving Special Education Services, 1996–1997	
Disabling Condition	**Percentage of Total School Enrollment***	**Percentage of Students with Disabilities Served**
Specific learning disabilities	5.53	51.1
Speech or language impairments	2.28	20.1
Mental retardation	1.16	11.4
Serious emotional disturbance	0.92	8.6
Other health impairments	0.34	3.1
Multiple disabilities	0.19	1.9
Hearing impairments	0.14	1.3
Orthopedic impairments	0.14	1.3
Autism	0.07	0.7
Visual impairments	0.05	0.5
Traumatic brain injury	0.02	0.2
Deaf-blindness	0.00	0.0
Total	10.84	100.0

*Percentages are based on disabled children aged 6–17 as a percentage of total school enrollment for kindergarten through twelfth grade.

SOURCE: Department of Education (1998).

Students who are learning disabled, speech impaired, mentally retarded, or emotionally disturbed most likely to be served under PL 101-476

the most common types of children with disabilities receiving services (91.2 percent of the total) were those classified as having a specific learning disability, a speech or language impairment, mental retardation, or a serious emotional disturbance.

WHAT ARE THE REGULAR CLASSROOM TEACHER'S RESPONSIBILITIES UNDER PL 101-476? Regular classroom teachers may be involved in activities required directly or indirectly by PL 101-476 in four possible ways: referral, assessment, preparation of the IEP, and implementation and evaluation of the IEP.

Referral Most referrals for assessment and possible special instruction are made by a child's teacher or his or her parents because they are the ones most familiar with the quality of the child's daily work and progress as compared to other children.

Multidisciplinary assessment team determines if student needs special services

Assessment The initial assessment procedures, which must be approved by the child's parents, are usually carried out by school psychologists who are certified to administer tests. If the initial conclusions of the school psychologist support the teacher's or parents' perception that the student needs special services, the **multidisciplinary assessment team** required under PL 101-476 will be formed. As the classroom teacher, you should be prepared to provide such information as the quality of the child's homework and test scores, ability to understand and use language,

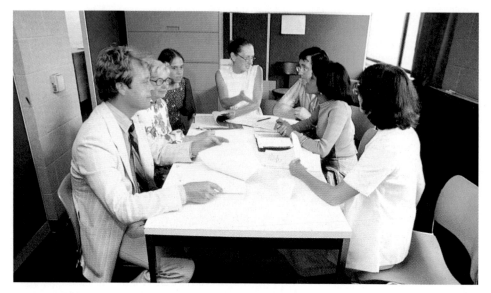

The decision as to whether a child qualifies for special education services under PL 101-476 is made largely on the basis of information supplied by the interdisciplinary assessment team. Classroom teachers typically contribute information about the child's academic and social behavior.

ability to perform various motor functions, alertness at different times of the day, and interpersonal relationships with classmates (Kubiszyn & Borich, 1996; Smith, 1998).

Preparation of the IEP   At least some, if not all, of the members of the assessment team work with the teacher (and the parents) in preparing the IEP. The necessary components of an IEP were described earlier, and they are illustrated in Figure 6.1.

| **Classroom teacher, parents, several specialists prepare IEP**

Implementation and Evaluation of the IEP   Depending on the nature and severity of the handicap, the student may spend part or all of the school day in a regular classroom or be placed in a separate class or school. If the student stays in a regular classroom, the teacher will be expected to put into practice the various instructional techniques listed in the IEP. Because the IEP is planned by a multidisciplinary team, you will be given direction and support in providing regular class instruction for students who have a disabling condition as defined under PL 101-476. The classroom teacher may also be expected to determine if the listed objectives are being met and to furnish evidence of attainment. Various techniques of instruction as well as approaches to evaluation that stress student mastery of individualized assignments will be discussed in several of the chapters that follow.

The types of atypical students you will sometimes be expected to teach in your classroom will vary. Some will be special education students who are being mainstreamed for a certain part of the school day. Others, although different from typical students in some noticeable respect, will not qualify for special education services under PL 101-476. The remainder of this chapter will describe atypical students from both categories and techniques for teaching them. Students with mental retardation, learning disabilities, and/or emotionally disturbance often require special forms of instruction, and we will focus on these categories in the remainder of this chapter. In addition, though not mentioned in PL 101-476, students who are gifted and talented require special forms of instruction, as we will also discuss.

Figure 6.1 Example of an Individualized Education Program (IEP)

INDIVIDUAL EDUCATIONAL PLAN _11/11/96_
DATE

STUDENT: Last Name _____ First _____ Middle _5.3_ _8 - 4 - 81_
School of Attendance _____ Home School _____ Grade Level Birthdate/Age
School Address _____ School Telephone Number

Child Study Team Members

L D Teacher
Homeroom   Case Manager   _Parents_
Name   Title   Name   Title
Facilitator
Name   Title   Name   Title
Speech
Name   Title   Name   Title

Summary of Assessment results

IDENTIFIED STUDENT NEEDS: _Reading from last half of_
DISTAR II - present performance level

LONG TERM GOALS: _To improve reading achievement level_
by at least one year's gain. To improve math
achievement to grade level. To improve
language skills by one year's gain.

SHORT TERM GOALS: _Master Level 4 vocabulary and reading_
skills. Master math skills in basic curriculum.
Master spelling words from Level 3 list. Complete
units 1-9 from Level 3 curriculum.

MAINSTREAM MODIFICATIONS: _____

White Copy—Cumulative Folder   Goldenrod Copy—Case Manager
Pink Copy—Special Teacher   Yellow Copy—Parent

Description of Services to Be Provided

Type of Service	Teacher	Starting Date	Amt. of time per day	OBJECTIVES AND CRITERIA FOR ATTAINMENT
SLD level III	LD Teacher	11-11-96	2½ hrs	_Reading: will know all vocabulary through the "Honeycomb" level. Will master skills as presented through Distar II. Will know 1 2 3 second-symbols presented in "Sound Way to Reading." Math: will pass all tests at Basic 4 level. Spelling: 5 words each week from level 3 lists Language: will complete Units 1 – 9 of the 4th grade language program. Will also complete supplemental units from "Language Step by Step."_

Mainstream Classes	Teacher	Amt. of time per day	OBJECTIVES AND CRITERIA FOR ATTAINMENT
		3½ hrs	_Out of seat behavior: Sit attentively and listen during mainstream class discussions. A simple management plan will be implemented if he does not meet this expectation. Mainstream modifications of Social Studies: will keep a folder in which he expresses through drawing the topics his class will cover. Modified district Social Studies curriculum. No formal testing will be made._

The following equipment and other changes in personnel, transportation, curriculum methods, and educational services will be provided: _Distar II Reading Program, Spelling Level 3, "Sound Way to Reading" Program, Vocabulary tapes_

Substantiation of least restrictive alternatives: _The planning team has determined academic needs are best met with direct SLD support in reading, math, language, and spelling_

ANTICIPATED LENGTH OF PLAN _1 yr._ The next periodic review will be held: _May 1997_
DATE/TIME/PLACE

☐ I approve this program placement and the above IEP
☐ I do not approve this placement and/or the IEP
☐ I request a conciliation conference

Form 2011

PARENT/GUARDIAN

Principal or Designee

Students with Mental Retardation

CLASSIFICATION OF CHILDREN WITH MENTAL RETARDATION

Despite the trend away from the rigid use of classification schemes in American education, the need to classify children with mental retardation has been recognized by the American Association on Mental Retardation (AAMR) in order to plan and finance special education for them. The AAMR applies the term **mental retardation** to individuals who have IQ scores of 67 and below and who have concurrent problems functioning in social environments. The AAMR uses the following classifications:

Mild retardation: IQ score between 67 and 52

Moderate retardation: IQ score between 51 and 36

Severe retardation: IQ score between 35 and 20

Profound retardation: IQ score of 19 and below

As a result of legal challenges to IQ testing and special class placement as well as to the trend toward mainstreaming, students classified as mildly retarded who were once separated are more likely now to be placed in regular classes. You probably will not encounter a great many mainstreamed children classified as moderately or severely retarded because of the specialized forms of care and instruction they need. You may, however, be asked to teach for at least part of the day one or more of the higher-scoring children with mild retardation.

CHARACTERISTICS OF CHILDREN WITH MILD RETARDATION[1]

Students who have below-average IQ scores follow the same general developmental pattern as their peers with higher IQ scores, but they differ in the rate and degree of development. Accordingly, students with low IQ scores may possess characteristics typical of students with average IQ scores who are younger than they are. One general characteristic of such students, therefore, is that they often appear immature compared with their age-mates. Immature students are likely to experience frustration frequently when they find they are unable to do things their classmates can do, and many students with mild retardation tend to have a low tolerance for frustration and a tendency toward low self-esteem, low confidence, and low motivation. These feelings in conjunction with the cognitive deficits outlined in the next paragraph sometimes make it difficult for the child with mild retardation to make friends and get along with peers of average ability.

Students with mild retardation may frustrate easily, lack confidence and self-esteem

The cognitive characteristics of children with mild retardation include a limited amount of knowledge about how one learns and the factors that affect learning (this concept is known as *metacognition* and will be discussed more fully in Chapter 8), a tendency to oversimplify concepts, limited ability to generalize, smaller memory capacity, shorter attention span, the inclination to concentrate on only one aspect of a learning situation and to ignore other relevant features, the inability to formulate learning strategies that fit particular situations, and delayed language development. Several of these deficits often operate in concert to produce or contribute to the learning problems of students with mild retardation. Take, for example, the problem of generalization (also known as transfer). This refers to the ability of a learner to take something that has been learned in one context, such as paper-and-pencil arithmetic skills, and use it to deal with a similar but different task, such as knowing whether one has received the correct change after making a purchase at a store. Students with mild mental retardation may not spontaneously exhibit transfer because (1) their metacognitive deficits limit their tendency to look for signs of similarity between two tasks, (2) their relatively short attention span prevents them from noticing similarities, and (3) their limited memory capacity and skills lessens their ability to recall relevant knowledge.

Students with mild retardation tend to oversimplify, have difficulty generalizing

These characteristics can be understood more completely if they are related to Jean Piaget's description of cognitive development. Middle and high school students with mild retardation may never move beyond the level of concrete operations. They may be able to deal with concrete situations but find it difficult to grasp abstractions, generalize from one situation to another, or state and test

---

[1] Many of the points in this section are based on a discussion of characteristics of mentally retarded children in *Exceptional Children and Youth* (1994), by Nancy Hunt and Kathleen Marshall; *Special Education: A Practical Approach for Teachers* (3d ed., 1995), by James Ysseldyke and Bob Algozzine; *Educating Exceptional Children* (8th ed., 1997), by Samuel Kirk, James Gallagher, and Nicholas Anastasiow; and *Introduction to Special Education* (3d ed., 1998), by Deborah Deutsch Smith.

hypotheses. Younger children with retardation tend to classify things in terms of a single feature.

The following Suggestions for Teaching take into account the characteristics just described, as well as points made by Nancy Hunt and Kathleen Marshall (1994, pp. 165–167); James Ysseldyke and Bob Algozzine (1995, pp. 306–338); Samuel Kirk, James Gallagher, and Nicholas Anastasiow (1997, pp. 218–223); and Deborah Deutsch Smith (1998, pp. 250–259).

SUGGESTIONS FOR TEACHING IN YOUR CLASSROOM

Instructing Students with Mild Retardation

1 As much as possible, try to avoid placing students with mild retardation in situations that are likely to lead to frustration. When, despite your efforts, such students indicate that they are close to their limit of frustration tolerance, encourage them to engage in relaxing change-of-pace pursuits or in physical activities.

2 Do everything possible to encourage a sense of self-esteem.

3 Present learning tasks that contain a small number of elements, at least some of which are familiar to students, and that can be completed in a short period of time.

4 Try to arrange what is to be learned into a series of small steps, each of which leads to immediate feedback.

5 Teach simple techniques for improving memory and consistently point out how use of these techniques leads to more accurate recall.

6 Devise and use record-keeping techniques that make it clear that assignments have been completed successfully and that progress is taking place.

1 **As much as possible, try to avoid placing students with mild retardation in situations that are likely to lead to frustration. When, despite your efforts, such students indicate that they are close to their limit of frustration tolerance, encourage them to engage in relaxing change-of-pace pursuits or in physical activities.**

Journal Entry
Helping Students with Mild Retardation Deal with Frustration

Since children with retardation are more likely to experience frustration than their more capable peers, try to minimize the frequency of such experiences in the classroom. Probably the most effective way to do this is to give students with mild retardation individual assignments so that they are not placed in situations where their work is compared with that of others. No matter how hard you try, however, you will not be able to eliminate frustrating experiences, partly because you will have to schedule some all-class activities and partly because even individual assignments may be difficult for a child with mild retardation to handle. If you happen to notice that such a student appears to be getting more and more bothered by an inability to complete a task, you might try to divert attention to a less demanding form of activity or have the student engage in physical exercise of some kind.

2 **Do everything possible to encourage a sense of self-esteem.**

Children with mild retardation are prone to devalue themselves because they are aware that they are less capable than their classmates at doing many things. One

Children with mild retardation are more likely to respond to instruction if they are presented with simple learning tasks and provided with immediate feedback.

way to combat this tendency toward self-devaluation is to make a point of showing that you have positive feelings about less capable students. If you indicate that you have positive feelings about an individual, that person is likely to acquire similar feelings about herself.

As you saw in Chapter 5, many teachers, usually without realizing it, tend to communicate low expectations to students of low ability. To avoid committing the same error, you might do one or more of the following: make it clear that you will allow plenty of time for all students to come up with an answer to a question, repeat the question and give a clue before asking a different question, remind yourself to give frequent personal attention to students with mild retardation, and/or try to convey to these students the expectation that they *can* learn. Perhaps the best overall strategy to use in building self-esteem is to help children with retardation successfully complete learning tasks. Suggestions 3 through 7 offer ideas you might use.

Journal Entry
Combating the
Tendency to
Communicate
Low Expectations

3 Present learning tasks that contain a small number of elements, at least some of which are familiar to students, and that can be completed in a short period of time.

Since students with retardation tend to oversimplify concepts, try to provide learning tasks that contain only a few elements, at least some of which have been previously learned. For example, you might ask middle or secondary school social studies students with mild retardation to prepare a report on the work of a single police officer, as opposed to preparing an analysis of law enforcement agencies (which might be an appropriate topic for the best student in the class).

Students with retardation tend to have a short attention span. If they are asked to concentrate on demanding tasks that lead to a delayed payoff, they are likely to become distracted or discouraged. Therefore, it is better to give a series of short assignments that produce immediate feedback than to use any sort of contract approach or

Journal Entry
Giving Students
with Mild Retar-
dation Simple
Assignments

**Give students with mild retar-
dation specific assignments
that can be completed quickly**

the equivalent in which the student is expected to engage in self-directed effort leading to a remote goal.

4 Try to arrange what is to be learned into a series of small steps, each of which leads to immediate feedback.

Students who lack confidence, tend to think of one thing at a time, are unable to generalize, and have a short memory and attention span usually respond quite positively to programmed instruction and certain forms of computer-assisted instruction (to be described more completely in Chapter 7). Some computer programs offer a systematic step-by-step procedure that emphasizes only one specific idea per step or frame. They also offer immediate feedback. These characteristics closely fit the needs of children who are mildly retarded. You might look for computer programs in the subject or subjects you teach or develop your own materials, perhaps in the form of a workbook of some kind.

5 Teach simple techniques for improving memory and consistently point out how use of these techniques leads to more accurate recall.

In Chapter 8 we will describe a set of memory aids called mnemonic devices. Used for thousands of years by scholars and teachers in different countries, most are fairly simple devices that help a learner organize information, encode it meaningfully, and generate cues that allow it to be retrieved from memory when needed. The simplest mnemonic devices are rhymes, first-letter mnemonics (also known as acronyms), and sentence mnemonics. For example, a first letter mnemonic or acronym for the Great Lakes is *HOMES: H*uron, *O*ntario, *M*ichigan, *E*rie, *S*uperior.

6 Devise and use record-keeping techniques that make it clear that assignments have been completed successfully and that progress is taking place.

Journal Entry
Giving Students
with Mild Retar-
dation Proof
of Progress

Students who are experiencing difficulties in learning are especially in need of tangible proof of progress. When, for instance, they correctly fill in blanks in a programmed workbook and discover that their answers are correct, they are encouraged to go on to the next question. You might use the same basic approach in more general ways by having students with retardation keep records of progress. (This technique might be used with *all* students in a class.) For example, you could make individual charts for primary grade students. As they successfully complete assignments, have them color in marked-off sections, paste on gold stars or the equivalent, or trace the movement of animal figures, rockets, or whatever toward a destination.

Students with Learning Disabilities

By far the greatest number of students who qualify for special education under PL 101-476 are those classified as learning disabled. According to Department of Education (1998) figures, the number of students identified as learning disabled increased from approximately 800,000 in 1976–1977 to 2,669,491 in 1996–1997. In the 1976–1977 school year students with learning disabilities accounted for about 24 percent of the handicapped population. By the 1996–1997 school year that estimate had grown to a little more than 51 percent. Especially because so many students are now classified as learning disabled, it is important to define and explore the characteristics of students with **learning disabilities**.

CHARACTERISTICS OF STUDENTS WITH LEARNING DISABILITIES

In the early 1960s groups of concerned parents called attention to a problem in American education: a significant number of students in public schools were experiencing difficulties in learning but were not eligible for special classes or remedial instruction programs. These children were not mentally retarded, deaf, blind, or otherwise disabled, but they were unable to respond to aspects of the curriculum presented in regular classrooms. In 1963 parents of such children formed the Association for Children with Learning Disabilities to call attention to the scope of these problems not traceable to any specific cause. Their efforts were rewarded in 1968 when the National Advisory Committee on the Handicapped of the U.S. Office of Education developed a definition of specific learning disabilities, which was utilized by Congress the following year in the Learning Disability Act of 1969. That definition was revised and inserted in PL 94-142 (the predecessor of PL 101-476). It stresses the following basic points:

1. The individual has a *disorder in one or more of the basic psychological processes*. (These processes refer to intrinsic prerequisite abilities such as memory, auditory perception, visual perception, and oral language.)
2. The individual has *difficulty in learning*, specifically in the areas of speaking, listening, writing, reading (word recognition skills and comprehension), and mathematics (calculation and reasoning).
3. A *severe discrepancy exists between the student's apparent potential for learning and low level of achievement*.
4. The problem is *not due primarily to other causes*, such as visual or hearing impairments, motor handicapped, mental retardation, emotional disturbance, or economic, environmental, or cultural disadvantage.

Learning disabilities: disorders in basic processes that lead to learning problems not due to other causes

In addition to these problems with cognitive processing and learning, many students with a learning disability (as well as students with mild mental retardation and students with emotional disturbance) have more poorly developed social skills than their nondisabled peers. Such students are more likely to ignore the teacher's directions, cheat, use profane language, disturb other students, disrupt group activities, and start fights. As a result, they are often rejected by the rest of the class, which contributes to lowered self-esteem and poor academic performance (Gresham & MacMillan, 1997).

Some people dismiss the notion of a learning disability as a fiction since everyone at one time or another has misread numbers, letters, and words; confused pronunciations of words and letters; and suffered embarrassing lapses of attention and memory. But students with learning disabilities really are different from others—in degree, mostly, rather than in kind. Although the nondisabled individual may occasionally exhibit lapses in basic information processing, the learning disabled individual does so consistently and with little hope of self-correction. The important point to keep in mind is that you need to know what a student with a learning disability (as well as a low-achieving non–learning disabled student) can and cannot do so that you can effectively remediate those weaknesses (Spear-Swerling & Sternberg, 1998).

PROBLEMS WITH BASIC PSYCHOLOGICAL PROCESSES

The fundamental problem that underlies a learning disability is, as the law states, "a disorder in one or more basic psychological processes." Although this phrase is somewhat vague, it generally refers to problems with how students receive information, process it, and express what they have learned. Specifically, many students with learning disabilities have deficits in perception, attention, memory encoding and storage, and metacognition.

Some students with learning disabilities have great difficulty perceiving the difference between certain sounds (*f* and *v*, *m* and *n*, for example) or letters (*m* and *n*, *b*, *p*, and *d*, for example). As a result, words that begin with one letter (such as *v*ase) are sometimes perceived and pronounced as if they begin with another letter (as in *f*ase). As you can no doubt appreciate from this simple example, this type of deficit makes learning to read and reading with comprehension a long and frustrating affair for some students.

Many students with learning disabilities also have difficulty with attention and impulse control—focusing on a task, noticing important cues and ideas, and staying with the task until it is completed. The source of the distraction may be objects and activities in the classroom, or it may be unrelated thoughts. In either case the student misses much of what the teacher says or what is on a page of text, or misinterprets directions. Children with extreme deficits in attention may be diagnosed as having **attention-deficit/hyperactivity disorder (ADHD).** For a student to be judged as having ADHD, the symptoms have to first appear before the age of seven, and they have to be displayed in several settings, such as at home, at school, and at play. The main symptoms of ADHD are impulsivity, distractibility, and hyperactivity. It is estimated that 3 to 5 percent of all children have ADHD, with boys outnumbering girls by six to one (American Psychiatric Association, 1994; Thompson, 1996). Services for children with ADHD can be funded under the "seriously emotionally disturbed" category, the "specific learning disabilities" category, or the "other health impaired" category of PL 101-476 (Lerner, Lowenthal, & Lerner, 1995).

Because so many students with learning disabilities have problems with perception and attention, they also have problems with accurate recall of information. Because accurate recall is heavily dependent on what gets stored in memory in the first place and where in memory information is stored (Hunt & Marshall, 1994), students who encode partial, incorrect, or unimportant information have memory problems.

Like students with mild retardation, many students with learning disabilities have a deficit in metacognitive skills (Hunt & Marshall, 1994). As a result, their learning activities are chaotic, like those of young children. For example, they may begin a task before they have thought through all of the steps involved.

Students with learning disabilities tend to be characterized as passive and disorganized: passive in the sense that they take few active steps to attend to relevant information, store it effectively in memory, and retrieve it when needed; and disorganized in the sense that their learning activities are often unplanned and subject to whatever happens to capture their attention at the moment.

Students with learning disabilities have problems with perception, attention, memory, metacognition

The following Suggestions for Teaching will give you some ideas about how to help students with learning disabilities improve their learning skills and feel better about themselves.

SUGGESTIONS FOR TEACHING IN YOUR CLASSROOM

Instructing Students with Learning Disabilities

1 Structure learning tasks to help students with learning disabilities compensate for weaknesses in psychological processes.

2 Capitalize on the natural resources that exist in your classroom to help students with learning disabilities improve academically, socially, and emotionally.

1 Structure learning tasks to help students with learning disabilities compensate for weaknesses in psychological processes.

Because of their weaknesses in basic psychological processes, students with learning disabilities are often distractible, impulsive, forgetful, disorganized, poor at comprehension, and unaware of the factors that affect learning. But these deficits can be moderated to some extent by implementing one or more of the procedures that follow.

Journal Entry
Helping Students with Learning Disabilities Improve Basic Learning Processes

EXAMPLES

■ For students who have difficulty distinguishing between similar-looking or -sounding stimuli (such as letters, words, or phrases), point out and highlight their distinguishing characteristics. For example, highlight the circular part of the letters *b, p,* and *d* and place a directional arrow at the end of the straight segment to emphasize that they have the same shape but differ in their spatial orientation. Or highlight the letters *t* and *r* in the words *though, thought,* and *through* to emphasize that they differ from each other by the absence or presence of one letter.

■ For students who are easily distracted, instruct them to place only the materials being used on top of the desk or within sight.

■ For students who seem unable to attend to important stimuli such as significant sections of a text page, show them how to underline or outline in an effort to distinguish between important and unimportant material. Or suggest that they use a ruler or pointing device under each line as they read so that they can evaluate one sentence at a time. To help them attend to important parts of directions, highlight or write key words and phrases in all capitals. For especially important tasks, you might want to ask students to paraphrase or repeat directions verbatim.

Help students with learning disabilities to reduce distractions, attend to important information

■ For students who have a short attention span, give brief assignments and divide complex material into smaller segments. After each short lesson segment, provide both immediate positive feedback and tangible evidence of progress. (Many sets of published materials prepared for use with students with learning disabilities are designed in just this way.)

■ To improve memory and comprehension of information, teach students memorization skills and how to relate new information to existing knowledge schemes to improve long-term storage and retrieval. Also, make frequent use of simple, concrete analogies and examples to explain and illustrate complex, abstract ideas. (We will describe several techniques for enhancing memory and comprehension in Chapter 8.)

■ To improve organization, suggest that students keep a notebook in which to record homework assignments, a checklist of materials needed for class, and books and materials that need to be brought home for studying and homework.

- To improve general awareness of the learning process, emphasize the importance of thinking about the factors that could affect one's performance on a particular task, of forming a plan before actually starting to work, and of monitoring the effectiveness of learning activities.

- Consider the variety of learning environments increasingly available through multimedia software programs. Some students with learning disabilities may respond better to a combination of visual and auditory information, while others may learn best in a hands-on setting. Multimedia programs provide options to address these different styles and also allow the student to control the direction and pace of learning. Some excellent examples for young children are the Living Books series (Broderbund).

2 Capitalize on the natural resources that exist in your classroom to help students with learning disabilities improve academically, socially, and emotionally.

Although you and the resource teacher will be the main sources of instruction and support for mainstreamed students, recognize that other sources of classroom support are almost always available. The other students in your class, for example, can supplement your instructional efforts. As we pointed out in the previous chapter, peer tutoring typically produces gains in achievement, interpersonal relationships, and attitudes toward subject matter. These effects have been documented for students with a learning disability as well as low-achieving students without a learning disability (Fuchs, Fuchs, Mathes, & Simmons, 1997). And don't overlook the benefits of having students with learning disabilities play the role of tutor. Giving students with disabilities the opportunity to tutor either a low-achieving classmate in a subject that is not affected by the student's disability or a younger student in a lower grade can produce a noticeable increase in self-esteem.

Another way to make use of the other students in your class is through cooperative learning. This technique was initially described in the last chapter and is described in more detail in Chapter 10. Like peer tutoring, which it incorporates, it also produces gains in achievement, interpersonal relationships, and self-esteem.

Finally, make use of the various ways in which information can be presented to students and in which students can respond. In addition to text material and lecturing, you can use films, computer-based presentations, picture charts, diagrams, and demonstrations. In addition to having students demonstrate what they have learned through paper-and-pencil tests and other written products, you can have them make oral presentations, produce pictorial products, create an actual product, or give a performance. Hands-on activities are particularly useful for students with ADHD.

Students with Emotional Disturbance

ESTIMATES OF EMOTIONAL DISTURBANCE

In a 1998 report to Congress on the implementation of PL 101-476, the Department of Education noted that 446,635 students were classified as seriously emotionally disturbed for the 1996–1997 school year. This figure accounted for 8.5

percent of all schoolchildren classified as handicapped and slightly less than 1 percent of the general school-age population. Not everyone agrees, however, that these figures accurately reflect the scope of the problem. Other estimates of the extent of serious emotional disturbances in the general school-age population range from 1 percent to 20 percent (Kirk, Gallagher, & Anastasiow, 1997). Frank Wood and Robert Zabel (1978) offer an explanation for these differences between estimates and classifications by suggesting that most identification procedures ask teachers to rate children in their classes at a particular point in time. Some identification procedures, however, stress recurrent problems. It seems possible, therefore, that, although perhaps one out of five students attending public schools may sometimes exhibit emotional problems, only two or three out of one hundred will display severe, persistent problems.

DEFINITIONS OF EMOTIONAL DISTURBANCE

Two other reasons that estimates of **emotional disturbance** vary are the lack of any clear descriptions of such forms of behavior and different interpretations of the descriptions that do exist. Children with *serious emotional disturbance* are defined in PL 101-476 in this way:

(I)   The term means a condition exhibiting one or more of the following characteristics over a long period of time and to a marked degree that adversely affects a child's educational performance:

(A)   An inability to learn that cannot be explained by intellectual, sensory, or health factors;

(B)   An inability to build or maintain satisfactory interpersonal relationships with peers and teachers;

(C)   Inappropriate types of behavior or feelings under normal circumstances;

Emotional disturbance: poor relationships, inappropriate behavior, depression, fears

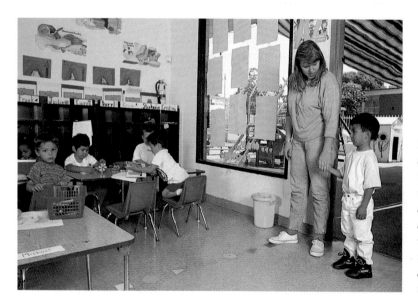

Students who have an emotional disturbance tend to be either aggressive or withdrawn. Because withdrawn students tend to be anxious and fearful about interpersonal relationships, they may need to be encouraged to interact with their classmates.

(D) A general pervasive mood of unhappiness or depression; or

(E) A tendency to develop physical symptoms or fears associated with personal or school problems.

(II) The term includes schizophrenia. The term does not apply to children who are socially maladjusted, unless it is determined that they have a serious emotional disturbance. (Office of the Federal Register, 1994, pp. 13–14)

Several special education scholars (for example, Kirk, Gallagher, & Anastasiow, 1997, pp. 278–280; Smith, 1998, pp. 328–330; Ysseldyke & Algozzine, 1995, pp. 345–346) point out the difficulties caused by vague terminology in distinguishing between students who have emotional disturbance and students who are normal. The phrase *a long period of time*, for example, is not defined in the law (although many special education experts use six months as a rough rule of thumb). Behaviors such as *satisfactory interpersonal relationships, a general pervasive mood*, and *inappropriate types of behavior or feelings under normal circumstances* are difficult to measure objectively and can often be observed in normal individuals. Since long-term observation of behavior is often critical in making a correct diagnosis of emotional disturbance, you can aid the multidisciplinary assessment team in this task by keeping a behavioral log of a child you suspect may have this disorder.

That many educators and psychologists use such terms as *emotionally disturbed, socially maladjusted,* and *behavior disordered* synonymously makes matters even more confusing. The term **behavior disorder** has many adherents and has been adopted by several states for two basic reasons. One reason is that it calls attention to the actual behavior that is disordered and needs to be changed. The second reason is that behaviors can be directly and objectively assessed. Although there are subtle differences between the terms *emotionally disturbed* and *behavior disorder*, they are essentially interchangeable, and you can probably assume that those who use them are referring to children who share similar characteristics. Because of the nature of bureaucracies, however, it may be necessary for anyone hoping to obtain special assistance for a child with what many contemporary psychologists would call a behavior disorder to refer to that child as *seriously emotionally disturbed* since that is the label used in PL 101-476.

Term *behavior disorder* focuses on behavior that needs to be changed, objective assessment

CHARACTERISTICS OF STUDENTS WITH A SERIOUS EMOTIONAL DISTURBANCE

Several classifications of emotional disturbance (or behavior disorders) have been made (see, for example, Achenbach & Edelbrock, 1983; Quay, 1986; Wicks-Nelson & Israel, 1991). Most psychologists who have attempted to classify such forms of behavior describe two basic patterns: externalizing and internalizing. Externalizing students are often aggressive, uncooperative, restless, and negativistic. They tend to lie and steal, to defy teachers, and to be hostile to authority figures. Sometimes they are cruel and malicious. Internalizing students, by contrast, are typically shy, timid, anxious, and fearful. They are often depressed and lack self-confidence. Teachers tend to be more aware of students who display aggressive disorders because their behavior often stimulates or forces reactions. The withdrawn student, however, may be more likely to develop serious emotional problems such as depression and may even be at risk of suicide during the adolescent years.

Students with behavior disorders tend to be either aggressive or withdrawn

In the next section are Suggestions for Teaching to help you teach both the withdrawn student and the aggressive student.

SUGGESTIONS FOR TEACHING IN YOUR CLASSROOM

Instructing Students with Emotional Disturbance[2]

1 Design the classroom environment and formulate lesson plans to encourage social interaction and co-operation.

2 Prompt and reinforce appropriate social interactions.

3 Train other students to initiate social interaction.

4 Design the classroom environment to reduce the probability of disruptive behavior.

5 Reinforce appropriate behavior, and, if necessary, punish inappropriate behavior.

6 Use group contingency-management techniques.

1 Design the classroom environment and formulate lesson plans to encourage social interaction and cooperation.

Students whose emotional disturbance manifests itself as social withdrawal may stay away from others on purpose (perhaps because they find social contacts threatening), or they may find that others stay away from them (perhaps because they have poorly developed social skills). Regardless of the cause, the classroom environment and your instructional activities can be designed to foster appropriate interpersonal contact.

Foster interpersonal contact among withdrawn students

EXAMPLES

■ Preschool and elementary school teachers can use toys and materials as well as organized games and sports that encourage cooperative play and that have a reduced focus on individual performance. Activities might include dress-up games or puppet plays; games might include soccer, variations of "it" (such as tag), and kickball or softball modified such that everyone on the team gets a turn to kick or bat before the team plays in the field.

Journal Entry
Activities and Materials That Encourage Cooperation

■ Elementary and middle school teachers can use one or more of several team-oriented learning activities. See *Cooperative Learning* (2d ed., 1995), by Robert Slavin, for details on using such activities as Student Teams-Achievement Divisions, Jigsaw, and Team Accelerated Instruction.

2 Prompt and reinforce appropriate social interactions.

Prompting and positive reinforcement are basic learning principles that will be discussed at length in Chapter 7. Essentially, a prompt is a stimulus that draws out a desired response, and positive reinforcement involves giving the student a positive reinforcer (which is something the student wants) immediately after a desired behavior. The aim is to get the student to behave that way again. Typical reinforcers include verbal praise, stickers (with pictures of gold stars and smiley faces, for instance), and small prizes (such as a pencil with the child's name engraved on it).

EXAMPLE

■ You can also set up a cooperative task or activity: "Marc, I would like you to help Carol and Raquel paint the scenery for next week's play. You can paint the trees and flowers, Carol will

---

[2] Most of these suggestions were derived from points made in Chapters 6 and 8 of *Strategies for Managing Behavior Problems in the Classroom* (3d ed., 1998), by Mary Margaret Kerr and C. Michael Nelson.

paint the grass, and Raquel will do the people." After several minutes say something like, "That's good work. I am really pleased at how well the three of you are working together." Similar comments can be made at intervals as the interaction continues.

3 Train other students to initiate social interaction.

In all likelihood you will have too many classroom responsibilities to spend a great deal of time working directly with a withdrawn child. It may be possible, however, using the steps that follow, to train other students to initiate contact with withdrawn students.

EXAMPLES

Journal Entry
Getting Students to Initiate Interaction with a Withdrawn Child

■ First, choose a student who interacts freely and well, who can follow your instructions, and who can concentrate on the training task for at least ten minutes. Second, explain that the goal is to get the withdrawn child to work or play with the helping student but that the helper should expect rejection, particularly at first. Role-play the actions of a withdrawn child so that the helper understands what you mean by rejection. Emphasize the importance of making periodic attempts at interaction. Third, instruct the helper to suggest games or activities that appeal to the withdrawn student. Fourth, reinforce the helper's attempts to interact with the withdrawn child.

4 Design the classroom environment to reduce the probability of disruptive behavior.

Use techniques to forestall aggressive or antisocial behavior

The best way to deal with aggressive or antisocial behavior is to nip it in the bud. This strategy has at least three related benefits. One benefit of fewer disruptions is that you can better accomplish what you had planned for the day. A second benefit is that you are likely to be in a more positive frame of mind than if you spend half the day acting as a referee. A third benefit is that, because of fewer disruptions and a more positive attitude, you may be less inclined to resort to physical punishment (which, as we will point out in Chapter 7, often produces undesirable side effects).

EXAMPLES

■ With student input, formulate rules for classroom behavior and penalties for infractions of rules. Remind all students of the penalties, particularly when a disruptive incident seems about to occur, and consistently apply the penalties when the rules are broken.

■ Place valued objects and materials out of reach when they are not needed or in use.

■ Minimize the aggressive student's frustration with learning by using some of the same techniques you would use for a child with mild retardation: break tasks down into small, easy-to-manage pieces; provide clear directions; and reinforce correct responses.

5 Reinforce appropriate behavior, and, if necessary, punish inappropriate behavior.

In suggestion 2 we described the use of positive reinforcement to encourage desired behavior. Reinforcement has the dual effect of teaching the aggressive student which behavior is appropriate and reducing the frequency of inappropriate behavior as it is replaced by desired behavior. Disruptive behavior will still occur, however. Three effective techniques for suppressing it while reinforcing desired behaviors are contingency contracts, token economies and fines, and time-out. Each of these techniques will be described in Chapter 7 of this book.

6 **Use group contingency-management techniques.**

Up to now we have suggested methods that focus on the aggressive student. In addition, you may want to reward the entire class when the aggressive student behaves appropriately for a certain period of time. Such rewards—which may be free time, special classroom events, or certain privileges—should make the aggressive student the hero and foster better peer relationships.

Gifted and Talented Students

Students who learn at a significantly faster rate than their peers or who possess superior talent in one or more areas also need to be taught in special ways if they are to make the most of their abilities. Unlike students with mental retardation, learning disabilities, and emotional disturbance, however, students with superior capabilities are not covered by PL 101-476. Instead, the federal government provides technical assistance to states and local school districts for establishing programs for superior students. Although most states have such programs, some experts in special education (for example, Horowitz & O'Brien, 1986) feel that they are not given the resources they need to adequately meet the needs of all gifted and talented students. The Suggestions for Teaching that follows a bit later reflect this situation. All of the suggestions are inexpensive to implement and require few additional personnel.

A definition of the term **gifted and talented** was part of a bill passed by Congress in 1988:

> The term *gifted and talented children and youth* means children and youth who give evidence of high performance capability in areas such as intellectual, creative, artistic, or leadership capacity, or in specific academic fields, and who require services or activities not ordinarily provided by the school in order to fully develop such capabilities. (Title IV-H.R.5, 1988, pp. 227–228)

Gifted and talented students show high performance in one or more areas

IDENTIFICATION OF GIFTED AND TALENTED STUDENTS

Eligibility for gifted and talented programs has traditionally been based on standardized test scores, particularly IQ tests. It was not uncommon in years past for students to have to achieve an IQ score of at least 130 to be admitted to such programs. But criticisms about the narrow range of skills covered by such tests (mainly Gardner's linguistic and logical-mathematical intelligences and Sternberg's analytical ability) has led most states to eliminate the use of a numerical cutoff score for identification (Cassidy & Johnson, 1986).

Although this is seen as a step in the right direction, critical weaknesses in the identification of gifted and talented children remain, particularly gifted children from minority cultures. One remaining problem is the historical emphasis on IQ. Achievement and mental ability are still often looked to as indicators of giftedness at the expense of such other relevant characteristics as motivation, creativity, leadership, and critical thinking ability (Feldhusen, 1998). A second problem is educators' unfamiliarity with ways of measuring human characteristics other than by standard-

Minorities underrepresented in gifted classes because of overreliance on test scores

ized tests. Checklists, rating scales, and nominations by peers and adults can also be used (Richert, 1997). A third problem is a general ignorance of characteristics that are more highly valued by a minority culture than by the majority culture. Some Native American tribes, for example, deemphasize the concept of giftedness because it runs counter to their belief that the welfare and cohesion of the group are more important than celebrating and nurturing the talents of any individual. The members of other tribes may place as much value on a child's knowledge of tribal traditions, storytelling ability, and artistic ability as they do on problem-solving ability and scientific reasoning (Callahan & McIntire, 1994). A child's giftedness may, therefore, be evident only when examined from the perspective of a particular culture. This may explain why only 2 percent of Native Americans can be found in classes for the gifted and talented (Winner, 1997).

CHARACTERISTICS OF GIFTED AND TALENTED STUDENTS

In one sense, gifted and talented students are like any other group of students. Some are healthy and well coordinated, whereas others are not. Some are extremely popular and well liked, but others are not. Some are well adjusted; others are not (Ysseldyke & Algozzine, 1995). But as a group, gifted and talented students are often noticeably different (see, for example, discussions by Piechowski, 1997 and Winner, 1997). Here are some of the main characteristics that many gifted and talented students share:

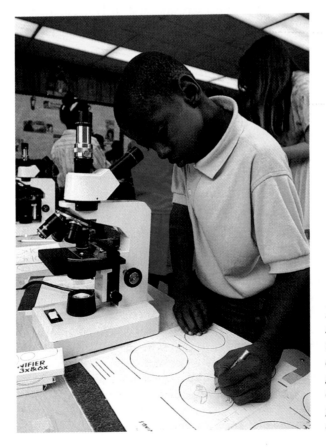

Because gifted and talented students understand and integrate abstract ideas more quickly than do their non-gifted classmates, they are capable of successfully completing tasks that older students routinely carry out.

1. They excel on tasks that involve language, abstract logical thinking, and mathematics.

2. They are faster at encoding information and retrieving it from memory.

3. They are highly aware of how they learn and the various conditions that affect their learning. As a result, they excel at transferring previously learned information and skills to new problems and settings.

4. They exhibit such high levels of motivation and task persistence that the phrase "rage to master" is sometimes used to describe their behavior.

5. They tend to be more solitary and introverted than average children.

6. They tend to have very intense emotional lives. They react with intense feelings, such as joy, regret, or sorrow, to a story, a piece of music, or a social encounter. They also tend to be emotionally sensitive and will sometimes surpass adults in their ability to notice and identify with the feelings of others.

Gifted and talented students differ from their nongifted peers intellectually and emotionally

For the most part gifted and talented students see themselves as they were just described. In comparison to intellectually average students, they have a moderately stronger academic self-concept but score at about the same level on measures of physical and social self-concepts (Hoge & Renzulli, 1993).

INSTRUCTIONAL OPTIONS

Gifted and talented students constantly challenge a teacher's skill, ingenuity, and classroom resources. While trying to instruct the class as a whole, the teacher is faced with the need to provide more and more interesting and challenging materials and ideas to the gifted student. In this section we will examine three possible solutions to this problem.

ACCELERATED INSTRUCTION   Accelerated instruction is often suggested as a solution to this problem. For many people, the phrase *accelerated instruction* means allowing the student to skip one or more grades, which often happens. But there are at least three other ways of accomplishing the same goal. The curriculum can be compressed, allowing gifted and talented students to complete the work for more than one grade during the regular school year; the school year can be extended by the use of summer sessions; and students can take college courses while still in high school.

Whatever the form of accelerated instruction, this is always a hotly debated topic, with pros and cons on each side. Two often quoted advantages for giving gifted students the opportunity to work on complex tasks are that (1) it keeps them from becoming bored with school, and (2) it produces more positive attitudes toward learning. On the negative side, two frequent arguments are that (1) a gifted student may have trouble with the social and emotional demands of acceleration, and (2) acceleration produces an undesirable sense of elitism among gifted students. (Benbow, 1991; Kulik & Kulik, 1984) As with all informed educational decisions, the unique needs of the individual and the situation must be considered before the best course of action can be determined.

GIFTED AND TALENTED CLASSES AND SCHOOLS   Some public school districts offer separate classes for gifted and talented students either as an alternative to accelerated instruction or as something that follows accelerated instruction. In addition, so-called magnet schools are composed of students whose average level of ability is higher than that found in a typical elementary, middle, or high school. Finally, many states sponsor high-ability high schools, particularly in mathematics and science.

Recent findings suggest that such placements do not produce uniformly positive results and should be made only after the characteristics of the student and the program have been carefully considered. In terms of achievement, the typical gifted student can expect to score moderately higher (about one-third of a standard deviation) on tests than comparable students who remain in heterogeneous classes (Kulik & Kulik, 1991). But the effects of separate class or school placement on measures of academic self-concept have been inconsistent; some researchers find them to be higher than those of students who remain in heterogeneous classes, whereas other researchers have found either no differences or declines (Hoge & Renzulli, 1993; Kulik & Kulik, 1991; Marsh, Chessor, Craven, & Roche, 1995).

Separate classes for gifted and talented students aid achievement but may lower academic self-concept of some students

ENRICHMENT TECHNIQUES AND PROGRAMS   In two books (Reis & Renzulli, 1985; Renzulli & Reis, 1985), Joseph Renzulli and Sally Reis describe three levels of curriculum enrichment for gifted and talented learners. The first level (type I enrichment) involves exploratory activities that are designed to expose students to topics, events, books, people, and places not ordinarily covered in the regular curriculum. The basic purpose of these activities is to stimulate new interests. Among the many suggestions Renzulli and Reis offer are having students view and write reports on films and videocassettes (such as *The Eagle Has Landed: The Flight of Apollo 11*) and having a local resident make a presentation on his occupation or hobby.

The second level (type II enrichment) involves instructional methods and materials that are aimed at the development of such thinking and feeling processes as thinking creatively, classifying and analyzing data, solving problems, appreciating, and valuing.

The third level (type III enrichment) consists of activities in which students investigate and collect data about a real topic or problem. For example, a student may decide to document the history of her school, focusing on such issues as changes in size, instructional materials and methods, and curriculum.

Several databases on the Internet are now devoted to long-distance education, enrichment, and tutoring. You might explore the Global Network Academy (http://www.gnacademy.org/), which offers on-line courses in a wide range of areas. The International Tutoring Foundation (http://edie.cprost.sfu.ca/it/programs. html), a nonprofit organization based at the University of Toronto, provides tutoring for all age and grade levels, including special programs for gifted students (as well as for students with disabilities).

The following Suggestions for Teaching provide ideas for working with gifted and talented students.

SUGGESTIONS FOR TEACHING IN YOUR CLASSROOM

Instructing Gifted and Talented Students

1 Consult with gifted and talented students regarding individual study projects, perhaps involving a learning contract.

2 Encourage supplementary reading and writing.

3 Have gifted students act as tutors.

1 Consult with gifted and talented students regarding individual study projects, perhaps involving a learning contract.

One of the most effective ways to deal with gifted students is to assign individual study projects. These assignments should probably be related to some part of the curriculum. If you are studying Mexico, for example, a gifted student could devote free time to a special report on some aspect of Mexican life that intrigues him. In making these assignments, you should remember that even very bright students may not be able to absorb, organize, and apply abstract concepts until they become formal thinkers. Thus, up until early middle school years, it may be preferable to keep these assignments brief rather than comprehensive.

Journal Entry
Individual Study for
Students Who Are
Gifted and Talented

To provide another variation of the individual study project, you could ask the gifted student to act as a research specialist and report on questions that puzzle the class. Still another individual study project is the creation of an open-ended, personal yearbook. Any time a gifted student finishes the assigned work, she might be allowed to write stories or do drawings for such a journal. When possible, however, unobtrusive projects are preferable. Perhaps you can recall a teacher who rewarded the fast workers by letting them work on a mural (or the equivalent) covering the side board. If you were an average student, you can probably attest that the sight of the class "brains" having the time of their lives was not conducive to diligent effort on the part of the have-nots sweating away at their workbooks. Reward assignments should probably be restricted to individual work on unostentatious projects.

Finally, you might set up independent study projects by using the contract approach (described more completely in Chapters 7 and 13). Consult with students on an individual basis and agree on a personal assignment that is to be completed by a certain date.

2 Encourage supplementary reading and writing.

Encourage students to spend extra time reading and writing. A logical method of combining both skills is the preparation of book reports. It is perhaps less threatening to call them book *reviews* and emphasize that you are interested in personal reaction, not in a précis or an abstract. Some specialists in the education of the gifted have suggested that such students be urged to read biographies and autobiographies. The line of reasoning here is that potential leaders might be inspired to emulate the exploits of a famous person. Even if such inspiration does not result, you could recommend life stories simply because they are usually interesting.

Journal Entry
Providing Gifted
and Talented
Students with
Opportunities for
Additional Reading
and Writing

If your school has a computer network, or is connected to the Internet, other possibilities for writing are e-mail exchanges with other students, siblings at college, or friends in different areas. Or a student may write a review of a World Wide Web site that she has discovered. If the appropriate software and support are available, students could be encouraged to create "home pages," or World Wide Web sites for themselves, either on a topic mutually selected with the teacher or on their personal interests (the latter would be much like a yearbook entry).

3 Have gifted students act as tutors.

Depending on the grade, subject, and personalities of those involved, gifted students might be asked to act occasionally as tutors, lab assistants, or the equivalent. Some bright students will welcome such opportunities and are capable of providing instruction in such a way that their peers do not feel self-conscious or humiliated. Others, however, may resent being asked to spend school time helping classmates and/or may lack skills in interpersonal relationships. If you do decide to ask a gifted student to function as a tutor, therefore, it would be wise to proceed tentatively and cautiously.

Using Technology to Assist Exceptional Students

There is perhaps no place in education today where technology is making as significant an impact as in the field of special education. Interpretations of least restrictive environments and other legislation have expanded the scope of technological services schools are required to provide for disabled students (Parette, Dunn, & Hoge, 1995). For instance, the Education of the Handicapped Act Amendments of 1980 (PL 99-457) mandate the provision of adapted technology for any need related to the learning or development of a child (Snider & Badgett, 1995).

As the laws related to the disabled have expanded during the past two decades, there has been a simultaneous proliferation in assistive technologies to help students with special learning needs succeed academically. **Assistive technology** refers to "any item, device, or piece of equipment that is used to increase, maintain, or improve the functional abilities of persons with disabilities" (PL 100-407, Technology Related Assistance for Individuals with Disabilities Act of 1988, 29 U.S.C. 2202, Section 3[2]; Holder-Brown & Parette, 1992). Such tools may range from less expensive low-tech equipment such as adapted spoons, joysticks, taped stories, adaptive switches, head pointing devices, and communication boards (message display devices that contain vocabulary choices from which the child can select an answer) to commercially developed high-tech devices such as screen magnifiers, speech synthesizers and digitizers, voice-recognition devices, touch screens, and alternative computer keyboards (Blackhurst, 1997; Messerer, 1997; Snider & Badgett, 1995).

Advances in technology to assist visually and hearing impaired students, to provide powered mobility for the physically impaired, and to offer augmented communication tools to those who lack the ability to communicate their needs to others are occurring worldwide (Howell, 1996; Parette, Hourcade, & VanBiervliet, 1993).

Federal legislation has led to the development of various assistive technologies

Technology for Students with Hearing Impairments

Hearing-impaired students can be assisted with technology tools in a number of ways, including: (1) closed captioning, (2) multimedia technologies, and (3) **electronic networking**. Recent laws have required television sets in the United States to be equipped with internal decoding circuitry for captioning of text on the screen so that it can be read, while placing pressure on educators to provide captioning within educational videotapes and television programs (Elwell, Reeve, & Hofmeister, 1992).

Multimedia programs and other technologies are emerging to help hearing-impaired students develop their sign language and lip-reading skills, vocabulary and reading comprehension, and spoken and written communication skills (Aedo, Miranda, Panetsos, Torra, & Martin, 1994). One highly visible electronic network-based classroom known as ENFI (Electronic Networks for Interaction) (Bruce, Peyton, & Batson, 1993) was developed in 1985 at Gallaudet University, a well-known school for the deaf in Washington, DC. Collaborative writing tools like Realtime Writer are included within ENFI to teach writing to hearing-impaired students by conducting all class discussion and interaction in electronic writing. Here, students and the teacher sit at computer terminals and compose messages at the bottom of their computer screens. Student work can be transmitted to all computer screens in the class, or it can be read by and discussed privately with the teacher.

TECHNOLOGY FOR STUDENTS WITH VISUAL IMPAIRMENTS

Closed captioning and Web-based conferencing tools are popular among deaf students; speech synthesizers and voice-recognition devices offer similar liberating assistance to the visually impaired (Messerer, 1997; Scrase, 1997). With speech synthesis, the user can select a word, sentence, or chunk of information from any written or scanned text and hear it pronounced by a speech synthesizer. For example, DECTalk is a high-quality speech synthesis program developed by Digital Equipment Corporation that analyzes, synthesizes, and converts plain text into high-quality speech, nearly as comprehensible as recorded speech. Using seven built-in voices, the DECTalk system provides on-line reading and computerized speech support (Leong, 1995). Voice recognition allows the visually impaired student to access computer files and different options by talking. In addition to speech synthesis and voice recognition, there are products for the visually impaired that enlarge the information on the computer screen or that magnify the image by attaching screens to the front of the monitor (Messerer, 1997).

TECHNOLOGY FOR STUDENTS WITH ORTHOPEDIC IMPAIRMENTS

For students who have physical limitations, pointing devices held in the mouth or attached to the head may provide the needed device control. Students with more limited fields of motion but acceptable fine motor skill may also benefit from condensed or mini keyboards that position the keys more closely together and require less strength to use (Snider & Badgett, 1995). For those students with less fine motor control, touch-sensitive expanded keyboards offer more space between keys and are often programmed to accept overlay plastic sheets for different applications or user needs.

TECHNOLOGY FOR STUDENTS WITH SPEECH OR LANGUAGE IMPAIRMENTS

Technology can also help individuals with communication impairments. Using computer software with a speech synthesizer and expanded keyboard, Teris Schery and Lisa O'Connor (1997) demonstrated positive effects of computer training in vocabulary, early grammar skills, and social communication among toddlers with Down syndrome as well as young children with severe language and behavioral disabilities. In a small pilot study, they later discovered that parent volunteers briefly trained in using this software can be more effective than a professional speech pathologist.

TECHNOLOGY FOR STUDENTS WITH LEARNING DISABILITIES

Whereas assistive technology is intended to compensate for or circumvent a disability, some instructional technologies are meant to help students with learning disabilities remediate their weaknesses (Raskind, 1993). Many new technology tools can help LD students spend less time concentrating on such surface-level task demands as the spelling and formatting of papers and more time analyzing problems, interpreting information, and reflecting on answers. According to David Kumar and Cynthia Wilson (1997), a variety of tools are now available for LD students to reduce the cognitive demands of a task by serving as external memory aids. For instance, talking calculators provide auditory feedback or confirmation of basic mathematical operations.

In the area of reading, some software programs can help young LD readers focus on basic phoneme identification and segmentation (Torgesen & Barker, 1995), while hypertext applications can help younger children develop prereading skills (Boone, Higgins, Notari, & Stump, 1996). For high school students, hypertext can create multiple ways to interact with text material and learn new information (Higgins, Boone, & Lovitt, 1996). For instance, Charles MacArthur and Jacqueline Haynes (1995) found that the reading comprehension of LD high school students was enhanced when the computer system included such features as speech synthesis, an on-line glossary, links between questions raised and the text, computer highlighting of main ideas, and supplemental summaries and explanations.

In the area of writing, Charles MacArthur (1996) notes that there are many tools for students with learning disabilities that can help them—and other students—with basic sentence generation, transcription, and revision. As indicated earlier, spelling, style, and grammar checkers can help raise student focus from the mechanical demands and surface-level concerns about task length requirements to higher-level text cohesion and integration issues. However, MacArthur (1994) cautions that technology by itself does not improve middle school LD student writing. Instead, he has found that sound instructional practices such as peer tutoring on the word-processed text raise the quality and number of student revisions and overall quality of their writing.

There are also tools for LD students to set writing goals, generate content, and plan and evaluate their writing (MacArthur, 1996). Personal data managers, for instance, might help LD students record writing deadlines, remember important due dates, and plan their writing schedules (Raskind, 1993). Computerized post-it notes, outlining aids, and semantic webbing tools, moreover, can also facilitate organization of their ideas prior to writing (Raskind, 1993). Additionally, computer prompting programs can help students brainstorm and organize ideas and reflect on audience needs (Bonk & Reynolds, 1992). Finally, electronic dictionaries, thesauruses, and encyclopedias also open up new vistas in LD student written communication (Skinner, Gillespie, & Balkam, 1997).

TECHNOLOGY FOR GIFTED AND TALENTED STUDENTS

Gifted students can also benefit from advances in instructional technology, such as distance education. Stanford University, for instance, has been experimenting with providing year-round, accelerated instruction in mathematics and physics to gifted high school students through the Education Program for Gifted Youth (EPGY) (Ravaglia, Suppes, Stillinger, & Alper, 1995). In addition to digitized lectures and on-line quizzes, students in EPGY can contact the instructors via e-mail, telephone project staff, attend discussion sessions at Stanford, and try out various physics experiments at home. Given all these supports, it is not surprising that students have done exceedingly well in this program.

SPECIAL EDUCATION TECHNOLOGY RECOMMENDATIONS AND PROJECTIONS

According to guidelines that have been proposed for the proper use of technology in special education classes, technology programs and products should: (1) be intuitive and straightforward to learn, (2) allow alternative ways to present and access information, (3) contain uncluttered screen displays with few font types, (4) require minimal keyboarding skills, (5) provide adequate praise and clear feedback, (6) include opportunities to review concepts, (7) embed learner control adaptable to the nature and degree of the disability, (8) contain only graphic elements that contribute to the instructional function of the program, (9) challenge and pique learner interest, and (10) be reliable, cost justifiable, easily transported, and useful across contexts (Gray, 1991; Larsen, 1995; Lee, 1987; Raskind, 1993). Although the preceding factors are important, Steen Larsen (1995) notes that the most critical issues relate to the pedagogical decisions surrounding the use of these tools, not necessarily what technology to choose.

What does the future hold? As we head into the next century, the widening spectrum of available technology for students with special needs will undoubtedly be paralleled by significant cost reductions, thereby increasing the number of students who can benefit from instructional services offered in schools (Parette et al., 1993). Advances in robotics, artificial intelligence, speech recognition, and virtual reality are bound to affect the education of students with special needs. Certainly, voice-operated computers, for instance, will increasingly help both visually and physically impaired students in the near future (Messerer, 1997). Speech synthesis technology, too, is likely to increase in sophistication and create more demand and opportunity for talking books (Torgesen & Barker, 1995). Clearly, such technological advances will demand that a growing number of students and teachers become proficient in the use of computers and other technologies of instruction (Hauser & Malouf, 1996; Skinner, Gillespie, & Balkam, 1997). Unfortunately, most teaching professionals currently lack sufficient training or experience in assistive and instructional technologies to help students with special needs (Holder-Brown & Parette, 1992).

RESOURCES FOR FURTHER INVESTIGATION

■ Ability Grouping

Additional discussions of ability grouping and alternatives to it can be found in a number of books and journal articles. For a comprehensive treatment of this topic, look at Crossing the Tracks: How "Untracking" Can Save America's Schools (1992), by Anne Wheelock. In Part 1, Wheelock describes the nature of tracking; its origins, prevalence, and negative effects; and alternative methods of organizing classrooms for the purpose of instruction. Part 2 describes how to organize and teach heterogeneous classrooms. Wheelock covers many of the same topics in Alternatives to Tracking and Ability Grouping (1994), but in far fewer pages (77 versus 285). The November 1995 (Vol. 77, No. 3) issue of Phi Delta Kappan contains several articles on tracking and its effects. For teachers who are committed to whole class instruction, a useful source of ideas is Teaching the Whole Class (4th ed., 1997), by Betty Lou Leaver.

■ Texts on the Education of Exceptional Children

The following books provide general coverage of the education of exceptional children: *Exceptional Children and Youth* (1994), by Nancy Hunt and Kathleen Marshall; *Educating Exceptional Children* (8th ed., 1997), by Samuel Kirk, James Gallagher, and Nicholas Anastasiow; *Special Education: A Practical Approach for Teachers* (3d ed., 1995), by James Ysseldyke and Bob Algozzine.

A book that emphasizes general teaching techniques for students with special needs is *Teaching Students with Learning and Behavior Problems* (3d ed., 1997), by Diane Pedrotty Rivera and Deborah Deutsch Smith. Part 1 describes the IEP process and general teaching skills that all teachers of students with special needs should possess. Part 2 presents techniques for managing disruptive behavior and teaching appropriate social skills. Part 3 describes techniques for improving reading, writing, mathematics, and study skills.

■ Mainstreaming and Inclusion

In *Effective Teaching Strategies That Accommodate Diverse Learners* (1998), Edward Kameenui and Douglas Carnine illustrate how various subjects (such as reading, writing, mathematics, science, social studies) can be effectively taught to groups of students who vary in cultural background, social class, and learning ability. Each chapter on teaching a particular subject matter is organized around six instructional principles whose effectiveness has been supported by research: Big Ideas, Conspicuous Strategies, Mediated Scaffolding, Primed Background Knowledge, Strategic Integration, and Judicious Review. *Successful Inclusive Teaching: Proven Ways to Detect and Correct Special Needs* (2d ed., 1997), edited by Joyce S. Choate, is a comprehensive treatment of how to accommodate special needs students in the regular classroom. Part 1 covers the legal issues surrounding mainstreaming and inclusion, the characteristics of students with disabilities, and basic principles of inclusive instruction. Part 2 describes how to use those basic principles to teach reading comprehension, language skills, writing, arithmetic, mathematical problem solving, science, and social studies. Part 3 covers classroom management.

The December 1994/January 1995 and February 1996 issues of *Educational Leadership* are devoted to the pros and cons of inclusion and to ways of teaching students with special needs in the regular classroom.

On-line information on the Americans with Disabilities Act can be found at **http://www.public.iastate.edu/~sbilling/ada.html**. Edlaw, a national legal organization and publisher, supports a site that follows developments in IDEA and legal requirements for educators and administrators of special education programs. It can be found at **http://www.edlaw.net/**.

■ Teaching Students with Mental Retardation

Specialized techniques for teaching students with mental retardation can be found in *Strategies for Teaching Students with Mild to Severe Mental Retardation* (1993), edited by Robert Gable and Steven Warren; and *Mental Retardation* (4th ed., 1994), by Mary Beirne-Smith, James Patton, and Richard Ittenbach.

Two excellent on-line sources of information about mental retardation and other types of disabilities are (1) The Arc of the United States, a national organization on mental retardation (**http://The Arc.org/welcome.html**); and (2) The University of Kansas Special Education Department (**http://www.sped.ukans.edu/**). In particular, check the link on the University of Kansas site that is labeled Disabilities Resources.

■ Teaching Students with Learning Disabilities

The following books provide information about the nature of learning disabilities and how to teach students with learning disabilities: *Learning Disabilities; Theories, Diagnosis, and Teaching Strategies* (7th ed., 1997), by Janet Lerner; *Students with Learning Disabilities* (5th ed., 1997), by Cecil Mercer; and *Learning Disabilities: Characteristics, Identification, and Teaching Strategies* (3d ed., 1998), by William Bender. Information on the nature and teaching of students with attention deficits is offered by Janet Lerner, Barbara Lowenthal, and Sue Lerner (1995) in *Attention Deficit Disorders: Assessment and Teaching*.

■ Teaching Students with Behavior Disorders

Information on the nature of behavior disorders and on how the regular classroom teacher can deal with such students can be found in *Antisocial Behavior in School: Strategies and Best Practices* (1995), by Hill Walker, Geoff Colvin, and Elizabeth Ramsey; *Teaching Students with Behavior Disorders: Techniques and Activities for Classroom Instruction* (2d ed., 1995), by Patricia Gallagher; and *Strategies for Managing Behavior Problems in the Classroom* (3d ed., 1998), by Mary Margaret Kerr and C. Michael Nelson.

■ Teaching Gifted and Talented Learners

These books describe various techniques to use in instructing gifted and talented learners: *Handbook of Gifted Education* (2d ed., 1997), edited by Nicholas Colangelo and Gary Davis; *Curriculum Development and Teaching Strategies for Gifted Learners* (2d ed., 1996), by C. June Maker and Aleene B. Nielson; *Programs and Practices in Gifted Education* (1992), edited by Sandra Berger; and *Teaching the Gifted Child* (4th ed., 1994), by James Gallagher and Shelagh Gallagher.

SUMMARY

1. Three early attempts at dealing with student variability were age-graded classrooms, ability grouping, and special class placement. Age-graded classrooms grouped together students who were roughly the same age. Ability grouping sorted normal students into separate classes according to mental ability test scores. Special class placement was used to separate normal students from those with mental and physical disabilities.

2. Sixty percent of all elementary schools and about 80 percent of all middle and high schools use some form of ability grouping.

3. The four currently popular approaches to ability grouping are between-class ability grouping, regrouping, the Joplin Plan, and within-class ability grouping. In one form or another, ability grouping is widely practiced in the United States.

4. Ability grouping is based on the assumptions that intelligence is genetically determined, is reflected by an IQ score, and is unchangeable and that instruction is more effective with homogeneous groups of students.

5. There is no research support for between-class ability grouping and limited support for regrouping. Moderately positive results have been found for the Joplin Plan as well as within-class ability grouping.

6. Students in low ability groups often receive lower-quality instruction.

7. In light of research findings on ability grouping, educators may choose to discontinue the use of between-class ability grouping, use only within-class grouping and the Joplin Plan, or discontinue all forms of ability grouping.

8. The Education for All Handicapped Children Act (Public Law 94-142) was enacted in 1975 to ensure that students with disabling conditions receive the same free and appropriate education as nondisabled students. It was last revised in 1990 as PL 101-476, the Individuals with Disabilities Education Act (IDEA).

9. Major provisions of PL 101-476 include the right to a free and appropriate public education, an appropriate and valid preplacement evaluation, the development of an individualized education program, the education of students with disabilities in the least restrictive environment (also known as mainstreaming), and procedural safeguards.

10. In some school districts mainstreaming has been extended to the point where students with disabilities are taught only in regular classrooms by regular and special education teachers. This practice is known as inclusion, or full inclusion.

11. The evidence on inclusion, although somewhat limited and inconsistent, indicates that the practice produces at least moderate benefits for some students with disabilities but has little beneficial effect on others.

12. Inclusion is likely to work best for those students with disabilities for whom the regular classroom is an appropriate setting and in those classrooms where the teacher uses instructional methods that are proven to be effective with a wide variety of learners.

13. The regular classroom teacher's responsibilities under PL 101-476 may include participation in referral, assessment, preparation of the IEP, and implementation of the IEP.

14. Children with mild mental retardation are likely to be mainstreamed for some part of the school day and week. They are likely to have a low tolerance for frustration, to lack confidence and self-esteem, to oversimplify matters, and to have difficulty generalizing from one situation to another.

15. Students with learning disabilities account for more than half of all students with disabilities. They have a disorder in one or more of such basic psychological processes as perception, attention, memory, and metacognition, which leads to learning problems not attributable to other causes.

16. The true number of schoolchildren with serious emotional disturbance is unknown because of variation in identification procedures, vague definitions of emotional disturbance, and differences in interpretation of definitions.

17. Most classifications of disturbed behavior focus on aggressive behavior or withdrawn behavior.

18. Students who are gifted and talented excel in performing tasks that require intellectual, creative, artistic, or leadership ability.

19. Minorities are underrepresented in gifted and talented classes because standardized test scores are emphasized at the expense of other indices such as creativity, leadership, communication skill, critical-thinking ability, and persistence.

20. The academic needs of students who are gifted and talented are usually met through accelerated instruction, placement in classes or schools for the gifted and talented, or classroom enrichment activities. Special classes and schools typically produce moderate achievement benefits but can also produce declines in academic self-concept.

21. A variety of adaptive technologies exist to help students compensate for and/or remediate disabilities. These include closed captioning, word processing within networked computers, speech synthesis, voice recognition, screen magnifiers, special keyboards, writing tools, and distance education.

KEY TERMS

between-class ability grouping *(176)*
regrouping *(177)*
Joplin Plan *(177)*
within-class ability grouping *(177)*
individualized education program
  (IEP) *(181)*
least restrictive environment *(181)*

mainstreaming *(182)*
inclusion *(182)*
full inclusion *(182)*
multidisciplinary assessment
  team *(187)*
mental retardation *(189)*
learning disabilities *(194)*

attention-deficit/hyperactivity disorder
  (ADHD) *(195)*
emotional disturbance *(198)*
behavior disorder *(199)*
gifted and talented *(202)*
assistive technology *(207)*
electronic networking *(207)*

DISCUSSION QUESTIONS

1. You probably experienced ability grouping, in one form or another, at the elementary and secondary levels. Try to recall the ability grouping used in your schools. Think about whether it might have been between-class grouping, regrouping, the Joplin Plan, or within-class grouping. Could you tell which group you were in? Did you have feelings about being in that group? How did you feel about classmates who were in other groups? Do you think this practice aided or hindered your educational progress? Why? Given your own experiences as a student and what you have learned from this chapter, would you advocate or employ some form of ability grouping for your own students someday?

2. Many regular classroom teachers say that although they agree with the philosophy behind PL 101-476, they feel that their training has not adequately prepared them for meeting the needs of students with disabling conditions. Would you say the same about your teacher education program? Why? If you feel that your training is not adequately equipping you to teach students who are mentally retarded, learning disabled, or emotionally disturbed, what might you do to prepare yourself better?

3. Relatively little money is spent on programs for the gifted and talented compared to the amounts made available for the disabled. Defenders of this arrangement sometimes argue that since money for educational programs is always short, and since gifted students have a built-in advantage rather than a disability, we *should* invest most of our resources in programs and services for the disabled. Do you agree or disagree? Explain why.

Learning and Instruction

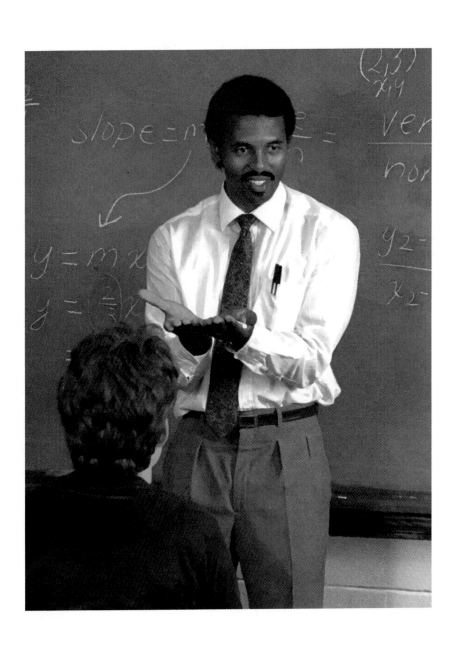

7 Behavioral and Social Learning Theories

Now that you are familiar with how students develop from preschool through high school, with some of the major ways in which students differ from one another, and with the main ways in which schools try to address student variability, it is time to examine what is perhaps the most fundamental and important aspect of schooling—the learning process. Since the primary reason why we have schools is to help children acquire the knowledge and skills that adults consider necessary for successful functioning in society, the instructional and curricular decisions that teachers make should be based on an understanding of how people learn. But as with most of the topics in this text, learning is a complex phenomenon that has been studied from different perspectives.

KEY POINTS

These key points will help you learn the important information in this chapter. To help you study, they also appear in the margins of the pages, next to the text where they are discussed.

Operant Conditioning

- Operant conditioning: voluntary response strengthened or weakened by consequences that follow

- Positive reinforcement: strengthen a target behavior by presenting a positive reinforcer after the behavior occurs

- Negative reinforcement: strengthen a target behavior by removing an aversive stimulus after the behavior occurs

- Punishment: weaken a target behavior by presenting an aversive stimulus after the behavior occurs

- Time-out: weaken a target behavior by temporarily removing a positive reinforcer after the behavior occurs

- Extinction: weaken a target behavior by ignoring it

- Spontaneous recovery: extinguished behaviors may reappear spontaneously

- Generalization: responding in similar ways to similar stimuli

- Discrimination: responding in different ways to similar stimuli

- Complex behaviors are shaped by reinforcing closer approximations to terminal behavior

- Fixed interval schedules: reinforce after regular time intervals

- Variable interval schedules: reinforce after random time intervals

- Fixed ratio schedules: reinforce after a set number of responses

- Variable ratio schedules: reinforce after a different number of responses each time

Educational Applications of Operant Conditioning Principles

- Programmed instruction: arrange material in small steps; reinforce correct responses

- CAI-taught students learn more with simulation programs than with drill-and-practice programs

- CAI works best for elementary grade students, low achievers, urban students

- Behavior modification: shape behavior by ignoring undesirable responses, reinforcing desirable responses

- Premack principle: required work first, then chosen reward

- Token economy is a flexible reinforcement system

- Contingency contracting: reinforcement supplied after student completes mutually agreed-on assignment

- Time-out works best with disruptive, aggressive children

- Punishment is likely to be ineffective because of temporary impact, side effects

Social Learning Theory

- People learn to inhibit or make responses by observing others

- Processes of observational learning: attention, retention, production, motivation

- Imitation is strengthened through direct reinforcement, vicarious reinforcement, self-reinforcement

- Self-efficacy: how capable one feels to handle particular kinds of tasks

- Self-efficacy influenced by past performance, persuasion, emotional reactions, observation of models

- Self-efficacy affects one's goals, thought processes, persistence, emotions

- Cognitive skills can be learned by observation of models

Using Computer-Assisted Instruction in Your Classroom

- Types of CAI programs: drill-and-practice, tutorial, problem solving, integrated learning systems

- Quality of CAI programs is generally poor

216

Since 1879, when the first laboratory devoted to the scientific study of human behavior was opened in Leipzig, Germany by Wilhelm Wundt, learning has been studied more extensively by more psychologists than any other aspect of human behavior. As a result, there are varied, seemingly conflicting, opinions about how teachers should arrange learning activities in classrooms. Such differences of opinion are not necessarily a problem since different theories and the approaches to teaching that flow from them complement, rather than compete with, one another. Think of these different theories as something like a jigsaw puzzle. To see the entire picture, you need to have all the pieces, and you need to know how to put them together. We hope that you will have some sense of how to do that by the end of this part.

This chapter is devoted to two theories of learning—a type of behavioral learning theory known as operant conditioning and social learning theory. Although different, they share certain assumptions about principles of learning. ■

Operant Conditioning

In 1913 with the publication of an article titled "Psychology as the Behaviorist Views It," the influential American psychologist John Watson argued that psychology would quickly lose credibility as a science if it focused on internal mental and emotional states that could not be directly observed or accurately measured. The solution was to study what could be directly observed and objectively and accurately measured—the external stimuli that people experienced and what people did in response. In a word, behavior. From this point until the late 1960s, behavioral theories of one sort or another dominated the psychology of learning and culminated in the work of B. F. Skinner.

BASIC NATURE AND ASSUMPTIONS

B. F. Skinner put together a theory that not only successfully combines many different ideas but also serves as the basis for a variety of applications to human behavior. Skinner's theory, **operant conditioning**, takes as its starting point that many of the voluntary responses of animals and humans are strengthened when they are reinforced (followed by a desirable consequence) and weakened when they are either ignored or punished. In this way organisms learn new behaviors and when to exhibit them and "unlearn" existing behaviors. The term *operant conditioning* refers to the fact that organisms learn to "operate" on their environment (make a particular response) in order to obtain or avoid a particular consequence. Some psychologists use the term *instrumental* since the behavior is instrumental in bringing about the consequence.

Most of the experiments on which the principles of operant conditioning are based involved an ingenious apparatus invented by Skinner and appropriately referred to as a Skinner box (see Figure 7.1). This is a small enclosure that contains only a bar (or lever) and a small tray. Outside the box is a hopper holding a supply of food pellets that are dropped into the tray when the bar is pressed under certain conditions.

A hungry rat is placed in the box, and when in the course of exploring its new environment, the rat approaches and then presses the bar, it is rewarded with a food pellet. The rat then presses the bar more frequently than it did before being rewarded. If food pellets are supplied under some conditions when the bar is pushed down—for example, when a tone is sounded—but not under others, the rat learns to discriminate one situation from the other, and the rate of bar pressing

Operant conditioning: voluntary response strengthened or weakened by consequences that follow

Figure 7.1 A Rat in a Skinner Box

The rat's behavior is reinforced with a food pellet when it presses the bar under conditions preselected by the experimenter. In the process of exploring the Skinner box, the rat is almost certain to touch the bar. When that occurs, the experimenter supplies a food pellet and bar-pressing behavior is reinforced. Eventually, the rat may be reinforced only when a particular sequence of actions (for example, pressing the bar five times in succession) is performed.

drops noticeably when the tone is not sounded. If a tone is sounded that is very close in frequency to the original tone, the rat generalizes (treats the two tones as equivalent) and presses the bar at the same rate for both. But if the food pellets are not given after the rat presses the bar, that behavior stops, or is extinguished.

The Skinner box's prominent role in operant conditioning experiments reflects Skinner's view of psychology as a natural science. One important assumption that underlies all natural sciences is that natural phenomena (such as weather patterns, earthquakes, and human behavior) may appear on the surface to be random but really operate according to set laws. What psychology needed, in Skinner's view, was the means by which a researcher could control the environment to observe the lawful and hence predictable influence of environmental factors on behavior.

A second assumption underlying Skinner's work is that a science develops most effectively when scientists study some phenomenon at its most simple, fundamental level. What is learned at this level can then be used to understand more complex processes.

A third assumption is that principles of learning that arise from experiments with animals *should* apply to humans. Note, however, the conditional phrasing of the last sentence. Although Skinner accepted the usefulness of animal research, he was always careful to point out that such principles needed to be tested again at the human level.

A fourth assumption is that a change in an organism's behavior pattern is the only basis for concluding that learning has occurred. Although admitting the existence of such internal processes as thoughts, motives, and emotions, Skinner had two objections to including them in his theoretical system. First, such processes have no place in the scientific study of learning since they cannot be directly observed or measured. Second, he believed that his experiments with rats in the Skinner box show that learning is caused not by internal processes but by the environmental consequences that follow behavior.

BASIC PRINCIPLES OF OPERANT CONDITIONING

To repeat the basic idea behind operant conditioning: all behaviors are accompanied by certain consequences, and these consequences strongly influence (some might say determine) whether these behaviors are repeated and at what level of intensity. In general, the consequences that follow behavior are either pleasant and desirable or unpleasant and aversive. Depending on conditions that we will discuss shortly, these consequences either increase (strengthen) or decrease (weaken) the likelihood that the preceding behavior will recur under the same or similar circumstances. When consequences strengthen a preceding behavior, *reinforcement* has taken place. When consequences weaken a preceding behavior, *punishment* and *extinction* have occurred. There are two forms of reinforcement and two forms of punishment. This section will describe both forms of reinforcement, both forms of punishment, extinction, and several related principles that can be applied to aspects of human learning.

POSITIVE REINFORCEMENT   Although the term *positive reinforcement* may be unfamiliar to you, the idea behind it probably is not. If you can recall spending more time studying for a certain subject because of a compliment from the teacher or a high grade on an examination, you have experienced positive reinforcement. Specifically, **positive reinforcement** involves strengthening a target behavior—that is, increasing and maintaining the probability that a particular behavior will be repeated—by presenting a stimulus (called a *positive reinforcer*) immediately after the behavior has occurred. Praise, recognition, and the opportunity for free play are positive reinforcers for many (but not all) students. The term *positive* as used by Skinner refers to the act of presenting a stimulus (think of positive as *adding* here); it does not refer to the pleasant nature of the stimulus itself. You will understand better why this distinction is very important as we consider the other form of reinforcement.

> **Positive reinforcement:
> strengthen a target behavior
> by presenting a positive
> reinforcer after the
> behavior occurs**

NEGATIVE REINFORCEMENT   People frequently have difficulty understanding the concept of negative reinforcement, most often confusing it with punishment,

Students are likely to be motivated to learn if they are positively reinforced for completing a project or task. Awards and praise from the teacher and one's peers are strong positive reinforcers for many students.

so we will examine it carefully here. The goal of **negative reinforcement** is the same as positive reinforcement—to *increase* the strength of a particular behavior. The method, however, is different. Instead of supplying a desirable stimulus, *one removes an unpleasant and aversive stimulus* whenever a target behavior is exhibited. As you study this definition, pay special attention to the removing action. Just as positive refers to adding, negative refers to the act of *removing* a stimulus. By removing something unwanted, you encourage the student to learn new behaviors.

> **Negative reinforcement: strengthen a target behavior by removing an aversive stimulus after the behavior occurs**

In everyday life negative reinforcement occurs quite frequently. A child picks up his clothes or toys to stop his parents' nagging. A driver uses a seat belt to stop the annoying buzzer sound. Later in the chapter we will describe how educators use negative reinforcement. We will also discuss its desirability relative to positive reinforcement.

PUNISHMENT   There are three procedures that reduce the likelihood of a particular behavior being repeated. The first is **punishment**, also known as Type I punishment, or presentation punishment. Punishment is defined by operant psychologists as the presentation of an aversive stimulus (such as scolding, paddling, ridiculing, or making a student write five hundred times "I will not chew gum in class") that reduces the frequency of a target behavior. From an operant perspective, you can claim to have punished someone else only if the target behavior is actually reduced in frequency. (Note that whether these methods of punishment do achieve their goal and are effective and whether they are ethical are other issues—ones that we will discuss later in this chapter.)

> **Punishment: weaken a target behavior by presenting an aversive stimulus after the behavior occurs**

Many people confuse negative reinforcement with punishment. Both involve the use of an aversive stimulus, but the effects of each are opposite. Remember that negative reinforcement strengthens a target behavior, whereas punishment weakens or eliminates a behavior.

TIME-OUT   The second procedure that decreases the frequency of or eliminates a target behavior is another form of punishment, called **time-out**. But instead of presenting an aversive stimulus, time-out *temporarily removes the opportunity to receive positive reinforcement*. (Time-out is sometimes called Type II punishment, or removal punishment.) For instance, a student who frequently disrupts classroom routine to get attention may be sent to sit in an empty room for five minutes. Removal from a reinforcing environment (as well as the angry tone of voice and facial expression that normally accompany the order to leave the classroom) is usually looked on as an aversive consequence by the individual being removed. An athlete who is suspended from competition is another example of this form of punishment.

> **Time-out: weaken a target behavior by temporarily removing a positive reinforcer after the behavior occurs**

EXTINCTION   A third consequence that weakens undesired behavior is extinction. **Extinction** occurs when a previously reinforced behavior decreases in frequency, and eventually ceases altogether, because reinforcement is withheld. Examples of extinction include a mother ignoring a whining child or a teacher ignoring a student who spontaneously answers a question without waiting to be called on. Both extinction and time-out are most effective when combined with other consequences, such as positive reinforcement. To help yourself define and remember the distinguishing characteristics of positive reinforcement, negative reinforcement, punishment, and extinction, study Table 7.1.

> **Extinction: weaken a target behavior by ignoring it**

SPONTANEOUS RECOVERY   When used alone, extinction is sometimes a slow and difficult means of decreasing the frequency of undesired behavior because ex-

Table 7.1	Conditions That Define Reinforcement, Punishment, and Extinction		
Type of Stimulus +	**Action +**	**Effect on Behavior =**	**Result**
Desirable	Present	Strengthen	Positive reinforcement
Aversive	Remove	Strengthen	Negative reinforcement
Aversive	Present	Weaken	Type I (presentation) punishment
Desirable	Remove	Weaken	Type II (removal) punishment (also called time-out)
Desirable	Withhold	Weaken	Extinction

Spontaneous recovery: extinguished behaviors may reappear spontaneously

tinguished behaviors occasionally reappear without having been reinforced (an occurrence known as **spontaneous recovery**). Under normal circumstances, however, the time between spontaneous recoveries lengthens, and the intensity of the recurring behavior becomes progressively weaker. If the behavior undergoing extinction is not terribly disruptive, and if the teacher (or parent, counselor, or supervisor) is willing to persevere, these episodes can sometimes be tolerated on the way to more complete extinction.

Generalization: responding in similar ways to similar stimuli

GENERALIZATION   When an individual learns to make a particular response to a particular stimulus and then makes the same or a similar response in a slightly different situation, **generalization** has occurred. For example, students who were positively reinforced for using effective study skills in history go on to use those same skills in chemistry, social studies, algebra, and so on. Or, to use a less encouraging illustration, students ignore or question a teacher's every request and direction because they have been reinforced for responding that way to their parents at home. The less similar the new stimulus is to the original, however, the less similar the response is likely to be.

Discrimination: responding in different ways to similar stimuli

DISCRIMINATION   When inappropriate generalizations occur, as in the preceding example, they can be essentially extinguished through discrimination training. Quite simply, in **discrimination** individuals learn to notice the unique aspects of seemingly similar situations (for example, that teachers are not parents, although both are adults) and to respond differently to each situation. Teachers can encourage this process by reinforcing only the desired behaviors (for instance, attention, obedience, and cooperation) and withholding reinforcement following undesired behaviors (such as inattention or disobedience).

SHAPING   Up to now, we have not distinguished relatively simple learned behaviors from more complex ones. A bit of reflection, however, should enable you to realize that many of the behaviors human beings learn (such as playing a sport or writing a term paper) are complex and are acquired gradually. The principle of **shaping** best explains how complex responses are learned.

Complex behaviors are shaped by reinforcing closer approximations to terminal behavior

In shaping, actions that move progressively closer to the desired *terminal behavior* (to use Skinner's term) are reinforced. Actions that do not represent closer approximations of the terminal behavior are ignored. The key to success is to take one step at a time. The movements must be gradual enough so that the person or animal becomes aware that each step in the sequence is essential. This process is typically called *reinforcing successive approximations to the terminal behavior*.

At least three factors can undermine the effectiveness of shaping. First, too much positive reinforcement for early, crude responses may reduce the learner's willingness to attempt a more complex response. Second, an expectation of too much progress too soon may decrease the likelihood of an appropriate response. If this results in a long period of nonreinforcement, what has been learned up to that point may be extinguished. For example, expecting a student to work industriously on a homework assignment for ninety minutes just after you have shaped forty-five minutes of appropriate homework behavior is probably too big a jump. If it is, the student may revert to her original level of performance owing to the lack of reinforcement. Third, delay in the reinforcement of the terminal behavior allows time for additional, unrelated behaviors to occur. When the reinforcement eventually occurs, it may strengthen one or more of the more recent behaviors rather than the terminal behavior.

SCHEDULES OF REINFORCEMENT

If you have been reading this section on basic principles carefully, you may have begun to wonder if the use of operant conditioning principles, particularly positive reinforcement, requires you to be present every time a desired response happens. If so, you might have some justifiable reservations about the practicality of this theory. The answer is yes, up to a point, but after that, no. As we have pointed out, when you are trying to get a new behavior established, especially if it is a complex behavior that requires shaping, learning proceeds best when every desired response is positively reinforced and every undesired response is ignored. This is known as a *continuous reinforcement* schedule.

Once the behavior has been learned, however, positive reinforcement can be employed on a noncontinuous, or intermittent, basis to perpetuate that behavior. There are four basic *intermittent reinforcement* schedules: fixed interval (FI), variable interval (VI), fixed ratio (FR), and variable ratio (VR). Each schedule produces a different pattern of behavior.

Fixed Interval Schedule

In this schedule, a learner is reinforced for the first desired response that occurs after a predetermined amount of time has elapsed (for example, five minutes, one hour, or seven days). Once the response has occurred and been reinforced, the next interval begins. Any desired behaviors that are made during an interval are ignored. The reinforced behavior occurs at a lower level during the early part of the interval and gradually rises as the time for reinforcement draws closer. Once the reinforcer is delivered, the relevant behavior declines in frequency and gradually rises toward the end of the next interval.

FI schedules of reinforcement occur in education when teachers schedule exams or projects at regular intervals. The grade or score is considered to be a reinforcer. As you are certainly aware, it is not unusual to see little studying or progress occur during the early part of the interval. However, several days before an exam or due date, the pace quickens considerably.

Variable Interval Schedule

If you would like to see a more consistent pattern of behavior, you might consider using a variable interval schedule. With a VI schedule, the length of time between reinforcements is essentially random but averages out to a predetermined interval. Thus, four successive reinforcements may occur at the following intervals: one week, four weeks, two weeks, five weeks. The average

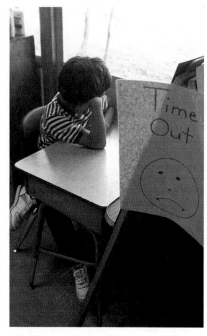

The time-out procedure recommended by behavior modification enthusiasts involves weakening an undesirable form of behavior (such as shoving on the playground) by temporarily removing positive reinforcement (by having the misbehaving student remain in a corner of the classroom for five minutes while the rest of the class continues to enjoy another activity).

Fixed interval schedules: reinforce after regular time intervals

Variable interval schedules: reinforce after random time intervals

interval is three weeks. Teachers who give surprise quizzes or who call on students to answer oral questions on the average of once every third day are invoking a variable interval schedule.

Fixed ratio schedules: reinforce after a set number of responses

Fixed Ratio Schedule.   Within this schedule, reinforcement is provided whenever a predetermined number of responses are made. A rat in a Skinner box may be reinforced with a food pellet whenever it presses a lever fifty times. A factory worker may earn $20 each time he assembles five electronic circuit boards. A teacher may reinforce a student with praise for every ten arithmetic problems correctly completed. FR schedules tend to produce high response rates since the faster the learner responds, the sooner the reinforcement is delivered. However, a relatively brief period of no or few responses occurs immediately after the reinforcer is delivered.

Variable ratio schedules: reinforce after a different number of responses each time

Variable Ratio Schedule.   Like a variable interval schedule, this schedule tends to eliminate irregularities in response rate, thereby producing a more consistent rate. This is accomplished through reinforcement after a different number of responses from one time to the next according to a predetermined average. If you decided to use a VR fifteen schedule, you might reinforce a desired behavior after twelve, seven, twenty-three, and eighteen occurrences, respectively (that is, after the twelfth, nineteenth, forty-second, and sixtieth desired behaviors). Because the occurrence of reinforcement is so unpredictable, learners tend to respond fairly rapidly for long periods of time. If you need proof, just watch people play the slot machines in Las Vegas.

Educational Applications of Operant Conditioning Principles

In the late 1940s when Skinner's daughter was in elementary school, he observed a number of instructional weaknesses that concerned him. These included the excessive use of aversive consequences to shape behavior (students studying to avoid a low grade or embarrassment in the classroom), an overly long interval between students taking tests or handing in homework and getting corrective feedback, and poorly organized lessons and workbooks that did not lead to specific goals. Skinner became convinced that if the principles of operant conditioning were systematically applied to education, all such weaknesses could be either reduced or eliminated.

That belief, which he then reiterated consistently until his death in 1990 (see, for example, Skinner, 1984), is based on four prescriptions that come straight from his laboratory research on operant conditioning: (1) be clear about what is to be taught, (2) teach first things first, (3) allow students to learn at their own rate, and (4) program the subject matter. This straightforward formulation became the basis for two educational applications: an approach to teaching that we now call computer-assisted instruction and a set of procedures for helping students learn appropriate classroom behaviors that is referred to as behavior modification. The next few sections will describe the nature of these applications and assess the extent to which they improve classroom learning.

COMPUTER-ASSISTED INSTRUCTION

THE PRECURSOR: SKINNER'S PROGRAMMED INSTRUCTION   The key idea behind Skinner's approach to teaching is that learning should be shaped. Programs of stimuli (material to be learned) and consequences should be designed to lead students step by step to a predetermined end result. In the mid-1950s Skinner turned this shaping approach into an innovation called **programmed instruction.**

When programmed materials were first made commercially available during the mid-1950s, they were designed to be presented to students in one of two ways: in book form or as part of mechanical teaching machines. The earliest teaching machines were simple mechanical devices. A program on a roll of paper was inserted in the machine, and the first statement or question was "framed" in a viewing window. (That is why the individual steps of a program are referred to as **frames**.) Today programmed instruction in book format is very uncommon, and the early mechanical teaching machines have been almost totally supplanted by the personal computer because computers can do everything the books or the machine could do—and far more.

Programmers begin developing a program by defining precisely what is to be learned (the terminal behavior). They then arrange facts, concepts, and principles in a logical sequence so that students will be adequately prepared for each frame, or numbered problem, when they reach it. Prompts are periodically provided to draw out the desired response, and the step size (the knowledge needed to go from frame to frame) is made small enough so that reinforcement occurs with optimal frequency. Feedback about the correctness of the response is given immediately, and students work through the program at their own pace.

> Programmed instruction: arrange material in small steps; reinforce correct responses

According to Skinner (1968, 1986), when programmed materials are well designed and appropriately used, they produce the following effects:

1. Reinforcement for the right answer is immediate.
2. The teacher can monitor each student's progress more closely.
3. Each student learns at his own rate, completing as many problems as possible within the allotted time.
4. Motivation stays high because of the high success level designed into the program.
5. Students can easily stop and begin at almost any point.
6. Learning a complex repertoire of knowledge proceeds efficiently.

DOES COMPUTER-ASSISTED INSTRUCTION AID LEARNING?   A teaching machine, either mechanical or electronic, is only as good as the instructional software program that runs it.[1] And as we point out on pages 245–246, high-quality instructional programs are the exception rather than the rule. With this caveat in mind, we now ask, How effective is **computer-assisted instruction (CAI)**, which is also known as computer-based instruction (CBI)? The answer to this question, like the answers to most of the questions posed in this book, is that it depends—in this

---

[1] In case you have never understood the terms *hardware* and *software* when used with reference to computers, *hardware* refers to the machine itself and other electronic devices, and *software* refers to the program language or instructions used to make the machine operate.

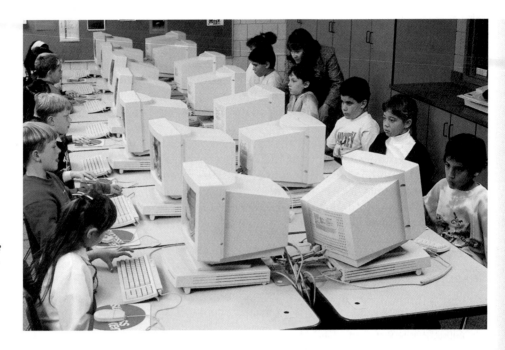

Computer-assisted instruction can help teachers shape new capabilities in students through the use of good quality drill-and-practice, tutorial, and simulation programs.

case, largely on the type of program with which students interact, the grade level of the students, and the ability level of the students.

In general, CAI-taught students have scored at about the 60th percentile on classroom achievement tests, while their conventionally taught (lecture/discussion/worksheets) peers have scored at the 50th percentile (Christmann, Badgett, & Lucking, 1997; Fletcher-Flinn & Gravatt, 1995). Researchers consider a difference of this magnitude to be relatively small.

CAI-taught students learn more with simulation programs than with drill-and-practice programs

CAI works best for elementary grade students, low achievers, urban students

The picture brightens considerably, however, when a more fine-grained analysis of the research is done. Compared to conventional instruction, CAI produces stronger effects for **simulation** programs (artificial environments that mimic the real world) than for **drill-and-practice programs** (Khalili & Shashaani, 1994), for elementary grade students than for middle school or high school students (Bangert-Drowns, Kulik, & Kulik, 1985; Kulik, Kulik, & Bangert-Drowns, 1985), for low-achieving students than for high-achieving students (Kulik, Kulik, & Bangert-Drowns, 1985; Bangert-Drowns, Kulik, & Kulik, 1985), for learning such complex cognitive skills as planning, problem solving, and reasoning than for learning subject matter (Liao, 1992), and for students who live in urban settings than for students who live in rural or suburban settings (Christmann, Lucking, & Badgett, 1997). For these comparisons, the advantage ranges from 18 to 28 percentile ranks.

These findings suggest that CAI, when properly designed and used, can effectively supplement a teacher's attempts to present, explain, apply, and reinforce knowledge and skills. The relatively high degree of structure inherent in CAI seems to be particularly helpful to low-achieving and younger students. These findings also reaffirm what was suggested in Chapter 1 about good teaching being partly an art and partly a science. Whenever you as a teacher apply any psychological principle in your classroom, you will need to ask yourself: For whom is this instructional technique likely to be beneficial? With what materials? For what outcome? As the options for using CAI expand, with more varied and complex programs available, the ability of teachers to answer these questions will become increasingly important.

BEHAVIOR MODIFICATION

Though applied in many ways, the term **behavior modification** basically refers to the use of operant conditioning techniques to (as the phrase indicates) modify behavior. Since those who use such techniques attempt to manage behavior by making rewards contingent on certain actions, the term *contingency management* is also sometimes used.

After Skinner and his followers had perfected techniques of operant conditioning in modifying the behavior of animals, they concluded that similar techniques could be used with humans. We will briefly discuss several techniques in this section that teachers may use to strengthen or weaken specific behaviors. Techniques applied in education to strengthen behaviors include shaping, token economies, and contingency contracts. Techniques that aim to weaken behaviors include extinction and punishment.

SHAPING   You may want to take a few minutes now to review our earlier explanation of shaping. Most attempts at shaping important classroom behaviors should include at least the following steps (Walker & Shea, 1999):

1. Select the target behavior.
2. Obtain reliable baseline data (that is, determine how often the target behavior occurs in the normal course of events).
3. Select potential reinforcers.
4. Reinforce successive approximations of the target behavior each time they occur.
5. Reinforce the newly established target behavior each time it occurs.
6. Reinforce the target behavior on a variable reinforcement schedule.

Behavior modification: shape behavior by ignoring undesirable responses, reinforcing desirable responses

To illustrate how shaping might be used, imagine that you are a third-grade teacher (or a middle or high school teacher) with a chronic problem: one of your students rarely completes more than a small percentage of the arithmetic (or algebra) problems on the worksheets you distribute in class, even though you know the student possesses the necessary skills. To begin, you decide that a reasonable goal would be for the student to complete at least 85 percent of the problems on a given worksheet. Next, you review the student's work for the past several weeks and determine that, on average, he completed only 25 percent of the problems per worksheet. Your next step is to select positive reinforcers that you know or suspect will work.

Reinforcers come in a variety of forms. Most elementary school teachers typically use such things as stickers, verbal praise, smiles, and classroom privileges (for example, feed the gerbil, clean the erasers). Middle school and high school teachers can use letter or numerical grades, material incentives (such as board games and computer games, as long as school policy and your financial resources allow it), and privately given verbal praise. With certain reservations, public forms of recognition can also be used. The reservations include the following: any public display of student work or presentation of awards should be made to several students at the same time (to avoid possible embarrassment among adolescents) (Emmer, Evertson, Clements, & Worsham, 1994); awards should be made without letter grades; and awards should be given with an awareness that public displays of recognition are not appropriate or comfortable for all cultures.

One popular shaping technique that has stood the test of time involves having students first list favorite activities on a card. Then they are told that they will be able to indulge in one of those activities for a stated period of time after they have completed a set of instructional objectives. This technique is sometimes called the **Premack principle** after psychologist David Premack (1959), who first proposed it. It is also called *Grandma's rule* since it is a variation of a technique that grandmothers have used for hundreds of years ("Finish your peas, and you can have dessert").

Once you have decided on a sequence of objectives and a method of reinforcement, you are ready to shape the target behavior. For example, you can start by reinforcing the student for completing five problems (25 percent) each day for several consecutive days. Then you reinforce the student for completing five problems and starting a sixth (a fixed ratio schedule). Then you reinforce the student for six completed problems and so on. Once the student consistently completes at least 85 percent of the problems, you provide reinforcement after every fifth worksheet on the average (a variable ratio schedule).

Although you control the classroom environment while students are in school, this accounts for only about half of their waking hours. Accordingly, parents might supplement your efforts at shaping behavior. The first step in a home-based reinforcement program is obtaining the parents' and student's formal agreement to participate. Then you typically send home a brief note or form on a regular basis (daily, weekly) indicating whether the student exhibited the desired behaviors. For example, in response to the items "Was prepared for class" and "Handed in homework," you would circle "yes" or "no." In response to a homework grade or test grade, you would circle the appropriate letter or percent correct designation. The parents are then responsible for providing the appropriate reinforcement or punishment (temporary loss of a privilege, for example). This procedure has been successful in both reducing disruptive classroom behavior and increasing academic performance (longer time on tasks and higher test scores, for example). Some studies suggest that it may not be necessary to target both areas, as improved academic performance often results in decreased disruptiveness (Kelley & Carper, 1988).

TOKEN ECONOMIES   A second technique used to strengthen behavior in the classroom, the **token economy**, was introduced first with people who had been hospitalized for emotional disturbances and then with students in special education classes. A token is something that has little or no inherent value but can be used to "purchase" things that do have inherent value. In society, money is our most ubiquitous token. Its value lies not in what it is made of but in what it can purchase—a car, a house, or a college education. By the same token (if you will excuse the pun), students can accumulate check marks, gold stars, or happy faces and "cash them in" at some later date for any of the reinforcers already mentioned.

One reason for the advent of the token economy approach was the limited flexibility of more commonly used reinforcers. Candies and cookies, for instance, tend to lose their reinforcing value fairly quickly when supplied continually. It is not always convenient to award free time or the opportunity to engage in a highly preferred activity immediately after a desired response. And social rewards may or may not be sufficiently reinforcing for some individuals. Tokens, however, can always be given immediately after a desirable behavior, can be awarded according to one of the four schedules mentioned earlier, and can be redeemed for reinforcers that have high reinforcing value.

Token economies are effective in reducing such disruptive classroom behaviors as talking out of turn, being out of one's seat, fighting, and being off task. They are also effective in improving academic performance in a variety of subject areas (Naughton & McLaughlin, 1995; Shook, LaBrie, Vallies, McLaughlin, & Williams,

---

Premack principle: required work first, then chosen reward

Token economy is a flexible reinforcement system

1990). Token economies have been used successfully with individual students, groups of students, entire classrooms, and even entire schools. Some studies have shown that awarding tokens for group efforts is at least as effective and possibly more effective than awarding them to individuals (McLaughlin & Williams, 1988). See the Case in Print on page 229 for an illustration of one token economy in action in a school system. Accordingly, token economies can be easily used in conjunction with the cooperative learning technique that was briefly mentioned in Chapter 5 and that will be described in detail in Chapter 10.

CONTINGENCY CONTRACTING　　A third technique teachers use to strengthen behavior is **contingency contracting**. A contingency contract is simply a more formal method of specifying desirable behaviors and consequent reinforcement. The contract, which can be written or verbal, is an agreement worked out by two people (teacher and student, parent and child, counselor and client) in which one person (student, child, client) agrees to behave in a mutually acceptable way, and the other person (teacher, parent, counselor) agrees to provide a mutually acceptable form of reinforcement. For example, a student may contract to sit quietly and work on a social studies assignment for thirty minutes. When the student is done, the teacher may reinforce the child with ten minutes of free time, a token, or a small toy.

> Contingency contracting: reinforcement supplied after student completes mutually agreed-on assignment

Contracts can be drawn up with all members of a class individually, with selected individual class members, or with the class as a whole. As with most contracts, provisions can be made for renegotiating the terms. Moreover, the technique is flexible enough to incorporate the previously discussed techniques of token economies and shaping. It is possible, for example, to draw up a contract that provides tokens for successive approximations to some target behavior (Bushrod, Williams, & McLaughlin, 1995).

EXTINCTION, TIME-OUT, AND RESPONSE COST　　The primary goal of behavior modification is to strengthen desired behaviors. Toward that end, techniques such as shaping, token economies, and contingency contracts are likely to be very useful. There will be times, however, when you have to weaken or eliminate undesired behaviors because they interfere with instruction and learning. For these occasions, you might consider some form of extinction. The most straightforward approach is to simply ignore the undesired response. If a student bids for your attention by clowning around, for instance, you may discourage repetition of that sort of behavior by ignoring it. It is possible, however, that classmates will not ignore the behavior but laugh at it. Such response-strengthening reactions from classmates will likely counteract your lack of reinforcement. Accordingly, you need to observe what happens when you try to extinguish behavior by not responding.

If other students are reinforcing a youngster's undesired behavior, you may want to apply the time-out procedure briefly discussed earlier. Suppose a physically active third-grade boy seems unable to keep himself from shoving classmates during recess. If verbal requests, reminders, or warnings fail to limit shoving, the boy can be required to take a five-minute time-out period immediately after he shoves a classmate. He must sit alone in the classroom for that period of time while the rest of the class remains out on the playground. Time-out appears to be most effective when it is used with aggressive, group-oriented children who want the attention of the teacher and their peers (Walker & Shea, 1999). The rules for the procedure should be clearly explained, and after being sentenced to time-out (which should last no more than five minutes), a child should be given reinforcement for

> Time-out works best with disruptive, aggressive children

Learning Is a Rewarding Experience for Some Students

Token economies are effective in reducing such disruptive behaviors as talking out of turn, being out of one's seat, fighting, and being off task. They are also effective in improving academic performance in a variety of subject areas. Token economies have been used successfully with individual students, groups of students, entire classrooms, and even entire schools. (p. 227)

STUDYING'S REWARDS
SACHA PFEIFFER
Boston Globe 1/3/96

NEWTON—Life, David Morris will tell you, is all about incentive.

Give him a scenario, be it the classroom or in the workplace, and the 18-year-old Newton North High School senior will give you an example of a society motivated by the prospect of gain—a better school, a better job, a better income.

Now, in a program designed by Morris, honor roll students at Newton North have an additional enticement: a coupon book containing more than $300 worth of gifts tailored to the teen-age appetite.

The book offers more than mere discounts and buy-one, get-one-free offers. Bearers are entitled to such things as free pizzas, ice cream, bagels, car washes, movie rentals, beeper services, health club visits and limousine rentals.

"All around us, there are different types of incentives, whether they are varsity letters or merit scholarships," said Morris, who, perhaps not surprisingly, is bound for the University of Pennsylvania's Wharton School of Business next fall. "So why not reward those students who think academics are important?"

The ultimate reward of the program, dubbed the Newton North High School Honor Roll Card Coupon Book, is a scholarship fund for college-bound seniors created by a $200 mandatory contribution from participating businesses.

The dual membership requirement for merchants presented a tough challenge to Morris and his small but growing sales staff.

"Most stores would immediately say, 'Wait, you want me to give money and a discount?'" recalled junior Noam Schimmel, who will run the program next year. "Their usual response was, 'Hi, thanks for calling, but that's a lot of money.'"

But hard work pays off, as the program's motto proclaims, and 50 merchants from Newton and beyond eventually agreed to participate. Collectively, those businesses made a $10,000 infusion to the fund last year—more than half of which was given to academically eligible, financially needy students.

The program, now entering its fourth grading period, weathered its share of criticism before getting off the ground.

"We had to ask ourselves if we were selling grades," said high school principal V. James Marini, echoing the concerns of educators who believe academic achievement should not be a material pursuit.

But recalling a discussion he had with Morris, Marini said the entrepreneurial student countered that young people are always told hard work will yield rewards. "How can you argue with that?" the principal said.

By the accounts of students, teachers and administrators, the program has been a roaring success, and may be a factor motivating some of Newton North's 1,800 high schoolers to study that extra hour. The school experienced a 37 percent jump in the number of seniors named to the honor roll last grading period, and a 21 percent increase among juniors.

The coupon book "definitely entices kids to want to succeed," said junior Daniel Steinberg. "If you give kids the book and say, 'Here, take this as a sign of your accomplishment,' you give them a better reason to feel better about themselves."

Even senior Josh Newman, who says he was skeptical that the book would catch on among students, now calls himself a coupon convert.

"I never thought it would work and I didn't think kids would even come pick the books up," admitted Newman, who said he has friends who raised their grades to become part of the program. "But the free stuff is great . . . and a larger amount of kids are trying harder in school because of it."

And, Morris boasts, not a penny of school or scholarship money was spent to run the program. All goods and services, from display easels to adhesive tapes, were donated. . . .

Student Schimmel says he is confident the program will continue with the same success when he takes it over next year.

"This program is a community-wide acknowledgment of academic achievement and educational excellence," said Schimmel. "It's an innovative way of saying, 'Thank you, good job.' And kids realize that beyond the little slice of pizza they got, there's something to perseverance and working hard."

Questions and Activities

1. Although the coupon book program had been in operation for only three grading periods at the time the article was written, it appeared to be quite successful. Do you think reinforcement programs like this one are likely to be successful over an extended period of time? Why or why not?

2. Students are typically given reinforcers by teachers in school-based token economies. Is there any reason that the behavior of teachers and administrators should not be reinforced by students when the occasion warrants? What might be the advantages (and disadvantages) of a token economy that runs in both directions?

3. The principal in this article is portrayed as being initially hesitant to implement the coupon book incentive program as it might have been perceived by some as the equivalent of bribing students to learn. But the student who created the program argued that it should be tried since adults constantly tell young people that if they work hard and succeed, they will be rewarded by society. These two views suggest that the token economy has potential advantages and disadvantages as a way to motivate students to learn. Based on the material in the chapter and your own experiences, write down as many advantages and disadvantages as you can think of.

agreeable, helpful behavior—for example, "Thank you for collecting all the playground balls so nicely, Tommy."

Another technique, **response cost**, is similar to time-out in that it involves the removal of a stimulus. It is often used with a token economy. With this procedure, a certain amount of positive reinforcement (for example, 5 percent of previously earned tokens) is withdrawn every time a child makes an undesired response. Anyone who has been caught exceeding the speed limit and been fined at least $50 can probably attest to the power of response cost as a modifier of behavior.

PUNISHMENT   Punishment is one of the most common behavior modification techniques, particularly when it takes the form of corporal punishment. It is also one of the most controversial. At the present time corporal punishment has been banned in twenty-seven states either by state law or by state department of education regulation (Evans & Richardson, 1995). The remaining twenty-three states either explicitly permit schools to physically punish students or are silent on the matter. In states that allow corporal punishment, local school districts may regulate, but not prohibit, its use. Where states have not addressed the issue, local districts may regulate the use of corporal punishment or ban it altogether.

Although corporal punishment is actually fairly widely used in classrooms where it is permitted, considerable laboratory evidence, collected from human and animal subjects, suggests that it is likely to be ineffective in modifying behavior. The following reasons are typically cited:

1. Mild punishment (which is the kind usually applied) does not permanently eliminate undesirable behaviors. At best, it suppresses them temporarily.

2. Punished behaviors may continue to occur when the punisher is not present.

3. Punishment may actually increase the strength of undesirable behavior. Many teachers assume that a public reprimand is aversive. But for some students, teacher and peer attention, regardless of the form it takes, acts as a positive reinforcer and thus tends to increase behaviors the teacher seeks to eliminate.

4. Punishment may produce undesirable emotional side effects. Just as a shocked rat comes to fear a Skinner box, punished children may perceive the teacher

> Punishment is likely to be ineffective because of temporary impact, side effects

and the school as objects to fear and avoid. The result is truancy, tardiness, and high levels of anxiety, all of which impair the ability to learn.

5. Punishers model a type of behavior (physical aggression) that they do not want students to exhibit.

6. To be effective, punishment must often be severe and must occur immediately after an undesirable response. Legal, ethical, and moral restrictions do not allow severe punishment.

SHOULD YOU USE BEHAVIOR MODIFICATION? This may seem a strange question to ask given the number of pages we have just spent covering behavior modification methods. Obviously, we feel that the results of decades of research on these techniques justify their use by teachers. Nevertheless, there are criticisms of behavior modification that are not adequately addressed by research findings and that you should carefully consider.

One criticism is that many students, including those in the primary grades, will eventually catch onto the fact that they get reinforced only when they do what the teacher wants them to do. Some may resent this and misbehave out of spite. Others may weigh the amount of effort required to earn a favorable comment or a privilege and decide the reinforcer isn't worth the trouble. Still others may develop a "What's in it for me?" attitude. That is, some students may come to think of learning as something they do only to earn an immediate reinforcer. The potential danger of using behavior modification over an extended period of time is that learning may come to an abrupt halt when no one is around to supply reinforcement (Kohn, 1993). (This point will be addressed by the next theory to be examined, social learning theory.)

A second major criticism is that behavior modification methods, because of their potential power, may lend themselves to inappropriate or even unethical uses. For example, teachers may shape students to be quiet and obedient because it makes their job easier, even though such behaviors do not always produce optimum conditions for learning.

In response to these criticisms, Skinner and other behavioral scientists (see Chance, 1993, for example) argue that if we do not systematically use what we know about the effects of stimuli and consequences on behavior, we will leave things to chance. In an uncontrolled situation some fortunate individuals will have a favorable chain of experiences that will equip them with desirable attitudes and skills, but others will suffer an unfortunate series of experiences that will lead to difficulties and disappointment. In a controlled situation it may be possible to arrange experiences so that almost everyone acquires desirable traits and abilities. What behavioral psychologists seem to be saying is that educators could be accused of being unethical for not making use of an effective learning tool. The challenge, of course, is to use it wisely.

Despite the popularity of operant conditioning among many American psychologists, a number of researchers, beginning in the 1940s, were eager to study types of human behavior that could not be readily explained in terms of principles of operant conditioning. They shared the desire of Skinner and his followers to study behavior as objectively as possible, but they wanted to analyze human behavior in social settings—to see how children acquire acceptable forms of social behavior (or become socialized). Together, these researchers contributed to the development of a set of ideas about human learning that borrowed from operant conditioning but was different from it as well. These ideas came to be called social learning theory.

Social Learning Theory

Albert Bandura, the acknowledged spokesperson for the social learning theory point of view, presents what is generally considered to be the definitive exposition of this theory in *Social Foundations of Thought and Action: A Social Cognitive Theory* (1986). In essence, **social learning theory** deemphasizes the role of reinforcement in learning by attributing initial changes in behavior to the observation and imitation of a model (which explains why social learning is also called **observational learning**).

In the sections that follow we will discuss some of the main features of Bandura's social learning theory and examine some of the research it has spawned. First, we will describe the various ways in which observational learning occurs: inhibition, disinhibition, facilitation, and true observational learning. Following this, we will describe the four processes that underlie observational learning: attention, retention, production, and motivation.

TYPES OF OBSERVATIONAL LEARNING EFFECTS

INHIBITION   In many instances we learn not to do something that we already know how to do because a model we are observing refrains from behaving, is punished for behaving, or does something different from what we intended to do. Consider the following example: a ten-year-old is taken to her first symphony concert by her parents. After the first movement of Beethoven's Fifth Symphony, she is about to applaud but notices that her parents are sitting quietly with their hands in their laps. She does the same.

DISINHIBITION   On occasion we learn to exhibit a behavior that is usually disapproved of by most people because a model does the same without being punished.

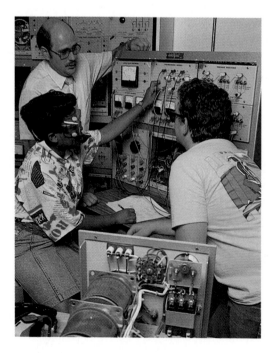

When teaching students a potentially dangerous skill, it is particularly important to remember the principles of observational learning noted by Bandura: make sure everyone is paying attention, have each student give a "dry run" demonstration, have students reproduce the correct procedures, and provide reinforcement for correct performance.

For example, a student attends his school's final football game of the season. As time expires, thousands of students run onto the field and begin tearing up pieces of turf to take home as a souvenir. Noticing that the police do nothing, the student joins in.

People learn to inhibit or make responses by observing others

FACILITATION   This effect occurs whenever we are prompted to do something that we do not ordinarily do because of insufficient motivation rather than social disapproval. For example, a college student attends a lecture on reforming the American education system. Impressed by the lecturer's enthusiasm and ideas, the student vigorously applauds at the end of the presentation. As several members of the audience stand and applaud, so does the student.

TRUE OBSERVATIONAL LEARNING   This effect occurs when we learn a new behavior pattern by watching and imitating the performance of someone else. A teenage girl learning how to hit a topspin forehand in tennis by watching her instructor do the same is an example of observational learning. The four processes that make this form of learning possible will be discussed next.

PROCESSES IN OBSERVATIONAL LEARNING

ATTENTION   Clearly, if learning is observational, paying attention to a model's behavior is a critical first step. What factors, then, affect the willingness of a child to observe and mimic the behavior of a model? The most important factor seems to be the degree of similarity between the model and the observer. On the basis of an extensive review and analysis of previous research, Dale Schunk (1987) drew the following conclusions about the effect of observer-model similarity on observational learning:

1. When children are concerned about the appropriateness of a behavior, or when they have self-doubts about their capabilities, they are more likely to model a peer than an older child or adult.

2. Age similarity seems less important for the learning of skills, rules, and novel responses than does the competence of the model. When children question the competence of peers, they tend to model the behavior of adults.

3. Children learn academic skills from models of either sex, but they are more apt to perform behaviors displayed by models whom they believe are good examples of their gender role.

4. Children who have a negative self-concept, or who have had learning problems in the past, are more likely to imitate a peer who exhibits some initial learning difficulties and overcomes them (a coping model) than a peer who performs flawlessly (a mastery model). Improvements in self-concept and achievement are more likely to occur in response to coping models than to master models.

RETENTION   Once we have noticed a model's behavior with the intention of imitating it, we must encode that behavior in memory. Encoding may encompass just the observed behaviors, or it may also include an explanation of why, how, and when something is done. In the case of behavior, the encoding may be visual (that is, mental pictures) and/or verbal. In the case of behavioral rules, the encoding will likely be in terms of verbal propositions. The benefit of encoding behavioral rules is the ability to generalize the response. Modeled behaviors may be unitary, terminal behaviors (for example, working on a problem until it is solved), or they may be components of a complex behavior (such as striking a golf ball with a golf club). Once the behavior has been modeled, the observer should have several opportunities to engage in overt and/or covert rehearsal.

PRODUCTION   Bandura divides production into (1) selecting and organizing the response elements, and (2) refining the response on the basis of informative feedback. The smooth operation of the production process is based on the assumption that the necessary response elements have been previously acquired (for example, gripping a golf club, addressing the ball, executing the swing, following through).

MOTIVATION   Like Skinner, Bandura acknowledges the motivational value of reinforcement and incorporates it into his theory. Unlike Skinner, however, Bandura thinks of reinforcement in broader terms. As a result, he talks about direct reinforcement, vicarious reinforcement, and self-reinforcement.

> Processes of observational learning: attention, retention, production, motivation

As part of observational learning, **direct reinforcement** occurs when an individual watches a model perform, imitates that behavior, and is reinforced (or punished) by the model or some other individual. A primary grade student, for example, may be told by the teacher to observe how a fellow student cleans up his desk at the end of the day. If that behavior is imitated, the teacher will praise the child. **Vicarious reinforcement** refers to a situation in which the observer anticipates receiving a reward for behaving in a given way because someone else has been so rewarded. A middle school student, for example, who observes that a classmate is praised by the teacher for completing an assignment promptly may strive to work quickly and diligently on the next assignment in anticipation of receiving similar praise. **Self-reinforcement** refers to a situation in which the individual strives to meet personal standards and does not depend on or care about the reactions of others. A high school student may strive to become as skillful as a classmate at word processing primarily because of an internal desire to prove that she can master that skill.

> Imitation is strengthened through direct reinforcement, vicarious reinforcement, self-reinforcement

THE EFFECT OF SELF-EFFICACY ON OBSERVATIONAL LEARNING AND BEHAVIOR

Unlike self-concept, which we described in Chapter 3 as the *overall*, or *global*, picture that people have of themselves, *self-efficacy* refers to how capable or prepared we believe we are for handling *particular* kinds of tasks (Bandura 1982, 1986, 1989). For example, a student may have a high level of self-efficacy for mathematical reasoning—a feeling that she can master any math task that she might encounter in a particular course—but have a low level of self-efficacy for critical analysis of English literature. There are at least two reasons for Bandura's interest (and for general interest as well) in this phenomenon: (1) an individual's level of self-efficacy can be influenced by several factors, one of which is observing the behavior of a model, and (2) self-efficacy appears to strongly affect a variety of behaviors.

> Self-efficacy: how capable one feels to handle particular kinds of tasks

FACTORS THAT AFFECT SELF-EFFICACY   One obvious way in which we develop a sense of what we can and cannot do in various areas is by thinking about how well we have performed in the past on a given task or a set of closely related tasks. If, for example, my friends are always reluctant to have me on their team for neighborhood baseball games, and if I strike out or ground out far more often than I hit safely, I will probably conclude that I just don't have whatever skills it takes to be a competitive baseball player. Conversely, if my personal history of performance in school is one of mostly grades of A and of consistently being among the top ten students, my sense of academic self-efficacy is likely to be quite high.

A second source of influence mentioned by Bandura—verbal persuasion—is also fairly obvious. We frequently try to convince a child, student, relative, spouse, friend, or coworker that he has the ability to perform some task at a creditable level, and he in turn frequently tries to convince us of the same thing. Perhaps you can recall feeling somewhat more confident about your ability to handle some task (like college classes) after having several family members and friends express their confidence in your ability.

A third source of influence is more subtle. It is the emotions we feel as we prepare to engage in a task. Individuals with low self-efficacy for science may become anxious, fearful, or restless prior to attending chemistry class or to taking an exam in physics. Those with high self-efficacy may feel assured, comfortable, and eager to display what they have learned. Some individuals are acutely aware of these emotional states and infer from them high or low capabilities for performing specific tasks.

Finally, our sense of self-efficacy may be influenced by observing the successes and failures of individuals with whom we identify—what Bandura refers to as vicarious experience. If I take note of the fact that a sibling or neighborhood friend who is like me in many respects but is a year older has successfully adjusted to high school, I may feel more optimistic about my own adjustment the following year.

> **Self-efficacy influenced by past performance, persuasion, emotional reactions, observation of models**

TYPES OF BEHAVIORS THAT ARE AFFECTED BY SELF-EFFICACY   Bandura has identified four types of behaviors that are at least partly influenced by an individual's level of self-efficacy: the goals and activities in which the person chooses to engage, the kind of thought processes she uses, how hard and how long she strives to achieve a goal, and the kinds of emotional reactions she experiences when she takes on certain tasks.

Individuals with a strong sense of self-efficacy, particularly if it extends over several areas, are more likely than others to consider a variety of goals and participate in a variety of activities. They may, for example, think about a wide range of career options, explore several majors while in college, take a variety of courses, participate in different sporting activities, engage in different types of social activities, and have a wide circle of friends.

One way in which the thinking of high self-efficacy individuals differs from that of their low self-efficacy peers is in their tendency to use higher-level thought processes (such as analysis, synthesis, and evaluation) to solve complex problems. Thus, in preparing a classroom report or a paper, low self-efficacy students may do little more than repeat a set of facts found in various sources (because of their belief that they are not capable of more), whereas high self-efficacy individuals discuss similarities and differences, inconsistencies and contradictions, and make evaluations about the validity and usefulness of the information they have found. Another difference is that high self-efficacy people are more likely to visualize themselves being successful at some challenging task, whereas low self-efficacy individuals are more likely to imagine disaster. This leads to differences in the next category of behaviors—motivation.

> **Self-efficacy affects one's goals, thought processes, persistence, emotions**

Those who rate their capabilities as higher than average can be expected to work harder and longer to achieve a goal than those who feel less capable. This difference should be particularly noticeable when individuals experience frustrations (poor-quality instruction, for example), problems (coursework being more difficult than anticipated), and setbacks (a serious illness). When faced with a challenging task, the high self-efficacy individual is more likely to experience excitement, curiosity, and an eagerness to get started rather than the sense of anxiety, depression, and impending disaster that many low self-efficacy individuals feel.

RESEARCH ON SOCIAL LEARNING THEORY

The research that has been stimulated by social learning theory supports Bandura's basic view that we can and do learn many types of behaviors by watching what other people do and the consequences they experience. In this section we will summarize several studies that, taken together, illustrate the wide range of this form of learning.

EFFECTS OF MODELING ON AGGRESSION   The essential principles of social learning theory as described by Bandura can be illustrated by a series of three classic experiments he carried out in the 1960s. In the first experiment (Bandura, Ross, & Ross, 1961), a child was seated at a table and encouraged to play with a toy. The model sat at a nearby table and either played quietly with Tinker Toys for ten minutes or played with the Tinker Toys for a minute and then played aggressively with an inflatable clown "Bobo" doll for several minutes, punching, kicking, and sitting on it and hitting it with a hammer. In a subsequent, structured play situation, children who did not observe a model as well as those who observed a nonaggressive model displayed little aggression. By contrast, children exposed to the aggressive model behaved with considerably more aggression toward the Bobo doll and other toys.

The second study (Bandura, Ross, & Ross, 1963a) obtained similar results in response to children viewing a film of either an adult or an adult dressed as a cartoon character engaging in aggressive behavior. The third study (Bandura, Ross, & Ross, 1963b) attempted to determine how rewarding the model for aggressive behavior would affect children's imitative behavior. In general, children were more aggressive after they saw an aggressive model positively rewarded than when the model was punished. These studies, as you may have realized, illustrate the disinhibition effect described earlier.

These three studies stimulated hundreds of other investigations of the same type, particularly because of the implication that viewing aggressive behavior in a film or television program would lead to violence. Reviews of this research, such as those by T. H. A. van der Voort (1986), have found that exposure to repeated scenes of violence *can* engender violent behavior if the right set of conditions is in place. These conditions include the nature of the television program being watched (if the violent behavior is realistic and appears to be justified by the circumstances), the characteristics of the individual child (some children are more aggressive than others), the child's family, the child's neighborhood, and the reactions of others who are watching the program with the child.

EFFECTS OF MODELING ON THE LEARNING OF COGNITIVE SKILLS   Since the main focus of classroom life is the learning of various cognitive skills, researchers interested in social learning theory began to wonder if cognitive skills could be learned through modeling and if such modeling would produce higher levels of achievement. A study by Dale Schunk (1981) provides an answer. Schunk arranged for nine-, ten-, and eleven-year-old children who had done poorly in math to receive one of two types of instruction. Children in the modeling condition received written materials that explained how to solve long-division problems, and they observed an adult model. While solving a series of problems, the model verbalized the underlying cognitive operations (such as estimating the quotient and multiplying the quotient by the divisor). The children then practiced what they had observed, with the

Cognitive skills can be learned by observation of models

researchers providing corrective modeling for any operations the youngsters failed to grasp. Children in the nonmodeling condition received the same written materials, which they studied on their own. When comprehension problems arose, these children were told to review the relevant section of the written instructions. In comparison to pretest scores, both treatments enhanced persistence, self-confidence, and accuracy of performance. The modeling condition, however, produced greater gains in accuracy than did the nonmodeling condition. (For more about how modeling aids the learning of cognitive skills, see Schunk and Zimmerman, 1997.)

Another illustration of how students learn what their teachers model (and do not learn what they do not model) was offered by Diane Miller (1993). She described a middle school math teacher who was upset because his students did not use such terms as *numerator* and *denominator* in their writings about fractions. Instead, they substituted the phrases *the number on the top* and *the number on the bottom*. But when the teacher was observed reviewing a unit on fractions, he never used the terms *numerator* and *denominator*. When asked after class why he had avoided using these two terms, he said that he thought he had used them and was quite surprised to learn otherwise.

EFFECTS OF MODELING ON SELF-EFFICACY Dale Schunk and Antoinette Hanson (1989) confirmed Bandura's contention that an individual's self-efficacy can be enhanced by watching a competent model. Nine- to twelve-year-old children whose math achievement was below the 35th percentile on a standardized test watched a videotape of a similar child receiving instruction in how to do subtraction with regrouping problems (i.e., borrowing) and then solving similar problems. In comparison to a group of similar children who saw a videotape of a teacher solving subtraction with regrouping problems and a group that did not see a model, those who saw a peer model had significantly higher self-efficacy ratings.

Now that you are familiar with operant conditioning and social learning theory, it is time to examine several Suggestions for Teaching derived from the principles and research findings that have just been discussed.

SUGGESTIONS FOR TEACHING IN YOUR CLASSROOM

Applying Behavioral Learning Theory and Social Learning Theory in the Classroom

1 Remain aware that behavior is the result of particular conditions.

2 Use reinforcement, and use it appropriately to strengthen behaviors you want to encourage.

3 Take advantage of knowledge about the impact of different reinforcement schedules to encourage persistent and permanent learning.

a. When students first attempt a new kind of learning, supply frequent reinforcement. Then supply rewards less often.

b. If you want to encourage periodic spurts of activity, use a fixed interval schedule of reinforcement.

4 Give students opportunities to make overt responses, and provide prompt feedback.

a. Require students to make frequent, overt, and relevant responses.

b. Provide feedback so that correct responses will be reinforced and students will become aware of and correct errors.

5 When students must struggle to concentrate on material that is not intrinsically interesting, use special forms of reinforcement to motivate them to persevere.

a. Select, with student assistance, a variety of reinforcers.

b. Establish, in consultation with individual students, an initial contract of work to be performed to earn a particular reward.

c. Once the initial reward is earned, establish a series of short contracts leading to frequent, immediate rewards.

6 Remember the basic processes of observational learning and make effective use of observation and imitation.

1 Remain aware that behavior is the result of particular conditions.

Unlike the controlled environment of a Skinner box, many causes of behavior in a real-life classroom may not be observable or traceable. You might as well accept the fact, therefore, that quite often you are going to be a haphazard shaper of behavior. Nevertheless, there will be times when you and your students may benefit if you say to yourself, "Now, there have to be some causes for that behavior. Can I figure out what they are and do something about changing things for the better? Am I doing something that is leading to types of behavior that are making life difficult for some or all of us in the room?" When you are engaging in such speculations, keep in mind that reinforcement strengthens behavior. And check to see if you are inadvertently rewarding students for misbehavior (by calling attention to them, for example, or failing to reinforce those who engage in desirable forms of behavior).

Journal Entry
Checking on Causes of Behavior

EXAMPLES

■ If you become aware that it takes a long time for your students to settle down at the beginning of a period and that you are reacting by addressing critical remarks specifically to those who dawdle the longest, ignore the dawdlers, and respond positively to those who are ready to get to work.

■ Let's say that you have given students thirty minutes to finish an assignment. To your dismay, few of them get to work until almost the end of the period, and you find that you have to do a lot of nagging to hold down gossip and horseplay. When you later analyze why this happened, you conclude that you actually encouraged the time-killing behavior because of the way you set up the lesson. The next time you give a similar assignment, tell the students that as soon as they complete it, they can have class time to work on homework, a term project, or the equivalent and that you will be available to give help or advice to those who want it.

2 Use reinforcement, and use it appropriately to strengthen behaviors you want to encourage.

Why would we remind you to do something as obvious as reinforce behaviors you want students to acquire and exhibit in the future? Wouldn't you do that almost automatically? Well, we certainly hope so, but statistics suggest otherwise. A large team of researchers headed by John Goodlad (1984) observed the classroom behavior of 1,350 teachers and 17,163 students in thirty-eight schools from seven sections of the country. What they found may surprise you. Teachers' praise of student work occurred about 2 percent of the observed time in the primary grades and about 1 percent of the time in high school.

Once you have resolved to reinforce desired behavior systematically, you need to be sure that you do it appropriately. Although reinforcement is a simple princi-

One of the basic principles of instruction derived from operant conditioning experiments is that teachers should provide elementary grade students with immediate reinforcement for correct responses.

ple that can be readily understood at an intuitive level, it has to be used in the right way to produce desired results. Paul Chance (1992) offers seven guidelines for the effective use of positive reinforcement:

Journal Entry
Ways to Supply
Reinforcement

- Use the weakest reward available to strengthen a behavior. In other words, don't use material rewards when you know that praise will be just as effective a reinforcer. Save the material rewards for that special behavior for which praise or other reinforcers may not be effective.

- When possible, avoid using rewards as incentives. What Chance means is don't get into the habit of automatically telling the student that if she does what you want, you will provide a specific reward. Instead, sometimes ask the student to do something (like work quietly or help another student), and then provide the reinforcer.

- Reward at a high rate in the early stages of learning and reduce the frequency of rewards as learning progresses.

- Reward only the behavior you want repeated. Although you may not realize it, students are often very sensitive to what is and is not being reinforced. If you decide that one way to encourage students to be more creative in their writing is to tell them not to worry about spelling and grammar errors, then don't be surprised to see many misspelled words and poorly constructed sentences. Or if you decide to reward only the three highest scorers on a test, reasoning that competition brings out the best in people, be prepared to deal with the fact that competition also brings out some of the worst in people (like cheating and refusing to help others).

- Remember that what is an effective reinforcer for one student may not be for another. For some students, comments such as "Very interesting point," "That's right," or "That was a big help" will strengthen the target behavior. But for others, something less overt, such as smiling encouragingly, may be just right.

- Set standards so that success is a realistic possibility for each student. Because classrooms are becoming increasingly diverse, you may have students whose English proficiency is limited or who have disabilities related to learning and intellectual functioning. One way to deal with such diversity is to reward students for making steady progress from whatever their baseline level of performance was at the beginning of the term.

- An often-mentioned goal of teachers is to have students become intrinsically motivated or to take personal pride and satisfaction in simply doing something well. You can use natural instructional opportunities to point this out— for example, explore with students how satisfying it is to write a clear and interesting story as they are writing.

3 **Take advantage of knowledge about the impact of different reinforcement schedules to encourage persistent and permanent learning.**

a. When students first attempt a new kind of learning, supply frequent reinforcement. Then supply rewards less often.

Keep in mind the impact of different schedules of reinforcement so that you can use the same techniques of reinforcement effectively in your classroom. For example, when students first try a new skill or type of learning, praise almost any genuine attempt, even though it may be inept. Then as they become more skillful, reserve your praise only for especially good performances. Avoid a set pattern of commenting on student work. Make favorable remarks at unpredictable intervals.

b. If you want to encourage periodic spurts of activity, use a fixed interval schedule of reinforcement.

Occasionally, you will want to encourage students to engage in spurts of activity since steady output might be too demanding or fatiguing. In such cases supply reinforcement at specified periods of time. For example, when students are engaging in strenuous or concentrated activity, circulate and provide praise and encouragement by following a set pattern that will bring you in contact with each student at predictable intervals.

4 **Give students opportunities to make overt responses, and provide prompt feedback.**

a. Require students to make frequent, overt, and relevant responses.

The tendency of teachers is to talk and to do so for large chunks of time. Those who advocate a programmed approach to teaching recommend that teachers limit the amount of information and explanation they give to students and substitute opportunities for students to overtly respond. In addition, the responses should be directly related to the objectives. If your objectives emphasize the application of concepts and principles, then most of the responses students are asked to make should be about applications. The reason for this suggestion is that the delivery of corrective feedback and other forms of positive reinforcement can be increased when students make frequent responses, thereby accelerating the process of shaping.

EXAMPLES

- Instead of lecturing for twenty to thirty minutes at a time about the development of science and technology in the twentieth century, present information in smaller chunks, perhaps eight to ten minutes at a time, and then ask students to describe how an everyday product or service grew out of a particular scientific principle.

- Periodically ask students to summarize the main points of the material you presented over the last several minutes.

Journal Entry
Ways to Supply Immediate Feedback

b. Provide feedback so that correct responses will be reinforced and students will become aware of and correct errors.

Research clearly shows that students who study material about a topic, answer a set of questions about that material, and are then told whether their responses are correct and why, score significantly higher on a subsequent test of that material than do students who receive no feedback. The difference was about three-fourths of a standard deviation, meaning that the average student who received no feedback scored at the 50th percentile whereas the average student who received feedback scored at the 77th percentile. Here are a couple of examples of how you can provide timely and useful feedback to students (Bangert-Drowns, Kulik, Kulik, & Morgan, 1991).

EXAMPLES

- Immediately after students read a chapter in a text, give them an informal quiz on the key points you listed. Then have them pair off, exchange quizzes, and correct and discuss them.

- As soon as you complete a lecture or demonstration, ask individual students to volunteer to read to the rest of the class what they wrote about the points they were told to look for. Indicate whether the answer is correct; and if it is incorrect or incomplete, ask (in a relaxed and nonthreatening way) for additional comments. Direct students to amend and revise their notes as they listen to the responses.

5 **When students must struggle to concentrate on material that is not intrinsically interesting, use special forms of reinforcement to motivate them to persevere.**

Journal Entry
Ways to Encourage Perseverance

For a variety of reasons, some students may have an extraordinarily difficult time concentrating on almost anything. And, as we all know, to master almost any skill or subject, we have to engage in a certain amount of tedious effort. Accordingly, you may sometimes find it essential to use techniques of behavior modification to help students stick to a task. If and when that time comes, you might follow these procedures.

a. Select, with student assistance, a variety of reinforcers.

A behavior modification approach to motivation appears to work most successfully when students are aware of and eager to earn a payoff. Because students react differently to rewards and because any reward is likely to lose effectiveness if used to excess, it is desirable to list several kinds of rewards and permit students to choose. Some behavior modification enthusiasts (for example, Walker & Shea, 1999) even recommend that you make up a *reinforcement preference list* for each student. If you allow your students to prepare individual reinforcement menus themselves, they should be instructed to list school activities they really enjoy doing. It would be wise, however, to stress that entrées on anyone's menu must be approved by you so that they will not conflict with school regulations or interfere with the rights of others. A student's reward menu might include activities such as these: read a book of one's choice, work on an art of craft project, or view a videotape in another room. A reinforcement menu can be used in conjunction with Grandma's rule (the Premack principle). Set up learning situations, particularly those that are not intrinsically appealing, by telling students that as soon as they finish their broccoli (for example, doing a series of multiplication problems), they can have a chocolate sundae (an item from their reinforcement menu).

b. Establish, in consultation with individual students, an initial contract of work to be performed to earn a particular reward.

Once you have established a list of payoffs, you might consult with students (on an individual basis, if possible) to establish a certain amount of work that must be completed for students to obtain a reward selected from the menu. Refer to Chapter 10 for Robert Mager's suggestions for preparing specific objectives. To ensure that students will earn the reward, the first contract should not be too demanding. For example, it might be something as simple as "successfully spell at least seven out of ten words on a list of previously misspelled words," or "correctly answer at least six out of ten questions about the content of a textbook chapter."

c. Once the initial reward is earned, establish a series of short contracts leading to frequent, immediate rewards.

The results of many operant conditioning experiments suggest that the frequency of reinforcement is of greater significance than the amount of reinforcement. Therefore, having students work on brief contracts that lead to frequent payoffs immediately after the task is completed is preferable to having them work toward a delayed, king-sized award.

6 Remember the basic processes of observational learning and make effective use of observation and imitation.

You can enhance learning of skills and promote desirable kinds of behavior if you take into account the four basic processes of observational learning: attention, retention, production, and motivation. If you plan to demonstrate the correct way to perform some skill or process, first make sure you have the attention of everyone in the class. (Techniques for securing attention will be discussed in the analysis of information processing in Chapter 8.) Then, after explaining what you are going to do (perhaps noting particular points students should look for), demonstrate. Immediately after you demonstrate, have all the students in the class try out the new skill to foster retention. Or, for complex skills, have them write down the steps to follow before they try the activity on their own. Finally, arrange for all the students to get feedback and experience satisfaction and/or reinforcement immediately after they imitate your behavior by proving to themselves that they can carry out the activity on their own.

Journal Entry
Modeling Desirable Behaviors

EXAMPLES

■ Show primary grade students how to solve multiplication problems by first placing a large, colorful poster on a bulletin board with a diagram of the process. Explain the diagram and then demonstrate how to solve some simple problems. As soon as you finish, hand out a worksheet containing several simple problems similar to those you just demonstrated.

- Have students work on the problems for a specified period of time and then secure their attention once again and demonstrate on the board the correct procedure for solving each problem. Have students correct their own papers as you demonstrate, point out that they now know how to do multiplication problems, and praise them for learning the skill so rapidly.

- In a high school business class, follow a similar procedure when showing students how to set up a word processor to type a form letter. Make sure everyone is paying attention. Demonstrate the correct procedure. Have students write down the steps they should follow to imitate your actions. Have them study the steps before setting up their own word processor. Have them reproduce the letter. Provide reinforcement to supplement their own satisfaction in having completed the task successfully.

- Select low-achieving students who have mastered a skill to demonstrate the skill to other low-achieving students.

- A final point to remember about observational learning is that, in the lower grades particularly, you will be an admired model your students will be inclined to imitate. If you are well organized and businesslike, but also thoughtful and considerate, your students may act that way themselves.

Using Computer-Assisted Instruction in Your Classroom

We mentioned earlier that under the right conditions computers can effectively supplement classroom instruction. If you are now thinking that you might like to use CAI in your own classroom, there are a few additional things you need to know before you get started. You should know something about the types of programs that exist, their general quality, and how you can identify the best available programs.

USES OF COMPUTERS

Perhaps the most general distinction that can be made about the use of computers in schools is *learning about computers* versus *learning with computers*. The first approach, used primarily at the high school level, emphasizes two things: understanding how computers work and learning how to use computers for such everyday purposes as word processing, data analysis, production of graphic material, and information organization. This "computer as a learning tool" (Taylor, 1980) approach is more typical of the cognitive approach to computers that is covered in the next chapter. The second approach, "computer as tutor" (Taylor, 1980), which is found in CAI software, aligns well with behavioral theory since it has students use the computer and instructional programs in fairly controlled conditions to master typical school subject matter (such distinctions in the use of computers will be discussed further in Chapter 10).

Types of CAI programs: drill and practice, tutorial, problem solving, integrated learning systems

CAI is typically found at the elementary and middle school levels (Hassett, 1984) and relies on one or more of the following types of programs: drill-and-practice, tutorials, and simulations and games. Such approaches may also be combined in more elaborate software packages called **integrated learning systems (ILS)**, which provide sequenced, self-paced learning, enrichment, and remediation activities in many different content areas. Table 7.2 notes the purpose and main features of drill-and-practice programs, tutorials, and simulations and games.

Table 7.2	Major Types of CAI Programs	
Type of Program	**Purpose**	**Main Features***
Drill and Practice	Practice knowledge and skills learned earlier to produce fast and accurate responses	• Presents many problems, questions, and exercises. • Checks answers and provides feedback. • Provides cues when student is not sure of correct responses. • Keeps track of errors. • Adjusts difficulty level of problems and questions to the proficiency level of the student.
Tutorial	Teach new information (e.g., facts, definitions, concepts) and skills	• New material presented in either linear or branching format. • Linear programs require all students to begin with first frame and work through subsequent frames in given sequence. Incorrect responses minimized by brief answers, small steps, and frequent prompts. • Branching programs allow students to respond to different sets of frames depending on correctness of responses. For incorrect responses, program provides supplementary material that attempts to reteach. • Dialogue programs mimic teacher-student interactions by presenting material, evaluating responses, and adjusting subsequent instruction by presenting either more difficult or easier material.
Problem-Solving Programs: Simulations and Games	Teach new information and skills and provide an opportunity to apply what was learned in a meaningful context that would otherwise be unavailable because of cost, physical danger, and time constraints	• Student uses newly learned and existing information to solve a realistic problem. • Settings may be realistic (e.g., piloting a plane), historical/adventure (e.g., guiding a wagon train across the Oregon Trail), or imaginary (e.g., colonizing a new world). • Students practice creating and testing hypotheses on effects of different variables on achieving a goal.

*Not all programs contain all of the listed features.

SOURCES: Grabe & Grabe (1998); Neill & Neill (1993).

Roy Clariana (1996) notes that integrated learning systems are now used in about 11 percent of all school districts and account for about 50 percent of all technology-related expenditures by schools. Such systems present information in a more sequenced and comprehensive fashion than traditional CAI programs. Integrated learning systems can, in fact, cover the content for an entire K-8 mathematics curriculum. They also allow students to go through tutorials at their own pace, track student progress across grade levels, and present students with appropriate remediation or enrichment activities.

Clariana's (1996) study of the impact of an ILS on the mathematics achievement of fifth graders produced more favorable results for concept learning than for computations and applications. This is an especially interesting finding, since CAI programs have been criticized for some time for not teaching concepts.

PROGRAM QUALITY

After the teacher, the most important elements in CAI are clearly the programs themselves. The quality of software your students use is more important than how much information the classroom computer can store, how many disk drives it has, how many columns of characters it can display on its screen, and so on.

Quality of CAI programs is generally poor

The unfortunate reality of educational software is that the not-so-good programs significantly outnumber the excellent ones. Why are good programs in such short supply? One reason is because their development requires a set of capabilities that are difficult to find in one person or among a small group of people. However, in recent years several large developers of educational software have successfully produced high-quality programs by including programmers, instructional designers, teachers, and students as members of their development teams.

Another reason that good CAI programs are in short supply is that a crucial step in the development process—the field test—is often eliminated. Even though a new program may have been revised several times by its author and reviewed by a panel of experts, its instructional effectiveness is still essentially unknown. The best way to identify and eliminate problems of design clarity, confusing steps or sequences, improper feedback, busy screens, overwhelming gimmicks, and so on, is to try the program out on a representative group of students. Although a field test strikes people as so obviously necessary that they just assume it is a standard part of instructional software development, it may not be. The use of field testing is one criterion to look for when you select an instructional program, and most developers will provide you with information on their testing process.

The importance of integrating learning principles into the design of instructional programs has been discussed by Julie Vargas (1986). She finds that poor-quality programs often overlook such basic operant conditioning principles as offering maximum opportunities for active responding, providing immediate feedback, and shaping behavior. Some drill-and-practice programs, for example, incorporate into their lessons a variety of attention-getting features (such as familiar tunes, trains that puff across the screen, or animal characters that make facial expressions) in an attempt to keep the student interested and motivated. But the more often these features are used, the greater time students spend watching them rather than practicing skills. As a result, it takes longer for basic cognitive skills (such as adding or multiplying numbers or recognizing and spelling words) to become automatic. Even worse, students may become distracted altogether from the goal of the drill if the motivational features are too numerous and compelling. It is also crucial to integrate learning principles in the use of programs. For instance, tutorials and simulations often put students in an environment that requires them to experiment or explore, and the teacher must be prepared to act as a guide to this learning, to provide prompts, and to model approaches to solving the problems found in the simulation. To help you evaluate the quality of instructional software you may one day want to use in your classroom, a checklist devised by Julie Vargas appears in Table 7.3.

Of course, publications and annual software guides can also help you in your software decisions. For example, you might obtain *Only the Best: Annual Guide to Highest-Rated Software* (1993), by Shirley Boes Neill and George Neill, or *The Latest and Best of TESS: The Educational Software Selector* (1993), by the Educational Products Information Exchange Institute (EPIE), a nonprofit organization. Such publications review software by subject matter and also evaluate particular features (for example, animation, sound, tutorials, etc.). Be sure to consult such guides when

Table 7.3	Eight Points to Consider When Choosing a CAI Program

1. Does the software require a high frequency of responding (as opposed to screens of material to read)? For tutorials and drills, how many problems does a student actually do in a 10-minute session?

2. Is the responding relevant to your goals? (Do students do what they are to learn?)

3. Do students have to respond to the critical parts of the problems?

4. Is most of the screen content necessary for the response, or does the program assume that students will learn content without having to respond overtly to it?

5. Does the screen ask students to discriminate between at least two responses?

6. Can students see their progress as they work with the program from day to day or session to session?

7. Are students mostly successful going through the program (as opposed to becoming frustrated)? Do they enjoy using the program?

8. For series, or lessons to be used repeatedly, does the program adjust according to the performance level or progress of the student?

SOURCE: Vargas (1986).

in the position of making software recommendations or decisions in your school as well as your home.

Before leaving this topic, a final cautionary note about all forms of computer-based instruction is in order. As enthusiastic as you and others may be about the potential of CAI, recognize that it cannot substitute or compensate for poor-quality classroom teaching. There is a set of skills all teachers need to master in order to integrate computers successfully in a classroom. As we noted in Chapter 1, and as Larry Cuban (1986) points out in a provocative book about the relationship between teachers and machines, successful teaching often depends on the ability of a live teacher to establish a positive emotional climate (by communicating interest, excitement, expectations, and caring), to monitor student actions and reactions (by "reading" students' verbal and nonverbal communications), and to orchestrate the sequence and pace of instructional events (by making additions, deletions, and modifications in lesson plans). If one thinks of the computer as simply another tool to work with, then each type of computer program—drills, tutorials, simulations, integrated learning systems—requires teachers to plan learning activities, interact with students, provide encouragement and feedback, and design assessments. Although acquiring these skills may be a challenge, many teachers feel that being able to give their students meaningful access to such powerful learning tools is a significant reward (Grabe & Grabe, 1998).

RESOURCES FOR FURTHER INVESTIGATION

■ B. F. Skinner

In three highly readable volumes: *Particulars of My Life* (1976), *The Shaping of a Behaviorist* (1979), and *A Matter of Consequences* (1983), B. F. Skinner describes his interests, aspirations, triumphs, and failures; the people and events that led him into psychology; and the forces that led him to devise operant conditioning.

A highly readable summary and critical analysis of Skinner's brand of operant conditioning can be found in Robert Nye, *What Is B. F. Skinner Really Saying?* (1979). According to Nye, "Two major thoughts accompanied the writing of this book: a growing sense of the importance of Skinner's work and the awareness that his ideas are often misjudged" (p. 4).

The Technology of Teaching (1968) is Skinner's most concise and application-oriented discussion of operant conditioning techniques related to pedagogy.

In *Walden Two* (1948), Skinner describes his conception of a utopia based on the application of science to human behavior. To get the full impact of the novel and of Skinner's ideas, you should read the entire book. However, if you cannot read the whole book at this time, Chapters 12 through 17, which describe the approach to child rearing and education at Walden Two, may be of special interest to you as a future teacher.

■ Behavior Modification

If the possibilities of behavior modification seem attractive, you may wish to examine issues of the journals *Behavior Modification*, *Behavior Research and Therapy*, *Child Behavior Therapy*, *Journal of Applied Behavior Analysis*, and *Journal of Behavioral Education*. If you browse through the education and psychology sections of your college bookstore, you are likely to find a number of books on behavior modification. Or you might look for these titles in the library: *Classroom Management for Elementary Teachers* (4th ed., 1997), by Carolyn Evertson, Edmund Emmer, Barbara Clements, and Murray Worsham; *Classroom Management for Secondary Teachers* (4th ed., 1997), by Edmund Emmer, Carolyn Evertson, Barbara Clements, and Murray Worsham; *Achieving Educational Excellence: Using Behavioral Strategies* (1986), by Beth Sulzer-Azaroff and G. Roy Mayer; and *Making It Till Friday: A Guide to Successful Classroom Management* (4th ed., 1989), by James Long, Virginia Frye, and Elizabeth Long. And, as the title suggests, *Beyond Behavior Modification: A Cognitive-Behavioral Approach to Behavior Management in the School* (3d ed., 1995), by Joseph Kaplan, goes beyond the typical behavior modification book. It includes chapters on assessing the classroom and school environment and teaching students how to use self-management, social, and stress-management skills.

■ Software Programs to Explore

The following are a few software programs whose excellence is generally recognized. They cover the range of drills, tutorials, simulations, and games.

Operation: Frog (Scholastic): allows students to simulate the dissection of a frog, complete with full graphics and video. Students can also "rebuild" the frog to practice locating its organs.

MathMagic (MindPlay Methods): offers an addition/subtraction drill program with an arcade game format, appropriate for elementary school students.

Oregon Trail (MECC): enables students to experience the journey from Independence, Missouri, to Oregon as the pioneers did in 1865. Students are responsible for stocking a wagon, avoiding obstacles on the trail, making decisions about how to cross rivers and catch food, and so forth.

SimCity, SimLife, SimAnt, and SimTower (Maxis): allow students to control a large number of variables in complex simulations. The simulations are challenging, but the extensive tutorials and touch of humor in the programs reduce the risk of frustration. Excellent for group work.

Where in the World Is Carmen Sandiego? (Broderbund): requires students to interpret clues, put new or known facts (such as the location of cities) to use, and problem solve creatively.

■ Internet Site for Social Learning

If you would like to pursue further information and materials relating to social learning, the Oregon Social Learning Center can be found at **www.oslc.org:80/**.

SUMMARY

1. Operant conditioning is a theory of learning devised by B. F. Skinner. It focuses on how voluntary behaviors are strengthened (made more likely to occur in the future) or weakened by the consequences that follow them.

2. Operant conditioning assumes that human behavior is a natural phenomenon that can be explained by a set of general laws, that the best way to understand complex behaviors is to analyze and study the components that make them up, that the results of animal learning studies are potentially useful in understanding human learning, and that learning is the ability to exhibit a new behavior pattern.

3. Basic learning principles that derive from Skinner's work are positive reinforcement, negative reinforcement, punishment (Type I, or presentation punishment), time-out (Type II, or removal punishment), extinction, spontaneous recovery, generalization, and discrimination.

4. Positive reinforcement and negative reinforcement strengthen behaviors. Punishment, time-out, and extinction weaken target behaviors.

5. Complex behaviors can be learned by the reinforcement of successive approximations to the terminal (final) behavior and by the ignoring of nonapproximate behaviors, a process called shaping.

6. Once a new behavior is well established, it can be maintained at that level by the supplying of reinforcement on an intermittent schedule. The four basic schedules are fixed interval, variable interval, fixed ratio, and variable ratio.

7. Skinner's interest in educational applications of operant conditioning grew out of his disappointment with the quality of instruction his daughter was receiving in public school.

8. One of the first educational applications of operant conditioning principles was programmed instruction. It involves presenting written material in small steps according to a predetermined sequence, prompting the correct response, and presenting positive reinforcement in the form of knowledge of results.

9. In recent years programmed materials have been designed for presentation by computer, an innovation generally referred to as computer-assisted instruction.

10. CAI has its strongest effect on simulation programs, elementary grade students, low-achieving students, urban students, and learning complex cognitive skills.

11. CAI can be an effective supplement to regular classroom instruction, when it is used appropriately.

12. Another application of operant conditioning principles is behavior modification. The goal of behavior modification is for the teacher to help students learn desirable behaviors by ignoring or punishing undesired behaviors and reinforcing desired ones. Techniques for achieving this goal include shaping, token economies, contingency contracts, extinction, and punishment.

13. Social learning theory, which was devised largely by Albert Bandura, explains how individuals learn by observing a model (who may or may not be reinforced for the behavior involved) and imitating the model's behavior.

14. The processes involved in social learning (also called observational learning) are attention, retention, production, and motivation (reinforcement). The reinforcement can come from observing someone else (direct), from anticipating that one will be treated as the model was (vicarious), or from meeting personal standards (self-reinforcement).

15. Self-efficacy refers to how capable people believe they are for handling a particular task.

16. An individual's sense of self-efficacy is likely to be affected by a combination of past performance, persuasive comments from others, emotional reactions about an imminent task, and observation of the behavior of models judged to be similar to the individual.

17. Self-efficacy can affect an individual's choice of goals and activities, thought processes, willingness to persist at difficult tasks, and emotional reactions.

18. Research suggests that many social behaviors, such as aggression, may be learned by imitation of a model. Many academic-related behaviors, such as persistence, self-confidence, cognitive skills, and self-efficacy, can also be learned by observing and imitating a model.

19. Computer-assisted instruction occurs mostly in the elementary and middle school grades.

20. The main types of CAI programs are drill and practice, tutorial, simulation, and integrated learning systems.

21. The quality of CAI programs is generally poor, making it imperative that teachers be aware of sources that offer informed evaluations of software.

KEY TERMS

operant conditioning *(217)*	shaping *(221)*	token economy *(227)*
positive reinforcement *(219)*	programmed instruction *(224)*	contingency contracting *(228)*
negative reinforcement *(220)*	frames *(224)*	response cost *(230)*
punishment *(220)*	computer-assisted instruction	social learning theory *(232)*
time-out *(220)*	(CAI) *(224)*	observational learning *(232)*
extinction *(220)*	simulation *(225)*	direct reinforcement *(234)*
spontaneous recovery *(221)*	drill-and-practice programs *(225)*	vicarious reinforcement *(234)*
generalization *(221)*	behavior modification *(226)*	self-reinforcement *(234)*
discrimination *(221)*	Premack principle *(227)*	integrated learning systems (ILS) *(243)*

DISCUSSION QUESTIONS

1. The theory of operant conditioning holds that we learn to respond or not respond to certain stimuli because our responses are followed by desirable or aversive consequences. How many of your own behaviors can you explain in this fashion? Why, for example, are you reading this book and answering these questions?

2. Many educators have a negative attitude toward operant conditioning because they feel it presents a cold, dehumanizing picture of human learning and ignores the role of such factors as free will, motives, and creativity. Did you feel this way as you read through the chapter? Do you think positive attributes of operant conditioning balance out possible negative aspects of the theory?

3. Skinner has argued that society too frequently uses aversive means to shape desired behavior (particularly punishment) rather than the more effective positive reinforcement. As you think about how your behavior has been shaped by your parents, teachers, friends, supervisors at work, law enforcement officials, and so on, would you agree or disagree with Skinner's observation? Can you think of some possible reasons we tend to use punishment more frequently than positive reinforcement?

4. Can you recall a teacher whom you admired so much that you imitated some aspects of her behavior (if not immediately, then sometime later)? What was it about this teacher that caused you to behave in the same way? How might you have the same effect on your students?

8 Information-Processing Theory

In the previous chapter we noted that operant conditioning emphasizes the role of external factors in learning. Behavioral psychologists focus on the nature of a stimulus to which a student is exposed, the response that the student makes, and the consequences that follow the response. They see no reason to speculate about what takes place in the student's mind before and after the response. The extensive Suggestions for Teaching in Your Classroom presented at the end of the chapter on behavioral learning theories serve as evidence that conclusions and principles based on analyses of external stimuli, observable responses, and observable consequences can be of considerable value to teachers.

But cognitive psychologists, meaning those who study how the mind works and influences be-

KEY POINTS

These key points will help you learn the important information in this chapter. To help you study, they also appear in the margins of pages, next to the text where they are discussed.

The Information-Processing View of Learning

- Information processing: how humans attend to, recognize, transform, store, retrieve information

A Model of Information Processing

- Sensory register: stimuli held briefly for possible processing
- Recognition: noting key features and relating them to stored information
- Attention: focusing on a portion of currently available information
- Information in long-term memory influences what we attend to
- Short-term memory: about seven bits of information held for about twenty seconds

- Maintenance rehearsal: hold information for immediate use
- Elaborative rehearsal: use stored information to aid learning
- Organizing material reduces number of chunks, provides recall cues
- Meaningful learning occurs when organized material is associated with stored knowledge
- Long-term memory: permanent storehouse of unlimited capacity
- Information in long-term memory organized as schemata
- Students remember much of what they learn in school, especially if mastery and active learning are emphasized

Metacognition

- Metacognition: our own knowledge of how we think
- Insight into one's learning processes improves with age

Helping Students Become Strategic Learners

- Strategy: plan to achieve a long-term goal

- Tactic: specific technique that helps achieve long-term goal
- Rote rehearsal not a very effective memory tactic
- Acronym: word made from first letters of items to be learned
- Acrostic: sentence made up of words derived from first letters of items to be learned
- Loci method: visualize items to be learned stored in specific locations
- Keyword method: visually link pronunciation of foreign word to English translation
- Mnemonic devices meaningfully organize information, provide retrieval cues
- Self-questioning improves comprehension, knowledge integration
- Taking notes and reviewing notes aid retention and comprehension
- Learning strategy components: metacognition, analysis, planning, implementation, monitoring, modification

- Reciprocal teaching: students learn to summarize, question, clarify, predict as they read

Suggestions for Teaching in Your Classroom

- Unpredictable changes in environment usually command attention
- Attention span can be increased with practice
- Distributed practice: short study periods at frequent intervals
- Serial position effect: tendency to remember items at beginning and end of a long list
- Concrete analogies can make abstract information meaningful

Technology as an Information-Processing Tool

- Computer-based technology helps students organize and represent ideas and comprehend text
- Hypermedia and multimedia tools produce both positive and negative results

havior, are convinced that it is possible to study nonobservable behavior, such as thought processes, in a scientific manner. Some cognitive psychologists focus on how people use what they know to solve different kinds of problems in different settings; their work will be discussed in the next chapter. Many cognitive psychologists are especially interested in an area of study known as **information-processing theory**, which seeks to understand how people acquire new information, how they store information and recall it from memory, and how what they already know guides and determines what and how they will learn.

Information-processing theory became a popular approach to the study of learning because it provided psychologists with a framework for investigating the role of a variable that behaviorism had ignored—the nature of the learner. Instead of being viewed as relatively passive organisms that respond in fairly predictable ways to environmental stimuli, learners were now seen as highly active interpreters and manipulators of environmental stimuli. The stage was set for psychology to study learning from a broader and more complicated perspective—namely, as an *interaction* between the learner and the environment. ■

The Information-Processing View of Learning

Information processing: how humans attend to, recognize, transform, store, retrieve information

Information-processing theory rests on a set of assumptions of which three are worth noting. First, information is processed in steps, or stages. The major steps typically include attending to a stimulus, recognizing it, transforming it into some type of mental representation, comparing it with information already stored in memory, assigning meaning to it, and acting on it in some fashion (Searleman & Herrmann, 1994). At an early processing stage, human beings encode information (represent it in thought) in somewhat superficial ways (as when they represent visual and auditory stimuli as true-to-life pictures and sounds) and at later stages in more meaningful ways (as when they grasp the gist of an idea or its relationship to other ideas). Second, there are limits on how much information can be processed at each stage. Although the absolute amount of information human beings can learn appears to be limitless, it must be acquired gradually. Third, the human information-processing system is interactive. Information already stored in memory influences and is influenced by perception and attention. We see what our prior experiences direct us to see, and, in turn, what we see affects what we know.

Thus, according to the information-processing view, learning results from an interaction between an environmental stimulus (the *information* that is to be learned) and a learner (the one who *processes*, or transforms, the information). What an information-processing psychologist wants to know, for instance, is what goes on in a student's mind as a teacher demonstrates how to calculate the area of a triangle or as the student reads twenty pages of a social studies text or responds to test questions. In the sense that contemporary information processing emphasizes the use of existing knowledge schemes to interpret new information and build new knowledge structures, it can be considered a *constructivist* view of learning (Mayer, 1996). (The next chapter presents a full description of the nature of constructivism and of the viewpoints most associated with it.)

We believe that you ought to read this chapter very carefully because the information-processing decisions you make affect when you learn, how much you learn, how well you learn—indeed, whether you learn at all. To give you an appreciation of the information-processing approach to learning and how it can help teachers and students do their jobs, the next section will describe several basic cognitive processes and their role in how people store and retrieve information. The section following that will describe research on selected learning tactics and discuss the nature of strategic learning.

A Model of Information Processing

As mentioned earlier, information-processing psychologists assume that people process new information in stages, that there are limits on how much information can be processed at each stage, and that previously learned information affects how and what people currently learn. Consequently, many psychologists think of information as being held in and transferred among three memory stores—a sensory register, a short-term store, and a long-term store. Each store varies as to the processes required to move information into and out of it, how much information it can hold, and for how long it can hold information. A symbolic representation of these memory stores and their associated processes appears in Figure 8.1. Called a *multi-store* model, it is based on the work of several theorists (for example, Atkinson & Shiffrin, 1968; Norman & Rumelhart, 1970). Note that our use of the term *memory stores* is not meant to suggest specific locations in the brain where information is held; it is simply a metaphorical device for classifying different memory phenomena.

Shortly after the introduction of multi-store models, information-processing theorists divided themselves into two groups. In one camp are those who believe that a multi-store model is the best way to explain a variety of memory phenomena. In the other camp are those who favor a theoretically leaner, single memory system. Although this debate has yet to be firmly resolved, the multi-store model is

Figure 8.1 An Information-Processing Model of Learning

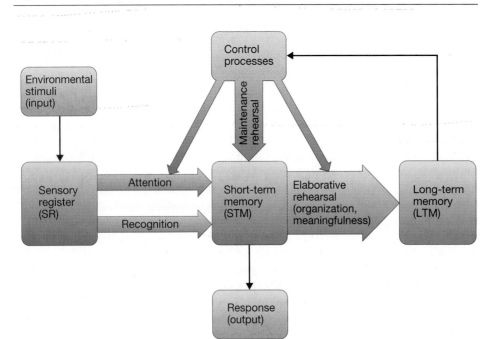

seen as having enough validity that it can be productively used to organize and present much of what is known about how humans store, process, and retrieve information from memory (Searleman & Herrmann, 1994; Spear & Riccio, 1994).

Control processes govern both the manner in which information is encoded and its flow between memory stores. These processes include *recognition, attention, maintenance rehearsal, elaborative rehearsal* (also called *elaborative encoding*), and retrieval. Elaborative rehearsal is a general label that includes a variety of organizational and meaning-enhancing encoding techniques. Each control process is associated primarily with a particular memory store. The control processes are an important aspect of the information-processing system for two reasons. First, they determine the quantity and quality of information that the learner stores in and retrieves from memory. Second, it is the learner who decides whether, when, and how to employ them. That the control processes are under our direct, conscious control will take on added importance when we discuss educational applications a bit later. Before we get to applications, however, we need to make you more familiar with the three memory stores and the control processes specifically associated with each of them.

THE SENSORY REGISTER AND ITS CONTROL PROCESSES

THE SENSORY REGISTER A description of how human learners process information typically begins with environmental stimuli. Our sense receptors are constantly stimulated by visual, auditory, tactile, olfactory, and gustatory stimuli. These experiences are initially recorded in the **sensory register (SR)**, the first memory store. It is called the sensory register because the information it stores is thought to be encoded in the same form in which it is originally perceived. The purpose of the SR is to hold information just long enough (about one to three seconds) for us to decide if we want to attend to it further. Information not selectively attended to and recognized decays or disappears from the system. At the moment you are reading these words, for example, you are being exposed to the appearance of letters printed on paper, to sounds in the place where you are reading, and to many other stimuli. The sensory register might be compared to an unending series of instant-camera snapshots or videotape segments, each lasting from one to three seconds before fading away. If you recognize and attend to one of the snapshots, it will be "processed" and transferred to short-term memory.

> Sensory register: stimuli held briefly for possible processing

THE NATURE OF RECOGNITION The process of **recognition** involves noting key features of a stimulus and relating them to already stored information. This process is interactive in that it depends partly on information extracted from the stimulus itself and partly on information stored in long-term memory. The ability to recognize a dog, for example, involves noticing those physical features of the animal that give it "dogness" (for example, height, length, number of feet, type of coat) and combining the results of that analysis with relevant information from long-term memory (such as that dogs are household pets, are walked on a leash by their owners, are used to guard property). To the degree that an object's defining features are ambiguous (as when one observes an unfamiliar breed of dog from a great distance) or a learner lacks relevant prior knowledge (as many young children do), recognition and more meaningful processing will suffer. Recognition of words and sentences during reading, for example, can be aided by such factors as clear printing, knowledge of spelling patterns, knowledge of letter sounds, and the frequency with which words appear in natural language. The important point to remember is that

> Recognition: noting key features and relating them to stored information

recognition and meaningful processing of information are most effective when we make use of all available sources of information (Driscoll, 1994).

One implication of this work to be discussed in more detail in this and other chapters is that, according to the information-processing view, elementary school students need more structured learning tasks than middle school or high school students. Because of their limited store of knowledge in long-term memory and narrow ability to logically relate what they do know to the task at hand, younger students should be provided with clear, complete, explicit directions and learning materials (see, for example, Doyle, 1983).

THE IMPACT OF ATTENTION   The environment usually provides us with more information than we can deal with at one time. From the multitude of sights, sounds, smells, and other stimuli impinging on us at a given moment, only a fraction are noticed and recorded in the sensory register. At this point yet another reduction typically occurs. We may process only one-third of the already-selected information recorded in the SR. We continually focus on one thing at the expense of something else. This selective focusing on a portion of the information currently stored in the sensory register is what we call **attention**.

> **Attention: focusing on a portion of currently available information**

As with any human characteristic, there are individual differences in attention. Some people can concentrate on a task while they are surrounded by a variety of sights and sounds. Others need to isolate themselves in a private study area. Still others have difficulty attending under any conditions. What explains these differences? Again, information from long-term memory plays an influential role. According to Ulric Neisser, "Perceivers pick up only what they have schemata for, and willy-nilly ignore the rest" (1976, p. 79). In other words, we choose what we will see (or hear) by using our prior knowledge and experiences (i.e., schemata) to anticipate the nature of incoming information. Students daydream, doodle, and write letters rather than listen to a lecture because they anticipate hearing little of value.

> **Information in long-term memory influences what we attend to**

Under normal circumstances, our environment contains a wealth of stimuli. Attending to and processing one of those stimuli usually means that the rest are ignored and not stored in memory.

Moreover, these anticipatory schemata are likely to have long-lasting effects. If someone asked you now to read a book about English grammar, you might recall having been bored by diagramming sentences and memorizing grammatical rules in elementary school. If that was the case, you might not read the grammar text very carefully. A basic challenge for teachers is to convince students that a learning task will be useful, enjoyable, informative, and meaningful. Later in this chapter we will present some ideas as to how this might be accomplished.

SHORT-TERM MEMORY AND ITS CONTROL PROCESSES

SHORT-TERM MEMORY   Once information has been attended to, it is transferred to **short-term memory (STM)**, the second memory store. Short-term memory can hold about seven unrelated bits of information for approximately twenty seconds. Although this brief time span may seem surprising, it can be easily demonstrated. Imagine that you look up and dial an unfamiliar phone number and receive a busy signal. If you are then distracted by something or someone else for fifteen to twenty seconds, chances are you will forget the number. Short-term memory is often referred to as *working memory* since it holds information we are currently aware of at any given moment and is the place where various encoding, organizational, and retrieval processes occur.

Working memory is increasingly being viewed as a critical component in our information-processing system. In the view of one researcher, working memory capacity may be equivalent to Spearman's *g* factor (intelligence as a general mental capability) and "is more highly related to learning, both short-term and long-term, than is any other cognitive factor" (Kyllonen, 1996, p. 73).

REHEARSAL   A severe limitation of short-term memory, as you can see, is how quickly information disappears or is forgotten in the absence of further processing. This problem can be dealt with through *rehearsal*. Most people think of rehearsal

Short-term memory: about seven bits of information held for about twenty seconds

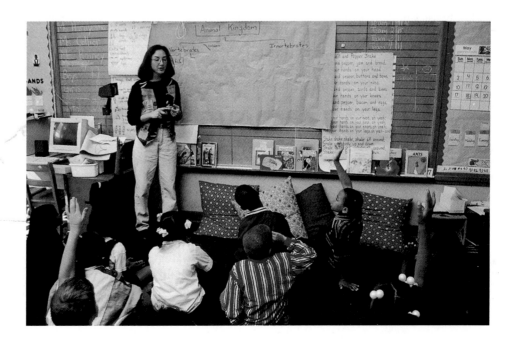

To help students encode information, teach them how to group objects and ideas according to some shared feature.

as repeating something over and over either in silence or out loud. The usual purpose for such behavior is to memorize information for later use, although occasionally we simply want to hold material in short-term memory for immediate use (for example, to redial a phone number after getting a busy signal). Rehearsal can serve both purposes, but not in the same way. Accordingly, cognitive psychologists have found it necessary and useful to distinguish two types of rehearsal: maintenance and elaborative.

Maintenance rehearsal (also called *rote rehearsal* or *repetition*) has a mechanical quality. Its only purpose is to use mental and verbal repetition to hold information in short-term memory for some immediate purpose. Although this is a useful and often-used capability (as in the telephone example), it has no effect on long-term memory storage.

Elaborative rehearsal (also called *elaborative encoding*) consciously relates new information to knowledge already stored in long-term memory. Elaboration occurs when we use information stored in long-term memory to add details to new information, clarify the meaning of a new idea, make inferences, construct visual images, and create analogies (King, 1992b). In these ways we facilitate both the transfer of information to LTM and its maintenance in STM. For example, if you wanted to learn the lines for a part in a play, you might try to relate the dialogue and behavior of your character to similar personal experiences you remember. As you strive to memorize the lines and actions, your mental "elaborations" will help you store your part in long-term memory so that you can retrieve it later. Elaborative rehearsal, whereby information from long-term memory is used in learning new information, is the rule rather than the exception. Mature learners don't often employ maintenance rehearsal by itself. The decision to use one or the other, however, depends on the demands you expect the environment to make on you. If you need to remember things for future use, use elaborative rehearsal; if you want to keep something in consciousness just for the moment, use rote rehearsal.

It is important for you to keep in mind that younger children may not use rehearsal processes in the same way as more mature learners. Kindergarten students rarely engage in spontaneous rehearsal. By the age of seven, however, children do typically use simple rehearsal strategies. When presented with a list of items, the average seven-year-old rehearses each word by itself several times. From the age of ten, rehearsal becomes more like that of an adult. Several items may be grouped together and rehearsed as a set.

So far, we have explained the effect of elaborative rehearsal in terms of relating new information to information already stored in long-term memory. That's fine as a very general explanation. But to be more precise, we need to point out that elaborative rehearsal is based on *organization* (as in the preceding example, where several items were grouped together on some basis and rehearsed as a set) and *meaningfulness* (as in the earlier example, where lines in a play were related to similar personal experiences).

ORGANIZATION   Quite often the information we want to learn is complex and interrelated. We can simplify the task by organizing several separate chunks of information into a few "clumps," or "chunks," of information, particularly when each part of a chunk helps us remember other parts. The value of organizing material was illustrated by an experiment (Bower, Clark, Lesgold, & Winzenz, 1969) in which two groups of subjects were asked to learn 112 words in four successive lists but under different conditions. One group was given each of the four lists for four trials in the hierarchical arrangement displayed in Figure 8.2. The other group was

> **Maintenance rehearsal: hold information for immediate use**

> **Elaborative rehearsal: use stored information to aid learning**

Figure 8.2 Hierarchical Arrangement of Words Produces Superior Recall

SOURCE: Bower et al. (1969).

Organizing material reduces
number of chunks, provides
recall cues

given the same lists and the same hierarchical tree arrangement, but the words from each list were randomly arranged over the four levels of the hierarchy. As you can see, through the first three trials the first group recalled more than twice as many words as the second and achieved perfect recall scores for the last two trials. The organized material was much easier to learn not only because there were fewer chunks to memorize but also because each item in a group served as a cue for the other items. When you decide to store pertinent material from this chapter in your long-term memory in preparation for an exam, you will find the job much easier if you organize what you are studying. To learn the various parts of the information-processing model under discussion, for instance, you might group the ideas being described under the various headings used in this chapter (as we do in the *Study Guide*).

MEANINGFULNESS	The meaningfulness of new information that one is about to learn has been characterized as "potentially the most powerful variable for explaining the learning of complex verbal discourse" (Johnson, 1975, pp. 425–426). According to David Ausubel (Ausubel, Novak, & Hanesian, 1978), **meaningful learning** occurs when a learner encounters clear, logically organized material and consciously tries to relate the new material to ideas and experiences stored in long-term memory. You might, for example, imagine yourself using learning theory principles to teach a lesson to a group of students. Or you might modify a previously constructed flow chart on the basis of new information. The basic idea behind meaningful learning is that the learner actively attempts to associate new ideas to existing ones. The questions that we pose to you at the end of each chapter, for example, are designed to foster meaningful encoding by getting you to relate text information to relevant prior experience.

> **Meaningful learning occurs when organized material is associated with stored knowledge**

Lev Vygotsky, the Russian psychologist we mentioned in Chapter 2, emphasized the role of teachers, parents, siblings, and other kinds of expert tutors in meaningful learning. Vygotsky pointed out that some of what we learn about the world in which we live comes from direct, unfiltered contact with stimuli. Touch a hot stove and you get burned. Insult or ridicule a friend and you are likely to have one less friend at the end of the day. The limitation of this kind of learning, which Vygotsky called *direct* learning, is that one is likely to miss the general lesson or principle that underlies the event. Consequently, Vygotsky favored *mediated* learning. A mediator is an individual, usually older, more knowledgeable and skilled, who selects stimuli to attend to, directs attention to certain aspects of the chosen stimulus, and explains why things are the way they are and why things are done in a certain way. Thus, parents explain to their children why it is not acceptable to hit or tease playmates, and teachers explain to students why it is necessary for them to learn how to use the concepts and rules of English grammar, plane geometry, and the like (Kozulin & Presseisen, 1995).

From a Vygotskian perspective, the main goal of instruction is to provide learners with the psychological tools they will need to engage in self-mediation. If individuals are to function effectively once they leave school, they have to learn how to look beyond the immediate situation and see how they can use new knowledge and skills in future situations. Psychologists refer to this process as transfer of learning, and we will discuss it at length in Chapter 9.

This brief description of meaningfulness and its role in learning contains a strong implication for teaching in culturally diverse classrooms. You can foster meaningful learning for students from other cultures by pointing out similarities between ideas presented in class and students' culture-specific knowledge. For example, you might point out that September 16 has the same significance to people of Mexican origin as July 4 has to U.S. citizens since the former date commemorates Mexico's revolution against and independence from Spain.

VISUAL IMAGERY ENCODING	Generating mental images of objects, ideas, and actions is a particularly powerful form of elaborative encoding. Like pictures, images can be said to be worth a thousand words because they contain a wealth of information in a compact, organized, and meaningful format. Such notable individuals as Albert Einstein (physics), Michael Faraday (physics), Sir Francis Galton (anthropology and genetics), James D. Watson (biochemistry), and Joan Didion (literature) have described how mental imagery played a significant role in their thinking and problem-solving efforts (Shepard, 1978).

Research has consistently shown that directing students to generate visual images as they read lists of words or sentences, several paragraphs of text, or lengthy text passages produces higher levels of comprehension and recall as compared to students who are not so instructed. Also, text passages that contain many concrete words and phrases are more easily understood and more accurately recalled than passages that contain more abstract than concrete ideas (Clark & Paivio, 1991). As we will see later in the chapter, visual imagery is an integral part of several effective study skills.

A popular explanation for the beneficial effect of imagery and concreteness is Allan Paivio's **dual coding theory** (Clark & Paivio, 1991). According to the dual coding theory, concrete material (such as pictures of familiar objects) and concrete words (such as *horse, bottle, water*) are remembered better than abstract words (such as *deduction, justice, theory*) because the former can be encoded two ways—as images and as verbal labels—whereas abstract words are only encoded verbally. This makes retrieval easier since a twice-coded item provides more potential retrieval cues than information that exists in only one form.

LONG-TERM MEMORY

We have already referred, in a general way, to the third memory store, **long-term memory (LTM)**, which is perhaps the most interesting of all. On the basis of neurological, experimental, and clinical evidence, most cognitive psychologists believe that the storage capacity of long-term memory is unlimited and that LTM contains a permanent record of everything an individual has learned, although some doubt exists about the latter point (see, for example, Loftus & Loftus, 1980).

Long-term memory: permanent storehouse of unlimited capacity

The neurological evidence comes from the work of Wilder Penfield (1969), a Canadian neurosurgeon who operated on more than one thousand patients who experienced epileptic seizures. To determine the source of the seizures, Penfield electrically stimulated various parts of the brain's surface. During this procedure, many patients reported vivid images of long-dormant events from their past. It was as if a neurological videotape had been turned on.

The experimental evidence, although less dramatic, is just as interesting. In a typical memory study (such as Tulving & Pearlstone, 1966), subjects receive a list of nouns to learn. After giving subjects ample opportunity to recall as many of the words as possible, researchers provide retrieval cues—for instance, category labels such as "clothing," "food," or "animals." In many cases cued subjects quickly recall additional items. Experiments on how well people recognize previously seen pictures have produced some startling findings. Thirty-six hours after viewing over 2,500 pictures, a group of college students correctly identified an average of about 2,250, or 90 percent (Standing, Conezio, & Haber, 1970). In fact, it has been estimated that if one million pictures could be shown, recognition memory would still be 90 percent or better (Standing, 1973). Finally, psychiatrists and psychotherapists have reported many case histories of individuals who have been helped to recall seemingly forgotten events through hypnosis and other techniques (Erdelyi & Goldberg, 1979).

HOW INFORMATION IS ORGANIZED IN LONG-TERM MEMORY   As you have seen, long-term memory plays an influential role throughout the information-processing system. The interests, attitudes, skills, and knowledge of the world that reside there influence what we perceive, how we interpret our perceptions, and whether we process information for short-term or long-term storage. In most instances retrieval of information from long-term memory is extremely rapid and accurate, like finding a book in a well-run library. Accordingly, we can conclude that information in long-term memory must be organized. The nature of this organization is a key area in the study of memory. The insights it provides help illuminate the encoding and retrieval processes associated with long-term memory.

Many cognitive psychologists believe that our store of knowledge in long-term memory is organized in terms of **schemata** (which is plural for *schema* and is related in meaning to Jean Piaget's *scheme*). Richard Anderson (1984) defines a schema as an abstract structure of information. It is abstract because it summarizes information about many different cases or examples of something, and it is structured because it represents how its own informational components are interrelated. Schemata give us expectations about objects and events (dogs bark, birds fly, students listen to their teachers and study industriously). When our schemata are well formed and a specific event is consistent with our expectation, comprehension occurs. When schemata are poorly structured or absent, learning is slow and uncertain. The following example should make this notion of schemata more understandable.

| Information in long-term memory organized as schemata

For most everyone raised in the United States, the word *classroom* typically calls to mind a scene that includes certain people (teacher, students), objects (desks, chalkboard, books, pencils), rules (attend to the teacher's instructions, stay in the classroom unless given permission to leave), and events (reading, listening, writing, talking, drawing). This is a generalized representation, and some classrooms may contain fewer or more of these characteristics. However, as long as students and teachers share the same basic classroom schema, each will generally know what to expect and how to behave in any given classroom. It is when people do not possess an appropriate schema that comprehension, memory, and behavior problems arise.

Because people interpret new information and experience on the basis of existing long-term memory schemes, and because no two people's schemes are identical, each person is likely to represent the same idea or experience in a unique fashion.

This notion was first investigated during the early 1930s by Sir Frederick Bartlett (1932), an English psychologist. In one experiment Bartlett had subjects read and recall a brief story, entitled "The War of the Ghosts," that was based on North American Indian folklore. Since Bartlett's subjects had little knowledge of Native American culture, they had difficulty accurately recalling the story; they omitted certain details and distorted others. The distortions were particularly interesting because they reflected an attempt to interpret the story in terms of the logic and beliefs of Western culture. Similar studies, conducted more recently with other kinds of reading materials, have reported similar results (di Sibio, 1982). The conclusion that Bartlett and other researchers have drawn is that remembering is not simply a matter of retrieving a true-to-life record of information. People often remember their *interpretations* or *constructions* of something read, seen, or heard. In addition, when they experience crucial gaps in memory, people tend to fill in these blanks with logical reconstructions of what they think must have been. People then report these reconstructions as memories of actual events (di Sibio, 1982).

These experiments and the Case in Print on page 262 vividly demonstrate the interactive nature of memory. What we know influences what we perceive and how we interpret and store those perceptions. And because our memories of specific events or experiences are assembled, constructed, and sometimes reassembled by the brain over time, accurate and complete recall of information we once stored is not always possible. As a teacher, then, you should pay deliberate attention to how your students use their background knowledge, helping them to use it as accurately and completely as possible to process new information.

HOW WELL DO WE REMEMBER WHAT WE LEARN IN SCHOOL?   Conventional wisdom (which is often wrong, by the way) holds that much of the information that we learn in school is forgotten soon after a unit of instruction or course has ended. You may have felt the same way yourself on more than one occasion. But is this belief true? To answer this question, George Semb and John Ellis (1994) reviewed the results of fifty-six research articles published between 1930 and 1993. Their main findings are very consistent with the information-processing principles that you have read about and should at least partially reassure you that you haven't been wasting your time all these years.

1. More than seven out of ten studies reported less than a 20 percent loss of what was learned when measured with a recognition task. One-half of the studies reported less than a 20 percent loss of what was learned when measured with free recall.

2. Subject matter that had a higher than average level of unfamiliar facts and associations (such as zoology, anatomy, and medical terminology) and for which students would have little relevant prior knowledge (such as electricity, mechanics, and linguistics) was associated with increased levels of forgetting.

3. Most of the forgetting of information occurred within four weeks after the end of a unit of instruction. Additional declines in recall occurred more slowly.

4. Less forgetting occurred among students who learned the material to a high level either by being required to achieve a high score on an exam before moving on to the next unit of instruction, by having to teach it to less knowledgeable students, or by taking advanced courses.

"Remembering" Things That Never Were

People often remember their interpretations or constructions of something read, seen, or heard. In addition, when they experience crucial gaps in memory, people tend to fill in these blanks with logical reconstructions of what they think must have been. People then report these reconstructions as memories of actual events. (p. 261)

YOU MUST REMEMBER THIS
SHARON BEGLEY WITH MARTHA BRANT
Newsweek 9/26/94

At first, Chris had only the foggiest recollection of getting lost in the Spokane shopping mall at the age of 5. His older brother, a psychology student at the University of Washington, was doing an experiment on memory; would Chris, 14, read this brief account of an incident from his childhood, and write down everything he could remember about it? After reading about getting lost in the mall, Chris wrote variations on "I sort of remember the stores." But a few weeks later, pressed by his brother, he offered a richly detailed narrative: "I think I went over to look at the toy store, the Kay-Bee store and, uh, we got lost. . . . and then this old man, I think he was wearing blue flannel, came up to me. . . . He was kind of old. He was kind of bald on top. . . . He had like a ring of gray hair . . ."

Chris had never been lost at a mall. But now he was sure that he had. . . .

Glimmers of how memories might be created out of mere wisps of suggestion began to emerge this summer, after a May conference at Harvard Medical School on the neurological bases of false memories. Start with how normal memory is thought to work: bits and pieces of an experience are parceled out to different regions of the brain. Memories of its sound settle in the auditory cortex, and memories of its appearance into the visual cortex . . . "Each neuron represents a little bit of the memory," explains psychologist James McClelland of the Center for the Neural Basis of Cognition in Pittsburgh. But all the scattered fragments remain physically linked. The job of assembling them falls to a part of the brain called the limbic system. Like a neural file clerk, it pulls disparate aspects of each memory from the separate file drawers scattered throughout the cortex, gathering them into a cohesive whole.

Whatever reason evolution had for creating this scheme, it practically guarantees people will "remember" things that never happened. For one thing, people routinely take perfectly accurate snippets and assemble them incorrectly. Sup-

pose you saw an accident in which a car ran a red light; a year later someone asks, "Remember when that guy ran the stop sign?" Neurons connected to the memory of the accident click in—but so do memories of stop signs. Time goes by. The next time you recall the accident, neurons holding memories of stop signs get activated, too—and suddenly you remember a car running a stop sign. Most chilling, says psychologist Michael Nash of the University of Tennessee, is that "there may be no structural difference between" a memory of a true event and a false one.

False memories commonly arise in a condition called "source amnesia." Thanks to the brain's frontal lobes, most people can distinguish the memory of a dream from the memory of a real event: these gelatinous folds of gray matter tag each incoming image with how, when and where it was acquired. But if the frontal lobes are damaged, their owners cannot remember where a memory came from, explains psychologist Daniel Schacter of Harvard. The patients retrieve bits and pieces of a memory—the face of an old teacher, a cinematic rape—and cannot distinguish which fragment came from where. "You could be remembering a dream, a fear or something someone talked about," says Schacter. "What gives the memory a feeling of authenticity is that authentic parts are included." Even in people with perfectly fine frontal lobes, a memory's origin deteriorates more quickly than its other aspects, says psychologist Stephen Ceci of Cornell University. (Do you remember your first day of kindergarten? Or is it your mother's endless recounting that you recall?) Source memory is also highly prone to suggestion—that the vision of a man by your bed is a real memory, for instance, and not an image drawn from hearing tales of abuse. "If you've imagined it enough and you lose the source of the information [your imagination]," says Ceci, "then you have a false memory."

Although not everyone is so suggestible—75 percent of the people in Loftus's lost-in-the-mall study refused to "remember" what had never been—certain conditions can make them do so. "Severe emotional stress overcomes internal checks on plausibility, and you are left with a false memory," says neurologist Marsel Mesulam of Northwestern University. From transcripts and session notes, Loftus, a psychologist at the University of Washington, found therapists who routinely told patients that if they cannot remember abuse, they should *imagine* it as an aid to memory. "Picture [your father] approaching the bed," one told her patient, Loftus reports. "Think about what happened in the bathtub," said another; "If you can't remember any details, just try to imagine what it must have been like." Many therapists also use hypnosis, which makes patients willing to internalize suggestions and to call any image they see a memory. "Under hypnosis," says psychiatrist David Spiegel of Stanford University, "you can create [memories] rather than retrieve them."

. . . Such skepticism about retrieved memories rankles people who counsel survivors of abuse. Harvard psychiatrist Judith Herman, for instance, says "scientists have no business using the term false memory. We have no way of judging independently [reports of] childhood experiences." That's OK if memories are used solely in therapy, and treated as mere expressions of the mind. But "memories" are sending people to jail: 700 civil and criminal cases have been filed based on retrieved memories of childhood abuse, according to the False Memory Syndrome Foundation. Some of the accused have been convicted and sentenced to 40 years, as in a case decided last week, based on nothing more substantial than retrieved memories. At least, the accusers thought they were memories.

Questions and Activities

1. Since people interpret experiences on the basis of their long-term memory schemes and, on occasion, add extraneous information to create a more meaningful and logical recollection, it is not surprising that disagreements occur about the details of an event. Teachers sometimes find themselves in such situations as, for example, when parents confront a teacher and demand to know why the teacher embarrassed their child in front of the rest of the class. The teacher is dumbfounded by the accusation and replies that she did no such thing. What might you do to avoid such confrontations by assuring that you and your students have a common understanding of important or sensitive events?

2. What kinds of classroom situations are most likely to be interpreted differently and hence remembered differently by teachers and students?

3. If you plan to have students view a film or videotape as part of a lesson, you may be able to demonstrate the phenomenon of false memory. Two weeks after students have viewed the film or tape, and without prior warning, announce that a prize will be awarded to the student who recalls the most information from the film. Have students write down as much as they can recall of what they saw and heard. Then give them a list of all the ideas that actually occurred in the film. Have them compare both lists and make a tally of both how many actual ideas they recalled *and* how many ideas they recalled that had never appeared.

Students remember much of what they learn in school, especially if mastery and active learning are emphasized

5. Less forgetting occurred in classes where students were more actively involved in learning (as in a geography field trip where students had to observe, sketch, record, and answer questions).

The instructional implications that flow from these findings include an emphasis on mastery learning, peer tutoring, frequent testing with corrective feedback, and forms of instruction that actively involve students in learning.

The discussion up to this point has focused on a general explanation of how people attend to, encode, store, and retrieve information. In a word, we have described some of the major aspects of *thinking*. During the last twenty years, researchers have inquired into how much knowledge individuals have about their own thought processes and what significance this knowledge has for learning. The term that was coined to refer to how much we know of our own thought processes is *metacognition*. As we will see, it plays a very important role in learning.

Metacognition

THE NATURE AND IMPORTANCE OF METACOGNITION

The notion of metacognition was proposed by developmental psychologist John Flavell (1976) to explain why children of different ages deal with learning tasks in different ways. For example, when seven-year-olds are taught how to remember pairs of nouns using both a less effective technique (simply repeating the words) and a more effective technique (imagining the members of each pair doing something together), most of these children will use the less effective technique when given a new set of pairs to learn. Most ten-year-olds, however, will opt to use the more effective method (Kail, 1990). The explanation for this finding is that the seven-year-old has not had enough learning experiences to recognize that some problem-solving methods are better than others. To the younger child, one means is as good as another. This lack of metacognitive knowledge makes true strategic learning impossible for young children.

One way to grasp the essence of metacognition is to contrast it with cognition. The term *cognition* is used to describe the ways in which information is processed—that is, the ways it is attended to, recognized, encoded, stored in memory for various lengths of time, retrieved from storage, and used for one purpose or another. **Metacognition** refers to our knowledge about those operations and how they might best be used to achieve a learning goal. As Flavell has put it:

> I am engaging in metacognition . . . if I notice that I am having more trouble learning A than B; if it strikes me that I should double-check C before accepting it as a fact; if it occurs to me that I had better scrutinize each and every alternative in any multiple-choice type task situation before deciding which is the best one; if I become aware that I am not sure what the experi-

Metacognition refers to the knowledge we have about how we learn. It is a key component of our ability to regulate our learning processes.

menter really wants me to do; if I sense that I had better make a note of D because I may forget it; if I think to ask someone about E to see if I have it right. Such examples could be multiplied endlessly. (1976, p. 232)

Metacognition: our own knowledge of how we think

Metacognition is obviously a very broad concept. It covers everything an individual can know that relates to how information is processed. To get a better grasp of this concept, you may want to use the three-part classification scheme proposed by Flavell (1987): knowledge of person variables, task variables, and strategy variables. An example of knowledge of person variables is that one is good at learning verbal material but poor at learning mathematical material. Another example is knowing that information not rehearsed or encoded is quickly forgotten. An example of knowledge of task variables is that passages with long sentences and unfamiliar words are usually harder to understand than passages that are more simply written. An example of knowledge of strategy variables is knowing that one should skim through a text passage before reading it to determine its length and difficulty level.

Lev Vygotsky believed that children acquire metacognitive knowledge and skills most effectively through direct instruction, imitation, and social collaboration in the following way:

1. Children are told by more experienced and knowledgeable individuals what is true and what is false, what is right and what is wrong, how various things should and should not be done, and why. ("Jason, don't touch that stove. It's hot and will give you a painful burn if you touch it.")

2. As opportunities arise, children use this knowledge to regulate their own behavior (saying out loud, "Hot stove. Don't touch.") as well as the behavior of others. If you have ever seen young children play "House" or "School" and faithfully mimic the dictates of their parents or teacher, then you have seen this process at work.

3. Children regulate their own behavior through the use of inner speech.

Vygotsky's analysis strongly suggests that providing children with opportunities to regulate their own and others' behavior, as in peer tutoring, is an excellent way to help them increase their metacognitive knowledge and skills and to improve the quality of their learning. Later in this chapter we describe one such program, reciprocal teaching. Working in pairs, students help each other improve their reading comprehension skills by first modeling comprehension processes (summarizing and questioning) and monitoring processes (clarifying and predicting), and then guiding their partner through each process. Programs like reciprocal teaching have produced high levels of learning, motivation, and transfer (Karpov & Haywood, 1998).

Recent research indicates significant differences in what younger and older children know about metacognition. What follows is a discussion of some of these differences.

AGE TRENDS IN METACOGNITION

Two reviews of research on metacognition (Duell, 1986; Kail, 1990) examined how students of different ages use memorization techniques and how well they understand what they are doing. Following are some of the reviews' key conclusions.

1. In terms of diagnosing task difficulty, most six-year-olds know that more familiar items are easier to remember than less familiar items and that a small set of items is easier to recall than a large set of items. What six-year-olds do not

yet realize is that the amount of information they can recall immediately after they study it is limited.

2. Similar findings have been obtained for reading tasks. Most second graders know that interest, familiarity, and story length influence comprehension and recall. However, they are relatively unaware of the effect of how ideas are sequenced, of the introductory and summary qualities of first and last paragraphs, and of the relationship between reading goals and tactics. Sixth graders, by contrast, are much more aware of the effects of these variables on comprehension and recall. Partly because of these differences in metacognitive knowledge, young children tend to treat reading as a task of decoding symbols rather than of constructing and comprehending meaning. Recent research has clearly shown that children's metacognitive awareness about reading is positively related to performance on a variety of reading tasks.

3. Most children know very little about the role their own capabilities play in learning. For example, not until about nine years of age do most children realize that their recall right after they study something is limited. Consequently, children through the third grade usually overestimate how much they can store in and retrieve from short-term memory. One likely reason for this developmental difference is that younger children base their prediction on irrelevant personal characteristics (such as "I'm pretty smart"), whereas older children focus more on relevant task characteristics.

4. There are clear developmental differences in how well students understand the need to tailor learning tactics to task demands. For example, four- and six-year-old children in one study cited by Robert Kail (1990) did not alter how much time they spent studying a set of pictures when they were told that a recognition test would follow either three minutes later, one day later, or one week later. Eight-year-olds did use that information to allocate less or more study time to the task. In another study, which we referred to earlier, children of various ages were trained to use interactive visual imagery to learn a list of concrete noun pairs. When given a similar task and left on their own, most of those below ten years of age reverted to the less effective technique of rote rehearsal.

5. In terms of monitoring the progress of learning, most children younger than seven or eight are not very proficient at determining when they know something well enough to pass a memory test. Also, most first graders typically don't know what they don't know. When given multiple opportunities to study and recall a lengthy set of pictures, six-year-olds chose to study pictures they had previously seen and recalled as well as ones they hadn't. Thus, they wasted time studying things they already knew. Third graders, by contrast, focused on previously unseen pictures.

The general conclusion that emerges from these findings is that the youngest school-age children have only limited knowledge of how their cognitive processes work and when to use them. Consequently, primary grade children do not systematically analyze learning tasks, formulate plans for learning, use appropriate techniques of enhancing memory and comprehension, or monitor their progress because they do not (some would say cannot) understand the benefits of doing these things. But as children develop and gain more experience with increasingly complex academic tasks, they acquire a greater awareness of metacognitive knowledge and its relationship to classroom learning. In this process teachers can assist

Insight into one's learning processes improves with age

their students and guide them toward maximum use of their metacognitive knowledge. To help you understand how, the next section will discuss learning tactics and strategies.

Helping Students Become Strategic Learners

With some effort and planning, a teacher can make logically organized and relevant lessons. However, this is only half the battle since students must then attend to the information, encode it into long-term memory, and retrieve it when needed. Getting students to use the attention, encoding, and retrieval processes discussed in the previous section is not always easy. The sad fact is that most children and adults are inefficient learners (as evidenced, for example, by Bond, Miller, & Kennon, 1987; Brown, Campione, & Day, 1981; Covington, 1985; Davies, 1984; Selmes, 1987; Simpson, 1984). Their attempts at encoding rarely go beyond rote rehearsal (for example, rereading a textbook chapter), simple organizational schemes (outlining), and various cueing devices (underlining or highlighting). When the nature of the learning task changes, few students think about changing their encoding techniques accordingly.

One reason for this state of affairs is that students are rarely taught how to make the most of their cognitive capabilities. In one study sixty-nine kindergarten through sixth-grade teachers were observed giving strategy instruction in only 9.5 percent of the times they were observed. Rationales for strategy use were given less than 1 percent of the time, and 10 percent of the teachers gave no strategy instructions at all. Moreover, the older the students were, the less likely they were to receive strategy instruction (Moely et al., 1992). Findings such as these are surprising, not to mention disappointing, since it is widely recognized that the amount of independent learning expected of students increases consistently from elementary school through high school and into college. The rest of this chapter will try to convince you that it need not be this way, at least for your students. The rise of information-processing theory has led researchers to study how cognitive processes can be taught to and used by students as learning tactics and strategies.

THE NATURE OF LEARNING TACTICS AND STRATEGIES

Strategy: plan to achieve a long-term goal

Tactic: specific technique that helps achieve long-term goal

A **learning strategy** is a general *plan* that a learner formulates for achieving a somewhat distant academic goal (like getting an A on your next exam). Like all strategies, it specifies what will be done to achieve the goal, where it will be done, and when it will be done. A **learning tactic** is a specific *technique* (like a memory aid or a form of notetaking) that a learner uses to accomplish an immediate objective (such as to understand the concepts in a textbook chapter and how they relate to one another). As you can see, tactics have an integral connection to strategies. They are the learning tools that move you closer to your goal. Thus, they have to be chosen so as to be consistent with the goals of a strategy. If you had to recall verbatim the preamble to the U.S. Constitution, for example, would you use a learning tactic that would help you understand the gist of each stanza or one that would allow for accurate and complete recall? It is surprising how often students fail to consider this point. Because understanding the different types and roles of tactics will help you better understand the process of strategy formulation, we will discuss tactics first.

TYPES OF TACTICS

Most learning tactics can be placed in one of two categories based on each tactic's intended primary purpose. One category, called *memory-directed tactics*, contains techniques that help produce accurate storage and retrieval of information. The second category, called *comprehension-directed tactics*, contains techniques that aid in understanding the meaning of ideas and their interrelationships (Levin, 1982). Within each category there are specific tactics from which one can choose. Because of space limitations, we cannot discuss them all. Instead, we have chosen to briefly discuss a few that are either very popular with students or have been shown to be reasonably effective. The first two, rehearsal and mnemonic devices, are memory-directed tactics. Both can take several forms and are used by students of almost every age. The last two, self-questioning and notetaking, are comprehension-directed tactics and are used frequently by students from the upper elementary grades through college.

REHEARSAL   The simplest form of rehearsal—rote rehearsal—is one of the earliest tactics to appear during childhood and is used by most everyone on occasion. It is not a particularly effective tactic for long-term storage and recall because it does not produce distinct encoding or good retrieval cues (although, as discussed earlier, it is a useful tactic for purposes of short-term memory). According to research reviewed by Kail (1990), most five- and six-year-olds do not rehearse at all. Seven-year-olds sometimes use the simplest form of rehearsal. By eight years of age, instead of rehearsing single pieces of information one at a time, youngsters start to rehearse several items together as a set. A slightly more advanced version, called *cumulative rehearsal*, involves rehearsing a small set of items for several repetitions, dropping the item at the top of the list and adding a new one, giving the set several repetitions, dropping the item at the head of the set and adding a new one, rehearsing the set, and so on. By early adolescence rehearsal reflects the learner's growing awareness of the organizational properties of information. When given a list of randomly arranged words from familiar categories, thirteen-year-olds will group items by category to form rehearsal sets. This version of rehearsal is likely to be the most effective because of the implicit association between the category members and the more general category label. If at the time of recall the learner is given the category label or can generate it spontaneously, the probability of accurate recall of the category members increases significantly.

MNEMONIC DEVICES   A **mnemonic device** is a memory-directed tactic that helps a learner transform or organize information to enhance its retrievability. Such devices can be used to learn and remember individual items of information (a name, a fact, a date), sets of information (a list of names, a list of vocabulary definitions, a sequence of events), and ideas expressed in text. These devices range from simple, easy-to-learn techniques to somewhat complex systems that require a fair amount of practice. Since they incorporate visual and verbal forms of elaborative encoding, their effectiveness is due to the same factors that make imagery and category clustering successful—organization and meaningfulness.

Although mnemonic devices have been described and practiced for over two thousand years, they were rarely made the object of scientific study until the 1960s (see Yates, 1966, for a detailed discussion of the history of mnemonics). Since that time, however, mnemonics have been frequently and intensively studied by researchers. In recent years there have been several reviews of mnemonics research (for example, Bellezza, 1981; Higbee, 1979; Pressley, Levin, & Delaney, 1982; Snowman, 1986). Table 8.1 provides descriptions, examples, and uses of five mnemonic devices: rhymes, acronyms, acrostics, the loci method, and the keyword method.

Rote rehearsal not a very effective memory tactic

Acronym: word made from first letters of items to be learned

Acrostic: sentence made up of words derived from first letters of items to be learned

Loci method: visualize items to be learned stored in specific locations

Keyword method: visually link pronunciation of foreign word to English translation

Table 8.1	Five Types of Mnemonic Devices		
Mnemonic	**Description**	**Example**	**Uses**
Rhyme	The items of information that one wants to recall are embedded in a rhyme that may range from one to several lines. A rhyme for recalling the names of the first 40 U.S. presidents, for example, contains 14 lines.	• Thirty days hath September, April, June, and November • Fiddlededum, fiddlededee, A ring around the moon is $\pi \times d$, If a hole in your sock you want repaired, Use the formula πr squared (to recall the formulas for circumference and area)	Recalling specific items of factual information
Acronym	The first letter from each to-be-remembered item is used to make a word. Often called the first-letter mnemonic.	• HOMES (for the names of the Great Lakes—Huron, Ontario, Michigan, Erie, Superior)	Recalling a short set of items, particularly abstract items, in random or serial order
Acrostic	The first letter from each to-be-remembered item is used to create a series of words that forms a sentence. The first letter of each word in the sentence corresponds to the first letters of the to-be-remembered items.	• Men Very Easily Make Jugs Serve Useful New Purposes (for the names of the 9 planets in our solar system—Mercury, Venus, Earth, Mars, Jupiter, Saturn, Uranus, Neptune, Pluto) • A Rat In The House May Eat The Ice Cream (to recall the spelling of the word *arithmetic*)	Recalling items, particularly abstract ones, in random or serial order
Method of Loci	Generate visual images of and memorize a set of well-known locations that form a natural series (such as the furniture in and the architectural features of the rooms of one's house). Second, generate images of the to-be-learned items (objects, events, or ideas) and place each in a separate location. Third, mentally walk through each location, retrieve each image from where it was placed, and decode into a written or spoken message. Loci (pronounced *low-sigh*) is the plural of *locus*, which means "place."	• To recall the four stages of Piaget's theory: For sensorimotor stage picture a car engine with eyes, ears, nose, and a mouth. Place this image in your first location (fireplace mantel). For preoperational stage, picture Piaget dressed in a surgical gown scrubbing up before an operation. Place this image in your second location (bookshelf). For concrete operational stage, picture Piaget as a surgeon cutting open a piece of concrete. Place this image in your third location (chair). For formal operational stage, picture Piaget as an operating room surgeon dressed in a tuxedo. Place this image in your fourth location (sofa).	Can be used by children, college students, and the elderly to recall lists of discrete items or ideas from text passages. Works equally well for free recall and serial recall, abstract and concrete items.
Keyword	Created to aid the learning of foreign language vocabulary, but is applicable to any task in which one piece of information has to be associated with another. First, isolate some part of the foreign word that, when spoken, sounds like a meaningful English word. This is the keyword. Then create a visual image of the keyword. Finally, form a compound visual image between the keyword and the translation of the foreign word.	• Spanish word *pato* (pronounced pot-o) means "duck" in English. Keyword is *pot*. Imagine a duck with a pot over its head or a duck simmering in a pot. • English psychologist Charles Spearman proposed that intelligence was composed of two factors—*g* and *s*. Keyword is "spear." Imagine a spear being thrown at a gas (for *g* and *s*) can.	For kindergarten through 4th grade, works best when children are given keywords and pictures. Can be used to recall cities and their products, states and their capitals, medical definitions, and famous people's accomplishments.

SOURCES: Atkinson (1975); Atkinson & Raugh (1975); Bellezza (1981); Carney, Levin, & Levin (1994); Raugh & Atkinson (1975); Yates (1966).

Why Mnemonic Devices are Effective   Mnemonic devices work so well because they enhance the encodability and retrievability of information. First, they provide a context (such as acronyms, sentences, mental walks) in which apparently unrelated items can be organized. Second, the meaningfulness of material to be learned is enhanced through associations with more familiar, meaningful information (for example, memory pegs or loci). Third, they provide distinctive retrieval cues that must be encoded with the material to be learned. Fourth, they force the learner to be an active participant in the learning process (Morris, 1977).

Mnemonic devices meaningfully organize information, provide retrieval cues

Why You Should Teach Students How to Use Mnemonic Devices   Despite the demonstrated effectiveness of mnemonic devices, many people argue against teaching them to students. They feel that students should learn the skills of critical thinking and problem solving rather than ways to reliably recall isolated bits of verbatim information. When factual information is needed, one can always turn to a reference source. Although we agree with the importance of teaching students to be critical thinkers and problem solvers, we feel this view is shortsighted for three reasons. First, it is very time-consuming to be constantly looking things up in reference books. Second, it ignores the fact that effective problem solving depends on ready access to a well-organized and meaningful knowledge base. Indeed, people who are judged to be expert in a particular field have an impressive array of factual material at their fingertips. Third, it focuses only on the "little idea" that mnemonic usage aids verbatim recall of bits of information. The "big idea" is that students come to realize that the ability to learn and remember large amounts of information is an acquired capability. Too often students (and adults) assume that an effective memory is innate and requires high intelligence. Once they realize that learning is a skill, students may be more inclined to learn how to use other tactics and how to formulate broad-based strategies.

SELF- AND PEER QUESTIONING   Since students are expected to demonstrate much of what they know by answering written test questions, self-questioning can be a valuable learning tactic. The key to using questions profitably is to recognize that different types of questions make different cognitive demands. Some questions require little more than verbatim recall or recognition of simple facts and details. If an exam is to stress factual recall, then it may be helpful for a student to generate such questions while studying. Other questions, however, assess comprehension, application, or synthesis of main ideas or other high-level information.

To ensure that students fully understood how to write comprehension-aiding questions, Alison King (1992b) created a set of question stems (see Table 8.2) that were intended to help students identify main ideas and think about how those ideas related to each other and to what the student already knew. When high school and college students used these question stems, they scored significantly better on tests of recall and comprehension of lecture material than did students who simply reviewed the same material. King (1994, 1998) also demonstrated that pairs of fourth- and fifth-grade students who were taught how to generate high-level questions and responses outperformed untrained students on tests that measured both comprehension and the ability to integrate text information with prior knowledge.

Self-questioning improves comprehension, knowledge integration

Self-questioning is a highly recommended learning tactic because it has a two-pronged beneficial effect. First, it helps students to better understand what they

Table 8.2	Self-Questioning Stems

What is a new example of . . . ?

How would you use . . . to . . . ?

What would happen if . . . ?

What are the strengths and weaknesses of . . . ?

What do we already know about . . . ?

How does . . . tie in with what we learned before?

Explain why . . .

Explain how . . .

How does . . . affect . . . ?

What is the meaning of . . . ?

Why is . . . important?

What is the difference between . . . and . . . ?

How are . . . and . . . similar?

What is the best . . . , and why?

What are some possible solutions to the problem of . . . ?

Compare . . . and . . . with regard to . . .

How does . . . cause . . . ?

What do you think causes . . . ?

SOURCE: From King A. (1992). "Facilitating Elaborative Learning Through Guided Student Generated Questioning," *Educational Psychologist, 27* (1), 111–126. Reprinted by permission of Lawrence Erlbaum Associates, Inc.

read. In order to answer the kinds of question stems suggested by King, students have to engage in such higher-level thinking processes as translating ideas into their own words (What is the meaning of . . . ? Explain why . . .), looking for similarities and differences (What is the difference between . . . and . . . ? How are . . . and . . . similar?), thinking about how ideas relate to one another (Compare . . . and . . . with regard to . . .) and to previously learned information (How does . . . tie in with what we learned before?), and evaluating the quality of ideas (What are the strengths and weaknesses of . . . ?). In short, answering high-level question stems leads to deeper processing of the reading material. Second, it helps students to monitor their comprehension. If too many questions cannot be answered or if the answers appear to be too superficial, this provides clear evidence that the student has not achieved an adequate understanding of the passage.

Studies that have examined the effect of responding to question stems on teacher-made classroom tests report very strong effects. The average student who responded to question stems while reading a passage scored at the 87th percentile on a subsequent test, while the average student who did not answer questions scored only at the 50th percentile. Differences of this magnitude do not appear in research studies very often and, in this case, argue very strongly for providing students with question stems and for teaching them how to construct their own questions and answers (Rosenshine, Meister, & Chapman, 1996). Discussion of the conditions that underlie effective self-questioning instruction can be found in articles by Bernice Wong (1985) and Zemira Mevarech and Ziva Susak (1993).

NOTETAKING   As a learning tactic, notetaking comes with good news and bad. The good news is that notetaking can benefit a student in two ways. First, the process of taking notes while listening to a lecture or reading a text leads to better retention and comprehension of the noted information than just listening or reading does. For example, Andrew Katayama (1997) found that college students who were given a set of partially completed notes for a text passage and told to fill in the blank spaces scored higher on a test of knowledge transfer than students who were given a complete set of notes. Second, the process of reviewing notes produces additional chances to recall and comprehend the noted material. The bad news is that we know very little at the present time about the specific conditions that make notetaking an effective tactic.

> **Taking notes and reviewing notes aid retention and comprehension**

This uncertainty as to what constitutes a good set of notes probably explains the results obtained by Alison King (1992a) in a comparison of self-questioning, summarizing, and notetaking. One group of students was given a set of question stems, shown how to generate good questions with them, and allowed to practice. A second group was given a set of rules for creating a good summary (identify a main idea or subtopic and related ideas, and link them together in one sentence), shown how to use them to create good summaries, and allowed to practice. A third group, however, was told to simply take notes as group members normally would in class. Both the self-questioning and summarizing groups scored significantly higher on an immediate and one-week-delayed retention test.

On the basis of this brief review, we would like to draw two conclusions. One is that students need to be systematically taught how to use learning tactics to make connections among ideas contained in text and lecture as well as between new and previously learned information. No one expects students to teach themselves to read, write, and compute. So why should they be expected to teach themselves how to use a variety of learning tactics? The second conclusion is that learning tactics should not be taught as isolated techniques, particularly to high school students. If tactics are taught that way, most students probably will not keep using them for very long or recognize that as the situation changes, so should the tactic. Therefore, as we implied at the start of this section, students should be taught how to use tactics as part of a broader learning strategy.

USING LEARNING STRATEGIES EFFECTIVELY

THE COMPONENTS OF A LEARNING STRATEGY   As noted, a learning strategy is a plan for accomplishing a learning goal. It consists of six components: metacognition, analysis, planning, implementation of the plan, monitoring of progress, and modification. To give you a better idea of how to formulate a learning strategy of your own, here is a detailed description of each of these components (Snowman, 1986, 1987).

> **Learning strategy components: metacognition, analysis, planning, implementation, monitoring, modification**

     1. *Metacognition.* In the absence of some minimal awareness of how we think and how our thought processes affect our academic performance, a strategic approach to learning is simply not possible. We need to know, at the very least, that effective learning requires an analysis of the learning situation, formulation of a learning plan, skillful implementation of appropriate tactics, periodic monitoring of our progress, and modification of things that go wrong. In addition, we need to know why each of these steps is necessary, when each step should be carried out, and how well prepared we are to perform each step. Without this knowledge, students who are taught one or more of the learning

Students can formulate strategic learning plans that identify and analyze the important aspects of a task. Then, they can tailor these plans to their own strengths and weaknesses as learners.

tactics mentioned earlier do not keep up their use for very long, nor do they apply the tactics to relevant tasks.

2. *Analysis.* Any workable plan must be based on relevant information. By thinking about the type of task that one must confront, the type of material that one has to learn, the personal characteristics that one possesses, and the way in which one's competence will be tested, the strategic learner can generate this information by playing the role of an investigative journalist and asking questions that pertain to what, when, where, why, who, and how. In this way the learner can identify important aspects of the material to be learned (what, when, where), understand the nature of the test that will be given (why), recognize relevant personal learner characteristics (who), and identify potentially useful learning activities or tactics (how).

3. *Planning.* Once satisfactory answers have been gained from the analysis phase, the strategic learner then formulates a learning plan by hypothesizing something like the following: "I know something about the material to be learned (I have to read and comprehend five chapters of my music appreciation text within the next three weeks), the nature of the test criterion (I will have to compare and contrast the musical structure of symphonies that were written by Beethoven, Schubert, and Brahms), my strengths and weaknesses as a learner (I am good at tasks that involve the identification of similarities and differences, but I have difficulty concentrating for long periods of time), and the nature of various learning activities (skimming is a good way to get a general sense of the structure of a chapter; mnemonic devices make memorizing important details easier and more reliable; notetaking and self-questioning are more effective ways to enhance comprehension than simple rereading). Based on this knowledge, I should divide each chapter into several smaller units that will take no longer than thirty minutes to read, take notes as I read, answer self-generated compare-and-contrast questions, use the loci mnemonic to memorize details, and repeat this sequence several times over the course of each week."

4. *Implementation of the plan*. Once the learner has formulated a plan, each of its elements must be implemented *skillfully*. A careful analysis and a well-conceived plan will not work if tactics are carried out badly. Of course, a poorly executed plan may not be entirely attributable to a learner's tactical skill deficiencies. Part of the problem may be a general lack of knowledge about what conditions make for effective use of tactics (as is the case with notetaking).

5. *Monitoring of progress*. Once the learning process is under way, the strategic learner assesses how well the chosen tactics are working. Possible monitoring techniques include writing out a summary, giving an oral presentation, working practice problems, and answering questions.

6. *Modification*. If the monitoring assessment is positive, the learner may decide that no changes are needed. If, however, attempts to memorize or understand the learning material seem to be producing unsatisfactory results, the learner will need to reevaluate and modify the analysis. This, in turn, will cause changes in both the plan and the implementation.

There are two points we would like to emphasize about the nature of a learning strategy. The first is that learning conditions constantly change. Subject matters have different types of information and structures, teachers use different instructional methods and have different styles, exams differ in the kinds of demands they make, and the interests, motives, and capabilities of students change over time. Accordingly, strategies must be *formulated* or constructed anew as one moves from task to task rather than *selected* from a bank of previously formulated strategies. The true strategist, in other words, is very mentally active.

The second point is that the concept of a learning strategy is obviously complex and requires a certain level of intellectual maturity. Thus, you may be tempted to conclude that, although *you* could do it, learning to be strategic is beyond the reach of most elementary and high school students. Research evidence suggests otherwise, however. A study of high school students in Scotland, for example, found that some students are sensitive to contextual differences among school tasks and vary their approach to studying accordingly (Selmes, 1987). Furthermore, as we are about to show, research in the United States suggests that elementary school youngsters can be trained to use many of the strategy components just mentioned.

RESEARCH ON LEARNING STRATEGY TRAINING   Research clearly shows that training students to use various tactics and strategies is a worthwhile use of the teacher's time. Students who were trained to use a single mnemonic technique outperformed nontrained students by a wide margin on subsequent tests of memory (86th percentile versus 50th percentile, respectively). The effect was particularly noticeable among primary grade and low-achieving students. A similar advantage was found for students who had been taught to use a variety of tactics and were tested for memory and low-level comprehension (75th percentile versus the control group's 50th percentile). Although the weakest effect was found in those studies where students were taught to approach learning in a more strategic fashion, these students nevertheless performed significantly better than students who were left to their own devices (70th percentile versus 50th percentile, respectively) (Hattie, Biggs, & Purdie, 1996).

Reciprocal teaching: students
learn to summarize, question,
clarify, predict as they read

A particularly effective strategy training program, as we mentioned earlier, is the *reciprocal teaching* (RT) program of Annemarie Palincsar and Ann Brown (1984). As the title of this program indicates, students learn certain comprehension skills by demonstrating them to each other. Palincsar and Brown trained a small group of seventh graders whose reading comprehension scores were at least two years below grade level to use the techniques of summarizing, self-questioning, clarifying, and predicting to improve their reading comprehension. These four methods were chosen because they can be used by students to improve *and* monitor comprehension.

During the early training sessions, the teacher explained and demonstrated the four methods while reading various passages. The students were then given gradually increasing responsibility for demonstrating these techniques to their peers, with the teacher supplying prompts and corrective feedback as needed. Eventually, each student was expected to offer a good summary of a passage, pose questions about important ideas, clarify ambiguous words or phrases, and predict upcoming events, all to be done with little or no intervention by the teacher. (This approach to strategy instruction, by the way, is based on Vygotsky's zone of proximal development concept that we first mentioned in Chapter 2.)

Palincsar and Brown found that the RT program produced two general beneficial effects. First, the quality of students' summaries, questions, clarifications, and predictions improved. Early in the program students produced overly detailed summaries and many unclear questions. But in later sessions concise summaries and questions dealing explicitly with main ideas were the rule. For example, questions on main ideas increased from 54 percent to 70 percent. In addition, the questions were increasingly stated in paraphrase form rather than as verbatim statements from the passage. Second, RT-trained students scored as well as a group of average readers on tests of comprehension (about 75 percent correct for both groups) and much better than a group taught how to locate information that might show up in a test question (75 percent correct versus 45 percent correct). Most impressively, these levels of performance held up for at least eight weeks after the study ended (no measures were taken after that point) and generalized to tests of social studies and science (20 percent correct prior to training versus 60 percent correct after training).

Subsequent research on the effectiveness of RT under both controlled and realistic conditions has continued to produce positive findings across a broad age spectrum (fourth grade through college). On the average, RT students have scored at the 62nd percentile on standardized reading comprehension tests (compared to the 50th percentile for the average control student) and at the 81st percentile rank on reading comprehension tests that were created by the experimenters (Alfassi, 1998; Carter, 1997; Rosenshine & Meister, 1994a).

The message of strategy training programs like reciprocal teaching is that knowledge of the learning process and the conditions that affect it should be as much a part of the curriculum as learning to read, write, and compute. Proponents have argued persuasively that mastery of traditional basic skills is influenced by the nontraditional but more basic skills of strategic reasoning (see, for example, Bracey, 1983). Accordingly, children should gradually be made aware of the general relationship between cognitive means and academic ends, the potential range of application of various learning tactics, how to determine if learning is proceeding as planned, and what to do if it is not.

In the following section we offer several Suggestions for Teaching that will help your students become more strategic and efficient learners.

SUGGESTIONS FOR TEACHING IN YOUR CLASSROOM

Helping Your Students Become Efficient Information Processors

1 Develop and use a variety of techniques to attract and hold attention, and give your students opportunities to practice and refine their skills in maintaining attention.

  a. Be aware of what will capture your students' attention.

  b. To maintain attention, emphasize the possible utility of learning new ideas.

  c. Teach students how to increase their span of attention.

2 Point out and encourage students to recognize that certain bits of information are important and can be related to what is already known.

3 Use appropriate rehearsal techniques, including an emphasis on meaning and chunking.

4 Organize what you ask your students to learn and urge older students to organize material on their own.

5 As much as possible, stress meaningfulness.

6 Demonstrate a variety of learning tactics and allow students to practice them.

  a. Teach students how to use various forms of rehearsal and mnemonic devices.

  b. Teach students how to formulate comprehension questions.

  c. Teach students how to take notes.

7 Encourage students to develop their metacognitive knowledge and skills by thinking about the various conditions that affect *how* they learn and remember.

---

1 Develop and use a variety of techniques to attract and hold attention, and give your students opportunities to practice and refine their skills in maintaining attention.

a. Be aware of what will capture your students' attention.

The ability to capture your students' attention is affected by characteristics of the information itself and by the learners' related past experiences. Learners are more likely to attend to things they expect to find interesting or meaningful. It is also true that human beings are sensitive to abrupt, sudden changes in their environment. Thus, anything that stands out, breaks a rhythm, or is unpredictable is almost certain to command students' attention.

Journal Entry
Techniques
for Capturing
Attention

| Unpredictable changes in environment usually command attention

EXAMPLES

■ Print key words or ideas in extralarge letters on the board.

■ Use colored chalk to emphasize important points written on the board.

■ When you come to a particularly important part of a lesson, say, "Now really concentrate on this. It's especially important." Then present the idea with intensity and emphasis.

■ Start off a lesson with unexpected remarks, such as "Imagine that you have just inherited a million dollars and . . . "

b. To maintain attention, emphasize the possible utility of learning new ideas.

Although it is possible to overdo attempts at making the curriculum relevant, it never hurts to think of possible ways of relating school learning to the present and future lives of students. When students realize that the basic purpose of school is to help them adapt to their environment, they are more apt to pay close attention to what you are trying to do.

Journal Entry
Techniques for
Maintaining
Attention

EXAMPLE

■ Teach basic skills—such as arithmetic computation, arithmetic reasoning, spelling, writing, and reading—as part of class projects that relate to students' natural interests (for example, keeping records of money for newspaper deliveries; measuring rainfall, temperature, and wind speed; writing letters to local television stations to express opinions on or request information about television shows).

c. Teach students how to increase their span of attention.

Journal Entry
Techniques for
Increasing Attention Span

Remember that paying attention is a skill that many students have not had an opportunity to refine. Give your students plenty of opportunities to practice and improve their ability to maintain attention.

Attention span can be increased with practice

EXAMPLES

■ Institute games that depend on maintaining attention, such as playing Simon Says, keeping track of an object hidden under one of several boxes (the old shell game), or determining whether two pictures are identical or different. At first, positively reinforce students for all correct responses. Then reinforce only for improvements in performance. Remind students that their success is a direct result of how well they pay attention.

■ Read a short magazine or newspaper story and ask students to report who, what, where, when, and why.

2 **Point out and encourage students to recognize that certain bits of information are important and can be related to what is already known.**

Attention is one control process for the sensory register; the other is recognition. Sometimes the two processes can be used together to induce students to focus on important parts of material to be learned. Sometimes you can urge your students to recognize key features or familiar relationships on their own.

EXAMPLES

■ Have students practice grouping numbers, letters, or classroom items according to some shared feature, such as odd numbers, multiples of five, letters with circles, or things made of wood.

Research findings demonstrate that notetaking in one form or another is an effective tactic for improving comprehension of text and lecture material. Consequently, students should be taught the basic principles that support effective notetaking.

■ Say, "This math problem is very similar to one you solved last week. Does anyone recognize something familiar about this problem?"

■ Say, "In this chapter the same basic point is made in several different ways. As you read, try to recognize and write down as many variations on that basic theme as you can."

3 Use appropriate rehearsal techniques, including an emphasis on meaning and chunking.

The power of chunking information into meaningful units was demonstrated in a study conducted with a single college student of average memory ability and intelligence (Ericsson, Chase, & Faloon, 1980). Over twenty months he was able to improve his memory for digits from seven to almost eighty. Being a track and field buff, he categorized three- and four-digit groups as running times for imaginary races. Thus, 3,492 became "3 minutes and 49.2 seconds, near world record time." Number groups that could not be encoded as running times were encoded as ages. These two chunking techniques accounted for almost 90 percent of his associations.

Journal Entry
Ways to Use Chunking to Facilitate Learning

    The main purpose of chunking is to enhance learning by breaking tasks into small, easy-to-manage pieces. To a large degree, students who are ten and older can learn to do this for themselves if you show them how chunking works. In addition, you can help by not requiring students to learn more than they can reasonably handle at one time. If you have a list of fifty spelling words to be learned, it is far better to present ten words a day, five days in a row, during short study periods than to give all fifty at once. This method of presentation is called **distributed practice**. In distributed practice, it is usually necessary to divide the material into small parts, which—because of the serial position effect—seems to be the best way for students to learn and retain unrelated material (for example, spelling words). The **serial position effect** refers to people's tendency to learn and remember the words at the beginning and end of a long list more easily than those in the middle. By using short lists, then, you in effect eliminate the hard-to-memorize middle ground. A description of the positive effect of distributed practice on classroom learning and an explanation of why educators do not make greater use of it have been offered by Frank Dempster (1988).

Distributed practice: short study periods at frequent intervals

Serial position effect: tendency to remember items at beginning and end of a long list

    Distributed practice may not be desirable for all learning tasks, however. If you ask students to learn roles in a play, short rehearsals might not be effective because students may have a difficult time grasping the entire plot. If you allow enough rehearsal time to run through a whole act, your students will be able to relate one speech to another and comprehend the overall structure of the play. When students learn by way of a few rather long study periods, spaced infrequently, psychologists call it **massed practice**.

    You might also tell your students about the relative merits of distributed versus massed practice. Robert Bjork (1979) has pointed out that most students not only are unaware of the benefits of distributed study periods but also go to considerable lengths to block or mass the study time devoted to a particular subject.

4 Organize what you ask your students to learn, and urge older students to organize material on their own.

At least some items in most sets of information that you ask your students to learn will be related to other items, and you will find it desirable to call attention to interrelationships. The Bower et al. (1969) experiment described earlier in which one

Journal Entry
Organizing Information into Related Categories

group of students was given a randomly arranged set of items to learn and another group was presented the same items in logically ordered groups illustrates the value of organization. By placing related items in groups, you reduce the number of chunks to be learned and also make it possible for students to benefit from cues supplied by the interrelationships between items in any given set. And by placing items in logical order, you help students grasp how information at the beginning of a chapter or lesson makes it easier to learn information that is presented later.

EXAMPLES

■ If students are to learn how to identify trees, birds, rocks, or the equivalent, group items that are related (for example, deciduous and evergreen trees). Call attention to distinctive features and to organizational schemes that have been developed.

■ Print an outline of a chapter on the board, or give students a duplicated outline, and have them record notes under the various headings. Whenever you give a lecture or demonstration, print an outline on the board. Call attention to the sequence of topics and demonstrate how various points emerge from or are related to other points.

5 As much as possible, stress meaningfulness.

Journal Entry
Ways to Stress
Meaningfulness

When you present material to be learned, emphasize the logic behind it and urge students to look for meaning on their own. Concrete analogies offer one effective way to add meaning to material. Consider someone who has no knowledge of basic physics but is trying to understand a passage about the flow of electricity through metal. For this person, statements about crystalline lattice arrays, free-floating electrons, and the effects of impurities will mean very little. However, such abstract ideas can be explained in more familiar terms. You might compare the molecular structure of a metal bar to a Tinker Toy arrangement, for example, or liken the effect of impurities to placing a book in the middle of a row of falling dominoes. Such analogies increase recall and comprehension (Royer & Cable, 1975, 1976).

Concrete analogies
can make abstract
information meaningful

EXAMPLES

■ Give students opportunities to express ideas in their own words and to relate new knowledge to previous learning.

■ When you explain or demonstrate, express complex and abstract ideas several different ways. Be sure to provide plenty of examples.

■ Construct essay tests and homework assignments that emphasize comprehension and application. Give credit for thoughtful answers even though they do not exactly match the answer you would have given.

■ For topics that are somewhat controversial (for example, nuclear energy, genetic engineering, pesticide use), require students to present both pro and con arguments.

6 Demonstrate a variety of learning tactics and allow students to practice them.

a. Teach students how to use various forms of rehearsal and mnemonic devices.

Journal Entry
Ways to Teach
Memory Tactics

At least two reasons recommend the teaching of rehearsal. One is that maintenance rehearsal is a useful tactic for keeping a relatively small amount of information active in short-term memory. The other is that maintenance rehearsal is one of a few tactics that young children can learn to use. If you do decide to teach rehearsal, we have two suggestions. First, remind young children that rehearsal is something that learners consciously decide to do when they want to remember things. Second, remind students to rehearse no more than seven items (or chunks) at a time.

Upper elementary grade students (fourth, fifth, and sixth graders) can be taught advanced forms of maintenance rehearsal, such as cumulative rehearsal, and forms of elaborative rehearsal, such as rehearsing sets of items that form homogeneous categories. As with younger students, provide several opportunities each week to practice these skills.

As you prepare class presentations or encounter bits of information that students seem to have difficulty learning, ask yourself if a mnemonic device would be useful. You might write up a list of the devices discussed earlier and refer to it often. Part of the value of mnemonic devices is that they make learning easier. They are also fun to make up and use. Moreover, rhymes, acronyms, and acrostics can be constructed rather quickly. You might consider setting aside about thirty minutes two or three times a week to teach mnemonics. First, explain how rhyme, acronym, and acrostic mnemonics work, and then provide examples of each (see Table 8.1). Once students understand how the mnemonic is supposed to work, have them construct mnemonics to learn various facts and concepts. You might offer a prize for the most ingenious mnemonic.

b. Teach students how to formulate comprehension questions.

We concluded earlier that self-questioning could be an effective comprehension tactic if students were trained to write good comprehension questions and given opportunities to practice the technique. We suggest you try the following instructional sequence:

Journal Entry
Ways to Teach
Comprehension
Tactics

1. Discuss the purpose of student-generated questions.
2. Point out the differences between knowledge-level questions and different types of comprehension-level questions (such as analysis, synthesis, and evaluation). An excellent discussion of these types can be found in the *Taxonomy of Educational Objectives, Handbook I: Cognitive Domain* (Bloom et al., 1956).
3. Explain and illustrate the kinds of responses that should be given to different types of comprehension-level questions.
4. Provide students with a sample paragraph and a set of high-level question stems. Have students formulate questions and responses either individually or in pairs.
5. Provide corrective feedback.
6. Give students short passages from which to practice.
7. Provide corrective feedback (André & Anderson, 1978–1979, King, 1994).

c. Teach students how to take notes.

Despite the limitations of research on notetaking, mentioned earlier, three suggestions should lead to more effective notetaking. First, provide students with clear, detailed objectives for every reading assignment. The objectives should indicate what parts of the assignment to focus on and how that material should

Journal Entry
Teaching Students
How to Take Notes

be processed (whether memorized verbatim, reorganized and paraphrased, or integrated with earlier reading assignments). Second, inform students that note-taking is an effective comprehension tactic when used appropriately. Think, for example, about a reading passage that is long and for which test items will demand analysis and synthesis of broad concepts (as in "Compare and contrast the economic, social, and political causes of World War I with those of World War II"). Tell students to concentrate on identifying main ideas and supporting details, paraphrase this information, and record similarities and differences. Third, provide students with practice and corrective feedback in answering questions that are similar to those on the criterion test.

7 Encourage students to develop their metacognitive knowledge and skills by thinking about the various conditions that affect *how* they learn and remember.

The very youngest students (through third grade) should be told periodically that such cognitive behaviors as describing, recalling, guessing, and understanding mean different things, produce different results, and vary in how well they fit a task's demands. For older elementary school and middle school students, explain the learning process more simply, focusing on the circumstances in which different learning tactics are likely to be useful. Then, have students keep a diary or log in which they note when they use learning tactics, which ones, and with what success. Look for cases where good performance corresponds to frequent reported use of tactics and positively reinforce those individuals. Encourage greater use of tactics among students whose performance and reported use of them are below average.

Although this same technique can be used with high school and college students, they should also be made aware of the other elements that make up strategic learning. Discuss the meaning of and necessity for analyzing a learning task, developing a learning plan, using appropriate tactics, monitoring the effectiveness of the plan, and implementing whatever corrective measures might be called for.

The next section describes several ways that you can use computer-based technology to improve your students' information processing skills.

Technology as an Information-Processing Tool

Although computer-based technology may have had its roots in behavioral learning theory, current technology is more likely to reflect an information-processing perspective. The programs and devices to be described in this section influence how we access, filter, represent, and evaluate knowledge. As the limitations of human memory and the difficulty of creating learning strategies have been clarified, computer-based technology has been called upon to help overcome these constraints and reduce the cognitive processing burden of complex tasks. For instance, technology might help someone better grasp an idea for a musical composition, see the structure of her writing plans, or watch chemical molecules react.

A myriad of computer tools exist today to support learners as they construct knowledge and design products. Robert Kozma (1987, p. 21) defines these tools as "software programs that use the control capabilities of the computer to amplify, extend, or enhance human cognition." Gavriel Salomon (1993) suggests that computer tools can assist humans in communication and expression; provide mental strategies that transform knowledge (for example, prompts or suggestions to integrate knowledge or draw a conclusion); and encourage learner manipulation and transformation of knowledge. He differentiates between computer tools that leave some lasting cognitive change or residue within the mind of the learner as a result of use and computer tools that simply enhance or speed up learner performance (for example, word processing tools). Both Salomon and Kozma argue that some computer tools act as cognitive tools by creating opportunities to generate hypotheses, browse and summarize data, organize information, depict causal relationships, and draw appropriate conclusions.

In this section we will examine technological tools that help students formulate and represent knowledge, acquire important knowledge and skills from different subject areas, provide multiple representations of knowledge, and regulate their own thinking.

TOOLS TO REPRESENT KNOWLEDGE

Over a decade ago David Olson (1985, p. 7) argued that "almost any form of human competence is a joint product of the resources of the mind and the potentials of those [computer] technologies." Naturally, the key to the success of such human-computer partnerships is the mindfulness displayed by the learner (Salomon, Perkins, & Globerson, 1991), which allows the performance to be more intelligent than would occur without the tool. As a result of this thinking skill partnership, complex or higher-order thinking processes are made more explicit or apparent to the learner and he or she can, over time, internalize these strategies.

One of the first pedagogical tools, the Learning Tool, was developed by Kozma (1987) over a decade ago. This program was designed to help students organize, chunk, link, and use knowledge that was gathered from a variety of sources. Tools for outlining and mapping out one's ideas as well as taking notes are available in the Learning Tool to augment the limitations of human working memory. Knowledge representation tools are designed to help students represent knowledge in multiple formats, organize and restructure knowledge, activate relevant prior knowledge, and efficiently retrieve information.

Computer-based technology helps students organize and represent ideas and comprehend text

TECHNOLOGY TOOLS FOR WRITING

In Robert Bangert-Drowns's (1993) review of more than thirty studies examining the effects of word processing on writing, he concluded that word processing without instructor guidance or relevant instructional activities may simply cause writers to write longer documents but not necessarily enhance the quality of their text. Students simply need more instructional guidance when using writing tools. Fortunately, tools like Writer's Workbench have proven effective at improving student editing and revising practices, while others, like Writer's Helper, use subprograms to force students to attend to prewriting, drafting, and revising. According to Mike Reed (1996), this division of writing into stages is helpful since studies show that good writers spend about 85 percent of their time prewriting and only 2 percent drafting their work, while average and less effective writers devote 98 percent of their time to drafting and nearly no time prewriting.

In addition to the tools just mentioned, there are prewriting tools such as IdeaFisher or Inspiration as well as notecards, outlining aids, journal writing supports, idea processors, and mind mapping or semantic webbing software (Kellogg, 1989; MacArthur, 1996). For revision, there are text analysis packages that check and correct one's writing style and format (for example, Grammatik and Microsoft Bookshelf) as well as computer prompting and metacognitive questioning tools to help one reflect on a written draft (Bonk & Reynolds, 1992; Zellermayer, Salomon, Globerson, & Givon, 1991). As mentioned in Chapter 2, prompts can provide less skilled and young writers with procedural support or strategic assistance for higher-level writing activities, such as creating paragraph transitions or checking for bias in one's writing. Research, in fact, reveals that computer prompts effectively move student concerns from lower-level spelling and grammar issues to higher-level idea generation and revision practices (Reynolds & Bonk, 1996; Zellermayer et al., 1991).

With the emergence of the World Wide Web, there are increasing opportunities for collaborative writing and the facilitation of audience awareness with interactive debate forums, peer mentor commenting windows, and on-line mentoring. Some programs, such as PREP Editor (now called Common Space), have been specifically designed for peer and instructor feedback on one's electronic documents (Neuwirth & Wojahn, 1996). And when students respond to such comments, their thinking processes become visible to the instructor. Other electronic writing tools exist to add layers of comments, arrows to signify text movements, and annotations that allow multiple users to make suggestions without directly affecting the underlying document.

Technology Tools for Reading

As with writing, electronic support systems have been used to increase student reading comprehension and metacognitive skill (Salomon, Globerson, & Guterman, 1989). A videodisk-based story or popular book (for example, *Jurassic Park*) can be segmented, replayed, debated, and compared to the original text version. Research on such tools indicates that student vocabulary can be enriched by anchoring student learning in these realistic and motivating contexts (Xin, Glaser, & Rieth, 1996). As indicated in previous chapters, with the emergence of voice recognition and speech synthesis, computers might highlight words being spoken or read them back to a writer, thereby increasing reading fluency.

Technology Tools for Science and Math

In mathematics and science, Marcia Linn (1992) and other prominent researchers have argued that students should spend less time manually calculating and plotting data and more time using technology to summarize and interpret data, look for trends, and predict relationships. Based on over ten years of research, Linn (1997) has created the Knowledge Integration Environment (KIE) to help students locate information on the World Wide Web, record and organize their findings and ideas in an electronic notebook, and participate in on-line discussions to make collaborative decisions about science. Like the writing tools mentioned earlier, the KIE notebook tool allows science students to organize and analyze evidence. Procedural guidance and hints are provided in the system to help students think critically and evaluate the evidence they gather.

As with the microcomputer-based laboratory equipment mentioned in Chapter 2, computer sensors and data logging devices connected to computers can quickly create graphs that help convey complex scientific information visually, as we describe shortly. Computer tools also exist for electronically dissecting animals and performing operations, exploring laws of physics, and conducting chemistry experiments (Snir, Smith, & Grosslight, 1993). CD-ROM resources can supply captivating animations of abstract microscopic events, video depictions of various chemical reactions, text information about potential hazards of these experiments, sample demonstrations and laboratory activities, and encyclopedias of teaching suggestions (Brooks & Brooks, 1996). In effect, with CD-ROMs and other technology, safety is no longer the overriding concern in a chemistry class. CD-ROMs might also be used to study such large-scale phenomena as hurricanes or winter storm patterns.

For mathematics and physics, the Calculator-Based Laboratory (CBL) from Texas Instruments provides "a data-collection system that uses probes, such as temperature, light, and voltage probes, to gather data into a **graphing calculator**" (Nicol, 1997, p. 86). CBLs convert information from sensors and probes into data that can be understood and graphed by the calculator. Students taking a math class might use this tool to represent and manipulate quadratic equations in algebra, visualize statistics and other information in geometry classes, and better understand derivatives and inequalities in calculus (Engebretsen, 1997; Ferrini-Mundy, & Lauten, 1994). In addition, there are computer tools that can be used to create sales forecast models and spreadsheets to track inventories for a local company, design truss structures in a physics class, or generate mathematical models of sports activities such as shooting a free throw (Murdick, 1996). This visualization and manipulation of data helps students investigate problems, tie the information together, perceive different aspects of problems, test real-life data and problems, and gain a sense of ownership over the learning process.

TECHNOLOGY TOOLS FOR ART AND MUSIC

As you may be aware, computer tools are also being used in the fine and performing arts. Art education, for instance, benefits from electronic tools that quickly erase or alter ideas. For instance, Jane Chia and Birnie Duthie (1993) provide examples of how electronic sketchpads, draw palettes, and paint packages can enhance the generation of elementary student visual imagery. For the music classroom, there are tools such as digital oscilloscopes that help students understand relationships between pitch and wavelength as well as software like KidsNotes that can emulate an electronic keyboard to help students develop pitch discrimination (Magnusson, 1996). In addition, CD technology can be used to present graphical representations of notes as they are played, sections of which can saved and compared to other verses of the same song or to other songs, thereby helping students understand themes and patterns in music. There are also a number of musical microworld tools that encourage students to construct and play their own music. Moreover, computer tools such as Musical Instrument Digital Interface (MIDI) (Reese, 1995) allow students to play a musical instrument and record it on a computer. Here students can explore concepts of pitch, duration, sound combination, repetition, and melody and engage in the process of musical thinking.

MULTIMEDIA TOOLS

As mentioned in Chapter 4, multimedia encyclopedias, databases, and libraries provide students with a wide variety of information resources. Simply put, multimedia tools offer multiple views (text, photographs, digitized video, animation, sound) on difficult concepts that can enrich student understanding of the topic (Toomey & Ketterer, 1995). The use of multimedia tools is related to such information-processing concepts as meaningful learning, the dual coding of information (Clark & Paivio, 1991), the use of visual imagery, and elaborative rehearsal. Like the mind, multimedia tools provide more than one way to retrieve or visit information; the richer or more dense the network or web of connections, the more likely one will comprehend the meaning.

HYPERMEDIA TOOLS

Hypermedia technology exists when multimedia information can be nonsequentially accessed, examined, and/or constructed by users, thereby enabling them to move from one information resource to another while controlling which options to take (Grabe & Grabe, 1998). Dispersed information fragments (called "nodes") are associated in hypermedia through "links" that reference one another or that help organize the resource. There are clear advantages to hypermedia, such as the richness of the network of ideas, the compact storage of information, the rapid nonlinear access to information, the flexible use of information, and learner control over the system. Not surprisingly, it has been suggested that hypermedia tools radically alter the way people read, write, compute, and perhaps even think (Nelson & Palumbo, 1992).

For such subjects as English literature, history, or teacher education, hypermedia tools can encourage the learner to see problems from multiple perspectives and develop more flexible knowledge structures (Spiro, Feltovich, Jacobson, & Coulson, 1991). Rand Spiro and his colleagues have used this concept to develop an instructional technique called "criss-crossing" the landscape. From this perspective, since there are multiple correct answers or plausible solutions that need to be explored by the learner from many directions, hypertexts can build "cognitive flexibility" (Spiro et al. 1991, p. 22) in the learner, while developing both cognitive processing skills and content knowledge. For instance, in your teacher education programs you might be given multiple case situations that are tailored around a common theme (for example, how to help to develop student self-concept).

Hypermedia tools in mathematics might include a video presentation, simple diagrams, digitized images of real-life phenomena, dynamic video clips or computer animation of problem sequences, definitions of terms, and computer prompts to go back and read the problem.

One science hypermedia tool, Microsoft Dinosaurs, contains an atlas that provides vital information about the location and movement of dinosaurs, a timeline that depicts changes in life forms over time, dinosaur movies that provide animations of dinosaur behavior, an index to search for topics, vocabulary tools, and a guided tour to learn how to use the hypermedia components of the tool (Shepardson & Britsch, 1996). In addition to being able to explore this information, the user of Microsoft Dinosaur can try out various games, such as dinosaur mystery episodes that contain currently debated questions about dinosaurs.

As multimedia and hypermedia technology spreads, it is likely that your students will be making such search and selection decisions on at least a daily basis. For instance, CD's and videodisks now provide text, still photographs, motion video, and games for children to dynamically explore newly discovered Mayan ruins, create multimedia presentations of zoo animals, confront life-and-death moral decisions, and better learn foreign languages (Kozma, 1991; Meskill, 1996). In terms of foreign or second language learning, Carla Meskill points out that students can control the rate and style of presentation to suit their own needs. For instance, a student learning the Russian language by watching a televison show from Moscow in a multimedia format might not only be able to view the broadcast but can have a copy of the verbatim text, an on-line Russian-English dictionary, links to related news stories and events, the capability to revisit earlier episodes, and a menu of other programs and commercials.

RESEARCH ON MULTIMEDIA AND HYPERMEDIA TECHNOLOGY   Do multimedia and hypermedia technology improve learning? David Ayersman's (1996) review of the initial research on hypermedia-based learning indicates that this tool has resulted in a number of positive outcomes, including a greater sense of control and personal freedom, increased intrinsic motivation, better recall of information and enhanced student listening comprehension, more effective study skills and strategies, greater individualization of learning, improved knowledge and skills, and more positive attitudes. But such preliminary findings have not been consistent across studies, as students' previous learning experiences in linear formats has not always been easy to overcome, nor are all commercially developed hypermedia software packages of high quality.

Other research indicates that multimedia environments can address individual learning preferences and expand the ways in which students can express themselves. Not surprisingly, student comprehension of hypermedia documents is positively affected when they use learning tactics such as comprehension monitoring, elaboration, and rehearsal (Davidson-Shivers, Rasmussen, & Bratton-Jeffery, 1997). One study has shown that students working on multimedia compositions in realistic environments can experience significant knowledge gains (Bonk, Hay, & Fischler, 1996).

On the negative side, students with poorly developed organizational skills can be distracted by multimedia environments that provide readily accessible graphics, animation, and sound. And although students can gain vital knowledge from information-rich hypermedia and multimedia tools, the research to date also clearly shows that they can end up disoriented, lacking in self-confidence, anxious, frustrated, overwhelmed, and confused (Morrell, Marchionini, & Neuman, 1993). Such research indicates that it is the pedagogical strategies and teacher guidance that often determine the difference between sophisticated student learning or casual browsing within these systems. Further, Daniel Shepardson and Susan Britsch (1996) caution that the hypermedia environment lacks the ability to negotiate meaning with the learner or involve him or her in a community of learners. Unfortunately, this is true of most multimedia and hypermedia learning tools.

| **Hypermedia and multimedia tools produce both positive and negative results** |

EFFECTS OF TECHNOLOGY ON METACOGNITION

When students select search topics and associated terms and then evaluate search results, they are making decisions about what information to read, thinking about knowledge interrelationships, and engaging in extensive self-questioning and note-taking (Kozma, 1991). When they create databases of related ideas or link information in multiple formats, they are making decisions and elaboratively encoding the information. These are important skills for the next century. But can computer-based instructional technology help students develop their metacognitive skills in addition to helping them learn content?

To answer this question, tools such as LOGO have been extensively explored for what they can offer in terms of student planning, error detection, comprehension monitoring, and other metacognitive skills. LOGO is a simple computer programming language that was designed to foster children's higher-order thinking and mathematical reasoning skills. Though initial studies were inconclusive, more research has found increases in metacognitive performance among elementary students when instructors mediate the learning environment (Lehrer & Littlefield, 1991) or when students work in pairs (Nastasi & Clements, 1994). Across a series of studies, in fact, Bonnie Nastasi and Douglas Clements (1993) have discovered that LOGO may facilitate higher-order thinking skills more effectively than certain types of CAI software. One recent study shows that simply having computers in the home or having access to them can promote metacognitive changes in the minds of preschool children (Fletcher-Flinn & Suddendorf, 1996). However, as alluded to in the discussion of scaffolding in Chapter 2, it is starting to become clear that computer environments combined with teacher guidance and explicit metacognitive training to plan, monitor, and evaluate learning seem to be the most effective means of developing children's self-regulatory skills and problem solving strategies.

RESOURCES FOR FURTHER INVESTIGATION

◼ The Nature of Information-Processing Theory

For more on how information-processing theory relates to teaching and learning, read Chapter 1 of *Cognitive Classroom Learning* (1986). Written by Thomas André and Gary Phye, and titled "Cognition, Learning, and Education," the chapter compares information processing with behavioral learning theory, describes the nature of memory stores and control processes, and discusses the value of an information-processing perspective for educational practice.

Another source of information is *The Cognitive Psychology of School Learning* (2d ed., 1993), by Ellen Gagné, Carol Walker Yekovich, and Frank Yekovich. The goal of these authors is to help educators use information-processing theory and research to answer the questions "What shall we teach?" and "How shall we teach?" Chapters 12–15 describe how to use this knowledge base to teach reading, writing, mathematics, and science, respectively.

A collection of ERIC (Education Resources Information Center) digests on information processing can be found at gopher://inet.ed.gov:12002/7waissrc%3A/EricDigests?information processing.

◼ Memory Structures and Processes

Norman Spear and David Riccio describe various aspects of memory structures and processes in *Memory: Phenomena and*

Principles (1994). As the title suggests, Alan Searleman and Douglas Herrmann cover the same ground, plus such additional topics as the role of social factors in memory, individual differences in memory, and changes in memory ability, in *Memory from a Broader Perspective* (1994). Alan Baddeley provides a detailed account of memory phenomena in *Human Memory: Theory and Practice* (rev. ed., 1998).

◼ Metacognition

If you would like to know more about the nature of metacognition and its role in memory, eyewitness testimony, and problem solving; its development in adulthood and old age; and the neuropsychology of metacognition, take a look at *Metacognition: Knowing About Knowing* (1994), edited by Janet Metcalfe and Arthur Shimamura. If teaching reading is going to be one of your future responsibilities, you may glean some useful ideas from Ruth Garner, *Metacognition and Reading Comprehension* (1987).

A collection of ERIC digests on metacognition can be found on-line at gopher://inet.ed.gov: 12002/7waissrc%3A/EricDigests?metacognitive strategies.

◼ Learning Tactics and Strategies

One of the most popular (and useful) memory improvement books available is *The Memory Book* (1974), by Harry

Lorayne and Jerry Lucas. They explain why and how you should think up ridiculous associations, offer suggestions for using substitute words, provide techniques for learning foreign and English vocabulary, and describe ways to remember names and faces.

Meredith Gall, Joyce Gall, Dennis Jacobsen, and Terry Bullock summarize underlying theories of information processing and motivation, outline why it is important to teach students study skills, and describe how a school or district can implement a study skills program in *Tools for Learning: A Guide to Teaching Study Skills* (1990).

Although written principally for college students and their instructors, *Learning to Learn: Making the Transition from Student to Life-Long Learner* (1998), by Kenneth A. Kiewra and Nelson F. DuBois, offers much of value to high school students and their teachers.

A complete list of projects on cognitive skills development approved by the Department of Education for national dissemination for elementary through high school educators is found on-line at the Department of Education's gopher server, **gopher://gopher.ed.gov:70/00/programs/NDN/edprog94/eptw10**. The site is maintained by the National Diffusion Network and is equivalent to its *Educational Programs That Work*, twentieth edition print catalogue.

■ Individual Differences in Memory

One of the most striking accounts of supernormal memory is provided by Alexander Luria, *The Mind of a Mnemonist: A Little Book About a Vast Memory* (1968). Luria describes his experiments and experiences over a period of almost thirty years with the man he refers to as S, who could recall nonsense material he had not seen for fifteen years. Charles Thompson, Thaddeus Cowan, and Jerome Frieman describe a series of studies done with Rajan Mahadevan, who earned a place in the *Guinness Book of World Records* by memorizing the first 31,811 digits of pi, in *Memory Search by a Memorist* (1993). Additional articles about people with unusually proficient memory capability can be found in *Memory Observed* (1982), edited by Ulric Neisser.

Robert Kail describes memory differences among normal children, as well as differences between normal and retarded children in *The Development of Memory in Children* (3d ed., 1990). Also briefly discussed is the phenomenon of the idiot savants—individuals who are below average on all measures of ability except one, in which they far surpass almost all other individuals—and the reliability of children's eyewitness testimony. Leon Miller describes musical savants, individuals with mental retardation, who can perfectly reproduce musical passages on an instrument after one hearing, in *Musical Savants: Exceptional Skill in the Mentally Retarded* (1989).

SUMMARY

1. Information-processing theory attempts to explain how individuals acquire, store, recall, and use information.

2. A popular model of information processing is composed of three memory stores and a set of control processes that determine the flow of information from one memory store to another. The memory stores are the sensory register, short-term memory, and long-term memory. The control processes are recognition, attention, maintenance rehearsal, elaborative rehearsal, and retrieval.

3. The sensory register holds information in its original form for two or three seconds, during which time we may recognize and attend to it further.

4. Recognition involves noticing key features of a stimulus and integrating those features with relevant information from long-term memory.

5. Attention is a selective focusing on a portion of the information in the sensory register. Information from long-term memory influences what we focus on.

6. Short-term memory holds about seven bits of information for about twenty seconds (in the absence of rehearsal). It is often called working memory because it is where various encoding, organizational, and retrieval processes occur.

7. Information can be held in short-term memory indefinitely through the use of maintenance rehearsal, which is rote repetition of information.

8. Information is transferred from short-term memory to long-term memory by the linking of the new information to related information in long-term memory. This process is called elaborative rehearsal.

9. Elaborative rehearsal is based partly on organization. This involves grouping together, or chunking, items of information that share some important characteristic.

10. Elaborative rehearsal is also based on meaningfulness. Meaningful learning occurs when new information that is clearly written and logically organized is consciously related to information the learner currently has stored in long-term memory.

11. Long-term memory is thought by some psychologists to be an unlimited storehouse of information from which nothing is ever lost.

12. Many psychologists believe the information in long-term memory is organized in the form of schemata. A schema is a generalized abstract structure of information. When schemata are absent or crudely formed, learning and recall problems occur.

13. Contrary to popular belief, students remember much of the information they learn in school, especially if it was well learned to start with and if it was learned in a meaningful fashion.

14. Metacognition refers to any knowledge an individual has about how humans think and how those processes can be used to achieve learning goals.

15. Metacognition increases gradually with experience. This helps explain why junior high and high school students are more flexible and effective learners than primary grade students.

16. A learning strategy is a general plan that specifies the resources one will use, when they will be used, and how one will use them to achieve a learning goal.

17. A learning tactic is a specific technique one uses to help accomplish an immediate task-related objective.

18. Most teachers provide little or no direct instruction to students in the formulation and use of strategies and tactics.

19. Learning tactics can be classified as memory directed or comprehension directed. The former are used when accurate storage and retrieval of information are important. The latter are used when comprehension of ideas is important.

20. Two types of memory-directed tactics are rehearsal and mnemonic devices. Since most forms of rehearsal involve little or no encoding of information, they are not very effective memory tactics. Because mnemonic devices organize information and provide built-in retrieval cues, they are effective memory tactics.

21. Popular mnemonic devices include rhymes, acronyms, acrostics, the loci method, and the keyword method.

22. Two effective comprehension tactics are self-questioning and notetaking.

23. The components of a learning strategy are metacognition, analysis, planning, implementation, monitoring, and modification.

24. Learning strategy training raises the reading comprehension scores of both average and below-average readers.

25. Contemporary computer-based technology supports information processing by helping students to organize and mentally represent ideas, write more clearly, better comprehend text, interpret mathematical data, and understand musical patterns.

KEY TERMS

information-processing theory *(251)*
sensory register (SR) *(253)*
recognition *(253)*
attention *(254)*
short-term memory (STM) *(255)*
maintenance rehearsal *(256)*
elaborative rehearsal *(256)*

meaningful learning *(258)*
dual coding theory *(259)*
long-term memory (LTM) *(259)*
schemata *(260)*
metacognition *(264)*
learning strategy *(267)*
learning tactic *(267)*

mnemonic device *(268)*
distributed practice *(278)*
serial position effect *(278)*
massed practice *(278)*
graphing calculator *(284)*

DISCUSSION QUESTIONS

1. Can you think of any personal, everyday experiences that illustrate the nature of one or more of the three memory stores? Have you recently, for instance, retrieved a long-dormant memory because of a chance encounter with an associated word, sound, or smell?

2. Information-processing psychologists have expressed disappointment that the results of their research on memory stores and processes, learning tactics, and learning strategies have not been widely implemented by teachers. Is this complaint consistent with your experience? Can you recall any instances when you were taught how to use a variety of learning tactics to formulate different strategies? How about out of school? Did you acquire any such skills without the help of a classroom teacher?

3. Many teachers have said that they would like to teach their students more about the nature and use of learning processes but that they don't have time because of the amount of subject material they must cover. What can you do as a teacher to avoid this pitfall?

4. A major problem in training students to use learning strategies and tactics is getting the youngsters to spend the time and effort required to master these skills. Suppose some students expressed their lack of interest, saying their own methods would be just as effective (although you know full well they would not be). How would you convince these students otherwise?

9 Constructivist Learning Theory, Problem Solving, and Transfer

When you begin to teach, you may devote a substantial amount of class time to having students learn information discovered by others. But the acquisition of a storehouse of facts, concepts, and principles is only part of what constitutes an appropriate education. Students must also learn how to *find*, *evaluate*, and *use* what they need to know to accomplish whatever goals they set for

KEY POINTS

These key points will help you learn the important information in this chapter. To help you study, they also appear in the margins of the pages, next to the text where they are discussed.

Meaningful Learning within a Constructivist Framework

- Constructivism: creating a personal interpretation of external ideas and experiences
- Bruner: discover how ideas relate to each other and to existing knowledge
- Construction of ideas aided by discussion and debate
- Cognitive constructivism emphasizes role of cognitive processes in meaningful learning
- Social constructivism emphasizes role of culture and social interaction in meaningful learning
- Scaffolding: provide student with enough help to complete a task; gradually decrease help as student becomes able to work independently
- Constructivism aided by cognitive apprenticeship, realistic tasks, multiple perspectives
- Constructivist-oriented teaching encourages creating new views; uses scaffolding, realistic tasks, and class discussion

The Nature of Problem Solving

- Well-structured problems: clearly stated, known solution procedures, known evaluation standards
- Ill-structured problems: vaguely stated, unclear solution procedures, vague evaluation standards
- Issues: ill-structured problems that arouse strong feelings
- Problem finding depends on curiosity, dissatisfaction with status quo
- Problem framing depends on knowledge of subject matter, familiarity with problem types
- Inert knowledge due to learning isolated facts under limited conditions
- Studying worked examples is an effective solution strategy
- Solve simpler version of problem first; then transfer process to harder problem
- Break complex problems into manageable parts
- Work backward when goal is clear but beginning state is not
- Evaluate solutions to well-structured problems by estimating or checking

Suggestions for Teaching in Your Classroom

- Comprehension of subject matter critical to problem solving

Transfer of Learning

- Early view of transfer based on degree of similarity between two tasks
- Positive transfer: previous learning makes later learning easier
- Negative transfer: previous learning interferes with later learning
- Specific transfer due to specific similarities between two tasks
- General transfer due to use of same cognitive strategies
- Low-road transfer: previously learned skill automatically applied to similar current task
- High-road transfer: formulate rule from one task and apply to related task
- Low-road and high-road transfer produced by varied practice at applying skills, rules, memory retrieval cues

Technology Tools for Knowledge Construction and Problem Solving

- Technology tools are available to help students construct knowledge, become better problem solvers themselves. In other words, students need to learn how to be effective problem solvers. One justification for teaching problem-solving skills in *addition* to ensuring mastery of factual information is that life in technologically oriented countries is marked by speedy change. New products, services, and social conventions are rapidly introduced and integrated into our lifestyles. Microcomputers, the Internet, cellular telephones, anticancer drugs, and in vitro fertilization, to name just a few examples, are relatively recent innovations that significantly affect the lives of many people.

But change, particularly rapid change, can be a mixed blessing. On the one hand, new products and services such as those just mentioned can make life more convenient, efficient, and enjoyable. On the other hand, they can make life more complicated and problematic. Factory automation, for example, promises increased efficiency and productivity (which contribute to our standard of living), but it also threatens the job security of thousands of workers. Advances in medical care promise healthier and longer lives, but they introduce a host of moral, ethical, legal, and economic problems.

The educational implication that flows from these observations is clear: if we are to benefit from our ability to produce rapid and sometimes dramatic change, our schools need to invest more time, money, and effort in teaching students how to be effective problem solvers. As Lauren Resnick, a past president of the American Educational Research Association, argues:

We need to identify and closely examine the aspects of education that are most likely to produce ability to adapt in the face of transitions and breakdowns. Rather than training people for particular jobs—a task better left to revised forms of on-the-job training—school should focus its efforts on preparing people to be good *adaptive learners*, so that they can perform effectively when situations are unpredictable and task demands change. (1987, p. 18)

Resnick's argument, which echoes many others, is not without some justification. According to estimates made by the Carnegie Foundation, big business spends up to $100 billion a year on corporate classrooms that try to develop the thinking skills corporate management believes the schools have failed to teach (Ruggiero, 1988).

Good problem solvers share two general characteristics: a well-organized, meaningful fund of knowledge and a systematic set of problem-solving skills. Historically, cognitive learning theories have been particularly useful sources of ideas for imparting both. In this chapter, then, we will examine the issue of meaningful learning from the perspective of a cognitive theory that we introduced in Chapter 2: constructivism. We will then go on to describe the nature of the problem-solving process and what you can do to help your students become better problem solvers. We will conclude by describing the circumstances under which learned capabilities are applied to new tasks, a process known as transfer of learning. ■

Meaningful Learning within a Constructivist Framework

Constructivism: creating a personal interpretation of external ideas and experiences

Constructivism, as you may recall, holds that meaningful learning occurs when people actively try to make sense of the world—when they construct an interpretation of how and why things are—by filtering new ideas and experiences through existing knowledge structures (referred to in Chapters 2 and 8 as schemes). For example, an individual who lives in a country that provides, for little or no cost, such social services as medical care, counseling, education, job placement and training,

Meaningful learning is more likely to occur when people use what they already know to interpret and make sense of new ideas.

and several weeks of paid vacation a year is likely to have constructed a rather different view of the role of government in people's lives than someone who lives in a country with a more market-oriented economy. To put it another way, meaningful learning is the active creation of knowledge structures (such as concepts, rules, hypotheses, and associations) from personal experience. In this section, we'll take a brief look at an early constructivist-oriented approach to learning, examine the nature of the constructivist model, and then put it all in perspective by considering the limits as well as the advantages of the constructivist perspective.

JEROME BRUNER AND DISCOVERY LEARNING: AN EARLY CONSTRUCTIVIST PERSPECTIVE

Constructivist explanations of learning are not new. Over the past seventy-five years, they have been promoted by such notable scholars as John Dewey, Jean Piaget, Lev Vygotsky, and Jerome Bruner. The constructivist perspective enjoyed a rebirth during the 1960s as a result of Russia becoming the first country to put a satellite (called *Sputnik*) in orbit around the earth in 1957. In an effort to catch up with and pass the Russians in space technology, a renewed emphasis was placed on alternative approaches to classroom learning and instruction, particularly in the areas of mathematics and science. Among the many ideas proposed in the 1960s for improving school learning was the **discovery learning** view of psychologist Jerome Bruner.

One of Bruner's major points was that too much school learning takes the form of step-by-step study of verbal or numerical statements or formulas that students can reproduce on cue but are unable to use outside the classroom. When students are presented with such highly structured materials as worksheets and other types of drill-and-practice exercises, Bruner argues, they become too dependent on others. Furthermore, they are likely to think of learning as something done only to earn a reward.

Instead of using techniques that feature preselected and prearranged materials, Bruner believes teachers should confront children with problems and help them seek solutions either independently or by engaging in group discussion. True learning, says Bruner, involves "figuring out how to use what you already know in order to go beyond what you already think" (1983, p. 183). Like Piaget, Bruner argues that conceptions that children arrive at on their own are usually more meaningful than those proposed by others and that students do not need to be rewarded when they seek to make sense of things that puzzle them. Bruner maintains, in addition, that when children are given a substantial amount of practice in finding their own solutions to problems, they not only develop problem-solving skills but also acquire confidence in their own learning abilities as well as a propensity to function later in life as problem solvers. They learn *how* to learn *as* they learn.

Bruner does not suggest that students should discover every fact or principle or formula they may need to know. Discovery is simply too inefficient a process to be used that widely, and learning from others can be as meaningful as personal discovery. Rather, Bruner argues that certain types of outcomes—understanding the ways in which ideas connect with one another, the possibility of solving problems on our own, and how what we already know is relevant to what we are trying to learn—are the essence of education and can best be achieved through personal discovery.

Bruner: discover how ideas relate to each other and to existing knowledge

As an example of this discovery approach, Bruner describes his approach to teaching geography in the elementary grades. Instead of having a group of fifth graders memorize a set of geography facts, he gave them blank outline maps that showed the location of rivers, lakes, mountains, valleys, plains, and so on. Their task was to figure out where the major cities, railways, and highways might be located. The students were not permitted to consult books or other maps; they had to figure out locations on their own by drawing on their prior knowledge and reasoning ability (Bruner, 1960).

CONSTRUCTIVISM TODAY

Contemporary constructivist theory has several variations, two of which we will describe shortly. But despite their differences, all the variations incorporate the following four facets.

FACETS OF CONSTRUCTIVISM   As we mentioned earlier, one facet of constructivism is that meaningful learning is the active creation of knowledge structures from personal experience. Each learner builds a personal view of the world by using existing knowledge, interests, attitudes, goals, and the like to select and interpret currently available information (Fosnot, 1996). As Rochel Gelman (1994) points out, this assumption highlights the importance of what educational psychologists call *entering behavior*—the previously learned knowledge and skill that students bring to the classroom.

Depending on the particular characteristics that are active in students when teachers present a lesson, students may ignore the information, attend to one or more parts of it, or add other information from their own experiences. Gelman vividly demonstrated this by asking fourth, fifth, and seventh graders to explain why there are two numbers in a fraction. Despite the fact that these students had been taught in the primary grades what the teachers deemed to be necessary prerequisite knowledge, many of them provided unsatisfactory answers, such as "Because if there weren't two numbers then you wouldn't have a fraction" and "The top one explains how many of the bottom ones there are." As many cognitive theorists have pointed out, if we do not try to get some sense of what students are bringing to a learning task, we may not be pleased with the understanding of it that they construct.

A second facet is that the essence of one person's knowledge can never be *totally* transferred to another person because knowledge is the result of a personal interpretation of experience that is influenced by such factors as the learner's age, gender, race, ethnic background, and knowledge base. When knowledge is transferred from one person to another, some aspects of it are invariably "lost in translation." The area of musical performance provides an apt illustration of this aspect of constructivism. Although a piano teacher can tell a student volumes about how and why a piece should be performed in a particular way, the teacher cannot tell the student *everything*. The interpretation of a composition is constructed from such factors as the performer's knowledge of the composer's personality and motives, the nature of the instrument or instruments for which the composition was written, and the nature of the music itself. Since performers assign different meanings to such knowledge, different (yet equally valid) interpretations of the same composition result. Think, for example, of the many different ways in which you have heard "The Star-Spangled Banner" sung. Although listeners may prefer one version over another, there is no one correct way to sing this song.

The third facet follows directly from the second. Does constructivism necessarily mean that everyone walks around with a personal, idiosyncratic view of the world and that consensus is impossible? A few minutes of reflection should tell you that the answer is no. And if you recall what you read in Chapter 5, you will recognize that the cultures and societies to which people belong channel and place limits on the views people have of the world around them. Consequently, individuals make observations, test hypotheses, and draw conclusions about a variety of events that are largely consistent with one another (Cognition and Technology Group at Vanderbilt, 1991; Duffy & Cunningham, 1996). Of course, there are many instances when people cannot reconcile their views and so "agree to disagree." For example, in 1995 the world observed the fiftieth anniversary of the atomic bombing of Hiroshima. Although everyone agreed on the basic facts of the event, there was sharp disagreement about why the bomb was dropped, whether it was necessary, and what exactly the anniversary should be observing. In matters such as these truth is where it always is for the constructivist—in the mind of the beholder.

The fourth and final facet of constructivism that we will discuss has to do with the formation and changing of knowledge structures. Additions to, deletions from, or modifications of these interpretations come mainly from the sharing of multiple perspectives. Systematic, open-minded discussions and debates are instrumental in helping individuals create personal views (Cunningham, 1991). As we have seen in previous chapters, scholars form and reform their positions on aspects of theory or research as a result of years of discussion and debate with colleagues. The debate between the Piagetians and the Vygotskians in Chapter 2 is a good example of this facet. Consequently, students need to be provided with the conditions that will allow them to construct their own interpretation of key information and experiences.

Construction of ideas aided by discussion and debate

TWO VARIATIONS ON A CONSTRUCTIVIST THEME   One view of meaningful learning that we described in Chapter 2, Jean Piaget's, holds that it is the natural result of an intrinsic drive to resolve inconsistencies and contradictions—that is, to always have a view of the world that makes sense in light of what we currently know. One contemporary variation of constructivism, **cognitive constructivism**, is an outgrowth of Piaget's ideas because it focuses on the cognitive processes that take place within individuals. In other words, an individual's conception of the "truth" of some matter (for example, birds and airplanes can both fly because they use the same aeronautical principles; high interest rates are bad because they discourage

Cognitive constructivism emphasizes role of cognitive processes in meaningful learning

companies from borrowing money and expanding their businesses; high interest rates are good because they provide more money to people who have investments in interest-bearing securities) is based on her ability, with teacher guidance, to effectively assimilate information into existing schemes and develop new schemes and operations (accommodation) in response to novel or discrepant ideas (Duffy & Cunningham, 1996; Fosnot, 1996).

The constructivist variation that is known as **social constructivism** holds that meaningful learning occurs when people are explicitly taught how to use the psychological tools of their culture (like language, mathematics, diagrams, and approaches to problem solving) and are then given the opportunity to use these tools to create a common, or shared, understanding of some phenomenon. Students are encouraged to engage in open-ended discussion with peers and the teacher about such things as the meaning of terms and procedures, the relationships among ideas, and the applicability of knowledge to specific contexts. This process is often referred to by social constructivists as *negotiating meaning*. This view has its roots in the writings of such individuals as the psychologist Lev Vygotsky and the educational philosopher John Dewey (Duffy & Cunningham, 1996; Hickey, 1997; Scheurman,1998).

Table 9.1 summarizes the characteristics of cognitive and social constructivism and the basic instructional approaches that flow from each of these variations. The main conditions that support an individual's attempt to construct personally meaningful knowledge are detailed in the next section.

CONDITIONS THAT FOSTER CONSTRUCTIVISM The fostering conditions that constructivists typically mention include a cognitive apprenticeship between student and teacher, a use of realistic problems and conditions, and an emphasis on multiple perspectives (Bednar et al., 1991).

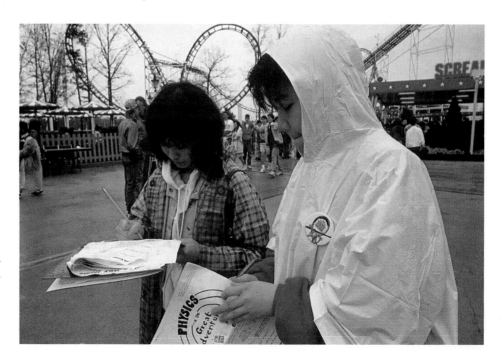

The constructivist view of learning holds that meaningful learning occurs when students have to use previously learned knowledge and skill to solve realistic problems in a realistic context.

Table 9.1	Cognitive and Social Constructivist Approaches to Learning and Teaching	
Approach	**Basic Characteristics**	**Instructional Implications**
Cognitive Constructivism	• Existing knowledge schemes and operations are modified by the addition (assimilation) of new ideas that are judged to be related. New knowledge schemes and operations are created (accommodation) to adapt to ideas and procedures that are inconsistent with existing schemes. • Assimilation and accommodation processes assumed to be innate and supported by opportunities to interact with peers and the physical environment.	• Teacher challenges students' current conceptions by presenting new ideas that do not quite fit (inducing disequilibrium). • Students work individually and together to construct new, more effective schemes. • Emphasis is on constructing personal meaning by developing new schemes.
Social Constructivism	• Learning initially occurs in the presence of and is influenced by more knowledgeable others. • The knowledge and skills that are acquired through the guidance of others are connected to existing schemes and gradually internalized, allowing the learner to become increasingly self-regulated and independent.	• Teacher helps students through scaffolded instruction to construct ideas using realistic, open-ended tasks. • Under teacher guidance, students work collaboratively to construct new conceptions. • Emphasis is on constructing and internalizing shared meaning.

Cognitive Apprenticeship   The first condition, that of a cognitive apprenticeship, was illustrated in Chapter 8 when we described the reciprocal teaching program of Annemarie Palincsar and Ann Brown (1984). Its main feature is that the teacher models a cognitive process that students are to learn and then gradually turns responsibility for executing the process over to students as they become more skilled. As you may recall from Chapter 2, providing such environmental supports as modeling, hints, leading questions, and suggestions, and then gradually removing them as the learner demonstrates increased competence is called *scaffolding*. Cognitive apprenticeships also occur in less formal circumstances, as when a child joins an existing peer group (like a play group), mostly watches at first what the other children do, and then gradually, with little explicit direction from the others, participates in one or more aspects of the task.

Scaffolding: provide student with enough help to complete a task; gradually decrease help as student becomes able to work independently

Situated Learning   The second condition, often called **situated learning** (or situated cognition) is that students be given learning tasks set in realistic contexts. A realistic context is one in which students must solve a meaningful problem by using a variety of skills and information. The rationale for this condition is twofold.

First, meaningful learning is the ability to use what one knows to function effectively (for example, learn new information, solve problems) in a given context (Duffy & Cunningham, 1996). Second, traditional forms of classroom learning and instruction, which are largely decontextualized in the sense that what students learn is relevant only to taking tests and performing other classroom tasks, leads to a condition that has been referred to as **inert knowledge**. That is, students fail to use what they learned earlier (such as mathematical procedures) to solve either real-life problems (such as calculating the square footage of the walls of a room in order to know how many rolls of wallpaper to buy) or other school-related problems because they don't see any relationship between the two. (We discuss the issue of inert knowledge and its relationship to transfer of learning later in this chapter.)

Inert knowledge due to learning isolated facts under limited conditions

An example of situated learning would be to use the game of baseball as a vehicle for middle school or high school students to apply aspects of science, mathematics, and sociology. Students could be asked to use their knowledge of physics to explain how pitchers are able to make the ball curve left or right or drop down as it approaches home plate. They could be asked to use their mathematical skills to figure out how far home runs travel. They could also be asked to read about the Negro Leagues and Jackie Robinson and discuss why it took until the early 1950s for major league baseball to begin integration. The Case in Print on page 298 provides a real-life example of how one teacher put the concept of situated learning into practice.

Constructivism aided by cognitive apprenticeship, realistic tasks, multiple perspectives

Multiple Perspectives   The third condition fostering constructivism is that students should view ideas and problems from multiple perspectives. The rationale for this condition is twofold: most of life's problems are multifaceted, and the knowledge base of experts is a network of interrelated ideas. The complex process of becoming an effective teacher is a good example of the need for multiple perspectives. As we mentioned in Chapter 1, being an effective teacher requires the mastery of many skills and disciplines so that classroom problems (such as why a particular student does not perform up to expectations) can be analyzed and attacked from several perspectives.

The following section provides an example of a constructivist-oriented teaching lesson.

AN EXAMPLE OF CONSTRUCTIVIST TEACHING   A first-grade teacher who wanted her students to understand the importance of using a standardized instrument, like a ruler, to make measurements decided to have them measure the size of the *Mayflower*, the boat that the English Pilgrims sailed in to the New World. After outlining the shape of the *Mayflower* in masking tape on the classroom floor, she began the lesson by saying, "Well, what should we do? Who has an idea?" By using probing questions to responses ("Why do you think the boat is three feet long?"), allowing for painful periods of silence, and pointing out dead ends (when the largest boy in class measured the boat the same way they measure the height of horses, in hands, the teacher suggested that the smallest girl in class do the same), this teacher subtly helped them construct the concept of a standard unit of measure and understand its importance (Schifter, 1996).

Constructivist-oriented teaching encourages creating new views; uses scaffolding, realistic tasks, and class discussion

The essence of a constructivist-oriented lesson is to provide students with realistic problems that cannot be solved with their current level of understanding and, by allowing them to interact mainly among themselves, to work out new understandings. It's important to emphasize the social nature of this approach. The experiences and ideas of others become springboards for further experimentation and

Constructing a Real Learning Experience

The fostering conditions that constructivists typically mention include a cognitive apprenticeship between student and teacher, a use of realistic problems and conditions, and an emphasis on multiple perspectives. . . . The second condition, often called situated learning, *is that students be given learning tasks set in realistic contexts. A realistic context is one in which students must solve a meaningful problem by using a variety of skills and information. (p. 295)*

SPIN DOCTORS
WILLIAM ALLEN
St. Louis Post-Dispatch 5/20/96

On an unseasonably cool, cloudy spring weekday at Six Flags Over Mid-America last month, Scott Lefton, a senior at Parkway Central High School, videotaped his friends as they madly twirled on the Hannibarrels spin ride.

Despite the drab weather, it wasn't a bad day for a romp in the amusement park.

But this wasn't just an end-of-the-year senior fling. The students on the ride held accelerometers, not souvenirs. And Lefton was videotaping a physics experiment, not a joy ride.

Lefton and the others went to Six Flags as part of its annual Physics Day. They analyzed the centrifugal force, potential energy and other physical properties of the Hannibarrels, bumper cars, roller coasters and other rides.

"At first we thought, 'What could be easier than figuring out little barrels spinning around in circles?'" said Drew Biscoe, one of the five members of Lefton's team. "Were we surprised."

Said a smiling Lefton: "I now know more about the Hannibarrels than I ever wanted to know."

More than 3,000 middle and high school students from around the St. Louis region made Six Flags their open-air classroom on April 19 and 26. They rode the rides with instruments to measure lengths, speeds and forces.

Lefton, Biscoe and other students in physics teacher Ron Schwarz's classes at Parkway Central were unusual in that they also brought video cameras. Each team in Schwarz's classes was assigned a ride to analyze, and they recorded images both on and off the ride.

That allowed them to take their study back to the classroom, feed the images into a computer and repeatedly analyze each aspect of the ride in painstaking detail.

"By videotaping, they have time to think about it and analyze it," Schwarz said. "And in some of these rides, many things are happening all at once."

"I want to see your proof of what's happening on your ride," Schwarz told one of his classes the next week.

Briscoe and his colleagues pushed the appropriate buttons to transfer their Hannibarrels images into a Macintosh computer. The computer digitized the sequence, meaning it recorded the video as a string of independent computerized pictures. Now the students could study what was happening in each frame.

"We're going to try to measure every physical force that you can experience on the ride," Lefton said.

It turns out that a lot of forces exert themselves in a Hannibarrel. First, all the barrels moved together in a circle on a spinning platform. Next, the barrels simultaneously took on their own independent spin—in some cases clockwise, in some counterclockwise.

To figure out the forces, the students analyzed the barrels' movements frame by frame. They figured in the readings from the on-board accelerometer, which gave them a measure of the barrels' changes in speed. They also studied clues revealed by the movements of a piece of foam dropped over the side of the barrel. "From this we can develop a plan of action to do our calculations," said Briscoe, whose team included exchange student Lubov Radchenko, from the St. Louis sister city of Samara, Russia.

They wrote and submitted their report completely on the computer. The report included a full description of the physics for the ride, a clip of the digitized video and a picture of all the team members.

Finally, each team reviewed the reports of the other teams. They got points for finding errors in other teams' analyses.

"The aim is to try to shoot down the physics of what everyone else did," Schwarz said, explaining that this is how scientists often approach one another's reports. "This way, they get to know one ride extremely well, and they have the benefit of the other groups' analyses of the other rides."

For the Parkway seniors, the Six Flags project was a chance to apply classroom lessons about the physics of motion learned during the fall semester.

"This takes it off the paper and makes it whole," said David Crowell, who worked on a team that analyzed acceleration of an antique car ride.

Kristin Virag's team analyzed the Ninja roller coaster. Virag said that as she fulfilled her role—taking measurements aboard the ride—she realized that the laws of physics are all around her, on amusement park rides as well as in everyday life. She had to overcome a bit of fear to do it, though.

"It was hard to gather the data," she said. "There were a lot of quick, jerky movements. But it went by very fast."

Whether the students go on in science in college or not, they retain a basic idea of how things work, Schwarz said. The Six Flags rides and the video and computer technology are key to bringing the textbook knowledge to life.

"This whole approach is different than giving them something and saying, 'Do it this way,'" Schwarz said. "Instead you just say, 'Tell me what's going on here.'

"It's hard, but when they're done they have a real sense of accomplishment, of putting it all together."

Questions and Activities

1. What principles of constructivist learning theory are reflected in the field trip the students in this story took to Six Flags Over Mid-America?

2. What other field-based projects can you think of that would accomplish the same objectives as the project described in this story? Describe where you would take students, what you would have them do, and what you would hope to accomplish.

3. The project described in this story was obviously made possible by the availability of videocameras and computers. If the school district in which you will work does not have such equipment, what nontechnological kinds of constructivist-oriented learning experiences can you design?

discussion. This approach also emphasizes the role of the teacher as artist. Since a teacher does not know beforehand what questions students will ask or what solutions they will propose, the teacher's questions and suggestions cannot be scripted in advance. They have to be generated on the spot, and they have to further the point of the lesson most of the time.

PUTTING CONSTRUCTIVISM IN PERSPECTIVE   Although constructivism has much to offer teachers, like any other theory, it does have its limitations. Here are a few you should keep in mind.

1. Because of constructivism's emphasis on guiding rather than telling, accepting different perspectives on issues and solutions to problems, modifying previous conceptions in light of new information, and creating an atmosphere that encourages active participation, it is almost impossible to create highly detailed lesson plans. Much of what teachers do depends on how students respond. Teaching from this perspective will place a premium on your teacher-as-artist abilities.

2. Recognize that students construct their own interpretations of things regardless of whether you teach from a constructivist perspective. You can provide students with a clear description of what you want them to learn, provide expert scaffolded instruction, and provide realistic tasks to which students can relate, and still find some students who have developed a very different idea of the purpose of the lesson.

3. Constructivism is not the only orientation to learning and teaching that you will ever need (nor is any other theory, for that matter). You need to know which theory or approach best fits which purposes and circumstances. Sometimes memorization of factual information is essential, and sometimes an instructional objective can be accomplished more efficiently (and just as effectively) with a clear and well-organized lecture (Airasian & Walsh, 1997).

There are many techniques you can use to foster meaningful learning within a constructivist framework. Several computer-based approaches are described at the end of this chapter. One that does not rely on computer technology but is particularly well suited to developing, comparing, and understanding different points of view is the classroom discussion (Rabow, Charness, Kipperman, & Radcliffe-Vasile, 1994; Schiever, 1991). Because this format also allows students to deal with realistic problems and to exercise cognitive skills taught by the teacher, it is an excellent general-purpose method for helping students construct a meaningful knowledge base. So let's turn our attention to some specific Suggestions for Teaching that describe how to use discussion to emphasize meaningful learning in your classroom.

SUGGESTIONS FOR TEACHING IN YOUR CLASSROOM

Using a Constructivist Approach to Meaningful Learning

1 Arrange the learning situation so that students are exposed to different perspectives of a problem or an issue.

   a. Ask students to discuss familiar topics or those that are matters of opinion.

   b. Provide necessary background information by asking all students to read all or part of a book, take notes on a lecture, or view a film.

2 Structure discussions by posing a specific question; by presenting a provocative, topic-related issue; or by asking students to choose topics or subtopics.

   a. In some cases encourage students to arrive at conclusions already reached by others.

   b. In other cases present a controversial topic for which there is no single answer.

3 If time is limited and if only one topic is to be covered, ask students to form a circle and have an all-class discussion.

   a. Ask questions that stimulate students to apply, analyze, synthesize, and evaluate.

   b. Allow sufficient time for initial responses and then probe for further information (if appropriate).

   c. When selecting students to recite, use techniques likely to sustain steady but nonthreatening attention. At the same time, guard against the temptation to call primarily on bright, articulate, assertive students.

4 If abundant time is available and if a controversial or subdivided topic is to be discussed, divide the class into groups of five or so and arrange for each member of each group to have eye contact with every other group member.

1 **Arrange the learning situation so that students are exposed to different perspectives on a problem or an issue.**

This is the crux of the discovery approach and the constructivist view of learning. The basic idea is to *arrange* the elements of a learning task and *guide* student actions so that students discover, or construct, a personally meaningful conception of a problem or issue. In some cases you may present a topic that is a matter of

Journal Entry
Ways to Arrange
for Discovery to
Take Place

A time-honored instructional technique that is consistent with constructivist learning principles and that exposes students to multiple points of view is the use of small-group discussions.

opinion or that all students are sure to know something about. In other cases you might structure the discussion by exposing all participants to the same background information.

a. Ask students to discuss familiar topics or those that are matters of opinion.

EXAMPLES

■ "What are some of the techniques that advertising agencies use in television commercials to persuade us to buy certain products?"

■ "What do you think is the best book you ever read, and why do you think so?"

b. Provide necessary background information by asking all students to read all or part of a book, take notes on a lecture, or view a film.

EXAMPLES

■ After the class has read *Great Expectations,* ask, "What do you think Dickens was trying to convey when he wrote this novel? Was he just trying to tell a good story, or was he also trying to get us to think about certain kinds of relationships between people?"

■ "After I explain some of the principles of electrical currents, I'm going to ask you to suggest rules for connecting batteries in series and in parallel. Then, we'll see how well your rules work."

2 Structure discussions by posing a specific question; by presenting a provocative, topic-related issue; or by asking students to choose topics or subtopics.

Journal Entry
Questions That Are Likely to Stimulate Productive Classroom Discussion

It is important to structure a discovery session by giving students something reasonably specific to discuss; otherwise, they may simply engage in a disorganized and desultory bull session. You might supply direction in the following ways.

a. In some cases encourage students to arrive at conclusions already reached by others.

Thousands of books provide detailed answers to such questions as "What is human about human beings? How did they get that way? How can they be made more so?" But constructivists believe that answers mean more when they are constructed by the individual, not supplied ready-made by others. As you look over lesson plans, therefore, you might try to select some questions for students to answer by engaging in discussion rather than by reading or listening to what others have already discovered. In searching for such topics, you might take into account the techniques described by Bruner. Here is a list of those techniques, together with an example of each one. In your Reflective Journal you might describe similar applications that you could use when you begin to teach. Keep in mind that students often acquire a deeper understanding of ideas and issues when they have had appropriate previous experience.

- *Emphasize contrast.* In an elementary school social studies unit on cultural diversity, say, "When you watch this film on Mexico, look for customs and ways of living that differ from ours. Then we'll talk about what these differences are and why they may have developed."
- *Stimulate informed guessing.* In a middle school unit on natural science, you might say, "Suppose we wanted to figure out some kind of system to classify trees so that we could later find information about particular types. What would be the best way to do it?" After students have developed a classification scheme, show them schemes developed by specialists.
- *Encourage participation.* In a high school political science class, illustrate the jury system by staging a mock trial. (Note that the use of a simulation satisfies the constructivist criterion of realistic tasks and contexts.)
- *Stimulate awareness.* In a high school English class, ask the students to discuss how the author developed the plot.

b. In other cases present a controversial topic for which there is no single answer.

Discussions might center on provocative issues about which there are differences of opinion. One caution here is to avoid topics (such as premarital sex or legalized abortion) that parents may not want discussed in school, either because they are convinced it is their prerogative to discuss them with their children or because they feel that students may be pressured to endorse your opinion because you assign grades. You should not avoid controversy, but neither should you go out of your way to agitate students and their parents.

Another caution is to avoid selecting issues that provoke more than they instruct. You may be tempted to present a highly controversial topic and then congratulate yourself at the end of the period if most students engaged in heated discussion. But if they simply argued enthusiastically about something that had nothing to do with the subject you are assigned to teach, you cannot honestly claim to have arranged an instructive exchange of ideas. A final caution relates to a characteristic of formal thought described in Chapter 2: there may be a tendency for secondary school students to engage in unrestrained theorizing when they first experience the thrill of being able to deal with hypotheses and possibilities. Thus, you may have to remind some students to take into account realities when they discuss controversial issues involving tangled background circumstances or conflicts of interest.

EXAMPLES

■ In a middle school science class, ask students to list arguments for and against attempting to alter the genetic code of human beings.

■ In a high school political science class, ask students to list arguments for and against democratic forms of government.

3 **If time is limited and if only one topic is to be covered, ask students to form a circle and have an all-class discussion.**

Journal Entry
Ways to Supervise Discussion Sessions

You may sometimes wish to have the entire class discuss a topic. Such discussions are most likely to be successful if all students have eye contact with one another. The simplest way to achieve this is to ask all students to form a circle. Next, invite responses to the question you have posed. As students make remarks, serve more as a moderator than as a leader. Try to keep the discussion on the topic, but avoid directing it toward a specific predetermined end result. If one or more students tend to dominate the discussion, say something like, "Kim and Carlos have given us their ideas. Now I'd like to hear from the rest of you." If an aggressive student attacks or belittles something said by a classmate, say something like, "It's good to *believe* in a point of view, but let's be friendly as we listen to other opinions. This is supposed to be a discussion, not an argument or a debate."

Factors that lead to successful or unsuccessful discussions are often idiosyncratic, but there are certain procedures you might follow to increase the likelihood of success.

a. Ask questions that stimulate students to apply, analyze, synthesize, and evaluate.

When you first structure a discussion session, but also when it is under way, take care to ask questions likely to elicit different points of view. If you ask students to supply information (for example, "When did Charles Dickens write *Great Expectations?*"), the first correct response will lead to closure. You may end up asking a series of questions leading to brief answers—the equivalent of a program or a fill-in exam. Meredith Gall (1970) reviewed dozens of studies of classroom recitation sessions and found consistent evidence that up to 80 percent of all questions asked by teachers stressed facts and knowledge. When one intends to encourage students to construct personally meaningful interpretations of the issues or to develop skills as deductive thinkers, it is preferable to ask questions likely to tap higher levels of thinking.

EXAMPLES

■ "You just learned how to calculate the area of a circle. Think of as many different ways as you can of how you might be able to use that bit of knowledge if you were a do-it-yourself homeowner." (Application)

■ "Last month we read a novel by Dickens; this month we read a play by Shakespeare. What are some similarities in the way each author developed the plot of his story?" (Synthesis)

b. Allow sufficient time for initial responses and then probe for further information (if appropriate).

Current research finds that many teachers fail to allow enough time for students to respond to questions. Quite often instructors wait only one second before repeating the question, calling on another student, or answering the question themselves. When teachers wait at least three seconds after asking a question, students are more likely to participate; their responses increase in frequency, length, and complexity; and their achievement improves. There are changes in teacher behavior as well. As a function of waiting longer, teachers ask more complex questions and have higher expectations for the quality of students' responses (Ormrod, 1999).

One possible explanation for improved student recitation when teachers wait longer for a response is that reflective thinkers have an opportunity to figure out what they want to say. But even impulsive thinkers probably welcome a few more seconds of thinking time. It seems logical to expect that snap answers will be more superficial than answers supplied after even a few seconds of reflection.

In addition to giving students ample time to make an initial response, you should encourage them to pursue an idea. If it seems appropriate, probe for further information or clarification of a point by asking students who give brief or incomplete answers to explain how or why they arrived at a conclusion or to supply additional comments.

EXAMPLE

■ "Well, Keesha, I'm sure a gardener might sometimes need to figure the area of a circle, but can you give a more specific example? If you can't think of one right away, put up your hand as soon as you can describe a specific situation where it would help to know the area of a circular patch of lawn or soil."

c. When selecting students to recite, use techniques likely to sustain steady but nonthreatening attention. At the same time, guard against the temptation to call primarily on bright, articulate, assertive students.

The way you moderate student contributions may not only determine how successful the discussion will be; it may also influence how students feel about themselves and each other. Jacob Kounin (1970) points out that when a teacher first names a student and then asks a question, the rest of the class may tend to turn its attention to other things. The same tendency to "tune out" may occur if a teacher follows a set pattern of calling on students (for example, by going around a circle). To keep all the students on their toes, therefore, you might ask questions first and then, in an unpredictable sequence, call on those who volunteer to recite, frequently switching from one part of the room to another. As you look around the room before selecting a volunteer, remember Skinner's criticism that a few students may make all the discoveries. Guard against the temptation to call primarily on students you expect to give good or provocative answers. Repeatedly ignoring students who may be a bit inarticulate or unimaginative may cause them and their classmates to conclude that you think they are incompetent. These students may then lose interest in and totally ignore what is taking place.

4 **If abundant time is available and if a controversial or subdivided topic is to be discussed, divide the class into groups of five or so and arrange for each member of each group to have eye contact with every other group member.**

A major limitation of any kind of discussion is that only one person can talk at a time. You can reduce this difficulty by dividing the class into smaller groups before asking them to exchange ideas. A group of about five seems to work best. If only two or three students are interacting with each other, the exchange of ideas may be

Journal Entry
Techniques for Arranging Small-Group Discussions

limited. If there are more than five, not all members will be able to contribute at frequent intervals.

One way to form groups, particularly if students have suggested subtopics, is to ask them to list in order their first three subject preferences. (Mention at the start that it is unlikely that all the students in the class will get their first choice.) Then, you can divide by referring to the lists. One advantage of this technique is that students embark on a discovery session with the feeling that they have chosen to do so. Another advantage is that you can arrange group membership to a certain extent since students won't know how many of their classmates listed a particular topic as first choice. You might break up potentially disruptive pairings and also spread around talkative, creative, and thoughtful students.

Another way to divide the class, particularly if all groups are to discuss the same topic, is to ask all students in a row to form a group. Or have the class count off from one to five. After all students have counted off, ask all "ones" to move to one part of the room, "twos" to another part, and so on. You can manage to achieve different assortments of students by having the class count off in different ways each time.

The Nature of Problem Solving

As with most of the topics covered in this book, an extensive amount of theorizing and research on problem solving has been conducted over the years. We will focus our discussion on the types of problems that students are typically required to deal with, the cognitive processes that play a central role in problem solving, and various approaches to teaching problem solving in the classroom.

Let's begin by asking what we mean by the terms *problem* and *problem solving*. Most, if not all, psychologists would agree that "a problem is said to exist when one has a goal and has not yet identified a means for reaching that goal" (Gagné, Yekovich, & Yekovich, 1993, p. 211). **Problem solving**, then, is the identification and application of knowledge and skills that result in goal attainment (Martinez, 1998). Although this definition encompasses a wide range of problem types, we will focus on three types that students frequently encounter both in school and out.

THREE COMMON TYPES OF PROBLEMS

In the first category are the well-structured problems of mathematics and science—the type of problems that students from kindergarten through middle school are typically required to solve. **Well-structured problems** are clearly formulated, can be solved by recall and application of a specific procedure (called an *algorithm*), and result in a solution that can be evaluated against a well-known, agreed-on standard (Hamilton & Ghatala, 1994). Examples of well-structured problems are

Well-structured problems: clearly stated, known solution procedures, known evaluation standards

$$5 + 8 =$$
$$732 - 485 =$$
$$8 + 3x = 40 - 5x$$
$$8 + 8x = 40$$
$$8x = 32$$
$$x = 4$$

Well-structured problems have a clear structure, can be solved by using a standard procedure, and produce solutions that can be evaluated against an agreed-on standard. They are the type of problem that students are asked to solve most frequently.

In the second category are the ill-structured problems often encountered in everyday life and in disciplines such as economics or psychology. **Ill-structured problems** are more complex, provide few cues pointing to solution procedures, and have less definite criteria for determining when the problem has been solved (Hamilton & Ghatala, 1994). Examples of ill-structured problems are how to identify and reward good teachers, how to improve access to public buildings and facilities for persons with physical handicaps, and how to increase voter turnout for primary and general elections.

Ill-structured problems: vaguely stated, unclear solution procedures, vague evaluation standards

The third category includes problems that are also ill-structured but differ from the examples just mentioned in two respects. First, these problems tend to divide people into opposing camps because of the emotions they arouse. Second, the primary goal, at least initially, is not to determine a course of action but to identify the most reasonable position. These problems are often referred to as **issues** (Ruggiero, 1988). Examples of issues are capital punishment, gun control, and nondenominational prayer in classrooms. Beginning with the freshman year in high school, students usually receive more opportunities to deal with ill-structured problems and issues.

Issues: ill-structured problems that arouse strong feelings

HELPING STUDENTS BECOME GOOD PROBLEM SOLVERS

Despite the differences that exist among well-structured problems, ill-structured problems, and issues, recent theory and research suggest that good problem solvers employ the same general approach when solving one or another of these problem types (see, for example, Bransford & Stein, 1993; Gagné, Yekovich, & Yekovich, 1993; Gick, 1986; Krulik & Rudnick, 1993; Nickerson, 1994; Ruggiero, 1988). When used to solve ill-structured problems or to analyze issues, this approach consists of five steps or processes (although the solution of well-structured problems may call only for the implementation of steps 2, 4, and 5):

1. Realize that a problem exists.
2. Understand the nature of the problem.
3. Compile relevant information.
4. Formulate and carry out a solution.
5. Evaluate the solution.

We will discuss each of these steps in the next few pages, along with some specific techniques that you can use to help your students become good problem solvers.

STEP 1: REALIZE THAT A PROBLEM EXISTS   Most people assume that if a problem is worth solving, they won't have to seek it out; it will make itself known. Like most assumptions, this one is only partly true. Well-structured problems are often thrust on us by teachers, in the form of in-class exercises or homework, or by supervisors at work. Ill-structured problems and issues, however, often remain hidden from most people. It is a characteristic of good problem solvers that they are more sensitive to the existence of problems than most of their peers (Okagaki & Sternberg, 1990).

Problem finding depends on curiosity, dissatisfaction with status quo

The keys to problem recognition, or *problem finding* as it is sometimes called, are curiosity and dissatisfaction. You need to question why a rule, procedure, or product is the way it is or to feel frustrated or irritated because something does not work as well as it might. The organization known as Mothers Against Drunk Driving, for example, was begun by a woman who, because her daughter had been killed in a traffic accident by a drunk driver, was dissatisfied with current, ineffective laws. This organization has been instrumental in getting state legislatures to pass laws against drunk driving that mandate more severe penalties. As another example, John Bransford and Barry Stein (1993) mention a business that, by taking a critical look at its record-keeping procedure, was able to eliminate the generation of 120 tons of paper per year.

Problem finding does not come readily to most people, possibly because schools emphasize solving well-structured problems and possibly because most people have a natural tendency to assume that things work as well as they can. Like any cognitive process, however, problem recognition can improve with instruction and practice. Students can be sensitized in a number of ways to the absence or flaws and shortcomings of products, procedures, rules, or whatever. We will make some specific suggestions about improving problem recognition and the other problem-solving processes a bit later in Suggestions for Teaching in Your Classroom.

STEP 2: UNDERSTAND THE NATURE OF THE PROBLEM   The second step in the problem-solving process is perhaps the most critical. The problem solver has to construct an *optimal* representation, or understanding, of the nature of a problem or issue. The preceding sentence stresses the word *optimal* for two reasons. First, most problems can be expressed in a number of ways. Written problems, for example, can be recast as pictures, equations, graphs, charts, or diagrams. Second, because the way we represent the problem determines the amount and type of solution-relevant information we recall from long-term memory, some representations are better than others. For obvious reasons, problem-solving researchers often refer to this process as **problem representation**, or **problem framing**.

To achieve an optimal understanding of a problem, an individual needs two things: a high degree of knowledge of the subject matter (facts, concepts, and principles) on which the problem is based and familiarity with that particular type of problem. This background will allow the person to recognize important elements (words, phrases, and numbers) in the problem statement and patterns of relationships among the problem elements. This recognition, in turn, will activate one or more solution-relevant schemes from long-term memory. It is just this level of knowledge of subject matter and problem types that distinguishes the high-quality problem representations of the expert problem solver from the low-quality representations of the novice. Experts typically represent problems in terms of one or more basic patterns or underlying principles, whereas novices focus on limited or superficial surface features of problems.

To give you a clearer idea of the nature and power of an optimal problem representation, consider the following situation. When novices are given a set of physics problems to solve, they sort them into categories on the basis of some noticeable feature. For example, they group together all problems that involve the use of an inclined plane or all the ones that involve the use of pulleys or all those that involve friction. Then, novices search their memory for previously learned information. The drawback to this approach is that although two or three problems may involve the use of an inclined plane, their solutions may depend on the application of different laws of physics. Experts, in contrast, draw on their extensive and well-organized knowledge base to represent groups of problems according to a common underlying principle, such as conservation of energy or Newton's third law (Gagné, Yekovich, & Yekovich, 1993; Gick, 1986).

An important aspect of the problem-solving process is the ability to activate relevant schemes (organized collections of facts, concepts, principles, and procedures) from long-term memory when they are needed. The more relevant and powerful the activated scheme is, the more likely it is that an effective problem solution will be achieved. But as many observers of education have pointed out, acquiring this ability is often easier said than done. John Bransford argues that standard educational practices produce knowledge that is *inert*. As mentioned earlier in the chapter, inert knowledge can be accessed only under conditions that closely mimic the original learning context (Bransford, Sherwood, Vye, & Rieser, 1986). Richard Feynman, a Nobel Prize–winning physicist, made the same observation in describing how his classmates at the Massachusetts Institute of Technology failed to recognize the application of a previously learned mathematical formula: "They didn't put two and two together. They didn't even know what they 'knew.' I don't know what's the matter with people: they don't learn by understanding; they learn by some other way—by rote, or something. Their knowledge is so fragile!" (1985, p. 36). To overcome this limitation of inert and fragile knowledge, teachers need to present subject matter in a highly organized fashion, and students need to learn more about the various conditions under which their knowledge applies.

STEP 3: COMPILE RELEVANT INFORMATION   For well-structured problems that are relatively simple and familiar (such as arithmetic drill problems), this step in the problem-solving process occurs simultaneously with problem representation. In the process of defining a problem, we very quickly and easily recall from long-term memory all the information that is needed to achieve a solution. As problems and issues become more complex, however, we run into two difficulties: the amount of information

Problem framing depends on knowledge of subject matter, familiarity with problem types

Inert knowledge due to learning isolated facts under limited conditions

relevant to the solution becomes too great to keep track of mentally, and there is an increasing chance that we may not possess all the relevant information. As a result, we are forced to compile what we know in the form of lists, tables, pictures, graphs, and diagrams, and so on and to seek additional information from other sources.

The key to using yourself as an information source is the ability to accurately retrieve from long-term memory information that will aid in the solution of the problem. We need to think back over what we have learned in other somewhat similar situations, make a list of some other form of representation of those ideas, and make a judgment as to how helpful that knowledge might be. Techniques for ensuring accurate and reliable recall were discussed in Chapter 8.

In addition to relying on our own knowledge and experience to solve problems, we can draw on the knowledge and experience of friends, colleagues, and experts. According to Vincent Ruggiero, "Investigating other people's views calls for little talking and a lot of careful listening. We do well, in such cases, to ask questions rather than make statements" (1988, p. 39). The main purpose of soliciting the views of others about solutions to problems and positions on issues is to identify the reasons and evidence those people offer in support of their positions. This skill of asking questions and analyzing responses is quite useful in debates and classroom discussions of controversial issues.

STEP 4: FORMULATE AND CARRY OUT A SOLUTION   When you feel you understand the nature of a problem or issue and possess sufficient relevant information, you are ready to attempt a solution. The first step is to consider which of several alternative approaches is likely to be most effective. The literature on problem solving mentions quite a few solution strategies. Because these solution strategies are very general in nature—they can apply to different kinds of problems in different content areas and offer only a general approach to solving a problem— they are referred to as **heuristics** (Martinez, 1998). We will discuss five heuristics that we think are particularly useful.

In order to become proficient at carrying out a proposed solution to a problem or evaluating the adequacy of a solution, students need many opportunities to practice these skills.

- *Study worked examples.* This approach may strike you as so obvious that it hardly merits attention. But it is worth mentioning for two reasons. First, obvious solution strategies are the ones that are most often overlooked. Second, it is a very effective solution strategy. Mary Gick (1986) cites almost a dozen studies in which learners improved their ability to solve a variety of problems by studying similar problems whose solutions had already been worked out. The beneficial effect is thought to be due to the learners' acquisition of a general problem schema.

  > **Studying worked examples is an effective solution strategy**

- *Work on a simpler version of the problem.* This is another common and very effective approach. Geometry offers a particularly clear example of working on a simpler problem. If you are having difficulty solving a problem of solid geometry (which involves three dimensions), work out a similar problem in plane geometry (two dimensions) and then apply the solution to the three-dimensional example (Nickerson, 1994; Polya, 1957). Architects and engineers employ this approach when they construct scaled-down models of bridges, buildings, experimental aircraft, and the like. Scientists do the same thing by creating laboratory simulations of real-world phenomena.

  > **Solve simpler version of problem first; then transfer process to harder problem**

- *Break the problem into parts.* The key to this approach is to make sure you break the problem into manageable parts. Whether you can do this will depend largely on how much subject-matter knowledge you have. The more you know about the domain from which the problem comes, the easier it is to know how to break a problem into logical, easy-to-handle parts.

  > **Break complex problems into manageable parts**

  At least two benefits result from breaking a problem into parts: doing so reduces the amount of information you have to keep in short-term memory to a manageable level, and the method used to solve one part of the problem can often be used to solve another part. Bransford and Stein (1993) use the following example to illustrate how this approach works.

  Problem: what day follows the day before yesterday if two days from now will be Sunday?

1. What is today if two days from now will be Sunday? (Friday)
2. If today is Friday, what is the day before yesterday? (Wednesday)
3. What day follows Wednesday? (Thursday)

- *Work backward.* This is a particularly good solution strategy to use whenever the goal is clear but the beginning state is not. Bransford and Stein (1993) offer the following example. Suppose you arranged to meet someone at a restaurant across town at noon. When should you leave your office to be sure of arriving on time? By working backward from your destination and arrival time (it takes about ten minutes to find a parking spot and walk to the restaurant; it takes about thirty minutes to drive to the area where you would park; it takes about five minutes to walk from your office to your car), you would more quickly and easily determine when to leave your office (about 11:15) than if you had worked the problem forward.

  > **Work backward when goal is clear but beginning state is not**

- *Solve an analogous problem.* If you are having difficulty solving a current problem, possibly because your knowledge of the subject matter is incomplete, it may be useful to think of a similar problem about a subject in which you are more knowledgeable. Solve the analogous problem and then use the same method to solve the current problem. In essence, this is a way of making the unfamiliar familiar.

Although solving analogous problems is a very powerful solution strategy, it can be difficult to employ, especially for novices. In our earlier discussion of understanding the problem, we made the point that novices represent problems on the basis of superficial features, whereas experts operate from knowledge of underlying concepts and principles. The same is true of analogies. Novices are more likely than experts to use superficial analogies (Gick, 1986).

STEP 5: EVALUATE THE SOLUTION   The last step in the problem-solving process is to evaluate the adequacy of the solution. For relatively simple, well-structured problems where the emphasis is on producing a correct response, two levels of evaluation are available to the problem solver. The first is to ask whether, given the problem statement, the answer makes sense. For example, if the problem reads $75 \times 5 = ?$ and the response is 80, a little voice inside the problem solver's head should say that the answer cannot possibly be right. This signal should prompt a reevaluation of the way the problem was represented and the solution procedure that was used (for example, "I misread the times sign as a plus sign and added when I should have multiplied"). The second level of evaluation is to use an alternative algorithm (a fixed procedure used to solve a problem) to check the accuracy of the solution. This is necessary because an error in the carrying out of an algorithm can produce an incorrect response that is "in the ballpark." For example, a common error in multiple-column subtraction problems is to subtract a smaller digit from a larger one regardless of whether the small number is in the minuend (top row) or the subtrahend (bottom row) (Mayer, 1987), as in

> **Evaluate solutions to well-structured problems by estimating or checking**

$$\begin{array}{r} 522 \\ -418 \\ \hline 116 \end{array}$$

Since this answer is off by only 12 units, it "looks right." The flaw can be discovered, however, by adding the answer to the subtrahend to produce the minuend.

The evaluation of solutions to ill-structured problems is likely to be more complicated and time consuming for at least two reasons. First, the evaluation should occur both before and after the solution is implemented. Although many flaws and omissions can be identified and corrected beforehand, some will slip through. There is much to be learned by observing the effects of our solutions. Second, because these problems are complex, often involving a dozen or more variables, some sort of systematic framework should guide the evaluation. Vincent Ruggiero suggests a four-step procedure (1988, pp. 44–46). The first step is to ask and answer a set of basic questions. Imagine, for example, that you have proposed a classroom incentive system (a token economy, perhaps) to enhance student motivation. You might ask such questions as, How will this program be implemented? By whom? When? Where? With what materials? How will the materials be obtained?

The second step is to identify imperfections and complications. Is this idea, for example, safe, convenient, efficient, economical, and compatible with existing policies and practices? The third step is to anticipate possible negative reactions from other people (such as parents and your school principal). The fourth step is to devise improvements.

The Suggestions for Teaching in Your Classroom section contains guidelines and examples that will help you improve the problem-solving skills of your students.

SUGGESTIONS FOR TEACHING IN YOUR CLASSROOM

Teaching Problem-Solving Techniques

1 Teach students how to identify problems.

2 Teach students how to represent problems.

3 Teach students how to compile relevant information.

4 Teach several methods for formulating problem solutions.

5 Teach students the skills of evaluation.

1 Teach students how to identify problems.

Since the notion of finding problems is likely to strike students as an unusual activity, you may want to introduce this skill in gradual steps. One way to start is to have students list different ways in which problems can be identified. Typical responses are to scan newspaper and magazine articles, observe customer and employee behavior in a store, watch traffic patterns in a local area, and interview local residents, including, for instance, teachers, business owners, police, clergy, or government officials. A next step is to have students carry out these suggested activities in order to gain an understanding of the status quo and to find out how people identify problems. They may learn, for example, that a principal periodically has lunch with a teacher in order to learn of conditions that decrease the teacher's effectiveness.

2 Teach students how to represent problems.

The ability to construct a good representation of a problem is based on a command of the subject matter surrounding the problem and familiarity with the particular type of problem. As the work of Jerome Bruner and David Ausubel indicates, students need to acquire a genuine understanding of many of the associations, discriminations, concepts, and rules of a discipline before they can effectively solve problems in that subject-matter area. Too often, students are taught to state principles on cue, but they reveal by further responses that they do not understand what they are saying. The classic illustration of this all too common trap was given by William James in his *Talks to Teachers:*

> A friend of mine, visiting a school, was asked to examine a young class in geography. Glancing at the book, she said: "Suppose you should dig a hole in the ground, hundreds of feet deep, how should you find it at the bottom—warmer or colder than on top?" None of the class replying, the teacher said: "I'm sure they know, but I think you don't ask the question quite rightly. Let me try." So, taking the book, she asked: "In what condition is the interior of the globe?" and received the immediate answer from half the class at once: "The interior of the globe is in a condition of igneous fusion." (1899, p. 150)

If these students had genuinely understood concepts and principles regarding the composition of the earth, instead of having simply memorized meaningless phrases, they would have been able to answer the original question.

| Comprehension of subject matter critical to problem solving

Different problem types lend themselves to particular forms of representation. Verbal reasoning problems that are based on relationships among categories, for example, can usually be represented by a set of intersecting circles known as a Venn diagram.

EXAMPLE PROBLEM

The government wants to contact all druggists, all gun store owners, and all parents in a town without contacting anyone twice. Based on the following statistics, how many people must be contacted?

Druggists	10
Gun store owners	5
Parents	3,000
Druggists who own gun stores	0
Druggists who are parents	7
Gun store owners who are parents	3

Solution Using Venn Diagram

The total number of people who must be contacted is 2990 + 7 + 3 + 3 + 2 = 3,005 (adapted from Whimbey & Lochhead, 1991, p. 102).[1]

Verbal reasoning problems that describe transactions can take the form of a flow diagram.

EXAMPLE PROBLEM

Sally loaned $7.00 to Betty. But Sally borrowed $15.00 from Estella and $32.00 from Joan. Moreover, Joan owes $3.00 to Estella and $7.00 to Betty. One day the women got together at

---

[1] Excerpts and diagrams in this section are from "Solution Using Venn Diagram," adapted from A. Whimbey and J. Lochhead, *Problem Solving and Comprehension*, Fifth Edition, (Hillside, NJ: Lawrence Erlbaum Associates, Inc., Publishers), p. 126. © 1991 reprinted by permission.

Betty's house to straighten out their accounts. Which woman left with $18.00 more than she came with?

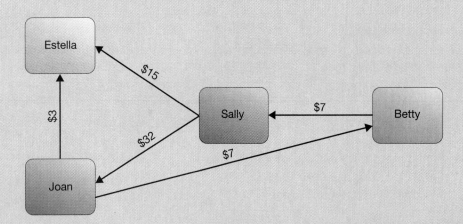

Solution Using Flow Diagram

From the diagram, it is clear that Estella left with $18.00 more than she came with (adapted from Whimbey & Lochhead, 1991, p. 126).

3 Teach students how to compile relevant information.

Good problem solvers start with themselves when compiling information to solve a problem or evidence to support a position on an issue. They recognize the importance of recalling earlier-learned information (metacognitive knowledge) and are adept at doing so (cognitive skill). Poor problem solvers, by contrast, lack metacognitive knowledge, cognitive skills, or both. If their deficiency is metacognitive, they make little or no effort to recall solution-relevant memories, even when the information was recently learned, because they do not understand the importance of searching long-term memory for potentially useful knowledge. Even if a student poor in problem solving recognizes the value of searching long-term memory for relevant information, he may still be handicapped because of inadequate encoding and retrieval skills.

To minimize any metacognitive deficiency, make sure your instruction in problem-solving methods emphasizes the importance of retrieving and using previously learned knowledge. To minimize retrieval problems, make sure *you* recall and implement the Suggestions for Teaching in Your Classroom that we offered in the preceding chapter.

If a student does not possess all the relevant information needed to work out a solution or to analyze an issue, you will have to guide her toward individuals and sources that can help. In referring students to individuals, select people who are judged to be reasonably knowledgeable about the subject, are careful thinkers, and are willing to share their ideas (Ruggiero, 1988). As an example, consider the issue of whether certain books (such as the novels *Catcher in the Rye*, by J. D. Salinger, and *Tom Sawyer*, by Mark Twain) should be banned from a school's reading list. In interviewing a knowledgeable person, students might ask questions like the following because they allow some insight into the individual's reasoning process and the evidence used to support his position:

- What general effects do you think characters in novels who rebel against adult authority have on a reader's behavior?
- Are certain groups of people, such as middle and high school students, likely to be influenced by the motives and actions of such characters? Why do you think so?
- Does a ban on certain books violate the authors' right to free speech?
- Does a book ban violate the principle of academic freedom? Why?
- Is it the proper role of a school board to prevent or discourage students from exposure to certain ideas during school hours?

If a reasonably informed person is not available, recognized authorities can often be interviewed by phone. If a student chooses this tactic, Ruggiero suggests calling or writing in advance for an appointment, preparing questions in advance, and asking permission to tape-record the interview.

Obviously, in addition to or in lieu of personal interviews, students can find substantial information in a good library. For example, you can steer them toward books by recognized authorities, research findings, court cases, and interviews with prominent individuals in periodicals. Although the Internet potentially contains a vast amount of information on any particular topic, warn students about using material gathered there indiscriminately. As with any medium, there are more and less reliable sources, and only material from reputable sources should be gathered. One additional benefit is that an extra layer of problem-solving activity is introduced when students must decide how to gather and evaluate online information.

4 Teach several methods for formulating problem solutions.

Earlier we mentioned five methods for formulating a problem solution: study worked examples, work on a simpler version of the problem, break the problem into parts, work backward, and solve an analogous problem. At the end of the chapter, under Resources for Further Investigation, we recommend several recently published books on problem solving that, taken together, provide numerous examples of each method. We encourage you to check out one or more of those references and other sources as demonstrations of worked problems and as opportunities for you to practice your own problem-solving skills so that you will be well prepared to teach each of these five methods.

5 Teach students the skills of evaluation.

Solutions to well-structured problems are usually evaluated through the application of an estimating or checking routine. Such procedures can be found in any good mathematics text. The evaluation of solutions to ill-structured problems and analyses of issues, however, is more complex and is less frequently taught. Ruggiero (1988) lists the following twelve habits and skills as contributing to the ability to evaluate complex solutions and positions:

- Being open-minded about opposing points of view.
- Selecting proper criteria of evaluation. Violations of this skill abound. A current example is the use of standardized achievement test scores to evaluate the quality of classroom instruction.

- Understanding the essence of an argument. To foster this skill, Ruggiero recommends that students be taught how to write a *précis*, which is a concise summary of an oral argument or a reading passage.

- Evaluating the reliability of sources.

- Properly interpreting factual data (for example, recognizing that an increase in a state's income tax rate from 4 to 6 percent is an increase not of 2 percent but of 50 percent).

- Testing the credibility of hypotheses. On the basis of existing data, hypotheses can range from highly improbable to highly probable.

- Making important distinctions (for instance, between preference and judgment, emotion and content, appearance and reality).

- Recognizing unstated assumptions (for example, that because two events occur close together in time, one causes the other; that what is clear to us will be clear to others; that if the majority believes something, it must be true).

- Detecting fallacies (for instance, stereotyping, faulty analogies, straw-man arguments [those that are easily refuted because they are deliberately weak], or overgeneralizing).

- Evaluating arguments.

- Making sound judgments.

- Recognizing when evidence is insufficient.

Transfer of Learning

Throughout Chapters 7, 8, and 9, we have indicated that classroom instruction should be arranged in such a way that students independently apply the knowledge and problem-solving skills they learn in school to similar but new situations. This capability is the main goal of problem-solving instruction and is typically valued very highly by educators (Halpern, 1998; Nickerson, 1994). Referred to as **transfer of learning**, it is the essence of being an autonomous learner and problem solver. In this section, we will examine the nature of transfer and discuss ways in which you can help bring it about.

THE NATURE AND SIGNIFICANCE OF TRANSFER OF LEARNING

THE THEORY OF IDENTICAL ELEMENTS   During the early 1900s, it was common practice for high school students and colleges to require that students take such subjects as Latin, Greek, and geometry. Because they were considered difficult topics to learn, mastery of them was expected to improve a student's ability to memorize, think, and reason. These enhanced abilities were then expected to facilitate the learning of less difficult subjects. The rationale behind this practice was that the human mind, much like any muscle in the body, could be exercised and made stronger. A strong mind, then, would learn things that a weak mind would not. This practice, known as the *doctrine of formal discipline*, constituted an early (and incorrect) explanation of transfer.

If teachers want students to apply what they learn in the classroom in other settings in the future, they should create tasks and conditions that are similar to those that students will encounter later.

In 1901 Edward Thorndike and Robert Woodworth proposed an alternative explanation of how transfer occurs. They argued that the degree to which knowledge and skills acquired in learning one task can help someone learn another task depends on how similar the two tasks are (if we assume that the learner recognizes the similarities). The greater the degree of similarity is between the tasks' stimulus and response elements (as in riding a bicycle and riding a motorcycle), the greater the amount of transfer will be. This idea became known as the **theory of identical elements** (Cox, 1997).

Early view of transfer based on degree of similarity between two tasks

POSITIVE, NEGATIVE, AND ZERO TRANSFER   In time, however, other psychologists (among them Ellis, 1965; Osgood, 1949) identified different types of transfer and the conditions under which each type prevailed. A useful distinction was made among positive transfer, negative transfer, and zero transfer (Ormrod, 1999).

The discussion up to this point has been alluding to **positive transfer**, defined as a situation in which prior learning aids subsequent learning. According to Thorndike's analysis, positive transfer occurs when a new learning task calls for essentially the same response that was made to a similar, earlier-learned task. The accomplished accordion player, for instance, probably will become a proficient pianist faster than someone who knows how to play the drums or someone who plays no musical instrument at all, all other things being equal. Similarly, the native English speaker who is also fluent in French is likely to have an easier time learning Spanish than is someone who speaks no foreign language.

Positive transfer: previous learning makes later learning easier

Negative transfer is defined as a situation in which prior learning interferes with subsequent learning. It occurs when two tasks are highly similar but require different responses. A tennis player learning how to play racquetball, for example, may encounter problems at first because of a tendency to swing the racquetball racket as if it were a tennis racket. Primary grade children often experience negative transfer when they encounter words that are spelled alike but pronounced differently (as in "I will *read* this story now since I *read* that story last week").

Negative transfer: previous learning interferes with later learning

Zero transfer is defined as a situation in which prior learning has no effect on new learning. It can be expected when two tasks have different stimuli and different responses. Learning to conjugate Latin verbs, for example, is not likely to have any effect on learning how to find the area of a rectangle.

SPECIFIC AND GENERAL TRANSFER The preceding description of positive transfer, although useful, is somewhat limiting because it is unclear whether transfer from one task to another is due to specific similarities or to general or nonspecific similarities. Psychologists (as described by Ellis, 1978, pp. 249–250) decide whether transfer is due to specific or general factors by setting up learning tasks such as the following for three different but equivalent groups of learners.

	Initial Task	Transfer Task
Group 1	Learn French	Learn Spanish
Group 2	Learn Chinese	Learn Spanish
Group 3		Learn Spanish

If on a Spanish test, group 1 scores higher than group 2, the difference is attributed to **specific transfer** of similarities between French and Spanish (such as vocabulary, verb conjugations, and sentence structure). If groups 1 and 2 score the same but both outscore group 3, the difference is attributed to nonspecific, or **general transfer**, of similarities between the two tasks since Chinese shares no apparent specific characteristics with French or Spanish. In this case it is possible that learners use cognitive strategies—such as imagery, verbal elaboration, and mnemonic devices—when learning a foreign language and that these transfer to the learning of other foreign languages. Such nonspecific transfer effects have also been demonstrated for other classroom tasks, such as problem solving and learning from text (Ellis, 1978; Royer, 1979).

> Specific transfer due to specific similarities between two tasks

> General transfer due to use of same cognitive strategies

CONTEMPORARY VIEWS OF SPECIFIC AND GENERAL TRANSFER

Gavriel Salomon and David Perkins (1989) offer a current treatment of specific and general transfer under the labels *low-road transfer* and *high-road transfer*, respectively.

LOW-ROAD TRANSFER **Low-road transfer** refers to a situation in which a previously learned skill or idea is almost automatically retrieved from memory and applied to a highly similar current task. For example, a student who has mastered the skill of two-column addition and correctly completes three-column and four-column addition problems with no prompting or instruction is exhibiting low-road transfer. Another example is a student who learns how to tune up car engines in an auto shop class and then almost effortlessly and automatically carries out the same task as an employee of an auto repair business. As you may have suspected, low-road transfer is basically a contemporary version of Thorndike and Woodworth's identical elements theory (Cox, 1997).

> Low-road transfer: previously learned skill automatically applied to similar current task

Two conditions need to be present for low-road transfer to occur. First, students have to be given ample opportunities to practice using the target skill. Second, practice has to occur with different materials and in different settings. The more varied the practice is, the greater is the range of tasks to which the skill can be applied. If, for example, you want students to be good notetakers, give them instruction and ample practice at taking notes from their biology, health, and English textbooks.

Once they become accomplished notetakers in these subjects, they will likely apply this skill to other subjects in an almost automatic fashion. The auto mechanic who has learned to change the spark plugs in a Chrysler, a Toyota, and a Mercedes-Benz should be able to do the same job as efficiently in a Ford, a Buick, or a Nissan. In essence, what we are describing is the behavioral principle of generalization. Since the transfer task is similar in one or more respects to the practice task, this type of transfer is also called *near transfer*. To understand how people transfer prior knowledge and skills to new situations that look rather different from the original task, we will need to explore the nature of high-road transfer.

HIGH-ROAD TRANSFER **High-road transfer** involves the conscious, controlled, somewhat effortful formulation of an "abstraction" (that is, a rule, a schema, a strategy, or an analogy) that allows a connection to be made between two tasks. For example, an individual who learns to set aside a certain number of hours every day to complete homework assignments and study for upcoming exams formulates the principle that the most efficient way to accomplish a task is to break it down into small pieces and work at each piece according to a set schedule. As an adult, the individual uses this principle to successfully deal with complex tasks at work and at home. As another example, imagine a student who, after much observation and thought, has finally developed a good sense of what school is and how one is supposed to behave there. In other words, this student has developed a school schema. Such a schema would probably be made up of actors (teachers and students), objects (desks, chalkboards, books, pencils), and events (reading, listening, writing, talking, drawing). Since this is an idealized abstraction, actual classrooms may contain fewer or greater numbers of these characteristics in varying proportions. Even so, with this schema a student could walk into any instructional setting (another school classroom, a training seminar, or a press briefing, for example) and readily understand what was going on, why it was going on, and how one should behave. Of course, with repeated applications of schemata, rules, strategies, and the like, the behaviors become less conscious and more automatic. What was once a reflection of high-road transfer becomes low-road transfer.

Gavriel Salomon and David Perkins (1989) refer to this deliberate, conscious, effortful formulating of a general principle or schema that can be applied to a variety of different-looking but fundamentally similar tasks as *mindful abstraction*. The *mindful* part of the phrase indicates that the abstraction must be thought about and fully understood for high-road transfer to occur. That is, people must be aware of what they are doing and why they are doing it. This is essentially training in metacognition. Recall our earlier discussion in this chapter (p. 308) of inert knowledge and Richard Feynman's observations of how his classmates at the Massachusetts Institute of Technology failed to recognize the application of a previously learned mathematical formula because it was initially learned for use only in that course.

TEACHING FOR LOW-ROAD AND HIGH-ROAD TRANSFER As we noted at the beginning of this section, transfer of previously learned knowledge and skill to new tasks and settings is a goal that is high on almost every teacher's list. Yet one study of classroom activity found that only seven percent of tasks required students to use information they had learned earlier (Bennett, Desforges, Cockburn, & Wilkinson, 1984). Perhaps most teachers feel they simply don't know how to teach for transfer. That need not be your fate. The following guidelines should produce greater levels of both low-road and high-road transfer.

High-road transfer: formulate rule from one task and apply to related task

1. Provide students with multiple opportunities for varied practice to help them develop a rich web of interrelated concepts.

2. Give students opportunities to solve problems that are similar to those they will eventually have to solve.

3. Teach students how to formulate for a variety of tasks general rules, strategies, or schemes that can be used in the future with a variety of similar problems.

4. Give students cues that will allow them to retrieve from memory earlier-learned information that can be used to make current learning easier.

5. Teach students to focus on the beneficial effects of creating and using rules and strategies to solve particular kinds of problems (Anderson, Reder, & Simon, 1996; Cox, 1997; Halpern, 1998; Salomon & Perkins, 1989).

> **Low-road and high-road transfer produced by varied practice at applying skills, rules, memory retrieval cues**

If there is one thing we hope you have learned from this discussion of transfer of learning, it is this: *if you want transfer, teach for transfer.* As you can see, students have to be carefully prepared and coached to use the information and skills they learn in school. If you expect transfer, be it low road or high road, to occur on its own, you will be disappointed most of the time.

Technology Tools for Knowledge Construction and Problem Solving

Wayne Nelson and David Palumbo (1992) warn that simply using hypermedia systems as a way to present or represent knowledge will probably not maximize student achievement. The full potential of such technology tools will more likely be achieved when learners are offered chances to construct, share, and revise knowledge in more open-ended environments. In effect, learners become producers, designers, or "authors of knowledge" (Lehrer, 1993).

For the K-12 classroom, knowledge construction and presentation tools such as HyperCard, Kid Pix Companion Slide Show, LinkWay, HyperStudio, PowerPoint, and ToolBook are frequently used. With such tools, students can link text, pictures, sound, and motion video using pages, cards, or slides of information that can be explored or replayed by others. Four projects that have successfully linked this constructivist principle of students as authors of knowledge to interactive technologies are HyperAuthor, Computer-Supported Intentional Learning Environments (CSILE), Learning Through Collaborative Visualization (CoVis), and The Adventures of Jasper Woodbury.

> **Technology tools are available to help students construct knowledge, become better problem solvers**

HYPERAUTHOR

Richard Lehrer (1993) has developed an interesting tool for knowledge construction called HyperAuthor. The rationale for HyperAuthor is based partly on John Dewey's progressive education idea to have students develop and design rather than receive knowledge (Lehrer, Erickson, & Connell, 1994). In HyperAuthor, there are tools for students to create and label their links, draw, design graphs or animations, and generate text. Lehrer (1993) points out that, as with the composing process, a hypermedia design project fosters the problem-solving skills of planning, finding and selecting information, organizing and representing that information, and, finally, evaluating and revising the design. In effect, students using Hyper-Author are constantly making decisions about what is important information, how to segment it, and how to organize and link it.

In one study (Lehrer, 1993), eighth-grade students used HyperAuthor to design hypermedia presentations during a six-week unit on the Civil War. Rather than attending a traditional class and relying on textbooks, HyperAuthor students designed their own electronic information about the Civil War. One result was that many students selected somewhat unusual topics, such as women or photographers of the Civil War, instead of the more traditional famous generals and battles. Another positive outcome was that enthusiasm for the project was so high that students were requesting access to the computers during study hall, after school, and on weekends. By the end of the project, these students developed an elaborate and deep understanding of the Civil War and came to view history as more of an interpretation than a collection of facts. Tests a year later indicated that these gains had been maintained compared to students taught in a traditional fashion.

A follow-up study involved ninth-grade students using HyperAuthor to design American history presentations. Once again, Lehrer et al. (1994) observed high student interest, task focus, planning, and concerted mental effort. The result was innovative and complex hypermedia documents about various aspects of American history. Long-term studies of *HyperAuthor* have revealed that, over time, students develop the ability to create and link hypermedia documents in ways that are useful for such other audiences as classmates, friends, and parents (Erickson & Lehrer, 1998).

COMPUTER-SUPPORTED INTENTIONAL LEARNING ENVIRONMENTS

Marlene Scardamalia and Carl Bereiter (1996, p. 10) ask us to "imagine a network of networks—people from schools, universities, cultural institutions, service organizations, businesses—simultaneously building knowledge within their primary groups while advancing the knowledge of others. We might call such a community network a knowledge-building society." For more than a decade, these researchers have developed and tested aspects of such a network with the Computer-Supported Intentional Learning Environments (CSILE) project (Scardamali & Bereiter, 1991). Based on years of research, CSILE was the first networking system supporting schools and students in knowledge building, collaboration, and inquiry.

The CSILE project is built around a set of learning tools that foster student goal setting, knowledge building, and active or intentional learning (Scardamalia, Bereiter, McLean, Swallow, & Woodruff, 1989). In an intentional learning environment, students learn how to set goals, generate and interrelate new ideas, link new knowledge to old, negotiate meaning with peers, and relate what was learned to other tasks. The product of these activities, like the product of any scientific inquiry, is then made available to other students.

The CSILE project allows students to create informational links, or "notes," in several ways (for example, text notes, drawings, graphs, pictures, timelines, and maps). CSILE also contains designated "cooperation" icons that encourage students to reflect on how their work links to others as well as idea browsing and linking tools for marking notes that involve or intend cooperation. In effect, through knowledge-building centers and public display of student work, the CSILE project grants more responsibility to students for their own learning while encouraging them to generate ideas, construct and negotiate knowledge with their peers, obtain peer feedback on their projects, consider ideas from different perspectives, and assume ownership over a product. Using this database system, students comment on the work of others, read responses to their hypotheses, or search for information posted by their peers under a particular topic title. For instance, a search for the word *whales* would call up all the work of students who assigned that word as a keyword in their CSILE contributions. In such a decentralized, free-flowing environment, no longer must the teacher initiate all discussion and coordinate turn taking (Scardamalia & Bereiter, 1991, 1996).

A new version of CSILE for the Web forces students to label their contribution to a topic prior to posting it (for example, *High-Level Question, New Learning, Plan, My Theory, What I Need to Understand, Conclusion, Synthesis*). Like the CoVis project mentioned next, the Web version of CSILE also encourages experts, parents, and community members to participate in the project. As such, it moves students from writing individual notes to jointly writing ideas to shared problems using discussion notes.

Studies show that students who use CSILE perform better on standardized language and reading tests, ask deeper questions, are more elaborate and coherent in their commentaries, demonstrate more mature beliefs about learning, and engage in discussions that are more committed to scientific progress (Scardamalia & Bereiter, 1996). The availability of a cooperation icon seems to foster greater peer commenting and cooperative efforts (Scardamalia & Bereiter, 1991), and students who make more conceptual progress with CSILE tend to be more problem- than fact-oriented (Oshima, Scardamalia, & Bereiter, 1996).

LEARNING THROUGH COLLABORATIVE VISUALIZATION

As indicated in Chapter 2, the emergence of computer networks has fostered global scientific data collection and sharing. Now, less skilled young learners can be apprenticed into fields like meteorology and environmental science through social interaction with experts and peers in a learning community. Many science projects are emerging that illustrate how to embed learning in real-world contexts by having students collect such data as rainfall, wind speed, and environmental pollutants, and share findings with peers. Such projects exemplify both the situated learning and social constructivist ideas outlined earlier in this chapter.

One such project is called Learning Through Collaborative Visualization (CoVis). One of the primary goals of CoVis is to foster project-based science learning, or "collaboratories" (Edelson, Pea, & Gomez, 1996, p. 158), which use computer networks so that students can access practicing scientists and scientific tools. The belief is that science is learned through participation and "learning-in-doing," not through preparation by someone else. As such, the project includes e-mail, news group discussions, listservs (Internet sites where individuals exchange information and ask questions about a specific topic), remote screen sharing, and communication with peers and scientists using both video and audio conferencing. Students' collaborative investigations might include such topics as weather forecasting, ozone depletion trends, global warming, and severe storms. Unlike conventional instruction, CoVis uses computer visualization tools to represent real-time data (for example, temperature as color, wind as vectors, and atmospheric pressure as contours).

CoVis researchers have also developed the Collaboratory Notebook, which serves as the key vehicle for students from different high schools to engage in scientific inquiries. Using this tool, students note their questions, plans, and hypotheses regarding their investigation. And as with the CSILE projects, CoVis students must label their individual contributions to the inquiry (for example, *Information,*

Commentary, Question, Conjecture, Evidence for, Evidence against, Plan, and *Step in the Plan*).

Since inception in 1992, the CoVis project has involved over one hundred teachers and three thousand students in innovative telecommunications projects meant to enhance science education. Preliminary research on CoVis revealed mixed success with the telecommunications tools, as some were easier and more practical to use than others (Gomez, Fishman, & Pea, in press). This research also indicated that teachers need assistance in developing assessment devices for student CoVis work, while students may need some help adapting to this new type of learning environment. Case studies have also found dramatic differences in adaptation and inventive use of CoVis between low and high socioeconomic schools (Shrader, Lento, Gomez, & Pea, 1997).

JASPER WOODBURY AND ANCHORED INSTRUCTION

A fourth project that attempts to foster constructivist principles while overcoming the inert knowledge problem mentioned earlier in the chapter comes from a group of researchers at Vanderbilt University called the Cognition and Technology Group at Vanderbilt (CTGV). During the past decade, CTGV researchers have devised and tested an interesting set of instructional materials that incorporate constructivist principles based on ideas of anchored instruction. **Anchored instruction** involves creating tasks that situate and focus student learning in interesting real-world contexts with many subproblems or issues (for example, making a business plan for the dunking booth at a school's fun fair) (Barron et al., 1995). Anchoring problems in a larger context helps students gain a meaningful understanding of the problems and perceive both critical aspects of problems and different points of view (CTGV, 1990).

The Adventures of Jasper Woodbury is an experimental video disk-based series designed to promote problem solving, reasoning, and effective communication among middle school students using anchored instruction. Each story in the series is a fifteen- to twenty-minute adventure that involves Jasper Woodbury and other characters. At the end of each story the characters are faced with a problem that students must solve before they are allowed to see how the characters in the video solved the problem. The basic design principles of such an approach are the video-based presentation, generative learning format, relevant and irrelevant data embedded within the problems, sufficient problem complexity, pairs of related adventures to promote transfer and generalization, links across the curriculum to multiple content areas, and episodes built around national learning standards (CTGV, 1993). The ability to replay video scenes on demand is also important.

The adventures are arranged in pairs so that the experimenters can assess how well students use the problem-solving skills they learned in the initial video. The first pair of adventures concerns planning a trip, the second pair involves using statistics to create a business plan, and the third pair focuses on meaningful uses of geometry. In the course of solving the problem posed in the video, students become involved in activities such as generating subgoals, identifying relevant information, cooperating with others, discussing the advantages and disadvantages of possible solutions, and comparing perspectives (CTGV, 1992a, 1992b).

Despite the complexity of these problems and the fact that Jasper students received less direct basic math instruction than control students, they performed quite well on standardized tests. On tests of basic math concepts such as units of time or distance, area, decimals, and fractions, both groups improved at the same rate. However, Jasper students scored significantly higher than the control students on word problems, tests of planning, and attitudes toward math, and they better appreciated complex challenges (CTGV, 1992a, 1992b).

An expanded version of this project has been made available on the Public Broadcasting System as the *Jasper Challenge Series*. Its purpose is to stimulate discussion of problems across classes, energize students by seeing how others work on the same problems, showcase student explanations, and attempt to build learning communities (Barron et al., 1995). In addition, these researchers have extended their anchored instruction research to create a Scientists-in-Action series meant to help students experience and better understand real-life science work (Goldman et al., 1996). A third new project by this group, the Little Planet Literacy Series, is a multimedia program that also uses anchored instruction to support children's decoding, writing, and recording of their own books (Secules, Cottom, Bray, & Miller, 1997).

TECHNOLOGY AND PROBLEM SOLVING

As we suggested in previous chapters, many commonly used technology tools—graphing calculators, spreadsheets, word processors, and databases—are, in effect, problem-solving facilitation devices, since studies show that they relieve students of low-level mental work, thereby facilitating the use of problem-solving strategies (Lambrecht, 1993). In fact, just working with computerized data can improve students' ability to see the relevance and sufficiency of information as well as judge the efficient and inefficient organization of information (White, 1987). Teachers also play an important role in fostering problem solving with technology, since student problem-solving skills in a technologically rich learning environment need to be mediated by the teacher's timely use of such task structuring devices as questioning, scaffolding, modeling, and pushing students to explore (Jarvela, 1995).

Given the importance of task structuring to facilitate problem formation, planning, and resolution in technology-intensive environments, Maria Cardelle-Elawar and Keith Wetzel (1995) developed a four-step model called IDEA in which young children (1) identify the problem posed by the computer, (2) describe what they have to find in this problem, (3) explore steps and strategies to solve this problem, and (4) assess success and failure and any progress in solving the problem. Initial research indicates that the IDEA strategy is successful in helping students in second and fourth grade monitor their learning and engage in better problem-solving practices.

RESOURCES FOR FURTHER INVESTIGATION

■ Constructivism

In *The Young Child as Scientist: A Constructivist Approach to Early Childhood Science Education* (1991), Christine Chaillé and Lory Britain start from the premise that young children learn and solve problems in much the same way as scientists do—they actively construct conceptions of the world on the basis of a constant process of theorizing and experimenting. From this perspective the authors describe how to create a constructivist learning environment for the purpose of teaching science to preschool and primary grade children.

Jacquiline Grennon Brooks and Martin G. Brooks discuss the call for constructivism in education, describe five guiding prinicples (with several examples of classroom applications), and describe how to create a constructivist classroom setting in their fairly brief (127 pages) and readable book, *In Search of Understanding: The Case for Constructivist Classrooms* (1993).

Constructivism in Education (1995), edited by Leslie Steffe and Jerry Gale, is a massive (550 pages) collection of chapters on various aspects of constructivism. Several chapters describe the relationship between constructivism and technology, and several others describe constructivist approaches to teaching science and mathematics.

For ideas about how to teach social studies from a constructivist perspective, see the January 1998 issue (vol. 62, no. 1) of *Social Education*.

Given the importance of interpersonal interaction to the constructivist position and the flexibility of classroom discussions as an instructional tool, you might want to read *William Fawcett Hill's Learning Through Discussion* (3d ed., 1994), by Jerome Rabow, Michelle Charness, Johanna Kipperman, and Susan Radcliffe-Vasile. A compact book at only 67 pages, it nevertheless provides a wealth of practical information on how to structure and run discussion groups in the classroom.

■ Problem-Solving Processes

In *Teaching Thinking Across the Curriculum* (1988), Vincent Ryan Ruggiero describes a model for solving problems and analyzing issues, discusses teaching objectives and methods, identifies obstacles to students' cognitive development, details assignments that can be used in a variety of courses, demonstrates how instructors can design additional course-specific thinking assignments, and offers guidelines for developing a thinking skills program.

Problem Finding, Problem Solving, and Creativity (1994), edited by Mark Runco, contains thirteen chapters that cover various aspects of problem solving. Several chapters discuss the often overlooked topic of problem finding.

Gary Woditsch designed *The Thoughtful Teacher's Guide to Thinking Skills* (1991) to help kindergarten through college teachers improve their students' thinking skills. According to the author, "Every page of this guide aims at classroom impact, regardless of whether that classroom happens to serve a college, a kindergarten, or somewhere in between. That impact is meant to flow from the reader's strengthened grasp of what constitutes and what advances skillful thought" (p.vii).

In *Reasoning and Problem Solving: A Handbook for Elementary School Teachers* (1993), Stephen Krulik and Jesse Rudnick discuss the nature of higher-order thinking skills, present a general approach to problem solving, provide steps teachers should follow when teaching problem solving, and offer hands-on materials and resources for problem-solving instruction.

In *The Art of Thinking* (4th ed., 1995), Vincent Ruggiero describes a four-part model for helping students become better thinkers and problem solvers. The chapters that describe each part ("Be Aware," "Be Creative," "Be Critical," "Communicate Your Ideas") are clearly written and contain a wealth of suggestions for classroom use.

SUMMARY

1. The constructivist view of learning holds that meaningful learing occurs when people use existing knowledge schemes and the viewpoints of others to interpret the world around them.

2. During the 1960s, Jerome Bruner proposed a constructivist view of learning that relied on giving students realistic problems for which they had to discover appropriate solutions.

3. The major aspects of constructivism are that meaningful learning occurs when people actively construct personal knowledge structures, that only part of a teacher's understanding of some concept or issue can be transferred to students through direct instruction, that the knowledge structures of different people have much in common, and that the formation and changing of knowledge structures come mainly from peer interaction.

4. A cognitive constructivist view, like that of Piaget, focuses on how individuals' cognitive structures influence the view of the world they construct.

5. A social constructivist view, like that of Vygotsky, focuses on how social processes influence the view of reality that students construct.

6. Three conditions that support constructivism are a cognitive apprenticeship between teacher and student, the use of realistic learning tasks (situated learning), and exposure to multiple perspectives.

7. The classroom discussion is an instructional technique that teachers can use to support a constructivist view of meaningful learning, for it allows students to share different perspectives of realistic problems.

8. The types of problems that students most often come into contact with are well-structured problems, ill-structured problems, and issues. Well-structured problems are clearly stated and can be solved by applying previously learned procedures, and their solutions can be accurately evaluated. Ill-structured problems are often vaguely stated, they cannot always be solved by applying previously learned procedures, and their solutions cannot always be evaluated against clear and widely accepted criteria. Issues are like ill-structured problems, but with two differences: they arouse strong emotions that tend to divide people into opposing camps, and they require that one determine the most reasonable position to take before working out a solution.

9. A general problem-solving model is composed of five steps: realize that a problem exists, understand the nature of the problem, compile relevant information, formulate and carry out a solution, and evaluate the solution.

10. The keys to realizing that a problem exists are to be curious about why things are the way they are and to be dissatisfied with the status quo.

11. Understanding the nature of a problem, also known as problem representation or problem framing, requires a high level of knowledge about the subject matter surrounding the problem and familiarity with the particular type of problem.

12. A problem solver can compile relevant information by searching long-term memory, retrieving solution relevant information, and representing that information as lists, tables, pictures, graphs, diagrams, and so on. In addition, friends, colleagues, and experts can be tapped for information.

13. A problem solver can formulate solutions by studying worked examples, working on a simpler version of the problem, breaking the problem into parts, working backward, or solving an analogous problem.

14. A problem solver can evaluate solutions for well-structured problems by estimating or checking and solutions for ill-structured problems by answering a set of basic questions that deal with who, what, where, when, why, and how; by identifying imperfections and complications; by anticipating possible negative reactions; and by devising improvements.

15. Transfer of learning occurs when the learning of new information or skills is influenced by previously learned information or skills.

16. An early view of transfer was based on Thorndike and Woodworth's theory of identical elements. This theory holds that transfer of learning is a function of how many elements two tasks have in common. The greater the similarity is, the greater is the degree of transfer.

17. Positive transfer occurs when a new learning task is similar to a previously learned task and calls for a similar response. Negative transfer occurs when a new learning task is similar to a previously learned task but calls for a different response. Zero transfer occurs when previously learned information or skills are so dissimilar to new information or skills that they have no effect on how quickly the latter will be learned.

18. Positive transfer that is due to identifiable similarities between an earlier-learned task and a current one is referred to as specific transfer. Positive transfer that is due to the formulation, use, and carryover of cognitive strategies from one task to another is referred to as general transfer.

19. A current view of specific transfer is called low-road transfer. It is produced by giving students many opportunities to practice a skill in different settings and with different materials.

20. A current view of general transfer is called high-road transfer. It is produced by teaching students how to formulate a general rule, strategy, or schema that can be used in the future with a variety of problems that are fundamentally similar to the original.

21. Students' knowledge construction and problem-solving skills can be improved through one of several computer- or CD-ROM-based programs.

KEY TERMS

discovery learning (292)
cognitive constructivism (294)
social constructivism (295)
situated learning (296)
inert knowledge (297)
problem solving (305)
well-structured problems (305)

ill-structured problems (306)
issues (306)
problem representation/framing (308)
heuristics (309)
transfer of learning (316)
theory of identical elements (317)
positive transfer (317)

negative transfer (317)
zero transfer (318)
specific transfer (318)
general transfer (318)
low-road transfer (318)
high-road transfer (319)
anchored instruction (323)

DISCUSSION QUESTIONS

1. According to constructivist theory, meaningful learning occurs when students are encouraged to think about how the basic ideas of a subject relate to one another and to what students already know, when learning is set in realistic contexts, and when students can work together to figure out the meaning of ideas. Can you recall a class in which the instructor made use of constructivist techniques? What did the instructor do? How did you react? Was the learning outcome more meaningful than for other classes? How could you tell? How might you use constructivist-oriented teaching techniques?

2. Critics of American education argue that contemporary students are poor problem solvers because they receive little systematic instruction in problem-solving processes. How would you rate the quantity and quality of the instruction you received in problem solving? In terms of the five steps discussed in this chapter, which ones were you taught? What can you do to ensure that your students become good problem solvers?

3. Educational psychologists who have studied transfer have said to teachers that if they want transfer, they should teach for transfer. What do you think this statement means?

10 Approaches to Instruction

This chapter is concerned with helping you answer two questions: What are my objectives? (or, What do I want students to know and be able to do after I complete a unit of instruction?) and How can I help students achieve those objectives? The ordering of these two questions is not arbitrary. Instructional planning should always begin with a description of what you want students to know and be able to do some weeks, or even months, after the beginning of an instructional unit. To appreciate why, suppose that you follow the common practice of many teachers and prepare lesson plans by examining texts and other curriculum materials in order to devise an instructional sequence. Probably your first inclination is to concentrate on what is going to happen tomorrow and to put off thinking about what is going to happen two weeks or a month ahead when the time comes to evaluate what students have learned. You might reason that there is no point in thinking about tests until it is time to prepare tests. Quite a few teachers operate in such a one-thing-at-a-time way, and you are probably familiar with the results—disorganized lessons, lectures, and assignments, followed by exams that may not have much to do with what you think you were supposed to have learned. You can avoid falling into that common trap by concentrating at the very beginning on what you want your students to be able to do at the end of a unit of study. If you decide in advance what you want your students to achieve, you can prepare lessons that logically lead to a particular result and also use evaluation techniques efficiently designed to determine what level of achievement has occurred.

Once you have a clear idea of what you are trying to accomplish with your students, you can consider how you are going to help get them there. Here is where you can use your knowledge of learning and motivation. After all, if the goal of teaching is to help students acquire and use a variety of knowledge and skills, what better way to do that than to use approaches and techniques that are consistent with what is known about how people learn and the conditions under which they learn best. The theories that underlie the approaches to instruction that are described in this chapter emphasize different aspects of the learning process, and each has been supported by research. Thus, no one theory is sufficiently comprehensive and powerful that you can rely exclusively on it as a guide for designing classroom instruction. To work effectively with the diversity of students you will almost certainly encounter,

you will need to use a variety of instructional approaches and techniques. For some objectives and students you may want to use a highly structured approach that is consistent with the principles of behavioral and social learning theories. For other objectives you may want to focus on helping students develop more effective learning and problem-solving skills. You may also want students to work productively in groups and to respond to you and to learning in positive ways and to develop positive feelings about themselves as students. And you will probably also want to integrate computer-based technology with one or more of these approaches.

As we have stressed throughout, computer-based instruction is playing an increasingly important role in education. It is currently being used to help students acquire a wide array of knowledge and skills, ranging from simple facts to complex problem solving, and its usefulness in the classroom is almost certain to grow. It may interest you to know that when teaching machines first became available for classroom use in the late 1950s and early 1960s, many teachers were skeptical about their ability to teach anything except the most simple and basic skills. And some teachers were so fearful that these devices would eventually replace them that they lobbied for legislation that would ban teaching machines from the classroom (Benjamin, 1988). How times have changed!

In the next section we will introduce you to the concept of instructional objectives. We will distinguish between goals and objectives, describe organizational schemes called taxonomies that help you decide what you want your students to learn, describe two methods for preparing objectives, discuss the importance of aligning your objectives with your instructional approach and the tests you create, and summarize the research on the effect of objectives on student achievement. ■

Devising and Using Objectives

CONTRASTING OBJECTIVES WITH EDUCATIONAL GOALS

One way to help you understand the nature of instructional objectives is to contrast them with something with which they are often confused: educational goals. Goals are relatively broad statements of what political and educational leaders would like to see schools accomplish. Perhaps the best-known set of educational goals are those in the U.S. Government's Goals 2000 program. Signed into law on March 31, 1994, by President William Clinton as the Goals 2000: Educate America Act, the program states that the following eight goals should be achieved by the year 2000:

> **Goals are broad, general statements of desired educational outcomes**

1. All children will be ready to learn when they start school.

2. At least 90 percent of all students will graduate from high school.

3. At the end of the fourth, eighth, and twelfth grades, students will demonstrate their competency in such subjects as English, mathematics, science, foreign languages, civics and government, economics, art, history, and geography. In addition, students will acquire the thinking skills that will allow them to become responsible citizens, independent learners, and productive workers.

4. Teachers will have access to continuing education programs that will help them improve their professional knowledge and skills.

5. U.S. students will be ranked first in the world in science and mathematics achievement.

6. All adults will be sufficiently literate, knowledgeable, and skilled to compete in a global economy and behave as responsible citizens.

7. All schools will be free of drugs, violence, the unauthorized presence of alcohol and guns, and will offer an environment conducive to learning.

8. All schools will have programs that encourage parents to participate in promoting the social, emotional, and academic growth of children.

The current status of the Goals 2000 program is described on a Website that is maintained by the U.S. Department of Education. It can be found at **http://www.ed.gov/G2K/**.

The Goals 2000 list clearly mentions skills, attitudes, and interests that are desirable, if not essential, for someone who hopes to live successfully and happily in America. Unfortunately, these statements do not provide very useful guidelines for teachers charged with the responsibility for achieving them. What, exactly, is meant by "thinking skills" or "being sufficiently literate, knowledgeable, and skilled"? And will these terms mean the same thing to every teacher? Thinking skills, for example, could be interpreted to mean everything from memorization to problem solving. Instructional objectives, in contrast to these broad educational goals, specify the kinds of observable and measurable student behaviors that make it possible for the underlying goals to be achieved. To give teachers both a common vocabulary and a system for writing different kinds of objectives, psychologists have created organizational schemes called taxonomies.

> **Instructional objectives specify observable, measurable student behaviors**

TAXONOMIES OF OBJECTIVES

Awareness of the vagueness of educational goals stimulated a group of psychologists who specialized in testing to seek a better way to describe educational objectives. After experimenting with various ways to prepare lists of objectives that would be more useful to teachers than vaguely worded sets of goals, the test specialists decided to develop taxonomies of educational objectives. A **taxonomy** is a classification scheme with categories arranged in hierarchical order. Because goals of education are extremely diverse (take another look at those in the Goals 2000 program), the decision was made to prepare taxonomies in three areas, or *domains:* cognitive, affective, and psychomotor. The taxonomy for the **cognitive domain** stresses knowledge and intellectual skills; the taxonomy for the **affective domain** concentrates on attitudes and values; and that for the **psychomotor domain** focuses on physical abilities and skills.

Taxonomy: categories arranged in hierarchical order

TAXONOMY FOR THE COGNITIVE DOMAIN   The taxonomy for the cognitive domain was prepared by Benjamin S. Bloom and several associates (1956). It consists of six hierarchically ordered levels of instructional outcomes: knowledge, comprehension, application, analysis, synthesis, and evaluation. The taxonomy is described as a hierarchy because it was reasoned that comprehension relies on prior mastery of knowledge or facts, application depends on comprehension of relevant ideas, and so on through the remaining levels. An abridged outline of the taxonomy for the cognitive domain follows.

Taxonomy of Educational Objectives: Cognitive Domain

1.00 *Knowledge.* Remembering previously learned information, such as facts, terms, procedures, and principles.

2.00 *Comprehension* Grasping the meaning of information by putting it into one's own words, drawing conclusions, or stating implications.

Cognitive taxonomy: knowledge, comprehension, application, analysis, synthesis, evaluation

3.00 *Application.* Applying knowledge to actual situations as in taking principles learned in math and applying them to laying out a baseball diamond or applying principles of civil liberties to current events.

4.00 *Analysis.* Breaking down objects or ideas into simpler parts and seeing how the parts relate and are organized. For example, discussing how the public and the private sectors differ or detecting logical fallacies in an argument.

5.00 *Synthesis.* Rearranging component ideas into a new whole. For example, planning a panel discussion or writing a comprehensive term paper.

6.00 *Evaluation.* Making judgments based on internal evidence or external criteria. For example, evaluating a work of art, editing a term paper, or detecting inconsistencies in the speech of a politician.

TAXONOMY FOR THE AFFECTIVE DOMAIN   In addition to arranging instructional experiences to help students achieve cognitive objectives, virtually all teachers are interested in encouraging the development of attitudes and values. To clarify the nature of such objectives, a taxonomy for the affective domain was prepared (Krathwohl, Bloom, & Masia, 1964). Affective objectives are more difficult to define, evaluate, or encourage than cognitive objectives because they are often demonstrated in subtle or indirect ways. Furthermore, certain aspects of value

Taxonomy of affective objectives stresses attitudes and values

The taxonomy of objectives for the cognitive domain calls attention to the fact that instructional outcomes can range from such basic capabilities as verbatim recall and comprehension to such higher-level capabilities as application of knowledge and skill, analysis of complex ideas into their component parts, synthesis of different ideas into an integrated whole, and evaluation of the quality of ideas.

development are sometimes considered to be more the responsibility of parents than of teachers. Finally, because values and attitudes involve a significant element of personal choice, they are often expressed more clearly out of school than in the classroom. The complete taxonomy for the affective domain stresses out-of-school values as much as, if not more than, in-school values. The following abridgment concentrates on the kinds of affective objectives you are most likely to be concerned with as a teacher. You will probably recognize, though, that there is not much you can do to substantially influence the kinds of objectives described in the higher levels of the taxonomy since they represent a crystallization of values formed by experiences over an extended period of time.

Taxonomy of Educational Objectives: Affective Domain

1.0 *Receiving (attending)*. Willingness to receive or attend.

2.0 *Responding*. Active participation indicating positive response or acceptance of an idea or policy.

3.0 *Valuing*. Expressing a belief or attitude about the value or worth of something.

4.0 *Organization*. Organizing various values into an internalized system.

5.0 *Characterization by a value or value complex*. The value system becomes a way of life.

TAXONOMY FOR THE PSYCHOMOTOR DOMAIN   Cognitive and affective objectives are important at all grade levels, but so are psychomotor objectives. Regardless of the grade level or subject you teach, at some point you are likely to want to help your students acquire physical skills of various kinds. In the primary grades, for example, you will want your students to learn how to print legibly. And in many subjects in middle school and in high school, psychomotor skills (for example, driving a car, playing a violin, adjusting a microscope, manipulating a computer keyboard, operating a power saw, throwing a pot) may be essential. Recognition of the importance of physical skills prompted Elizabeth Simpson (1972) to prepare a taxonomy for the psychomotor domain. An abridged version of the taxonomy follows.

Taxonomy of Educational Objectives Psychomotor Domain

1.0 *Perception*. Using sense organs to obtain cues needed to guide motor activity.

2.0 *Set*. Being ready to perform a particular action.

3.0 *Guided response*. Performing under the guidance of a model.

4.0 *Mechanism*. Being able to perform a task habitually with some degree of confidence and proficiency. For example, demonstrating the ability to get the first serve in the service area 70 percent of the time.

5.0 *Complex or overt response*. Performing a task with a high degree of proficiency and skill. For example, typing all kinds of business letters and forms quickly with no errors.

6.0 *Adaptation*. Using previously learned skills to perform new but related tasks. For example, using skills developed while using a word processor to do desktop publishing.

7.0 *Origination*. Creating new performances after having developed skills. For example, creating a new form of modern dance.

Using these taxonomies will help you avoid two common instructional failings: ignoring entire classes of outcomes (usually affective and psychomotor) and overemphasizing the lowest level of the cognitive domain. According to Benjamin S. Bloom, organizer and driving force of the team that prepared the first taxonomy:

> After the sale of over one million copies of the *Taxonomy of Educational Objectives—Cognitive Domain* [Bloom et al., 1956] and over a quarter of a century of use of this domain in preservice and in-service teacher training, it is estimated that over 90% of test questions that U.S. public school students are *now* expected to answer deal with little more than information. Our instructional material, our classroom teaching methods, and our testing methods rarely rise above the lowest category of the Taxonomy—knowledge. (1984, p. 13)

The next section describes how you can write and profitably use objectives.

WAYS TO STATE AND USE OBJECTIVES

Many psychologists have offered suggestions for writing and using objectives, but the following discussion is limited to recommendations made by two of the most influential writers on the subject: Robert F. Mager and Norman E. Gronlund.

MAGER'S RECOMMENDATIONS FOR USE OF SPECIFIC OBJECTIVES   With the publication of a provocative and unorthodox little treatise titled *Preparing Instructional Objectives* (1962, 1997), Mager sparked considerable interest in the use of objectives. Mager emphasizes the importance of objectives by pointing out that

> If you don't know where you're going, the best-made maps won't help you get there. . . . Without a way to communicate your instructional objectives to others:
>
> • You wouldn't be able to decide which instructional content and procedures would help you to accomplish your objectives.

Psychomotor taxonomy outlines steps that lead to skilled performance

Most test questions stress knowledge, ignore higher levels of cognitive taxonomy

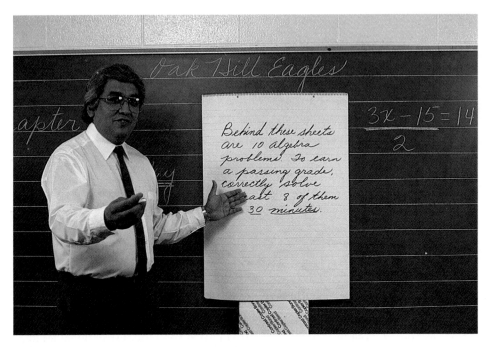

Mager recommends that teachers use objectives that identify the behavioral act that indicates achievement, define conditions under which the behavior is to occur, and state the criterion of acceptable performance.

- You wouldn't be able to create measuring instruments (tests) that tell you whether your students had become competent enough to move on.

- And your students wouldn't be able to decide for themselves when to stop practicing. (1997, p. vi)

Mager then offers these suggestions for writing **specific objectives** of instruction:

1. Describe what you want learners to be doing when demonstrating achievement and indicate how you will know they are doing it.

2. In your description, identify and name the behavioral act that indicates achievement, define the conditions under which the behavior is to occur, and state the criterion of acceptable performance.

3. Write a separate objective for each learning performance.

Mager: state specific objectives that identify act, define conditions, state criteria

Here are some examples of the types of objectives Mager recommends:

Correctly solve at least seven addition problems consisting of three two-digit numbers within a period of three minutes.

Correctly answer at least four of the five questions on the last page of story booklet 16 in the Reading Comprehension series of booklets.

Given pictures of ten trees, correctly identify at least eight as either deciduous or evergreen.

Correctly spell at least 90 percent of the words on the list handed out last week.

Given an electric typewriter or a computer and word processing program, set it up to type a business letter (according to the specifications provided) within two minutes.

Note that the criterion of acceptable performance can be stated as a time limit, a minimum number of correct responses, or a proportion of correct responses.

Mager's proposals were widely endorsed immediately after the publication of *Preparing Instructional Objectives*, but in time it became apparent that the very specific kinds of objectives he recommended were most useful in situations where students were asked to acquire knowledge of factual information or to learn simple skills. Norman E. Gronlund concluded that a different type of objective was more appropriate for more complex and advanced kinds of learning.

GRONLUND'S RECOMMENDATIONS FOR USE OF GENERAL OBJECTIVES

Gronlund (1995) has developed a two-step procedure for writing a more general type of objective. He suggests that teachers follow this procedure:

1. Examine what is to be learned with reference to lists of objectives such as those included in the three taxonomies. Use such lists to formulate **general objectives** of instruction that describe types of behavior students should exhibit in order to demonstrate that they have learned.

Gronlund: state general objectives, list sample of specific learning outcomes

2. Under each general instructional objective, list up to five *specific learning outcomes* that begin with an *action verb* and indicate specific, observable responses. These sets of specific learning outcomes should provide a representative sample of what students should be able to do when they have achieved the general objective.

If you were teaching an educational psychology course and you wanted to write a Gronlund-type objective that reflected an understanding of the four stages of Piaget's theory of cognitive development, it might look like this:

1. The student will understand the characteristics of Piaget's four stages of cognitive development.

   1.1 Describe in his or her own words the type of thinking in which students at each stage can and cannot engage.

   1.2 Predict behaviors of students of different ages.

   1.3 Explain why certain teaching techniques would or would not be successful with students of different ages.

If you wanted to cover the same outcome with a list of Mager-type objectives, it might look like this:

1. Given a list of the names of each of Piaget's four stages of cognitive development, the student, within twenty minutes, will describe in his or her own words two problems that students at each stage should and should not be able to solve.

2. Given a videotape of kindergarten students presented with a conservation-of-volume problem, the student will predict the response of 90 percent of the students.

3. Given a videotape of fifth-grade students presented with a class inclusion problem, the student will predict the response of 90 percent of the students.

4. Given eight descriptions of instructional lessons, two at each of Piaget's four stages, the student will be able to explain in each case why the lesson would or would not succeed.

Gronlund gives several reasons for beginning with general objectives. First, most learning activities are too complex to be described in terms of a specific objective for every learning outcome, as proposed by Mager. Second, the kind of specific objective advocated by Mager may tend to cause instructors and students to concentrate on memorizing facts and mastering simple skills. As indicated earlier, these types of behaviors are at the lowest levels of the taxonomies of objectives. Third, specific objectives can restrict the flexibility of the teacher. Gronlund's objectives allow performance criteria to be kept separate from the objective so a teacher can revise performance standards as needed without having to rewrite the objective. This feature is useful if the same behavior is to be evaluated several times over the course of a unit of instruction, with successively higher levels of performance required. A fourth and final reason is that general objectives help keep you aware that the main target of your instructional efforts is the general outcome (such as comprehension, application, or analysis).

To illustrate the differences between general objectives and specific outcomes, Gronlund has prepared lists of phrases and verbs that can be used in writing each type of objective for each of the levels of all three taxonomies of educational objectives. These lists can be found in Chapter 4 of Gronlund's *How to Write and Use Instructional Objectives* (5th ed., 1995) and in Appendix E of Linn and Gronlund's *Measurement and Assessment in Teaching* (7th ed., 1995).

ALIGNING OBJECTIVES WITH INSTRUCTION AND ASSESSMENT

Deciding in advance what you want your students to achieve by drawing from the various levels of the taxonomies and formulating instructional methods to help them master those objectives will be a largely wasted effort if you fail to recognize that the tests you create must also fit those objectives and methods.

As we discuss in Chapter 13, there are several types of classroom assessment methods, each of which is most useful for measuring only *certain* outcomes. Multiple-choice, short-answer, and true-false tests are useful for measuring mastery of basic factual knowledge. For objectives that emphasize the comprehension, analysis, and synthesis levels of Bloom's Taxonomy, essay questions that call for students to summarize, compare, and contrast would be more useful. For objectives that reflect a constructivist orientation, paper-and-pencil tests are likely to be much less useful than requiring students to solve a complex problem, create a product over an extended period of time, or work productively with a small group of peers on a project. (This type of testing is called performance assessment and is discussed in Chapters 13 and 14.)

Here's a small example of how things can go wrong if you don't align your tests with both your objectives and instructional methods. If you tell students that you want them to organize information into logical structures, integrate ideas into broad themes, and make connections with knowledge learned elsewhere, and then teach them how to think along those lines but load your tests with short-answer and multiple-choice items that require rote memorization, don't be surprised when students simply memorize facts. From their perspective, the content and level of the test items are the real objectives.

One final comment about alignment. In the first paragraph we referred to the tests you *create* rather than the tests you *use*. These two terms imply a subtle but important distinction. The best way to assure alignment between objectives, teaching approach, and assessment is for you to be the creator of the assessment. If you use a test that has been designed by somebody else, such as a standardized test, it is almost a certainty that some of the items will not match your objectives or instructional approach.

EVALUATIONS OF THE EFFECTIVENESS OF OBJECTIVES

Do students learn more when their teachers provide them with clearly written objectives? The answer is yes, but only under certain conditions. Reviews of research on the effectiveness of objectives (for example, Faw & Waller, 1976; Klauer, 1984; Melton, 1978) lead to the following conclusions:

Objectives work best when students are aware of them

1. Objectives seem to work best when students are aware of them, treat them as directions to learn specific sections of material, and feel they will aid learning.
2. Objectives seem to work best when they are clearly written and the learning task is neither too difficult nor too easy.
3. Students of average ability seem to profit more from being given objectives than do students of higher or lower ability.
4. Objectives lead to an improvement in intentional learning (what is stressed as important) but to a decline in incidental learning (not emphasized by the teacher). General objectives of the type recommended by Gronlund seem to lead to more incidental learning than do specific objectives of the type recommended by Mager.

As we mentioned at the beginning of the chapter, once you have decided what it is you want your students to learn, you need to decide which approaches you will use to help them achieve those objectives. Our use of the term *approaches* is deliberate. To repeat what we said at the beginning of the chapter, different approaches to instruction are based on different theories of learning and motivation, and given the complexity of the learning process and the diversity of learners in most classrooms, no one theory can be used for all instructional purposes and for all students. So as you read through the next several sections, try to imagine how you might use each of them over the course of a school year.

The Behavioral Approach to Teaching: Direct Instruction

For behavioral psychologists, learning means acquiring new behaviors, and new behaviors are learned because of the role played by external stimuli. Thus, a behavioral approach to teaching involves arranging and implementing those conditions that make it highly likely that a desired response will occur in the presence of a particular stimulus (such as reading a sentence fluently, accurately using the correct mathematical operations when faced with a long-division problem, and giving the correct English translation to a paragraph written in Spanish). Perhaps the most popular approach to teaching that is based on behavioral theory is direct instruction (although the label *explicit teaching* is sometimes used).

THE NATURE OF DIRECT INSTRUCTION

The underlying philosophy of **direct instruction** is that if the student has not learned, the teacher has not effectively taught. This approach calls for the teacher to keep students consistently engaged in learning basic skills and knowledge through the design of effective lessons, corrective feedback, and opportunities for practice. It is most frequently used in the teaching of basic skills (for example, reading, mathematical computation, writing) and subject matter (for example, science, social studies, foreign language vocabulary) in the primary and elementary grades but is also used to teach remedial classes at the middle school and high school levels. It is felt to be most useful for young learners, slow learners, and all learners when the material is new and difficult to grasp at first. Although there are several variations of direct instruction, the following represents a synthesis of descriptions offered by George Adams and Sigfried Engelmann (1996), Bruce Joyce and Marsha Weil (1996), Barak Rosenshine (1987), and Barak Rosenshine and Carla Meister (1994b).

when to use

The main characteristics of direct instruction include:

1. Focusing almost all classroom activity on learning basic academic knowledge and skills. Affective and social objectives, such as improved self-esteem and learning to get along with others, are either deemphasized or ignored.

2. Having the teacher make all instructional decisions, such as how much material will be covered at one time, whether students work individually or in groups, and whether students work on mathematics during the morning and social studies during the afternoon.

3. Keeping students working productively toward learning new academic knowledge and skills (usually called being on-task) as much as possible.

4. Maintaining a positive classroom climate by emphasizing positive reinforcement and avoiding the use of aversive consequences.

Direct instruction: focus on learning basic skills, teacher makes all decisions, keep students on-task, emphasize positive reinforcement

The goal of direct instruction is to have students master basic skills because students who mislearn information require substantially more time and effort to relearn concepts than would have been the case had they learned them correctly in the first place.

For obvious reasons, direct instruction is a highly structured approach to teaching and is often referred to as *teacher-directed* or *teacher-led instruction*.

THE COMPONENTS OF DIRECT INSTRUCTION

Bruce Joyce and Marsha Weil (1996) identify five general components, or phases, that make up direct instruction: orientation, presentation, structured practice, guided practice, and independent practice. These components are not derived just from theory. They reflect the techniques that effective teachers at all grade levels have been observed to use.

Journal Entry
Using a Direct Instruction Approach

ORIENTATION   During the orientation phase the teacher provides an overview of the lesson, explains why students need to learn the upcoming material, relates the new subject either to material learned during earlier lessons or to their life experience, tells students what they will need to do to learn the material, and tells students what level of performance they will be expected to exhibit.

PRESENTATION   The presentation phase initially involves explaining, illustrating, and demonstrating the new material. As with all forms of instruction based on operant conditioning, the lesson is broken down into small, easy-to-learn steps to ensure mastery of each step in the lesson sequence. Numerous examples of new concepts and skills are provided, and, consistent with social leaning theory, the teacher demonstrates the kind of response students should strive for (such as a particular pronunciation of foreign vocabulary, a reading of a poem or story, the steps

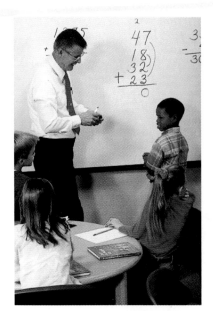

Teachers who subscribe to direct instruction emphasize efficient learning of basic skills through the use of structured lessons, positive reinforcement, and extensive practice.

Direct instruction involves structured, guided, and independent practice

in mathematical operations, or how to analyze a novel for theme, character, setting, etc.). To assist comprehension, and where appropriate, material can be presented pictorially (for example, slides, videotapes, videodisks, on computer) or graphically (as a concept map, or a timeline, or in table form). At the first sign of difficulty, additional explanations are given. The last step of the presentation phase is to evaluate students' understanding. This is typically done through a question-and-answer session in which the questions call for specific answers as well as explanations of how students formulated their answers. Some sort of system is used to ensure that all students receive an equal opportunity to respond to questions. Throughout the lesson efforts are made to stay on-task and avoid nonproductive digressions.

STRUCTURED, GUIDED, AND INDEPENDENT PRACTICE The last three phases of the direct instruction model all focus on practice, although with successively lower levels of assistance. Joyce and Weil (1996) refer to these three phases as *structured practice, guided practice,* and *independent practice.* Since the level of teacher assistance is gradually withdrawn, you may recognize this progression as an attempt to apply the behavioral principle of shaping. You may also recognize it as the constructivist principle of scaffolding.

Structured practice involves the greatest degree of teacher assistance. The teacher leads the entire class through each step in a problem or lesson so as to minimize incorrect responses. Visual displays, such as overhead transparencies, are commonly used during structured practice as a way to both illustrate and help students recall the components of a lesson. As the students respond, the teacher reinforces correct responses and corrects errors. During guided practice students work at their own desks on problems of the type explained and demonstrated by the teacher. The teacher circulates among the students, checking for and correcting any errors. When students can correctly solve at least 85 percent of the problems given to them during guided practice, they are deemed ready for independent practice. Students are encouraged to practice on their own either in class or at home. Although the teacher continues to assess the accuracy of the students' work and provide feedback, it is done on a more delayed basis.

GETTING THE MOST OUT OF PRACTICE

Joyce and Weil (1996) offer the following suggestions to help make practice effective.

1. Shape student learning by systematically moving students from structured practice to guided practice to independent practice.

2. Schedule several relatively short but intense practice sessions as this typically produces more learning than fewer but longer sessions. For primary grade students, several five- to ten-minute sessions scattered over the day are likely to produce better results than the one or two thirty- to forty-minute sessions that middle school or high school students can tolerate.

3. Carefully monitor the accuracy of students' responses during structured practice to reinforce correct responses and correct unacceptable responses. The reason for this suggestion comes straight out of operant conditioning research. As you may recall from Chapter 7, Skinner found that new behaviors are learned most rapidly when correct responses are immediately reinforced and incorrect responses are eliminated. When a learner makes incorrect responses that are not corrected, they become part of the learner's behavioral repertoire and impede the progress of subsequent learning.

4. To ensure the high degree of success that results in mastery of basic skills, students should not engage in independent practice until they can respond correctly to at least 85 percent of the examples presented to them during structured and guided practice.

5. Practice sessions for any lesson should be spread over several months. The practice of some teachers to not review a topic once that part of the curriculum has been covered usually leads to a lower quality of learning. Once again, distributed practice produces better learning than massed practice.

6. Space practice sessions close together during structured practice but further and further apart for guided practice and independent practice.

EFFECTIVENESS OF DIRECT INSTRUCTION

George Adams and Sigfried Engelmann (1996) conducted a review of thirty-seven studies of direct instruction and reported strong effects. On average, DI students scored at the 81st percentile on an end-of-unit exam whereas their conventionally taught peers scored at the 50th percentile. Positive effects for direct instruction have also been found for teaching reading comprehension and writing strategies to students with learning disabilities (Gleason, 1995), for teaching phonemic awareness skills (the ability to identify letter sounds, blends, and sequences of letters in words) to young children (Spector, 1995), for producing high levels of on-task behavior and low levels of disruptive behavior among third graders with behavior disorders (Nelson, 1996), and for increasing standardized achievement test scores among ethnic and racial minority second grade students (Brent & DiObilda, 1993).

| **Direct instruction helps students learn basic skills**

USING TECHNOLOGY TO SUPPORT BEHAVIORAL APPROACHES TO INSTRUCTION

The computer-based approach to instruction that uses behavioral learning principles emphasizes specific performance objectives, breaking learning down into small steps, shaping student success, using immediate feedback and consistent rewards, and predefining assessment techniques. Learning is viewed much like an industrial assembly line: information is transferred efficiently from a computer program to a waiting student. Most of the drill-and-practice CAI tools and integrated learning systems mentioned in Chapter 7 fit within this framework (Van Dusen & Worthen, 1995) as would multimedia technology if used simply to embellish a lecture with new pictures or sounds. Although this approach to the use of technology in instruction may be perceived as rote, boring, and dehumanizing, it can prove valuable if you are interested in accurate and efficient learning of basic facts and skills.

The Cognitive Approach to Teaching: Facilitating Meaningful and Self-Directed Learning

The focus of cognitive learning theories is the mind and how it works. Hence, cognitive psychologists are primarily interested in studying those mental processes that expand our knowledge base and allow us to understand and respond to the world differently. In this section we will lay out two approaches to instruction that are based on different forms of cognitive theory: information processing and constructivism. The information-processing approach to teaching involves implementing those conditions that help students effectively transfer information from the "outside" (a text or lecture, for example) to the "inside" (the mind), while the constructivist approach focuses on providing students opportunities to create their own meaningful view of reality.

THE NATURE AND ELEMENTS OF AN INFORMATION-PROCESSING APPROACH

As we noted in Chapter 8, information-processing theory focuses on how human beings interpret and mentally manipulate the information they encounter. In most instances, we attend to some things (or parts of things) and not others, we mentally change the form and organizational properties of information, we integrate information into existing bodies of knowledge, we retrieve certain aspects of stored information, and we use that information to solve a variety of everyday problems. The research evidence that has been generated over the past thirty-five to forty years in this field supports the following view of learning:

1. Information moves through a series of mental storehouses that vary in the way in which information is stored and for how long.

2. Learning occurs gradually because of limits on how much information we can attend to and think about at any point in time.

3. What we know strongly influences what we learn.

4. We can exert a great deal of control over the cognitive processes that result in learning.

In sum, for information to be meaningfully learned it must be attended to, its critical features must be noticed, and it must be coded in an organized and meaningful way so as to make its retrieval more likely (Corno, 1986; Marx & Winne, 1987; Pressley, Woloshyn, & Associates, 1995).

The approach to teaching that flows from information-processing theory has two main parts. First, design lessons and gear teaching behaviors to capitalize on what is known about the learning process. As you will see, this part of the information-processing approach has much in common with the behavioral approach that we just covered. Both approaches direct you to structure the classroom environment in a certain way (and to use some of the same tactics) to improve the effectiveness and efficiency of learning. Second—and this is what makes the information-processing approach unique—make students aware of how they learn and how they can use those processes to improve their classroom performance. Following are several suggestions for helping students become more effective processors of classroom instruction.

Information-processing approach: design lessons around principles of meaningful learning, teach students how to learn more effectively

Journal Entry
Using an Information-Processing Approach to Instruction

COMMUNICATE CLEAR GOALS   In Chapter 8 we pointed out that motivation for learning is highest when students can relate new information to what they already know and to out-of-school experiences. The ability to make these links is what makes learning in general, and school learning in particular, meaningful. The first question that students ask themselves when they take a new course, encounter a new topic, or are asked to learn a new skill is, "Why do I have to learn this?" Unfortunately, many teachers seem unaware of the need to clearly explain to students the immediate and larger purposes of learning most of a school's curriculum. Seymour Sarason (1993), who has written extensively and persuasively about the problems of education (including teacher education) and the need for reform, notes that "although that kind of question occurs to every child, I have never heard a student ask that question out loud, just as I have never observed a teacher address the issue" (p. 224). But some teachers do recognize the value of communicating clear goals. Margaret Metzger (1996), a veteran high school teacher, notes that teachers have to convince students that what they learn in school is important and relevant to their lives outside of school, both now and in the future.

At the beginning of each lesson, then, tell students what you want them to accomplish, why you think it's important that they learn this knowledge or skill, and how you are going to assess their learning. If you intend to use paper-and-pencil tests, tell them what content areas will be covered, what kinds of questions you will include (in terms of the levels of Bloom's Taxonomy), and how many of each type of question will be on the test. Without this information students will be unable to formulate a rational approach to learning and studying since they will be forced to guess about these features. They may, for example, take your general directive to "learn this material for the test" as a cue to memorize when you expected them to be able to explain ideas in their own words. If you intend to use performance measures, tell students the conditions under which they will have to perform and what criteria you will use to judge their performance.

> **Tell students what you want them to learn, why, and how they will be tested**

USE ATTENTION-GETTING DEVICES   Information-processing theory holds that material not attended to is not processed, and material that is not processed is not stored in memory. Consequently, you should use (but not overuse) a variety of attention-getting devices. The suggestion we just made to explain the purpose of a lesson, what students will be held accountable for learning, and how student learning will be assessed will likely capture the attention of some students. But once you

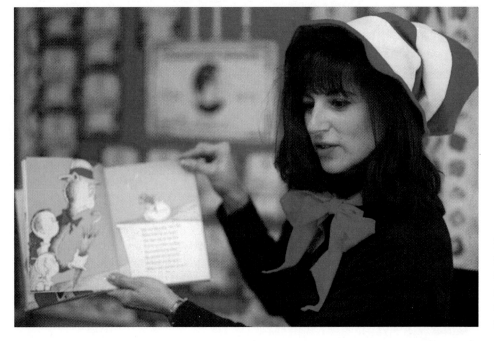

One implication of the information processing approach to instruction is to use attention-getting devices since information not attended to will not be learned.

are into a lesson, you may need to repeatedly gain and maintain students' attention. Toward that end, you can use one or more of the following devices:

- Orally emphasize certain words or phrases by raising or lowering your voice or by using sound effects.
- Use dramatic gestures.
- Write key words and phrases in colored chalk and/or capital letters.
- Underline key words and phrases.
- When discussing the work of important people, whether it be in science, math, social studies, or history, dress up to look like the person and speak as you think the person might have spoken.

EMPHASIZE ORGANIZATION AND MEANINGFULNESS   Research studies have repeatedly found that students learn and recall more information when it is presented in an organized format and a meaningful context. Information is organized when the components that make it up are linked together in some rational way. If you teach high school physics, you can organize material according to major theories or basic principles or key discoveries, depending on your purpose. For history, you can identify main ideas and their supporting details and/or describe events as a chain of causes and effects. Just about any form of organization would be better than having students memorize names, dates, places, and other facts as isolated fragments of information.

A popular method for organizing and spatially representing the relationships among a set of ideas is *concept mapping*. This technique involves specifying the ideas that make up a topic and indicating with lines how they relate to one another. Figure 10.1 is a particularly interesting example of both organized knowledge and a constructivist view of learning. (We will take a further look at this latter angle when we discuss constructivist approaches.)

Present organized and meaningful lessons   As we pointed out in Chapter 8, meaningful learning results in richer and more stable memory representations and occurs more readily when information can be related to familiar ideas and experiences. Several techniques that are known to facilitate meaningful learning are:

- Using some form of overview or introduction that provides a meaningful context for new material
- Using concrete examples and analogies to illustrate otherwise abstract ideas
- Using visually based methods of representing information, such as maps, graphs, three-dimensional models, and illustrations
- Stressing practical applications and relationships to other subjects. (Recall from the discussion in Chapter 4 that this tactic is used to help adolescent girls remain interested in science.)

PRESENT INFORMATION IN LEARNABLE AMOUNTS AND OVER REALISTIC TIME PERIODS   A common mistake that teachers make is to assign students too much information to learn for the amount of time that has been budgeted. The result is that some things are either not learned or are learned superficially. To avoid this outcome, keep in mind two facts you now know about the nature of information processing. One, the number of new ideas students can think about in working memory at any point in time is limited. Two, students need time and repeated exposure to new ideas in order to analyze, understand, and integrate them into existing

Figure 10.1 Two Concept Maps Constructed from Identical Concepts

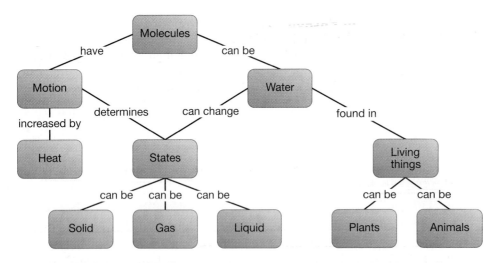

SOURCE: Novak and Gowin, 1984.

knowledge schemes. One instructional recommendation that flows from this analysis is the same as one of the recommendations for direct instruction—break lessons into small, manageable parts and don't introduce new topics until you have evidence that students have learned the current material. A second recommendation is to build into lessons opportunities for students to write about, discuss, and use the ideas they are learning about. By monitoring the accuracy of their responses, you will also have the information you need to judge whether it is time to introduce new ideas. Finally, arrange for relatively short practice sessions spread over several weeks rather

Present new information in small chunks

than one or two long practice sessions since distributed practice leads to better learning than massed practice.

FACILITATE ENCODING OF INFORMATION INTO LONG-TERM MEMORY   High-quality learning rarely occurs when students adopt a relatively passive orientation. As we pointed out in Chapter 8, many students do little more than read assigned material and record ideas in verbatim form. They spend little time thinking about how ideas within topics and between topics relate to one another or to concepts they have already learned. One reason is that many students simply do not know what else to do with information. Another reason is that teachers do little to support the kind of encoding that results in more meaningful forms of learning. Recall the study we mentioned in Chapter 8 that found that primary through middle school teachers provided students with suggestions for processing information less than 10 percent of the time and explanations for the suggestions they did give less than 1 percent of the time. To help your students encode information for more effective storage in and retrieval from long-term memory, incorporate the following techniques into your classroom instruction:

- Present information through such different media as pictures, videotape, audiotape, live models, and manipulation of physical objects.
- Use lots of examples and analogies (to foster elaboration).
- Prompt students to elaborate by asking them to put ideas in their own words, relate new ideas to personal experience, and create their own analogies.

PRACTICE WHAT YOU PREACH   As we pointed out in Chapter 7, a great deal of learning takes place by observing and imitating a model. Since teachers are generally perceived by students as being competent, in a high-status occupation, and having power, their behaviors are likely to be noticed and imitated. This is especially true when the behaviors that teachers model are important to a student's classroom success. If you are convinced that how students process information plays a major role in how well they learn that information, then you should clearly and explicitly demonstrate how to analyze a task, formulate a learning plan, use a variety of learning tactics (such as mnemonics, summarizing, self-questioning, notetaking, concept mapping), monitor the effectiveness of those tactics, and make changes when the results are unsatisfactory.

THE NATURE AND ELEMENTS OF A CONSTRUCTIVIST APPROACH

In Chapters 2 and 9 we noted that the essence of constructivist theory is that people learn best by creating their own understanding of reality. Using such characteristics as existing knowledge, attitudes, values, and experiences as filters, people interpret current experience in a way that seems to make sense to them at the time. As Figure 10.1 demonstrates, by constructing two different concept maps from an identical set of concepts, knowledge can be organized in any number of ways, and the scheme one creates will reflect one's purpose or focal point. Thus, some students understand that the Jane Austen novel *Sense and Sensibility* is as much a satire of the paternalistic class system of 1800s England as it is a love story, while other students see it only as a love story, and a boring one at that. The goal of constructivist-oriented teaching, then, is to provide a set of conditions that will lead students to construct a view of reality that both makes sense to them and addresses the essence of your objectives.

A brief description of four of the more prominent elements that help define a constructivist-oriented classroom follows. Although two of these elements reflect a social constructivist orientation, bear in mind that the goal of both cognitive and social constructivism is the same: to help students become more effective thinkers and problem solvers by helping them construct richer and more meaningful schemes. A social constructivist orientation simply gives greater weight to the role of social interaction in this process.

PROVIDE SCAFFOLDED INSTRUCTION WITHIN THE ZONE OF PROXIMAL DEVELOPMENT   To quickly review what we said in Chapter 2, the zone of proximal development (ZPD) is the difference between what a learner can accomplish without assistance and what can be accomplished with assistance. As an example, consider the case of a youngster who has been given her first bicycle. Since the child has no experience with balancing herself on a two-wheeled bike, her parents know she will fall quite a few times before learning how to balance, steer, and peddle at the same time. To avoid injury and loss of motivation, one parent holds the bike upright and helps the child steer in a straight line while she figures out how to monitor her balance and make the necessary adjustments. This is done initially at very low speeds with the parent firmly holding the frame of the bike. Gradually, the child is allowed to peddle faster and the parent loosens his grip on the bike. Eventually, the parent does little more than run alongside the bike, and then withdraws altogether.

Journal Entry
Using a Constructivist Approach to Instruction

This common example illustrates two related points about teaching from a constructivist (particularly a social constructivist) perspective: instruction should demand more than what a student is capable of doing independently and, because of these demands, instruction should be scaffolded. That is, teachers should provide just enough support, through such devices as explanations, modeling, prompting, offering clarifications, and verifying the accuracy of responses, that the learner can successfully complete the task. As students indicate that they have begun to internalize the basic ideas and procedures of the lesson, the scaffolding is gradually withdrawn (Roehler & Cantlon, 1997).

PROVIDE OPPORTUNITIES FOR LEARNING BY DISCOVERY   By its very nature, constructivism implies the need to let students discover things for themselves. But what things? According to Jerome Bruner, whose pioneering work we mentioned at the beginning of Chapter 9, the process of discovery should be reserved for those outcomes that allow one to be an autonomous, self-directed learner. These include understanding how ideas connect with one another, knowing how to analyze and frame problems, asking appropriate questions, recognizing when what we already know is relevant to what we are trying to learn, and evaluating the effectiveness of our strategies. The case we cited in Chapter 9 of the first-grade teacher who wanted her students to understand the importance of using a standardized measuring instrument is a good example of how these outcomes can be learned by guided discovery.

Constructivist approach: students discover how to be autonomous, self-directed learners

FOSTER MULTIPLE VIEWPOINTS   Given the basic constructivist premise that all meaningful learning is constructed and that everyone uses a slightly different set of filters with which to build their view of reality, what we refer to as knowledge is actually a consensus of slightly different points of view. Thus, another element of a constructivist approach to teaching is to help students understand that different

Meaningful learning aided by exposure to multiple points of view

views of the same phenomena exist and that they can often be reconciled to produce a broader understanding. In Chapter 9 we described how classroom discussions can be used for this purpose. Computer-based technology, such as e-mail, as well as regular mail, can be used to increase both the number and the diversity of individuals with whom students can interact. In one elementary classroom, students from a small town in Indiana exchanged stories, letters, and photographs with a similar classroom of students from Northern Ireland. This exchange awakened students to differences between them that ranged from the trivial (dates are written differently in Europe) to the significant (differences in car ownership by families and the constant presence of army patrols carrying loaded weapons) (Duffy & Cunningham, 1996).

The technique of cooperative learning is another way to expose students to peers who may have different views about the "right" way to do something or the "truth" of some matter and help them forge a broader understanding that is acceptable to all members of the group. Consider, for example, a group of college students who, as part of a science methods course, were asked to figure out how to generate electricity for a home using windmills but not batteries. Some members of the group were stumped because their conception of a battery was limited to things like car batteries and batteries for toys and electronic devices. But other members of the group maintained that a battery could be defined as any device that stored energy, such as a spring or a tank of hot water, thereby helping the rest of the group to see a different and broader truth (Brooks & Brooks, 1993). In the last major section of this chapter, we describe cooperative learning in considerable detail.

EMPHASIZE RELEVANT PROBLEMS AND TASKS   Can you recall completing a class assignment or reading a chapter out of a textbook that had no apparent relevance to anything that concerned you? Not very interesting or exciting, was it? Unfortunately, too many students perceive too much of schooling in that light. One constructivist remedy is to create interest and relevance by posing problems or assigning tasks that are both challenging and realistic. A basic purpose for emphasizing problems and tasks that are relevant to the lives of students is to overcome the problem of inert knowledge mentioned in Chapter 9. Constructivists believe that the best way to prepare students to function effectively in real-life contexts is to embed tasks in contexts that come as close as possible to those of real life (Duffy & Cunningham, 1996).

Problems can be challenging either because the correct answer is not immediately apparent or because there is no correct answer. The ill-structured problems and issues that we described in Chapter 9 are, by their nature, challenging and realistic and do not have solutions that everyone perceives as being appropriate and useful. But if you assign students an ill-structured task to investigate, pose it in such a way that they will see its relevance. For example, instead of asking high school students to debate the general pros and cons of laws that restrict personal freedoms, have them interview their community's mayor, chief of police, business owners, and peers about the pros and cons of laws that specify curfews for individuals under a certain age and that prohibit such activities as loitering and the purchase of alcohol and tobacco. Since many adolescents consider themselves mature enough to regulate their own behavior, analyzing and debating laws that are intended to restrict certain adolescent behaviors is likely to produce a fair amount of disequilibrium.

The technology section that follows presents some additional ideas for embedding learning in realistic settings.

USING TECHNOLOGY TO SUPPORT COGNITIVE APPROACHES TO INSTRUCTION

As educators begin to understand and address cognitive learning theories, the focus of computer technology is shifting from remediating learner skill deficiencies and rehearsing basic skills to finding ways to help the learner build, extend, and amplify new knowledge (Pea, 1985).

HELPING STUDENTS PROCESS INFORMATION   In the 1980s, new types of CAI programs were developed based on cognitive theories of how we acquire complex cognitive skills (Cognition and Technology Group at Vanderbilt, 1996). At that time, there was a focus on an information-processing approach that took into account student memory constraints, learning strategies, metacognitive skill, and the need to represent ideas hierarchically. An information-processing approach to instruction, therefore, uses technology to minimize the cognitive demands of a task; help learners form schemas, or patterns, of information; extend or augment thinking in new directions; and supply information overviews and memory cues (Kozma, 1987). The programs for outlining and notetaking mentioned in Chapter 8 are consistent with this approach as are electronic encyclopedias (for example, Grolier's Multimedia Encyclopedia) and hypermedia databases that contain conceptual resources like timelines, information maps, and overviews.

> Technology supports a cognitive approach to instruction by helping students code, store, and retrieve information

INTELLIGENT TUTORING SYSTEMS   The cognitive approach has recently been taken a step further by **intelligent tutoring systems**, computer tools that provide individualized guidance by comparing the problem-solving history of the user with models of expert performance. Ken Koedinger and John Anderson (1993), for instance, have developed the Geometry Tutor to help students understand the process of solving geometry problems. This program can help students visually represent the problem, generate goal statements, and search through the problem for the "given" information. Instead of simply providing feedback about whether an answer or step is "right" or "wrong," these "intelligent" tools build up elaborate cognitive models of the user that map out his or her problem-solving decisions and compare the decisions to those of experts (Cognition and Technology Group at Vanderbilt, 1996). Such information is used to determine the learner's level of conceptual development and make decisions about the timing, content, and order of hints that the system provides to help the student solve the problem.

DISCOVERY AND EXPLORATORY ENVIRONMENTS   Computers are not just tools to transmit or represent information for the learner; they also provide environments that allow for discoveries and insights. In such an **exploratory environment**, students might explore exciting information resources on the Web (see the Case in Print on page 350 about on-line expeditions), enter simulations or microworlds like LOGO, browse and rotate objects in a hypermedia or Web database, and use imaging technologies to explore inaccessible places (for example, underwater canyons or planet surfaces) (Woolsey & Bellamy, 1997). For instance, the Geometric Supposer, mentioned in Chapter 2, is an exploratory tool with which students can construct, manipulate, and measure different geometric figures and relationships. Such simulated environments, or microworlds, allow students the chance to explore relationships among variables or concepts and build personal models of how things work.

Microcomputer-based laboratory (MBL) equipment, also mentioned in Chapter 2, allows students to make predictions, test hypotheses, and interpret the results. MBLs and other devices that create exploratory environments enable students to try out many potential solution paths and problem-solving strategies without fear of being wrong, while learning how to solve problems. There are now, for example, exploratory modeling programs for learning key principles of economics, solving difficult physics problems, exploring the behavior of ant colonies, and analyzing molecular models of proteins and DNA (Barowy & Laserna, 1997; Doerr, 1996.)

GUIDED LEARNING   Although students can use modeling programs and simulations to plan experiments, take measurements, analyze data, and graph findings, there is still a need for teacher scaffolding and guidance in support of the learning process (de Jong & van Joolingen, 1998). In fact, most educational experts emphasize teacher-guided approaches when using technology (Toomey & Ketterer, 1995). In these **guided learning** environments, teachers might help students set goals, ask questions, encourage discussions, and provide models of problem-solving processes. In technology environments for social studies, for instance, Lee Ehman and his colleagues found that the teachers who were most successful at fostering problem solving provided a sense of structure, or metacognitive guidance, for their students (Ehman, Glenn, Johnson, & White, 1992). Such teachers provided a clear road map of the unit at the beginning, clear expectations and sequencing of activities, continued reinforcement and guidance, teacher modeling, opportunities for students to practice problem-solving steps, reflection on learning, and regular checking and sharing of student progress. (Note how this approach combines elements of the behavioral and information-processing approaches.)

One guided learning environment, the Higher Order Thinking Skills program (HOTS), focuses on higher-order thinking skills among at-risk youth (Pogrow, 1990). HOTS was designed around active learning, Socratic questioning, and reflection activities in using computers. Instead of the rote computer-based drills that these students would normally receive, they are prompted to reflect on their decision-making process while using computer tools. Teachers do not give away the answers but, instead, draw out key concepts by questioning students or telling them to go back and read the information on the computer screen. The developer of HOTS, Stanley Pogrow, calls this "controlled floundering," or leading students into frustration so that they have to reflect on the information on the screen to solve a problem. In effect, the learning dialogues and conversations between the teacher and student are the keys to learning here, not student use of the computer, since small-group discussion allows students to compare strategies and reflect on those that work.

PROBLEM- AND PROJECT-BASED LEARNING   Another way to implement constructivist trends in education is to use technology for problem-based learning (PBL), an instructional method that requires learners to develop solutions to real-life problems (Cognition and Technology Group at Vanderbilt, 1996). When using PBL with technology, students can plan and organize their own research while working collaboratively with others. In contrast to case-based learning, which is often used to test student knowledge after presenting information, PBL is used to help students

Making Learning a (Virtual) Adventure

Computers are not just tools to transmit or represent information for the learner; they also provide environments that allow for discoveries and insights. In such an exploratory environment, students might explore exciting information resources on the Web . . . (p. 348)

TEACHERS SPIN A WORLD WIDE WEB OF VIRTUAL VOYAGES

CHRISTINA PINO-MARINA
USA Today 9/29/98

For the 52.7 million students who started school this fall, an adventurous field trip could be just a mouse-click away.

Kids connected to the Internet can watch a team of AfricaQuest researchers climb Mount Kilimanjaro.

They can follow five explorers of GlobaLearn.com as they document a 4,000-mile drive across the USA. Students can research rain forests, oceans and wildlife while interacting with scientists taking part in expeditions run by The Jason Project, Scholastic and Sites*ALIVE*!

Such on-line odysseys took shape in the early '90s and are playing an increasing role in public, private and home-school curricula across the nation.

Fourth-grade teacher Cynthia Thomas says these virtual field trips have changed her academic approach after 22 years in her profession.

"It just made me fall in love with teaching again," says Thomas, of Oak Hill Elementary in Austin, Texas. The school of 820 students has one Internet connection. Students there will focus on AfricaQuest this year. "It is so exciting for me to take these kids to different places," she says.

There are a host of educational Web sites, but teachers say that K–12 students get excited by the interactive nature of on-line expeditions.

"A textbook is two-dimensional," says Linda Hiller, a technology specialist at Long Branch Elementary School in Arlington, Va. "When you are following somebody on the Internet, you can go where they go and discover with them. It makes a powerful impact on the students." The 435 K–5 students at Hiller's school follow GlobaLearn.com.

Educational projects like those run by GlobaLearn, AfricaQuest, The Jason Project, Scholastic and Sites*ALIVE*! will offer several social and scientific courses of study throughout the school year.

The subject matter varies on each Web site, but the projects are linked in their mission to engage and educate students through technology.

"We're providing teachers with a multimedia toolbox, not only to excite students but to help teachers become more involved in the classroom," says Tim Armour, executive director of The Jason Project, which focuses on the study of rain forests in 1998.

Kids can learn about remote places and communicate with explorers, researchers and scientists during on-line chats or satellite broadcasts. The credentials these experts bring to the on-line odysseys are part of the appeal for students.

Oceanographer Robert Ballard's location of the sunken Titanic in 1985 sparked the interest of young students before the advent of the World Wide Web and creation of The Jason Project.

AfricaQuest team leader Dan Buettner is famous for having set world records while biking across three continents. Rich Wilson, founder of Sites*ALIVE*! producer Ocean Challenge, captivated students when he broke a 140-year-old sailing record in 1993, rounding Cape Horn in 69 days and 20 hours in a great clipper ship.

But qualifications of on-line experts aside, some critics still question the educational value of the Internet and President Clinton's goal of having the nation's classrooms wired to the information superhighway by 2000.

David Gelernter, a computer science professor at Yale University, says the Internet is a distraction that encourages children to develop short attention spans.

"We have schools that are already failing miserably," says Gelernter. "It is more important for children to learn the basics—to read, to understand math, to use the library."

Gelernter says that, while the Internet has encouraged a resurgence of written communication, teachers should steer clear of the "escape hatch into cyberspace" that will never replace the value of well-written textbooks.

A recent study by Market Data Retrieval, an independent research firm, supports Gelernter's belief that the Internet does not necessarily help students. A random survey of 6,000 teachers, librarians and computer coordinators found that

86.6% believe that Internet use by kids in grades 3–12 does not improve classroom performance.

In 1998, the Federal Communications Commission will allocate $1.275 billion for school Internet connections, a 43% cut from the proposed $2.25 billion.

Nevertheless, many teachers will continue to use educational expeditions to motivate students. "Whether we like it or not, this is a technological world," Hiller says.

At M.V. Leckie Elementary School in Washington, D.C., teacher Hilda Taylor helps her students make connections to the world of technology.

Last year's fifth grade class was introduced to the study of sea plankton through The Jason Project. Afterward, Taylor took her students on a field trip to Echo Hill, Md., where they did science projects on marsh life.

"Before seeing The Jason Project, I didn't even know there was such a thing as plankton," says 11-year-old Jamal Hansberry, who observed the tiny animals and plants in a test tube during the field trip. Jamal says he was inspired as he watched a live broadcast—which he called "better than TV."

Schoolmate Joshua Franklin, 13, agrees. "You get to ask scientists a lot of questions," he says. And unlike TV, "No one will tell you to turn if off."

Vicarious Adventures

Online Expeditions for kindergarten through 12th-grade students:

- www.classroom.com
  Oct.–Nov. 1998. An eight-person team of scientists and researchers bicycle 1,500 miles through Africa's Great Rift Valley, as part of AfricaQuest. Online students help decide the route. **Cost:** $95 per classroom.

- www.scholastic.com
  Nov.–Dec. 1998. Expedition to Costa Rica will focus on the study of endangered leatherback sea turtles. **Cost:** $2,500 per school per year. (Project not yet in operation).

- www.globalearn.com
  Sept.–Dec. 1998. Five explorers travel 4,000 miles across the United States, covering the cities, people, and historical events that shape the nation. **Cost:** Free, $95 for optional class manuals.

- www.jasonproject.org
  Sept. 98–March 1999. Jason X, a team of scientists and students, do a comparative study of U.S. and Peruvian rain forests. Classrooms interact with scientists on the Internet and via satellite in specific sites. **Cost:** $400 for five teachers and 150 students per year.

- www.sitesalive.com
  Sept. 1998–June 1999. Simultaneous expeditions cover rain forests, wetlands and the ocean in Australia, Mexico and Turks and Caicos Islands. Includes an interactive field trip of 35 students aboard the ship Concordia. **Cost:** $499 per school per year.

SOURCE: © Copyright 1998 *USA Today*. Reprinted with permission.

Questions and Activities

1. David Gelernter, the computer science professor from Yale mentioned in the article, was highly critical of the Internet. He called it "a distraction that encourages children to develop short attention spans." Why do you think he holds this belief? Do you think his conclusion is valid?

2. Assume that Professor Gelernter's assertion is correct. Is this a fault of the technology or the way in which it is used? Why do you think so? (Before answering, you might want to read the following section on guided learning.)

3. The article notes that almost 87 percent of six thousand teachers, librarians, and computer coordinators do not believe that Internet use leads to improved classroom performance. Criticisms like these are often based on observations of a few cases and anecdotal evidence offered by others (whose weaknesses we discussed in Chapter 1). Before accepting such conclusions at face value, you should search several research literature databases (like ERIC and PsycINFO) to see what researchers have found about the effects of technology on student learning.

learn the material by developing their own positions on the material rather than hearing about someone else's position. Although PBL has its roots in medical and business school settings, the emergence of technologies for student exploration and knowledge construction has made this approach feasible with K–12 populations.

Technology can be used to support a learner-centered, problem-based approach to learning in which students create knowledge by designing and carrying out experiments and projects.

John Savery and Thomas Duffy (1996) point to eight constructivist principles that can guide those interested in using PBL, including anchoring learning in larger tasks or problems, supporting the learner in developing ownership of the overall problem or task, designing authentic tasks at students' developmental level, providing sufficient task complexity, allowing student ownership of the process used to develop a solution, encouraging teacher questioning and other challenges, testing ideas in a learning community, and providing opportunities for reflection. Students can be given a problem (for example, What caused the flooding in the Midwest in 1993 and what should be done to prevent floods in the future?), or they can generate questions as a class or small group. In either case, the problem must be perceived as real and not simplified into a prespecified set of readings or objectives.

In addition to PBL, science educators are advocating the use of technology within project-based learning in schools since it attempts to link students' learning to real-life situations while fostering deeper processing of information. Project-based learning provides structure by giving students a project or a problem, along with project goals and deadlines. According to Ronald Marx, Phyllis Blumenfeld, Joseph Krajcik, and Elliot Soloway (1997), the key components of project-based science include:

- driving questions (for example, instead of asking what the atmosphere of Mars is like, one should ask, "What kinds of environments could be built on Mars for humans to survive?")
- feasible real-world investigations (for example, "Is this lake dying?")
- tangible products (multimedia documents, posters, group presentations, etc.)
- group collaboration (for example, sharing and negotiating ideas, drawing on expertise of others, and extending the thinking of group members)
- the use of technology tools (to visualize dynamic relationships like cloud cover at night, collect data on a stream or lake, publish student work on the Web, etc.)

However, Marx et al. (1997) also admit that there are concerns and problems with these projects, such as the time required for deep exploration of ideas, meeting existing curriculum standards, balancing classroom management concerns with student exploration, designing proper assessments, and a lack of teacher training in how to scaffold instruction and effectively use technology tools.

SITUATED LEARNING   As you may recall from Chapter 9, situated learning, or situated cognition, is the concept that knowledge is closely linked to the environment in which it is acquired. The more true to life the task, therefore, the more meaningful the learning. Technology can play a key role in providing access to a wide variety of real-world learning situations (Derry & Lesgold, 1996). For instance, computer-based instructional technology can apprentice students into real work settings by providing access to authentic data and the tools to manipulate that data. According to Sasha Barab, Ken Hay, and Thomas Duffy (1998), tools like the videos in the Jasper Woodbury project mentioned in the last chapter as well as the simulations discussed briefly in Chapter 2 and again in this chapter illustrate how technology can influence instructional practices using situated cognition. Simulations like the Chelsea Bank simulation project (Hawley & Duffy, 1997) situate students in real-life events by placing them in certain defined roles (for example, bank teller, bank manager) and giving them problems to solve with various pieces of information (for example, bank manuals, account information, and materials submitted by the customer). With rich multimedia stories or episodes to draw upon, student recall is enhanced and the chance that students will simply acquire inert knowledge is lessened.

The Humanistic Approach to Teaching: Student-Centered Instruction

The **humanistic approach** pays particular attention to the role of noncognitive variables in learning, specifically, students' needs, emotions, values, and self-perceptions. It assumes that students will be highly motivated to learn when the learning material is personally meaningful, when they understand the reasons for their own behavior, and when they believe that the classroom environment supports their efforts to learn, even when they struggle. Consequently, a humanistic approach to teaching strives to help students better understand themselves and to create a supportive classroom atmosphere that activates the inherent desire all human beings have to learn and fulfill their potential (Groeben, 1994; Maslow, 1987; Rogers, 1983).

The relevance of a humanistic approach to teaching may not be immediately apparent to everyone, but it is easy to support. First, we've known for some time that learning is as much influenced by how students feel about themselves as by the cognitive skills they possess. When students conclude that the demands of a task are beyond their current level of knowledge and skill (what we referred to in Chapter 7 as a low sense of self-efficacy), they are likely to experience such debilitating emotions as anxiety and fear. Once these negative self-perceptions and emotions are created, the student has to divert time and energy from the task at hand to figuring out how to deal with them. And the solutions that students formulate are not always appropriate. Some may, for instance, decide to reduce their efforts and settle for whatever passing grade they can get. Others may give up entirely by cutting class, not completing homework assignments, and not studying for tests. A considerable amount of research from the health field has shown that people are more likely to use positive methods of coping with the stress of illness and disease when they perceive their environment to be *socially supportive*. The small amount of comparable research that exists on classroom learning suggests a similar outcome (Boekarts, 1993).

Second, this approach has the implicit support of teachers and parents. High on their list of desired educational outcomes is for students to develop positive feelings about themselves and about learning and to perceive school as a place where they will be supported in their efforts to develop new knowledge and skills.

PIONEERS OF THE HUMANISTIC APPROACH

The humanistic approach to teaching was proposed during the 1960s principally by Abraham Maslow, Carl Rogers, and Arthur Combs.

MASLOW: LET CHILDREN GROW   Abraham Maslow's approach to the study of human behavior was unique for its time. While most of his colleagues studied the psychological processes of people who were having problems dealing with the demands and stresses of everyday life (as Sigmund Freud had done), Maslow decided that more could be learned by studying the behavior of especially well-adjusted people, whom he referred to as *self-actualizers*. Self-actualizers, be they children, adolescents, or adults, have an inherent need for experiences that will help them fulfill their potential.

In Chapter 15 of *Toward a Psychology of Being* (2d ed., 1968), Maslow describes forty-three basic propositions that summarize his views. Some of the most significant of these propositions are as follows: Each individual is born with an essential inner nature. This inner nature is shaped by experiences and by unconscious thoughts and feelings, but it is not *dominated* by such forces. Individuals control much of their own behavior. Children should be allowed to make many choices about their own development. Parents and teachers play a significant role in preparing children to make wise choices by satisfying their physiological, safety, love, belonging, and esteem needs, but they should do this by helping and letting children grow, not by attempting to shape or control the way they grow. (A more detailed outline of Maslow's view is presented in Chapter 11.)

> **Maslow: help students develop their potential by satisfying their needs**

ROGERS: LEARNER-CENTERED EDUCATION   Carl Rogers was a psychotherapist who pioneered a new approach to helping people cope more effectively with their problems. He called it *client-centered* (or *nondirective*) therapy, to stress the fact that the client, rather than the therapist, should be the central figure and that the therapist was not to tell the patient what was wrong and what should be done about it.

As he practiced this person-centered approach, Rogers came to the conclusion that he was most successful when he did not attempt to put up a false front of any kind; established a warm, positive, acceptant attitude toward his clients; and was able to sense their thoughts and feelings. Rogers concluded that these conditions set the stage for successful experiences with therapy because clients became more self-accepting and aware of themselves. Once individuals acquired these qualities, they were inclined and equipped to solve personal problems without seeking the aid of a therapist (1967, pp. 53–54).

In addition to functioning as a therapist, Rogers served as a professor. Upon analyzing his experiences as an instructor, he concluded that the person-centered approach to therapy could be applied just as successfully to teaching. He thus proposed the idea of **learner-centered education**—that teachers should try to establish the same conditions as do person-centered therapists. Rogers argues (1980, pp. 273–278) that the results of learner-centered teaching are similar to those of person-centered therapy: students become capable of educating themselves without the aid of direct instruction from teachers.

Rogers: establish conditions that allow self-directed learning

COMBS: THE TEACHER AS FACILITATOR   Arthur Combs assumed that "all behavior of a person is the direct result of his field of perceptions at the moment of his behaving" (1965, p. 12). From this assumption it follows that the way a person perceives herself or himself is of paramount importance and that a basic purpose of teaching is to help each student develop a positive self-concept. He observed, "The task of the teacher is not one of prescribing, making, molding, forcing, coercing, coaxing, or cajoling; it is one of ministering to a process already in being. The role required of the teacher is that of facilitator, encourager, helper, assister, colleague, and friend of his students" (1965, p. 16). Combs elaborated on these points by listing six characteristics of good teachers: (1) they are well informed about their subject; (2) they are sensitive to the feelings of students and colleagues; (3) they believe that students can learn; (4) they have a positive self-concept; (5) they believe in helping all students do their best; and (6) they use many different methods of instruction (1965, pp. 20–23).

Taken together, the observations of Maslow, Rogers, and Combs lead to a conception of education in which teachers trust pupils enough to permit them to make many choices about their own learning. At the same time, teachers should be sensitive to the social and emotional needs of students, empathize with them, and respond positively to them. Finally, teachers should be sincere, willing to show that they, too, have needs, and experience positive feelings about themselves and what they are doing.

TEACHING FROM A HUMANISTIC ORIENTATION

Teachers who adopt a humanistic orientation seek to create a classroom atmosphere in which students believe that the teacher's primary goal is to understand the student's needs, values, motives, and self-perceptions, and to help the student learn. This atmosphere is established primarily by the teacher expressing genuine interest in and acceptance of the student. The teacher avoids giving the impression that he or she would like the student better if only the student dressed more appropriately, had a more positive attitude toward learning, associated with a different group of peers, and so on. In this kind of setting, students will be more inclined to openly discuss their feelings about and problems with learning and related issues. The teacher is then in a position to help students figure out better approaches to their schoolwork and relationships with others. The teacher does not tell students what to do but guides them to the correct action. Because the students' perceptions and decisions are the central focus, this approach is often referred to as either *student-directed* or *nondirective* (Joyce & Weil, 1996).

Humanistic approach addresses needs, values, motives, self-perceptions

To illustrate this approach, consider the case of a student who is unhappy about a poor grade on a test. The instinctive reaction of most teachers would be to explain how to study and prepare for the next test. The humanistically oriented teacher instead asks the student to describe his interest in the subject matter, how capable a learner the student feels himself to be, how well the student understands the subject, under what conditions the student studies, whether the student feels the teacher's instruction to be clear and well organized, and so on. To help students understand their feelings and the role they play in learning, the teacher may disclose some of her own feelings. For example, the teacher may tell this hypothetical student, "When I've had a bad day and feel as if I've let my students down, I sometimes question my ability as a teacher. Is that how you feel?" Once these self-perceptions have been raised and clarified, the teacher encourages the student to suggest a solution to the problem (Joyce & Weil, 1996).

THE HUMANISTIC MODEL

According to Bruce Joyce and Marsha Weil (1996), the nondirective model is made up of the following components:

1. *Defining the helping situation.* The topic that the student wants to discuss is identified, and the student is told that he or she is free to express any and all feelings that relate to the topic.

2. *Exploring the problem.* If the teacher has been able to establish the atmosphere of trust just described, it is assumed that students will be willing to describe the problem and any associated feelings. The teacher does not attempt to diagnose the student's problem but attempts to understand the situation as the student experiences it and then reflects this understanding back to the student. The teacher functions more as a resource, facilitator, and guide than as a director.

3. *Developing insight.* The student uses the information gained from exploring the problem to understand how various perceptions, emotions, beliefs, and behaviors cause various effects (such as a belief that one lacks ability leading to incomplete homework assignments and lack of interest in the subject, or a need for affiliation leading to more socializing than studying).

4. *Planning and decision making.* The teacher helps the student identify alternative behaviors and how they will be carried out.

5. *Integration.* The student reports on actions taken, their effects, and plans for future actions.

> **Journal Entry**
> Using a Humanistic Approach to Instruction

EFFECTIVENESS OF HUMANISTIC EDUCATION

After reviewing several dozen studies, John Swisher, Judith Vickery, and Peggy Nadenichek (1983) concluded that humanistic instructional techniques were much more likely to produce positive outcomes than negative outcomes. Most of these studies reported gains for classroom management (reductions in problem behaviors and tardiness, increases in attendance), achievement, attitudes toward school, self-esteem, creativity, communication skills, and social awareness (an important outcome given the current emphasis on multicultural programs).

D. B. Matthews (1991) found that eighth graders who learned in a relaxed atmosphere, where student suggestions about various school functions were sought, showed higher levels of intrinsic motivation for reading, social studies, and science than eighth graders who learned in a more structured and teacher-directed environment.

According to research reviewed by Alfie Kohn (1993b), children who were allowed to participate in decisions about what will be done, when, and for how long scored higher on standardized tests than children who were simply told what to do. In another study, when second graders were allowed to choose which tasks they would work on, they tended to complete more tasks in less time than did students who were not allowed to choose. Finally, inner-city minority children whose sense of self-determination was strengthened had higher attendance rates and scores on a test of basic skills than students from conventional classrooms.

USING TECHNOLOGY TO SUPPORT HUMANISTIC APPROACHES TO INSTRUCTION

Using technology to support a humanistic approach to teaching may seem like a contradiction in terms. But, as we noted earlier and will do so again in this section, educational technology is becoming more learner-centered in both its design and its use.

LEARNER-CENTERED EDUCATION   As we move from the relatively passive and predetermined approach of computer-assisted instruction of the 1960s and 1970s, learning with technology is now best viewed as a learner-centered process involving peers, teachers, experts, and other learning resources (Bonk, Hay, & Fischler, 1996; Sandholtz, Ringstaff, & Dwyer, 1997).

The learner-centered psychological principles from the American Psychological Association (American Psychological Association, 1997), mentioned in Chapter 1, focus on helping learners meaningfully construct and represent their knowledge, creating challenging and novel learning environments that help students link new information to old, achieving complex learning goals, and building thinking and reasoning strategies. They also emphasize fostering curiosity and intrinsic motivation, nurturing social interaction and interpersonal relationships, recognizing individual differences in learning, and setting appropriately high and challenging learning standards and goals. Technology can help achieve all of these goals.

Learner-centered technology tools can link concepts to everyday experiences, guide students in the problem-solving process, encourage learners to think more deeply, facilitate unique knowledge construction, and provide opportunities for social interaction and dialogue. For example, graphing calculators, handheld computers, and microcomputer laboratory equipment allow students to depict data collected from a polluted stream or pond. Prompts embedded in a word processing program encourage reflection on one's report about that environmental problem. Finally, computer conferencing on the Web allows these same students to engage in discussions about their findings with same age peers far beyond their own classroom. A key strength of emerging technology environments is that they place the responsibility for learning in the hands of the learner, thereby enabling him or her to ask personally relevant questions, pursue needed knowledge, and generally be more self-directed.

The Social Approach to Teaching: Teaching Students How to Learn from Each Other

Classroom tasks can be structured so that students are forced to compete with one another, work individually, or cooperate with one another to obtain the rewards that teachers make available for successfully completing these tasks. Traditionally, competitive arrangements have been assumed to be superior to the other two in increasing motivation and learning. But reviews of the research literature by David Johnson and Roger Johnson (Johnson & Johnson, 1995; Johnson, Johnson, & Smith,

1995) found cooperative arrangements to be far superior in producing these benefits. In this section we will describe cooperative, competitive, and individual learning arrangements; identify the elements that make up the major approaches to cooperative learning; and examine the effect of cooperative learning on motivation, achievement, and interpersonal relationships. We would also like to point out that cooperative learning methods are fully consistent with social constructivism since they encourage inquiry, perspective sharing, and conflict resolution.

TYPES OF CLASSROOM REWARD STRUCTURES

COMPETITIVE STRUCTURES   Competitive goal structures are typically norm referenced. The traditional practice of grading on the curve predetermines the percentage of A, B, C, D, and F grades regardless of the actual distribution of test scores. Because only a small percentage of students in any group can achieve the highest rewards and because this accomplishment must come at some other students' expense, competitive goal structures are characterized by negative interdependence. Students try to outdo one another, view classmates' failures as an advantage, and come to believe that the winners deserve their rewards because they are inherently better (Johnson, Johnson, & Holubec, 1994; Johnson, Johnson, & Smith, 1995).

Some researchers have argued that competitive reward structures lead students to focus on ability as the primary basis for motivation. This orientation is reflected in the question "Am I smart enough to accomplish this task?" When ability is the basis for motivation, competing successfully in the classroom may be seen as relevant to self-esteem (since nobody loves a loser), difficult to accomplish (since only a few can succeed), and uncertain (success depends on how everyone else does). These perceptions may cause some students to avoid challenging subjects or tasks, to give up in the face of difficulty, to reward themselves only if they win a competition, and to believe that their own successes are due to ability, whereas the successes of others are due to luck (Ames & Ames, 1984; Dweck, 1986).

| Competitive reward structures may decrease motivation to learn

INDIVIDUALISTIC STRUCTURES   Individualistic goal structures are characterized by students working alone and earning rewards solely on the quality of their own efforts. The success or failure of other students is irrelevant. All that matters is whether the student meets the standards for a particular task (Johnson, Johnson, & Holubec, 1994; Johnson, Johnson, & Smith, 1995). For example, thirty students working by themselves at computer terminals are functioning in an individual reward structure. According to Carole Ames and Russell Ames (1984), individual structures lead students to focus on task effort as the primary basis for motivation (as in "I can do this if I try"). Whether a student perceives a task as difficult depends on how successful she has been with that type of task in the past.

COOPERATIVE STRUCTURES   Cooperative goal structures are characterized by students working together to accomplish shared goals. What is beneficial for the other students in the group is beneficial for the individual and vice versa. Because students in cooperative groups can obtain a desired reward (such as a high grade or a feeling of satisfaction for a job well done) only if the other students in the group also obtain the same reward, cooperative goal structures are characterized by positive interdependence. Also, all groups may receive the same rewards, provided they meet the teacher's criteria for mastery. For example, a teacher might present a lesson on map reading, then give each group its own map and a question-answering exercise. Students then work with each other to ensure that all know how to inter-

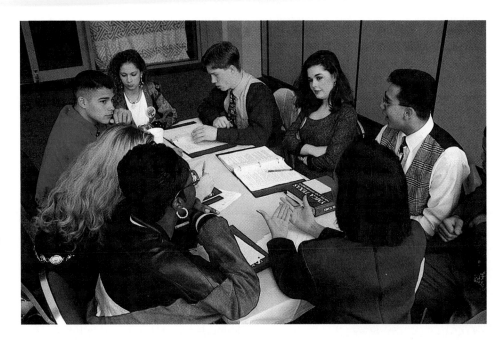

Cooperative reward structures are more likely to motivate almost all students in a class to study and develop positive attitudes toward learning than are competitive or individualistic arrangements.

pret maps. Each student then takes a quiz on map reading. All teams whose average quiz scores meet a preset standard receive special recognition (Johnson, Johnson, & Holubec, 1994; Johnson, Johnson, & Smith, 1995; Slavin, 1995).

Cooperative structures lead students to focus on effort and cooperation as the primary basis of motivation. This orientation is reflected in the statement "We can do this if we try hard and work together." In a cooperative atmosphere, students are motivated out of a sense of obligation: one ought to try, contribute, and help satisfy group norms (Ames & Ames, 1984). William Glasser points out that student motivation and performance tend to be highest for such activities as band, drama club, athletics, the school newspaper, and the yearbook, all of which require a team effort (Gough, 1987).

ELEMENTS OF COOPERATIVE LEARNING

Journal Entry
Using a Social
Approach to
Instruction

Over the past twenty-five years different approaches to cooperative learning have been proposed by different individuals. The three most popular are those of David Johnson and Roger Johnson (Johnson, Johnson, & Holubec, 1994), Robert Slavin (1994, 1995), and Shlomo Sharan and Yael Sharan (Sharan, 1995; Sharan & Sharan, 1994). To give you a general sense of what cooperative learning is like and to avoid limiting you to any one individual's approach, the following discussion is a synthesis of the main features of each approach.

GROUP HETEROGENEITY   The size of cooperative-learning groups is relatively small and as heterogeneous as circumstances allow. The recommended size is usually four to five students. At the very least, groups should contain both males and females and students of different ability levels. If possible, different ethnic backgrounds and social classes should be represented as well.

GROUP GOALS/POSITIVE INTERDEPENDENCE   A specific goal, such as a grade or a certificate of recognition, is identified for the group to attain. Students are told that they will have to support one another because the group goal can be achieved only if each member learns the material being taught (in the case of a task that culminates in an exam) or makes a specific contribution to the group's effort (in the case of a task that culminates in a presentation or a project).

PROMOTIVE INTERACTION   This element is made necessary by the existence of positive interdependence. Students are shown how to help one another overcome problems and complete whatever task has been assigned. This may involve episodes of peer tutoring, temporary assistance, exchanges of information and material, challenging of one another's reasoning, feedback, and encouragement to keep one another highly motivated.

INDIVIDUAL ACCOUNTABILITY   This feature stipulates that each member of a group has to make a significant contribution to achieving the group's goal. This may be satisfied by achieving a minimal score on a test, having the group's test score be the sum or average of each student's quiz scores, or having each member be responsible for a particular part of a project (such as doing the research and writing for a particular part of a history report).

INTERPERSONAL SKILLS   Positive interdependence and promotive interaction are not likely to occur if students do not know how to make the most of their face-to-face interactions. And you can safely assume that the interpersonal skills most students possess are probably not highly developed. As a result, they have to be taught such basic skills as leadership, decision making, trust building, clear communication, and conflict management. The conflict that arises over differences of opinion, for example, can be constructive if it is used as a stimulus to search for more information or to rethink one's conclusions. But it can destroy group cohesion and productivity if it results in students stubbornly clinging to a position or referring to one another as "stubborn," "dumb," or "nerdy."

EQUAL OPPORTUNITIES FOR SUCCESS   Because cooperative groups are heterogeneous with respect to ability and their success depends on positive interdependence, promotive interaction, and individual accountability, it is important that steps be taken to ensure that all students have an opportunity to contribute to their team. You can do this by awarding points for degree of improvement over previous test scores, having students compete against comparable members of other teams in a game- or tournament-like atmosphere, or giving students learning assignments (such as math problems) that are geared to their current level of skill.

TEAM COMPETITION   This may seem to be an odd entry in a list of cooperative-learning components, especially in light of the comments we made earlier about the ineffectiveness of competition as a spur to motivation and learning. But we're not being contradictory. The main problem with competition is that it is rarely used appropriately. When competition occurs between well-matched competitors, is done in the absence of a norm-referenced grading system, and is not used too frequently, it can be an effective way to motivate students to cooperate with each other.

DOES COOPERATIVE LEARNING WORK?

The short answer to this question is yes. In the vast majority of studies, forms of cooperative learning have been shown to be more effective than noncooperative re-

> Cooperative learning characterized by heterogeneous groups, positive interdependence, promotive interaction, individual accountability

ward structures in raising the levels of variables that contribute to motivation, in raising achievement, and in producing positive social outcomes.

EFFECT ON MOTIVATION   Because a student's sense of self-esteem can have a strong effect on motivation (a point we made in the last chapter), this variable has been examined in several cooperative-learning studies. The results are encouraging, yet confusing. Slavin (1995) found that in eleven of fifteen studies, cooperative learning produced bigger increases in some aspect of self-esteem (general self-esteem, academic self-esteem, social self-esteem) than the noncooperative method with which it was compared. But these effects were not consistent across studies. Some researchers reported increases in academic self-esteem or social self-esteem, but others found no effect. Adding to the confusion is the conclusion drawn by Johnson and Johnson (1995) that cooperative learning consistently produces higher self-efficacy scores than do competitive or individualistic conditions. Such inconsistencies may reflect weaknesses in the self-esteem instruments that were used (self-ratings are not always accurate), weaknesses in the designs of the studies (many cooperative-learning studies last anywhere from a few days to a few weeks, yet changes in self-esteem happen slowly), or differences in specific cooperative-learning programs. Perhaps future research will clarify this issue.

Another way in which cooperative learning contributes to high levels of motivation is in the proacademic attitudes that it fosters among group members. Slavin (1995) cites several studies in which students in cooperative-learning groups felt more strongly than did other students that their groupmates wanted them to come to school every day and work hard in class.

Probably because of such features as promotive interaction and equal opportunities for success, cooperative learning has been shown to have a positive effect on motivation-inducing attributions. Students in cooperative-learning groups were more likely to attribute success to hard work and ability than to luck (Slavin, 1995).

A strong indicator of motivation is the actual amount of time students spend working on a task. Most studies have found that cooperative-learning students spend significantly more time on-task than do control students (Johnson, Johnson, & Smith, 1995; Slavin, 1995).

EFFECT ON ACHIEVEMENT   Slavin (1995) examined several dozen studies that lasted four or more weeks and that used a variety of cooperative-learning methods. Overall, students in cooperative-learning groups scored about one-fourth of a standard deviation higher on achievement tests than did students taught conventionally. This translates to an advantage of 10 percentile ranks (60th percentile for the average cooperative-learning student versus 50th percentile for the average conventionally taught student). But the beneficial effect of cooperative learning varied widely as a function of the particular method used. The best performances occurred with two techniques called Student Teams-Achievement Divisions and Teams-Games-Tournaments. (Both are described in Chapter 11.) The cooperative-learning features that seem to be most responsible for learning gains are group goals and individual accountability.

David Johnson, Roger Johnson, and Karl Smith (1995) also reviewed much of the cooperative-learning literature but drew a somewhat different conclusion. They found that the test scores of students in the cooperative-learning groups were about two-thirds of a standard deviation higher than the test scores of students in competitive or individualistic situations. This translates to an advantage of 25 percentile ranks (75th versus 50th). It's not clear why Slavin's analysis produced a somewhat lower estimate of the size of the advantage produced by cooperative learning. It may be due in part to differences in the studies cited by each; Slavin focused on studies lasting at least four weeks. It may also be due to differences in the cooperative techniques used by various researchers.

In addition to achievement outcomes, researchers have also assessed the impact of cooperative learning on problem solving. Given the complex nature of problem solving and the multiple resources that a cooperative group has at its disposal, one would logically expect cooperative learning to have a positive effect on this outcome as well. This hypothesis was confirmed by Zhining Qin, David Johnson, and Roger Johnson (1995). After reviewing forty-six studies, they concluded that students of all age levels (elementary, secondary, college, adult) who worked cooperatively outscored students who worked competitively. The average student in a cooperative group solved more problems correctly than 71 percent of the students who worked competitively.

EFFECT ON SOCIAL RELATIONSHIPS   In most studies students exposed to cooperative learning were more likely than students who learned under competitive or individualistic conditions to name a classmate from a different race, ethnic group, or social class as a friend or to label such individuals as "nice" or "smart." In some studies the friendships that were formed were deemed to be quite strong. A similar positive effect was found for students with mental disabilities who were mainstreamed. Finally, the cooperation skills that students learn apparently transfer. Cooperative-learning students were more likely than other students to use the cooperative behaviors they were taught when they worked with new classmates (Johnson & Johnson, 1995; Slavin, 1995).

Students who learn cooperatively tend to be more highly motivated to learn because of increased self-esteem, the proacademic attitudes of groupmates, appropriate attributions for success and failure, and greater on-task behavior. They also score higher on tests of achievement and problem solving and tend to get along better with classmates of different racial, ethnic, and social class backgrounds. This last outcome should be of particular interest to those of you who expect to teach in areas marked by cultural diversity.

Why Does Cooperative Learning Work?

When researchers attempt to explain the widespread positive effects that are typically found among studies of cooperative learning, they usually cite one or more of the following explanations (Slavin, 1995).

MOTIVATIONAL EFFECT   The various features of cooperative learning, particularly positive interdependence, are highly motivating because they encourage such achievement-oriented behaviors as trying hard, attending class regularly, praising the efforts of others, and receiving help from one's groupmates. Learning is seen as an obligation and a valued activity because the group's success is based on it and one's groupmates will reward it.

COGNITIVE-DEVELOPMENTAL EFFECT   According to Lev Vygotsky, collaboration promotes cognitive growth because students model for each other more advanced ways of thinking than any would demonstrate individually. According to

Jean Piaget, collaboration among peers hastens the decline of egocentrism and allows the development of more advanced ways of understanding and dealing with the world.

COGNITIVE ELABORATION EFFECT   As we saw in Chapter 8, new information that is elaborated (restructured and related to existing knowledge) is more easily retrieved from memory than is information that is not elaborated. A particularly effective means of elaboration is explaining something to someone else.

Now that you have read about the behavioral, cognitive, humanistic, and social approaches to instruction, you should take a few minutes to study Table 10.1. It summarizes the basic emphasis of each approach and allows you to compare them for similarities and differences.

Table 10.1	Behavioral, Cognitive, Humanistic, and Social Approaches to Instruction
Behavioral (Direct Instruction)	Teacher presents information efficiently. Student accepts all information transmitted by teacher and textbook as accurate and potentially useful. Emphasis is on acquiring information in small units through clear presentations, practice, and corrective feedback and gradually synthesizing the pieces into larger bodies of knowledge.
Cognitive (Information Processing)	Teacher presents and helps students to process information meaningfully. Student accepts all information transmitted by teacher and textbook as accurate and potentially useful. Emphasis is on understanding relationships among ideas, relationships between ideas and prior knowledge, and on learning how to effectively control one's cognitive processes.
Cognitive (Constructivist)	Teacher helps students to construct meaningful and adaptive knowledge structures by requiring them to engage in higher levels of thinking such as classification, analysis, synthesis, and evaluation; providing scaffolded instruction within the zone of proximal development; embedding tasks in realistic contexts; posing problems and tasks that cause uncertainty, doubt, and curiosity; exposing students to multiple points of view; and allowing students the time to formulate a consensus solution to a task or problem.
Humanistic	Teacher creates a classroom environment that addresses students' needs, helps students understand their attitudes toward learning, promotes a positive self-concept in students, and communicates the belief that all students have value and can learn. Goal is to activate the students' inherent desire to learn and grow.
Social	Teacher assigns students to small, heterogeneous groups and teaches them how to accomplish goals by working together. Each student is accountable for making a significant contribution to the achievement of the group goal. Because of its emphasis on peer collaboration, this approach is consistent with a social constructivist view of learning.

USING TECHNOLOGY TO SUPPORT SOCIAL APPROACHES TO INSTRUCTION

SOCIAL CONSTRUCTIVIST LEARNING   While the cognitive constructivist looks to find tools to help the child's mind actively construct relationships and ideas, the social constructivist looks as well for tools that help children negotiate ideas and findings in a community of peers. For instance, some point out that it is not just the quality of a computer simulation or microworld that determines the degree to which students will become more like expert scientists, but rather it is the social activities and talk between students and teachers in that environment that is central to student learning (Roschelle, 1996). Idit Harel and Seymour Papert (1990) add that children need to design or construct tangible, external products that can be discussed or shared. Still others emphasize the need to incorporate communication technology to help learners negotiate and share meaning (Riel, 1993). As a teacher, you might attempt to foster rich conversations and collaborations among your students by incorporating computer networks, on-line information services, e-mail, discussion groups, bulletin boards, chat lines, collaborative Websites and pages, or electronic newsletters and journals.

> **Successful technology applications are embedded in an active social environment**

COOPERATIVE AND COLLABORATIVE LEARNING   Cooperative learning is fairly well structured, with assigned roles, tasks, and procedures to help students learn material covered in a classroom setting; a related concept, **collaborative learning**, allows the students themselves to decide on their roles and use their individual areas of expertise to help investigate problems (Marx, Blumenfeld, Krajcik, & Soloway, 1997). As noted throughout this book, with the emergence of the World Wide Web and telecommunications technologies that enable students to publish and share their work internationally, there is no shortage of cooperative and collaborative learning opportunities (Harasim, Hiltz, Teles, & Turoff, 1995). Networking technologies can be used for many cooperative and collaborative tasks, including:

- Collecting data for group science projects (Marx et al., 1997)
- Sharing video and text messages and ideas with peers and experts in a multimedia bulletin board (Woolsey & Bellamy, 1997)
- Asking questions of explorers as students explore the environment (Bonk & Sugar, 1998)
- Explaining theories and findings from excavations of simulated archaeological or geological sites (Woolsey & Bellamy, 1997)
- Engaging in global peace projects and simulations to build students' appreciation and knowledge of world events and problems (Rottier, 1995)
- Gathering and sharing data on current events in one's community (for example, the weather) (Bonk, Hay, & Fischler, 1996; Dede, 1996)
- Creating plays with sister schools (Sauer, 1994)
- Designing hypermedia "metastacks" that visually depict how all student hypermedia projects relate to one another (Scholten & Whitmer, 1996)
- Practicing reading and writing in a foreign language (Meagher, 1995)
- Giving peer feedback on writing assignments and reports (Hirtle, 1996)
- Cross-age mentoring (Dede, 1996)

- Communicating with electronic pen pals in other countries (Bradsher, 1996)
- Sharing artwork with students from schools around the world (Copen, 1995)

As noted in both Chapters 2 and 5, the emergence of computer networking technologies is creating many interesting opportunities for students to enter into virtual communities with peers from other schools and countries and share and discuss various data and ideas. The National Geographic Kids Network, for instance, involves research teams of ten or more classes from the United States and over forty other countries collecting real-world data (for example, acid rain samples). With the collection of raw data, each participant is actually making a vital contribution to project success. In some global projects, students not only see how their peers in troubled parts of the world are affected by international events, but they can actually make an impact on their lives (Copen, 1995; Meagher, 1995). Of course, success requires finding suitable partners, sharing background information, establishing clear goals and roles, coordinating schedules, tracking participation, having technology access across sites, facilitating group interaction, establishing a division of labor, building trust between sites, sustaining student progress and momentum with encouraging feedback, determining how credit is divided, and perhaps even changing one's teaching approach (Kimball, 1995). Given these constraints, it is important for teachers to reflect on the purpose and scope of a collaborative technology project before deciding to initiate one (Hirtle, 1996).

RESOURCES FOR FURTHER INVESTIGATION

■ Mager and Gronlund on Objectives

If you would like to read Robert Mager's complete description of his recommendations for writing specific objectives, peruse his brief paperback *Preparing Instructional Objectives* (3d ed., 1997). Norman Gronlund explains his approach to using objectives in *How to Write and Use Instructional Objectives* (5th ed., 1995) and in *Measurement and Assessment in Teaching* (7th ed., 1995), which he coauthored with Robert Linn.

■ Direct Instruction

In *Research on Direct Instruction: 25 Years Beyond DISTAR* (1996), Gary Adams and Siegfried Engelmann cover the origins of Direct Instruction (by capitalizing the term *Direct Instruction* Adams and Engelmann seek to distinguish the original and highly structured approach that was devised by Engelmann in 1964 from the more generic approach that was described in this chapter), its features, myths about its nature, and a review of research results on its effects. Appendix A provides a list of Direct Instruction programs for reading, language arts, writing, spelling, mathematics, and science that can be purchased from Science Research Associates (800-843-8855) and videodisk programs in math and science that can be purchased from BFA Educational Media (800-221-1274).

■ The Cognitive Approach to Instruction

In *Cognitive Strategy Instruction That Really Improves Children's Academic Performance* (2d ed., 1995), Michael Pressley, Vera Woloshyn, and others describe how to use information-processing principles to design cognitive strategy instruction for beginning reading, reading comprehension, vocabulary, spelling, writing, mathematics, science, and learning facts.

Scaffolding Student Learning: Instructional Approaches and Issues (1997), edited by Kathleen Hogan and Michael Pressley, contains five chapters that describe and illustrate with actual classroom examples how to use scaffolding for a variety of instructional outcomes.

■ The Humanistic Approach to Instruction

William W. Purkey and John M. Novak describe a humanistic approach to teaching called "invitational learning" in *Inviting School Success: A Self-Concept Approach to Teaching, Learning, and Democratic Practice* (3d ed., 1996). If you would like to sample a variety of descriptions and interpretations of humanistic education, examine *Readings in Values Clarification* (1973), edited by Howard Kirschenbaum and Sidney B. Simon, or *Humanistic Education Sourcebook* (1975), edited by Donald A. Read and Sidney B. Simon.

■ Cooperative Learning

The New Circles of Learning: Cooperation in the Classroom and School (1994), by David W. Johnson, Roger T. Johnson, and Edythe Johnson Holubec, is a brief (105 pages) and readable description of the basic elements of the authors' version of cooperative learning. In *Cooperative Learning* (2d ed., 1995), Robert E. Slavin describes the cooperative learning techniques that he favors, analyzes the research evidence that supports their use, and provides detailed directions on how to use them. Lynda Baloche provides numerous examples of how to use cooperative learning techniques in *The Cooperative Classroom: Empowering Learning* (1998).

Cooperative learning is sufficiently flexible that it can be used at all levels of education. Four books that describe how to use cooperative methods for specific grade levels are: *Cooperative Learning in the Early Childhood Classroom* (1991), by Harvey C. Foyle, Lawrence Lyman, and Sandra A. Thies; *Cooperative Learning in the Elementary Classroom* (1993), by Lawrence Lyman, Harvey C. Foyle, and Tara S. Azwell; *Cooperative Learning in Middle-Level Schools* (1991), by Jerry Rottier and Beverly J. Ogan; and *Secondary Schools and Cooperative Learning* (1995), edited by Jon E. Pederson and Annette D. Digby.

SUMMARY

1. Goals, like those found in the federal government's Goals 2000 program, are broad, general statements of desired educational outcomes. Because of their general language, they mean different things to different people and cannot be precisely measured.

2. The vagueness of such goals stimulated psychologists to specify educational outcomes as specific, clearly stated objectives and to organize objectives as taxonomies in each of three domains: cognitive, affective, and psychomotor.

3. The taxonomy for the cognitive domain that was prepared by Bloom and several associates is composed of six levels: knowledge, comprehension, application, analysis, synthesis, and evaluation.

4. The taxonomy for the affective domain that was prepared by Krathwohl and several associates is composed of five levels: receiving, responding, valuing, organization, and characterization by a value or value complex.

5. The taxonomy for the psychomotor domain that was prepared by Simpson is composed of seven levels: perception, set, guided response, mechanism, complex or overt response, adaptation, and origination.

6. Most teachers use test questions that measure knowledge-level objectives, largely ignoring higher-level outcomes.

7. Mager states that well-written objectives should specify what behaviors the learner will exhibit to indicate mastery, the conditions under which the behavior will be exhibited, and the criteria of acceptable performance.

8. Gronlund believes that complex and advanced kinds of learning do not lend themselves to Mager-type objectives. Complex outcomes are so broad in scope that it is impractical to ask students to demonstrate everything they have learned. Instead, Gronlund suggests that teachers first state a general objective and then specify a sample of related specific outcomes.

9. Objectives must be consistent with the instructional approach one uses and the types of tests one creates.

10. Objectives work best when students are aware of them and understand their intent, when they are clearly written, when they are provided to average students for tasks of average difficulty, and when intentional learning is measured.

11. Direct instruction is an approach to instruction that is derived from behavioral learning theory. Lessons are broken down into small steps, the teacher models the desired behavior, material is presented in a variety of formats, students are given extensive opportunities to practice, and feedback is given consistently.

12. An information-processing approach to teaching is based on knowledge of how information is meaningfully processed and attempts to teach students how to be self-directed learners. Teachers should communicate their goals clearly, use attention-getting devices, present information in organized and meaningful ways, present information in relatively small chunks over realistic time periods, use instructional techniques that facilitate encoding of information in long-term memory, make sure that test items reflect both objectives and actual classroom instruction, and model effective learning processes.

13. A constructivist approach to teaching is based on the view that meaningful learning occurs when students are encouraged and helped to create the knowledge schemes that produce a broad understanding of ideas and lead to self-directed learning. Key elements of the constructivist approach include scaffolded instruction within a student's zone of proximal development, learning by discovery, exposure to multiple points of view, and use of relevant and realistic problems and tasks.

14. A humanistic approach to teaching assumes all students will be motivated to learn if the classroom environment satisfies their basic needs, strengthens their self-concept, provides assistance in learning new ideas and skills, and allows them to direct their learning experiences.

15. A social approach to learning focuses on teaching students how to learn from one another in a cooperative environment. For students to be able to work together

successfully, the following conditions are necessary: heterogeneous groups, achievement of group goals by having students help one another to achieve individual goals, holding each student responsible for making a significant contribution to the group goal, development of interpersonal skills, giving each student an opportunity to succeed, and allowing for competition among teams.

Cooperative learning is successful because it raises the motivation levels of students, promotes cognitive growth, and encourages meaningful learning.

16. Technology tools can be used to support behavioral, information processing, learner-centered, and social approaches to instruction.

KEY TERMS

instructional objectives *(330)*
taxonomy *(331)*
cognitive domain *(331)*
affective domain *(331)*
psychomotor domain *(331)*

specific objectives *(334)*
general objectives *(335)*
direct instruction *(337)*
intelligent tutoring systems *(348)*
exploratory environments *(348)*

guided learning *(349)*
humanistic approach *(353)*
learner-centered education *(355)*
collaborative learning *(364)*

DISCUSSION QUESTIONS

1. Based on the content of this chapter and your own experiences as a student, do you agree that writing objectives and providing them to students are worthwhile expenditures of a teacher's time and effort? If so, then what steps will you take to ensure that, unlike many teachers today, you will make writing objectives a standard part of your professional behavior?

2. One criticism of writing objectives is that it limits the artistic side of teaching. That is, objectives lock teachers into a predetermined plan of instruction and eliminate the ability to pursue unplanned topics or interests. Can you respond to this criticism by recalling a teacher who provided you and your classmates with objectives but was still enthusiastic, flexible, spontaneous, and inventive?

3. Research cited in Chapter 8 noted that instruction in how to effectively process information is rarely provided to students by elementary grade teachers, despite its demonstrated effectiveness in study after study. One

reason is that teacher education programs typically provide little or no coursework on information processing and learning strategy instruction. Is this true of your program? Why? What can you do when you teach to make full use of information processing principles?

4. Can you recall any teachers who practiced the humanistic techniques suggested by Maslow, Rogers, and Combs? Did you like these teachers? Did you feel as if you learned as much from them as from other teachers? Would you model yourself after such teachers?

5. Have you ever experienced a competitive reward structure in school? Were your reactions to it positive or negative? Why? Would you use it in your own classroom? For what purpose and under what circumstances?

6. Have you ever experienced a cooperative reward structure in school? Were your reactions to it positive or negative? Why? Would you use it in your own classroom? For what purpose and under what circumstances?

Creating a Positive Learning Environment

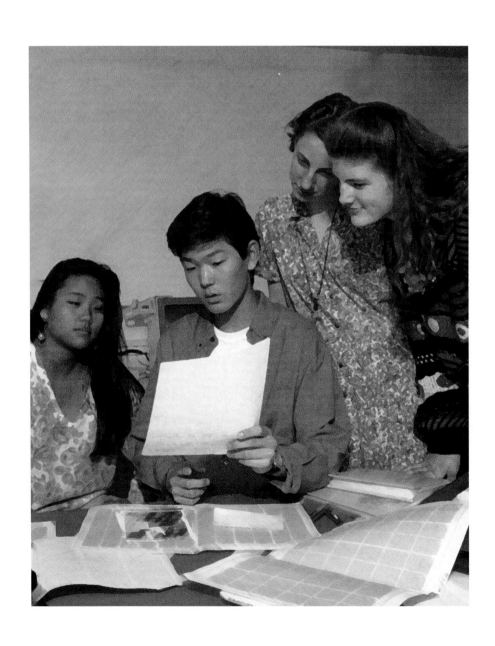

11 Motivation

Teaching is very much like putting together a puzzle. You first have to identify the pieces and then figure out how to construct them into a meaningful whole. This book is designed to help you identify the relevant pieces that make up the effective teaching puzzle and give you some ideas for using them in a coordinated fashion. In Part I, for example, you learned the importance of understanding how students develop socially, emotionally, and cognitively; what students are like at different ages; and how they differ from one another. In Part II, you were introduced to those pieces of the puzzle that pertain to the learning process and how different views of learning can

KEY POINTS

These key points will help you learn the important information in this chapter. To help you study, they also appear in the margins of pages, next to the text where they are discussed.

Behavioral Views of Motivation

- Behavioral view of motivation: reinforce desired behavior
- Social learning view of motivation: identification, imitation, vicarious reinforcement
- Extrinsic motivation occurs when learner does something to earn external reward
- Intrinsic motivation occurs when learner does something to experience inherently satisfying results
- Excessive use of external rewards may lead to temporary behavior change, materialistic attitudes, decreased intrinsic motivation
- Intrinsic motivation undermined by rewarding performance when interest is high, rewards held out in advance, quality of performance ignored

- Intrinsic motivation enhanced when reward is given according to predetermined standard or is consistent with individual's level of skill
- Give rewards sparingly, especially on tasks of natural interest

Cognitive Views of Motivation

- Cognitive-developmental view of motivation: strive for equilibration; master the environment
- Need for achievement revealed by desire to attain goals that require skilled performance
- High-need achievers prefer moderately challenging tasks
- Low-need achievers prefer very easy or very hard tasks
- Unsuccessful students attribute success to luck, easy tasks; failure, to lack of ability
- Successful students attribute success to effort, ability; failure, to lack of effort
- Students with entity beliefs motivated to get high grades, avoid failure

- Students with incremental beliefs motivated to meaningfully learn, improve skills
- Often difficult to arouse cognitive disequilibrium
- Need for achievement difficult to assess on basis of short-term observations
- Faulty attributions difficult to change due to beliefs about ability

The Humanistic View of Motivation

- People are motivated to satisfy deficiency needs only when those needs are unmet
- Self-actualization depends on satisfaction of lower needs, belief in certain values
- When deficiency needs are not satisfied, person likely to make bad choices
- Encourage growth choices by enhancing attractions, minimizing dangers
- Teachers may be able to satisfy some deficiency needs but not others

The Role of Self-Perceptions in Motivation

- Self-concept is description of self; self-esteem is value we place on that description
- High self-esteem due to being competent at valued tasks, reinforcement from others
- Self-esteem declines when students move from elementary grades to middle school and from middle school to high school
- Self-efficacy affects choice of goals, expectations of success, attributions for success and failure
- Raise self-esteem by helping students become better learners

Motivating Students with Technology

- Technology can be used to support both extrinsic and intrinsic motivation
- Technology increases intrinsic motivation by making learning more interesting and meaningful

be used to guide the type of instruction you provide. The puzzle pieces in this part deal with the importance of establishing a classroom environment that will motivate students to learn and of maintaining that positive atmosphere over time.

The last four chapters provided you with several explanations of how people learn and suggested related approaches for helping students achieve objectives. In this chapter we will try to answer the question of *why* students strive (or don't strive) for academic achievement—that is, what motivates students? The importance of motivation was vividly pointed out by Larry Cuban, a Stanford University professor of education who returned to teach a high school class for one semester after a sixteen-year absence. Of this experience, he says, "If I wanted those students to be engaged intellectually, then every day—and I *do* mean *every* day—I had to figure out an angle, a way of making connections between whatever we were studying and their daily lives in school, in the community, or in the nation" (1990, pp. 480–481). Cuban's comment about the importance of motivating students is as applicable to the elementary and middle school teacher as it is to the high school teacher. Researchers have consistently found that interest in school in general decreases the most between fourth and fifth grades, while interest in specific subjects decreases the most between sixth and seventh grades. Declines in motivation have also been found among girls when they move from a kindergarten through eighth-grade school to a traditional high school setting (Anderman & Maehr, 1994).

Motivation is typically defined as the forces that account for the selection, persistence, intensity, and continuation of behavior. Nevertheless, many teachers have at least two major misconceptions about motivation that prevent them from using this concept with maximum effectiveness. One misconception is that some students are unmotivated. Strictly speaking, that is not an accurate statement. As long as a student chooses goals and expends a certain amount of effort to achieve them, he is, by definition, motivated. What teachers really mean is that students are not motivated to behave in the way teachers would like them to behave. The second misconception is that one person can directly motivate another. This view is inaccurate because motivation comes from within a person. What you *can* do, with the help of the various motivation theories discussed in this chapter, is create the circumstances that *influence* students to do what you want them to do (Maehr & Meyer, 1997).

Many factors determine whether the students in your classes will be motivated or not motivated to learn. You should not be surprised to discover that no single theoretical interpretation of motivation explains all aspects of student interest or lack of it. Different theoretical interpretations do, however, shed light on why some students in a given learning situation are more likely to want to learn than others. Furthermore, each theoretical interpretation can serve as the basis for the development of techniques for motivating students in the classroom. Several theoretical interpretations of motivation—some of which are derived from discussions of learning presented earlier—will now be summarized. ■

Behavioral Views of Motivation

OPERANT CONDITIONING AND SOCIAL LEARNING THEORY

THE EFFECT OF REINFORCEMENT In Chapter 7 we discussed Skinner's emphasis on the role of reinforcement in learning. After demonstrating that organisms tend to repeat actions that are reinforced and that behavior can be shaped by reinforcement, Skinner developed the technique of programmed instruction to make it

Providing students with positive reinforcers after they exhibit a desired response may serve to motivate them to make the same response in the future, because the reinforcer tells students that their responses are acceptable.

possible for students to be reinforced for every correct response. Supplying the correct answer—and being informed by the program that it *is* the correct answer—motivates the student to go on to the next frame, and as the student works through the program, the desired terminal behavior is progressively shaped.

Following Skinner's lead, many behavioral learning theorists devised techniques of behavior modification. Students are motivated to complete a task by being promised a reward of some kind. Many times the reward takes the form of praise or a grade. Sometimes it is a token that can be traded in for some desired object, and at other times the reward may be the privilege of engaging in a self-selected activity.

Behavioral view of motivation: reinforce desired behavior

Operant conditioning interpretations of learning help reveal why some students react favorably to particular subjects and dislike others. For instance, some students may enter a required math class with a feeling of delight, while others may feel that they have been sentenced to prison. Skinner suggests that such differences can be traced to past experiences. He would argue that the student who loves math has been shaped to respond that way by a series of positive experiences with math. The math hater, in contrast, may have suffered a series of negative experiences.

THE POWER OF PERSUASIVE MODELS   Social learning theorists, such as Albert Bandura, call attention to the importance of observation, imitation, and vicarious reinforcement (expecting to receive the same reinforcer that we see someone else get for exhibiting a particular behavior). A student who identifies with and admires a teacher of a particular subject may work hard partly to please the admired individual and partly to try becoming like that individual. A student who observes an older brother or sister reaping benefits from earning high grades may strive to do

Social learning view of motivation: identification, imitation, vicarious reinforcement

the same with the expectation of experiencing the same or similar benefits. A student who notices that a classmate receives praise from the teacher after acting in a certain way may decide to imitate such behavior to win similar rewards. As we pointed out in Chapter 7, both vicarious reinforcement and direct reinforcement can raise an individual's sense of self-efficacy for a particular task, which, in turn, leads to higher levels of motivation.

LIMITATIONS OF THE BEHAVIORAL VIEW

Extrinsic motivation occurs when learner does something to earn external reward

Although approaches to motivation based on positive reinforcement are often useful, you should be aware of the disadvantages that can come from overuse or misuse of such techniques. Most of the criticisms of the use of reinforcement as a motivational incentive stem from the fact that it represents **extrinsic motivation**. That is, the learner decides to engage in an activity (such as participate in class, do homework, study for exams) to earn a reward that is not inherently related to the activity (such as receive praise from the teacher, earn a high grade, or enjoy the privilege of doing something different). By contrast, students under the influence of **intrinsic motivation** study a subject or acquire a skill because it produces such inherently positive consequences as becoming more knowledgeable, competent, and independent.

Intrinsic motivation occurs when learner does something to experience inherently satisfying results

Although extrinsic motivation is widespread in society (individuals are motivated to engage in many activities because they hope to win certificates, badges, medals, public recognition, prizes, or admiration from others), this approach has at least three potential dangers. First, changes in behavior may be temporary. As soon as the extrinsic reward has been obtained, the student may revert to such earlier behaviors as studying inconsistently, turning in poor-quality homework, and disrupting class with irrelevant comments and behaviors. Second, students may develop a materialistic attitude toward learning. They may think (or say), "What tangible reward will I get if I agree to learn this information?" If the answer is "none," they may decide to make little or no effort to learn it. Third, giving students extrinsic rewards for completing a task may lessen whatever intrinsic motivation they may have for that activity (Kohn, 1993).

Excessive use of external rewards may lead to temporary behavior change, materialistic attitudes, decreased intrinsic motivation

This last disadvantage, which is referred to as the *undermining effect,* has been extensively investigated by researchers. It appears that giving students rewards may indeed decrease their intrinsic motivation for a task, but only when (1) initial interest in the activity is very high, (2) the rewards used are not reinforcers (meaning they do not increase the desired behavior), (3) the rewards are held out in advance as incentives, and, most important, (4) the rewards are given simply for engaging in an activity (Cameron & Pierce, 1994; Eisenberger & Cameron, 1996; Ryan & Deci, 1996).

Intrinsic motivation undermined by rewarding performance when interest is high, rewards held out in advance, quality of performance ignored

However, there are two instances in which external rewards may enhance intrinsic motivation. First, when rewards are given according to some predetermined standard of excellence, when the task is moderately challenging, and when the reward is relatively large, intrinsic interest in the task is likely to increase. Second, intrinsic motivation can be enhanced when the task is moderately challenging and the size of the reward is consistent with the individual's perceived level of skill. If a student wins first prize in a science fair, for example, and believes that her project was truly superior to those of the other participants, a large reward may cause the student to maintain a strong interest in science (Pintrich & Schunk, 1996).

Intrinsic motivation enhanced when reward is given according to predetermined standard or is consistent with individual's level of skill

Taken as a whole, these results strongly suggest that teachers should avoid the indiscriminate use of rewards for influencing classroom behavior, particularly when an activity seems to be naturally interesting to students. Instead, rewards should be used to provide students with information about their level of competence on tasks they have not yet mastered (Lepper, Keavney, & Drake, 1996; Pintrich & Schunk, 1996).

Give rewards sparingly, especially on tasks of natural interest

Cognitive Views of Motivation

Cognitive views stress that human behavior is influenced by the way people think about themselves and their environment. The direction that behavior takes can be explained by four influences: the inherent need to construct an organized and logically consistent knowledge base, one's expectations for successfully completing a task, the factors that one believes account for success and failure, and one's beliefs about the nature of cognitive ability.

THE IMPACT OF COGNITIVE DEVELOPMENT

This view is based on Jean Piaget's principles of equilibration, assimilation, accommodation, and schema formation, which we discussed in Chapter 2. Piaget proposes that children possess an inherent desire to maintain a sense of organization and balance in their conception of the world (equilibration). A sense of equilibration may be experienced if a child assimilates a new experience by relating it to an existing scheme, or the child may accommodate by modifying an existing scheme if the new experience is too different.

In addition, individuals will repeatedly use new schemes because of an inherent desire to master their environment. This explains why young children can, with no loss of enthusiasm, sing the same song, tell the same story, and play the same game over and over and why they repeatedly open and shut doors to rooms and cupboards with no seeming purpose. It also explains why older children take great delight in collecting and organizing almost everything they can get their hands on and why adolescents who have begun to attain formal operational thinking will argue incessantly about all the unfairness in the world and how it can be eliminated (Stipek, 1998).

Cognitive-developmental view of motivation: strive for equilibration; master the environment

THE NEED FOR ACHIEVEMENT

Have you ever decided to take on a moderately difficult task (like take a course on astronomy even though you are a history major and have only a limited background in science) and then found that you had somewhat conflicting feelings about it? On the one hand, you felt eager to start the course, confident that you would be pleased with your performance. But on the other hand, you also felt a bit of anxiety because of the small possibility of failure. Now try to imagine the opposite situation. In reaction to a suggestion to take a course outside your major, you flat out refuse because the probability of failure seems great, while the probability of success seems quite small.

In the early 1960s John Atkinson (1964) proposed that such differences in achievement behavior are due to differences in something called the *need for achievement*. Atkinson described this need as a global, generalized desire to attain goals that require some degree of competence. He saw this need as being partly innate and partly the result of experience. Individuals with a high need for achievement have a stronger expectation of success than they do a fear of failure for most

Need for achievement revealed by desire to attain goals that require skilled performance

tasks and therefore anticipate a feeling of pride in accomplishment. When given a choice, high-need achievers seek out moderately challenging tasks because they offer an optimal balance between challenge and expected success. By contrast, individuals with a low need for achievement avoid such tasks because their fear of failure greatly outweighs their expectation of success, and they therefore anticipate feelings of shame. When faced with a choice, they typically opt either for relatively easy tasks because the probability of success is high or rather difficult tasks because there is no shame in failing to achieve a lofty goal.

Atkinson's point about taking fear of failure into account in arranging learning experiences has been made more recently by William Glasser in *Control Theory in the Classroom* (1986) and *The Quality School* (1990). Glasser argues that for people to succeed at life in general, they must first experience success in one important aspect of their lives. For most children, that one important part should be school. But the traditional approach to evaluating learning, which emphasizes comparative grading (commonly called "grading on the curve"), allows only a minority of students to achieve A's and B's and feel successful. The self-worth of the remaining students (who may be quite capable) suffers, which depresses their motivation to achieve on subsequent classroom tasks (Covington, 1985).

EXPLANATIONS OF SUCCESS AND FAILURE: ATTRIBUTION THEORY

Some interesting aspects of success and failure are revealed when students are asked to explain why they did or did not do well on some task. The four reasons most commonly given stress ability, effort, task difficulty, and luck. To explain a low score on a math test, for example, different students might make the following statements:

> "I just have a poor head for numbers." (Lack of ability)
> "I didn't really study for the exam." (Lack of effort)
> "That test was the toughest I've ever taken." (Task difficulty)
> "I guessed wrong about which sections of the book to study." (Luck)

Because students *attribute* success or failure to the factors just listed, research of this type contributes to what is referred to as **attribution theory**.

Students with long histories of academic failure and a weak need for achievement typically attribute their success to easy questions or luck and their failures to lack of ability. Ability is a stable attribution (that is, people expect its effect on achievement to be pretty much the same from one task to another), while task difficulty and luck are both external attributions (in other words, people feel they have little control over their occurrence). Research has shown that stable attributions, particularly ability, lead to expectations of future success or failure, whereas internal attributions (those under personal control) lead to pride in achievement and reward attractiveness following success or lead to shame following failure. Because low-achieving students attribute failure to low ability, future failure is seen as more likely than future success. In addition, ascribing success to factors beyond one's control diminishes the possibility of taking pride in achievement and of placing a high value on rewards. Consequently, satisfactory achievement and reward may have little effect on the failure-avoiding strategies that poor students have developed over the years.

Success-oriented students (high-need achievers), in contrast, typically attribute success to ability and effort and failure to insufficient effort. Consequently, failure does not diminish expectancy of success, feelings of competence, or reward

---

Margin notes:

High-need achievers prefer moderately challenging tasks

Low-need achievers prefer very easy or very hard tasks

Unsuccessful students attribute success to luck, easy tasks; failure, to lack of ability

Successful students attribute success to effort, ability; failure, to lack of effort

attractiveness for these students. They simply resolve to work harder in the future (Graham & Weiner, 1993).

BELIEFS ABOUT THE NATURE OF COGNITIVE ABILITY

Throughout the primary and elementary grades, most children believe that academic ability is closely related to effort; if one works hard, one succeeds and becomes "smarter." But as these same children reach the middle school and high school grades, many of them adopt a different view. Cognitive ability now comes to be seen as a trait—a fixed, stable part of a person that basically cannot be changed. It is not uncommon, for example, to hear older children and adolescents talk about peers who do or do not have "it" (Anderman & Maehr, 1994). Why this change occurs, and why it occurs in some individuals but not others, is not entirely known, but the increased emphasis on norm-referenced grading procedures (meaning the performance of every student in class is compared to the performance of every other student in that class to determine who gets which grades, a practice we will discuss in Chapters 13 and 14) is suspected of playing a major role. One casualty of this belief is motivation for learning.

Carol Dweck, who has done extensive research on this topic (see, for example, Cain & Dweck, 1995; Henderson & Dweck, 1990), has found that students can be placed into one of two categories based on their beliefs about the nature of cognitive ability. On the one hand are students who subscribe to what Dweck calls an *entity theory* because they talk about intelligence (another term for cognitive ability) as if it were a thing, or an entity, that has fixed characteristics. On the other hand are students who believe that intelligence can be improved through the use of new thinking skills. Dweck describes these students as subscribing to an *incremental theory* to reflect their belief that intelligence can be gradually improved by degrees or increments.

Students who believe that intelligence is an unchangeable thing are primarily motivated to prove their ability by getting high grades and praise and by avoiding

Students who attribute success to effort and failure to insufficient effort are more motivated to continue learning than are students who cite task difficulty and luck to explain their successes and failures.

Students who believe that success in the classroom is based on intellectual skills that can be improved with practice are likely to be more motivated to participate in class and persist in the face of difficulties than are students who believe that intelligence is a fixed capacity.

Students with entity beliefs motivated to get high grades, avoid failure

low grades and criticism. They report feeling bright or capable when they do not make major mistakes on a test or assignment or when they are among the first students to turn in a paper. If their confidence in their ability is low, they are likely to avoid challenging tasks. If avoidance is not possible, they become discouraged at the first sign of difficulty. This, in turn, produces anxiety, ineffective problem solving, and withdrawal from the task (as a way to avoid concluding that one lacks ability and thereby maintain some self-esteem). According to attribution theory, entity theorists should continue this pattern since success is not attributed to effort, but failure is attributed to low ability.

Those who believe that intelligence is a fixed trait and who are highly confident of their ability are likely to demonstrate such mastery-oriented behaviors as seeking challenges and persisting in the face of difficulty. Both high-confidence and low-confidence entity theorists strive to achieve high grades in order to be praised for their brightness. When confronted with a new task, their initial thought is likely to be "Am I smart enough to do this?" They may forgo opportunities to learn new ideas and skills if they think they will become confused and make mistakes (Mueller & Dweck, 1998).

Students with incremental beliefs motivated to meaningfully learn, improve skills

Students with incremental beliefs tend to be motivated to acquire new and more effective cognitive skills. They seek challenging tasks and do not give up easily because they see obstacles as a natural part of the learning process. They often tell themselves what adults have told them for years—"Think carefully," "Pay attention," and "Try to recall useful information that was learned earlier." They seem to focus on the questions "How do you do this?" and "What can I learn from this?" Errors are seen as opportunities for useful feedback.

LIMITATIONS OF COGNITIVE VIEWS

COGNITIVE DEVELOPMENT Although cognitive development theory can be useful as a means for motivating students, it has a major limitation: it is not always easy or even possible to induce students to experience a cognitive disequilibrium sufficient to stimulate them to seek answers. This is particularly true if an answer can be found only after comparatively dull and unrewarding information and skills are mastered. (How many elementary school students, for example, might be expected to experience a self-impelled urge to learn English grammar or to acquire skill in mathematics?) You are likely to gain some firsthand experience with the difficulty of arousing cognitive disequilibrium the first time you ask students to respond to what you hope will be a provocative question for class discussion. Some students may experience a feeling of intellectual curiosity and be eager to clarify their thinking, but others may stare out the window or do homework for another class.

Often difficult to arouse cognitive disequilibrium

NEED FOR ACHIEVEMENT Perhaps the major problem that teachers have in using Atkinson's theory of need for achievement is the lack of efficient and objective instruments for measuring its strength. Although you could probably draw reasonably accurate conclusions about whether a student has a high or low need for achievement by watching that student's behavior over time and in a variety of situations, you may not be in a position to make extensive observations. And the problem with short-term observations is that a student's achievement orientation may be affected by more or less chance circumstances. A student might do well on a first exam in a course, for example, because the teacher gave in-class time for study and happened to offer advice at a crucial point during the study period. The high score on that test might inspire the student to work for an A in that class. But if that

Need for achievement difficult to assess on basis of short-term observations

exam happened to be scheduled the day after a two-week bout with the flu, the student might not be well prepared and could end up with a C or D grade. Such a poor performance might cause the student to forget about the A and concentrate instead on obtaining a C.

ATTRIBUTION THEORY AND BELIEFS ABOUT ABILITY   The major implication of the idea that faulty attributions are at least partly responsible for sabotaging students' motivation for learning is to teach students to make more appropriate attributions. But this is likely to be a substantial undertaking requiring a concerted, coordinated effort. One part of the problem in working with students who attribute failure to lack of ability is that ability tends to be seen as a stable factor that is relatively impervious to change. The other part of the problem is that the same students often attribute their success to task difficulty and luck, two factors that cannot be predicted or controlled because they are external and random. Ideas about how to teach students to make more appropriate attributions for success and failure can be found in *Enhancing Motivation: Change in the Classroom* (1976), by Richard deCharms. An additional limitation is that attribution training is not likely to be fully effective with elementary school children. For them, two individuals who learn the same amount of material are equally smart despite the fact that one person has to work twice as long to achieve that goal. Older children and adolescents, however, have a better grasp of the concept of efficiency; they see ability as something that influences the amount and effectiveness of effort (Stipek, 1998).

| Faulty attributions difficult to change due to beliefs about ability

The Humanistic View of Motivation

Abraham Maslow earned his Ph.D. in a psychology department that supported the behaviorist position. After he graduated, however, he came into contact with Gestalt psychologists (a group of German psychologists whose work during the 1920s and 1930s laid the foundation for the cognitive theories of the 1960s and 1970s), prepared for a career as a psychoanalyst, and became interested in anthropology. As a result of these various influences, he came to the conclusion that American psychologists who endorsed the behaviorist position had become so preoccupied with overt behavior and objectivity that they were ignoring other important aspects of human existence (hence the term *humanistic* to describe his views). When Maslow observed the behavior of especially well-adjusted persons—or *self-actualizers*, as he called them—he concluded that healthy individuals are motivated to *seek* fulfilling experiences.

MASLOW'S THEORY OF GROWTH MOTIVATION

Maslow describes seventeen propositions, discussed in Chapter 1 of *Motivation and Personality* (3d ed., 1987), that he believes would have to be incorporated into any sound theory of *growth motivation* (or *need gratification*). Referring to need gratification as the most important single principle underlying all development, he adds that "the single, holistic principle that binds together the multiplicity of human motives is the tendency for a new and higher need to emerge as the lower need fulfills itself by being sufficiently gratified" (1968, p. 55). He elaborates on this basic principle by proposing a five-level hierarchy of needs. *Physiological* needs are at the bottom of the hierarchy, followed in ascending order by *safety, belongingness and love, esteem*, and *self-actualization* needs (see Figure 11.1). This order reflects differences in the relative strength of each need. The lower a need is in the hierarchy, the greater is its strength because when a lower-level need is activated (as in the case of extreme hunger or fear for one's physical safety), people will stop trying to satisfy a higher-level need (such as esteem or self-actualization) and focus on satisfying the currently active lower-level need (Maslow, 1987).

The first four needs (physiological, safety, belongingness and love, and esteem) are often referred to as **deficiency needs** because they motivate people to act only when they are unmet to some degree. Self-actualization, by contrast, is often called a **growth need** because people constantly strive to satisfy it. Basically, **self-actualization** refers to the need for self-fulfillment—the need to develop all of one's potential talents and capabilities. For example, an individual who felt she had the capability to write novels, teach, practice medicine, and raise children would not feel self-actualized until all of these goals had been accomplished to some minimal degree. Because it is at the top of the hierarchy and addresses the potential of the whole person, self-actualization is discussed more frequently than the other needs.

Maslow originally felt that self-actualization needs would automatically be activated as soon as esteem needs were met, but he changed his mind when he encountered individuals whose behavior did not fit this pattern. He concluded that individuals whose self-actualization needs became activated held in high regard such values as truth, goodness, beauty, justice, autonomy, and humor (Feist, 1990).

In addition to the five basic needs that compose the hierarchy, Maslow describes cognitive needs (such as the needs to know and to understand) and aesthetic needs (such as the needs for order, symmetry, or harmony). Although not part of the basic hierarchy, these two classes of needs play a critical role in the satisfaction of basic needs. Maslow maintains that such conditions as the freedom to investigate and learn, fairness, honesty, and orderliness in interpersonal relationships are critical

People are motivated to satisfy deficiency needs only when those needs are unmet

Self-actualization depends on satisfaction of lower needs, belief in certain values

Figure 11.1 Maslow's Hierarchy of Needs

Self-actualization (e.g., maximizing one's potential)

Esteem (e.g., respect)

Belongingness and love (e.g., acceptance, affection)

Safety (e.g., nurturance, money)

Physiological (e.g., food, water, oxygen)

SOURCE: Maslow (1943).

because their absence makes satisfaction of the five basic needs impossible. (Imagine, for example, trying to satisfy your belongingness and love needs or your esteem needs in an atmosphere characterized by dishonesty, unfair punishment, and restrictions on freedom of speech.)

IMPLICATIONS OF MASLOW'S THEORY

The implications of Maslow's theory of motivation for teaching are provocative. One down-to-earth implication is that a teacher should do everything possible to see that the lower-level needs of students are satisfied so that they are more likely to function at the higher levels. Students are more likely to be primed to seek satisfaction of the esteem and self-actualization needs, for example, if they are physically comfortable, feel safe and relaxed, have a sense of belonging, and experience self-esteem.

Only when the need for self-actualization is activated is a person likely to choose wisely when given the opportunity. Maslow emphasizes this point by making a distinction between *bad choosers* and *good choosers*. When some people are allowed freedom to choose, they seem consistently to make wise choices. Most people, however, frequently make self-destructive choices. An insecure student, for example, may choose to attend a particular college more on the basis of how close it is to home than on the quality of its academic programs.

> **When deficiency needs are not satisfied, person likely to make bad choices**

Growth, as Maslow sees it, is the result of a never-ending series of situations offering a free choice between the attractions and dangers of safety and those of growth. If a person is functioning at the level of growth needs, the choice will ordinarily be a progressive one. Maslow adds, however, that "the environment (parents, therapists, teachers) . . . can help by making the growth choice positively attractive and less dangerous, and by making the regressive choice less attractive and more costly" (1968, pp. 58–59). This point can be clarified by a simple diagram Maslow uses to illustrate a situation involving choice (1968, p. 47).

Enhance the dangers		Enhance the attraction
Safety	◄─── Person ───►	Growth
Minimize the attractions		Minimize the dangers

This diagram emphasizes that if you set up learning situations that impress students as dangerous, threatening, or of little value, they are likely to play it safe, make little effort to respond, or even try to avoid learning. If, however, you make learning appear appealing, minimize pressure, and reduce possibilities for failure or embarrassment, your students are likely to be willing, if not eager, to do an assigned task.

> **Encourage growth choices by enhancing attractions, minimizing dangers**

LIMITATIONS OF MASLOW'S THEORY

Although Maslow's speculations are thought-provoking, they are also sometimes frustrating. You may conclude, for instance, that awareness of his hierarchy of needs will make it possible for you to do an excellent job of motivating your students, only to discover that you don't know exactly how to apply what you have learned. Quite often, for example, you may not be able to determine precisely which of a student's needs are unsatisfied. Even if you *are* quite sure that a student lacks interest in learning because he feels unloved or insecure, you may not be able to do much about it. A girl who feels that her parents do not love her or that her peers do not accept her may not respond to your efforts. And if her needs for love, belonging, and esteem are not satisfied, she is less likely to be in the mood to learn.

> **Teachers may be able to satisfy some deficiency needs but not others**

Then again, there will be times when you can be quite instrumental in helping satisfy certain deficiency needs. The development of self-esteem, for example, is closely tied to successful classroom achievement for almost all students. Although you may not be able to feed students when they are hungry or protect them from physical danger, you can always take steps to help them learn more effectively.

The Role of Self-Perceptions in Motivation

Current interest in the effects of self-perceptions on school motivation and achievement runs high and seems to have been prompted by such developments as a better understanding of the nature of self-concept and self-esteem, the introduction by Albert Bandura of the self-efficacy concept, advances in the measurement of self-perceptions, and the consistent finding of a positive relationship among self-perceptions, motivation, and school achievement. Much of this interest can be traced to ideas published during the 1960s and 1970s by psychologists such as Abraham Maslow, Carl Rogers, and Arthur Combs. These individuals stressed that how students saw and judged themselves and others played an important part in determining how motivated they were and how much they learned.

In Chapter 3 we introduced and briefly discussed the notions of self-concept, self-esteem, and self-efficacy as important aspects of children's emotional and cognitive development. In Chapter 7 we described in even more detail the nature of self-efficacy and its role in learning. We review each of these concepts in Table 11.1 because of their relationship to motivation.

THE ROLE OF SELF-CONCEPT/SELF-ESTEEM IN MOTIVATION AND LEARNING

Over the years researchers have consistently found a moderately positive relationship (called a correlation) between measures of self-esteem and school achievement.

Students who have a positive self-concept tend to be intrinsically motivated. They have a high level of curiosity, are interested in schoolwork, and prefer moderately challenging tasks.

Table 11.1	Comparing Self-Concept, Self-Esteem, and Self-Efficacy	
Type of Self-Perception	**Characteristics**	**Examples**
Self-Concept	• The nonevaluative picture people have of themselves. • Made up of components that are hierarchically arranged. For example, academic self-concept = verbal self-concept + mathematical self-concept + science self-concept, etc.	• "I am a sixth grader." • "I am five feet one inch tall." • "My favorite subject is history."
Self-Esteem	• The evaluative judgments we make of the various components of our self-concept. • Self-concept describes who you are; self-esteem indicates how you feel about that identity.	• "I'm pretty smart at math." • "I'm not attractive because my nose is too big for my face." • "I'm disappointed that most people don't like me." • "I'm satisfied with how well I speak and understand a foreign language."
Self-Efficacy	• The evaluative judgments we make of how capable we think we are at organizing and carrying out a specific course of action.	• "I believe I can learn how to use a computer program." • "I'll never be able to figure out how to solve quadratic equations."

SOURCES: Bandura (1986); Beane (1994); Harter (1988); Marsh, Byrne, & Shavelson (1992); Pajares (1996); Schunk (1995).

Self-concept is description of self; self-esteem is value we place on that description

Students who score relatively high on measures of self-esteem tend to have higher-than-average grades. But, as the saying goes, correlation does not imply causation. The fact that students with high self-esteem scores tend to have high grades is not sufficient grounds for concluding that high self-esteem causes high achievement. It is just as plausible that high achievement causes increased self-esteem or that increases in both variables are due to the influence of a third variable. Recent work on the antecedents and consequences of self-esteem has begun to shed some light on what causes what.

Susan Harter (1988), on the basis of her own research and that of others, proposes the causal explanation depicted in Figure 11.2. Harter believes that achieving an acceptable level of competence in school, valuing academic success (which most students do), and being given support and positive feedback for one's academic accomplishments by parents, teachers, and friends are the primary determinants of a positive self-concept (high self-esteem). A positive self-concept contributes, in turn, to feeling satisfied and pleased about one's accomplishments, which contributes to the development of intrinsic motivation. Such students are likely to be curious about many things, to find schoolwork interesting, and to prefer moderately challenging tasks. This motivational orientation leads to high levels of achievement, which maintain high levels of self-esteem, and so on.

High self-esteem due to being competent at valued tasks, reinforcement from others

Figure 11.2 Causes and Consequences of Academic Self-Esteem

SOURCE: Adapted from Harter (1988).

In contrast, children with relatively low levels of achievement see themselves as less competent than their peers and tend to feel badly about their performance. This attitude leads to a more extrinsic motivation orientation in which students show little interest or pleasure in classroom learning, avoid challenging tasks when they have the opportunity to do so, and reduce their efforts in subjects where they are having difficulty keeping up with others. This, of course, leads to low grades and a perpetual pattern of low self-esteem, low motivation, and low grades.

In one study Harter found that seventh graders who placed a high value on academic success but who felt their learning skills weren't developing rapidly enough for them to keep up with teachers' demands had lower levels of self-esteem than did peers who were able to tell themselves that school success wasn't that important. The fact that Harter found this phenomenon among seventh graders is noteworthy given the often-cited declines in motivation that occur when students move from the elementary to the middle school or junior high grades and from the middle school or junior high to the high school grades. These transitions require students to deal with a larger and less familiar peer group, several teachers who are seen only for a short time each day, greater academic demands, and a more competitive reward system (Anderman & Maehr, 1994; Lipka, Hurford, & Litten, 1992).

> Self-esteem declines when students move from elementary grades to middle school and from middle school to high school

THE ROLE OF SELF-EFFICACY IN MOTIVATION AND LEARNING

An individual's sense of self-efficacy can affect motivation to learn in at least three ways, each of which we will discuss briefly.

CHOICE OF LEARNING GOALS   One way is by influencing the kind of learning goals a student chooses. According to one scheme, students may choose a task mastery, ego/social, or work-avoidant goal. Task mastery goals involve doing what is necessary to meaningfully learn the information and skills that have been assigned. They are chosen more often by students with high levels of self-efficacy than by students with low levels of self-efficacy. In pursuit of task mastery goals, high efficacy students will use a variety of encoding techniques, do more organizing of information to make it meaningful, review and practice more frequently, monitor their understanding more closely, and formulate more effective learning strategies. Ego/social goals involve doing what is necessary to please the teacher and one's parents. This may mean memorizing large amounts of information to get a high test grade without necessarily understanding the ideas or how they relate to each other or doing assignments neatly and exactly according to directions. Students who choose ego/social goals tend to have lower levels of self-efficacy. Work-avoidant goals involve, as the term suggests, trying to get by with as little work as possible. This goal is also selected more often by students with low levels of self-efficacy (Schunk, 1995).

OUTCOME EXPECTATIONS   A second way in which self-efficacy can affect motivation is in terms of the outcomes that students expect. Those with high levels of self-efficacy more often expect a positive outcome. As a result, they tend to be more willing to use the more complex and time-consuming learning skills mentioned previously and to persist longer in the face of difficulties. Those with lower levels of self-efficacy are more likely to expect a disappointing outcome, tend to use simpler learning skills, and are likely to give up more quickly when tasks demand greater cognitive efforts (Bandura, 1993; Schunk, 1995).

Recent research (Urdan, Midgley, & Anderman, 1998) has linked low levels of academic self-efficacy to what are called *self-handicapping behaviors* among fifth-grade students. As just about any teacher with at least a few years experience will tell you, some students unconsciously sabotage or handicap their chances for doing well in class. They put off getting started on homework or projects until the last minute, they study superficially for an exam, and they get involved in many in-school and out-of-school nonacademic activities. The purpose of such self-handicapping behavior is to be able to blame the circumstances rather than one's ability if school performance is unacceptable. Teachers may unwittingly encourage such behaviors, even in students whose sense of self-efficacy is at least adequate, by using a norm-referenced grading system. Because students are compared with one another to determine the top, middle, and low grades, this system encourages students to attribute their grades to a fixed ability. And students who have doubts about their ability are more likely to engage in self-handicapping behaviors.

ATTRIBUTIONS   A third way in which self-efficacy influences motivation is through the reasons students cite to explain why they succeeded or failed at a task. Those with a high level of self-efficacy for a subject are likely to attribute failure to insufficient effort (and so vow to work harder the next time) but credit their success to a combination of ability and effort. Their low self-efficacy peers are likely to explain their failures by saying that they just don't have the ability to do well in this subject, but they will chalk their successes up to an easy task or luck. As we pointed out earlier in this chapter, this attribution pattern undercuts motivation since it ascribes success to unstable factors that cannot be controlled but ascribes failure to a stable factor that is internal and often viewed as unchangeable (Bandura, 1993; Schunk, 1995).

> Self-efficacy affects choice of goals, expectations of success, attributions for success and failure

IMPLICATIONS OF RESEARCH ON SELF-PERCEPTIONS

According to current research, enhanced self-esteem does not lead to higher levels of motivation and achievement, but higher levels of achievement can increase future motivation and self-esteem. Furthermore, there is essentially no support for the

Raise self-esteem by helping students become
better learners

claims made by the designers of special curriculum programs that they can raise students' levels of self-esteem. A major implication that follows from these two statements is that educators should focus instead on altering the entire school environment so as to maximize the amount of meaningful learning that takes place (Beane, 1994; Kohn, 1994). We have already offered several suggestions for doing just that in Chapters 7, 8, and 9. We will offer some additional suggestions in Chapter 13 when we discuss mastery learning. And, as you will see from this chapter's Case in Print (page 386), which describes one solution to altering a whole school environment, sometimes the most effective way to enhance students' self-perceptions is to start with teachers' ideas about students' competence.

LIMITATIONS OF THE SELF-PERCEPTIONS APPROACH

One problem with using students' views of themselves as a way of influencing their motivation and learning is the lack of useful, commercially prepared measures of self-efficacy and self-esteem. Most of the available instruments assess global self-concept/global self-esteem. But the more narrow the measure of self-perception is (such as math self-esteem, self-efficacy for understanding medieval literature), the better it predicts motivation and achievement. One solution to this limitation is to prepare the same kinds of instruments that researchers use. This is not as difficult as it might seem. Some researchers use a relatively small set of questions ("How good are you at math?" "If you were to rank all the students in your math class from the worst to the best, where would you put yourself?" "Compared to your other school subjects, how good are you at math?") and ask students to rate themselves on a 7-point scale that may range from "not at all good" to "very good" (Stipek, 1998).

Another problem is that whatever success you may have in changing the sense of self-esteem and self-efficacy of students is likely to be slow in coming. This conclusion follows from two others. One is that changes in self-perception are best made by helping students become more effective learners than by constantly telling them they should feel good about themselves. The second conclusion is that learning how to use the cognitive skills that result in meaningful learning takes time because of their complexity and the doubts that some students will have about their ability to master these skills.

Motivating Students with Technology

EXTRINSIC VERSUS INTRINSIC MOTIVATION

Earlier in this chapter, we contrasted the behavioral, or extrinsic, approach to motivation with various cognitive, or intrinsic, approaches. Our goal was not to demonstrate that one approach is inherently superior to the other but to point out how and when both approaches can profitably be used to support classroom learning. A parallel situation exists with regard to the motivating effects of technology. Behavioral psychologists, for example, argue that students who work on computer-based drill-and-practice programs are motivated by the immediate feedback they receive and the steady progress they make. Cognitive psychologists argue that involving students in fantasy environments or in authentic tasks that are directed to audiences beside the teacher is intrinsically motivating because such programs and tasks give

Helping Teachers Develop Students' Self-Efficacy, Self-Esteem, and Motivation

Achieving an acceptable level of competence in school, valuing academic success . . . and being given support and positive feedback for one's academic accomplishments by parents, teachers, and friends are the primary determinants of a positive [academic] self-concept (high [academic] self-esteem). A positive self-concept contributes, in turn, to feeling satisfied and pleased about one's accomplishments, which contributes to the development of intrinsic motivation. (p. 382)

INSTITUTING EFFICACY: SELF-ESTEEM PRINCIPLES MAY BE TESTED AT BURKE HIGH

ESTHER SHEIN
Boston Sunday Globe 6/18/95

One of the first calls Steven Leonard made when he was named headmaster of Boston's Jeremiah E. Burke High School was to the Lexington-based Efficacy Institute. Leonard, who earlier this month was given the formidable task of helping the Burke regain its accreditation, has trained at the institute himself, and he was confident it could help his teachers.

His confidence is based not just on his own experience. Since it was founded 10 years ago, the Efficacy Institute has trained some 20,000 teachers in 64 school districts across the state. Its teaching is based on the principle that intelligence is a developmental process, not something a person is born with. It tries to instill the notion in teachers that all students have the ability to learn when teachers believe in the students' capabilities and the students are given confidence.

If he can come up with the $300 per-person training fee for the institute's four-day training sessions, Leonard said, Efficacy training will be a requirement for all teachers who remain at the Burke next fall.

"Efficacy is part of the solution," he said in a recent interview. "After you eliminate . . . the staff people that can't perform or don't want to perform in ways that are essential to educating children, you get to the realization that, in many, if not most, cases, teachers have been left in the lurch as far as

professional development in teaching the contemporary child."

Efficacy founder Jeff Howard said he will work closely with Leonard to train the Burke's teachers. But he said the city, in turn, needs to make an investment in the school building to show the students it cares about their welfare.

"The City of Boston ought to be ashamed of how it's treated that building," said Howard, a Harvard-educated social psychologist, "and the deplorable conditions the faculty has had to work under."

Another hurdle, Howard said, is helping teachers overcome a high level of frustration. They have become demoralized, he said, because society no longer views the teaching profession as prestigious.

"It's a terrible state for teachers to be in," he said. "They desperately want to be great teachers again—everybody wants to be effective in their work—and our secret weapon is that we help them feel effective again."

Another burden placed on teachers, Howard said, is the notion that there's an "unequal distribution of intelligence, and that the kinds of kids that go to inner-city schools . . . don't have a lot of intelligence."

That, he said, puts teachers "in a tough situation. They're given these kids that nobody thinks can learn much, and then they're given the mandate that they have to teach them."

Efficacy's role, according to Howard, is to "explode that bind. The underlying premise is all wrong." All students can learn, he said, if they are perceived to have the right attitude. But before that can happen, he said, the teachers' own attitude has to change.

"They have the capacity to be some of the best professionals in American society," Howard said of the teachers. "They have potential to be creative, disciplined, highly skilled, lifelong learners, but they have to believe in themselves and the kids. American society makes that hard; we make it easy."

Mia Roberts, director of community services for the institute, said much of the frustration lies in the fact that "kids come into school now with lots of other needs," including emotional and health issues.

Consequently, she said, the teachers become "educators, counselors, psychologists and moms and dads all rolled into one . . . and that can be very overwhelming."

Efficacy stresses, she said, that "all people are capable of brilliance and no one has limits. Human capabilities . . . can be developed throughout life."

That idea has become almost a religious belief for Jesse Solomon, a math teacher at Brighton High School who first learned about the institute while doing a college internship there.

"Having someone unconditionally believe in your intelligence can only be a positive thing," he said. "It turns kids around at best, and allows them small successes at worst."

Solomon believes he has always had a positive attitude toward his students, but he said Efficacy helped him translate that into action.

"Everything you see in your classroom sends a million messages a day," Solomon said, including messages about high expectations. But if those messages come from someone who believes in them, he said, the students are more likely to perform effectively.

Solomon recalled a middle-school student he taught for two years. For no particular reason, Solomon said, the student did poorly his first year.

"Showing him that I had a belief in him that wasn't going to go away . . . caused him to put in hard work," Solomon

said. "He came to school every day, and he graduated as a competent and confident student, more so than when I first met him."

Solomon attributes the turnaround to the student's increased motivation level and the desire to "make himself get smarter. The work has to be well-designed and supported, but I think that's the only way to get smarter."

Solomon said Efficacy also taught him the importance of creating networks with other teachers.

"No change or reform is going to come without those networks," he said. Calling teaching "a very isolated profession," Solomon said it would be cathartic for teachers to meet once a week after school to discuss issues such as dealing with students, developing curricula together or even reading articles about education.

"Often," he said, "there's no built-in time to share what you do professionally or no time to discuss their craft."

. . . The new headmaster said his challenge is to change the misperception that "some kids make it and some kids don't, and those who flunk are dumb . . . and the kids who make it are smart."

Leonard said Efficacy helps teachers understand that, many times, what's perceived as their failure is really "the failure of school systems and the university community to prepare teachers to do the job of urban education in 1995."

Even the best teachers will be deemed ineffective if they're asked to perform at levels that "exhaust their physical or mental resources, and right now that's what's being asked of many teachers—especially in urban environments—where issues of poverty are becoming more demanding and resources are decreasing."

Questions and Activities

1. The philosophy of the Efficacy Institute is that students' intellectual capabilities can be improved through systematic efforts that combine high-quality instruction and positive feedback from teachers about students' competence. This is the same idea as Dweck's incremental theory of intelligence. Do you share that belief? If so, what evidence can you cite in support of it? If you don't share that belief, can you explain why not?

2. Mia Roberts, the director of community services for the Efficacy Institute, noted that one of the challenges for teachers is that "kids come into school now with lots of other needs," and that these needs include emotional and health issues. As we pointed out earlier in the chap-

ter, Maslow's theory suggests that as long as a person's deficiency needs are unmet, growth needs will not be activated. One implication of this analysis is that teachers need to be aware of students' unmet deficiency needs. What steps can you take to increase the likelihood that you will notice and attend to a student's physiological, safety, belongingness, and esteem needs?

3. If you have the opportunity to work with a low-achieving student, systematically provide the type of positive feedback described in the article and note any subsequent changes in the student's behavior. Ask the student whether his or her self-efficacy and beliefs about intelligence changed as a function of your comments.

students a sense of confidence, personal responsibility, and control over their own learning (Collins, 1996).

Despite the differences in these two approaches to motivation, they are not mutually exclusive. Some of the most innovative and effective technological aids to learning combine both approaches. For example, the Jasper Challenge Series that we mentioned in Chapter 9 tries to engage intrinsic motivation by giving students control over and responsibility for how they collect, analyze, and use the data presented by the program and by embedding the task in a realistic context. Extrinsic rewards include class announcements of accomplishments, student demonstrations of problem-solving strategies, teacher praise for correct problem solutions, and feedback and encouragement from peers in other schools about one's problem solutions (Barron et al., 1995; Cognition and Technology Group at Vanderbilt, 1996). Other types of extrinsic rewards that can be used in conjunction with other technology-based approaches to learning include membership in multimedia clubs, special computer events and fairs for parents or the community, and certificates of recognition.

Technology can be used to support both extrinsic and intrinsic motivation

CAN TECHNOLOGY INCREASE MOTIVATION TO LEARN?

Now that we've established that computer-based technology can accommodate both extrinsic and intrinsic approaches to motivation, we can look at whether it does, in fact, increase students' motivation to learn.

Critics of computer-based learning argue that any observed increases in student motivation are likely to be short term and due largely to the novelty of the medium. But several studies have demonstrated that the use of computer-based instruction increases students' intrinsic motivation and performance. Diana Cordova and Mark Lepper (1996) found that rich fantasy contexts, personalization, and provision for student choice within children's software not only fosters intrinsic motivation and deeper engagement in learning but also boosts the amount that students learn, their perceived level of competence, and their levels of aspiration. In fact, in one four-month study, kindergarten children remained on-task about 90 percent of the time for the entire length of the study (Bergin, Ford, & Hess, 1993).

A decade-long evaluation of the Apple Classrooms of Tomorrow (ACOT) project by Judith Haymore Sandholtz, Cathy Ringstaff, and David Dwyer (1997) revealed that once the novelty factor has worn off, at least five factors affect student engagement with technology. First, motivation remains high when technology use is appropriate for the assignment and when teachers treat educational technology as one of many possible instructional tools. Second, technology must be integrated, or immersed, into the curriculum, not treated as a separate subject. Third, students are more engaged when using the computer as a tool than when the computer is mostly used as a drill-and-practice tutor. Fourth, teachers must adjust their use of technology to student ability levels; tasks that are too hard are likely to be frustrating, and tasks that are too simple are likely to be boring. Fifth, teachers must be willing to allow students more control over their own learning by using projects and interdisciplinary forms of learning.

USING MULTIMEDIA AND HYPERMEDIA TO INCREASE MOTIVATION

As indicated previously, the images, text, sound, video, and animation of multimedia and hypermedia can help gain student attention and make learning more relevant, thereby fostering a sense of learner control and intrinsic motivation (Becker & Dwyer, 1994).

Research shows that multimedia presentations are more motivating than print materials for middle school and high school children (Small & Ferreira, 1994). Interviews with elementary grade children suggest that they find it fun and interesting to use animation, create sound files, manipulate graphics, draw images, and design slides for their own computer projects (Gouzouasis, 1994). In foreign language learning, combining text and spoken words enhances the performance and motivation of elementary grade students (Jakobsdottir & Hooper, 1995).

Technology increases intrinsic motivation by making learning more interesting and meaningful

One form of multimedia, CD-ROM storybooks, allows young children a chance to pursue topics of interest and learn at their own pace and with their personal learning style (Glasgow, 1997). Since a CD-ROM can store 500,000 pages of text, or about 600 megabytes of information, large collections of literature can be contained on a single disk. With some of these tools, children not only read or listen to a story, but they can even create their own storybook presentations or songs, complete with pictures, words, and sounds. Such activities encourage active involvement in learning and the development of children's imaginations.

For slightly older children, CD-ROMs like Where in the World Is Carmen Sandiego? can teach research and geography skills as students track a gang of thieves who have stolen some of the world's greatest treasures from across the globe (Carroll, Knight, & Hutchinson, 1995). Motivators here include the humorous format, the challenge of following clues as a detective would, to eventually issue a warrant and complete an arrest, and amassing the points awarded for correct capture. Similar motivating materials can also be found for high school biology, social studies, and most other subject areas (see, for example, White, 1995).

USING CONSTRUCTIVIST-ORIENTED TECHNOLOGY TO INCREASE MOTIVATION

Common computer application tools—word processors, databases, simulations, telecommunications, spreadsheets, outlining tools, three-dimensional charts and graphs, and presentation tools—can also be used to motivate students. Databases might inspire students to search and sort through information while creating reports and knowledge bases, and simulations offer various gamelike features and immediate feedback. Such tools can be combined for enhancing student motivation through multimedia project presentations or interactive exhibits placed in local museums (Carver, 1995). Imagine technology projects where students are so motivated to complete them that they arrive at school at 6 A.M. and remain long past 4 P.M. (Ebert & Strudler, 1996; Lehrer, 1993).

As mentioned in Chapters 2 and 10, Geometer's Geometric Supposer can motivate students to learn mathematics by allowing them to invent, explore, and question various geometric properties and relationships (Schwartz, 1995). Similarly, a new program called Cocoa from the Apple Research Laboratory allows children to build their own simulations by designing objects and then creating and combining rules for the behavior of those objects on the screen (Woolsey & Bellamy, 1997). For instance, a student might draw a school of fish on the screen and then make decisions about the way they swim, the food they eat, and what they do if any of them run into a wall or another fish. Research on such constructivist tools, in particular LOGO, demonstrates that they can increase student **locus of control**, which is the perception that positive and negative events are under one's control (Bernhard & Siegel, 1994), as well as student willingness to accept challenges (Tyler & Vasu, 1995). These tools can also increase student motivation and perceived competence (Nastasi & Clements, 1994).

As mentioned in previous chapters, Web-based conferencing, e-mail, on-line chats, and electronic bulletin boards and discussion forums increase motivation to learn since they provide students access to information and communities that previously were beyond the boundaries of their classrooms and offer unique opportunities to collect meaningful, real-life data.

Electronic mail is often used to heighten student interest and motivation through pen pal projects that link students in different countries or locales or to coordinate interschool projects (Barr, 1994). Students in Oklahoma, for instance, might ask their new Japanese friends about earthquakes, while the Japanese students might ask what a tornado is like. Celeste Oakes (1996) described how she used e-mail with her first-grade class in Nevada to correspond with students in Alaska, ask questions of space shuttle astronauts, collaboratively write stories with students from other schools, and write letters to Santa Claus. In any of these projects, it is critical to have icebreaking activities, goals that relate to key objectives, and ground rules for collaboration (for example, time length, targeted deadlines, final project guidelines, and plans for culminating activities).

WHAT DOES THE FUTURE PROMISE?

There are a number of technologies emerging today that you may want to use to motivate student learning. For instance, Walter Rankin (1997) suggests that cyberjournals, or writing and researching on the Web, may not only be motivational but may also improve student writing skills. In addition, taking a course in high school on the Web might prove motivating for students since they can participate any time and any place, while their teachers might come from anywhere in the world (Tinker & Haavind, 1996).

Other motivational devices that will likely be common in the not-too-distant future include animated tutors, also called **intelligent agents** (for example, a Native American guide in an American history database), to help students use a program, electronically search for information, or schedule daily activities.

Though the computer-generated three-dimensional environment known as virtual reality (VR) is still in the early stages of development, some claim that it may have even greater motivational impact during the next decade than multimedia technology did during the 1990s (Chiou, 1994–1995; McLellan, 1996b). Why? Imagine the motivation simulated external worlds will offer when they allow students to explore previously inaccessible things or places (for example, a strand of DNA, the surface of Mars, etc.), access knowledge in a virtual library, practice surgical procedures on virtual cadavers, write virtual papers with contributors who have yet to be born, visualize unseen phenomena like air pressure, interact with historical figures representing different viewpoints within simulated negotiations, and touch and rotate museum artifacts (Pantelidis, 1993). Although headgear and data gloves are synonymous with virtual reality, it is important to recognize that VR now includes a number of computer desktop applications to help make learning experiences more realistic and meaningful (Hedberg & Alexander, 1994; McLellan, 1996b). For example, Sasha Barab and his colleagues have used VR programming languages to have high school students design plays (actors, props, scenes, soundtracks, etc.) as well as develop interactive scales of the solar system so they can better grasp issues of time, size, and distance (Barab, Hay, & Duffy, 1998).

Now that you are familiar with the various theories about and approaches to motivation, it is time to consider in the Suggestions for Teaching that follow how these ideas can be converted into classroom practice.

SUGGESTIONS FOR TEACHING IN YOUR CLASSROOM

Motivating Students to Learn

1 Use behavioral techniques to help students exert themselves and work toward remote goals.

2 Make sure that students know what they are to do, how to proceed, and how to determine when they have achieved goals.

3 Do everything possible to satisfy deficiency needs—physiological, safety, belongingness, and esteem.

    a. Accommodate the instructional program to the physiological needs of your students.

    b. Make your room physically and psychologically safe.

    c. Show your students that you take an interest in them and that they belong in your classroom.

    d. Arrange learning experiences so that all students can gain at least a degree of esteem.

4 Direct learning experiences toward feelings of success in an effort to encourage an orientation toward achievement, a positive self-concept, and a strong sense of self-efficacy.

    a. Make use of objectives that are challenging but attainable and, when appropriate, that involve student input.

    b. Provide knowledge of results by emphasizing the positive.

5 Try to encourage the development of need achievement, self-confidence, and self-direction in students who need these qualities.

    a. Use achievement-motivation training techniques.

    b. Use cooperative-learning methods.

6 Try to make learning interesting by emphasizing activity, investigation, adventure, social interaction, and usefulness.

---

1 **Use behavioral techniques to help students exert themselves and work toward remote goals.**

Journal Entry
Using Behavior Modification Techniques to Motivate

Maslow's hierarchy of needs calls attention to the reasons that few students come to school bursting with eagerness to learn. Only students with all their deficiency needs satisfied are likely to experience a desire to know and understand. But even growth-motivated students may not fully appreciate the need to master certain basic skills before they can engage in more exciting and rewarding kinds of learning. And as we noted earlier, the information that appropriately administered reinforcement provides about one's level of competence contributes to high levels of self-esteem. Accordingly, you may often need to give your students incentives to learn. Techniques you might use for this purpose were described in Chapter 7. They include shaping, modeling, token economies, and contingency contracting.

EXAMPLES

■ Arrange for students to observe that classmates who persevere and complete a task receive a reinforcer of some kind. (But let this occur more or less naturally. Also, don't permit students who have finished an assignment to engage in attention-getting or obviously enjoyable self-chosen activities; those who are still working on the assignment may become a bit resentful and therefore less inclined to work on the task at hand.)

■ Draw happy faces on primary grade students' papers, give check marks as students complete assignments, write personal comments acknowledging good work, and assign bonus points.

■ Develop an individual reward menu, or contract, with each student based on the Premack principle (Grandma's rule). After passing a spelling test at a particular level, for example, each student might be given class time to work on a self-selected project.

■ When making use of such motivational techniques, you might do your best to play down over-tones of manipulation and materialism. Point out that rewards are used in almost all forms of endeavor to induce people to work toward a goal. Just because someone does something to earn a reward does not mean that the activity should never be indulged in for intrinsic reasons. For example, athletes often compete to earn the reward of being members of the best team, but they still enjoy the game.

2 Make sure that students know what they are to do, how to proceed, and how to determine when they have achieved goals.

Journal Entry
Ways to Arrange
Short-Term Goals

Many times students do not exert themselves in the classroom because they say they don't know what they are supposed to do. Occasionally such a statement is merely an excuse for goofing off, but it may also be a legitimate explanation for lack of effort. Recall from Chapter 8 that knowing what one is expected to do is important information in the construction of a learning strategy. You should use the techniques described in Chapter 10 to take full advantage of the values of instructional objectives. In terms of motivation, objectives should be clear, understood by all members of the class, and attainable in a short period of time. For reasons illustrated by behavioral theorists' experiments with different reinforcement schedules, students are more likely to work steadily if they are reinforced at frequent intervals. If you set goals that are too demanding or remote, lack of reinforcement during the early stages of a unit may derail students, even if they started out with good intentions. Whenever you ask students to work toward a demanding or remote goal, try to set up a series of short-term goals.

EXAMPLE

■ One way to structure students' learning efforts is to follow the suggestions offered by Raymond Wlodkowski for drawing up a personal contract. He recommends that such a contract should contain four elements. A sample contract from Wlodkowski (1978, p. 57) is presented here, with a description of each element in brackets.

Date _____

1. Within the next two weeks I will learn to multiply correctly single-digit numbers ranging between 5 and 9, for example, 5 x 6, 6 x 7, 7 x 8, 8 x 9, 9 x 5. [What the student will learn]

2. When I feel prepared, I will ask to take a mastery test containing 50 problems from this range of multiplication facts. [How the student can demonstrate learning]

3. I will complete this contract when I can finish the mastery test with no more than three errors. [The degree of proficiency to be demonstrated]

4. My preparation and study will involve choosing work from the workbook activities, number games, and filmstrip materials. [How the student will proceed]

Signed _____

3 Do everything possible to satisfy deficiency needs—physiological, safety, belongingness, and esteem.

a. Accommodate the instructional program to the physiological needs of your students.

Journal Entry
Ways to Satisfy
Physiological
Needs

EXAMPLES

■ Be aware that your students may occasionally be hungry or thirsty. (This point sounds obvious, but it is frequently forgotten.) If conditions allow, permit snacks on an individual basis, or have a routine or occasional nonroutine snack break.

■ Have a change of pace or a break when appropriate. With young children, make allowance for a flexible naptime.

Theorists like Abraham Maslow, who argue that deficiency needs such as be-longingness and self-esteem must be satisfied before students will be motivated to learn, call attention to the importance of positive teacher-student relationships in the classroom.

- Schedule demanding activities when students are fresh; schedule relaxing activities toward the end of a period or day.
- Be prepared for greater restlessness before lunch and just before dismissal time at the end of the day.
- Make a habit of checking the room temperature. Ask students if the room is too warm or too cool.

Journal Entry
Ways to Satisfy
Safety Needs

b. Make your room physically and psychologically safe.

The need for safety is likely to be satisfied by the general classroom climate you establish, although physical factors of safety may be involved, particularly with young students. In one kindergarten, for example, several children were worried about the possibility of fire after seeing television news coverage of a fire in a school. In most cases, however, you can best ensure safety by establishing a relaxed, secure classroom environment.

EXAMPLES

- If you see that a student fears something (for example, bullies on the playground, fire, enclosed places), explain that you will offer protection or that adequate precautionary measures have been taken.
- Establish a classroom atmosphere in which students know what to expect and can relax about routines. Do everything you can to make your room a place that is psychologically safe. Be alert to things you do that are unnecessarily threatening. Try to see classroom assignments and activities from your students' point of view in an effort to detect anxiety-producing situations.
- As much as possible, establish classroom routines in which students can take the initiative. Don't require recitation; wait for students to volunteer. Don't force students to participate in new activities; let them try such activities when they feel ready.

Journal Entry
Ways to Satisfy
Belongingness
Needs

c. Show your students that you take an interest in them and that they belong in your classroom.

EXAMPLES

- Learn and use names as fast as you can.
- Keep detailed records for individual students and refer to specific accomplishments.

- Whenever possible, schedule individual tutorial or interview sessions so that you can interact with all students on a one-to-one basis. If a student is absent because of an extended illness, send a get-well card signed by the entire class.
- To encourage class spirit, schedule group planning sessions or sharing activities.

d. Arrange learning experiences so that all students can gain at least a degree of esteem.

Journal Entry
Ways to Satisfy
Esteem Needs

EXAMPLES

- Play down comparisons; encourage cooperation and self-competition. (Evaluation techniques that encourage self-competition will be provided in Chapter 14 in an analysis of mastery learning.)
- Permit students to work toward individual goals.
- Provide opportunities to students who possess culture-specific talents (such as storytelling, singing, dancing, or weaving) to demonstrate and teach them to others.
- Give unobtrusive individual assistance to students who are experiencing problems.

4 Direct learning experiences toward feelings of success in an effort to encourage an orientation toward achievement, a positive self-concept, and a strong sense of self-efficacy.

To feel successful, an individual must first establish goals that are neither so low as to be unfulfilling nor so high as to be impossible and then know that the goals have been achieved. This is a two-step process: establishing goals and receiving knowledge of results.

a. Make use of objectives that are challenging but attainable and, when appropriate, that involve student input.

Journal Entry
Ways to Encourage Students to
Set Their Own
Objectives

Although in many instructional situations, you may find it necessary to set goals yourself, when it is possible and instructionally appropriate, you can use goals to heighten motivation as well. In these instances you are likely to get a better reaction if you invite your students to participate in selecting objectives or at least in thinking along with you as you explain why the objectives are worthwhile. This will tend to shift the emphasis from extrinsic to intrinsic motivation.

To help students suggest appropriate objectives, you may want to use the techniques recommended by Robert Mager (discussed in Chapter 10). You might assist your students in stating objectives in terms of a time limit, a minimum number of correct responses, a proportion of correct responses, or a sample of actions.

EXAMPLES

- "How many minutes do you think you will need to outline this chapter? When you finish, we'll see that film I told you about."
- "George, you got six out of ten on this spelling quiz. How many do you want to try for on the retest?"

b. Provide knowledge of results by emphasizing the positive.

Journal Entry
Ways to Supply
Positive Feedback

To experience success (as a basis for establishing a realistic level of aspiration), your students must receive detailed information about their performance. Comments on the quality of a presentation, participation in a debate, papers and projects of various kinds, or answers on an exam may make the difference between feelings of success and feelings of failure. Accordingly, you should do

your best to comment favorably on successful performance and avoid calling   ✓
attention to failure, particularly the kind that is already apparent.

Jere Brophy (1981), however, suggests that classroom teachers rarely use
praise as an effective or desirable form of reinforcement. Brophy recommends
that teachers use praise in the following ways:

- As a spontaneous expression of surprise or admiration. ("Why, Juan! This
  report is really excellent!")

- As compensation for criticism or as vindication of a prediction. ("After
  your last report, Lily, I said I knew you could do better. Well, you *have*
  done better. This is really excellent.")

Praise

- As an attempt to impress all members of a class. ("I like the way Nguyen
  just put his books away so promptly.")

- As a transition ritual to verify that an assignment has been completed.
  ("Yes, Maya, that's very good. You can work on your project now.")

- As a consolation prize or as encouragement to students who are less capable than others. ("Well, Josh, you kept at it, and you got it finished. Good
  for you!")

In an effort to help teachers administer praise more effectively, Brophy drew
up the guidelines for effective praise listed in Table 11.2.

**5 Try to encourage the development of need achievement, self-confidence,
and self-direction in students who need these qualities.**

Despite your efforts to provide appropriate incentives, gratify deficiency needs, enhance the attractions of growth choices, and arrange learning experiences to produce a realistic level of aspiration and a feeling of success, some of your students
will still lack confidence in their ability to learn. In such cases you may try to help
students acquire a general motive to achieve.

a. Use achievement-motivation training techniques.

A technique described by John Nicholls (1979) allows students opportunities to
schedule their own classroom learning. For example, students can be given responsibility for deciding when to work on a particular assignment and for how long.
This gives them the feeling they are working on a task because they want to, not
because someone told them to. According to Nicholls, researchers have found
greater continuing interest in learning tasks under self-evaluation and greater fre-
quencies of assignment completion when opportunities for self-scheduling were
increased. As we mentioned in the previous section, research also suggests that
well-designed technology tools can contribute to a student's sense of self-direction
and self-efficacy because of the opportunities they provide for decision making.

b. Use cooperative-learning methods.

As we pointed out in Chapters 5 and 10, cooperative-learning methods have
proven effective in increasing motivation for learning and self-esteem, redirect-
ing attributions for success and failure, fostering positive feelings toward classmates, and increasing performance on tests of comprehension, reasoning, and
problem solving (Johnson & Johnson, 1995; Johnson, Johnson, & Smith, 1995;
Slavin, 1995). Accordingly, you may want to try one or more of the cooperative-
learning techniques described by David Johnson and Roger Johnson (Johnson,

Table 11.2	Guidelines for Effective Praise

Effective Praise	Ineffective Praise
1. Is delivered contingently	1. Is delivered randomly or unsystematically
2. Specifies the particulars of the accomplishment	2. Is restricted to global positive reactions
3. Shows spontaneity, variety, and other signs of credibility; suggests clear attention to the student's accomplishment	3. Shows a bland uniformity, which suggests a conditional response made with minimal attention
4. Rewards attainment of specified performance criteria (which can include effort criteria, however)	4. Rewards mere participation, without consideration of performance process or outcomes
5. Provides information to students about their competence or the value of their accomplishments	5. Provides no information at all or gives students information about their status
6. Orients students toward better appreciation of their own task-related behavior and thinking about problem solving	6. Orients students toward comparing themselves with others and thinking about competing
7. Uses students' own prior accomplishments as the context for describing present accomplishments	7. Uses the accomplishments of peers as the context for describing students' present accomplishments
8. Is given in recognition of noteworthy effort or success at tasks that are difficult (for *this* student)	8. Is given without regard to the effort expended or the meaning of the accomplishment (for *this* student)
9. Attributes success to effort and ability, implying that similar successes can be expected in the future	9. Attributes success to ability alone or to external factors such as luck or easy task
10. Leads students to expend effort on the task because they enjoy the task and/or want to develop task-relevant skills	10. Leads students to expend effort on the task for external reasons—to please the teacher, win a competition or reward, etc.
11. Focuses students' attention on their own task-relevant behavior	11. Focuses students' attention on the teacher as an external authority figure who is manipulating them
12. Fosters appreciation of and desirable attributions about task-relevant behavior after the process is completed	12. Intrudes into the ongoing process, distracting attention from task-relevant behavior

SOURCE: Brophy (1981).

Johnson, & Holubec, 1994) and Robert Slavin (1995). To familiarize you with these methods, we will briefly describe the Student Teams-Achievement Divisions (STAD) method devised by Slavin and his associates at Johns Hopkins University.

STAD is one of the simplest and most flexible of the cooperative-learning methods, having been used in grades 2 through 12 and in such diverse subject areas as math, language arts, social studies, and science. As with other cooperative-learning methods, students are assigned to four- or five-member groups, with each group mirroring the makeup of the class in terms of ability, background, and gender. Once these assignments are made, a four-step cycle is initiated: teach, team study, test, and recognition. The teaching phase begins with the presentation of material, usually in a lecture-discussion format. Students should be told what it is they are going to learn and why it is important. During team study, group members work cooperatively with teacher-provided worksheets and answer sheets. Next, each student *individually* takes a quiz. Using a scoring system that ranges from 0 to 30 points and reflects degree of individual improvement over previous quiz scores, the teacher scores the papers. Each team receives one of three recognition awards, depending on the average number of points earned by the team. For example, teams that average 15 to 19 improvement points receive a GOODTEAM certificate, teams that average 20 to 24 improvement points receive a GREATTEAM certificate, and teams that average 25 to 30 improvement points receive a SUPERTEAM certificate. Another cooperative learning method, Teams-Games-Tournaments, is similar to STAD except that students compete in academic tournaments instead of taking quizzes.

The cooperative methods developed by the Johnsons are similar to those developed by Slavin, but with two exceptions: these methods place a greater emphasis on teaching students how to productively work together, and they recommend using team grades, rather than certificates or other forms of recognition, as positive reinforcers.

6 Try to make learning interesting by emphasizing activity, investigation, adventure, social interaction, and usefulness.

More than twenty-five years ago, May Seagoe suggested an approach to motivation that is based on students' interests and that is consistent with many of the motivation

May Seagoe found that students respond with interest to school situations that are active, investigative, adventurous, social, and useful. Having members of a fifth-grade class play the roles of state government officials is an activity that includes almost all these features.

theories and technology tools mentioned in this chapter. Among the "points of appeal that emerge from studies of specific interests," she lists the following:

> (a) the opportunity for overt bodily *activity*, for manipulation, for construction, even for observing the movement of animals and vehicles of various sorts; (b) the opportunity for *investigation*, for using mental ingenuity in solving puzzles, for working problems through, for creating designs, and the like; (c) the opportunity for *adventure*, for vicarious experiences in make believe, in books, and in the mass media; (d) the opportunity for *social assimilation*, for contacts with others suitable to the maturity level of the child (ranging from parallel play to discussion and argument), for social events and working together, for human interest and humanitarianism, and for conformity and display; and (e) the opportunity for use of the new in real life, making the new continuous with past experience and projecting it in terms of future action. (1970, p. 25)

One approach that incorporates most or all of these features, and that can be used with preschool and primary grade children, is the project approach. Lillian Katz and Sylvia Chard (1989) define a project as an in-depth study of a particular topic that one or more children undertake and that extends over a period of days or weeks. Projects may involve an initial discussion that captures the students' interest (for example, discussing how a house is built); dramatic play; drawing, painting, and writing; group discussions; field trips; construction activities; and investigation activities. Because projects are based on children's natural interests and involve a wide range of activities, they are more likely to be intrinsically motivating.

As you think about how you are going to organize your lesson plans for each day and each period, you might ask yourself: "Are there ways that I can incorporate activity, investigation, adventure, social interaction, and usefulness into this presentation?" "Are there projects that I can assign to students, particularly as cooperative groups, that incorporate most of these features?" Here are some examples of techniques you might use.

ACTIVITY

- Have several students go to the board. Give a rapid-fire series of problems to be solved by those at the board as well as those at their desks. After five problems, have another group of students go to the board, and so on.

- Think of ways to move out of the classroom legitimately every now and then. Teach geometry, for instance, by asking the class to take several balls of string and lay out a baseball diamond on the side lawn of the school.

Journal Entry
Ways to Make
Learning Active

INVESTIGATION

- In elementary grade classrooms (and in some middle school and high school classrooms), set up a variety of learning centers with themes such as library, games, social science, cultural appreciation, and computer use, and organize these with provocative displays and materials. For example, your social science center could be stocked with maps, charts, and documents (Charles, 1972). Your computer center might include educational software such as CD-I (compact discs that connect to a television set and contain programs with which students can interact), CD-ROM, and database programs; student-created publications made with desktop publishing or word processing programs; a computer equipped with modem, communications software, Internet or commercial on-line service access; and lists of appropriate and interesting on-line sites.

- In middle school and high school classrooms, you might arrange centers that pertain to different aspects of a single subject. In a science class, for example, you might have an appreci-

Journal Entry
Ways to Promote
Investigation

ation center stressing aesthetic aspects of science, a display center calling attention to new developments in the field, a library center consisting of attractive and provocative books, and so on.

Journal Entry
Ways to Make Learning Seem Adventurous

ADVENTURE

■ Occasionally, use techniques that make learning entertaining and adventurous. Such techniques might be particularly useful when you introduce a new topic. You might employ devices used by advertisers and the creators of *Sesame Street,* for instance. Use intensity, size, contrast, and movement to attract attention. Make use of color, humor, exaggeration, and drama to introduce a new unit. Use one or more of the computer-based approaches to learning discussed in the last section (such as hypermedia, multimedia, and telecommunications projects as well as adventure-based simulations). Take students by surprise by doing something totally unexpected.

■ The night before you introduce a new unit, redecorate part of the room. Then ask the class to help you finish it.

■ Arrange a "Parade of Presidents" in which each student selects a president of the United States and presents a State of the Union message to the rest of the class, with the rest of the class taking the part of members of Congress.

■ Hand out a dittoed sheet of twenty questions based on articles in each section of a morning newspaper. Students compete against themselves to discover how many of the questions they can answer in the shortest period of time. (Typical questions: "Why is the senator from Mississippi upset?" "Who scored the most points in the UCLA–Notre Dame basketball game?" "What did Lucy say to Charlie Brown?")

Journal Entry
Ways to Make Learning Social

SOCIAL INTERACTION

■ Have students pair off and ask each other questions before an exam. Do the same with difficult-to-learn material by suggesting that pairs cooperate in developing mnemonic devices, preparing flashcards, and engaging in the like to help each other master information.

■ Organize an end-of-unit extravaganza in which individuals and groups first present or display projects and then celebrate by having refreshments.

Journal Entry
Ways to Make Learning Useful

USEFULNESS

■ Continually point out that what is being learned can be used outside of class. Ask students to keep a record of how they use what they learn outside of class.

■ Develop exercises that make students aware that what they are learning has transfer value. Have students in an English class write a job application letter, for instance; have math students balance a checkbook, fill out an income tax form, or work out a yearly budget; have biology students think about ways they can apply what they have learned to avoid getting sick.

RESOURCES FOR FURTHER INVESTIGATION

■ Surveys of Motivational Theories

In a basic survey text, *Motivation to Learn: From Theory to Practice* (3d ed., 1998), Deborah Stipek discusses reinforcement theory, social cognitive theory, intrinsic motivation, need for achievement theory, attribution theory, and perceptions of ability. In Appendix 2-A, she presents a rating form and scoring procedure with which teachers can identify students who may have motivation problems. Appendix 3-A is a self-rating form that teachers can use to keep track of how often they provide rewards and punishments.

A useful summary of motivation theories and techniques can be found in the Worcester Polytechnic Institute's Website for teacher development, at **http://www.wpi.edu/~isg_501/motivation.html**.

■ Self-Perceptions

In *When the Kids Come First* (1987), James Beane and Richard Lipka describe the kinds of organizational, curricular, and instructional features that contribute to positive self-perceptions among middle school students. The same two authors cover the same issue, but in more detail and over a wider age range (childhood through adulthood), in *Self-Concept, Self-Esteem, and the Curriculum* (1986).

Four studies on the relationship between self-esteem and achievement done recently at the University of Queensland in Australia can be found on-line at **http://www.cltr.uq.oz.au:8000/nllia/rd531**. These studies focus on language learning in particular and are of interest because of their currency and detail.

The on-line psychology library at the University of California, Berkeley, is an excellent resource for researching further aspects of motivation and self-perception. It is located at **gopher://library.berkeley.edu:70/00/resdbs/educ/psycinfo**.

■ Motivational Techniques for the Classroom

Eager to Learn (1990), by Raymond Wlodkowski and Judith Jaynes, is a good source of classroom application ideas. Techniques for motivating students from diverse cultural backgrounds are described by Raymond Wlodkowski and Margery Ginsberg in *Diversity and Motivation: Culturally Responsive Teaching* (1995b). *Motivating Students to Learn: Overcoming Barriers to High Achievement* (1993), edited by Tommy Tomlinson, devotes four chapters to elementary school and four chapters to high school motivation issues.

Two sources of information on motivation techniques and suggestions for teaching are found at Columbia University's Institute for Learning Technologies, which contains documents, papers, and unusual projects and activities that could be used to increase student motivation; and at Northwestern University's Institute for Learning Sciences Engines for Education on-line program, which allows educators to pursue a number of questions about students, learning environments, and successful teaching through a hyperlinked database. The Institute for Learning Technologies is found at **http://www.ilt.columbia.edu/ilt/**. The Institute for Learning Sciences is found at **http://www.ils.nwu.edu/**.

SUMMARY

1. Motivation is the willingness to expend a certain amount of effort to achieve a particular goal.

2. Behavioral views of motivation are based on the desire of students to obtain a positive reinforcer (in the case of operant conditioning theory) or to imitate an admired individual because of vicarious reinforcement (in the case of social learning theory).

3. A potential limitation of operant conditioning theory is its emphasis on extrinsic sources of motivation. The learner is motivated to attain a goal in order to receive a reward that is not inherently related to the activity. This may produce only temporary changes in behavior, a materialistic attitude toward learning, and an undermining of whatever intrinsic motivation a student may have for a particular task.

4. The condition that is most likely to undermine a student's intrinsic interest in a task is rewarding the student for simply engaging in an activity regardless of the quality of the student's response. Thus, teachers should reward students only for significant behaviors that require the skilled use of recently learned information and skills.

5. Cognitive views of motivation emphasize the effect of various kinds of thinking on students' academic behavior.

6. The cognitive development view holds that people are inherently driven to overcome gaps, inconsistencies, or contradictions between what they know and what they experience.

7. Atkinson proposes that people are motivated by a need for achievement, which is a general desire to attain goals that require some degree of competence. An individual's level of need is determined by the extent to which he emphasizes an expectation of success or a fear of failure. Individuals with a high need to achieve have a greater expectation of success than they do a fear of failure. They prefer moderately difficult tasks because such tasks provide an optimal balance between the possibility of failure and the expectation of success. Individuals with a low need to achieve are dominated by a fear of failure. Consequently, they prefer either very easy tasks (because success is assured) or very difficult tasks (because there is no shame in failing to do well at them).

8. Research on attribution theory found marked differences between high achievers and low achievers. High achievers attribute success to ability and effort and failure to insufficient effort. Low achievers attribute success to luck or task difficulty and failure to lack of ability.

9. Some students are less motivated than others because they subscribe to what Dweck calls an entity theory of cognitive ability. Because they believe that intelligence is a fixed capacity, they tend to avoid challenging tasks if uncertain of success. Students who subscribe to an incremental theory tend to pursue more meaningful learning opportunities because they think of intelligence as something that can be improved through experience and corrective feedback.

10. One limitation of the cognitive view is that teachers may not always find it possible to induce a sense of disequilibrium in students.

11. A problem with need for achievement theory is the lack of instruments with which to measure it and the unreliability of short-term observations.

12. A limitation of attribution theory and beliefs about ability is the difficulty of changing students' faulty attribution patterns and beliefs about the nature of cognitive ability.

13. Maslow's humanistic view of motivation is based on a person satisfying a hierarchical sequence of deficiency needs (physiological, safety, belongingness and love, and esteem) so that the individual can satisfy her self-actualization needs.

14. A limitation of the humanistic view is that the teacher may not always find it possible to identify a student's unmet deficiency needs or to satisfy them once they are identified.

15. Factors that appear to determine one's level of self-esteem are being competent at a valued task and being given support and positive feedback for one's accomplishments from significant others. High self-esteem contributes to feeling satisfied about one's accomplishments, which leads to the development of intrinsic motivation.

16. Declines in self-esteem have been found in some students when they move from the elementary to the middle school or junior high grades and from the middle school or junior high to the high school grades.

17. A student's level of self-efficacy—how capable one believes one is to perform a particular task—affects motivation by affecting the learning goals that are chosen, the outcome the student expects, and the attributions the student makes for success and failure.

18. Since self-esteem and self-efficacy are most directly affected by performance accomplishments, teachers should arrange instruction to maximize learning for all students.

19. Technology tools such as hypermedia, multimedia, simulations, databases, problem-solving programs, and telecommunications (e-mail, electronic bulletin boards, Web-based conferencing) have been shown to have a beneficial effect on students' motivation to learn because they make learning interesting and meaningful.

KEY TERMS

extrinsic motivation *(373)*
intrinsic motivation *(373)*
attribution theory *(375)*

deficiency needs *(379)*
growth need *(379)*
self-actualization *(379)*

locus of control *(389)*
intelligent agents *(390)*

DISCUSSION QUESTIONS

1. At the beginning of this chapter, we drew a distinction between extrinsic motivation (doing something solely to obtain a reward offered by someone else) and intrinsic motivation (doing something solely because it brings pleasure or satisfaction). What percentage of your behavior do you think stems from intrinsic motivation? From extrinsic motivation? Do you think it is possible to change this ratio? How? Are any of your ideas applicable to the classroom?

2. Maslow states that for individuals to be motivated to satisfy self-actualization needs, deficiency needs have to

be satisfied first. Has this been the case in your own experience? If not, how was it different?

3. Students with a high need to achieve usually attribute success to effort and ability and failure to lack of effort. If you think of yourself as fitting this pattern, how did you get this way? Is there anything from your own experiences that you can use to help students develop this attributional pattern?

12 Classroom Management

By now you have no doubt begun to realize what we pointed out in Chapter 1—teaching is a complex enterprise. It is complex for the following reasons:

- Students vary in their physical, social, emotional, cognitive, and cultural characteristics.
- Learning occurs gradually and only with extensive and varied practice.
- Different students learn at different rates.

- Systematic preparations have to be made to ensure that students master the objectives that teachers lay out.
- Students are motivated to learn (or not learn) by different factors.
- Learning can be measured and evaluated in a variety of ways.

If not managed properly, an endeavor as complex as teaching can easily become chaotic. As a

KEY POINTS

These key points will help you learn the important information in this chapter. To help you study, they also appear in the margins of pages, next to the text where they are discussed.

Authoritarian, Laissez-Faire, and Authoritative Approaches to Classroom Management

- Authoritative approach to classroom management superior to permissive and authoritarian approaches

Preventing Problems: Techniques of Classroom Management

- Ripple effect: group response to a reprimand directed at an individual
- Teachers who show they are "with it" head off discipline problems

- Being able to handle overlapping activities helps maintain classroom control
- Teachers who continually interrupt activities have discipline problems
- Keeping entire class involved and alert minimizes misbehavior
- Identify misbehavers; firmly specify constructive behavior
- Well-managed classroom: students complete clear assignments in busy but pleasant atmosphere
- Effective teachers plan how to handle classroom routines
- During first weeks, have students complete clear assignments under your direction
- Manage behavior of adolescents by making and communicating clear rules and procedures

Suggestions for Teaching in Your Classroom: Techniques of Classroom Management

- Establish, call attention to, and explain class rules the first day
- Establish a businesslike but supportive classroom atmosphere

Techniques for Dealing with Behavior Problems

- Use supportive reactions to help students develop self-control
- Give criticism privately; then offer encouragement
- I-message: tell how you feel about an unacceptable situation
- Determine who owns a problem before deciding on course of action
- No-lose method: come to mutual agreement about a solution to a problem

Suggestions for Teaching in Your Classroom: Handling Problem Behavior

- Be prompt, consistent, reasonable when dealing with misbehavior

Violence in American Schools

- Incidents of crime and serious violence occur relatively infrequently in public schools
- Male aggressiveness due to hormonal and cultural factors
- Middle school and junior high boys with low grades may feel trapped
- Misbehavior of high school students may reveal lack of positive identity
- School violence can be reduced by improving student achievement levels
- Violence less likely when students invited to participate in making decisions

result, students are likely to become confused, bored, uninterested, restless, and perhaps even disruptive. But a well-managed classroom is not what many people think—students working silently at their desks (or in front of their computers), speaking only when spoken to, and providing verbatim recitations of what the teacher and textbook said. Such a classroom is incompatible with the contemporary views of learning and motivation described in Chapters 7–11. If some of your goals are for students to acquire a meaningful knowledge base, to become proficient problem solvers, and to learn how to work productively with others, then you have to accept the idea that these goals are best met in classrooms that are characterized by a fair amount of autonomy, physical movement, and social interaction (McCaslin & Good, 1992).

To help you accomplish these goals *and* keep student behavior within manageable bounds, we describe in this chapter a general approach to classroom management that is related to an effective parenting style, various techniques that you can use to prevent behavior problems from occurring, and a set of techniques for dealing with misbehavior once it has occurred. In addition, we analyze the issue of school violence and summarize various approaches to reducing its frequency. ■

Authoritarian, Laissez-Faire, and Authoritative Approaches to Classroom Management

You may recall from Chapter 3 that Diana Baumrind (1971, 1991) found that parents tended to exhibit one of four styles in managing the behavior of their children: authoritarian, laissez-faire (or permissive), authoritative, or rejecting-neglecting. The first three of these styles have been applied to a teacher's actions in the classroom. We will quickly review Baumrind's categories and then take a brief look at how teachers' approaches to management, too, can be characterized by these styles. Authoritarian parents establish rules for their children's behavior and expect them to be blindly obeyed. Explanations of why a particular rule is necessary are almost never given. Instead, rewards and punishments are given for following or not following rules. Laissez-faire parents represent the other extreme. They impose few controls. They allow their children to make many basic decisions (such as what to eat, what to dress, when to go to bed) and provide advice or assistance only when asked. Authoritative parents provide rules but discuss the reasons for them, teach their children how to meet them, and reward children for exhibiting self-control. Authoritative parents also cede more responsibility for self-governance to their children as the children demonstrate increased self-regulation skills. This style, more so than the other two, leads to internalization of the parents' norms and to maintenance of intrinsic motivation for following them in the future.

You can probably see the parallel between Baumrind's work and classroom management. Teachers who adopt an authoritarian style tend to have student compliance as their main goal ("Do what I say because I say so") and make heavy use of rewards and punishments to produce that compliance. Teachers who adopt a permissive style rely heavily on students identifying with and respecting them as their main approach to classroom management ("Do what I say because you like me and respect my judgment"). Teachers who adopt an authoritative style have as their main goal students who can eventually regulate their own behavior. By explaining the rationale for classroom rules and by adjusting those rules as students demonstrate the ability to appropriately govern themselves, authoritative teachers hope to convince students that adopting the teacher's norms for classroom behavior as their own will lead to the achievement of valued academic goals ("Do what I say because doing so will help you learn more"). The students of authoritative teachers better understand the need for classroom rules and tend to operate within them most of the time (McCaslin & Good, 1992).

> **Authoritative approach to classroom management superior to permissive and authoritarian approaches**

The next part of this chapter will describe guidelines you might follow to establish and maintain an effective learning environment.

Preventing Problems: Techniques of Classroom Management

KOUNIN'S OBSERVATIONS ON GROUP MANAGEMENT

Interest in the significance of classroom management was kindled when Jacob Kounin wrote a book titled *Discipline and Group Management in Classrooms* (1970). Kounin noted that he first became interested in group management when he reprimanded a college student for blatantly reading a newspaper in class. Kounin was struck by the extent to which the entire class responded to a reprimand directed at only one person, and he subsequently dubbed this the **ripple effect**. Chances are you can recall a situation when you were diligently working away in a classroom and the teacher suddenly became quite angry at a disruptive classmate. If you felt a bit tense after the incident (even though your behavior was blameless) and tried to give the impression that you were a paragon of student virtue, you have had personal experience with the ripple effect.

> **Ripple effect: group response to a reprimand directed at an individual**

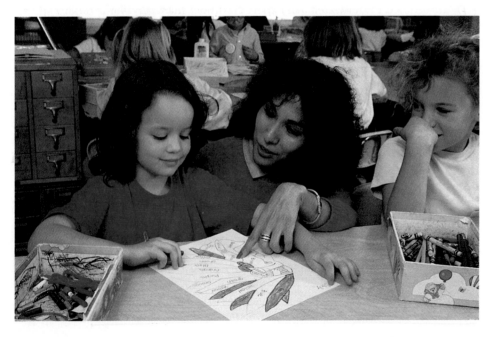

Jacob Kounin found that teachers who were "with it" could deal with overlapping situations, maintained smoothness and momentum in class activities, used a variety of activities, kept the whole class involved, and had few discipline problems.

Once his interest in classroom behavior was aroused, Kounin supervised a series of observational and experimental studies of student reactions to techniques of teacher control. In analyzing the results of these various studies, he came to the conclusion that the following classroom management techniques appear to be most effective.

1. *Show your students that you are "with it."* Kounin coined the term **withitness** to emphasize that teachers who prove to their students that they know what is going on in a classroom usually have fewer behavior problems than teachers who appear to be unaware of incipient disruptions. An expert at classroom management will nip trouble in the bud by commenting on potentially disruptive behavior before it gains momentum. An ineffective teacher may not notice such behavior until it begins to spread and then perhaps hopes that it will simply go away. At first glance Kounin's suggestion that you show that you are with it might seem to be in conflict with operant conditioning's prediction that nonreinforced behavior will disappear. If the teacher's reaction is the only source of reinforcement in a classroom, ignoring behavior may cause it to disappear. In many cases, however, a misbehaving student gets reinforced by the reactions of classmates. Therefore, ignoring behavior is much less likely to lead to extinction of a response in a classroom than in controlled experimental situations.

2. *Learn to cope with overlapping situations.* When he analyzed videotapes of actual classroom interactions, Kounin found that some teachers seemed to have one-track minds. They were inclined to deal with only one thing at a time, and this way of proceeding caused frequent interruptions in classroom routine. One primary grade teacher observed by Kounin, for example, was working with a reading group when she noticed two boys on the other side of the room poking each other. She abruptly got up, walked over to the boys, berated them at length, and then returned to the reading group. By the time she returned, however, the children in the reading group had become bored and listless and were tempted to engage in mischief of their own.

   Kounin concluded that withitness and skill in handling overlapping activities seemed to be related. An expert classroom manager who is talking to children in a reading group, for example, might notice two boys at the far side of the room who are beginning to scuffle with each other. Such a teacher might in midsentence tell the boys to stop and make the point so adroitly that the attention of the children in the reading group does not waver.

3. *Strive to maintain smoothness and momentum in class activities.* This point is related to the previous one. Kounin found that some teachers caused problems for themselves by constantly interrupting activities without thinking about what they were doing. Some teachers whose activities were recorded on videotape failed to maintain the thrust of a lesson because they seemed unaware of the rhythm of student behavior (that is, they did not take into account the degree of student inattention and restlessness but instead moved ahead in an almost mechanical way). Others flip-flopped from one activity to another. Still others would interrupt one activity (for example, a reading lesson) to comment on an unrelated aspect of classroom functioning ("Someone left a lunch bag on the floor"). There were also some who wasted time dwelling on a trivial incident (making a big fuss because a boy lost his pencil). And a few teachers delivered individual, instead of group, instructions ("All right, Charlie, you go to the board. Fine. Now, Rebecca, you go to the board"). All these types of teacher behavior tended to interfere with the flow of learning activities.

4. *Try to keep the whole class involved, even when you are dealing with individual students.* Kounin found that some well-meaning teachers had fallen into a pattern of calling on students in a predictable order and in such a way that the rest of the class served as a passive audience. Unless you stop to think about what you are doing during group recitation periods, you might easily fall into the same trap. If you do, the "audience" is almost certain to become bored and may be tempted to engage in troublemaking activities just to keep occupied. Some teachers, for example, call on students to recite by going around a circle, or going up and down rows, or by following alphabetical order. Others call on a child first and then ask a question. Still others ask one child to recite at length (read an entire page, for example). All these techniques tend to spotlight one child in predictable order and cause the rest of the class members to tune out until their turn comes. You are more likely to maintain interest and limit mischief caused by boredom if you use techniques such as the following:

Journal Entry
Ways to Keep
the Whole Class
Involved

- Ask a question, and after pausing a few seconds to let everyone think about it, pick out someone to answer it. With subsequent questions, call on students in an unpredictable order so that no one knows when he or she will be asked to recite. (If you feel that some students in a class are very apprehensive about being called on, even under relaxing circumstances, you can either ask them extremely easy questions or avoid calling on them at all.)

Keeping entire class involved and alert minimizes misbehavior

- If you single out one child to go to the board to do a problem, ask all other students to do the same problem at their desks, and then choose one or two at random to compare their work with the answers on the board.

- When dealing with lengthy or complex material, call on several students in quick succession (and in unpredictable order) and ask each to handle one section. In a primary grade reading group, for example, have one child read a sentence; then pick someone at the other side of the group to read the next sentence and so on.

- Use props in the form of flashcards, mimeographed sheets, or workbook pages to induce all students to respond to questions simultaneously. Then, ask students to compare answers. (One ingenious elementary school teacher observed by Kounin had each student print the ten digits on cards that could be inserted in a slotted piece of cardboard. She would ask a question such as "How much is 8 and 4?"; she would pause a moment while the students arranged their answers in the slots and then say, "All show!")

5. *Introduce variety, and be enthusiastic, particularly with younger students.* After viewing videotapes of different teachers, Kounin and his associates concluded that some teachers seemed to fall into a deadly routine much more readily than others. They followed the same procedure day after day and responded with the same, almost reflexive comments. At the other end of the scale were teachers who introduced variety, responded with enthusiasm and interest, and moved quickly to new activities when they sensed that students either had mastered or were satiated by a particular lesson. It seems logical to assume that students will be less inclined to sleep, daydream, or engage in disruptive activities if they are exposed to an enthusiastic teacher who varies the pace and type of classroom activities.

6. *Be aware of the ripple effect. When criticizing student behavior, be clear and firm, focus on behavior rather than on personalities, and try to avoid angry outbursts.* If you take into account the suggestions just made, you may be able to reduce the

amount of student misbehavior in your classes. Even so, some behavior problems are certain to occur. When you deal with these, you can benefit from Kounin's research on the ripple effect. On the basis of observations, questionnaires, and experimental evidence, he concluded that "innocent" students in a class are more likely to be positively impressed by the way the teacher handles a misbehavior if the following conditions exist:

Identify misbehavers; firmly specify constructive behavior

- The teacher identifies the misbehaver and states what the unacceptable behavior is. ("Jorge! Don't flip that computer disk at Jamal.")
- The teacher specifies a more constructive behavior. ("Please put the computer disk back in the storage box.")
- The teacher explains why the deviant behavior should cease. ("If the computer disk gets broken or dirty, no one else will be able to use it, and we'll have to try to get a new one.")
- The teacher is firm and authoritative and conveys a no-nonsense attitude. ("All infractions of classroom rules will result in an appropriate punishment—no ifs, ands, or buts.")
- The teacher does not resort to anger, humiliation, or extreme punishment. Kounin concluded that extreme reactions did not seem to make children behave better. Instead, anger and severe reprimands upset them and made them feel tense and nervous. ("Roger, I am deeply disappointed that you used obscene language in your argument with Michael. Such behavior is simply unacceptable in my classroom.")
- The teacher focuses on behavior, not on personality. (Say, "Ramona, staring out the window instead of reading your textbook is unacceptable behavior in my classroom" rather than "Ramona, you're the laziest student I have ever had in class.")

UNIVERSITY OF TEXAS STUDIES OF GROUP MANAGEMENT

Stimulated by Kounin's observations, members of the Research and Development Center for Teacher Education at the University of Texas at Austin instituted a series of studies on classroom management. The basic procedure followed in most studies was to first identify very effective and less effective teachers by using a variety of criteria (often stressing student achievement). Then classroom management techniques used by very effective teachers were analyzed in detail. In some studies (for example, Brophy, 1979; Good, 1982), basic characteristics of well-managed classrooms were described. They can be summarized as follows:

1. Students know what they are expected to do and generally experience the feeling that they are successful doing it.

Well-managed classroom: students complete clear assignments in busy but pleasant atmosphere

2. Students are kept busy engaging in teacher-led instructional activities.
3. There is little wasted time, confusion, or disruption.
4. A no-nonsense, work-oriented tone prevails, but at the same time there is a relaxed and pleasant atmosphere.

These conclusions can be related to information presented in earlier chapters. The first point can be interpreted as supporting the use of instructional objectives that are stated in such a way that students know when they have achieved them. The next three points stress student productivity under teacher guidance and a no-nonsense, work-oriented atmosphere. These outcomes are more likely when teachers use procedures recommended by behavioral and cognitive psychologists.

Another set of studies carried out by the Texas researchers led to two recent books on group management, one for elementary school teachers (Evertson, Emmer, Clements, & Worsham, 1997) and the other for secondary school teachers (Emmer, Evertson, Clements, & Worsham, 1997). You may wish to examine the appropriate book for your grade level (complete titles and names of authors are given in Resources for Further Investigation), but for now we will provide the following summary of basic keys to management success stressed in both volumes.

1. On the first day with a new class, very effective teachers clearly demonstrate that they have thought about classroom procedures ahead of time. They have planned first-day activities that make it possible for classroom routine to be handled with a minimum of confusion. They also make sure students understand why the procedures are necessary and how they are to be followed.

2. A short list of basic classroom rules is posted and/or announced, and students are told about the penalties they will incur in the event of misbehavior.

3. During the first weeks with a new group of students, effective teachers have students engage in whole-group activities under teacher direction. Such activities are selected to make students feel comfortable and successful in their new classroom.

4. After the initial shakedown period is over, effective teachers maintain control by using the sorts of techniques described by Kounin: they show they are with it, cope with overlapping situations, maintain smoothness and momentum, and avoid ignoring the rest of the class when dealing with individual students.

5. Effective teachers give clear directions, hold students accountable for completing assignments, and give frequent feedback.

Effective teachers plan how to handle classroom routines

During first weeks, have students complete clear assignments under your direction

MANAGING THE MIDDLE, JUNIOR HIGH, AND HIGH SCHOOL CLASSROOM

Most of the classroom management techniques and suggestions we have discussed so far are sufficiently general that they can be used in a variety of classroom settings and with primary through secondary grade students. Nevertheless, teaching preadolescents and adolescents is sufficiently different from teaching younger students that the management of the middle school, junior high, and high school classroom requires a slightly different emphasis and a few unique practices.

Classroom management has to be approached somewhat differently in the secondary grades (and in those middle schools that change classes several times a day) because of the segmented nature of education for these grades. Instead of being in charge of the same twenty-five to thirty students all day, most junior high or high school teachers (and some middle school teachers) are responsible for as many as five different groups of twenty-five to thirty students for about fifty minutes each. This arrangement results in a wider range of individual differences, a greater likelihood that these teachers will see a wide range of behavior problems, and a greater concern with efficient use of class time.

Because of the special nature of adolescence, relatively short class times, and consecutive classes with different students, middle school, junior high, and high school teachers must concentrate their efforts on preventing misbehavior. Edmund

Because middle school, junior high, and high school students move from one teacher to another every fifty minutes or so, it is important to establish a common set of rules that govern various activities and procedures and to clearly communicate the reasons for those rules.

Emmer, Carolyn Evertson, Barbara Clements, and Murray Worsham (1997), in *Classroom Management for Secondary Teachers* (4th ed.), discuss how teachers can prevent misbehavior by carefully organizing the classroom environment, establishing clear rules and procedures, and delivering effective instruction.

According to Emmer and his associates, the physical features of the classroom should be arranged to optimize teaching and learning. They suggest an environment in which (1) the arrangement of the seating, materials, and equipment is consistent with the kinds of instructional activities the teacher favors; (2) high traffic areas, such as the teacher's desk and the pencil sharpener, are kept free of congestion; (3) the teacher can easily see all students; (4) frequently used teaching materials and student supplies are readily available; and (5) students can easily see instructional presentations and displays.

In too many instances teachers spend a significant amount of class time dealing with misbehavior, rather than with teaching and learning, either because students are never told what is expected of them or because rules and procedures are not communicated clearly. Accordingly, Emmer et al. suggest that classroom rules be specifically stated, discussed with students on the first day of class, and, for seventh, eighth, and ninth grades, posted in a prominent place. Sophomores, juniors, and seniors should be given a handout on which the rules are listed. Some examples of these basic rules follow:

Bring all needed materials to class.

Be in your seat and ready to work when the bell rings.

Respect and be polite to all people.

Do not talk or leave your desk when someone else is talking.

Respect other people's property.

Obey all school rules.

You may also want to allow some degree of student participation in rule setting. You can ask students to suggest rules, arrange for students to discuss why certain classroom rules are necessary, and perhaps allow students to select a few rules. This last suggestion should be taken up cautiously, however. Because middle school and secondary teachers teach different sets of students, having a different set of rules for each class is bound to cause confusion for you and hard feelings among some students. You may find yourself admonishing a student for breaking a rule that applies to a different class, and some students will naturally want to know why they cannot do something that is allowed in another class.

In addition to rules, various procedures need to be formulated and communicated. Procedures differ from rules in that they apply to a specific activity and are usually directed at completing a task rather than completing a behavior. To produce a well-run classroom, you will need to formulate efficient procedures for beginning-of-the-period tasks (such as taking attendance and allowing students to leave the classroom), use of materials and equipment (such as the encyclopedia, dictionary, and pencil sharpener), learning activities (such as discussions, seatwork, and group work), and end-of-the-period tasks (such as handing in seatwork assignments, returning materials and equipment, and making announcements).

Much of what Jacob Kounin, Carolyn Evertson, and Edmund Emmer mention in relation to the characteristics of effective instruction has been described in earlier chapters. For example, they recommend that short-term (daily, weekly) and long-term (semester, annual) lesson plans be formulated and coordinated, that instructions and standards for assignments be clear and given in a timely manner, that feedback be given at regular intervals, and that the grading system be clear and fairly applied. As the next section illustrates, technology can help you carry out these tasks in a highly efficient and effective manner.

Manage behavior of adolescents by making and communicating clear rules and procedures

TECHNOLOGY TOOLS FOR CLASSROOM MANAGEMENT

A large part of classroom management involves such routine tasks as taking attendance, completing forms, maintaining student records, tracking student progress, and settling disputes. Although effectively carrying out such tasks is part of what makes a classroom well managed, they can be both tedious and time consuming. Fortunately, technology tools now exist to help teachers keep records of student progress, organize teaching notes, create lesson plans and timelines, send individualized notes to students, update attendance records, and generate electronic study guides (Allen, 1996; Dattilo, Stout, & Watrous, 1991). Computer technology can help teachers create test question banks and individual tests (including alternate forms), as well as record, calculate, and graph student grades. Moreover, teachers can employ database, word processing, and spreadsheet files to maintain class rosters, develop seating charts, create professional-looking handouts and worksheets, and note missing student work. Still other classroom management tools can aid teachers in rethinking and redesigning basic classroom layouts and space utilization (Holzberg, 1995).

Teachers can also rely on samples of prior student work posted to a classroom's or school's Website to lessen anxiety or confusion about how an assignment should be carried out. To avoid more significant behavioral problems, teachers might use software packages that teach anger control, conflict resolution, and better peer relationships (Allen, 1996).

In addition to using computer technology to assist in classroom activities and overall organization, teachers can use it to monitor and assess student progress. For instance, through the use of local area networks a teacher can monitor student progress from his or her workstation without interrupting student work. Second, individual keypad systems can immediately and anonymously tally and graph student responses to teacher or class questions (Fischer, 1996). Third, in "smart lectern" systems, a teacher can remotely control technology presentation equipment, thereby allowing him or her additional mobility within the classroom in order to check on student work.

CENTRALIZED INFORMATION SYSTEMS   The tools mentioned so far are designed for a single teacher's use in a single classroom. Centralized student information systems are designed to be used by all teachers in a school (O'Lone, 1997). With such systems, teachers can take attendance for their own records and have that information simultaneously transferred to a central administration computing system. In return, teachers have automatic access to this information as well as that related to student special needs, test results, and pertinent family data. Centralized information systems allow teachers and administrators to more efficiently access records of infractions and action taken, and any notes, photos, or other information that might aid them with difficult decisions regarding student behavioral problems (O'Lone, 1997).

INTEGRATED LEARNING SYSTEMS   As mentioned in Chapter 7, an integrated learning system (ILS) adjusts the difficulty of the instructional activity according to student ability level, while offering teachers a great deal of detail about student academic progress and performance. Developers of these systems also claim that they individualize instruction, continually monitor student activities, provide useful instructional feedback, accurately summarize student performance, and accelerate student learning.

Lani Van Dusen and Blaine Worthen (1995) found that integrated learning systems increase student engaged time by nearly 20 percent over traditional forms of instruction and have the potential to allow teachers to create user friendly and informative reports as well as reduce the need for teacher-scored assignments. However, most teachers do not use ILS reports. In addition, they lack training in selecting and scheduling valuable learning events and integrating ILS activities across subject matter domains (Jones, 1994). Teachers also lack sufficient training to help students interpret computer feedback and progress reports. Not surprisingly, then, many teachers view integrated learning systems as a supplemental resource, not as an essential part of the curriculum. Thomas Callister and Faith Dunne (1992) further warn that such systems can effectively shift instructional decision making from the instructor to the developers of the system, thereby lowering the status of teachers from instructional experts to managers of a fairly rigid system. Instead of allowing technology to disempower teachers, however, Van Dusen and Worthen (1995) argue that teachers need to think about how ILS technology, or any technology for that matter, fits into their plans for student instruction and assessment and how it might help them shift their role from dispenser of information to student coach or learning guide.

NEW CLASSROOM ROLES FOR TEACHERS   Technology-intensive environments offer a chance to rethink the teaching and learning process from a student viewpoint. A recent conference among the top twenty-five educational technology innovators in K–12 education found general agreement among participants that technology will drastically change the classroom management and instructional role of teachers (Eakin, 1997). When students are more engaged, active, and responsible for their own learning, teachers in technology-intensive environments can begin to assume the roles of facilitator and consultant.

What happens to the classroom management duties of teachers when schools adopt technology? Carolyn Keeler's (1996) study of thirteen elementary classrooms engaged in a school-wide computer implementation project revealed that students were more on-task, self-managed, and engaged than before. As technology tools provided greater insight into student thought processes, the teachers, in turn, became more interested in individual students and their progress. Given the perceived improvements in student motivation and behavior as well as increases in student responsibility for their own learning, these teachers stated that they would most likely not return to the instructional techniques that they used prior to project implementation. In effect, technology significantly changed the teaching/learning environment of this school.

John Mergendoller (1996) argues that although many technology tools and ideas simplify everyday tasks, they also create new and more difficult managerial and instructional roles for teachers. According to him, "American teachers will need to become experts in the management of complex classroom social interactions and the scaffolding of individual student learning" (p. 45). Clearly, as schools combine various technology tools and systems, your classroom management procedures and disciplinary decisions will no doubt be highly complex, yet, at the same time, vitally important to student success.

The following Suggestions for Teaching will help you become an effective manager of student behavior in the classroom.

SUGGESTIONS FOR TEACHING IN YOUR CLASSROOM

Techniques of Classroom Management

1 Show you are confident and prepared the first day of class.

2 Think ahead about how you plan to handle classroom routine and explain basic procedures the first few minutes of the first day.

3 Establish class rules, call attention to them, and explain why they are necessary.

4 Begin class work the first day with an instructional activity that is clearly stated and can be completed quickly and successfully.

5 During the first weeks with a new group of students, have them spend most of their time engaging in whole-class activities under your direction.

6 Give clear instructions, hold students accountable for carrying them out, and provide frequent feedback.

7 Continually demonstrate that you are competent, well prepared, and in charge.

8 Be professional but pleasant and try to establish a businesslike but supportive classroom atmosphere.

1 Show you are confident and prepared the first day of class.

The first few minutes with any class are often crucial. Your students will be sizing you up, especially if they know you are a new teacher. If you act scared and unsure of yourself, you will probably be in for trouble. Even after years of experience, you may find that confronting a roomful of strange students for the first time is a bit intimidating. You will be the center of attention and may feel the equivalent of stage fright. To switch the focus of attention and to begin identifying your students as individuals rather than as a threatening audience, you might consider using this strategy. Hand out 4-by-6-inch cards as soon as everyone is seated and ask your students to write down their full names, the names they prefer to be called, what their hobbies and favorite activities are, and a description of the most interesting experience they have ever had. (For primary grade students who are unable to write, substitute brief oral introductions.)

1st day activity

As they write, you will be in a position to make a leisurely scrutiny of your students as individuals. Recognizing that you are dealing with individuals should reduce the tendency to feel threatened by a group. Perhaps you have read about singers who pick out a single, sympathetic member of the audience and sing directly to her. The sea of faces as a whole is frightening. The face of the individual is not. Even if you are not bothered by being the center of attention, you might still consider using this card technique to obtain information that you can use to learn names rapidly and to individualize instruction. Whatever you do during the first few minutes, it is important to give the impression that you know exactly what you are doing. The best way to pull that off is to be thoroughly prepared.

Journal Entry
Planning How to
Handle Routines

2 Think ahead about how you plan to handle classroom routine and explain basic procedures the first few minutes of the first day.

The Texas researchers found that very effective teachers demonstrated from the first moment with a new group of students that they knew how to handle the details of their job. They also conveyed the impression that they expected cooperation. To demonstrate that you are a confident, competent instructor, you should plan exactly how you will handle classroom routines. You will pick up at least some ideas about the details of classroom management during student-teaching experiences, but it might be worth asking a friendly experienced teacher in your school for advice about tried-and-true procedures that have worked in that particular school. (You might also read one of the books on classroom management recommended at the end of this chapter.)

Try to anticipate how you will handle such details as taking attendance, assigning desks, handing out books and materials, permitting students to go to the restroom during class, and so forth. If you don't plan ahead, you will have to come up with an improvised policy on the spur of the moment, and that policy might turn out to be highly inefficient or in conflict with school regulations.

3 Establish class rules, call attention to them, and explain why they are necessary.

Establish, call attention to, and explain class rules the first day

Very effective teachers observed by the Texas researchers demonstrated an authoritative approach to classroom management by explaining class rules the first day of school. Some teachers list standard procedures on a chart or bulletin board; others simply state them the first day of class. Either technique saves time and trouble later because all you have to do is refer to the rule when a transgression occurs. The alternative to this approach is to interrupt the lesson and disturb the whole class while you make a hurried, unplanned effort to deal with a surprise attack. Your spur-of-the-moment reaction may turn out to be clumsy and ineffective.

When you introduce rules the first day, take a positive, nonthreatening approach. If you spit rules out as if they were a series of ultimatums, students may feel

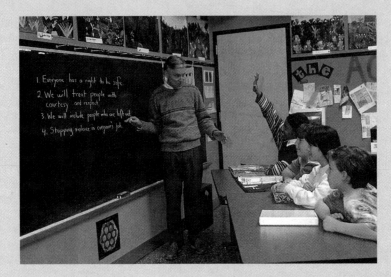

Research has shown that effective teachers call attention to and explain class rules on the first day of class.

you have a chip on your shoulder, which the unwritten code of the classroom obligates them to try knocking off. One way to demonstrate your good faith is to invite the class to suggest necessary regulations and explain why they should be established. Whatever your approach, encourage understanding of the reasons for the rules. You can make regulations seem desirable, rather than restrictive, if you discuss why they are needed. Reasonable rules are much more likely to be remembered and honored than pronouncements that seem to be the whims of a tyrant.

EXAMPLES

- "During class discussion, please don't speak out unless you raise your hand and are recognized. I want to be able to hear what each person has to say, and I won't be able to do that if more than one person is talking."

- "During work periods, I don't mind if you talk a bit to your neighbors. But if you do it too much and disturb others, I'll have to ask you to stop."

- "If you come in late, go to your desk by walking along the side and back of the room. It's disturbing—and not very polite—to walk between people who are interacting with each other."

4 Begin class work the first day with an instructional activity that is clearly stated and can be completed quickly and successfully.

When selecting the very first assignment to give to a new class, refer to the suggestions for preparing instructional objectives proposed by Robert Mager and Norman Gronlund (Chapter 10) and arrange a short assignment that can be successfully completed before the end of the period. Clearly specify what is to be done, and perhaps state the conditions and criteria for determining successful completion. In addition, mention an activity (such as examining the assigned text) that students should engage in after they have completed the assignment. In the elementary grades, you might give a short assignment that helps students review material covered in the preceding grade. At the secondary level, pick out an initial assignment that is short, interesting, and does not depend on technical knowledge.

EXAMPLES

- "Your teacher from last year told me that most of you were able to spell all of the words on the list I am going to read. Let's see if you can still spell those words. If you have trouble with certain ones, we can work together to come up with reminders that will help you remember the correct spelling."

- ■ "The first chapter in our natural science text for this fall is about birds. I want you to read the first ten pages, make a list of five types of birds that are described, and prepare your own set of notes about how to recognize them. At 10:30 I am going to hold up pictures of ten birds, and I want you to see if you can correctly identify at least five of them."

- ■ In a high school history class, ask students to write a brief description of a movie they have seen that depicted historical events. Then ask them to indicate whether they felt the film interpretation was accurate.

5 During the first weeks with a new group of students, have them spend most of their time engaging in whole-class activities under your direction.

The very effective teachers observed by the Texas researchers followed the strategy just described, which makes sense when you stop to think about it. You can't expect students to adjust to the routine of a new teacher and classroom in just a few days. Accordingly, it would be wise to make sure students have settled down before asking them to engage in relatively unstructured activities like discovery learning. Furthermore, group discussions or cooperative-learning arrangements usually work out more successfully when the participants have a degree of familiarity with one another and a particular set of background factors (such as a chapter in a text). Thus, as you plan activities during the first weeks with a new class, prepare instructional objectives that ask students to complete assignments under your direction. Postpone using the techniques just mentioned until later in the report period.

6 Give clear instructions, hold students accountable for carrying them out, and provide frequent feedback.

All three of these goals can be achieved by making systematic use of instructional objectives as described in Chapter 10 and by putting into practice the model of instruction described throughout this book.

7 Continually demonstrate that you are competent, well prepared, and in charge.

As students work at achieving instructional objectives, participate in group discussions, or engage in any other kind of learning activity, show them that you are a competent classroom manager. Arrange periods so that there will be a well-organized transition from one activity to the next, maintain smoothness and momentum, and don't waste time. Use a variety of teaching approaches so that you please some of your students some of the time, and use techniques recommended by behavioral, cognitive, and humanistic psychologists. Show you are with it by being alert for signs of mischief or disruptive behavior, and handle such incidents quickly and confidently by using the techniques described later in this chapter and in Chapter 15.

8 Be professional but pleasant and try to establish a businesslike but supportive classroom atmosphere.

If you establish classroom routines in a competent fashion and keep your students busy working to achieve clearly stated instructional objectives, you should be able to establish a no-nonsense, productive atmosphere. At the same time, you should strive to make your room an inviting and pleasant place to be. Keep in mind the points made in Chapters 3 and 11 regarding the importance of self-esteem, self-efficacy, and interpersonal relationships. Put yourself in the place of students thrust into a strange classroom with an unfamiliar instructor. Try to identify with your students so that you can appreciate how they feel if they do or say something embarrassing or have difficulty with class work.

Establish a businesslike but supportive classroom atmosphere

One of the best ways to get students to respond positively to you and make them feel welcome in your classroom is to learn their names as quickly as possible (even if you have five sections of secondary school students to teach). To accomplish this feat, refer to the cards mentioned in point 1. Use the information that students have provided, perhaps supplemented by your own notes or sketches about distinctive physical and facial features, to establish associations between names and faces. Before and after every class period the first few days, flip through your pile of cards, try to picture the appearance of the students, and practice using their names. Refer to the description of mnemonic devices in Chapter 8. Once you have learned a student's name, use it as often as possible to maintain the memory trace. Greet students by name as they come in the door, use their names when asking them to recite or carry out some task, and speak to them personally when you hand back assignments.

Another way to make students feel at home in your classroom is to try establishing a feeling of class spirit. One way to do this is to have a brief *sharing* period—similar to the sharing time you may remember from your kindergarten days—at the beginning of each period. Invite students to describe recent interesting experiences they have had or to give announcements about extracurricular activities. If a member of the class is injured in an accident or suffers a lengthy illness, buy a get-well card and have every member of the class sign it before sending it off.

Techniques for Dealing with Behavior Problems

If you follow the procedures just discussed, you should be able to establish a well-managed classroom. As noted at the beginning of this chapter, however, you are likely to encounter occasional incidents of misbehavior. Even if you do everything possible to prevent problems from developing, you are still likely to have to deal with disruptive behavior. Therefore, techniques for handling disruptive behavior, the extent of disciplinary problems, and some of the factors that lead to misbehavior are topics that merit attention.

INFLUENCE TECHNIQUES

In *Mental Hygiene in Teaching* (1959), Fritz Redl and William Wattenberg describe a list of behavior management interventions called *influence techniques*. This list was modified by James Walker and Thomas Shea in *Behavior Management: A Practical Approach for Educators* (1999). In the following sections and subsections, based on the ideas of both sets of individuals, we will offer specific examples roughly reflecting a least-direct to most-direct ordering. Some of these examples are based on ideas noted by Redl and Wattenberg; some are based on the ideas of Walker and Shea; some are the results of reports by students and teachers; some are based on personal

Signals such as staring at a misbehaving student or putting a finger to one's lips are examples of the influence techniques suggested by Redl and Wattenberg.

Journal Entry
Signals to Use
to Nip Trouble in
the Bud

Use supportive reactions to help students develop self-control

experience. You might use the Journal Entries to pick out or devise techniques that seem most appropriate for your grade level or that you feel comfortable about.

The value of these techniques is that they appeal to self-control and imply trust and confidence on the part of the teacher. However, they may become ineffective if used too often, and that is why so many different techniques will be described. The larger your repertoire is, the less frequently you will have to repeat your various gambits and ploys.

PLANNED IGNORING   As we pointed out in Chapter 7, you might be able to extinguish inappropriate attention-seeking behaviors by merely ignoring them. Such behaviors include finger snapping, body movements, book dropping, hand waving, and whistling. If you plan to use this technique, make sure the student is aware that he is engaging in the behavior and that the behavior does not interfere with the efforts of other students.

EXAMPLE

- Carl has recently gotten into the habit of tapping his pencil on his desk as he works on an assignment as a way to engage you in a conversation that is unrelated to the work. The next several times Carl does this, do not look at him or comment on his behavior.

SIGNALS   In some cases a subtle signal can put an end to budding misbehavior. The signal, if successful, will stimulate the student to control herself. (Note, however, that this technique should not be used too often and that it is effective only in the early stages of misbehavior.)

EXAMPLES

- Clear your throat.
- Stare at the offender.
- Stop what you are saying in midsentence and stare.
- Shake your head (to indicate no).
- Say, "Someone is making it hard for the rest of us to concentrate" (or the equivalent).

PROXIMITY AND TOUCH CONTROL   Place yourself close to the misbehaving student. This makes a signal a bit more apparent.

EXAMPLES

- Walk over and stand near the student.
- With an elementary grade student, it sometimes helps if you place a gentle hand on a shoulder or arm.

INTEREST BOOSTING   Convey interest in the misbehavior. This relates the signal to schoolwork.

EXAMPLES

- Ask the student a question, preferably related to what is being discussed. (Questions such as "Ariel, are you paying attention?" or "Don't you agree, Ariel?" invite wisecracks. *Genuine* questions are to be preferred.) Go over and examine some work the student is doing. It often helps if you point out something good about it and urge continued effort.

HUMOR   Humor is an excellent, all-around influence technique, especially in tense situations. However, remember that it should be *good*-humored humor—gentle and benign rather than derisive. Avoid irony and sarcasm.

EXAMPLES

- "Shawn, for goodness sake, let that poor pencil sharpener alone. I heard it groan when you used it just now."

Perhaps you have heard someone say, "We're not laughing at you; we're laughing *with* you." Before you say this to one of your students, you might take note that one second grader who was treated to that comment unhinged the teacher by replying, "I'm not laughing."

HELPING OVER HURDLES   Some misbehavior undoubtedly occurs because students do not understand what they are to do or lack the ability to carry out an assignment.

EXAMPLES

- Try to make sure your students know what they are supposed to do.
- Arrange for students to have something to do at appropriate levels of difficulty.
- Have a variety of activities available.

PROGRAM RESTRUCTURING   In Chapter 1 we noted that teaching is an art because lessons do not always proceed as planned and must occasionally be changed in midstream. The essence of this technique is to recognize when a lesson or activity is going poorly and to try something else.

> **Journal Entry**
> Using Alternative
> Activities to Keep
> Students On-Task

EXAMPLES

- "Well, class, I can see that many of you are bored with this discussion of the pros and cons of congressional term limits. Let's turn it into a class debate instead, with the winning team getting 50 points toward its final grade."
- "I had hoped to complete this math unit before the Christmas break, but I can see that most of you are too excited to give it your best effort. Since today is the last day before the break, I'll postpone the lesson until school resumes in January. Let's do an art project instead."

ANTISEPTIC BOUNCING   Sometimes a student will get carried away by restlessness, uncontrollable giggling, or the like. If you feel that this is nonmalicious behavior and due simply to lack of self-control, ask the student to leave the room. (You may have recognized that antiseptic bouncing is virtually identical to the *time-out* procedure described by behavior modification enthusiasts.)

EXAMPLES

- "Nancy, please go down to the principal's office and sit on that bench outside the door until you feel you have yourself under control."
- Some high schools have "quiet rooms"—supervised study halls that take extra students any time during a period, no questions asked.

PHYSICAL RESTRAINT   Students who lose control of themselves to the point of endangering other members of the class may have to be physically restrained. However, such restraint should be protective, not punitive, that is, don't shake or hit. This technique is most effective with younger children; such control is usually not appropriate at the secondary level.

EXAMPLE

- If a boy completely loses his temper and starts to hit another child, lead him gently but firmly away from the other students, or sit him in a chair, and keep a restraining hand on his shoulder.

DIRECT APPEALS   When appropriate, point out the connection between conduct and its consequences. This technique is most effective if done concisely and infrequently.

EXAMPLES

- "We have a rule that there is to be no running in the halls. Scott forgot the rule, and now he's down in the nurse's office having his bloody nose taken care of. It's too bad Mr. Harris opened his door just as Scott went by. If Scott had been walking, he would have been able to stop in time."

- "If everyone would stop shouting, we'd be able to get this finished and go out to recess."

CRITICISM AND ENCOURAGEMENT   On those occasions when it is necessary to criticize a particular student, do so in private if possible. When public criticism is the only possibility, do your best to avoid ridiculing or humiliating the student. Public humiliation may cause the child to resent you or hate school, to counterattack, or to withdraw. Because of the ripple effect, it may also have a negative impact on innocent students (although nonhumiliating public criticism has the advantage of setting an example for other students). One way to minimize the negative after-effects of criticism is to tack on some encouragement in the form of a suggestion as to how the backsliding can be replaced by more positive behavior.

Give criticism privately; then offer encouragement

EXAMPLES

- If a student doesn't take subtle hints (such as stares), you might say, "Levar, you're disturbing the class. We all need to concentrate on this." It sometimes adds punch if you make this remark while you are writing on the board or helping some other student.

- Act completely flabbergasted, as though the misbehavior seems so inappropriate that you can't comprehend it. A kindergarten teacher used this technique to perfection. She would say, "Adam! Is that you?" (Adam has been belting Lucy with a shovel.) "I can't believe my eyes. I wonder if you would help me over here." Obviously, this gambit can't be used too often, and the language and degree of exaggeration have to be altered a bit for older students. But indicating that you *expect* good behavior and providing an immediate opportunity for the backslider to substitute good deeds can be very effective.

DEFINING LIMITS   In learning about rules and regulations, children go through a process of testing the limits. Two-year-olds particularly, when they have learned how to walk and talk and manipulate things, feel the urge to assert their independence. In addition, they need to find out exactly what the house rules are. (Does Mommy *really* mean it when she says, "Don't take the pots out of the cupboard"? Does Daddy *really* mean it when he says, "Don't play with that hammer"?) Older children do the same thing, especially with new teachers and in new situations. The technique of defining limits includes not only establishing rules (as noted earlier) but also enforcing them.

EXAMPLES

- Establish class rules, with or without the assistance of students, and make sure they are understood.

- When someone tests the rules, show that they are genuine and that there *are* limits.

POSTSITUATIONAL FOLLOW-UP   Classroom discipline occasionally has to be applied in a tense, emotion-packed atmosphere. When this happens, it often helps to have a postsituational discussion—in private if an individual is involved, with the whole class if it was a groupwide situation.

EXAMPLES

- In a private conference: "Leila, I'm sorry I had to ask you to leave the room, but you were getting kind of carried away."

- "Well, everybody, things got a bit wild during those group work sessions. I want you to enjoy yourselves, but we practically had a riot going, didn't we? And that's why I had to ask you to stop. Let's try to hold it down to a dull roar tomorrow."

MARGINAL USE OF INTERPRETATION   Analysis of behavior can sometimes be made *while* it is occurring rather than afterward. The purpose here is to help students become aware of potential trouble and make efforts to control it.

EXAMPLE

- To a restless and cranky prelunch class, you might say, "I know that you're getting hungry and that you're restless and tired, but let's give it all we've got for ten minutes more. I'll give you the last five minutes for some free visiting time."

I-MESSAGES

In *Teacher and Child*, Haim Ginott offers a cardinal principle of communication: "Talk to the situation, not to the personality and character" (1972, p. 84). Instead of making derogatory remarks about the personalities of two boys who have just thrown bread at each other, Ginott suggests that as a teacher you deliver an **I-message** explaining how you feel. Don't say, "You are a couple of pigs"; say, "I get angry when I see bread thrown around. This room needs cleaning." According to Ginott, guilty students who are told why a teacher is angry will realize the teacher is a real person, and this realization will cause them to strive to mend their ways. Ginott offers several examples of the cardinal principle of communication in Chapter 4 of *Teacher and Child*. And in Chapter 6 he offers some observations on discipline. Seek alternatives to punishment. Try not to diminish a misbehaving student's self-esteem. Try to provide face-saving exits.

Journal Entry
Using I-Messages

I-message: tell how you feel about an unacceptable situation

PROBLEM OWNERSHIP

In *TET: Teacher Effectiveness Training* (1974), Thomas Gordon suggests that teachers try to determine who *owns* a problem before they decide how to handle that problem. If a student's misbehavior (such as disrupting the smooth flow of instruction with inappropriate comments or joking remarks) results in the teacher feeling annoyed, frustrated, or angry at not being able to complete a planned lesson, the teacher owns the problem and must respond by doing something to stop the disruptive behavior. But if a student expresses anger or disappointment about some classroom incident (getting a low grade on an exam), that student owns the problem.

Gordon suggests that failure to identify problem ownership may cause teachers to intensify difficulties unwittingly, even as they make well-intended efforts to diminish them. If a student is finding it difficult to concentrate on schoolwork because her needs are not satisfied, the situation will not be ameliorated if the teacher orders, moralizes, or criticizes. According to Gordon, such responses act as roadblocks to finding solutions to student-owned problems because they tend to make the student feel resentful and misunderstood.

The preferred way to deal with a student who owns a problem is to use what Gordon calls **active listening**. The listener is *active* in the sense that interest is shown

Journal Entry
Speculating about Problem Ownership

Determine who owns a problem before deciding on course of action

and the talker is encouraged to continue expressing feelings; the listener does *not* actively participate by interpreting, explaining, or directing. The listener *does* respond, however, by recognizing and acknowledging what the student says.

For teacher-owned problems—those that involve misbehavior that is destructive or in violation of school regulations—Gordon agrees with Ginott that I-messages are appropriate. Instead of ordering, threatening, moralizing, using logic, offering solutions, or commenting on personal characteristics, teachers should explain why they are upset. Proof of the effectiveness of I-messages takes the form of anecdotes reported in *TET* and provided by teachers who used the technique successfully. A principal of a continuation school for dropouts, for example, reported that a group of tough boys responded very favorably when he told them how upset he became when he saw them break some bottles against the school wall.

Almost invariably the anecdotes reported in *TET* refer to the success of a teacher's first try at delivering an I-message. It seems likely that at least part of the technique's success the first time it is used could be attributed to surprise or novelty. But it is also possible that extensive use of the technique might stir up, rather than calm down, troublemakers. Instead of saying, "Gee! We never realized you felt that way!" they might say, "We're getting awfully tired of hearing about your troubles!"

No-Lose Method

Journal Entry
Trying the No-Lose Method

Thomas Gordon (1974) also urges teachers to try resolving conflicts in the classroom by using the **no-lose method**. If either person in a conflict loses, there is bound to be resentment. If you tell a girl who is fooling around during a work period that she must settle down or stay after school, *she* loses. If you make a halfhearted and unsuccessful effort to control her and then try to cover up your failure by ignoring her and working with others, *you* lose. In Gordon's method, the preferred procedure is to talk over the problem and come up with a mutually agreeable compromise solution. He offers this six-step procedure for coming up with no-lose solutions, a procedure that is similar to the one we described in Chapter 9:

No-lose method: come to mutual agreement about a solution to a problem

1. Define the problem.
2. Generate possible solutions.
3. Evaluate the solutions.
4. Decide which solution is best.
5. Determine how to implement the solution.
6. Assess how well the solution solved the problem. (1974, p. 228)

To put this procedure into practice with an individual, you might approach a boy who is disruptive during a work period and engage in a dialogue something like this:

You: You're making such a ruckus over here by talking loudly and shoving others that I can't hear the group I'm working with.

Student: I think this workbook junk is stupid. I already know how to do these problems. I'd rather work on my science project.

You: Well, suppose we try this. You do one page of problems. If you get them all correct, we'll both know you can do them, and you should be free to work on your science project. If you make some mistakes, that means you need more practice. Suppose you do a page and then ask me to check it. Then we can take it from there. How does that sound?

Some general guidelines you might consider when you find it necessary to resort to disciplinary techniques appear in Suggestions for Teaching in Your Classroom.

SUGGESTIONS FOR TEACHING IN YOUR CLASSROOM

Handling Problem Behavior

1 Have a variety of influence techniques planned in advance.

2 Be prompt, consistent, and reasonable.

3 Avoid threats.

4 Whenever you have to deal harshly with a student, make an effort to reestablish rapport.

5 When you have control, ease up some.

1 Have a variety of influence techniques planned in advance.

You may save yourself a great deal of trouble, embarrassment, and strain if you plan ahead. When first-year teachers are asked which aspects of teaching bother them most, classroom control is almost invariably near the top of the list. Perhaps a major reason is that problems of control frequently erupt unexpectedly, and they often demand equally sudden solutions. If you lack experience, your shoot-from-the-hip reactions may be ineffective. Initial attempts at control that are ineffective tend to reinforce misbehavior, and you will find yourself trapped in a vicious circle. Yet this sort of trap can be avoided if specific techniques are devised ahead of time. Being familiar with several of the techniques mentioned in the preceding section will prepare you for the inevitable difficulties that arise.

However, if you find yourself forced to use prepared techniques too often, some self-analysis is called for. How can you prevent so many problems from developing? Frequent trouble is an indication that you need to work harder at motivating your class. Also, check on your feelings when you mete out punishment. Teachers who really like students and want them to learn consider control techniques a necessary evil and use them only when they will provide a better atmosphere for learning. If you find yourself looking for trouble or perhaps deliberately luring students into misbehaving, or if you discover yourself gloating privately or publicly about an act of punishment, stop and think. Are you using your power to build up your ego or giving vent to personal frustration rather than paying attention to your students' needs?

2 Be prompt, consistent, and reasonable.

No attempt to control behavior will be effective if it is remote from the act that provokes it. If a troublemaker is to comprehend the relationship between behavior and counterreaction, one must quickly follow the other. Don't postpone dealing with misbehaving students or make vague threats to be put into effect sometime in the future (such as not permitting the students to attend an end-of-the-year event). By that time, most students will have forgotten what they did wrong. They then feel resentful and persecuted and may conclude that you are acting out of sheer malice. A frequent reaction is more misbehavior in an urge to get even. (In such situations guilty students

Journal Entry
Being Prompt, Consistent, and Reasonable in Controlling the Class

are not likely to remember that you are the one doing the evening up.) However, retribution that is too immediate, that is applied when a student is still extremely upset, may also be ineffective. At such times it is often better to wait a bit.

Being consistent about classroom control can save a lot of time, energy, and misery. Strictness one day and leniency the next, or roughness on one student and gentleness with another, invite all students to test you every day just to see whether this is a good day or a bad day or whether they can get away with something more frequently than others do. Establishing and enforcing class rules are an excellent way to encourage yourself to be consistent.

Be prompt, consistent, reasonable when dealing with misbehavior

Harshness in meting out retribution encourages, rather than discourages, more extreme forms of misbehavior. If students are going to get into a lot of trouble for even a minor offense, they will probably figure they should get their money's worth. Several hundred years ago in England all offenses—from picking pockets to murder—were punishable by death. The petty thief quickly became a murderer; it was a lot easier (and less risky) to pick the pocket of a dead man and, since the punishment was the same, eminently more sensible. The laws were eventually changed to make punishment appropriate to the degree of the offense. Keep this in mind when you dispense justice.

3 Avoid threats.

If at all possible, avoid a showdown in front of the class. In a confrontation before the whole group, you are likely to get desperate. You may start out with a "Yes, you will," "No, I won't" sort of duel and end up making a threat on the spur of the moment. Frequently, you will not be able to make good on the threat, and you will lose face. It's far safer and better for everyone to settle extreme differences in private. When two people are upset and angry with each other, they look silly at best and completely ridiculous at worst. You lose a great deal more than a student does when this performance takes place in front of the class. In fact, a student may actually gain prestige by provoking you successfully.

Perhaps the worst temptation of all is to try getting back at the entire class by making a blanket threat of a loss of privilege or detention. It hardly ever works and tends to lead to a united counterattack by the class. One elementary school teacher had the reputation of telling her students at least once a year that they would not be allowed to participate in the Spring Play-Day if they didn't behave. By the time students reached this grade, they had been tipped off by previous students that she always made the threat but never carried it out. They behaved accordingly.

Journal Entry
Ways to Reestablish Rapport

4 Whenever you have to deal harshly with a student, make an effort to reestablish rapport.

If you must use a drastic form of retribution, make a point of having a confidential conference with your antagonist as soon as possible. Otherwise, she is likely to remain an antagonist for the rest of the year. It's too much to expect chastised students to come to you of their own volition and apologize. You should set up the conference and then explain that the punishment has cleared the air as far as you are concerned. You shouldn't be surprised if a recalcitrant student doesn't respond with signs or words of gratitude. Perhaps some of the causes of misbehavior lie outside of school, and something you did or said may have been merely the last straw. Even if you get a sullen reaction, at least indicate your willingness to meet punished students more than halfway.

At the elementary level, you can frequently make amends simply by giving the child some privilege—for example, passing out paper or being hall monitor at recess. One teacher made it a point to praise a child for some positive action shortly after a severe reprimand.

5 **When you have control, ease up some.**

It is extremely difficult, if not impossible, to establish a controlled atmosphere after allowing anarchy. Don't make the mistake of thinking you will be able to start out without any control and suddenly take charge. It may work, but in most cases you will have an armed truce or a cold war on your hands. It is far better to adopt the authoritative approach of starting out on the structured side and then easing up a bit after you have established control.

Violence in American Schools

HOW SAFE ARE OUR SCHOOLS?

You have probably read or heard reports about the frequency of crime in the United States, particularly among juveniles. One recent report noted that of all persons arrested for serious crimes, 43 percent were between the ages of seven and eighteen, despite the fact that this age group accounts for only 20 percent of the population. The peak age for committing crime among this group is fourteen (Wiles & Bondi, 1993). Since the kinds of behaviors one observes in schools tend to reflect trends in society at large, it is natural that a certain amount of violent behavior occurs on school grounds and during school hours. However, schools are still relatively safe places. One basis for that claim is that the most common types of school-based conflicts fall into a few time-honored categories: verbal harassment (name calling, insults, teasing), verbal arguments, and physical fights (hitting, kicking, scratching, and pushing). Most of the fights do not involve serious injury or violations of law (Johnson & Johnson, 1996). Second, a national survey of over 1,200 U.S. public schools conducted during the 1996–1997 school year found relatively low levels of violence and crime (Heaviside, Rowand, Williams, & Farris, 1998). In question-and-answer form, here are the main findings from that survey.

- Do criminal incidents occur in most schools? Yes, but not very frequently. Thirty-seven percent of schools reported five or fewer crimes while an additional 20 percent reported six or more crimes for the 1996–1997 school year.

Incidents of crime and serious violence occur relatively infrequently in public schools

- Is it accurate to say that acts of crime and violence have reached epidemic proportions in U.S. schools? No. Forty-three percent of public schools reported no incidents of crime and, as just indicated, an additional 37 percent reported five or fewer crimes. Only 10 percent of all public schools reported one or more incidents of serious violent crime (murder, rape, suicide, robbery, a physical attack or fight involving a weapon).

- Are some schools more likely to experience crime and violence than other schools? Yes. Violence is more likely to occur in middle schools and high schools than in elementary schools.
- Are schools addressing the problem of crime and violence? Yes. Eighty-four percent of schools restrict access to their buildings, 11 percent have either a security guard or metal detectors plus restricted access, and 2 percent have a full-time guard and metal detector checkpoints. Only 3 percent reported using no security measures. In terms of prevention, 78 percent of schools reported having a violence prevention or reduction program.

These findings suggest that most teachers and students are likely to be physically safe in their own classrooms and school buildings. Nevertheless, school violence can occur in any school and at any time. Accordingly, you should be aware of the various explanations of school violence and the steps that can be taken to reduce its frequency.

ANALYZING REASONS FOR VIOLENCE

PHYSIOLOGICAL FACTORS   The research just cited noted that the level of violence was highest in secondary schools with a high proportion of male students. One of the clear-cut gender differences that has been repeatedly supported by consistent evidence (reviewed by Parke & Slaby, 1983) is that males are more aggressive than females. Although the cause of this difference cannot be traced precisely, it is likely due to hormonal as well as cultural factors. *Hormone* in the Greek means "to arouse" or "to urge on," which reflects the fact that these substances are released in the bloodstream and arouse reactions in various parts of the body. The male sex hormone androgen arouses high energy and activity levels. Moreover, because of long-established cultural expectancies, males in our society are encouraged to assert themselves in physical ways. As a result, tendencies toward high energy and activity levels aroused by male sex hormones may be expressed in the form of aggressiveness against others.

Male aggressiveness due to hormonal and cultural factors

GENDER-RELATED CULTURAL FACTORS   As noted in the discussion of age-level characteristics in Chapter 3, there is also evidence that young girls in our society are encouraged to be dependent and to be eager to please adults, while young boys are encouraged to assert their independence (Block, 1973; Fagot, 1978). Furthermore, it appears that boys are more likely than girls to be reinforced for assertive and illegal forms of behavior. Martin Gold and Richard Petronio (1980, p. 524) speculate that delinquency in our society seems to have a masculine character. They suggest that the range of delinquent behavior that will be admired by peers is narrower for females than for males and that boys are more likely to achieve recognition by engaging in illegal acts. The same reasoning may well apply to disruptive behavior in the classroom. A boy who talks back to the teacher or shoves another boy in a skirmish in the cafeteria is probably more likely to draw a favorable response from peers than is a girl who exhibits the same behavior. Thus, there are a variety of factors that predispose boys to express frustration and hostility in physical and assertive ways.

ACADEMIC FACTORS   Boys also seem more likely than girls to experience feelings of frustration and hostility in school. For a variety of reasons (more rapid maturity, desire to please adults, superiority in verbal skills) girls earn higher grades, on the average, than boys do. A low grade almost inevitably arouses feelings of resent-ment and anger. In fact, any kind of negative evaluation is a very direct threat to a student's self-esteem. Thus, a middle school, junior high, or high school boy who has received an unbroken succession of low grades and is unlikely to graduate may experience extreme frustration and anger. Even poor students are likely to be aware that their chances of getting a decent job are severely limited by the absence of a high school diploma.

At the same time, high school students who have never developed successful study habits and who are saddled with a low grade-point average may feel that they can do nothing about the situation unless there is a continuation school or the equivalent to attend. Older high school boys who do not have opportunities to at-tend special schools can escape further humiliation by dropping out of school; but middle school and junior high boys cannot legally resort to the same solution, which may partially explain why violent acts are twice as frequent in seventh, eighth, and ninth grades as in the upper grades.

Middle school and junior high boys with low grades may feel trapped

PSYCHOSOCIAL FACTORS   Other explanations of disruptive classroom behavior are supplied by Erik Erikson's observations on identity, which we discussed in Chapter 2. A teenager who has failed to make a clear occupational choice, who is confused about gender roles, or who does not experience acceptance "by those who count" may decide to establish a negative identity. Instead of striving to behave in ways that parents and teachers respond to in positive ways, negative identity teenagers may deliberately engage in opposite forms of behavior (Lowry, Sleet, Duncan, Powell, & Kolbe, 1995).

James Marcia's identity status concept (1980, 1991), discussed in Chapter 2, may also help you understand why certain students cause problems in class. Indi-viduals in foreclosure who have accepted parental values may well be model stu-dents. Those in a moratorium state who are experiencing identity crises of different kinds may feel impelled to release frustration and anger. But even students who are not experiencing identity problems, either because they are too young to be con-cerned or because they have resolved their identity conflicts, may misbehave be-cause they need to release frustration and tension.

Misbehavior of high school students may reveal lack of positive identity

SCHOOL ENVIRONMENT FACTORS   So far we have mentioned the role of hor-monal, gender-related cultural, academic, and personality factors in school violence. Each of these explanations places the responsibility for violent behavior largely or entirely on the individual. Other explanations focus instead on schools that are poorly designed and do not meet the needs of their students. Violent behavior, in this view, is seen as a natural (though unacceptable) response to schools that are too large, impersonal, and competitive; that do not enforce rules fairly or consistently; that use punitive ways of resolving conflict; and that impose an unimaginative, non-meaningful curriculum on students (Lowry et al., 1995). Dona Kagan (1990) re-ports that students who are at risk of dropping out of school believe that their teachers neither care about them nor consider them capable of academic success. Ironically, the self-esteem and motivation of a large proportion of these students improve after they leave school to the extent that they enroll in General Equiva-lency Diploma or job training programs. Similar observations on the characteristics of schools that have low levels of violence are stressed by Eugene Howard, an au-thority on school climate and discipline, who writes:

Schools with positive climates are places where people care, respect, and
trust one another; and where the school as an institution cares, respects, and

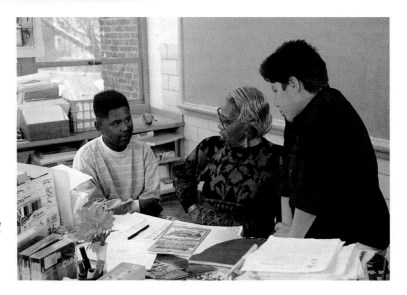

Research findings indicate that impersonal and punitively oriented schools have higher than average levels of school violence. Consequently, one preventive technique suggested by some experts is to involve students in some aspects of school and classroom decision-making and to treat students with respect.

trusts people. In such a school people feel a high sense of pride and ownership which comes from each individual having a role in making the school a better place. . . . Schools with positive climates are characterized by people-centered belief and value systems, procedures, rules, regulations, and policies. (1981, p. 8)

REDUCING SCHOOL VIOLENCE

CLASSROOM TACTICS   Several analyses of school violence (for example, Howard, 1981; Kagan, 1990; Zwier & Vaughan, 1984) suggest that academic achievement and school atmosphere can play a significant role in reducing school violence. To foster respectable levels of achievement by as many students as possible, teachers can make effective use of carefully selected objectives, help students establish at least short-term goals, use efficient instructional techniques (such as those advocated by behavioral theorists), teach students how to use learning strategies, and implement a mastery approach. If you show that students who do not do well on the first try at an assignment will receive your help and encouragement to improve their performance, you may be able to convert at least some resentment into a desire to achieve.

School violence can be reduced by improving student achievement levels

At the same time, it appears that students should be invited to participate in making at least some decisions about what is to be studied and about school and classroom rules. Constructivist techniques and contingency contracts, for example, permit some self-direction by students. Such tactics may ease students' fears that schooling is impersonal and that they have no control over what happens to them. As humanistic psychologists have argued, students seem to respond more positively to schooling when they are treated as individuals, when their feelings and opinions are taken into account, and when they are invited to participate in making decisions about how the school and the classroom function.

PROGRAMS TO REDUCE VIOLENCE AND IMPROVE DISCIPLINE   Several states and many school districts have initiated programs to make schools safer places for students and teachers. One such program is the just community at the

Birch Meadow Elementary School in Reading, Massachusetts (Murphy, 1988). The goal of the just community at Birch Meadow was to help students take responsibility for reducing undesirable behaviors (such as petty bickering among students, the development of cliques, and graffiti on restroom walls) and for promoting more desirable actions (such as cooperative learning, cleanup activities, and the organization of fund-raising events).

Implementation of the just community concept involves two types of activities: circle meetings and student councils. Circle meetings are held in each classroom. The first meeting occurs on the first day of the school year and is devoted to establishing classroom rules and punishments. Subsequent meetings can be called at any time to deal with such issues as unfair treatment of some students by others (or by the teacher), classroom safety, and revisions of classroom rules. There were two student councils at Birch Meadow: one (the primary council) for kindergarten through grade 3 and the other (the intermediate council) for grades 4 and 5. Each class selects a representative to serve on the council. The councils meet separately with the principal in alternating weeks to decide on ways to make the atmosphere of the school more enjoyable. For example, the primary council conducted a playground cleanup campaign, and the intermediate council raised money to purchase an American flag for the school auditorium.

Violence less likely when students invited to participate in making decisions

A somewhat different approach to decreasing physical violence, particularly between students, is the Resolving Conflict Creatively Program (RCCP). Created by Linda Lantieri in 1985, the goal of the program is to teach students how to use nonviolent conflict resolution techniques in place of their more normal and more violent methods. Students are trained by teachers to monitor the school environment (such as the playground, the cafeteria, and hallways) for imminent or actual physical confrontations between students. For example, picture two students who are arguing about a comment that struck one as an insult. As the accusations and counter accusations escalate, one student threatens to hit the other. At that moment one or two other students who are wearing T-shirts with the word *mediator* printed across the front and back intervene and ask if the two students would like help in resolving their problem. The mediating students may suggest that they all move to a quieter area where they can talk. The mediators then establish certain ground rules, such as each student gets a turn to talk without being interrupted and that name calling is not allowed.

The goal of the RCCP is to teach students that they should listen to one another when disputes arise and actively work toward peaceful solutions. The program is currently being used in school districts in New York City, Anchorage, New Orleans, southern California, and New Jersey and is described by Lantieri as the largest school-based program of its kind in the country. In schools where the program has been implemented, teachers have noted less physical violence in their classrooms, fewer insults and verbal put-downs, and greater spontaneous use of conflict resolution skills (Lantieri, 1995).

A review of research on various types of conflict resolution programs concluded that students who have not been trained in how to appropriately settle conflicts among themselves tend to leave their conflicts unresolved by ignoring the other student, suppressing an aggressive response, or coercing the other student to behave in a desired manner ("If you don't stop spreading rumors about me I'll see to it that nobody has anything to do with you."). After training, students are more likely to resolve conflicts through the use of discussion and negotiation procedures that produce mutually acceptable agreements. In comparison to untrained students, students who use conflict resolution procedures tend to have a more positive atti-

One approach to reducing school violence is to train students to mediate disputes between other students.

tude toward school, increased self-esteem, and fewer discipline problems and suspensions (Johnson & Johnson, 1996).

An innovative approach to reducing school violence by modifying the school environment is being tried by a large high school in Baltimore, Maryland. Patterson High School used to be a typical, large (two thousand students) urban high school. There were numerous instances of vandalism, fighting, gambling, cutting classes, and verbal abuse directed at teachers. On some days the attendance rate was as low as 50 percent. But a dramatic change occurred after the school was reorganized into six self-contained units. One part of the building is devoted to a ninth-grade Success Academy in which teachers and students work in small groups. The rest of the building houses five Career Academies that combine a college-oriented curriculum with career interests. Each academy has about three hundred students, its own entrance, its own administrator, its own guidance counselor, and is separated from the other academies by walls and doors.

Students who would normally be suspended or transferred for discipline problems have to attend an after-hours program at Patterson High called the Twilight School. Students are placed in small classes and receive help from teachers and counselors in resolving their academic and behavioral problems.

Daily average attendance has risen to 80 percent, the promotion rate to ninth grade has increased from 35 percent to 80 percent, transfer requests from teachers are virtually nonexistent, the school is graffiti-free, and most faculty describe the school environment as being like a big family and conducive to learning (McPartland, Jordan, Letgers, & Balfanz, 1997).

A description of how conflict resolution and other violence reduction programs are being implemented in the schools is presented in the Case in Print on page 430.

USING TECHNOLOGY TO KEEP STUDENTS IN SCHOOL

As we pointed out earlier, students who exhibit poor academic performance and believe that their teachers don't care about them are prone to engage in disruptive and violent behavior. They are also at-risk for dropping out of school. About 25 percent of U.S. public school students (50 percent or more in some urban areas) drop out of school, costing the U.S. economy about $100 billion in direct costs and lost revenue (Braun, 1993). According to an analysis by Ludwig Braun (1993), these costs and the dropout rate could be reduced substantially by spending about $1,000 per student annually on technology to promote higher levels of student motivation and learning. Here are a few examples of how some schools have used technology to reduce student absenteeism and the dropout rate.

- To entice potential dropouts to stay in school and become eligible either for college or gainful employment, regular schools have made extensive use of such attractive technologies as camcorders, videocassette recorders, CD-ROMs, videodisks, satellite dishes, video editing equipment, and multimedia facilities. Alternative schools have used many of the same technologies to recruit truant students back to school, even on holidays and summer vacations (Braun, 1993).

- The Carrollton City School System in rural western Georgia reduced its dropout rate from 19 percent to 6 percent in just a few years, while increasing student use of library media and motivation to learn. The types of technology used by the Carrollton City Schools included self-paced instructional

Violent behavior, in this view, is seen as a natural (though unacceptable) response to schools that are too large, impersonal, and competitive; that do not enforce rules fairly or consistently; that use punitive ways of resolving conflict; and that impose an unimaginative, nonmeaningful curriculum on students. . . . Several states and many school districts have initiated programs to make schools safer places for students and teachers. (pp. 426–427)

PATHWAYS TO PEACE
MICKEY BACA
Merrimack Valley Sunday 3/5/95

At the Kelley Elementary School in Newburyport [MA], a fourth grader who flares up in anger is moved to a separate area of the room surrounded by restful scenes and posters. He is given drawing materials and earphones to listen to relaxation tapes until he cools off enough to discuss what sent him up the anger "escalator."

At Triton Regional School in Salisbury, two eighth graders involved in a shoving match in the hall sit down with a pair of student mediators to analyze what led to the scuffle. After nearly two hours, they emerge with a written agreement on how to avoid future strife.

At Newburyport's Nock Middle School, a couple of fifth graders who sometimes clash because one's mother buys her clothes at K-Mart rather than the more trendy Gap find themselves working together to solve a burglary case in a group lesson designed to build cooperation and understanding.

Like their counterparts around the country, local schools are turning to a variety of techniques to try to combat intolerance and violence in their students. . . .

. . ."There's a real culture in our society that reinforces violence," says Susan Fallon, health coordinator at Triton. "We're trying to create a culture that reinforces nonviolence."

For the past three years, the Triton School District—which includes Salisbury, Rowley and Newbury—has been training its staff and passing on to its students the latest techniques in violence prevention. Teachers have attended seminars on something called "conflict resolution skills"—methods to resolve disputes through nonviolent means such as better communication, collaboration and compromise. The idea, according to former state Rep. Barbara Hildt of Amesbury, who works in violence prevention and is participating in the Partnership effort, is to give students strategies to better manage anger, listen more, "talk about problems, not people," offer choices and work with others on problem solving.

Triton also has a peer mediation program in which students are trained to act as impartial middlemen in student conflicts to root out and hopefully defuse their causes. . . .

"They provide a neutral way to clarify what the problem is," says Fallon. "And to help each side understand the other's point of view.". . .

Under peer mediation at Triton, school staff advising the mediators take referrals about fights between students or even about conflicts that could lead to fights eventually. The referrals can come from a teacher, parent, bus driver, hallway monitor or a student who is either being picked on or perhaps has a friend facing conflict, according to Fallon. Mediation augments, but doesn't replace, regular school disciplinary consequences to violence. . . .

Staff advisors decide what's appropriate for mediation. Some things—like harassment cases or any kind of dating violence—are not, Fallon says. . . .

Fallon says one indication she sees that Triton's commitment to anti-violence training is paying off is the kids' willingness to use the relatively new peer mediation option. She and other educators say kids like the idea of sitting down with their peers rather than with adults to resolve their differences.

What's more, Fallon says, the results of mediation sessions are encouraging. "It can be truly moving. You can see some tough kids becoming choked up."

Over in Newburyport, where anti-violence training is less developed in the schools, officials have mixed reactions to the training trend.

Doug Lay, principal at the Nock Middle School, says some schools seem to have a positive track record with such training, but it's hard to say how effective things like conflict resolution training will be in the long run in changing middle school kids' views towards violence.

"I don't see that it's ever going to resolve all of the conflicts," he says.

What it will do, Lay says, is build a common vocabulary for nonviolent problem-solving and spell out ways to break down conflicts more objectively.

Given that framework, kids are willing to work at solving conflicts, Lay finds, and have also shown more of a willingness to seek the help of an adult when facing problems.

. . . [Newburyport High School] Principal Mary Lanard . . . sees a clear need for it at the high school, she says, particularly in the area of teaching kids to tolerate diversity.

"We're looking at ways we can make it easier for kids who are coming from other schools or who are different," Lanard says. "I think we're trying to make the school more humane."

At the elementary school level, Chris Morton, a fourth grade teacher at the Kelley School, a strong proponent of violence prevention training, says her students have been quick to pick up the conflict resolution lessons they've been getting since last year.

"I think we know it works when we begin seeing kids solve problems without violence," she says, noting that she does hear her students using the terminology of conflict resolution.

Morton says Newburyport elementary schools have also begun a unique "time out" process that really seems to help students better manage their anger. An area of the classroom is set up away from the rest of the class where angry students go to cool off and get in control by listening to relaxation tapes. The area also features posters that remind kids to do things like count backwards from 10 when they feel themselves getting angry.

For the most part, she says, kids are able to calm down in 15 or 20 minutes and are then ready to talk about the problem. . . .

One program that Lay says has been effective in promoting understanding and stemming conflicts at his school is an effort started last year, called Prime Time. Under that program, the school's student population is divided up into groups of roughly 16 that meet three mornings a week for 45 minutes.

Group advisors, including teachers and Lay himself, lead the groups in exercises that emphasize group cohesiveness, encourage students to share their thoughts and feelings and look at issues like peer pressure and conflict.

Like other area school officials, Lay doesn't see racial or cultural differences as a source of conflict among his students. His school population, and the population through Essex County, is pretty homogeneous in that respect.

What he does see is economic prejudices and stereotypes fueling conflict, Lay notes.

"Kids making fun of each other's clothing. Do you buy at the Gap or do you buy at K-Mart? You end up with a potentially polarized population."

The most important thing Lay believes school programs should teach kids is tolerance and respect of diversity. . . .

After only a year, Prime Time seems to be working. Lay says there's a lot more cohesiveness and a lot less tension and conflict among students this year.

Questions and Activities

1. According to two educators interviewed in this article, student-based conflict resolution strategies are not appropriate for dealing with certain types of problems and may not effectively resolve other types of conflicts. Do you agree with this view? If you do agree, what types of problems should student mediators not try to resolve? Why? Where peer mediation is appropriate, with which types of conflicts is it likely to be unsuccessful? Why? If you do not agree that peer mediation has its limits, explain why.

2. Although peer mediation is an attractive method for helping students peacefully resolve conflicts, it may not work effectively below a certain grade level. Review the discussion in Chapter 2 of Piaget's theory of cognitive development, note the lowest grade level below which you would not institute this type of program, and explain why.

3. Relate what you learned in Chapter 4 and elsewhere in this book about teaching in a culturally diverse classroom to the comments about diversity in this article. Do you agree with the educator who says that the most important things school programs can teach are tolerance and respect for diversity? Why or why not? As a classroom teacher with an awareness of issues related to cultural or economic diversity, how could you augment some of the strategies and policies described in this article?

4. To test the feasibility of peer mediation, try acting as a go-between the next time two friends or family members have a disagreement (with their permission of course). Ask each party to describe the source of the conflict, why the two parties have different views, what their feelings are, and what ideas they might have for resolving it.

modules, a graphics art laboratory, a TV studio, a career center, a computer-aided design laboratory, increased computer networking, desktop video-conferencing, televisions, videocassette recorders, and overhead projectors (Mitchell, 1996).

- Several schools have used electronic publishing centers, labs, integrated learning systems, and various other technology-oriented instructional media to increase student attendance, raise achievement, and actually bring dropouts back to school. One project used modems, telecommunications software, and laptop computers to help homebound students and those who have extensive absentee records stay in school (Peck & Catello, 1990).

- Television, audio- and video-conferencing, and the World Wide Web are particularly useful technologies for helping students with high absentee rates, such as the children of migrant workers, to take courses and complete their schooling (Peck & Catello, 1990).

Although computer-based technology can be used in a number of creative ways to combat the problems of low achievement, disruptive behavior, absenteeism, and dropping out of school, we don't want to leave you with the impression that these are relatively simple problems for which technology is an all-purpose solution. We have, after all, spent the last twelve chapters showing you that school learning and instruction are rather complex phenomena. Technology is but a tool. And, as with any tool, its effectiveness is largely determined by how well educators understand its strengths, its limitations, and how it can best be used in combination with other resources to serve various purposes.

RESOURCES FOR FURTHER INVESTIGATION

■ Classroom Management

Even though the second edition of *Mental Hygiene in Teaching*, by Fritz Redl and William Wattenberg, was published in 1959, it includes a particularly clear, concise, and well-organized analysis of influence techniques. Many of the techniques described have been used by teachers for years and will continue to be used as long as an instructor is asked to supervise a group of students.

More recent analyses of classroom control techniques can be found in *Classroom Management and Discipline* (1995), by Paul Burden; *Classroom Management for Elementary Teachers* (4th ed., 1997), by Carolyn Evertson, Edmund Emmer, Barbara Clements, and Murray Worsham; *Classroom Management for Secondary Teachers* (4th ed., 1997), by Edmund Emmer, Carolyn Evertson, Barbara Clements, and Murray Worsham; *Behavior Management: A Practical Approach for Educators* (7th ed., 1999), by James Walker and Thomas Shea; and *Elementary Classroom Management: Lessons from Research and Practice* (2d ed., 1997), by Carol Weinstein and Andrew Mignano Jr.

Discussions of classroom management that emphasize particular approaches or techniques can also be found. For instance, James Cangelosi emphasizes the use of methods that foster student cooperation in *Classroom Management*

Strategies: Gaining and Maintaining Students' Cooperation (3d ed., 1997); and William Purkey and David Strahan emphasize the use of invitational learning in *Positive Discipline: A Pocketful of Ideas* (1986).

On-line resources for classroom management include Teacher Talk, a World Wide Web site maintained by the Indiana University Center for Adolescent Studies at **http://education.indiana.edu/cas/tt/tthmpg.html**. The site is a journal with articles on many topics, including coverage of classroom management. In particular, it includes a self-survey to help you determine your classroom management style. The survey can be found at **http://education.indiana.edu/cas/tt/v1i2/what/html**.

Teachers Edition Online is another resource with tips for classroom management (including a "Tip of the Day"), answers to teacher questions, and sample lesson plans. It's found at **http://www.teachnet.com/**.

Teachers Helping Teachers provides a "bulletin board" of postings by teachers about particular topics, including classroom management. Many of these first-person comments are insightful and relevant to most beginning teachers. The site can be found at **http://www. pacificnet.net/~mandel/**.

The AskERIC on-line database contains a large number of resources for classroom management. The searchable database is found at **http://ericir.sunsite.syr.edu/**. It can be searched for articles, ERIC digests, postings from newsgroups and classroom-related listservs, and so forth.

School Violence

For information on how to reduce school violence through the use of behavior modification techniques, psychodynamic and humanistic interventions, and the teaching of prosocial values and behaviors, read *School Violence* (1984), by Arnold Goldstein, Steven Apter, and Berj Harootunian. *Victimization in Schools* (1985), by Gary Gottfredson and Denise Gottfredson, describes research conducted at the Center for Social Organization of Schools at Johns Hopkins University on the

nature and frequency of school violence; it also discusses possible solutions. And, finally, Chester Quarles describes how teachers can try to prevent school violence and deal with it when it does happen in *Staying Safe at School* (1993).

There are a number of on-line resources dedicated to educating educators, parents, and students about violence and its effects. One unusual site is Danger High, a simulation in which students are confronted with somewhat realistic situations and must solve problems. Developed by the Metro Nashville Police Department on a National Institute of Justice grant, it can be found at **http://www.nashville.net/ ~police/dangerhi/**.

Summary

1. Just as parents adopt either an authoritarian, laissez-faire (permissive), authoritative or rejecting-neglecting approach to raising children, teachers adopt approaches to managing the behavior of students. The authoritative approach, which revolves around explaining the rationale for classroom rules and adjusting those rules as students demonstrate the ability for self-governance, produces the highest level of desirable student behavior.

2. Kounin, one of the early writers on classroom management, identified several effective classroom management techniques. He emphasized being aware of the ripple effect, cultivating withitness, coping with overlapping activities, maintaining the momentum of a lesson, keeping the whole class involved in a lesson, using a variety of instructional techniques enthusiastically, focusing on the misbehavior of students rather than on their personalities, and suggesting alternative constructive behaviors.

3. Researchers at the University of Texas found that in well-managed classrooms students know what they are expected to do and do it successfully, are kept busy with teacher-designated activities, and exhibit little confusion or disruptive behavior. Such classrooms are marked by a work-oriented yet relaxed and pleasant atmosphere.

4. Classroom management can be made easier by using technology tools to carry out such tasks as test construction, record keeping, developing seating arrangements, analyzing space utilization, and monitoring student work. Software programs exist that teach students how to resolve conflicts nonviolently.

5. Redl and Wattenberg proposed a set of behavior management methods in 1959 called influence techniques that were designed to help teachers deal with classroom misbehavior.

6. Ginott suggests that teachers use I-messages when responding to misbehavior. These are statements that indicate to students how the teacher feels when misbehavior occurs. The aim is to comment on the situation rather than on the personality and character of the student.

7. Gordon recommends that teachers determine who owns a problem, use active listening when the student owns the problem, and resolve conflicts by using the no-lose method. The no-lose method involves discussing problem behaviors with the misbehaving student and formulating a mutually agreeable compromise solution.

8. Despite reports in the media about school-based crime and violence, classrooms and school buildings are relatively safe environments. Most schools report no or few instances of crime, and only 10 percent of schools report one or more instances of serious violent crime.

9. Possible explanations for misbehavior and violence, particularly among boys at the junior high and high school levels, include high levels of the male sex hormone androgen, a culture that encourages male aggression and independence, feelings of resentment and frustration over low levels of achievement, and difficulty in establishing a positive identity.

10. Other explanations for school violence focus on the characteristics and atmosphere of schools that are so large that they seem impersonal, that emphasize competition, that do not enforce rules fairly or consistently, that use punishment as a primary means of resolving conflict, and that offer a curriculum perceived as unimaginative and nonmeaningful.

11. Steps that classroom teachers can take to reduce school violence include providing students with well-conceived objectives, helping students set short-term goals, using instructional techniques derived from behavioral learning theories, teaching students how to use learning strategies, using a mastery approach, and allowing students to make some decisions about classroom rules and what is to be studied.

12. Schoolwide programs that may reduce violence and improve behavior are the just community, in which students are given responsibility for reducing undesirable behavior and increasing the frequency of desirable behavior; the Resolving Conflict Creatively Program, in which students mediate disputes between other students to prevent physical violence; and dividing large, impersonal high schools into relatively small, self-contained units.

13. Some school districts have been able to reduce their absenteeism and dropout rates by getting students interested in using technological aids to learning.

KEY TERMS

ripple effect *(404)*   I-message *(420)*   no-lose method *(421)*
withitness *(405)*   active listening *(420)*

DISCUSSION QUESTIONS

1. Can you recall any classes in which you experienced Kounin's ripple effect? Since this phenomenon simultaneously affects the behavior of several students, would you consider using it deliberately? Why?

2. Haim Ginott and Thomas Gordon recommend that when responding to misbehavior, teachers speak to the behavior and not the character of the student. How often have you seen this done? If it strikes you as a good approach that is not practiced often enough, what steps will you take to use it as often as possible with your own students?

3. Do you agree with the argument raised earlier that school violence can be caused by a nonmeaningful, unimaginative curriculum? If so, what can you do to make the subjects you teach lively, interesting, and useful?

Assessment of Students

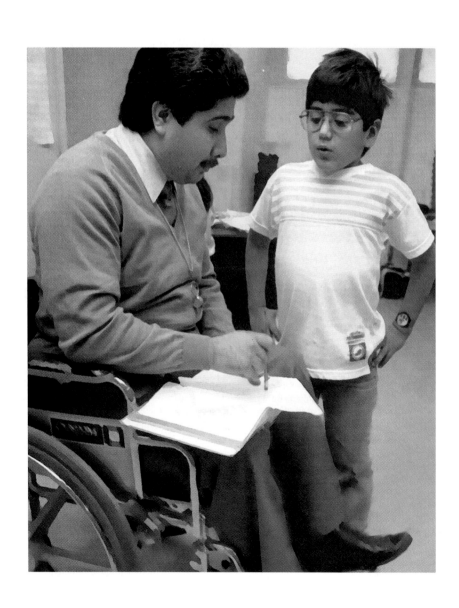

13 Assessment of Classroom Learning

The first three parts of this book discuss three major aspects of the teacher's role: understanding student differences and how to properly address them (Chapters 2 through 6), understanding the learning process and how to use that knowledge to formulate effective approaches to instruction (Chapters 7 through 10), and establishing a positive learning environment by influencing motivation to learn and creating an orderly classroom (Chapters 11 and 12). This next and last part, assessing performance, is as significant an aspect of the teacher's role as the first three. Virtually everyone connected with public schools—from students to teachers and administrators to state education officials to members of Congress—is keenly interested in knowing how much

KEY POINTS

These key points will help you learn the important information in this chapter. To help you study, they also appear in the margins of pages, next to the text where they are discussed.

The Role of Assessment in Teaching

- Measurement: assigning numbers to things according to rules to create a ranking
- Evaluation: making judgments about the value of a measure
- Summative evaluation: measure achievement; assign grades
- Formative evaluation: monitor progress; plan remedial instruction
- Tests can positively affect many aspects of students' learning
- Moderate testing produces more learning than no testing or infrequent testing

Ways to Measure Student Learning

- Written tests measure degree of knowledge about ideas
- Selected-response tests objectively scored and efficient but usually measure lower levels of learning
- Short-answer tests easy to write but measure lower levels of learning
- Essay tests measure higher levels of learning but are hard to grade consistently
- Performance tests measure ability to use knowledge and skills to solve realistic problems, create products
- Performance tests may vary in degree of realism
- Reliability and validity of performance tests not yet firmly established

Ways to Evaluate Student Learning

- Norm-referenced grading: compare one student to others
- Norm-referenced grading based on absence of external criteria
- Norm-referenced grading can be used to evaluate advanced levels of learning
- Criterion-referenced grading: compare individual performance to stated criteria
- Criterion-referenced grades provide information about strengths and weaknesses
- Mastery approach: give students multiple opportunities to master goals at own pace

Improving Your Grading Methods: Assessment Practices to Avoid

- Be aware of and avoid faulty measurement and grading practices

Technology for Classroom Assessment

- Digital portfolio: collection of work that is stored and illustrated electronically
- Special rubrics needed to assess electronic portfolios and presentations

Suggestions for Teaching in Your Classroom: Effective Assessment Techniques

- Necessary to obtain a representative sample of behavior when testing
- Table of specifications helps ensure an adequate sample of content, behavior
- Elementary grade students tested as much for diagnostic, formative evaluation purposes as for summative purposes
- Rating scales and checklists make evaluations of performance more systematic
- Item analysis tells about difficulty, discriminability of multiple-choice items

436

and how well students have learned. In this and the next chapter we describe a twofold process for assessing student learning: using teacher-made tests to assess mastery of the teacher's specific objectives and using professionally prepared standardized tests to measure the extent of a student's general knowledge base and aptitudes. Although the items that make up teacher-made and standardized tests can be very similar, if not identical, the construction of each type of instrument, the conditions under which they are administered, and the purposes for which each are used are all quite different. ■

The Role of Assessment in Teaching

Assessing student learning is something that every teacher has to do, usually quite frequently. Written tests, book reports, research papers, homework exercises, oral presentations, question-and-answer sessions, science projects, and artwork of various sorts are just some of the ways in which teachers measure student learning, with written tests accounting for about 45 percent of a typical student's course grade (Green & Stager, 1986–1987). It is no surprise, then, that the typical teacher can spend between one-third and one-half of her class time engaged in one or another type of measurement activity (Stiggins, 1997). Yet despite the amount of time teachers spend assessing student learning, it is a task that most of them dislike and that few do well. One reason is that many teachers have little or no in-depth knowledge of assessment principles (Crooks, 1988; Hills, 1991). Another reason is that the role of assessor is seen as being inconsistent with the role of teacher (or helper). Since teachers with more training in assessment use more appropriate assessment practices than do teachers with less training (Green & Stager, 1986–1987), a basic goal of this chapter is to help you understand how such knowledge can be used to reinforce, rather than work against, your role as teacher. Toward that end, we will begin by defining what we mean by the term *assessment* and by two key elements of this process, *measurement* and *evaluation*.

WHAT IS ASSESSMENT?

Broadly conceived, classroom assessment involves two major types of activities: collecting information about how much knowledge and skill students have learned (measurement) and making judgments about the adequacy or acceptability of each student's level of learning (evaluation). Both the measurement and the evaluation aspects of classroom assessment can be accomplished in a number of ways. The most common way that teachers determine how much learning has occurred is to have students take exams, respond to oral questions, do homework exercises, write papers, solve problems, create products, and make oral presentations. Teachers can then evaluate the scores from those activities by comparing them either to one another or to an absolute standard (such as an A equals 90 percent correct). In this chapter we will explain and illustrate the various ways in which you can measure and evaluate student learning with assessments that you create and administer on a regular basis.

Measurement: assigning numbers to things according to rules to create a ranking

MEASUREMENT   Measurement is the assignment of numbers to certain attributes of objects, events, or people according to a rule-governed system. For our purposes, we will limit the discussion to attributes of people. For example, we can measure someone's level of typing proficiency by counting the number of words the person accurately types per minute or someone's level of mathematical reasoning by counting the number of problems correctly solved. In a classroom or other group situation, the rules that are used to assign the numbers will ordinarily create a ranking that reflects how much of the attribute different people possess (Linn & Gronlund, 1995).

EVALUATION   Evaluation involves using a rule-governed system to make judgments about the value or worth of a set of measures (Linn & Gronlund, 1995). What does it mean, for example, to say that a student answered eighty out of one hundred earth science questions correctly? Depending on the rules that are used, it could mean that the student has learned that body of knowledge exceedingly well and is ready to progress to the next unit of instruction or, conversely, that the student has significant knowledge gaps and requires additional instruction.

> **Evaluation: making judgments about the value of a measure**

WHY SHOULD WE ASSESS STUDENTS' LEARNING?

This question has several answers. We will use this section to address four of the most common reasons for assessment: to provide summaries of learning, to provide information on learning progress, to diagnose specific strengths and weaknesses in an individual's learning, and to motivate further learning.

SUMMATIVE EVALUATION   The first, and probably most obvious, reason for assessment is to provide to all interested parties a clear, meaningful, and useful summary or accounting of how well a student has met the teacher's objectives. When testing is done for the purpose of assigning a letter or numerical grade, it is often called summative evaluation since its primary purpose is to sum up how well a student has performed over time and at a variety of tasks.

> **Summative evaluation: measure achievement; assign grades**

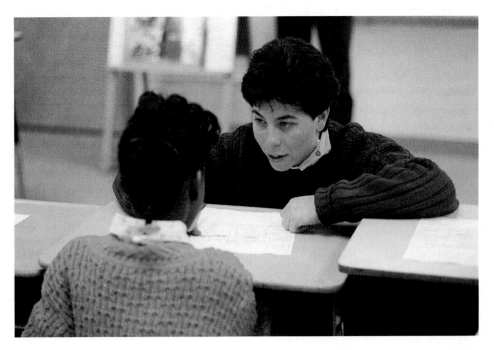

Classroom assessments serve several purposes. They provide information about the extent to which students have acquired the knowledge and skills that have recently been taught, they indicate whether students are understanding and keeping up with the pace of instruction, they may identify the particular cause of a student's learning difficulties, and they help students effectively regulate their study efforts.

FORMATIVE EVALUATION   A second reason for assessing students is to monitor their progress. The main things that teachers want to know from time to time are whether students are keeping up with the pace of instruction and are understanding all of the material that has been covered so far. For students whose pace of learning is either slower or faster than average or whose understanding of certain ideas is faulty, you can introduce supplementary instruction (a workbook or a computer-based tutorial program), remedial instruction (which may also be computer based), or in-class ability grouping (recall that we discussed the benefits of this arrangement in Chapter 6). Because the purpose of such assessment is to facilitate, or form, learning and not to assign a grade, it is usually called **formative evaluation**.

> **Formative evaluation: monitor progress; plan remedial instruction**

DIAGNOSIS   A third reason follows from the second. If you discover a student who is having difficulty keeping up with the rest of the class, you will probably want to know why in order to determine the most appropriate course of action. This purpose may lead you to construct an assessment (or to look for one that has already been made up) that will provide you with specific diagnostic information.

EFFECTS ON LEARNING   A fourth reason for assessment of student performance is that it has potentially positive effects on various aspects of learning and instruction. As Terence Crooks points out, classroom assessment guides students' "judgment of what is important to learn, affects their motivation and self-perceptions of competence, structures their approaches to and timing of personal study (e.g., spaced practice), consolidates learning, and affects the development of enduring learning strategies and skills. It appears to be one of the most potent forces influencing education" (1988, p. 467).

> **Tests can positively affect many aspects of students' learning**

Proof of Crooks's contention that classroom testing helps students consolidate their learning (despite students' arguments to the contrary) was examined by Robert Bangert-Drowns, James Kulik, and Chen-Lin Kulik (1991). They analyzed the results of forty studies conducted in actual classrooms and drew the following conclusions:

1. Students who were tested more frequently (six or seven tests over the course of a semester) scored about one-fourth of a standard deviation higher on a final exam than did students who were tested less frequently. (See Chapter 14 for a discussion of standard deviations.) This translated to an advantage of 9 percentile ranks for the more frequently tested students.

2. The advantage was even larger (20 percentile ranks) when students who were tested several times were compared to students who were never tested.

> **Moderate testing produces more learning than no testing or infrequent testing**

3. As students took more tests over the course of a semester, they generally scored higher on a final exam, but the increases became successively smaller for each additional test. The benefit of taking multiple tests seemed to peak by the sixth or seventh test.

Ways to Measure Student Learning

Just as measurement can play several roles in the classroom, teachers have several ways to measure what students have learned. Which type of measure you choose will depend, of course, on the objectives you have stated. For the purposes of this discussion, objectives can be classified in terms of two broad categories: knowing *about* something (for example, that knots are used to secure objects, that dance is a form of social expression, that microscopes are used to study things too small to be seen by the naked eye) and knowing *how to do* something (for example, tie a square knot, dance the waltz, operate a microscope). Measures that attempt to assess the range and accuracy of someone's knowledge are usually called written tests. And measures that attempt to assess how well somebody can do something are often referred to as performance tests. Again, keep in mind that both types have a legitimate place in a teacher's assessment arsenal. Which type is used, and to what extent, will depend on the purpose or purposes you have for assessing students. In the next two sections, we will briefly examine the nature of both types.

WRITTEN TESTS

As we indicated at the beginning of this chapter, teachers spend a substantial part of each day assessing student learning, and much of this assessment activity involves giving and scoring some type of written test. Most written tests are composed of one or more of the following item types: selected response (multiple-choice, true-false, and matching, for example), short-answer, and essay. They are designed to measure how much people know about a particular subject. In all likelihood, you have taken hundreds of these types of tests in your school career thus far. In the next couple of pages, we will briefly describe the main features, advantages, and disadvantages of each test.

Written tests measure degree of knowledge about ideas

SELECTED-RESPONSE TESTS   Selected-response tests are so named because the student reads a relatively brief opening statement (called a stem) and selects one of the provided alternatives as the correct answer. Selected-response tests are typically made up of multiple-choice, true-false, or matching items. Quite often all three item types are used in a single test.

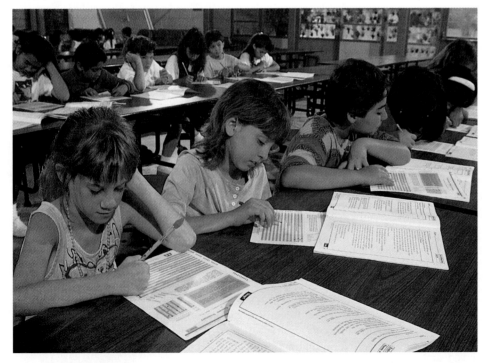

Most of the tests that students take are written tests composed of multiple-choice and short-answer items. Written tests are efficient in that many items can be asked in a short space of time and they can be quickly and reliably scored. But they tend to be used to measure the lowest level of Bloom's taxonomy.

Characteristics   Selected-response tests are sometimes called "objective" tests because they have a simple and set scoring system. If alternative (b) of a multiple-choice item is keyed as the correct response and the student chose alternative (d), the student is marked wrong, regardless of how much the teacher wanted the student to be right. Selected-response tests are typically used when the primary goal is to assess what might be called *foundational knowledge*. This is the basic factual information and cognitive skills that students need in order to do such high-level tasks as solve problems and create products (Stiggins, 1997).

Advantages   A major advantage of selected-response tests is efficiency—a teacher can ask many questions in a short period of time. Another advantage is ease and reliability of scoring. With the aid of a scoring template (such as a multiple-choice answer sheet that has holes punched out where the correct answer is located), many tests can be quickly and uniformly scored.

Disadvantages   Because items that reflect the lowest level of Bloom's Taxonomy (verbatim knowledge) are the easiest to write, most teacher-made tests are composed almost entirely of knowledge-level items (a point we made initially in Chapter 10). As a result, students focus on verbatim memorization rather than on meaningful learning. Another disadvantage is that although we get some indication of what students know, such tests tell us nothing about what students can do with that knowledge.

Selected-response tests objectively scored and efficient but usually measure lower levels of learning

SHORT-ANSWER TESTS   As their name implies, short-answer tests require a brief written response from the student.

Characteristics   Instead of *selecting* from one or more alternatives, the student is asked to *supply* from memory a brief answer consisting of a name, word, phrase, or symbol. Like selected-response tests, short-answer tests can be scored quickly, accurately, and consistently, thereby giving them an aura of objectivity. They are primarily used for measuring foundational knowledge.

Advantages   Short-answer items are relatively easy to write, so a test, or part of one, can be constructed fairly quickly. They allow for either broad or in-depth assessment of foundational knowledge since students can respond to many items within a short space of time. Since students have to supply an answer, they have to recall, rather than recognize, information.

Disadvantages   Short-answer tests have the same basic disadvantages as selected-response tests. Because short-answer items ask only for short verbatim answers, students are likely to limit their processing to that level, and these items provide no information about how well students can use what they have learned. In addition, unexpected but plausible answers may be difficult to score.

Short-answer tests easy to write but measure lower levels of learning

ESSAY TESTS   Essay items require students to organize a set of ideas and write a somewhat lengthy response to a broad question.

Characteristics   The student is given a somewhat general directive to discuss one or more related ideas according to certain criteria. One example of an essay question is "Compare operant conditioning theory and information-processing theory in terms of basic assumptions, typical research findings, and classroom applications."

Advantages   Essay tests reveal how well students can recall, organize, and clearly communicate previously learned information. When well written, essay tests call on such higher-level abilities as analysis, synthesis, and evaluation. Because of these demands, students are more likely to try to meaningfully learn the material on which they are tested.

Disadvantages   Consistency of grading is likely to be a problem. Two students may have essentially similar responses, yet receive different letter or numerical grades. These test items are also very time consuming to grade. And because it takes time for students to formulate and write responses, only a few questions at most can be given.

Essay tests measure higher levels of learning but are hard to grade consistently

PERFORMANCE TESTS

In recent years many teachers and measurement experts have argued that the typical written test should be used far less often because it reveals little or nothing of the depth of students' knowledge and how students use their knowledge to work through questions, problems, and tasks. The solution that these experts have proposed is to use one or more of what are called performance tests.

WHAT ARE PERFORMANCE TESTS?

Performance tests require students to use a wide range of knowledge and skills over an extended period of time to complete a task or solve a problem under more or less realistic conditions. At the low end of the realism spectrum, students may be asked to construct a map, interpret a graph, or write an essay under highly standardized conditions. That is, everyone completes the same task in the same amount of time and under the same conditions. At the high end of the spectrum, students may be asked to conduct a science experiment, produce a painting, or write an essay under conditions that are similar to those of real life. For example, students may be told to produce a compare-and-contrast essay on a particular topic by a certain date, but the resources students choose to use, the number of revisions they make, and when they work on the essay are left unspecified. When performance testing is conducted under such realistic conditions, it is also called *authentic assessment* (Baker, O'Neil, & Linn, 1993; Meyer, 1992). Per-

Performance tests measure ability to use knowledge and skills to solve realistic problems, create products

Performance tests assess how well students complete a task under realistic conditions.

haps the clearest way to distinguish between traditional paper-and-pencil tests (like multiple-choice tests) and performance tests is to say that the former measure how much students *know* whereas the latter measure what students *can do* with what they know. In the sections that follow we will first define four different types of performance tests and then look at their most important characteristics.

TYPES OF PERFORMANCE TESTS   Currently, there are four ways in which the performance capabilities of students are typically assessed: direct writing assessments, portfolios, exhibitions, and demonstrations.

Direct Writing Assessments   These tests ask students to write about a specific topic ("Describe the person whom you admire the most, and explain why you admire that person.") under a standard set of conditions. Each essay is then scored by two or more people according to a set of defined criteria.

Portfolios   A portfolio may contain one or more pieces of a student's work, some of which demonstrate different stages of completion. For example, a student's writing portfolio may contain business letters; pieces of fiction; poetry; and an outline, rough draft, and final draft of a research paper. Through the inclusion of various stages of a research paper, both the process and the end product can be assessed. Portfolios can also be constructed for math and science as well as for projects that combine two or more subject areas. Often the student is involved in the selection of what is included in his portfolio. The portfolio is sometimes used as a showcase to illustrate exemplary pieces, but it also works well as a collection of pieces that represent a student's typical performances. In its best and truest sense, the portfolio functions not just as a housing for these performances but also as a means of self-expression, self-reflection, and self-analysis for an individual student (Hebert, 1998; Templeton, 1995).

Exhibitions   Exhibitions involve just what the label suggests—a showing of such products as paintings, drawings, photographs, sculptures, videotapes, and models. As with direct writing assessments and portfolios, the products a student chooses to exhibit are evaluated according to a predetermined set of criteria.

Demonstrations   In this type of performance testing, students are required to show how well they can use previously learned knowledge or skills to solve a somewhat unique problem (such as conducting a scientific inquiry to answer a question, interpreting a graph, or diagnosing the cause of a malfunctioning engine and describing the best procedure for fixing it) or perform a task (such as reciting a poem, performing a dance, or playing a piece of music). Figure 13.1 shows a performance item for graph interpretation, the partially correct response of a student, and the corrective feedback offered by two classmates.

CHARACTERISTICS OF PERFORMANCE TESTS   Performance tests are different from traditional written tests in that they require the student to make an active response, are more like everyday tasks, contain problems that involve many variables, are closely related to earlier instructional activities, use scoring guides that clearly specify the criteria against which responses will be evaluated, and emphasize formative evaluation.

Emphasis on Active Responding   As we pointed out previously, the goal of performance testing is to gain some insight into how competently students can

Figure 13.1 Example of a Performance Assessment: Interpreting a Graph

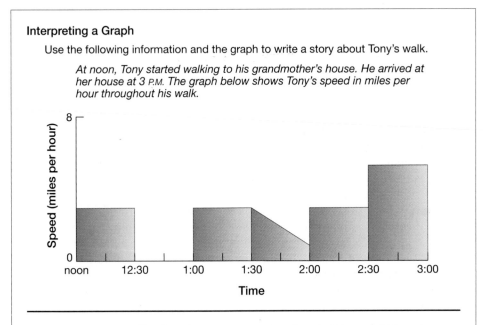

Interpreting a Graph

Use the following information and the graph to write a story about Tony's walk.

At noon, Tony started walking to his grandmother's house. He arrived at her house at 3 P.M. The graph below shows Tony's speed in miles per hour throughout his walk.

Write a story about Tony's walk. In your story, describe what Tony might have been doing at the different times.

Tony left his grandmother's house at noon. He made a stop at 12:30 to get a bite to eat Taco Bell. From 12:30 to 1:00 he stopped to rest on a bench at the park. From 1:00 to 1:30 he continued his walk. So Tony decided to stop at a friend house from 1:30 to 2:00. From 2:00 to 2:30 he continued his walk. Finally he arrived back at his grandmothers.

Students critique the response:

Because while he was at a friends house he was going 3 miles per hour. Also he didn't say when he sped up they didn't say.

Watch the chart when you write and put in minor details as well. Plus you can watch your speed.

SOURCE: Parke and Lane (1997).

carry out various tasks. Consequently, such tests focus on processes (that is, the underlying skills that go into a performance), products (an observable outcome such as a speech or a painting), or both. For example, a speech teacher may be interested in assessing how well students use gestures, pauses, and changes in voice pitch and volume; the accuracy and comprehensiveness of the content of their speeches; or both (Linn & Gronlund, 1995). A science teacher may want to know if students can use their knowledge of electric circuitry to determine the types of electrical elements that are inside a set of boxes (Shavelson & Baxter, 1992).

Degree of Realism   Although performance tests strive to approximate everyday tasks, not every test needs to be or can be done under the most realistic circumstances. How realistic the conditions should be depends on such factors as time, cost, availability of equipment, and the nature of the skill being measured. Imagine, for example, that you are a third-grade teacher and one of your objectives is that students will be able to determine how much change they should receive after making a purchase in a store. If this is a relatively minor objective, or if you do not have a lot of props available, you might simply demonstrate the situation with actual money and ask the students to judge whether the amount of change received was correct. If, however, you consider this to be a major objective and you have the props available, you might set up a mock store and have each student make a purchase using real money (Gronlund, 1998).

Performance tests may vary in degree of realism

Emphasis on Complex Problems   To properly assess how well students can use foundational knowledge and skills in a productive way, the questions and problems they are given should be sufficiently open-ended and ill-structured (Wiggins, 1993). The problems contained in *The Adventures of Jasper Woodbury* program that we described in Chapter 9 are good examples of complex and somewhat ill-structured tasks. They have several interrelated parts, provide few cues as to how the problem might be solved, and contain some uncertainty about what constitutes an appropriate solution.

Close Relationship Between Teaching and Testing   All too often students walk out of an exam in a state of high frustration (if not anger) because the content and format of the test seemed to have little in common with what was covered in class and the way in which it was taught. It's the old story of teaching for one thing and testing for something else. Performance testing strives for a closer match between teaching and testing. For example, if in giving an oral book report, a student is expected to speak loudly and clearly enough for everyone to hear, to speak in complete sentences, to stay on the topic, and to use pictures or other materials to make the presentation interesting, the student needs to be informed of these criteria, and classroom instruction should be organized around them. By the same token, the assessment of students' performances should be limited to just the criteria emphasized during instruction (Egeland, 1996–1997; McTighe, 1996–1997). One reason that proponents of performance testing push for this feature is because it has always been a standard part of successful programs in sports and the arts. Football coaches, for example, have long recognized that if they want their quarterback to know when during a game to attempt a pass and when not to (the equivalent of a final exam), they must provide him with realistic opportunities to practice making this particular type of decision. Perhaps you recall our mentioning in Chapter 9 that realistic and varied practice are essential if students are to transfer what they learn in an instructional setting to an applied setting.

Use of Scoring Rubrics   A **rubric** is a scoring guide that specifies the criteria used to distinguish acceptable from unacceptable responses, describes the qualitative levels or categories into which the responses will be sorted, and specifies how the responses will be scored (as separate elements or holistically). For writing tasks, which are probably the most common performance measures, some commonly used criteria include organization, grammatical usage, spelling, and use of supporting detail (Popham, 1997). An example of a scoring rubric for a written report is provided in Table 13.1.

Creating and using scoring rubrics is highly desirable for at least two reasons. First, they increase the objectivity, consistency, and efficiency of scoring. Second, they help teachers match their instructional activities to the demands of the performance

Table 13.1	Scoring Rubric for a Written Report			
Criteria	**Quality**			
Purposes	The report explains the key purposes of the invention and points out less obvious ones as well.	The report explains all the key purposes of the invention.	The report explains some of the purposes of the invention but misses key purposes.	The report does not refer to the purposes of the invention.
Features	The report details both key and hidden features of the invention and explains how they serve several purposes.	The report details the key features of the invention and explains the purposes they serve.	The report neglects some features of the invention or the purposes they serve.	The report does not detail the features of the invention or the purposes they serve.
Critique	The report discusses the strengths and weaknesses of the invention and suggests ways in which it can be improved.	The report discusses the strengths and weaknesses of the invention.	The report discusses either the strengths or weaknesses of the invention but not both.	The report does not mention the strengths or the weaknesses of the invention.
Connections	The report makes appropriate connections between the purposes and features of the invention and many different kinds of phenomena.	The report makes appropriate connections between the purposes and features of the invention and one of two phenomena.	The report makes unclear or inappropriate connections between the invention and other phenomena.	The report makes no connections between the invention and other things.

SOURCE: Goodrich (1996–1997).

measure—the goal we discussed in the previous section. By providing students with verbal descriptions and examples of the desired performance or product, teachers clearly communicate to students the types of behaviors that represent the range from unacceptable to exceptional performance (Goodrich, 1996–1997; Wiggins 1993). As we noted in Chapter 8, planning and monitoring are two components of strategic learning. Thus, if you want to help students be strategic learners, provide them with the measurement conditions that make that behavior possible. Although this type of preparation is unfortunately not a common part of everyday classroom testing, it is typically used in the performing arts, the studio arts, athletics, and vocational education. One proponent of performance testing cited the old farm adage, "You don't fatten the cattle by weighing them" to make this point. He then went on to note, "If we expect students to improve their performance on these new, more authentic measures, we need to engage in 'performance-based instruction' on a regular basis" (McTighe, 1996–1997, p. 7).

Use of Formative Evaluation   Earlier we pointed out that tests can be used as a source of feedback to help students improve the quality of their learning efforts. Because many real-life performances and products are the result of several feedback and revision cycles, performance testing often includes this feature as well. As anyone who has ever done any substantial amount of writing can tell you (and your author is no exception), a satisfactory essay, story, or even personal letter is not produced in one attempt. Usually, there are critical comments from oneself and others and subsequent attempts at another draft. If we believe that the ability to write well, even among people who do it for a living, is partly defined by the ability to profitably use feedback, why should this be any different for students (Wiggins, 1993)? Some specific forms of formative assessment are dress rehearsals, practice tests, reviews of writing drafts, and peer response groups (McTighe, 1996–1997).

SOME CONCERNS ABOUT PERFORMANCE ASSESSMENT

There is no question that alternative assessment methods have excited educators and will be used with increasing frequency in future years. But some of the same features that make these new assessment methods attractive also create problems that may or may not be solvable. For example, evaluating portfolios, exhibits, and demonstrations is time consuming, labor intensive, and expensive. In addition, there are questions about the reliability (consistency of performance) and validity (how accurately the test measures its target) of such measures. It is difficult to obtain reliable and valid measures of some characteristic by judging the quality of portfolios, performances, and exhibitions because there is as yet no consensus as to what a portfolio should include, how large a portfolio should be, what standards should be used to judge products and performances, and whether all students should be assessed under precisely the same conditions (Linn, 1994; Terwilliger, 1997; Wiggins, 1993; Worthen, 1993).

> **Reliability and validity of performance tests not yet firmly established**

The few research findings currently available suggest that the proponents of performance assessment have their work cut out for them. Richard Shavelson and Gail Baxter (1992) investigated the reliability and validity of different kinds of science assessments for fifth and sixth graders. The good news was that several raters had little problem agreeing on the quality of students' performances as they worked through three science investigations (a form of reliability known as *interrater reliability*). The troubling news was that students' scores were very inconsistent from task to task (thereby producing a relatively low level of a form of reliability known as *internal consistency*). Thus, to get a clear picture of whether a student understands the use of basic scientific principles, understands how to do scientific projects of a particular type, or can only complete the particular science project that is contained in the assessment, a number of tasks may be needed. This calls the feasibility of performance assessment into question since it becomes even more expensive and time consuming.

John Herman, Maryl Gearhart, and Eva Baker (1993) found that the writing portfolios of first-, third-, and fourth-grade children could be consistently scored by trained raters and that the same rating scale could be used to score different types of writing products. But they also reported two troubling findings. One was that the pieces students wrote in class for inclusion in their portfolios were scored higher than a narrative they wrote in thirty minutes under standardized conditions (an example of a direct writing assessment). The researchers could not determine which writing sample was a better estimate of students' writing ability. The second problem was that overall portfolio scores were substantially higher than the aggregate scores of the individual items that made up the portfolio—truly a case of the whole being greater than the sum of its parts. Whatever the cause of this effect, it suggests that those who are selected to rate portfolios need to be given rational, clear, and comprehensive directions.

Despite these problems, the Case in Print on page 448 illustrates why performance tests have become so popular among educators, including primary grade teachers.

Those Who Can, Perform

In recent years many teachers and measurement experts have argued that the typical written test should be used far less often because it reveals little or nothing of the depth of students' knowledge and how students use their knowledge to work through questions, problems, and tasks. The solution that these experts have proposed is to use one or more of what are called performance tests. (p. 442)

TEACHERS LOOK FOR NEW WAYS TO MEASURE LEARNING
DALE SINGER
St. Louis Post-Dispatch 1/26/98

Congratulations! You've been invited to Joe's birthday party along with Stephanie and Andrea and will get some of those terrific chocolate-chunk cookies baked by his grandmother.

But there's one problem: You have 15 cookies for four partygoers. What is the best way to share?

In the past, second-graders faced with this question on a test would be able to choose the right answer from a set of possibilities. As tests move away from multiple choice in favor of judging how well students can solve problems—and describe how they came up with their answers—cooking up the proper response is more difficult.

As teachers discovered in a recent workshop, devising properly phrased questions—ones that fairly and accurately test what they are designed to test—isn't so easy either.

"I left that meeting feeling kind of frustrated," said Melanie Avery, a teacher at Robinson School in Kirkwood, who came up with the cookie question along with Judith Joerding, a second-grade teacher at Airport School in the Ferguson-Florissant district. "I felt we needed to go back and really rethink that question and make sure we are addressing the higher-level thinking that performance assessment is supposed to address."

"When Melanie and I got together and designed the task," Joerding added, "we wanted the children to use problem-solving skills. The world they're going to live in won't necessarily have one correct answer. They're going to need different ways and strategies to solve a problem."

Cookies, Clay and Marshmallows

Before such thinking became popular, anyone faced with the cookie dilemma probably would have had choices like this:

- (a) 3 cookies each.
- (b) 4 cookies each.
- (c) 5 cookies each.
- (d) 3¾ cookies each.

Students who came up with the right answer—in this case (d), if the goal was to make sure each person had an equal cookie ration—didn't necessarily know how to divide 15 by four. They could have guessed or used real-life substitutes like clay or marshmallows to eliminate some wrong options.

As new tests are born, students in Missouri will have to do more than simply fill in a correct answer. They'll have to explain how they got there and why they think their choice is right. The change is designed to show how they can turn the basic knowledge they have into real problem-solving skills instead of simply the ability to take tests.

"You could really psych out the test," said Bill Foster about the multiple-choice variety. Foster is director of professional development schools at the School of Education of the University of Missouri at St. Louis. "If you'd memorized a lot, you could easily pick out the answer. It's like bench engineers who are surprised by new graduates who don't know how to approach a problem and come up with a creative solution. They know a lot of facts and theories, but they don't know how to use them."

Foster and Mike Fulton, an assistant to the superintendent of the Pattonville School District for planning and assessment, are helping develop the techniques needed to test such skills. Their Show-Me Classroom Performance Assessment Project brings together teachers from across Missouri, under a grant from the Department of Elementary and Secondary Education, to devise ways to determine how well students are learning what the state's education standards demand.

"We want them to think in ways so that if they can do these kind of activities," Fulton said, "they should be able to do well on the test."

Bake More Cookies

That's where Joe and his birthday cookies come in. Avery, Joerding and other teachers met on a recent Saturday at Holman Middle School, 11055 St. Charles Rock Road in St. Ann, to go over questions they had devised earlier and the answers their students had given in the classroom. Responses didn't always match expectations.

For example, the cookie question was phrased this way:

"Now you will need to figure out a way to share the cookies among the FOUR of you."

Even though they knew elementary division, few students used precision to give each child 3¾ cookies. Most used more creative solutions, like giving Joe extra cookies because he was the guest of honor; or letting Joe's mother share the feast, giving each person three cookies; or baking more cookies so that the bigger batch would let everyone share equally.

Such answers may be resourceful, but the teachers had to determine whether they really responded to the question. They also had to determine what grade to give each response, based on a four-point scale, with each level responding to certain criteria.

Matching each answer to a grade was slippery work, but for such tests to be meaningful when they are given to a large group of students, both the questions and the grading scale must be uniformly understood.

"You have to make sure you come up with tasks where the question you ask is not phrased in a way that will allow confusion," said Foster. "It's not fair to students to have them guessing what you want. It should be clear to them the kind of thing you are looking for."

Creativity within Limits

Teachers also wanted to make sure students had room to use their imaginations to come up with different ways to reach their conclusion, within the proper limits. Creativity doesn't mean anything goes; there may not be just one right answer, but students' responses have to fit what the question is asking and what skills the test is trying to assess.

Questions and Activities

1. Performance-based assessment has the advantage of requiring students to demonstrate both their understanding of information and their ability to use it to solve problems. But what are the disadvantages of this testing format? Can they be reduced or overcome? How?

2. For students to do well on a performance-based test, they have to be able to recognize that previously learned information is relevant to the problem they are working on and to accurately retrieve that information either from memory or from a reference source. This is essentially a problem of transfer of learning (which we discussed in Chapter 9). What should teachers do to maximize the probability that transfer will occur when students take performance-based tests?

3. The teachers mentioned in this article discovered that writing good performance-based assessment items is not necessarily an easy task. Since some amount of specialized knowledge about assessment is necessary to write good test items, and since you will be responsible someday for creating both paper-and-pencil and performance tests, you might think about how you will acquire the knowledge and skill that helps one produce good tests. If your program offers a classroom measurement course that is not required, you would be wise to consider adding it to your program.

Ways to Evaluate Student Learning

Once you have collected all the measures you intend to collect—for example, test scores, quiz scores, homework assignments, special projects, and laboratory experiments—you will have to give the numbers some sort of value (the essence of evaluation). As you probably know, this is most often done by using an A to F grading scale. There are two general ways to approach this task. One approach involves comparisons among students. Such forms of evaluation are called norm-referenced since students are identified as average (or normal), above average, or below average. An alternative approach is called criterion-referenced because performance is interpreted in terms of defined criteria. Although both approaches can be used, we favor criterion-referenced grading for reasons we will mention shortly.

NORM-REFERENCED GRADING

A **norm-referenced grading** system assumes that classroom achievement will naturally vary among a group of heterogeneous students because of differences in such characteristics as prior knowledge, learning skills, motivation, and aptitude (to be discussed in Chapter 14). Under ideal circumstances (hundreds of scores from a diverse group of students), this variation produces a bell-shaped, or "normal," distribution of scores that ranges from low to high, has few tied scores, and has only a very few low scores and only a very few high scores. For this reason, norm-referenced grading procedures are also referred to as "grading on the curve."

THE NATURE OF NORM-REFERENCED GRADING   Course grades, like standardized test scores (see Chapter 14), are determined through a comparison of each student's level of performance to the normal, or average, level of other, similar students in order to reflect the assumed differences in amount of learned material. The comparison may be to all other members of the student's class that year, or it may be to the average performance of several classes stretching back over several years. It is probably better for teachers to use a broad base of typical student performance made up of several classes as grounds for comparison than to rely on the current class of students. Doing so avoids two severe distorting effects: when a single class contains many weak students, those with more well-developed abilities will more easily obtain the highest grades; and when the class has many capable students, the relatively weaker students are virtually predestined to receive low or failing grades (Gronlund, 1998; Kubiszyn & Borich, 1996).

Norm-referenced grading: compare one student to others

The basic procedure for assigning grades on a norm-referenced basis involves just a few steps. First, determine what percentage of students will receive which grades. If, for example, you intend to award the full range of grades, you may decide to give A's to the top 15 percent, B's to the next 25 percent, C's to the middle 35 percent, D's to the next 15 percent, and F's to the bottom 10 percent. Second, arrange the scores from highest to lowest. Third, calculate which scores fall in which category and assign the grades accordingly.

Of course, many other arrangements are also possible. How large or small you decide to make the percentages for each category will depend on such factors as the nature of the students in your class, the difficulty of your exams and assignments, and your own sense of what constitutes appropriate standards. Furthermore, a norm-referenced approach does not necessarily mean that each class will have a normal distribution of grades or that anyone will automatically fail. For example, it is possible for equal numbers of students to receive A's, B's, and C's if you decide to limit your grading system to just those three categories and award equal numbers of each grade. A norm-referenced approach simply means that the grading symbols being used indicate one student's level of achievement relative to other students.

Proponents of norm-referenced grading typically point to the absence of acceptable external criteria for use as a standard for evaluating and grading student performance. In other words, there is no good way to externally determine how much learning is too little, just enough, or more than enough for some subject. And if there is no amount of knowledge or set of behaviors that must be mastered by all students, then grades may be awarded on the basis of relative performance among a group of students (Gronlund, 1998).

Norm-referenced grading based on absence of external criteria

STRENGTHS AND WEAKNESSES OF NORM-REFERENCED GRADING   There are at least two circumstances under which it may be appropriate to use norm-referenced measurement and evaluation procedures. You might, for example, wish to formulate a two-stage instructional plan in which the first stage involves helping all students master a basic level of knowledge and skill in a particular subject. Performance at this stage would be measured and evaluated against a predetermined standard (such as 80 percent correct on an exam). Once this has been accomplished, you could supply advanced instruction and encourage students to learn as much of the additional material as possible. Since the amount of learning during the second stage is not tied to a predetermined standard, and since it will likely vary because of differences in motivation and learning skills, a norm-referenced approach to grading can be used. This situation also fits certain guidelines for the use of competitive reward structures (discussed in Chapter 10) since everyone starts from the same level of basic knowledge.

Norm-referenced measurement and evaluation are also applicable in cases where students with the best chances for success are selected for a limited-enrollment program from among a large pool of candidates. One example is the selection of students for honors programs who have the highest test scores and grade-point averages (Gronlund, 1998).

The main weakness of the norm-referenced approach to grading is that there are few situations in which the typical public school teacher can appropriately use it. Either the goal is not appropriate (as in mastery of certain material and skills by all students or diagnosis of an individual student's specific strengths and weaknesses), or the basic conditions cannot be met (classes are too small and/or homogeneous). When a norm-referenced approach is used in spite of these weaknesses, communication and motivation problems are often created. Consider the example of a group of high school sophomores having a great deal of difficulty mastering German vocabulary and grammar. The students may have been underprepared, the teacher may be doing a poor job of organizing and explaining the material, or both factors may be at work. At any rate, the top student averages 48 percent correct on all of the exams, quizzes, and oral recitations administered during the term. That student and a few others with averages in the high 40s will receive the A's. Although these fortunate few may realize their knowledge and skills are incomplete, others are likely to falsely conclude that these students learned quite a bit about the German language since a grade of A is generally taken to mean superior performance.

At the other extreme we have the example of a social studies class in which most of the students are doing well. Because the students were well prepared by previous teachers, used effective study skills, were exposed to high-quality instruction, and were strongly motivated by the enthusiasm of their teacher, the final test averages ranged from 94 to 98 percent correct. And yet the teacher who uses a norm-referenced scheme would assign at least A's, B's, and C's to this group. Not only does this practice seriously damage the motivation of students who worked hard and performed well, but it also miscommunicates to others the performance of students who received B's and C's (Airasian, 1997).

CRITERION-REFERENCED GRADING

A **criterion-referenced grading** system permits students to benefit from mistakes and to improve their level of understanding and performance. Furthermore, it establishes an individual (and sometimes cooperative) reward structure, which fosters motivation to learn to a greater extent than other systems.

Norm-referenced grading can be used to evaluate advanced levels of learning

Norm-referenced grading systems should rarely, if ever, be used in schools since there are few circumstances that warrant their use and they are likely to depress the motivation of all but the highest scoring students.

THE NATURE OF CRITERION-REFERENCED GRADING Under a criterion-referenced system, grades are determined through comparison of the extent to which each student has attained a defined standard (or criterion) of achievement or performance. Whether the rest of the students in the class are successful or unsuccessful in meeting that criterion is irrelevant. Thus, any distribution of grades is possible. Every student may get an A or an F, or no student may receive these grades. For reasons we will discuss shortly, very low or failing grades may occur less frequently under a criterion-referenced system.

> Criterion-referenced grading: compare individual performance to stated criteria

A common version of criterion-referenced grading assigns letter grades on the basis of the percentage of test items answered correctly. For example, you may decide to award an A to anyone who correctly answers at least 85 percent of a set of test questions, a B to anyone who correctly answers 75 to 84 percent, and so on down to the lowest grade. To use this type of grading system fairly, which means specifying realistic criterion levels, you would need to have some prior knowledge of the levels at which students typically perform. You would thus be using normative information to establish absolute, or fixed, standards of performance. However, although norm-referenced and criterion-referenced grading systems both spring from a normative database (that is, from comparisons among students), only the former system uses those comparisons to directly determine grades.

STRENGTHS AND WEAKNESSES OF CRITERION-REFERENCED GRADING Criterion-referenced grading systems (and criterion-referenced tests) have become increasingly popular in recent years primarily because of the following advantages. First, such tests and grading systems provide more specific and useful information about student strengths and weaknesses than do norm-referenced grading systems. Parents and teachers are more interested in knowing that Carol Anne received an A on an earth science test because she mastered 92 percent of the objectives for that unit than they are in knowing that she received an A on a test of the same material because she outscored 92 percent of her classmates. Second, criterion-referenced grading systems promote motivation to learn because they hold out the promise that all students who have sufficiently well-developed learning skills and who receive good-quality instruction can master most of a teacher's objectives (Gronlund, 1998).

> Criterion-referenced grades provide information about strengths and weaknesses

One weakness of the criterion-referenced approach to grading is that the performance standards one specifies (such as a grade of A = 90 percent correct) are arbitrary and may be difficult to justify to parents and colleagues. (Why not 87 percent correct for an A? Or 92 percent?) A second weakness is that although a teacher's standards may appear to be stable from one test to another (90 percent correct = an A for all tests), they may in reality fluctuate as a result of unnoticed variation in the difficulty of each test and the quality of instruction (Gronlund, 1998).

Finally, we would like to alert you to a characteristic of criterion-referenced evaluation that is not a weakness but is, unfortunately, a fact of educational life that you may have to address. In a variety of subtle and sometimes not so subtle ways, teachers are discouraged from using a criterion-referenced approach to grading because it tends to produce higher test scores than a norm-referenced approach. The reason for the higher scores is obvious and quite justified. When test items are based solely on the specific instructional objectives that teachers write, and when those objectives are clear and provided to students, students know what they need to learn and what they need to do to meet the teacher's objectives. Also, because students' grades do not depend on how well their classmates perform but only on how well they perform, motivation for learning tends to be higher. The result is that students tend to learn more and to score higher on classroom tests. So why should this happy outcome be a cause for concern? Because individuals who are not well versed in classroom measurement and evaluation may believe that the only reason large numbers of students achieve high grades is because the teacher has lower standards than other teachers. Consequently, you may find yourself in a position of having to defend the criteria you use to assign grades. As Tom Kubiszyn and Gary Borich point out, "It is a curious fact of life that everyone presses for excellence in education, but many balk at marking systems that make attainment of excellence within everyone's reach" (1996, p. 180).

A particular criterion-referenced approach to grading is often referred to as a mastery approach because it allows students multiple opportunities to learn and demonstrate their mastery of instructional objectives. This approach stems in large part from the work of John Carroll (1963) and Benjamin Bloom (1968, 1976) on the concept of *mastery learning*. The basic idea behind mastery learning is that most students can master most objectives if they are given good-quality instruction, sufficient time to learn, and are motivated to continue learning.

Journal Entry
Trying a Mastery Approach to Grading

MASTERY

ELEMENTS OF A MASTERY APPROACH TO GRADING   The following suggestions can be adapted for use at any grade level and any subject area.

1. Go through a unit of study, a chapter of a text, or an outline of a lecture and pick out what you consider to be the most important points—that is, those points you wish to stress because they are most likely to have later value or are basic to later learning.

2. List these points in the form of a goal card, instructional objectives (as described by Robert Mager [1997] or Robert Linn and Norman Gronlund [1995]), key points, or the equivalent. If appropriate, arrange the objectives in some sort of organized framework, perhaps with reference to the relevant taxonomy of educational objectives (see Chapter 10).

3. Distribute the list of objectives at the beginning of a unit. Tell your students that they should concentrate on learning those points and that they will be tested on them.

4. Consider making up a study guide in which you provide specific questions relating to the objectives and a format that students can use to organize their notes.

5. Use a variety of instructional methods and materials to explain and illustrate objectives-related ideas.

6. Make up exam questions based on the objectives and the study guide questions. Try to write several questions for each objective.

7. Arrange these questions into at least two (preferably three) alternate exams for each unit of study.

8. Make up tentative criteria for grade levels for each exam and for the entire unit or report period (for example, A—not more than one question missed on any exam; B—not more than two questions missed on any exam; C—not more than four questions missed on any exam).

9. Test students either when they come to you and indicate they are ready or when you feel they have all had ample opportunity to learn the material. Announce all exam dates in advance and remind students that the questions will be

based only on the objectives you have mentioned. Indicate the criteria for different grade levels and emphasize that any student who fails to meet a desired criterion on the first try will have a chance to take an alternate form of the exam.

10. Grade and return the exams as promptly as possible, go over questions briefly in class (particularly those that caused problems for more than a few students), and offer to go over exams individually with students. Allow for individual interpretations and give credit for answers you judge to be logical and plausible, even if they differ from the answers you expected.

11. Schedule alternate exams and make yourself available for consultation and tutoring the day before. (While you are giving alternate exams, you can administer the original exam to students who were absent.)

12. If students improve their score on the second exam but still fall below the desired criterion, consider a safety valve option: invite them to provide you with a completed study guide (or the equivalent) when they take an exam the second time, or give them an open-book exam on the objectives they missed to see whether they can explain them in terms other than those of a written examination. If a student fulfills either of these options satisfactorily, give credit for one extra answer on the second exam.

13. To supplement exams, assign book reports, oral reports, papers, or some other kind of individual work that will provide maximum opportunity for student choice. Establish and explain the criteria you will use to evaluate these assignments but stress that you want to encourage freedom of choice and expression. (Some students will thrive on free choice, but others are likely to feel threatened by open-ended assignments. To allow for such differences, provide specific directions for those who need them and general hints or a simple request that "original" projects be cleared in advance for the more independent thinkers.) Grade all reports Pass or Do Over and supply constructive criticism on those you consider unsatisfactory. Announce that all Do Over papers can be reworked and resubmitted within a certain period of time. Have the reports count toward the final grade—for example, three reports for an A, two for a B, one for a C. (In addition, students should pass each exam at the designated level.) You might also invite students to prepare extra papers to earn bonus points to be added to exam totals.

This basic technique will permit you to work within a traditional A to F framework, but in such a way that you should be able, without lowering standards, to increase the proportion of students who do acceptable work. An example of a mastery-oriented, criterion-referenced approach to grading appears in Figure 13.2.

Improving Your Grading Methods: Assessment Practices to Avoid

Earlier in this chapter we noted that the typical teacher has little systematic knowledge of assessment principles and as a result may engage in a variety of inappropriate testing and grading practices. We hope that the information in this chapter will help you become more proficient than most of your colleagues at these tasks. (In addition, we strongly encourage you to take a course in classroom assessment if you

Figure 13.2 Page from a Teacher's Grade Book and Instructions to Students: Mastery Approach Featuring + or − Grading

	First Exam		Second Exam		Third Exam		Project 1	Project 2	Project 3	Extra Project	Grade
	1st Try	2nd Try	1st Try	2nd Try	1st Try	2nd Try					

	1st Exam		2nd Exam		3rd Exam		Exam Total Points	Projects			Extra Project	Grade
	1st Try	2nd Try	1st Try	2nd Try	1st Try	2nd Try		1	2	3		
Adams, Ann	16	18	17	18	18			P	P	P		
Baker, Charles	13	14	14		10	14		P				
Cohen, Matthew	14	16	15	16	17			P	P			
Davis, Rebecca	19		19		20			P	P	P		
Evans, Deborah	16	18	17	18	16	18		P	P	P		
Ford, Harold	15	16	17		15			P	P			
Grayson, Lee	10	13	12	14	12	15		P				
Hood, Barbara	16		17		15			P	P			
Ingalls, Robert	16	18	16		15			P	P			
Jones, Thomas	11	14	12	16	15			P				
Kim, David	18		19		19			P	P	P		
Lapine, Craig	14	16	18		16			P	P			
Moore, James	17		17		17			P	P			
Nguyen, Tuan	17	18	19		16	17		P	P	P		
Orton, John	10	10	11		9							
Peck, Nancy	14	15		14				P				
Quist, Ann	16	18	17	18	18			P	P	P		
Richards, Mary	16		17		15			P	P			
Santos, Maria	13		15		14			P				
Thomas, Eric	15	16	15	17	15			P	P			
Wong, Yuen	14		15		16			P				
Vernon, Joan	11	14	13	14	12	14		P				
Zacharias, Saul	18	18	17		16	19		P	P	P		

Instructions for Determining Your Grade in Social Studies

Your grade in social studies this report period will be based on three exams (worth 20 points each) and satisfactory completion of up to three projects.

Here are the standards for different grades:

A—Average of 18 or more on three exams, plus three projects at Pass level

B—Average of 16 or 17 on three exams, plus two projects at Pass level

C—Average of 14 or 15 on three exams, plus one project at Pass level

D—Average of 10 to 13 on three exams

F—Average of 9 or less on three exams

Another way to figure your grade is to add together points as you take exams. This may be the best procedure to follow as we get close to the end of the report period. Use this description of standards as a guide:

A—At least 54 points, plus three projects at Pass level

B—48 to 53 points, plus two projects at Pass level

C—42 to 47 points, plus one project at Pass level

D—30 to 41 points

F—29 points or less

If you are not satisfied with the score you earn on any exam, you may take a different exam on the same material in an effort to improve your score. (Some of the questions on the alternate exam will be the same as those on the original exam; some will be different.) Projects will be graded P (Pass) or DO (Do Over). If you receive a DO on a project, you may work to improve it and hand it in again. You may also submit an extra project, which may earn up to 3 points of bonus credit (and can help if your exam scores fall just below a cutoff point). As you take each exam and receive a Pass for each project, record your progress on this chart.

have not already done so.) To reinforce what you have learned here, we will now describe some of the more common inappropriate testing and grading practices committed by teachers. The following list is based largely on the observations of Robert Lynn Canady and Phyllis Riley Hotchkiss (1989) and John Hills (1991).

1. *Worshiping averages.* Some teachers mechanically average all scores and automatically assign the corresponding grade, even when they know an unusually low score was due to an extenuating circumstance. Allowances can be made for physical illness, emotional upset, and the like; students' lowest grade can be dropped, or they can repeat the test on which they performed most poorly. Although objectivity in grading is a laudatory goal, it should not be practiced to the extent that it prevents you from altering your normal procedures when your professional judgment indicates an exception is warranted.

Another shortcoming of this practice is that it ignores measurement error. No one can construct the perfect test, and no person's score is a true indicator of knowledge and skill. Test scores represent estimates of these characteristics. Accordingly, giving a student with an average of 74.67 a grade of D when 75 is the minimum needed for a C pretends the test is more accurate than it really is. This is why it is so important to conduct an item analysis of your tests. If you discover several items that are unusually difficult, you may want to make allowances for students who are a point or two from the next highest grade (and modify the items if you intend to use them again). We describe a simple procedure for analyzing your test items in the next Suggestions for Teaching section.

2. *Using zeros indiscriminately.* The sole purpose of grades is to communicate to others how much of the curriculum a student has mastered. When teachers also use grades to reflect their appraisal of a student's work habits or character, the validity of the grades is lessened. This occurs most dramatically when students receive zeros for assignments that are late (but are otherwise of good quality), incomplete, or not completed according to directions and for exams on which they are suspected of cheating. This is a flawed practice for two reasons. First, and to repeat what we said in point 1, there may be good reasons that projects and homework assignments are late, incomplete, or different from what was expected. You should try to uncover such circumstances and take them into account. The second reason for not automatically giving zeros is that they cause communication problems. If a student who earns grades in the low 90s for most of the grading period is given two zeros for one or more of the reasons just mentioned, that student could easily receive a D or an F. Such a grade is not an accurate reflection of what was learned. If penalties are to be given for work that is late, incomplete, or not done according to directions and for which there are no extenuating circumstances, they should be clearly spelled out far in advance of the due date, and they should not seriously distort the meaning of the grade. For students suspected of cheating, for example, a different form of the exam can be given.

3. *Providing insufficient instruction before testing.* For a variety of reasons, teachers occasionally spend more time than they had planned on certain topics. In an effort to "cover the curriculum" prior to a scheduled exam, they may significantly increase the pace of instruction or simply tell students to read the remaining material on their own. The low grades that typically result from this practice will unfortunately be read by outsiders (and this includes parents) as a deficiency in students' learning ability when in fact they more accurately indicate a deficiency in instructional quality.

Be aware of and avoid faulty measurement and grading practices

4. *Teaching for one thing but testing for another*. This practice takes several forms. For instance, teachers may provide considerable supplementary material in class through lecture, thereby encouraging students to take notes and study them extensively, but base test questions almost entirely on text material. Or if teachers emphasize the text material during class discussion, they may take a significant number of questions from footnotes and less important parts of the text. A third form of this flawed practice is to provide students with simple problems or practice questions in class that reflect the knowledge level of Bloom's Taxonomy but to give complex problems and higher-level questions on a test. Remember what we said at the end of Chapter 9: if you want transfer, then teach for transfer.

5. *Using pop quizzes to motivate students*. If you recall our discussion of reinforcement schedules from Chapter 7, you will recognize that surprise tests represent a variable interval schedule and that such schedules produce a consistent pattern of behavior in humans under certain circumstances. Being a student in a classroom is not one of those circumstances. Surprise tests produce an undesirable level of anxiety in many students and cause others to simply give up. If you sense that students are not sufficiently motivated to read and study more consistently, consult Chapter 11 for better ideas on how to accomplish this goal.

6. *Keeping the nature and content of the test a secret*. Many teachers scrupulously avoid giving students any meaningful information about the type of questions that will be on a test or what the test items will cover. The assumption that underlies this practice is that if students have been paying attention in class, have been diligently doing their homework, and have been studying at regular intervals, they will do just fine on a test. But they usually don't—and the main reason can be seen in our description of a learning strategy (Chapter 8). A good learning strategist first analyzes all of the available information that bears on attaining a goal. But if certain critical information about the goal is not available, the rest of the strategy (planning, implementing, monitoring, and modifying) will suffer.

7. *Keeping the criteria for assignments a secret*. This practice is closely related to the previous one. Students may be told, for example, to write an essay on what the world would be like if all diseases were eliminated and to give their imagination free rein in order to come up with many original ideas. But when the papers are graded, equal weight is given to spelling, punctuation, and grammatical usage. If these aspects of writing are also important to you and you intend to hold students accountable for them, make sure that fact is clearly communicated to them.

8. *Shifting criteria*. Teachers are sometimes disappointed in the quality of students' tests and assignments and decide to change the grading criteria as a way to "shock" students into more appropriate learning behaviors. For example, a teacher may have told students that mechanics will count for one-third of the grade on a writing assignment. But when the teacher discovers that most of the papers contain numerous spelling, punctuation, and grammatical errors, she may decide to let mechanics determine one-half of the grade. As we indicated before, grades should not be used as a motivational device or as a way to make up for instructional oversights. There are far better ways to accomplish these goals.

In recent years, a number of technological formats and products have been developed to make the task of classroom assessment easier, more informative, and less prone to error. The next section describes several of these formats and products.

Technology for Classroom Assessment

At the beginning of this chapter, we mentioned that assessment activities can account for anywhere from 33 to 50 percent of a teacher's time. This large investment in time is partly due to the importance of assessment in both teaching and learning, but it is also related to the fact that many assessment activities involve time-consuming methods of creating, administering and scoring tests, and analyzing and recording scores. Fortunately, recent developments in computer-based technology now allow for the efficient creation of test-item banks, assembling of examinations, maintaining of student records, and generation of reports (Baker & O'Neil, 1995; Kumar & Helgeson, 1995). Test-item banks, for instance, can now store information related to date of entry, author, references, type of item (for example, true-false), cognitive skill addressed, and item difficulty.

Assessment technology also makes it possible for teachers to record student interviews and observations in portable and hand-held computers, scan student work into portfolios, diagnose student misconceptions, track student solutions, and generate multidimensional displays or profiles of students' progress (Altschuld, 1995).

ELECTRONIC GRADEBOOKS

As indicated in Chapter 12, electronic gradebooks can store records of student test performance, compute test averages and cumulative averages, weight scores, note students with particular scores or characteristics, and print grade reports with standard as well as specific student comments (Vockell & Fiore, 1993). Edward Vockell and Douglas Fiore (1993) found that speed, accuracy, customizability, and organization are the key advantages of these systems. However, they also admit that there are distinct disadvantages to electronic gradebooks, such as incorrect data entry, system impersonality, and inflexibility with absent students and special situations. For more flexibility in electronic record keeping, Vockell and Fiore recommend the use of database and spreadsheet programs since they permit assessment records to be tailored to a teacher's specific needs.

As on-line instructional activities and courses proliferate, teachers will increasingly need to know how to use grading mechanisms designed for both World Wide Web and videoconferencing courses. Fortunately, there are systems on the Web that can grade student tests and offer feedback, recommend remediation, show Web references for information related to missed items, and keep the student from progressing to new lessons until mastery has been achieved (Dickinson, 1997). Additionally, these Web test systems can be password protected and date and time restricted to prevent unauthorized access and cheating.

TECHNOLOGY-BASED PERFORMANCE ASSESSMENT

As you may recall from our earlier discussion, performance assessments give students the opportunity to demonstrate how well they can use the knowledge and skills that were the focus of an instructional unit to carry out realistic and meaningful tasks. Computer-based technology is an excellent vehicle for this purpose. You can require students to use computer programs and Web-based resources to carry out such tasks as preparing documentaries on weather-related issues, determining energy use in taking a shower or cooking a meal, and determining the impact of a recycling plan on land fill use (Okey, 1995). Clearly, no matter what subject you will teach, you will have numerous performance assessment options.

Computer-based simulation is another potentially useful form of technology-based performance assessment. While simulations help students grasp the complexity of such real-life tasks as developing buildings or cities, operating a nuclear reactor, or running a factory, they can also be used to assess how well students have grasped such important issues as time, safety, and complexity (Kumar & Helgeson, 1995). Computer-based simulations also maintain full records of student performance and reveal approaches to solutions that may not have been apparent in more traditional forms of assessment (Baker & O'Neil, 1995; Shavelson & Baxter, 1992).

Technology tools like hypermedia, with text, audio, video, and graphics components, also offer opportunities for students to demonstrate their ability to solve real-world problems in a number of content areas. Ivan Baugh (1994), for instance, notes that students investigating concepts such as biomes and ecosystems could (1) construct hypermedia stacks such as encyclopedias and pictorial atlases on CD-ROM, (2) record narrative voice-overs for such segments, (3) use telecommunications to exchange information with people living near those environments, (4) use videodisks to provide illustrations of food chains in action, (5) digitize videotape taken from the local environment, (6) type environmental reports, newspapers, and brochures in a word processor, and (7) create replayable, brief movies about the different locales that link to other hypermedia or word processing documents.

DIGITAL PORTFOLIOS

Although technology-based performance assessments typically focus on student use of a particular skill at a particular point in time, electronic, or digital, portfolios document student performance over an extended period of time and across skill areas (Okey, 1995). Terry Wiedmer (1998, p. 586) defines a **digital portfolio** as "a purposeful collection of work, captured by electronic means, that serves as an exhibit of individual efforts, progress, and achievements in one or more areas." In their digital portfolios, students can create, store, and manage various products and processes that they want to document and perhaps showcase.

Digital portfolios are similar in purpose to the more traditional portfolios, but they extend beyond paper versions because they can include such things as sound effects, audio and video testimonials, voice-over explanations of a student's thinking process as a project is worked on, special visual effects such as animation, movies of how the student used recently learned knowledge to produce a product (such as using mathematical principles to help build a homeless shelter), and diagrams and drawings to indicate growth over a period of time.

It is very important that each student portfolio submission be linked to self-reflections about why the item was selected, since "without time for reflection, the digital portfolio might be no different from a paper portfolio filed away in a locked cabinet" (Niguidula, 1997, p. 28). This opportunity for self-reflection is a key advantage of digital portfolios: they allow students to demonstrate what they know, how they came to know it, how their knowledge increased and evolved over time, and what they have accomplished with that knowledge. David Berliner (1992) points out that portfolios, in contrast to other forms of assessment, are more representative

Digital portfolio: collection of work that is stored and illustrated electronically

of the range of learning experiences and curriculum activities that students are exposed to during a given year or unit.

Finally, John Mergendoller (1996, p. 44) argues that digital portfolios may "stimulate a redefinition of student assessment and a reconsideration of the role of assessment in teaching and learning. The payoff is not the ability to digitize student performances, but the design of meaningful evaluative criteria, the application of those criteria to performances in a reliable manner, the understanding and communication of student strengths and weaknesses, and finally, the use of this knowledge to support continued student learning."

It is important to give some thought to the software needed to produce a worthwhile digital portfolio. Harry Grover Tuttle (1997) argues that high-quality portfolio software should have options for inputting student introductions, district goals and competencies, numerous types of student work, teacher evaluations and feedback, student reflections, and summaries of student achievements. (For a listing of K–12 evaluation software and related Internet sites, see Johnson, 1996–1997.)

Following are some specific examples of the types of information a student might put in an electronic portfolio (Milone, 1995; Moersch & Fisher, 1995; O'Lone, 1997; Tuttle, 1997):

- *digitized pictures and scanned images*: photos of the student and/or objects he or she has created, artwork, models, science experiments over time, fax exchanges with scientists, spelling tests, math work, self-assessment checklists

- *documents*: electronic copies of student writing, reflection journals, publications, copies of Web pages created, and teacher notes and observations

- *audio recordings*: persuasive speeches, poetry readings, rehearsals of foreign language vocabulary, readings of select passages, self-evaluations, interviews or voice notes regarding the rationale for work included

- *videotapes*: student or teams of students engaged in science experiments and explaining their steps, student performances in physical education or the performing arts.

- *multimedia presentations*: QuickTime movies of interdisciplinary projects

Perhaps you are wondering if the school district where you will teach will be able to afford such technologies. Although some schools rely on CD-ROMs and laser disks to create student portfolios, other schools are adopting low-cost options such as having students use audiotape, videotape, and computer diskettes to create multimedia books, biographies, science projects, and math story problems (D'Ignazio, 1994). To further reduce costs, students might narrate their own work, use low-cost or free clip art, and personally shoot all video materials. Although producing exhibits that students can put on display in the classroom or community is currently the ultimate goal, in the near future student electronic portfolios might be used for college entrance files and to help students test out of various college entrance requirements (Tuttle, 1997; Wiedmer, 1998).

RUBRICS FOR ELECTRONIC PORTFOLIOS AND PRESENTATIONS   With all the information a digital portfolio might contain, how can a classroom teacher fairly and efficiently assess student learning? First of all, electronic writing, just like paper-based compositions, can be assessed holistically in a general impression rating. It can also be analyzed with specific criteria such as whether the work is insightful, well organized, clear, focused, relevant, sequentially flowing, persuasive, inspirational, and original (see Bonk & Cummings, 1998). In terms of the process of electronic research, Rich Lehrer (1993) suggests assessing student ability to use electronic databases, locate and select information, segment information into useful categories, and interpret and summarize information from multiple sources. For hypermedia or multimedia designs, he recommends evaluating the structure of student presentations, the rationale for including different information, the use of multiple ways of representing information, any consideration of audience, the division of labor within a group, and product changes in response to previous evaluations. There are also rubrics for analyzing the mechanics of student hypermedia presentations (for example, ability to explain the project, amount of eye contact with the audience, voice, use of examples, text and screen clarity, organization, visual aids, etc.; see Pate, Homestead, & McGinnis, 1993).

PERFORMANCE AND PORTFOLIO ASSESSMENT PROBLEMS

Special rubrics needed to assess electronic portfolios and presentations

We would be remiss not to point out the problems often associated with technology-based performance and portfolio assessment. High-quality performance assessments require extensive time, special equipment, careful planning, and continued modification (O'Neil, 1992; Shavelson & Baxter, 1992). Student performance in these assessments varies widely, thereby requiring a substantial number of tasks to better estimate a student's achievement. Electronic portfolios can overload teachers with work since they can become large, complex, and time consuming to grade fairly (Moersch & Fisher, 1995).

Staff development and teacher training are additional barriers to effective use of performance assessment and digital portfolios. But with proper training, teachers may begin to ask whether technology-based school and classroom assessment plans are practical, cost effective, and qualitatively better than traditional assessments.

The following Suggestions for Teaching should help you properly implement the assessment concepts and research findings presented in this chapter.

SUGGESTIONS FOR TEACHING IN YOUR CLASSROOM

Effective Assessment Techniques

1 As early as possible in a report period, decide when and how often to give tests and other assignments that will count toward a grade and announce tests and assignments well in advance.

2 Prepare a content outline and/or a table of specifications of the objectives to be covered on each exam, or otherwise take care to obtain a systematic sample of the knowledge and skill acquired by your students.

3 Consider the purpose of each test or measurement exercise in light of the developmental characteristics of the students in your classes and the nature of the curriculum for your grade level.

4 Decide whether a written test or a performance test is most appropriate.

5 Make up and use a detailed answer key or rubric.

a. Evaluate each answer by comparing it to the key or rubric.

b. Be willing and prepared to defend the evaluations you make.

6 During and after the grading process, analyze questions and answers in order to improve future exams.

1 **As early as possible in a report period, decide when and how often to give tests and other assignments that will count toward a grade and announce tests and assignments well in advance.**

Journal Entry
Announcing Exams
and Assignments

If you follow the suggestions for formulating objectives presented in Chapter 10, you should be able to develop a reasonably complete master plan that will permit you to devise a course outline even though you have only limited experience with teaching and/or a text or unit of study. In doing so, you will have not only a good sense of the objectives you want your students to achieve but also the means by which achievement will be assessed.

Before the term actually starts is a good time to block out the number of tests you will give in that term. Recall that research cited earlier has shown that students who take six or seven tests per term (two or three per grading period) learn more than students who are tested less frequently or not at all. Don't assume, however, that if giving three tests per grading period is good, then giving five or six tests is better. A point of diminishing returns is quickly reached after the fourth test.

If you announce at the beginning of a report period when you intend to give exams or set due dates for assignments, you not only give students a clear idea of what they will be expected to do, but you also give yourself guidelines for arranging lesson plans and devising, administering, and scoring tests. (If you will be teaching elementary students, it will be better to announce exams and assignments for a week at a time rather than providing a long-range schedule.)

For the most part it is preferable to announce tests well in advance. Pop quizzes tend to increase anxiety and tension and to force students to cram on isolated sections of a book on a day-by-day and catch-as-catch-can basis. Simple homework assignments or the equivalent are more likely to encourage more careful and consistent study than pop quizzes. When tests are announced, it is useful to students to know exactly what material they will be held responsible for, what kinds of questions will be asked, and how much tests will count toward the final grade. Research indicates that students who are told to expect (and who receive) an essay test or a multiple-choice test score slightly higher on an exam than students who do not know what to expect or who are led to expect one type of test but are given another type (Lundeberg & Fox, 1991).

In order for students to effectively plan how they will master your objectives, they need to know as early as possible how many tests they will have to take, when the tests will occur, what types of items each test will contain, and what content they will be tested on.

For term papers or other written work, list your criteria for grading the papers (for example, how much emphasis will be placed on style, spelling and punctuation, research, individuality of expression). In laboratory courses most students prefer a list of experiments or projects and some description of how they will be evaluated (for example, ten experiments in chemistry, fifteen drawings in drafting, five paintings in art, judged according to posted criteria).

Journal Entry
Using a Table of Specifications

2 **Prepare a content outline and/or a table of specifications of the objectives to be covered on each exam, or otherwise take care to obtain a systematic sample of the knowledge and skill acquired by your students.**

The more precisely and completely goals are described at the beginning of a unit, the easier and more efficient assessment (and teaching) will be. The use of a clear outline will help ensure an adequate sample of the most significant kinds of behavior.

When the time comes to assess the abilities of your students, you can't possibly observe and evaluate all relevant behavior. You can't listen to more than a few pages of reading by each first grader, for example, or ask high school seniors to answer questions on everything discussed in several chapters of a text. Because of the limitations imposed by large numbers of students and small amounts of time, your evaluation will have to be based on a sample of behavior—a three- or four-minute reading performance and questions covering points made in only a few sections of text material assigned for an exam. It is therefore important to try to obtain a representative, accurate sample.

Necessary to obtain a representative sample of behavior when testing

Psychologists who have studied measurement and evaluation often recommend that as teachers prepare exams they use a **table of specifications** to note the types and numbers of test items to be included so as to ensure thorough and systematic coverage. You can draw up a table of specifications by first listing along the left-hand margin of a piece of lined paper the important topics that have been covered. Then insert appropriate headings from the taxonomy of objectives for the cognitive domain (or for the affective or psychomotor domain, if appropriate) across the top of the page. An example of such a table of specifications for the information discussed so far in this chapter is provided in Figure 13.3. A computer spreadsheet program such as Microsoft Excel is an ideal tool for creating a table of specifications. Doing your work on the computer gives you the ability to save and modify it for future use.

Table of specifications helps ensure an adequate sample of content, behavior

Test specialists often recommend that you insert in the boxes of a table of specifications the percentage of test items that you intend to write for each topic and each type of objective. This practice forces you to think about both the number and the relative importance of your objectives before you start teaching or writing test items. Thus, if some objectives are more important to you than others, you will have a way of ensuring that these are tested more thoroughly. If, however, a test is going to be brief and emphasize all objectives more or less equally, you may wish to put a check mark in each box as you write questions. If you discover that you are overloading some boxes and that others are empty, you can take steps to remedy the situation. The important point to realize is that by taking steps to ensure that your tests cover what you want your students to know, you will be increasing the tests' validity.

For reasons to be discussed shortly, you may choose not to list all of the categories in the taxonomy for all subjects or at all grade levels. Tables of specifications that you draw up for your own use, therefore, may contain fewer headings across the top of the page than those in the table illustrated in Figure 13.3.

**Figure 13.3 Example of a Table of Specifications for Material Covered
            So Far in This Chapter**

Topic	Objectives					
	Knows	Comprehends	Applies	Analyzes	Synthesizes	Evaluates
Nature of measurement and evaluation						
Purposes of measurement and evaluation						
Types of written tests						
Nature of performance tests						

3 **Consider the purpose of each test or measurement exercise in light of the
developmental characteristics of the students in your classes and the nature of the curriculum for your grade level.**

In addition to considering different uses of tests and other forms of measurement
when you plan assessment strategies, you should think about the developmental
characteristics of the students you plan to teach and the nature of the curriculum
at your grade level. As noted in the discussion of Jean Piaget's theory in Chapter 2,
there are significant differences among preoperational, concrete operational, and
formal thinkers. Furthermore, because primary grade children are asked to master a
curriculum that is substantially different from the curriculum upper elementary
and secondary school students are expected to learn, different forms of measurement should be used at each level.

Primary grade children are asked to concentrate on learning basic skills, and
their progress—or lack of it—will often be apparent even if they are not asked to
take tests. A second grader who can read only a few words, for instance, will reveal
that inability each time she is asked to read. Upper elementary grade and middle
school students are asked to improve and perfect their mastery of skills in reading,
writing, and arithmetic and also to study topics in the sciences, social studies, and
other subjects. Their success in dealing with many subjects, learning materials, and
tests often depends on skill in reading. A fifth grader who is a slow reader, for instance, might not be able to get through an assigned chapter or answer all the
questions on a multiple-choice test in the allotted time. Because performance in
several subjects must be reported, many separate assessments have to be made. In
all of the elementary grades, there is usually an emphasis on helping as many students as possible master the curriculum. Thus, tests may be used as much to diag-

**Elementary grade students
tested as much for diagnostic,
formative evaluation purposes
as for summative purposes**

nose weaknesses and chart improvement (a formative evaluation function) as to establish grades.

At the secondary level, many subjects are arranged in sequence; in addition, the process of identifying students most likely to go on to college begins at this time. Thus, comparisons of students become more systematic and direct. It is often desirable (or necessary) to discover if a student who takes Math I, for instance, is ready to go on to Math II. Colleges and universities may request that high schools establish particular grading standards to facilitate the selection of candidates who apply for admission. If a school does not maintain sufficiently high standards, graduates may encounter problems when they apply for admission to certain institutions of higher learning.

Journal Entry
Using Different
Types of Test
Items

4 Decide whether a written test or a performance test is most appropriate.

As you think about which types of questions to use in a particular situation, consider the student characteristics and curriculum differences noted earlier. In the primary grades, you may not use any written tests in the strict sense. Instead you might ask your students to demonstrate skills, complete exercises (some of which may be similar to completion tests), and solve simple problems (often on worksheets). In the upper elementary and middle school grades you may need to use or make up dozens of measurement instruments since many subjects must be graded. Accordingly, it may be necessary to make extensive use of completion, short-answer, and short-essay items that can be printed on the board or on a ditto master. If you find it impossible or impractical to make up a table of specifications for each exam, at least refer to instructional objectives or a list of key points as you write questions. At the secondary level, you might do your best to develop some sort of table of specifications for exams not only to ensure measurement of objectives at various levels of the taxonomy but also to remind yourself to use different types of items.

In certain elementary and middle school subjects and in skill or laboratory subjects at the secondary level, performance tests may be more appropriate than written tests. At the primary grade level, for instance, you may be required to assign a grade in oral reading. In a high school home economics class, you may grade students on how well they produce a garment or a soufflé. In a woodshop class, you may base a grade on how well students construct a piece of furniture. In such cases you can make evaluations more systematic and accurate by using rating scales and checklists and by attempting to equate (or at least take into account) the difficulty level of the performance to be rated.

Rating scales and checklists make evaluations of performance more systematic

To evaluate a product such as a garment or piece of furniture, you might use a checklist that you devised and handed out at the beginning of a course. Such a checklist should state the number of possible points that will be awarded for various aspects of the project—for example, accuracy of measurements and preparation of component parts, neatness of assembly, quality of finishing touches, and final appearance. To evaluate a performance, you might use the same approach, announcing beforehand how heavily you intend to weigh various aspects of execution. In music, for instance, you might note possible points to be awarded for tone, execution, accuracy, and interpretation. For both project and performance tasks, you might multiply the final score by a difficulty factor. (You have probably seen television coverage of Olympic events in which divers and gymnasts have their performance ratings multiplied by such a difficulty factor.)

5 **Make up and use a detailed answer key or rubric.**

Journal Entry
Preparing a
Detailed Key

a. Evaluate each answer by comparing it to the key or rubric.

One of the most valuable characteristics of a test is that it permits comparison of the permanently recorded answers of all students to a fixed set of criteria. A complete key or rubric not only reduces subjectivity; it can also save you much time and trouble when you are grading papers and/or defending your evaluation of questions.

For short-answer, true-false, matching, or multiple-choice questions, you should devise your key as you write and assemble the items. With planning and ingenuity, you can prepare a key that will greatly simplify grading. For essay questions, you should also prepare answers as you write the questions. If you ask students to write answers to a small number of comprehensive essay questions, you are likely to maximize the consistency of your grading process by grading all answers to the first question at one sitting, then grading all answers to the second question, and so on. However, if a test consists of eight or ten short-essay items (which can usually be answered in a half-hour or so), you would have to do too much paper shuffling to follow such a procedure. One way to speed up the grading of short-essay exams (so that you can evaluate up to thirty tests in a single session of forty minutes or so) is to use plus or minus grading. If you use a point scale to grade short-essay answers, you will spend an agonizing amount of time deciding just how much a given answer is worth. But with practice, you should be able to write short-essay questions and answers (on your key) that can be graded plus or minus.

To develop skill in writing such questions, make up a few formative quizzes that will not count toward a grade. Experiment with phrasing questions that require students to reveal that they either know or don't know the answer. Prepare

The onerous chore of grading papers can be speeded up and simplified if plus-minus grading is used.

your key as you write the questions. When the time comes to grade papers, simply make a yes or no decision about the correctness of each answer. With a felt-tip pen, make a bold check over each satisfactory answer on an exam and simply tally the number of checks when you have read all the answers. (Counting up to eight or ten is obviously a lot quicker and easier than adding together various numbers of points for eight or ten answers.) Once you have developed skill in writing and evaluating short-essay questions that can be graded plus or minus, prepare and use summative exams. If you decide to use this type of exam, guard against the temptation to write items that measure only knowledge. Use a table of specifications, or otherwise take steps to write at least some questions that measure skills at the higher levels of the taxonomy for the cognitive domain.

b. Be willing and prepared to defend the evaluations you make.

You will probably get few complaints if you have a detailed key, and when exams are returned, you can explain to the class how each answer was graded. To a direct challenge about a specific answer to an essay or short-essay question, you might respond by showing complainers an answer that received full credit and inviting them to compare it with their own.

Perhaps the best way to provide feedback about responses to multiple-choice questions is to prepare a feedback booklet (see the Study Guide that accompanies this text for an example). As you write each multiple-choice question, also write a brief explanation as to why you feel the answer is correct and why the distractors are incorrect. If you follow this policy (which takes less time than you might expect), you can often improve the questions as you write your defense of the answer. If you go a step farther (to be described in the next point), you can obtain information to use in improving questions after they have been answered. This is a good policy to follow with any exam, multiple choice or otherwise.

Journal Entry
Analyzing Test
Items

6 **During and after the grading process, analyze questions and answers in order to improve future exams.**

If you prepare sufficient copies of feedback booklets for multiple-choice exams, you can supply them to all students when you hand back scored answer sheets (and copies of the question booklets). After students have checked their papers and identified and examined questions that were marked wrong, invite them to select up to three questions that they wish to challenge. Even after they read your explanation in the feedback booklet, many students are likely to feel that they selected a different answer than you did for logical and defensible reasons. Permit them to write out a description of the reasoning behind their choices. If an explanation seems plausible, give credit for the answer. If several students chose the same questions for comment, you have evidence that the item needs to be revised. (It's also possible that the information reflected in the item was not directly related to your objectives or was poorly taught.)

If you follow the procedure of supplying feedback booklets, it is almost essential to prepare at least two forms of every exam. After writing the questions, arrange them into two tests. Make perhaps half of the questions the same, half unique to each exam. (If you have enough questions, you might prepare three forms.) If you teach multiple sections, give the first form to period 1, the next form to period 2, and thereafter use the forms in random order. This procedure will reduce the possibility that some students in later classes will have advance information about most of the questions on the test. (Having two or more forms also equips you to use a mastery approach.)

If you find that you do not have time to prepare feedback booklets, you might invite students to select three answers to defend as they record their choices when taking multiple-choice exams. This will supply you with information about ambiguous questions, even though it will not provide feedback to students. It may also provide you with useful information about how well the items were written.

Turning back to multiple-choice questions, you may also want to use simple versions of item-analysis techniques that measurement specialists use to analyze and improve this type of item. These techniques will allow you to estimate the difficulty level and discriminating power of each item. Discriminating power is the ability of a test item to distinguish students who have learned that piece of information from students who have not. To do so, try the following steps suggested by Norman Gronlund (1998):

Item analysis tells about difficulty, discriminability of multiple-choice items

- Rank the test papers from highest score to lowest score.

- Select approximately the top one-third and call this the upper group. Select approximately the bottom one-third and call this the lower group. Set the middle group of papers aside.

- For each item, record the number of students in the upper group and in the lower group who selected the correct answer and each distracter as follows:

Item 1 Alternatives	A	B*	C	D	F
Upper Group	0	6	3	1	0
Lower Group	3	2	2	3	0

* = correct answer

- Estimate the item difficulty by calculating the percentage of students who answered the item correctly. The difficulty index for the preceding item is 40 percent ($8/20 \times 100$). Note that the smaller the percentage is, the more difficult the item is.

- Estimate the item discriminating power by subtracting the number in the lower group who answered the item correctly from the number in the upper group and divide by one-half of the total number of students included in the item analysis. For the preceding example, the discrimination index is 0.40 ($6 - 2 \div 10$). When the index is positive, as it is here, it indicates that more students in the upper group than in the lower group answered the item correctly. A negative value indicates just the opposite.

As you can see, this type of item analysis is not difficult to do, nor is it likely to be very time consuming. It is important to remember, however, that the benefits of item analysis can quickly be lost if you ignore certain limitations. One is that you will be working with relatively small numbers of students. Therefore, the results of item analysis are likely to vary as you go from class to class or from test to test with the same class. Because of this variation, you should retain items that a measurement specialist would discard or revise. In general, you should retain multiple-choice items whose difficulty index lies between 50 and 90 percent and whose discrimination index is positive (Gronlund, 1998). Another limitation is that you may have objectives that everyone must master. If you do an effective job of teaching these objectives, the corresponding test items are likely to be answered correctly by nearly every student. These items should be retained rather than revised to meet arbitrary criteria of difficulty and discrimination.

RESOURCES FOR FURTHER INVESTIGATION

■ Suggestions for Constructing Written and Performance Tests

For specific suggestions on ways to write different types of items for paper-and-pencil tests of knowledge and on methods for constructing and using rating scales and checklists to measure products, performances, and procedures, consult one or more of the following books: *Measurement and Evaluation in Teaching* (7th ed., 1995), by Robert Linn and Norman Gronlund; *Assessment of Student Achievement* (6th ed., 1998), by Norman Gronlund; *Classroom Assessment: What Teachers Need to Know* (2d ed.,1999), by W. James Popham; *Student-Centered Classroom Assessment* (2d ed., 1997), by Richard Stiggins; and *Classroom Assessment* (3d ed., 1997), by Peter Airasian.

Two books that are devoted exclusively to performance assessment are *Becoming Reflective Students and Teachers with Portfolios and Authentic Assessments* (1994), by Scott Paris and Linda Ayres; and *Authentic Assessment in Action* (1995), by Linda Darling-Hammond, Jacqueline Ancess, and Beverly Falk. The latter book describes the effect that performance-based assessments had on teachers and students in five schools.

The most extensive on-line database of assessment information is the ERIC/AE Test Locater, which is found at **http://educsrvb.educ.cua.edu/testcol.htm**. It includes numerous topics, reviews of tests, suggestions and digests relating to alternative assessment, and standards and policymaking information concerning the evaluation and assessment of students.

The Center on Learning, Assessment, and School Structure provides in-service workshops, professional development seminars, printed materials, and videotapes aimed at improving student assessment and curriculum design. The center is headed by Grant Wiggins, a noted scholar on assessment. Its Website, which can be found at **http://www.classnj.org**, contains assessment-related ideas, resources, and projects. Their mailing address and telephone number are 65 South Main Street, Building B, Box 210, Pennington, NJ 08534; 609/730-1199.

■ Writing Higher-Level Questions

As Benjamin Bloom and others point out, teachers have a disappointing tendency to write test items that reflect the lowest level of the taxonomy—knowledge. To avoid this failing, carefully read Part 2 of *Taxonomy of Educational Objectives: The Classification of Educational Goals, Handbook I: Cognitive Domain* (1956), edited by Benjamin Bloom, Max Englehart, Edward Furst, Walker Hill, and David Krathwohl. Each level of the taxonomy is clearly explained and followed by several pages of illustrative test items.

■ Analyzing Test Items

Norman Gronlund briefly discusses item-analysis procedures for norm-referenced and criterion-referenced tests in Chapter 7 of *Assessment of Student Achievement* (6th ed., 1998). For norm-referenced multiple-choice tests, these include procedures for assessing the difficulty and discriminating power of each item and the effectiveness of each alternative answer. For criterion-referenced tests, they include a measure for assessing the effects of instruction. More detailed discussions of item-analysis procedures can be found in Chapter 8 of *Educational Testing and Measurement: Classroom Application and Practice* (5th ed., 1996), by Tom Kubiszyn and Gary Borich.

Question Mark Software, based in Britain, produces a software program that can help teachers generate quality test items. Information on the software can be found at **http://www.qmark.com** or by calling the U.S. distributor at 800/863-3950.

SUMMARY

1. Classroom assessment, which involves the measurement and evaluation of student learning, accounts for anywhere between one-third and one-half of a teacher's class time.

2. Measurement involves ranking individuals according to how much of a particular characteristic they possess. Evaluation involves making judgments about the value or worth of a set of measures.

3. Teachers give tests and assign grades to communicate to others how well students have mastered the teacher's objectives, to find out if students are keeping up with and understanding the learning material, to diagnose students' strengths and weaknesses, and to positively affect students' approaches to studying.

4. Research indicates that students who take four to six exams a term learn more than students who take fewer or no exams.

5. Written tests are used to measure how much knowledge people have about some topic. Test items can be classified as selected response (multiple choice, true-false, matching), short answer, and essay.

6. Selected-response tests are efficient to administer and score but tend to reflect the lowest level of the cognitive domain taxonomy and provide no information about what students can do with the knowledge they have learned.

7. Short-answer tests measure recall, rather than recognition, of information and allow for comprehensive coverage of a topic, but they have the same disadvantages as selected-response tests.

8. Essay tests measure such high-level skills as analysis, synthesis, and evaluation but are difficult to grade consistently, are time consuming to grade, and allow only limited coverage of material.

9. Performance tests are used to measure how well students use basic knowledge to perform a particular skill or produce a particular product under somewhat realistic conditions.

10. Performance tests are characterized by active responding, realistic conditions, complex problems, a close relationship between teaching and testing, use of scoring rubrics, and use of test results for formative evaluation purposes.

11. It has not yet been demonstrated that student performances and products can be measured reliably (consistently) and validly (accurately).

12. When grades are determined according to a norm-referenced system, each student's level of performance is compared to the performance of a group of similar students. A norm-referenced scheme is used by those who feel that external criteria for determining the adequacy of performance are unavailable.

13. In a criterion-referenced grading system, each student's level of performance is compared to a predetermined standard.

14. A mastery approach to criterion-referenced measurement and evaluation, which is based on the concept of mastery learning, allows students multiple opportunities to pass tests.

15. The potential benefits of measurement and evaluation activities can be undermined by any one of several inappropriate testing and grading practices.

16. Classroom assessment can be made easier through the use of such technological products and formats as test-item banks, electronic gradebooks, simulation programs, hypermedia, videodisks, telecommunications, and digital portfolios.

17. To be sure that the number of various types of items on a test is consistent with your instructional objectives, prepare a table of specifications.

18. For primary and elementary grade students, the formative evaluation purpose of tests should be emphasized at least as much as the summative purpose.

19. Item-analysis procedures exist to determine the difficulty and discriminability of multiple-choice items.

KEY TERMS

measurement *(437)*
evaluation *(438)*
summative evaluation *(438)*
formative evaluation *(439)*

performance tests *(442)*
rubric *(445)*
norm-referenced grading *(450)*
criterion-referenced grading *(451)*

digital portfolio *(459)*
table of specifications *(463)*

DISCUSSION QUESTIONS

1. Because students in American schools feel considerable pressure to obtain high grades, a significant number of them feel driven to cheat. Knowing that you will almost certainly have to give tests and assign grades on one basis or another, what might you do to reduce your students' tendency to cheat?

2. Although performance assessment is a relatively new development in education, it has been used for some years in the fine arts, athletics, and vocational education. Have you ever taken any kind of performance assessment as a student? Did you feel that it accurately reflected what you had learned? To what extent would

you use performance measures for such academic subjects as writing, math, science, and social studies? Why?

3. Over the last ten to twelve years you have probably taken hundreds of classroom tests. What types of tests best reflected what you learned? Why?

4. A norm-referenced approach to grading is often called grading on the curve. Have you ever taken a class in which grades were determined in this fashion? Did you feel that your grade accurately reflected how much you had learned? If not, explain why the grade was too low or too high.

Understanding and Using Standardized Tests

14

Because standardized assessment of scholastic aptitude and achievement is such a popular practice in the United States (as well as in many other countries), this chapter will focus on the nature of standardized tests, how they are used to assess student variability, and how these test results can be employed in putting together effective instructional programs for students. As we will see, the use of standardized tests to assess variability and guide the subsequent placement of students into different instructional programs is truly a double-edged sword: it has the potential to harm students as well as help them. ■

KEY POINTS

These key points will help you learn the important information in this chapter. To help you study, they also appear in the margins of pages, next to the text where they are discussed.

Standardized Tests

- Standardized tests: items presented and scored in standard fashion; results reported with reference to standards

- Basic purpose of standardized test is to obtain accurate, representative sample of some aspect of a person

- Standardized test scores used to identify strengths and weaknesses, plan instruction, select students for programs

- Reliability: similarity between two rankings of test scores obtained from the same individual

- Validity: how accurately a test measures what users want it to measure

- Content validity: how well test items cover a body of knowledge and skill

- Predictive validity: how well a test score predicts later performance

- Construct validity: how accurately a test measures a particular attribute

- Meaningfulness of standardized test scores depends on representativeness of norm group

- Formal testing of young children is inappropriate because of rapid developmental changes

- Achievement tests measure how much of a subject or skill has been learned

- Diagnostic achievement tests designed to identify specific strengths and weaknesses

- Competency tests determine if potential graduates possess basic skills

- Aptitude tests measure predisposition to develop advanced capabilities in specific areas

- Norm-referenced tests compare one student with others

- Criterion-referenced tests indicate degree of mastery of objectives

- Percentile rank: percentage of scores at or below a given point

- Standard deviation: degree of deviation from the mean of a distribution

- z score: how far a raw score is from the mean in standard deviation units

- T score: how far a raw score is from the mean in numerical terms

- Stanine score: student performance indicated with reference to a 9-point scale based on normal curve

A Critical Look at the Misuses of Standardized Tests

- Overreliance on test scores can bar gifted and talented minority children from special programs

- Test scores inappropriately used to evaluate quality of teachers, schools, school districts

- Test score pollution: test-related practices that cause test scores to vary independent of what test measures

Authentic and Performance-Based Assessments

- Performance-based tests used in statewide assessments because of accountability pressures, limitations of standardized tests

Standardized Testing and Technology

- Clarity of test standards aided by putting examples on CD-ROM, computer files, videotape

- Computer adaptive testing: computers determine sequence and difficulty level of test items

Standardized Tests

NATURE OF STANDARDIZED TESTS

The kinds of assessment instruments described in this chapter are typically referred to as **standardized tests**, although the term *published tests* is sometimes used (because they are prepared, distributed, and scored by publishing companies or independent test services). You have almost certainly taken several of these tests during your academic career, and so you are probably familiar with their appearance and general characteristics. They are called standardized tests for the following reasons:

> **Standardized tests: items presented and scored in standard fashion; results reported with reference to standards**

1. They are designed by people with specialized knowledge and training in test construction.
2. Every person who takes the test responds to the same items under the same conditions.
3. The answers are evaluated according to the same scoring standards.
4. The scores are interpreted through comparison to the scores obtained from a group (called a norm group) that took the same test under the same conditions or (in the case of some achievement tests) to a predetermined standard.

The basic purpose of giving a standardized test is to obtain an *accurate and representative sample* of how much of some characteristic a person possesses (such as knowledge of a particular set of mathematical concepts and operations). The benefit of getting an accurate measure from a test is obvious. When standardized tests are well designed, they are likely to be more accurate measures of a particular characteristic than nonstandardized tests. Standardized tests measure a *sample* of the characteristic since a comprehensive measure would be too expensive, time consuming, and cumbersome to administer (Walsh & Betz, 1995).

> **Basic purpose of standardized test is to obtain accurate, representative sample of some aspect of a person**

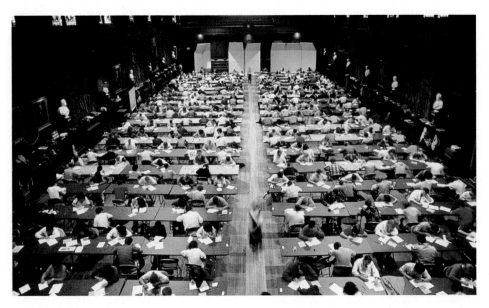

When high school seniors take exams such as the Scholastic Aptitude Test (or the equivalent) the results are reported in terms of norm-referenced scores. Each student's performance is compared to that of the sample of students who made up the standardization group when the test was devised.

PREVALENCE OF STANDARDIZED TESTING

No one knows for certain how many students are tested in a given year or how many tests the typical student takes because comprehensive and unambiguous data are not available. (If a student takes an achievement battery that covers four subjects, does that count as one test or four?) Nevertheless, Walter Haney, George Madaus, and Robert Lyons (1993) provide low and high estimates of such usage on the basis of late-1980s data for four kinds of testing: state-mandated testing programs, school district testing programs, testing of special populations, and college admissions testing. On the low end, they estimate that slightly more than 143 million students a year were tested and that the average child took 2.7 tests per year. On the high end, they estimate that just over 395 million students a year were tested and that the average child took 5.4 tests per year. In either case it is clear that American schools engage in a substantial amount of standardized testing.

USES OF STANDARDIZED TESTS

Standardized test scores used to identify strengths and weaknesses, plan instruction, select students for programs

Historically, standardized test scores, particularly achievement tests, have been used by educators for a variety of instructionally related purposes. Teachers, guidance counselors, and principals have used test data to identify general strengths and weaknesses in student achievement, inform parents of their child's general level of achievement, plan instructional lessons, group students for instruction, and recommend students for placement in special programs. To cite just one example, when a child moves to a different neighborhood within a city or a different city within a state or a different part of the country, it is highly desirable to have some idea as to what the child knows about basic subjects. Standardized achievement tests do an effective job of providing information about the mastery of general subject matter and skills and thus can be used for planning, grouping, placement, and instructional purposes.

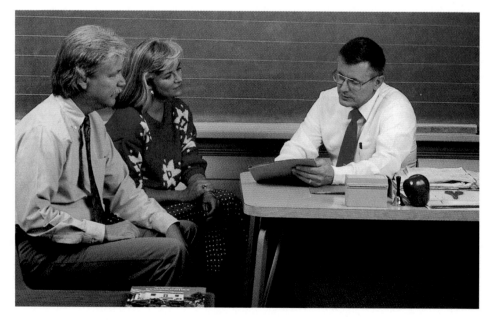

When properly used, standardized test scores can keep parents, students, and educators aware of a student's general level of achievement, and they can help teachers and administrators make decisions about placing students in special programs.

When you read the test profiles that report how students in your classes have performed on standardized tests, you will get a general idea of some of your students' strengths and weaknesses. If certain students are weak in particular skill areas and you want to help them overcome those weaknesses, test results *may* give you *some* insights into possible ways to provide remedial instruction. If most of your students score below average in certain segments of the curriculum, you will know that you should devote more time and effort to presenting those topics and skills to the entire class. You can and should, of course, supplement what you learn from standardized test results with your own tests and observations in order to design potentially effective forms of remedial or advanced instruction. The Case in Print titled "Measuring Up to the Norm" on page 475 highlights the views of educators in one state on standardized tests and how they use the scores.

CRITERIA FOR EVALUATING STANDARDIZED TESTS

Like most things, standardized tests vary in quality. To use test scores wisely, you need to be an informed consumer—to know what characteristics distinguish well-constructed from poorly constructed tests. Four criteria are widely used to evaluate standardized tests: reliability, validity, normed excellence, and examinee appropriateness. Each of these criteria will be explained individually.

RELIABILITY   A basic assumption that psychologists make about human characteristics (such as intelligence and achievement) is that they are relatively stable, at least over short periods of time. For most people this assumption seems to be true. Thus, you should be able to count on a test's results being consistent, just as you might count on a reliable worker doing a consistent job time after time. This stability in test performance is known as **reliability**. It is one of the most important characteristics of standardized tests and can be assessed in a number of ways.

To illustrate the importance of reliability, imagine that you wish to form cooperative learning groups for mathematics. Since these types of groups should be composed of five to six students who differ on a number of characteristics, including achievement, you use the students' most recent scores from a standardized mathematics test to assign two high, medium, and low achievers to each group. One month later the children are retested, and you now find that many of those who scored at the top initially (and who you thought were very knowledgeable about mathematics) now score in the middle or at the bottom. Conversely, many students who initially scored low now have average or above-average scores. What does that do to your confidence in being able to form heterogeneous groups based on scores from this test? If you want to be able to consistently differentiate among individuals, you need to use an instrument that performs consistently.

Psychologists who specialize in constructing standardized tests assess reliability in a variety of ways. One method is to administer the same test to the same people on two occasions and measure the extent to which the rankings change over time. This approach results in *test-retest reliability*. Another method is to administer two equivalent forms of a test to the same group of students at the same time. This approach results in *alternate-form reliability*. A third approach is to administer a single test to a group of students, create two scores by dividing the test in half, and measure the extent to which the rankings change from one half to the other. This method results in *split-half reliability* and measures the internal consistency of a test.

Measuring Up to the Norm

When you read the test profiles that report how students in your classes have performed on standardized tests, you will get a general idea of some of your students' strengths and weaknesses. If certain students are weak in particular skill areas and you want to help them overcome those weaknesses, test results may give you some insights into possible ways to provide remedial instruction. If most of your students score below average in certain segments of the curriculum, you will know that you should devote more time and effort to presenting those topics and skills to the entire class. You can and should, of course, supplement what you learn from standardized test results with your own tests and observations in order to design potentially effective forms of remedial or advanced instruction. (p. 474)

TEST SCORES SHOW; WHAT DO THEY TELL?

DALE SINGER
St. Louis Post-Dispatch 12/14/97

Do MMATs, MAPs and ACTs show whether students are learning their ABCs?

Not everyone thinks so. Still, in a nation that avidly amasses statistics on everything from sports to snowfall to sex, report cards and test results inevitably invite comparisons. Like kids on the playground eagerly asking each other, "Whadja get?" parents check the latest numbers for their district and their child's school to see how things stack up.

If the test in question is a good one, results can provide a valid picture for how a particular student or class performed on a particular day. Its value beyond that, though, is the subject of lively debate, particularly when it comes to measuring one school or district against another.

"There's very little way to look at 10 different kinds of data and do anything with it," said John Crowell, assistant superintendent for the Ritenour School District.

"There are so many variables at this moment with this topic of assessment, not only in the St. Louis area but across Missouri, that you end up creating more mass confusion than answers. You're going to have apples to oranges to bananas."

Comparing different tests may pose a problem, but test scores themselves can be a valid and valuable way to make sure schools are serving students as well as possible, said Bill Elder. He is a research associate at the Office of Social and Economic Data Analysis at the University of Missouri, which tracks test scores and other statistics.

Elder said scores cannot be the sole measure of a school's success, because so much of what affects student learning occurs outside the classroom. Still, he said, using the scores to measure progress is worthwhile.

Elder said no district should use test scores to excuse poor performance. Instead, he said, the scores should be used as explanations for where problems exist.

"An excuse is something you point to as a factor that you say is influencing achievement and you don't do anything different from what you are doing now," he said. "If it's an explanation, you say these are factors that need to be addressed as a community, because the school after all is part of the community.

"Some sort of standardized testing makes sense from that point of view. It's dangerous to get caught up in a simple kind of comparison, because it doesn't take into account these other factors. But it's also dangerous to ignore these scores, because that puts the children at risk."

Complicating the issue is how tests keep changing. For 10 years, Missouri students' progress was measured with the Basic Essential Skills Test, or the BEST. Then came the Missouri Mastery and Achievement Test, or MMAT, introduced in 1987.

As part of the process that began with the Outstanding Schools Act of 1993, the MMAT is being phased out over the next few years by the Missouri Assessment Program, or MAP. It is designed to gauge how well students are meeting the 73 academic standards adopted by the state Board of Education in January 1996.

Orlo Shroyer, Missouri's assistant commissioner of education for instruction, said the new test is designed to show not only what students know but also how well they can use it.

"When we get out of school," he said, "we all become problem solvers and decision makers at some level. We need to be able to take what we have learned and become those problem solvers and decision makers."

While the MAP will be given by all 525 of Missouri's districts to students in grades 4, 8 and 10, the MMAT has not been used everywhere, or even in the same grades where it is given. Some districts use other exams such as the Iowa or Stanford tests.

The variety reflects what Kent King, coordinator of supervision for the Department of Elementary and Secondary Education, calls the state's strong tradition of local control of education—a tradition that is fading.

"Missouri has not mandated testing programs or a lot of things that some states do," said King. "The MMAT has been required, but there's also been an exemption, so districts have had the option not to do that.

"With the age of accountability as strong as it is, and with the development of a new assessment system, we're not going to give options. School districts all will administer that test (the MAP), so there will be comparison data out there."

What the data will compare, and which numbers should be used, are other questions that make some educators leery of holding one district up against another.

Even with the MMAT, King explained, the data can be compared at least three different ways. One is with the actual scores on tests, figured by how many questions a student gets right. Some questions are worth more than others, so it's not just a simple matter of counting up correct answers.

Another is using what is called the median student mastery rate: figuring the score for the median students in any particular group, where as many students scored above that number as scored below it. A third method determines how many students scored in the top 40 percent, as measured by a scale based on the first year the test was given.

Each method has its value, King said, but each gauges achievement in a slightly different way.

Plus, he said, the tests are limited in what they measure, and how well they do the job.

"You probably can't always look at an individual student and determine that on a certain day he knew certain things," King said, "because a lot of things impact those test scores. He may have had a fight with his brother or a fight with his mom that morning, and a lot of things become more important than the test."

Crowell, the assistant superintendent at Ritenour, argues that testing can do little more than capture certain skills at a certain time.

"Tests don't measure an entire educational program," he said. "They are just designed to measure the particular skills that the test purports to measure. It's a snapshot of how kids did that one particular day, at one point in the year.

"Having it be the only thing you're making decisions on wouldn't be educationally sound."

Questions and Activities

1. This article states that "test scores can be a valid and valuable way to make sure schools are serving students as well as possible." What kinds of content validity evidence, predictive validity evidence, and construct validity evidence (all three forms of evidence are described in the next section) would a test's author have to present in order to support the inference that high (or low) test scores largely reflect the efforts of the teachers and administrators in helping students learn?

2. State-mandated assessments are often referred to as high-stakes testing because the scores are frequently used to praise or criticize both the teachers and the administrators of a school district. Using standardized test scores for this purpose leads many teachers to gear their instruction to the content of the test, a process that is known as measurement-driven instruction. What are the pros and cons of allowing the content of tests to influence classroom instruction? (HINT: Think about the points we made in Chapter 10 about the role of objectives.)

3. If the state in which you live or attend college has a statewide assessment program, interview several teachers at different grade levels to learn what they think of such testing programs. Make a note of the techniques they use to address the demands of high-stakes standardized testing programs.

**Reliability: similarity between
two rankings of test scores
obtained from the
same individual**

Regardless of which method is used to assess reliability, the goal is to create two rankings of scores and to see how similar the rankings are. This degree of consistency is expressed as a correlation coefficient (abbreviated with a lower-case *r*) that ranges from 0 to 1. Well-constructed standardized tests should have correlation coefficients of about 0.95 for split-half reliability, 0.90 for test-retest reliability, and 0.85 for alternate-form reliability (Kubiszyn & Borich, 1996). Bear in mind, however, that a particular test may not report all three forms of reliability and that reliabilities for subtests and for younger age groups (kindergarten through second grade) are likely to be lower than these overall figures.

**Validity: how accurately a
test measures what users
want it to measure**

VALIDITY   A second important characteristic of a test is that it accurately measures what it claims to measure. A reading comprehension test should measure just that—nothing more, nothing less. Whenever we speak of a test's accuracy, we are referring to its **validity**. Since most of the characteristics we are interested in knowing something about (such as arithmetic skills, spatial aptitude, intelligence, and knowledge of the American Civil War) are internal and hence not directly observable, tests are indirect measures of those attributes. Therefore, any test-based conclusions we may draw about how much of a characteristic a person possesses, or any predictions we may make about how well a person will perform in the future (on other types of tests, in a job, or in a specialized academic program, for example), are properly referred to as *inferences*. So when we inquire about the validity of a test by asking, "Does this test measure what it claims to measure?" we are really asking, "How accurate are the inferences that I wish to draw about the test taker?" (See, for example, Messick, 1989.) The degree to which these inferences can be judged accurate, or valid, depends on the type and quality of the supporting evidence that we can muster. Three kinds of evidence that underlie test-based inferences are content validity evidence, predictive validity evidence, and construct validity evidence.

A standardized test that is considered to be valid measures what it claims to measure and allows educators to make reasonably accurate predictions about how well students perform academically in the near future.

Content Validity Evidence   This kind of evidence rests on a set of judgments about how well a test's items reflect the particular body of knowledge and skill (called a *domain* by measurement specialists) about which we want to draw inferences. If a test on the American Civil War, for example, contained no items on the war's causes, its great battles, or the years it encompassed, some users might be hesitant to call someone who had achieved a high score knowledgeable about this topic. Then again, other users might not be nearly so disturbed by these omissions (and the inference that would be drawn from the test score) if they considered such information to be relatively unimportant.

| Content validity: how well test items cover a body of knowledge and skill |

Predictive Validity Evidence   This evidence allows us to make probabilistic statements about how well students will behave in the future ("Based on his test scores, there is a strong likelihood that Yusef will do well in the creative writing program next year"). Many colleges, for example, require students to take the American College Testing Program (ACT) or the Scholastic Assessment Test (SAT) and then use the results (along with other information) to predict each prospective student's grade-point average at the end of the freshman year. All other things being equal, students with higher test scores are expected to have higher grade-point averages than students with lower test scores and thus stand a better chance of being admitted.

| Predictive validity: how well a test score predicts later performance |

Construct Validity Evidence   This evidence indicates how accurately a test measures a theoretical description of some internal attribute of a person. Such attributes—for example, intelligence, creativity, motivation, and anxiety—are called *constructs* by psychologists. To illustrate the nature of construct validity, we will use a hypothetical theory of intelligence called the Perfectly Valid theory. This theory holds that highly intelligent individuals should have higher-than-average school grades now and in the future, demonstrate superior performance on tasks that involve abstract reasoning, and be able to distinguish worthwhile from nonworthwhile goals. They may or may not, however, be popular among their peers. If the Perfectly Valid theory is accurate and if someone has done a good job of constructing an intelligence test based on this theory (the Smart Intelligence Test), people's scores on the Smart Test should vary in accordance with predictions derived from the Perfectly Valid theory. We should see, for example, a strong positive relationship, or correlation, between intelligence quotient (IQ) scores and grade-point average but no relationship between IQ scores and measures of popularity. As more and more of this type of evidence is supplied, we can feel increasingly confident in drawing the inference that the Smart Intelligence Test is an accurate measure of the Perfectly Valid theory of intelligence.

| Construct validity: how accurately a test measures a particular attribute |

NORMED EXCELLENCE   For a test score to have any meaning, it has to be compared to some yardstick, or measure of performance. Standardized tests use the performance of a norm group as the measure against which all other scores are compared. A norm group is a sample of individuals carefully chosen so as to reflect the larger population of students for whom the test is intended. In many cases the larger population consists of all elementary school children or all high school children in the United States. The norm group must closely match the larger population it represents on such major demographic variables as age, sex, race, region of country, family income, and occupation of head of household. These variables are considered major because they are strongly associated with differences in school performance. If, for example, the U.S. Census Bureau reports that 38 percent of all

Hispanic-American males between the ages of six and thirteen live in the southwestern region of the country, a good test constructor testing in the Southwest will try to put together a norm group that contains the same percentage of six- to thirteen-year-old Hispanic-American males.

As you might suspect, problems of score interpretation arise when the major demographic characteristics of individuals who take the test are not reflected in the norm group. Suppose you were trying to interpret the score of a fourteen-year-old African-American male on the EZ Test of Academic Achievement. If the oldest students in the norm group were twelve years of age and if African-American children were not part of the norm group, you would have no way of knowing if your student's score is below average, average, or above average, compared to the norm.

EXAMINEE APPROPRIATENESS Because developing a standardized test is a substantial undertaking that requires a considerable investment of money, time, and expertise, most tests of this type are designed for nationwide use. But the curriculum in school districts in different types of communities and in different sections of the country varies to a considerable extent. Therefore, it is important to estimate how appropriate a given test is for a particular group of students. When you are estimating the content validity of a test, you should pay attention not only to how well the questions measure what they are supposed to measure, but also to whether they are appropriate in terms of level of difficulty and the vocabulary and characteristics of your students. For example, the administration of readiness tests to preschool and kindergarten children to determine whether they are ready to begin school or should be promoted to first grade has been heavily criticized on the basis of examinee appropriateness. A major problem with the use of tests for the making of admission and retention decisions in the early grades is their low reliability. Young children change physically, socially, emotionally, and intellectually so rapidly that many of them score very differently when retested six months later (Schultz, 1989).

TYPES OF STANDARDIZED TESTS

In this section we will examine two major categories of standardized tests—achievement tests and aptitude tests—each of which has several varieties. We will also examine two approaches to the interpretation of test scores—norm referenced and criterion referenced.

ACHIEVEMENT TESTS One type of standardized test that you probably took during your elementary school years was the **single-subject achievement test**, designed to assess how much you had learned—or achieved—in a particular basic school subject. The very first standardized test you took was probably designed to evaluate aspects of reading performance. Then at intervals of two years or so, you probably worked your way tensely and laboriously through **achievement batteries** designed to assess your performance in reading as well as math, language, and perhaps other subjects. During your high school years, you may have taken one or more achievement batteries that evaluated more sophisticated understanding of basic reading-writing-arithmetic skills as well as course content in specific subjects.

At some point during your elementary school years, you may also have been asked to take a **diagnostic test**, a special type of single-subject achievement test intended to identify the source of a problem in basic subjects and perhaps in study skills as well.

Marginal notes:

Meaningfulness of standardized test scores depends on representativeness of norm group

Formal testing of young children is inappropriate because of rapid developmental changes

Achievement tests measure how much of a subject or skill has been learned

Diagnostic achievement tests designed to identify specific strengths and weaknesses

Depending on when and where you graduated from high school, you may have been asked to take a **competency test** a few months before the end of your senior year. Competency tests came into use in the mid-1970s when it was discovered that many graduates of American high schools were unable to handle basic skills. In many school districts, therefore, students were asked to prove that they were competent in reading, writing, and arithmetic before they were awarded diplomas.

You may have earned some of your college credits by taking the College-Level Examination Program, a **special-purpose achievement test**. Depending on the state in which you choose to teach, you may be required to take and pass another special-purpose achievement test, the National Teacher Examination, before being granted a teaching certificate.

> Competency tests determine if potential graduates possess basic skills

APTITUDE TESTS   An aptitude is an underlying predisposition to respond to some task or situation in a particular way; it makes possible the development of more advanced capabilities (Snow, 1992). The word *aptitude* is derived from the Middle English *apte*, which meant "to grasp" or "to reach" and is related to the French *apropos*, which means "appropriate," "fitting," or "suited to a purpose." For the last several decades, aptitudes have come to be identified entirely with cognitive predispositions, and **aptitude tests**, designed to indicate the level of knowledge and skill a student could acquire with effective instruction, have become increasingly common. Thus, there are now a number of somewhat general tests of **scholastic aptitude** (the cognitive skills deemed most likely to predict a student's ability to cope with academic demands), like the intelligence tests we described in Chapter 4 and the familiar SAT, and many specific tests of aptitude, such as tests of musical aptitude, mechanical aptitude, and spatial relations. However, Richard Snow (1992) argues for a broader conception of aptitude that also includes affective and motivational predispositions. In his scheme, which we find attractive, such characteristics of people as extroversion, conformity, independence, production of mental images, attention span, beliefs, and fear of failure would also be considered aptitudes because they are fairly broad and stable predispositions to respond to tasks in certain ways.

> Aptitude tests measure predisposition to develop advanced capabilities in specific areas

Further, some contemporary psychologists argue that we should stop trying to distinguish between aptitude (or ability) and achievement and should abandon the view that one's ability is the cause of one's achievement. Robert Sternberg (1998), for example, notes that the items that appear in various mental ability tests (such as vocabulary, reading comprehension, verbal analogies, arithmetic problem solving, and determining similarities) are often the focus of classroom instruction and are the same types of items that appear on many achievement tests. Second, he notes that achievement test scores are as good predictors of ability test scores as ability test scores are predictors of achievement test scores. Rather than thinking of such aptitudes as verbal reasoning, mathematical reasoning, spatial orientation, and musical aptitude as largely inherited capabilities that are responsible for the level of expertise one develops in a particular area, he prefers to think of aptitudes as various forms of *developing* expertise.

NORM-REFERENCED TESTS   Most of the achievement and aptitude tests just described are referred to as **norm-referenced tests** since one's performance is evaluated with reference to norms—the performance of others—established when the final form of the test was administered to the sample of students who made up the standardization group. After taking an achievement battery in the elementary grades, for example, you were probably told that you had performed as well on reading comprehension questions as 80 percent (or whatever) of all of the students

> Norm-referenced tests compare one student with others

who took the test. If you take the Graduate Record Exam (GRE), you will be told how far from the average score of 500 you are (in terms of a score to be described shortly). Thus, you will learn just where you stand in a distribution of scores arranged from lowest to highest. Tests that are constructed according to norm-referenced criteria tend to cover a broad range of knowledge and skill but have relatively few items for each topic or skill tested. But in the last twenty years or so, an alternative approach to reporting achievement scores has been developed.

Criterion-referenced tests indicate degree of mastery of objectives

CRITERION-REFERENCED TESTS   A different approach to reporting achievement test scores is used by **criterion-referenced tests**. When a test is scored in this manner, an individual's performance is not compared with the performance of others. Instead, students are evaluated according to how well they have mastered specific objectives in various well-defined skill areas. Because of this feature, you may find criterion-referenced tests more useful than norm-referenced tests in determining who needs how much additional instruction in what areas (provided, of course, that the test's objectives closely match your own). The criterion-referenced approach is intended to reduce overtones of competition and emphasize mastery of objectives at a rate commensurate with students' abilities. Tests that have criterion-referenced scoring systems tend to cover less ground than norm-referenced tests but contain more items for the objectives they do assess. Because norm-referenced and criterion-referenced scoring systems provide different types of information about student achievement, many testing companies provide both types of scores.

A new development in criterion-referenced testing has occurred within several states. In states such as Kentucky, statewide assessment systems that are known as **performance-based or authentic assessment** are being put into place in an attempt to counter some of the disadvantages of traditional norm-referenced standardized testing. We will look at these new tests in greater detail at the end of this chapter.

INTERPRETING STANDARDIZED TEST SCORES

Scores on the most widely used standardized tests are typically reported on student profile forms that summarize and explain the results. Although most profiles contain sufficient information to make it possible to interpret scores without additional background, you should know in advance about the kinds of scores you may encounter, particularly since you may be asked to explain scores to students as well as to their parents.

GRADE EQUIVALENT SCORES   The **grade equivalent score** interprets test performance in terms of grade levels. A student who makes a grade equivalent score of 4.7 on an achievement test, for example, got the same number of items right on this test as the average fourth grader in the standardization group achieved by the seventh month of the school year. The grade equivalent score was once widely used at the elementary level, but because it may lead to misinterpretations, this score is not as popular as it once was. One problem with grade equivalent scores is the tendency to misinterpret a score above a student's actual grade level as an indication that the student is capable of consistently working at that level. This kind of assumption might lead parents or perhaps teachers themselves to consider accelerated promotion. Remember that although such scores may show that a student did somewhat better on the test than the average student a grade or two above her, they do not mean that the student tested has acquired knowledge of all the skills covered in the grade that would be skipped.

PERCENTILE RANKS   Probably the most widely used score for standardized tests is the **percentile rank**. This score indicates the percentage of students who are at and below a given student's score. It provides specific information about relative position. Students earning a percentile rank of 87 did as well as or better than 87 percent of the students in the particular normative group being used. They did not get 87 percent of the questions right—unless by coincidence—and this is the point parents are most likely to misunderstand. Parents may have been brought up on the percentages grading system, in which 90 or above was A, 80 to 90 was B, and so on down the line. If you report that a son or daughter has a percentile rank of 50, some parents are horrorstruck or outraged, not understanding that the child's score on this test is average, not a failure. In such cases the best approach is to emphasize that the percentile rank tells the percentage of cases at or below the child's score. You might also talk in terms of a hypothetical group of 100; for example, a child with a percentile rank of 78 did as well as or better than 78 out of every 100 students who took the test.

Although the percentile rank gives simple and direct information on relative position, it has a major disadvantage: the difference in achievement among students clustered around the middle of the distribution is often considerably less than the difference among those at the extremes. The reason is that *most* scores are clustered around the middle of most distributions of large groups of students. The difference in raw score (number of items answered correctly) between students at percentile ranks 50 and 51 may be 1 point. But the difference in raw score between the student ranked 98 and one ranked 97 may be 10 or 15 points because the best (and worst) students scatter toward the extremes. This quality of percentile ranks means that ranks on different tests cannot be averaged. To get around that difficulty, standard scores are often used.

> **Percentile rank: percentage of scores at or below a given point**

STANDARD SCORES   Standard scores are expressed in terms of a common unit—the **standard deviation**. This statistic indicates the degree to which scores in a group of tests (a distribution) differ from the average, or mean. (The *mean* is the arithmetical average of a distribution and is calculated by adding all scores and dividing the total by the number of scores.) The standard deviation is most valuable when it can be related to the normal probability curve. Figure 14.1 shows a normal probability curve indicating the percentage of cases to be found within 3 standard deviations above and below the mean. The **normal curve** is a mathematical concept that depicts a hypothetical bell-shaped distribution of scores. Such a perfectly symmetrical distribution rarely, if ever, occurs in real life. However, since many distributions of human characteristics and performance closely *resemble* the normal distribution, it is often assumed that such distributions are typical enough to be treated as "normal." Thus, information derived by mathematicians for the hypothetical normal distribution can be applied to the approximately normal distributions that are found when human attributes are measured. When very large numbers of students are asked to take tests designed by specialists who go to great lengths to cancel out the impact of selective factors, it may be appropriate to interpret the students' scores on such tests with reference to the normal curve.

> **Standard deviation: degree of deviation from the mean of a distribution**

For purposes of discussion, and for purposes of acquiring familiarity with test scores, it will be sufficient for you to know about two of the standard scores that are derived from standard deviations. One, called a **z score**, tells how far a given raw score is from the mean in standard deviation units. A z score of −1.5, for example, would mean that the student was 1.5 standard deviation units below the mean. Be-

> **z score: how far a raw score is from the mean in standard deviation units**

Figure 14.1 The Normal Probability Curve

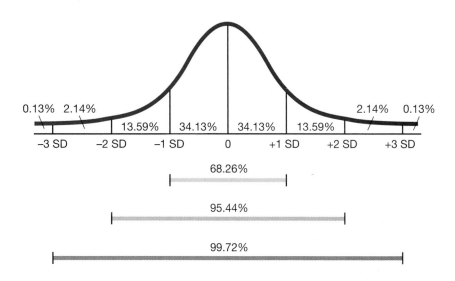

cause some z scores (such as the one in the example just given) are negative and involve decimals, **T scores** are often used instead. T scores range from 0 to 100 and use a preselected mean of 50 to get away from negative values. Most standardized tests that use T scores offer detailed explanations, either in the test booklet or on the student profile of scores, of how they should be interpreted. In fact, many test profiles adopt the form of a narrative report when explaining the meaning of all scores used.

To grasp the relationship among z scores, T scores, and percentile ranks, examine Figure 14.2. The diagram shows each scale marked off below a normal curve. It supplies information about the interrelationships of these various scores, provided that the distribution you are working with is essentially normal. In a normal distribution, for example, a z score of +1 is the same as a T score of 60 or a percentile rank of 84; a z score of −2 is the same as a T score of 30 or a percentile rank of about 2. (In addition, notice that the distance between the percentile ranks clustered around the middle is only a small fraction of the distance between the percentile ranks that are found at the ends of the distribution.)

STANINE SCORES During World War II, air force psychologists developed a statistic called the **stanine score** (an abbreviation of "standard nine-point scale"), reflecting the fact that it is a type of standard score and divides a population into nine groups. Each stanine is one-half of a standard deviation unit, as indicated in Figure 14.3.

When stanines were first introduced on test profiles reporting the performance of public school children on standardized tests, they were often used to group students. (Students in stanines 1, 2, and 3 would be placed in one class; those in 4, 5, and 6 in another class; and so on.) For the reasons given in Chapter 6 and later in this chapter, grouping has become a highly controversial issue in American schools. Consequently, stanine scores are now used to indicate relative standing. They are easier to understand than z scores or T scores since any child or parent can understand that

Figure 14.2 Relationship Among z Scores, T Scores, and Percentile Ranks

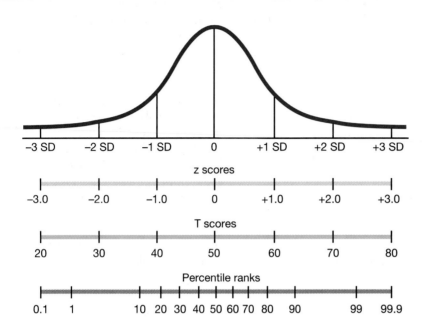

stanines represent a 9-point scale with 1 as the lowest, 5 as the average, and 9 as the highest. Furthermore, unlike percentile ranks, stanine scores can be averaged. In those cases when it is desirable to have more precise information about relative standing, however, percentile ranks may be more useful, even though they cannot be averaged.

LOCAL AND NATIONAL NORMS   Percentile ranks and stanines are often used when local norms are prepared. As noted in our earlier description of how standardized tests are developed, the norms used to determine a student's level of perform-

Figure 14.3 Percentage of Cases in Each Stanine (with Standard Deviation Units Indicated)

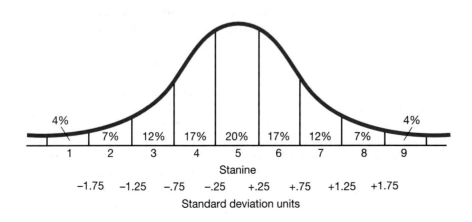

ance are established by asking a representative sample of students to take the final form of the test. Inevitably, there will be differences between school systems (in texts used and the time during a school year or years when certain topics are covered, for instance). Accordingly, some test publishers report scores in terms of local as well as national norms. Each student's performance is thus compared not only with the performance of the members of the standardization group but also with the performance of all students in the same school system.

At the beginning of this section, we pointed out that standardized tests can be used in several ways to support the instructional goals of a school and a teacher. In instances where teachers fully understand the characteristic being measured; where reliable, valid, and well-normed tests are readily available; and where teachers know how to appropriately interpret test results, this strategy for dealing with individual differences can work quite well, particularly when it is supplemented with teacher observations and informal assessments. Effective remedial reading and math programs, for example, are based to a large extent on scores from diagnostic reading and math tests. But when the characteristic being measured and the nature of the test are poorly understood, misuses occur and inappropriate decisions and controversy often result. In the next section we'll take a look at two ways in which standardized tests are misused.

A Critical Look at the Misuses of Standardized Tests

Two types of misuse of standardized testing stand out as particularly important. First, we will look at the discriminatory judgments that have been made about certain groups of children when standardized test scores are the sole or primary basis for making educational decisions. Second, we will look at how standardized test scores have been used to make inappropriate judgments about the quality of teachers or school systems.

POTENTIAL DISCRIMINATORY MISUSE OF STANDARDIZED TESTS

On the average, American children who come from upper- and middle-SES homes perform better in school and on standardized tests than do children who come from lower-SES homes. Some critics of tests argue that improperly used test scores perpetuate or increase such differences. Some cite the overrepresentation of minority-group students in programs for the mentally retarded and their underrepresentation in programs for the gifted and talented as examples of how overreliance on a narrow range of test scores can harm students. Selection for gifted and talented programs is often based largely on classroom performance, standardized achievement test scores, and intelligence test scores. But talented members of minorities often hold values about school and academic achievement that differ from the norm. Their classroom performance and test scores may suffer as a result, thereby making them ineligible for these programs (Whitmore, 1987).

Consider Sioux children, for example. If they succeed in school, their Sioux peers think of them as lacking in independent thought, spontaneity, and creativity. Many Cherokee youngsters do not believe that success in school will have a positive impact on the quality of their lives on the reservation (Brantlinger & Guskin,

Overreliance on test scores can bar gifted and talented minority children from special programs

Some critics of standardized tests argue that such tests are biased in favor of children from middle-class homes and against children from lower SES and/or minority group backgrounds.

1985). Gifted and talented lower-SES African-American children may not embrace such traditional middle-class values as deferring immediate gratification (as in "Study first; then go out and play"), accepting the importance of symbolic indicators of success (such as grades or test scores), and focusing on the future (as in "Learning geometry and trigonometry now will help you become an engineer later") (Frasier, 1987; Stronge, Lynch, & Smith, 1987).

Misuse of test scores occurs even with children whose abilities lie in the mainstream. Ellen Winner (1997) describes the case of a young boy, Jonathan, who began to talk at nine months and was reading at the second-grade level and speaking with the vocabulary of an eight-year-old at two and a half years of age. When Jonathan was five years old his parents tried to get him admitted into the local school district's gifted and talented program. Because Jonathan found the items on the IQ test too easy, he refused to complete them. When his mother tried to explain the reason for Jonathan's behavior, school officials responded that there was nothing wrong with the test and that Jonathan probably wasn't as bright as the mother thought. As a result, Jonathan's parents had to enroll him in a private school for gifted children.

Defenders of standardized tests maintain that tests, if used and interpreted properly, can help *reduce* differences in academic performance. If a test accurately reveals that a student is below average in ability, for example, it is often wise to acknowledge that fact and arrange instructional experiences accordingly. If teachers assume that no differences in ability exist, they might be inclined to expose all students to the same sequences of educational experiences presented in the same way. In such a situation more capable and better-prepared students are likely to thrive, and less capable students with inadequate backgrounds are likely to fall further and further behind. Busing, Head Start and Follow-Through programs, continuation schools, and equal opportunity and affirmative action regulations are all based on the premise that some American children are raised in learning environments that are less desirable than others and that such students need assistance if they are to compete against more favored age-mates.

The basic issue here is whether reliance on standardized test scores, particularly ability or aptitude scores, helps or harms students. You should recognize that this issue cannot be resolved to everyone's satisfaction. Every psychologist, teacher, parent, lawyer, or legislator must take his or her own position on the basis of available evidence. Our view is that standardized tests can benefit students if those who use the scores understand fully both the nature of the characteristic being measured and the nature of the test.

AVOIDING TEST SCORE MISINTERPRETATION AND TEST SCORE POLLUTION

Over the last several years various individuals and groups have expressed strong dissatisfaction with the levels of achievement demonstrated by many students. To rectify matters, many of these individuals and groups feel that at least two things should be done. First, schools should provide tangible evidence (meaning scores from standardized tests) that students are mastering much of the curriculum to which they are exposed. Second, teachers whose students score at or above the norm on standardized achievement tests should be rewarded, while teachers whose students score below the norm should not be rewarded or should even be punished.

These pressures have led to an increase in the frequency of testing and to additional (and inappropriate) uses of standardized test scores. Many principals, for example, evaluate the quality of teachers' instruction on the basis of how the students in those classes score (above the norm, around the norm, below the norm). Schools, school districts, and states are likewise evaluated by superintendents, boards of education, state departments of education, legislatures, and the press.

Test scores inappropriately used to evaluate quality of teachers, schools, school districts

The use of standardized achievement test scores to draw inferences about how well teachers, schools, school districts, and states educate their children is inappropriate because the tests were not designed to support such use. There are many factors that are not assessed by these instruments, such as the physical facilities of a school and a student's home environment, that help determine the quality of teaching and learning (Feuer, Fulton, & Morison, 1993). The pressure to test more often (at least once every year in many districts) and to produce ever-increasing scores affect the students as well. By the time students get to high school, many have become suspicious and cynical about the purpose of standardized testing. Low achievers, in particular, become so anxious about their performance that they either cheat or approach the test with a blasé attitude. The result, of course, is that the test loses much of its validity (Paris, Lawton, Turner, & Roth, 1991). Nevertheless, principals and especially teachers feel compelled to raise students' scores as high as possible. The steps that some educators take to deal with this pressure result in a phenomenon called *test score pollution* (Haladyna, Nolan, & Haas, 1991).

Test score pollution: test-related practices that cause test scores to vary independent of what test measures

Test score pollution refers to test-related practices that cause scores to go up or down but that are unrelated to what the test measures. Coaching students with items similar to those on the test, developing a curriculum based on the content of the test, dismissing low-achieving students on the day the test is given, and helping students choose the correct response to one or more questions are examples of practices that contribute to test score pollution. These practices result in a meaningless score in the same way that students not taking a test seriously does. If you knew that Mr. Wallace engaged in some of the test score polluting practices just mentioned but that Ms. Chang did not, and if the students in Mr. Wallace's class scored at the 74th percentile on a test of English grammar, whereas the students in Ms. Chang's class scored at the 57th percentile, would you be willing to conclude that Mr. Wallace's students learned more English grammar than did Ms. Chang's students? Of course not. But suppose you had no knowledge of Mr. Wallace's teaching and testing practices? Perhaps now you see the problems that are created with these practices, particularly when test scores are used to compare teachers, schools, and school districts.

Although the likelihood of your engaging in any of the test score polluting practices just mentioned is small, you should recognize that teachers are acutely aware of the pressure to raise scores. Consider, for example, the following exchange reported by Mary Lee Smith between a primary grade teacher and an interviewer concerning the use of scores from the Iowa Test of Basic Skills (ITBS):

Interviewer: Do the ITBS scores ever get used against you?

Teacher: Well, the first year I used Math Their Way [a program designed for conceptual understanding of math concepts through the manipulation of concrete materials], I was teaching a second grade class and they scored at grade level. But other second grades in that school scored higher than grade level, and I had to do an awful lot of talking before they allowed me to use that program again.

Interviewer: So they were willing to throw out the program on the basis of the scores. How did you feel?

Teacher: I was angry. I was really angry because so many of the things I had taught those children about math were not on the test—were not tested by the test. And, indeed, the following year they did extremely well in the third grade. I had no children who were in any of the low math classes and a great many of my children were in the advanced classes doing better than some of the children who had scored higher than they had on the ITBS. (1991, p. 8)

According to figures cited by Thomas Haladyna, Susan Nolan, and Nancy Haas (1991), 8.5 percent of secondary level teachers and 10 percent of elementary grade teachers engaged in the highly unethical practice of teaching students the actual items from the current year's test. In addition, 8 percent of the elementary teachers reported deviating from a test's standard directions or increasing the amount of time allotted to students.

Authentic and Performance-Based Assessments

As we noted at the beginning of this chapter, standardized testing is a prominent part of the American school experience; the typical student may take two or more such tests per year. But many educators have been dissatisfied for some time with the information that traditional standardized achievement tests provide and are experimenting with alternatives. These alternatives, which we described in Chapter 13, are commonly referred to as either performance-based assessment or authentic assessment. In this section, we will briefly examine how performance-based tests are being used in state-mandated assessment programs and why they are being increasingly looked to as a replacement for the traditional standardized achievement test. Figure 14.4 provides an example of a performance-based item that measures ability to use arithmetic knowledge to solve a realistic problem.

In recent years several states have moved to statewide assessments that are either primarily or totally performance-based. Vermont's assessment program, for example, is based entirely on the evaluation of math and writing portfolios. Kentucky requires writing portfolios and performances in science, social studies, and mathematics. Maryland's program incorporates performance assessments of writing and reading comprehension (O'Neil, 1992). Three reasons why performance assessment

Figure 14.4 Example of a Performance-Based Item

1. Bus Ride – A friend of yours, who just moved to the United States, must ride the bus to and from school each day. The bus ride costs 50 cents. Your friend must have exact change and must use only nickels, dimes, and quarters. Your friend has a problem because she does not yet understand our money, and she does not know how to count our money.

   Help your friend find the right coins to give to the bus driver. Draw and write something on a whole sheet of paper that can help her. She needs a sheet of paper that can show which combinations of coins can be used to pay for the 50-cent bus ride.

Sample Student Answer 1

Systematic List

5	10	25
0	0	2
1	2	1
3	1	1
5	0	1
0	5	0
2	4	0
4	3	0
6	2	0
8	1	0
10	0	0

5 = *nickle*
10 = *dime*
25 = *quarter*

The chart reads across row by row. The number indicates how many of each coin.

Ex

1	2	1

1 nickle
2 dimes
1 quarter

Sample Student Answer 2

$$(10) + (10) + (10) + (10) + (10) = 20\cancel{p}$$

$$\begin{array}{r} (25) \\ + (25) \\ \hline 50\cancel{p} \end{array}$$

1	3	1
25	5	10	20

SOURCE: Shepard & Bliem (1995).

is becoming a popular format for statewide assessments are noted in the following sections.

REASONS FOR THE GROWTH OF PERFORMANCE TESTING

EMPHASIS ON ACCOUNTABILITY   As far back as the 1960s, groups of parents, teachers, and educational critics were calling for better ways to define and measure student achievement than traditional norm-referenced written tests could provide. Two responses that were popular in the 1960s and 1970s were the specification

Because traditional standardized tests provide little or no information on how well students can use the knowledge they have acquired in school, educators are increasingly using performance tests. Popular types of performance tests include compiling portfolios of writing and math assignments, making a product, and conducting scientific experiments.

of student outcomes in terms of behavioral objectives and the use of criterion-referenced tests. In the 1980s many states mandated that students pass minimal competency tests before being awarded a high school diploma. In the 1990s an increased emphasis was placed on performance assessment as a way to determine the extent to which educational goals are being achieved (Stiggins, 1997).

LIMITATIONS OF STANDARDIZED TESTS   Traditional norm-referenced multiple-choice tests are designed to measure generally accepted goals rather than the specific objectives to which a school or district might subscribe. Consequently, these tests assess a broad array of basic factual knowledge and skills in order to appeal to the greatest number of school districts. Subject areas are not assessed in depth, and no evidence is collected as to what students can do with the knowledge they acquire. In addition, these tests do not allow teachers the opportunity to probe the reasoning behind a response (Worthen, 1993). These limitations probably explain why most parents prefer performance-based assessments over norm-referenced standardized tests: they provide the same kind of useful information about their child's capabilities as does a conference with the teacher or seeing graded examples of their child's work (Shepard & Bliem, 1995).

Performance-based tests used in statewide assessments because of accountability pressures, limitations of standardized tests

DISSATISFACTION WITH LEVELS OF ACHIEVEMENT   A basic assumption on which conventional standardized testing rests is that individuals who achieve high scores have learned a variety of facts, concepts, principles, and procedures that they will be able to apply in other settings. But this assumption is not always true. For example, you may recall from Chapter 9 the anecdote by Richard Feynman (1985), a Nobel Prize–winning physicist, about the inability of his classmates at the Massachusetts Institute of Technology to recognize a specific application of a general mathematical formula they all had learned in a previous class. He referred to his classmates' knowledge as "fragile." John Bransford, an educational psychologist, has observed the same inability among many students and characterizes them as having "inert knowledge" (Bransford, Sherwood, Vye, & Rieser, 1986).

The gap between expectation and result started becoming apparent in the 1970s. Colleges and businesses complained that many high school and college graduates were not prepared to handle the tasks given to them by instructors or supervisors because of an inability to productively use whatever knowledge and skill they had acquired in school. Colleges felt compelled to establish learning skills programs, and the business community spent hundreds of millions of dollars a year to teach new employees the thinking skills it felt the schools had neglected. Performance testing is expected to help teachers produce more students who can use what they know to solve a variety of problems in various settings because it emphasizes a closer relationship between teaching and testing.

In the next section we describe how recent developments in technology are making it easier to prepare students for standardized assessments, administer the tests, and score students' responses.

Standardized Testing and Technology

Given the prevalence of standardized testing and the large amount of money that schools spend on testing programs, it is not too surprising that technology tools exist for a wide range of assessment formats including the standard true-false, multiple-choice, and fill-in-the-blank questions as well as alternative assessments such as essay writing, debate forums, simulations, and electronic exhibitions of student work. As we discuss in this section, technology can be used in all phases of testing, including preparing students for standardized tests, administering tests, and scoring students' responses.

USING TECHNOLOGY TO PREPARE STUDENTS FOR ASSESSMENTS

For students to perform well on standardized tests, they need to have a clear understanding of the standards that will be used to evaluate their responses (as we noted in Chapter 10), and they need to be adequately prepared to meet those standards. As national educational standards are proposed for disciplines such as mathematics, science, reading, writing, and even physical education, the role of technology in the preparation and assessment of students is steadily increasing. In physical education, for instance, standards related to demonstrating competency in many movement forms and applying what one has learned to improve motor skills in an area could be addressed by: (1) using CD-ROM videos to model proper tennis techniques, (2) converting video of golf swings to a digitized video file, (3) employing heart monitors to assess and graph targeted heart rates in an aerobics class, (4) comparing printouts from one's performance on fitness equipment to fitness goals as well as to previous accomplishments, and (5) videotaping athletic performances of peers and presenting hypermedia summaries and suggestions of what one has learned (Baugh, 1994; Mohnsen, 1997).

Clarity of test standards aided by putting examples on CD-ROM, computer files, videotape

Another way professional organizations, states, school districts, and teachers in any discipline electronically communicate their standards and student performance goals is through the use of electronic exemplars (Lavigne & Lajoie, 1996). For instance, weak and strong examples of a skill might be posted to the Web to make performance criteria visible and provide a model for students to discuss and debate.

And with the rise of technology on the Web for condensing and replaying audio and video files, segments from videotapes of expert or targeted performances might also be digitized and placed into a library of electronic performance standards.

USING TECHNOLOGY TO ASSESS MASTERY OF STANDARDS

In addition to using technology to model standards, technology can also be used to assess whether certain standards have been met. For instance, test developers at American College Testing (ACT) have created a computerized writing assessment, piloted with more than thirteen thousand students, that asks examinees to edit several 225-word passages on a computer screen (Davey, Godwin, & Mittelholtz, 1997). Instead of flagging errors for students and giving them lists of alternative corrections, this system requires the examinee to determine if a writing problem exists. In selecting from four alternative ways of rewriting each passage segment, the test taker must move the cursor to the section of text that he or she thinks needs to be changed and select from alternatives related to grammar, organization, or style of that section. ACT's experience indicates that less effective writers tend to replace errors with new ones or introduce entirely new errors to the manuscript. Although students can go back and revise the text on multiple occasions, at this point only their final products are judged, not their writing processes and decision-making strategies. Nevertheless, these types of problem-finding tests will add another dimension to both standardized and classroom testing and perhaps speed up college or even high school placement decisions.

National testing services are also interested in using technology to grade essay exam questions since human judgment on national tests is fairly subjective, costly, and cursory. Ellis Page (1994) has developed a technology tool, Project Essay Grade (PEG), to show that computers can rate student essays as well as or better than humans. According to Page and Nancy Petersen (1995), recent versions of this tool evaluate such complex and important writing variables as content, organization, style, and creativity, in addition to mechanics and document length. In one experiment, Page took hundreds of twelfth-grade student writing samples from the 1988 and 1990 National Assessment of Writing Progress to show that computer scoring is superior to human scoring, even when there are multiple human raters on each essay. Computer scoring is not only quicker and more economical, but apparently it is more accurate and statistically informative than human ratings (Page & Petersen, 1995). Page argues that the increased use of grammar and style checkers in word processors, combined with the exploding power of technology and simultaneous falling costs, signals a bright future for computer assessment of essay exams and other forms of writing. Given the millions of essays rated each year by the Educational Testing Service alone and the growing reliance on essay writing in future SATs and GREs, computer-rated essays may soon become commonplace in standardized testing.

COMPUTER ADAPTIVE TESTING

Technology has also changed the very nature of some tests. Instead of subjecting every student to the same sequence of test items, **computer adaptive testing (CAT)** adjusts item difficulty and sequence to the ability level and responses of the examinee (Helgeson & Kumar, 1993). With immediate feedback and developmentally appropriate assistance, the student can recover from erroneous steps and get back on

Computer adaptive testing: computers determine sequence and difficulty level of test items

track to solve the problem, thereby exhibiting knowledge that ordinarily would remain hidden (Singley & Taft, 1995).

As followers of Vygotsky would propose, such diagnostic tests can reveal both the current level of a student's performance and his or her potential with a bit of support. And the more diagnostic information one has about student conceptual and skill deficiencies, the greater the chance for teachers to differentiate student zones of development and determine how to successfully work with each student (Zehavi, 1997). In addition to the immediate feedback and individualization provided by CAT, it is highly flexible, avoids human error in rating, reduces the number of examination proctors, awards partial credit, follows a student's pace or rhythm, and takes less time to complete (Singley & Taft, 1995; Trentin, 1997). In effect, computer technology can help create personalized tests that would be too time consuming and complex for a human to develop. On the downside, however, these complex testing systems are available only for certain types of cognitive skills (for example, memory tasks) and are often limited by computer hardware availability (Trentin, 1997).

In the next section we offer several Suggestions for Teaching that will help you and your students appropriately use standardized test scores.

SUGGESTIONS FOR TEACHING IN YOUR CLASSROOM

Using Standardized Tests

1 Before you give a standardized test, emphasize that students should do their best and give them suggestions for taking such tests.

2 Examine the test booklet and answer sheet in advance so that you are familiar with the test.

3 Be cautious when interpreting scores and always give the student the benefit of the doubt.

4 Do your best to control the impact of negative expectations.

5 Be prepared to offer parents clear and accurate information about their children's test scores.

Journal Entry
Explaining Test-
Taking Skills

1 **Before you give a standardized test, emphasize that students should do their best and give suggestions for taking such tests.**

For maximum usefulness, scores on standardized tests should be as accurate a representation of actual ability as possible.

Accordingly, the day before a standardized test is scheduled, tell your students that they should do their best. Emphasize that the scores will be used to help them improve their school performance and will provide useful feedback to you about the quality of your instruction. If you're thinking about ignoring this suggestion because you don't believe that students will score significantly higher on a standardized test in response to a simple pep talk, you might want to reconsider. In one study (Brown & Walberg, 1993), primary and elementary grade students were urged to do as well as possible on the Mathematics Concepts subtest of the Iowa Test of Basic Skills because their scores would be useful to them, to their teacher, and to their parents. Compared to a comparable group of students who received standard instructions, the average student scored about 12 percentile ranks (about one-third of a standard deviation) higher.

You may be able to partly reduce the anxiety and tension that are almost inevitable under formal testing conditions by giving some test-taking hints in advance. Robert Linn and Norman Gronlund note the following tips that might be stressed (depending on the type of test and the grade level of the student):

1. Listen to or read directions carefully.
2. Listen to or read test items carefully.
3. Set a pace that will allow time to complete the test.
4. Bypass difficult items and return to them later.
5. Make informed guesses rather than omit items.
6. Eliminate as many alternatives as possible on multiple-choice items before guessing.
7. Follow directions carefully when marking the answer sheet (for example, be sure to darken the entire space).
8. Check to be sure the item number and answer number match when marking an answer.
9. Check to be sure the appropriate response is marked on the answer sheet.
10. Go back and check the answers if time permits. (1995, p. 430)

2 Examine the test booklet and answer sheet in advance so that you are familiar with the test.

Ideally you might take the test yourself so that you become thoroughly familiar with what your students will be doing. If there are any aspects of recording answers that are especially tricky, you might mention these when you give your test-taking skills presentation or when you hand out examination booklets and answer sheets.

3 Be cautious when interpreting scores and always give the student the benefit of the doubt.

Journal Entry
Interpreting
Test Scores

The profiles or reports you will receive a few weeks after a test has been administered will contain information that is potentially beneficial to you and to your students. If misused or misinterpreted, however, the information is potentially harmful. Misinterpretations of scores can lead to complaints by parents. Therefore, as you examine the scores concentrate on ways you can make positive use of the results. Look for areas of weakness in student performance that need special attention. At the same time, do your best to avoid forming negative expectations. Chances are that the overall test scores will often reinforce your own impressions of the general abilities of students. You can't help forming such impressions, and they can work to the advantage of students. If a student has had trouble with almost every assignment and classroom test you have given, it is often the case that test scores will reflect that level of performance. If such a student scores higher than expected, however, you might ask yourself if your expectations for that student have been too low and make a resolution to give extra help and encouragement, using the test scores to provide direction.

If a student's test scores are lower than you expected them to be, examine them to discover areas of weakness but guard against thinking, "Well, I guess he had me fooled. He's not as sharp as I thought he was. Maybe I had better lower grades a notch on the next report card." There are many reasons a student may not do well on a test (for example, anxiety, fatigue, illness, worry about some home or school interpersonal situation), and scores may not be an accurate reflection of current capability. Thus, whenever there is a discrepancy between test scores and observed classroom performance, always assume that the more favorable impression is the one to use as an indication of general capability. Try to use indications of below-average performance in constructive ways to help students overcome inadequacies.

4 Do your best to control the impact of negative expectations.

As you peruse student test scores, do your best to resist the temptation to label or categorize students, particularly those who have a consistent pattern of low scores. Instead of succumbing to thoughts that such students are incapable of learning, you might make an effort to concentrate on the idea that they need extra encouragement and individualized attention. Use the information on test profiles to help them overcome their learning difficulties, not to justify fatalistically ignoring their problems.

5 Be prepared to offer parents clear and accurate information about their children's test scores.

For a variety of reasons, misconceptions about the nature of standardized tests are common. As a result, many parents do not fully understand what their children's scores mean. Parent-teacher conferences are probably the best time to correct misconceptions and provide some basic information about the meaning of standardized test scores. In an unobtrusive place on your desk, you might keep a brief list of points to cover as you converse with each parent. In one way or another you should mention that test scores should be treated as *estimates* of whatever was measured (achievement, for example). There are two reasons for representing test scores in this fashion. First, tests do not (indeed, they cannot) assess everything that students know or that makes up a particular capability. Standardized achievement tests, for example, tend to cover a relatively broad range of knowledge but do not assess any one topic in great depth. Therefore, students may know more than their scores suggest. Second, all tests contain some degree of error because of such factors as vaguely worded items, confusing directions, and low motivation on the day the test is administered.

Remember that a student's test score reflects the extent to which the content of that test has been mastered at about the time the test was taken. A student may have strengths and weaknesses not measured by a particular test, and because of changes in such characteristics as interests, motives, and cognitive skills, test scores can change, sometimes dramatically. The younger the student is and the longer the interval is between testings (on the same test), the greater the likelihood that a test score will change significantly.

What a test score means depends on the nature of the test. If an intelligence or a scholastic aptitude test was taken by your students, point out that such tests measure the current status of those cognitive skills that most closely relate to academic success. Also mention that IQ scores are judged to be below average, average, or above average on the basis of how they compare to the scores of a norm group. You might use personal wealth as an analogy to illustrate this last point. Whether someone is considered poor, financially comfortable, or wealthy depends on how much money everyone else in that person's reference group possesses. A net worth of $100,000 is considered wealthy in some circles but barely adequate in others.

If you are discussing achievement test scores, make sure you understand the differences among diagnostic tests, norm-referenced tests, and criterion-referenced tests. Scores from a diagnostic achievement test can be used to discuss a student's strengths and weaknesses in such skills as reading, math, and spelling. Scores from a norm-referenced achievement test can be used to discuss general strengths and weaknesses in one or more content areas. For achievement tests that provide multiple sets of norms, start your interpretation at the most local level (school norms, ideally) since they are likely to be the most meaningful to parents, and then move to a more broad-based interpretation (district, state, or national norms). Scores from a criterion-referenced achievement test can be used to discuss how well a student has mastered the objectives on which the test is based. If there is a close correspondence between the test's objectives and those of the teacher, the test score can be used as an indicator of how much the student has learned in class.

The instructional decisions you make in the classroom will be *guided* but not dictated by the test scores. Many parents fear that if their child obtains a low score on a test, she will be labeled a slow learner by the teacher and will receive less attention than higher-scoring students. This is a good opportunity to lay such a fear to rest in two ways. First, note that test scores are but *one* source of information about students. You will also take into account how well they perform on classroom tests, homework assignments, and special projects as well as in classroom discussions. Second, emphasize that you are committed to using test scores not to classify students but to help them learn.

RESOURCES FOR FURTHER INVESTIGATION

■ Technical and Specialized Aspects of Testing

For more information about standardized tests and how to appropriately use the information they provide, consult one or more of these books: *Psychological Testing* (7th ed., 1997), by Anne Anastasi and Susan Urbina; *Essentials of Psychological Testing* (5th ed., 1990), by Lee Cronbach; *Essentials of Educational Measurement* (5th ed., 1991), by Robert Ebel and David Frisbie; *Measurement and Assessment in Teaching* (7th ed., 1995), by Robert Linn and Norman Gronlund; and *Tests and Assessment* (3d ed., 1995), by W. Bruce Walsh and Nancy Betz.

For information about issues surrounding the testing of minority students, examine *Assessment and Instruction of Culturally and Linguistically Diverse Students with or At-Risk of Learning Problems: From Research to Practice* (1997), by Virginia Gonzalez, Rita Brusca-Vega, and Thomas Yawkey; *Multicultural Assessment Perspectives for Professional Psychology* (1993), by Richard Dana; and *Assessment and Placement of Minority Students* (1991), by Ronald Samuda and associates.

■ Critiques of Standardized Testing

A critical view of the nature of standardized tests and how they might be changed can be found in *Standardized Tests and Our Children: A Guide to Testing Reform* (1990), by the organization FairTest.

References for Evaluating Standardized Tests

To obtain the information necessary for evaluating standardized tests, examine *Ninth Mental Measurements Yearbook* (1985), edited by James Mitchell, Jr.; *Tenth Mental Measurements Yearbook* (1989), edited by Jane Close Conoley and Jack Kramer; and *Test Critiques* (Vols. 1–8) (1984–1991), edited by Daniel Keyser and Richard Sweetland. You may have to check earlier editions of *Mental Measurements Yearbook* and *Test Critiques* for information on a specific test since there are far too many tests available for either publication to review in a single edition.

Some additional on-line resources for you to explore include the ERIC Clearinghouse on Assessment and Evaluation at **http://ericae.net/**. This site includes a test locator, links to other assessment-oriented Websites, an on-line assessment library, and an assessment-oriented listserv.

The American Educational Research Association provides a Code of Fair Testing Practices at **http://aera.net/resource/resource.html**. The code can also be reached at **gopher://vmsgopher.cua.edu/00gopher_root_eric_ae%3a%5b_tc%5d_code.txt**.

The National Center for Fair and Open Testing (more commonly known as FairTest) is an advocacy group whose goal is the development of fair, open, and educationally sound standardized tests. Its home page can be found at **http://www.fairtest.org/index.htm**. Under a menu titled "FairTest Programs" you will find a "K–12 Testing" page with several links to fact sheets and publications.

SUMMARY

1. Standardized tests are designed by people with specialized training in test construction, are given to everyone under the same conditions, are scored the same for everyone, and are interpreted with reference either to a norm group or a set of predetermined standards.

2. The purpose of giving a standardized test is to obtain an accurate and representative sample of some characteristic of a person, since it is impractical to measure that characteristic comprehensively.

3. Standardized tests are typically used to identify students' strengths and weaknesses, inform parents of their child's general level of achievement, plan instructional lessons, and place students in special groups or programs.

4. One of the most important characteristics of a standardized test is its reliability—the similarity between two rankings of test scores obtained from the same individuals.

5. Another important characteristic of standardized tests is validity. A valid test accurately measures what its users intend it to measure and allows us to draw appropriate inferences about how much of some characteristic the test taker possesses. Three types of evidence that contribute to accurate inferences are content validity evidence, predictive validity evidence, and construct validity evidence.

6. A third important characteristic of a standardized test is its norm group—a sample of students specially chosen and tested so as to reflect the population of students for whom the test is intended. The norm group's performance becomes the standard against which scores are compared.

7. Standardized achievement tests measure how much has been learned about a particular subject. The major types of achievement tests are single subject, batteries, diagnostic, competency, and special purpose.

8. Diagnostic tests identify specific strengths and weaknesses in basic learning skills.

9. Competency tests measure how well high school students have acquired such basic skills as reading, writing, and computation.

10. Aptitude tests estimate an individual's predisposition to acquire additional knowledge and skill in specific areas with the aid of effective instruction.

11. Tests that use a norm-referenced scoring system compare an individual's score to the performance of a norm group.

12. Tests that use a criterion-referenced scoring system judge scores in terms of mastery of a set of objectives.

13. Percentile rank indicates the percentage of scores that are at or below a person's score.

14. A z score is a standard score that indicates how far in standard deviation units a raw score is from the mean.

15. A T score is a standard score that indicates in whole positive numbers how far a raw score is from the mean.

16. A stanine score indicates in which of nine normal-curve segments a person's performance falls.

17. When test scores are the sole or primary basis for making educational decisions, unfair practices can result. For example, in some areas lower-SES and ethnic minority students are overrepresented in classes for the mentally retarded and underrepresented in classes for the gifted and talented.

18. In recent years test scores have been inappropriately used to assess the quality of instruction provided by teachers, schools, school districts, and entire states.

19. This constant pressure on educators to raise test scores to please critics has led to test score pollution—test preparation and test-taking practices that artificially inflate or deflate scores.

20. In recent years several statewide assessment programs have replaced their traditional norm-referenced, multiple-choice achievement tests with one or more types of performance tests. A performance test assesses how well students can use the knowledge and skill they have learned in the classroom to solve different types of problems and complete various tasks.

21. Technology can aid in preparing students for standardized tests and in administering and scoring the tests.

KEY TERMS

standardized tests *(472)*
reliability *(474)*
validity *(477)*
norm group *(478)*
single-subject achievement test *(479)*
achievement battery *(479)*
diagnostic test *(479)*
competency test *(480)*

special-purpose achievement test *(480)*
aptitude tests *(480)*
scholastic aptitude *(480)*
norm-referenced test *(480)*
criterion-referenced test *(481)*
performance-based or authentic
  assessment *(481)*
grade equivalent score *(481)*

percentile rank *(482)*
standard deviation *(482)*
normal curve *(482)*
z score *(482)*
T score *(483)*
stanine score *(483)*
test score pollution *(487)*
computer adaptive testing *(492)*

DISCUSSION QUESTIONS

1. If you are like most people, you took a variety of standardized tests throughout your elementary and high school years. The results of those tests were probably used to help determine what you would be taught and how. Do you think that those tests adequately reflected what you had learned and were capable of learning and, therefore, were always used in your best interest? What can you do to increase the chances you will use test scores to help *your* students fulfill their potential?

2. Think about norm-referenced tests and criterion-referenced tests. Which do you think you prefer? Why?

Can you describe a set of circumstances in which a norm-referenced test would be clearly preferable to a criterion-referenced test and vice versa?

3. If you had to tell parents about the results of a standardized test, which type of score could you explain most clearly: raw score, percentile rank, z score, T score, or stanine score? Which do you think would be most informative for parents? For you as a teacher? If you do not understand completely the one that you think most informative, what can you do about this situation?

Becoming a Better Teacher by Becoming a Reflective Teacher

As you know from personal experience, some teachers are much more effective than others. Take a moment and think back to as many teachers as you can remember. How many of them were really outstanding in the sense that they established a favorable classroom atmosphere, were sensitive to the needs of students, and used a variety of techniques to help you learn? How many of them did an adequate job but left you bored or indifferent most of the time? How many of them made you dread entering their classrooms because they were either ineffective teachers or insensitive or even cruel in dealing with you and your classmates? Chances are you remember just a few outstanding teachers and had at least one who was incompetent or tyrannical (and perhaps several of them). You probably know from your experiences as a student that ineffective or vindictive teachers are often dissatisfied with themselves and with their jobs. It seems logical to assume a circular relationship in such cases: unhappy teachers often do a poor job of instruction; teachers who do a poor job of instruction are likely to be unhappy.

If you hope to be an effective teacher who enjoys life in the classroom (most of the time), you must be well prepared and willing to work. You will need a wide variety of skills, sensitivity to the needs of your students, and awareness of many instructional techniques. Each chapter in this book was written to help you acquire these various skills, sensitivities, and techniques. In addition, you will need to develop the reflective attitudes and abilities that help you formulate thoughtful instructional goals and plans, implement those plans, observe their effects, and judge whether your goals were met. This last chapter offers some suggestions you might use to enhance such attitudes and abilities. ■

Improving Your Teaching and Reflection Skills

Scholars who study instructional processes often liken the role of the classroom teacher to that of an orchestra conductor. Jere Brophy and Carolyn Evertson, for example, note that "effective teaching involves *orchestration* of a large number of factors, continually shifting teaching behavior to respond to continually shifting needs" (1976, p. 139). They also note that "the most successful teachers looked upon themselves as diagnosticians and problem solvers" (1976, p. 45). Taken together, these two comments emphasize the point that to be consistently effective, you will need to observe and analyze what you do in the classroom and use different approaches with different groups of students.

There are a number of ways you can strive to become a more reflective and effective teacher. You might ask for students' evaluations or suggestions, employ peer or self-assessment techniques, or use a Reflective Journal to both troubleshoot your teaching and systematically analyze your goals and techniques. Each of these will be discussed separately.

STUDENT EVALUATIONS AND SUGGESTIONS

In many respects students are in a better position to evaluate teachers than anyone else. They may not always be able to analyze *why* what a teacher does is effective or ineffective (even an experienced expert observer might have difficulty doing so), but they know, better than anyone else, whether they are responding and learning. Furthermore, students form their impressions after interacting with a teacher for hundreds or thousands of hours. Most principals or other adult observers may watch a teacher in action for only a few minutes at a time. It makes sense, therefore, to pay attention to and actively solicit opinions from students.

As a matter of fact, it will be virtually impossible for you to ignore student reactions. Every minute that school is in session, you will receive student feedback in the form of attentiveness (or lack of it), facial expressions, restlessness, yawns, sleeping, disruptive behavior, and the like. If a particular lesson arouses either a neutral or a negative reaction, this should signify to you that you need to seek a better way to present the same material in the future. If you find that you seem to be spending much of your time disciplining students, it will be worth your while to evaluate why and to find other methods.

In addition to analyzing the minute-by-minute reactions of your students, you may find it helpful to request more formal feedback. After completing a unit, you might say, "I'd like you to tell me what you liked and disliked about the way this unit was arranged and give me suggestions for improving it if I teach it again next year."

A more comprehensive and systematic approach is to distribute a questionnaire or evaluation form and ask students to record their reactions anonymously. You might use a published form or devise your own. In either case a common format involves listing a series of statements and asking students to rate them on a 5-point scale. Some of the published forms use special answer sheets that make it possible to tally the results electronically. One disadvantage of many rating-scale evaluation forms is that responses may not be very informative unless you can compare your ratings to those of colleagues. If you get an overall rating of 3.5 on "makes the subject matter interesting," for example, you won't know whether you need to work on that aspect of your teaching until you discover that the average rating of other teachers of the same grade or subject was 4.2. Another disadvantage is that published evaluation forms may not be very helpful unless all other teachers use the same rating scale. Fortunately, this may be possible in school districts that use a standard scale to obtain evidence for use in making decisions about retention, tenure, and promotion.

Another disadvantage of many rating scales is indicated by the phrase *leniency problem*. Students tend to give most teachers somewhat above-average ratings on most traits. Although leniency may soothe a teacher's ego, wishy-washy responses do not provide the information needed to improve pedagogical effectiveness. To get

Figure 15.1 The Descriptive Ranking Form for Teachers

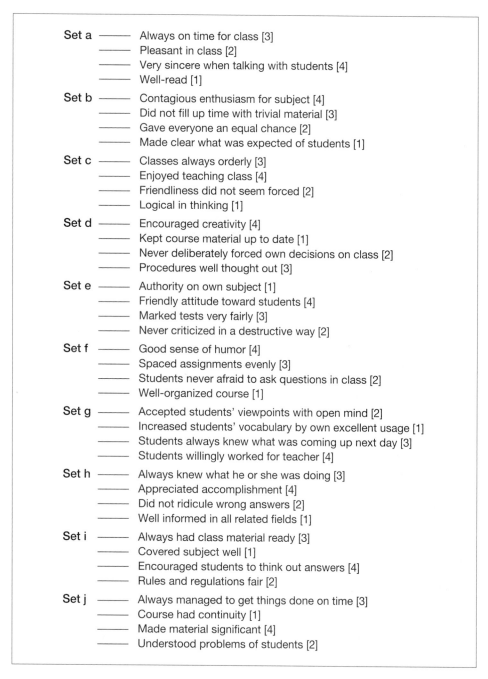

Set a
— Always on time for class [3]
— Pleasant in class [2]
— Very sincere when talking with students [4]
— Well-read [1]

Set b
— Contagious enthusiasm for subject [4]
— Did not fill up time with trivial material [3]
— Gave everyone an equal chance [2]
— Made clear what was expected of students [1]

Set c
— Classes always orderly [3]
— Enjoyed teaching class [4]
— Friendliness did not seem forced [2]
— Logical in thinking [1]

Set d
— Encouraged creativity [4]
— Kept course material up to date [1]
— Never deliberately forced own decisions on class [2]
— Procedures well thought out [3]

Set e
— Authority on own subject [1]
— Friendly attitude toward students [4]
— Marked tests very fairly [3]
— Never criticized in a destructive way [2]

Set f
— Good sense of humor [4]
— Spaced assignments evenly [3]
— Students never afraid to ask questions in class [2]
— Well-organized course [1]

Set g
— Accepted students' viewpoints with open mind [2]
— Increased students' vocabulary by own excellent usage [1]
— Students always knew what was coming up next day [3]
— Students willingly worked for teacher [4]

Set h
— Always knew what he or she was doing [3]
— Appreciated accomplishment [4]
— Did not ridicule wrong answers [2]
— Well informed in all related fields [1]

Set i
— Always had class material ready [3]
— Covered subject well [1]
— Encouraged students to think out answers [4]
— Rules and regulations fair [2]

Set j
— Always managed to get things done on time [3]
— Course had continuity [1]
— Made material significant [4]
— Understood problems of students [2]

SOURCE: Cosgrove (1959).

around the leniency problem and to induce students to give more informative reactions, forced-choice ratings are often used. Figure 15.1 shows a forced-choice rating form, the Descriptive Ranking Form for Teachers, developed by Don Cosgrove (1959). This form is designed to let teachers know how students perceive their skill in four areas of performance: (1) knowledge and organization of subject matter, (2) adequacy of relations with students in class, (3) adequacy of plans and procedures in class, and (4) enthusiasm in working with students. If you decide to use this form, omit the numbers in brackets that follow each statement when you prepare copies for distribution to students. On your own copy of the form, write in those numbers and use them to prepare your score in each of the four categories.

To calculate your index of effectiveness in each category of the Descriptive Ranking Form for Teachers, assign a score of 4 to the phrase in each group that is ranked 1, a score of 3 to the phrase marked 2, and so on. Then add together the scores for all phrases identified by the parenthetical number 1 and do the same for the other sets of phrases. The cluster of phrases that yields the highest score is perceived by your students to be your strongest area of teaching; the cluster that yields the lowest score is considered to be your weakest. A total of 30 points for all phrases indicated by the parenthetical number 1, for example, means that you ranked high in category 1 (knowledge and organization of subject matter). If, however, you get only 12 points for phrases identified by the parenthetical number 4, you will need to work harder at being enthusiastic when working with students.

Quite often a homemade form that covers specific points regarding your personal approach to teaching will provide useful information. You might ask a series of questions about specific points (Were there enough exams? Did you think too much homework was assigned?). Or you can ask students to list the three things they liked best, the three things they liked least, and what they would suggest you do to improve the way a particular unit is taught. When you ask students to respond to questions like these, not only do you usually get feedback about teaching techniques, but you also get ideas you might use to improve your teaching skill. (On a rating scale, if rated below average on an item such as "Examinations are too difficult," you may not know *why* you were rated low or what you might do to change things for the better.)

PEER AND SELF-ASSESSMENT TECHNIQUES

OBSERVATION SCHEDULES   Although your students can supply quite a bit of information that can help you improve your teaching, they cannot always tell you about technical flaws in your instructional technique. This is especially true with younger students. Accordingly, you may wish to submit to a detailed analysis of your approach to teaching. Several observation schedules have been developed for this purpose. The Flanders Interaction Analysis Categories (Flanders, 1970) is perhaps the most widely used teacher behavior schedule, but ninety-eight others are described in *Mirrors for Behavior III: An Anthology of Observation Instruments* (1974), edited by Anita Simon and E. Gil Boyer.

As the title of the Flanders schedule indicates, it stresses verbal interactions between teacher and students. The following ten categories are listed on a record blank:

- accepts feelings
- praises or encourages
- uses student ideas
- asks questions
- lectures

- gives directions
- criticizes
- pupil talk—response
- pupil talk—initiation
- silence or confusion

A trained observer puts a check mark opposite one of these categories every three seconds during a period when teacher and students are interacting verbally.

Soliciting comments about the effectiveness of one's teaching methods from students and colleagues and reflecting on these comments is an excellent way to become a better teacher.

Once the observation is completed, it is a simple matter to tally checks and determine the percentage of time devoted to each activity. Then, if a teacher discovers that a substantial amount of time was spent in silence or confusion and that only a tiny fraction of interactions involved praise or encouragement, she can make a deliberate effort to change for the better.

Perhaps the biggest problem with such observational approaches is the need for a trained observer. But it would be possible to team up with another teacher and act as reciprocal observers if you feel that a detailed analysis of your teaching style would be helpful.

AUDIOTAPED LESSONS   If it is not possible for you to team up with a colleague, you might consider trying to accomplish the same goal through the use of audiotape. Your first step should be to decide which classes or parts of classes you want to record, for how long, and on what day of the week. The goal should be to create a representative sample of the circumstances under which you teach. Then, you should inform your students that you intend to tape-record a sample of your lessons over a period of several weeks to study and improve your instructional methods and that you will protect their confidentiality by not allowing anyone but you to listen to the tapes. Then you can analyze the tapes according to the same categories that make up the Flanders instrument as well as any others that might be of interest.

When this method was used with ten secondary student teachers, significant improvements were achieved in such behaviors as amount of time used for bringing a lesson to closure, waiting for students to formulate answers to questions (commonly referred to as wait-time), and making positive statements. The impact of listening to yourself as an outsider would can be appreciated from the following comment by one student teacher: "Now I'm just so much more aware of waiting. Before, I would address all questions to the class and whoever wanted could blurt out the answer. Whereas, now, I'm much more conscious of calling a name and waiting for a response for that person" (Anderson & Freiberg, 1995, p. 83).

REFLECTIVE LESSON PLANS Finally, you may want to try something called reflective lesson plans (Ho, 1995). To do so, follow these four steps:

1. Divide a sheet of paper in half. Label the left-hand side "Lesson Plan." Label the right-hand side "Reflective Notes."

2. On the lesson plan side, note relevant identifying information (fourth period English, January 23, 9:00 A.M.; honors algebra; fourth-grade social studies), the objectives of the lesson, the tasks that are to be carried out in chronological order, the materials and equipment that are to be used, and how much time has been allotted for this lesson.

3. On the reflective notes side, write your thoughts about the worthwhileness of the objective that underlies the lesson, the adequacy of the materials, and how well you performed the basic mechanics of teaching as soon as possible after the lesson.

4. Make changes to the lesson plan based on your analysis of the reflective notes.

DEVELOPING A REFLECTIVE JOURNAL

Seymour Sarason (1993), who has written extensively about schooling and school reform, points out what may seem obvious but is often missed in practice: every teacher should be an expert in both subject matter and how children learn in classrooms. The goal, and the challenge, is to figure out how to present the subject matter so that students understand it, remember it, and use it. To do that, you must constantly prepare, observe, and reflect on the results of your actions. The Reflective Journal that we mentioned in Chapter 1 and that is described in this section is intended to help you begin that process in a systematic way.

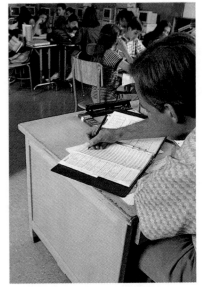

We recommend that you develop a Reflective Journal for two basic purposes: (1) to serve as a repository of instructional ideas and techniques that you have either created from your own experiences or gleaned from other sources, and (2) to give yourself a format for recording your observations and reflections on teaching. These two purposes can be separate from each other or, if you choose, related to each other in a cycle of reflectivity that we will describe. As you read this section, refer to Figure 15.2 for an illustration of how a journal page might look.

The form your Reflective Journal takes will probably change over the years to reflect your experiences and changing needs. But to begin, we suggest that you organize your first journal around the marginal notes in each chapter that are labeled "Journal Entry." Use the Journal Entries as just what their name implies—page headings in your Reflective Journal. To allow room for both the expansion of your teaching ideas and the inclusion of your ongoing reflections, you might purchase a three-ring binder so that pages can be added or dropped. Alternatively, if you have regular access to a computer, you might want to create your Reflective Journal on electronic files, which would give you unlimited capacity for interaction and expansion.

Research has shown that keeping a personal journal about one's teaching activities and outcomes helps teachers improve their effectiveness because it forces them to focus on what they do, why they do it, and what kinds of results are typically obtained.

Under each heading, you can develop a two-part page or multipage entry. As was illustrated in the top half of Figure 15.2, the first part should contain your own teaching ideas, custom-tailored from the Suggestions for Teaching sections of the chapters of this book and from personal experience and other sources to fit the grade level and subjects you expect to teach.

To illustrate, let's use the Journal Entry from page 505, "Ways to Teach Comprehension Tactics." First, search your memory for techniques used by your former teachers. Did your fifth-grade teacher, for instance, have a clever way of relating

Figure 15.2 Sample Page for Your Reflective Journal

Journal Entry: *Ways to Teach Comprehension Tactics*
Source: *Chapter 8—Information-Processing Theory*

Ideas for Instruction

Note: All the ideas you list here will pertain to the particular journal entry/instructional goal for this journal page.

- *Customized suggestions for teaching—those points, principles, activities, and examples taken from the text and the Suggestions for Teaching that are most relevant to your own situation.*

- *Ideas generated from past experiences as a student.*

- *Ideas provided by professional colleagues.*

- *Ideas collected from student-teaching experiences.*

- *Ideas gathered from methods textbooks.*

Reflections: Questions and "Restarter" Suggestions for Instruction

Reflective Question (to focus observation of my teaching and my students' learning):
Do my students have difficulty understanding the meaning of what they read or of what I present in class?

(Record your ongoing reflections, observations, and analytic notes about your instruction and your students' learning of this topic here. If necessary, you may need to "jump-start" or reorient your instruction. One possible idea follows.)

Suggested Action: *Schedule a series of sessions on how to study. Explain the purpose of various comprehension tactics and provide opportunities for students to practice these skills on material they have been assigned to read. Give corrective feedback.*

---

new information to ideas that you had learned earlier in order to make the new information easier to understand? Describe the technique so you will remember to try it yourself. Did a high school teacher have an ingenious way of displaying the similarities and differences among a set of ideas? Exactly how did she or he do it? After you exhaust your own recollections, ask roommates or classmates if they can remember any successful ways that their teachers made learning easier.

Next, examine the examples opposite the Journal Entry. Which ones seem most appropriate for the grade level and subject you will be teaching? Jot them down. Do any of the examples suggest variations you can think of on your own? Write them down before you forget them.

Finally, add ideas that you pick up in methods classes or during your student-teaching experience. If you see a film in a methods class that shows how a teacher helps students understand a particular point, describe it in your journal. If your master teacher uses a successful technique to clarify difficult-to-understand material, record it. If you follow some or all of these suggestions for using the Journal Entries, you will have a rich source of ideas to turn to when you discover that your students seem confused and anxious because of poor comprehension and you find yourself wondering if there is anything you can do about it.

With this part of the journal under way, you should feel reasonably well prepared when you first take charge of a class. But given the complexity of classroom teaching, lessons or techniques that looked good on paper do not always produce the intended effect. This is the point at which you need to reflect on and analyze what you are doing and how you might bring about improvements. On the bottom half of your journal page, write in question form what the nature of the problem seems to be. Then try to identify the cause (or causes) of the problem and at least one possible solution. You can use this suggestion to get restarted or headed in a new direction with your teaching. If, for example, some of your students still have difficulty comprehending what they read despite the comprehension-enhancing techniques that you embedded into your lessons, you might reread Chapter 8, as well as other articles and books on information processing, and decide that your students really need systematic instruction in how to use various comprehension-directed learning tactics.

IS REFLECTION AND JOURNAL WRITING EFFECTIVE?   Recent research found that student teachers who were given questions as reflective prompts (for example, Why was this event significant? How did you react to this event? Why did you react that way? What did you learn from this event?) were more likely to note the reasons for their actions and to make judgments about the adequacy of their efforts than were those who were not given such prompts. According to one student teacher:

> After your lesson, you may say, "It's over," and you may not think about it again. But with the reflective logs, you are forced to sit down and really think about what was something significant about the class and what did you do about it? So, I think it is important. Because if this assignment wasn't there, I probably would just go on and forget about the lesson, and this is not a good thing to do. (Tsangaridou & O'Sullivan, 1994, p. 23)

If we haven't yet convinced you of the value of keeping a Reflective Journal, perhaps the experiences of two veteran teachers will. Middle school teacher Linda Van Wagenen used both a personal portfolio and a Reflective Journal to analyze and improve the quality of her instruction (Van Wagenen & Hibbard, 1998). She compiled a portfolio of her efforts to achieve certain teaching goals and used that to examine her effectiveness. She judged her first two efforts to be unsatisfactory because they were largely descriptive; they emphasized what she had done and ignored what effects those efforts had on her students (self-assessment), what she thought about the quality of her own instruction (self-evaluation), or what she planned to do next (self-regulation). Her third attempt focused on ways to motivate students to improve their performance in persuasive and expository writing. She identified a set of steps that would help her understand the problem and produce improvements. Evidence of her successes and failures made up the portfolio. In addition, she also kept a Reflective Journal because she felt it would help her stay focused on finding a solution to the problem she wanted to solve and would stimulate attempts at self-evaluation and self-regulation. The result of this third attempt was judged to be much more useful than either of her first two efforts. In addition to addressing the question "What did I do?," she also addressed the questions "What did I learn?" and "Now what will I do?"

Lynne Streib, who has taught kindergarten, first, and second grade for the Philadelphia, Pennsylvania, schools for over twenty years, had this to say about journal writing:

> I am a teacher. I write about my work, about teaching, and about researching my teaching through my journal. I enjoy writing, but teaching must be at the center of any other work that I do; my research and writing must directly feed my teaching. Keeping a journal has been a realistic way for me to learn about, inquire into, collect data about, and enhance my practice as well as to learn about and plan for the children. Although writing in my journal each day takes time, it is economical and is the genre most compatible with my style of writing, my way of teaching, and my way of thinking.
>
> Since 1980, I have kept some kind of journal. . . . I continue to keep a journal for a variety of reasons. First and most important, it helps me with my teaching. When used in certain ways, the journal allows me to look closely at the curriculum. As I teach, I wonder how my thinking and my students' thinking evolve over time. I wonder what I have valued and what the children are interested in and value. Lesson plans don't tell me this, but the journal does. My journal is a place for planning, for raising questions, for figuring things out, and for thinking. (Streib, 1993, pp. 121–122)

The Case in Print on page 508 describes a portfolio-type of Reflective Journal that some teacher education programs require their students to compile and that the students are using to demonstrate to potential employers their readiness to teach.

USING TECHNOLOGY FOR REFLECTION

Throughout this book we have described how you can use various technology tools to help your students become more effective learners. Now it's time to consider how you can use such technologies as the World Wide Web, videoconferencing, and Web-based conferencing to help you think about and improve your own teaching skills.

A major source of frustration for teachers is the limited intellectual and social contact they have with one another (Sarason, 1993). Certainly during school hours there are few opportunities for teachers to engage in meaningful discussions about teaching and learning. And after school, many teachers are either busy grading papers and making lesson plans or are at home with their families. Computer-based technologies can help break down this sense of isolation by providing forums for teachers to discuss instructional ideas and problems from any location and at any time. You can begin that process now by using the World Wide Web to discuss ideas and field experiences with peers in this country and others. (Bonk, Malikowski, Angeli, & East, 1998; Thurston, Secaras, & Levin, 1997). Electronic reflections can also take place in private journals that are accessible only by an instructor or a trusted friend. Later, when you have a full-time teaching position, you can use the Web to discuss such issues as teaching philosophy and common classroom problems and their solutions and to explore relevant resources (such as the many Websites devoted to K–12 instruction).

Starting a Reflective Journal Now Pays Off in the Future

Seymour Sarason (1993), who has written extensively about schooling and school reform, points out what may seem obvious but is often missed in practice: every teacher should be an expert in both subject matter and how children learn in classrooms. The goal, and the challenge, is to figure out how to present the subject matter so that students understand it, remember it, and use it. To do that, you must constantly prepare, observe, and reflect on the results of your actions. The Reflective Journal . . . that is described in this section is intended to help you begin that process in a systematic way. (p. 504)

PORTFOLIOS GIVE PROSPECTIVE TEACHERS AN EDGE WHEN THEY INTERVIEW FOR JOBS

VALERIE SCHREMP
St. Louis Post-Dispatch 12/14/97

Katherine Karoby, professor of education at Webster University, often tells a story about a student who showed up to a job interview with a teaching portfolio in her lap. The principal asked, "How would you teach reading in the second grade?"

"I would tell you," said the student, "But I would like to show you." She pulled a videotape from her portfolio, pulled in a VCR cart, popped in the tape, pressed play and got the job.

Karoby and the employed teacher are not alone in their testimony. Colleges, student teachers and even the Missouri Department of Elementary and Secondary Education are also praising portfolios. Teacher portfolios may contain videotapes, photos of bulletin boards and sample lesson plans.

The portfolios accomplish three things: they show the state Board of Education that a school is producing worthy teachers; they give students a record of growth over their college careers; and they show what a teacher can do.

Starting in fall 1998, Missouri will require education colleges to start portfolio programs. Every five years, to ensure the quality of an education program, the state will examine randomly selected portfolios from at least 10 percent of a program's students.

"Before, we focused on things like making sure institutions offered appropriate courses and hours," said Mike Lucas, head of certification for the Missouri Department of Elementary and Secondary Education. "Just because a student takes courses for x number of hours doesn't mean the individual has the competency to teach."

Several of Missouri's 34 teacher-educating colleges have already launched portfolio programs. So have Illinois colleges, though the state board does not require them.

Fontbonne College required this year's freshmen education students to begin portfolios. It even sells oversized, three-ring binders in its school bookstore as "start-up kits." Webster University wants to put portfolios on CD-ROM.

The University of Missouri at St. Louis, which placed 450 student teachers last year, uses portfolios to help grade students in education classes. Kathie Heywood, associate dean for academic affairs, said the education professors at first doubted the value of the portfolios. They feared students would put only their best pieces in them, presenting a false picture.

So they encourage students to include examples from the science lesson gone awry, or the behavior management plan that just didn't cut it in a high school class. That way, professors can help students correct their work or advise them not to go into teaching.

When students start looking for jobs, they can put together a professional portfolio, full of their best pieces to show off on interviews.

Principals notice. Phillip Silsby, principal of Belleville West High School, has seen just a few portfolios but called them effective. This year, he hired a counselor who had a portfolio of newspaper clips about a career education program she started at another school.

Jim Schwab, principal of Carollton Oaks Elementary in the Pattonville School District, says about one out of three applicants comes into an interview with a portfolio. "I look through them more out of courtesy than anything," he said. "But if two people come in with equal interviewing skills and equal credentials, a portfolio would certainly give them an edge."

One teacher interviewed at the school a couple of years ago, toting what Schwab called an impressive portfolio, full of creative ideas and projects. "That definitely put her over the top," he said. He hired her to teach third grade.

Questions and Activities

1. This article describes how prospective teachers are using portfolios to demonstrate their teaching skills to prospective employers. If this technique impresses you, start now to create your own portfolio. Save assignments from different classes, particularly those that required several steps to complete. As this article indicates, you can include videotapes, photographs, and newspaper articles, was well as the traditional written format.

2. In addition to using portfolios as a job-seeking technique, you can use them to practice reflective teaching. Think about how you can combine the Reflective Journal described in this chapter with a portfolio.

In addition to on-line conferencing, educational researchers and teacher education programs are experimenting with multimedia and hypermedia programs that feature case-based learning formats that encourage new models of teaching, learning, and assessment among both preservice and practicing teachers (Fitzgerald, Wilson, & Semrau, 1997; Krajcik et al., 1996; Lambdin, Duffy, & Moore, 1997). Some researchers are relying on video-based stories to provide a context or situation for teacher reflection and introduce both to a more constructivist teaching orientation. Tools already exist for selecting and displaying problem cases and situations, recording preliminary case solutions, browsing through expert commentary and supplemental case information, exploring library materials for case solutions and alternative cases, and provoking student reflection. And with technology's replay capabilities, a preservice teacher like you could use these multimedia cases to identify key instructional decisions in planning or conducting a lesson. After watching a video sequence a second or third time for critical teaching decisions, you might post some reflection notes or compare that situation to another. Perhaps more importantly, such tools are not only useful for individual exploration, they also promote rich conversations among teachers.

Due to changes in teaching approaches and the rise of computer-based technology, the training ground for preservice teachers is exploding with possibilities. If innovative, student-centered ideas can be implemented with technology tools in teacher training programs, future teachers will be simultaneously exposed to both the tools and the teaching practices of the twenty-first century. Perhaps both telecommunications and hypermedia learning environments can develop into safe harbors for preservice teachers to try out their instructional ideas and reflect on their early field experiences. You may, in fact, find yourself currently using such tools during your preservice teacher training. Hopefully, as such technology becomes infused into teacher education programs, you and other future teachers will enter the teaching profession equipped with the pedagogical skills needed to innovatively and successfully incorporate technology into your instruction.

RESOURCES FOR FURTHER INVESTIGATION

■ Reflective Teaching

Among the many recently published books on reflection in teaching, you might take a look at *Interwoven Conversations: Learning and Teaching Through Critical Reflection* (1991), by Judith Newman. Written in an interesting narrative form, this book describes the author's inquiry into her own pedagogical assumptions, teaching practices, and contradictions between beliefs and practices. Another book is *Teachers and Teaching: From Classroom to Reflection* (1992), edited by Tom Russell and Hugh Munby. The four topics covered by this book are "Reflection in Teaching," "Reflection in Cases in Teaching," "Narrative in Reflection," and "Reflection in the

Context of Teacher Education." Chapter 1 of *Reflective Teaching for Student Empowerment* (1993), by Dorene Ross, Elizabeth Bondy, and Diane Kyle, describes the essence of reflective teaching, explains why reflection is essential in teaching, and describes the knowledge and skills one must learn in order to teach reflectively. Judy Eby notes that her book, *Reflective Planning, Teaching, and Evaluation: K–12* (1994), is intended to help beginning and practicing teachers improve their performance through a process of self-discovery. The first five chapters of *Becoming a Reflective Teacher* (1994), by Leonard Kochendorfer, are designed to help readers reflect on and challenge their concepts of schooling and teaching. The last three chapters describe a model of teacher-based action research that teachers can use to investigate the validity of their conclusions. Finally, *Reports from the Classroom: Cases for Reflection* (1995), by Sarah Huyvaert, presents thirty-two case reports, each written by a practicing classroom teacher. Each report describes a classroom incident between either the teacher and a student, the teacher and an administrator, or the teacher and another teacher. Following the incident the teacher reflects on how the incident was handled (sometimes well, but sometimes not).

Glossary

accommodation   The process of creating or revising a scheme to fit a new experience. (*See* **schemes**)

achievement batteries   Sets of tests designed to assess performance in a broad range of subjects.

active listening   A way of dealing with a problem-owning student by showing interest and encouraging the talker to continue expressing feelings.

adaptation   The process, described by Piaget, of creating a good fit or match between one's conception of reality and one's real-life experiences. (*See* **assimilation** *and* **accommodation**)

adolescent egocentrism   The introspective, inward turning of a high school student's newly developed powers of thought, with a tendency to project one's self-analysis onto others. (*See* **egocentrism**)

adventure learning   A type of learning wherein students might participate in real-life expeditions, virtual field trips, historical reenactments, and local adventures in their community, typically in structured activities with students from other schools.

affective domain taxonomy   A classification of instructional outcomes that concentrates on attitudes and values.

anchored instruction   Method of embedding important information or skills in authentic problem-solving situations and meaningful contexts for prolonged student exploration. (*See* **inert knowledge; situated learning**)

aptitude tests   Tests intended to give educators some idea of the level of knowledge and skill a student could acquire with effective instruction.

assimilation   The process of fitting new experience into an existing scheme. (*See* **schemes**)

assistive technology   Any item, device, or piece of equipment, from low-tech equipment such as taped stories to more sophisticated technologies such as voice-recognition and speech-synthesis devices, that is used to increase, maintain, or improve the functional abilities of persons with disabilities.

attention   The selective focusing on a portion of the information currently stored in the sensory register. (*See* **sensory register**)

attention-deficit/hyperactivity disorder (ADHD)   A disorder that begins in childhood, is marked by abnormally high levels of impulsive behavior, dis-

tractibility, and motor activity, and leads to low levels of learning.

attribution theory   A body of research into the ways that students explain their success or failure, usually in terms of ability, effort, task difficulty, and luck.

authentic assessment   (*See* **performance-based assessment**)

authoritarian parents   Parents who make demands and wield power without considering their children's point of view.

authoritative parents   Parents who provide models of competence to be imitated, based on confidence in their own abilities.

behavior disorder   (*See* **emotional disturbance**)

behavior modification   The use of operant conditioning techniques to modify behavior, generally by making rewards contingent on certain actions. (Also called *contingency management. See* **operant conditioning**)

between-class ability grouping   Assigning students of similar learning ability to separate classes based on scores from standardized intelligence or achievement tests.

bilingual/immersion   An approach to bilingual education in which instruction is provided in both the minority language and the majority language to all students. (Also called *dual language* or *two-way bilingual*)

CD-ROM   Compact disk-read only memory is a form of multimedia technology that can store large collections of information (500,000 pages, or 600 megabytes of data) in a digital format on a single CD.

cognitive apprenticeship   A relationship in which help and guidance is provided by a mentor or expert practitioner to a learner that enables him or her to master a task and gradually participate in a culture or community. (*See* **teleapprenticeship**)

cognitive constructivism   A form of constructivist learning theory that emphasizes the role of assimilation and accommodation in constructing an understanding of the world in which one lives. (*See* **assimilation, accommodation, constructivism**)

cognitive domain taxonomy   A classification scheme of instructional outcomes that stresses knowledge and intellectual skills, including comprehension, application, analysis, synthesis, and evaluation. (Also called *Bloom's taxonomy*)

collaborative learning   Activities for which groups of learners use and combine their individual talents and areas of expertise to investigate problems, negotiate ideas, generate knowledge, and design products. (*See* **cooperative learning**)

competency test   A test to determine a student's ability to handle basic subjects.

computer adaptive testing (CAT)   A testing technique in which a computer program adapts the difficulty of questions to the ability level of the examinee based on his or her responses, thereby resulting in a reduction in test length and greater efficiency.

computer-assisted instruction (CAI)   Teaching methods that use interactive software as an aid to learning.

computer conferencing   An on-line discussion group typically organized by topic that can provide students with access to information, viewpoints, and communities beyond the boundaries of their classrooms.

concept mapping   A technique for identifying and visually representing on paper the ideas that comprise a section of text and the ways in which they relate to each other.

conservation   The recognition that certain properties stay the same despite a change in appearance or position.

constructivism   The view that meaningful learning is the active creation of knowledge structures, rather than a mere transferring of objective knowledge from one person to another.

contingency contracting   A behavior-strengthening technique that specifies desirable behaviors and consequent reinforcement.

cooperative learning   An approach that uses small heterogeneous groups for purposes of mutual help in the mastery of specific tasks.

criterion-referenced grading   A system in which grades are determined on the basis of whether each student has attained a defined standard of achievement or performance.

criterion-referenced tests   Tests in which students are evaluated according to how well they have mastered specific objectives in various well-defined skill areas.

cultural pluralism   A set of tenets based on three principles: 1) every culture has its own internal coherence, integrity, and logic; 2) no culture is inherently better or worse than another; and 3) all persons are to some extent culture-bound.

culture   A description of the ways a group of people perceives the world; formulates beliefs; evaluates objects, ideas, and experiences; and behaves.

decentration   The ability to think of more than one quality of an object or problem at a time. (*See* **perceptual centration**)

deficiency needs   The first four levels (physiological, safety, belongingness or love, and self-esteem) in Maslow's hierarchy of needs, so called because these needs cause people to act only when they are unmet to some degree.

depression   An emotional disorder characterized by self-deprecation, crying spells, and suicidal thoughts, afflicting between 7 to 28 percent of all adolescents.

diagnostic test   A single-subject achievement test intended to identify the source of a problem in basic subjects and perhaps in study skills. (*See* **single-subject achievement test**)

digital portfolio   A multimedia collection of student work that documents individual expertise, achievement, accomplishments, and growth in one or more areas over extended periods of time. (Also called *electronic portfolio*)

direct instruction   An approach to instruction that emphasizes the efficient acquisition of basic skills and subject matter through lectures and demonstrations, extensive practice, and corrective feedback.

direct reinforcement   A situation in which an individual watches a model perform, imitates the behavior, and is reinforced by the model or some other individual.

discovery learning   A teaching strategy that encourages children to seek solutions to problems either on their own or in group discussion.

discrimination   A process in which individuals learn to notice the unique aspects of seemingly similar situations, and thus learn different ways of responding.

distributed practice   The practice of breaking up learning tasks into small, easy-to-manage pieces that are learned over several relatively brief sessions.

drill-and-practice programs   Computer programs that help students practice skills and learn factual information.

dual coding theory   A theory of elaboration that states that concrete objects and words are remembered better than abstract information because they are coded in memory as both visual images and verbal labels, whereas abstract words are only encoded verbally.

early language development The phase of language learning in which children tend to stick to their own rules, despite efforts to correct them.

early-maturing boy A boy whose early physical maturation typically draws favorable adult responses and promotes confidence and poise, thus contributing to leadership and popularity with peers. (*See* **late-maturing boy**)

early-maturing girl A girl whose early physical maturation typically makes her socially out of step with her peers. (*See* **late-maturing girl**)

educational psychology The branch of psychology that specializes in understanding how different factors affect the classroom behavior of both teachers and students.

egocentrism The difficulty a young child may find in taking another person's point of view.

elaborative rehearsal A process that consciously relates new information to knowledge already stored in long-term memory. (Also called *elaborative encoding. See* **long-term memory**)

electronic mentoring The use of technology by experts, instructors, and peers to provide various forms of support or assistance (for example, hints, questions, explanations, simplifications, examples, etc.) to help the learner understand a concept or complete a task that may ordinarily be out of reach. (*See* **teleapprenticeship**)

electronic networking Systems that support digital communication between connected computers.

electronic portfolio (*See* **digital portfolio**)

emotional disturbance An emotional condition in which inappropriate aggressive or withdrawal behaviors are exhibited over a long period of time and to a marked degree, adversely affecting a child's educational performance.

empirical learning The use of noticeable characteristics of objects and events by young children to form spontaneous concepts.

epigenetic principle The notion that a child's personality develops as the ego progresses through a series of interrelated stages, much as the human body takes shape during its fetal development.

equilibration The tendency to organize schemes to allow better understanding of experiences. (*See* **schemes**)

ethnic group A collection of people who identify with one another on the basis of such characteristics

as ancestral origin, race, religion, language, values, political or economic interests, and behavior patterns.

evaluation The use of a rule-governed system to make judgments about the value or worth of a set of measures.

exploratory environments Electronic environments that provide students with materials and resources to discover interesting phenomena and construct new insights; for example, computer simulations. (Also called *discovery environments. See* **discovery learning**)

extinction The weakening of a target behavior by ignoring it.

extrinsic motivation A form of incentive based on a system of rewards not inherent in a particular activity. (*See* **intrinsic motivation**)

field-dependent style A learning style in which a person's perception of and thinking about a task or problem is strongly influenced by such contextual factors as additional information and other people's behavior.

field-independent style A learning style in which a person's perception of and thinking about a task or problem is influenced more by the person's knowledge base than by the presence of additional information or other people's behavior.

foreclosure status An adolescent identity status marked by the unquestioning endorsement of parents' goals and values.

formative evaluation A type of assessment that monitors a student's progress in order to facilate learning rather than assign a grade.

frames The individual steps in a teaching program. (*See* **programmed instruction**)

full inclusion The practice of eliminating pull-out programs (those outside the classroom) and providing regular teachers with special training, so as to keep special needs students in regular classrooms. (Also called *inclusion*)

gender bias The tendency of teachers to respond differently to male and female students when there is no educationally sound reason for doing so.

gender roles An awareness among young children that shows up clearly in the toys and activities that boys and girls prefer.

generalization The learned ability to respond in similar ways to similar stimuli.

general objectives Objectives that use the three taxonomies (cognitive, affective, and psychomotor) to describe types of behavior that would demonstrate a student's learning. (*See* **taxonomy**)

general transfer   A situation in which prior learning aids subsequent learning due to the use of similar cognitive strategies.

gifted and talented student   A student who shows unusual ability in a variety of ways and who may require services not ordinarily provided by his or her school.

grade equivalent score   A measurement that interprets test performance in terms of grade levels.

graphing calculator   An electronic device used to gather, manipulate, and represent data, thereby helping students make connections between mathematical symbols and real-world events.

growth need   A yearning for personal fulfillment that people constantly strive to satisfy. (*See* **self-actualization**)

growth spurt   The rapid and uneven physical growth that besets adolescents during the middle school years.

guided learning   Environments where teachers, experts, or more knowledgeable peers support student inquiry by helping students set plans and goals, ask questions, discuss issues, solve problems, and reflect on strategies and solutions. (Also called *guided discovery learning. See* **cognitive apprenticeship** *and* **constructivism**)

heuristics   General approaches to solving problems, such as studying worked examples and breaking problems into parts, that can be applied to different subject areas.

high-road transfer   A situation involving the conscious, controlled, somewhat effortful formulation of an "abstraction" (that is, a rule, a schema, a strategy, or an analogy) that allows a connection to be made between two tasks.

humanistic approach   An approach to instruction that emphasizes the effect of student needs, values, motives, and self-perceptions on learning.

hypermedia   A technology that combines multimedia and hypertext so that the learner can nonsequentially access and explore interesting and important information resources. (*See* **hypertext** *and* **multimedia**)

hypertext   A system of linking text in a nonlinear way, thereby enabling users to jump from one section of text to another section of the same document or to other documents, often through pressing highlighted or "hot" words.

identity   A relatively stable conception of where and how one fits into a society that is strongly influenced by the perception of one's physical appearance, the goals one establishes and achieves, and recognition from significant others in the environment.

identity achievement status   An adolescent identity status marked by self-chosen commitments with respect to at least some aspects of identity.

identity diffusion status   An adolescent identity status marked by the avoidance of choices pertaining to jobs, roles, or values, and the readiness to change one's position in response to negative or positive feedback.

identity status   A style or approach that adolescents adopt to deal with such identity-related issues as career goal, gender-role orientation, and religious beliefs. James Marcia identified four identity statuses: identity diffusion, moratorium, foreclosure, and identity achievement.

ill-structured problems   Vaguely stated problems with unclear solution procedures and vague evaluation standards. (*See* **well-structured problems**)

I-message   A first-person statement by a teacher that emphasizes the teacher's feelings about a situation rather than his or her feelings about the students.

impulsive   A learning style in which students respond relatively quickly to questions or tasks for which there is no obvious correct answer or solution.

inclusion   An extension of the least restrictive environment provision of PL 101-476 in which students with disabilities are placed in regular classrooms for the entire school day and receive some instruction and support from a special education teacher. (*See also* **full inclusion**)

individualized education program (IEP)   A written statement describing an educational program designed to meet the unique needs of a child with a particular disability.

inert knowledge   Information, typically memorized verbatim, that is unconnected, lacking in context, and not readily accessible for application to real-world tasks. (*See* **anchored instruction; drill-and-practice programs; meaningful learning; situated learning**)

information-processing theory   An area of study that seeks to understand how people acquire, store, and recall information, and how their current knowledge guides and determines what and how they will learn.

instructional objectives Statements written by teachers that specify the knowledge and skills students should be able to exhibit after a unit of instruction.

integrated learning systems (ILS) Computer-based instructional systems that provide sequenced and self-paced learning activities to students in many different content areas as well as appropriate remediation or enrichment activities.

intelligence The ability of an individual to use a variety of cognitive and noncognitive capabilities to formulate goals, logically work toward achieving those goals, and adapt to the demands of the environment.

intelligent agents Computer programs or tools that perform tasks and provide various forms of performance support for users (for example, printing files, analyzing large databases, pronouncing difficult words, scheduling daily activities). (Also called *animated tutors* or *knowbots*)

intelligent tutoring systems Computer tools that attempt to provide timely and individualized guidance by comparing the problem-solving histories of the user with models of expert performance in that domain.

Internet (*See* **World Wide Web**)

interpersonal reasoning The ability to understand the relationship between motives and behavior among a group of people.

intrinsic motivation A form of incentive inherent in a particular activity, such as the positive consequence of becoming more competent or knowledgeable. (*See* **extrinsic motivation**)

irreversibility The inability of a young child to mentally reverse physical or mental processes, such as pouring water from a tall, thin glass back into a short, squat one.

issues Ill-structured problems that arouse strong feelings. (*See* **ill-structured problems**)

Joplin Plan An ability grouping technique that combines students of different grade levels according to their standardized test scores. (*See* **regrouping**)

late-maturing boy A boy whose delayed physical maturation typically causes inferiority feelings and leads to bossy and attention-getting behavior. (*See* **early-maturing boy**)

late-maturing girl A girl whose delayed physical maturation typically makes her more poised than others her age and elicits praise from elders, thus conferring leadership tendencies. (*See* **early-maturing girl**)

learner-centered education An educational philosophy in which the teacher helps guide students to meaningfully construct knowledge and monitor their own learning by emphasizing student choice, responsibility, challenge, intrinsic motivation, and ownership of the learning process.

learning disability Problems in otherwise mentally fit students who are unable to respond to certain aspects of the curriculum presented in regular classrooms because of disorders in one or more basic psychological processes.

learning strategy A general plan that a learner formulates for achieving a somewhat distant academic goal.

learning style A consistent tendency or preference to respond to a variety of intellectual tasks and problems in a particular fashion.

learning tactic A specific technique that a learner uses to accomplish an immediate learning objective.

least restrictive environment A requirement under the 1994 Code of Federal Regulations that disabled children be provided with education in the least restrictive setting possible, usually by including them in regular classrooms. (*See* **mainstreaming**)

locus of control The tendency to perceive positive and negative events as being either under one's control (that is, internal) or due to outside factors and circumstances (that is, external).

long-term memory (LTM) Storehouse of permanently recorded information in an individual's memory.

loss of voice The tendency of adolescent females to suppress their true beliefs about issues and either claim that they have no opinion or state what they think others want to hear because of socialization practices.

low-road transfer A situation in which a previously learned skill or idea is almost automatically retrieved from memory and applied to a highly similar current task. (*See* **high-road transfer**)

mainstreaming The policy of placing students with disabilities in regular classes.

maintenance rehearsal A rather mechanical process that uses mental and verbal repetition to hold information in short-term memory for some immediate purpose. Also called *rote rehearsal* or *repetition*. (*See* **short-term memory**)

massed practice An approach to learning that emphasizes a few long, infrequently spaced study periods.

mastery learning An approach that assumes most students can master the curriculum if certain conditions are established: (a) sufficient aptitude, (b) sufficient ability to understand instruction, (c) a willingness to persevere, (d) sufficient time, and (e) good-quality instruction.

meaningful learning When new information or learning activities are made relevant by relating them to personal interests and prior experiences or knowledge.

measurement The assignment of numbers to certain attributes of objects, events, or people according to a rule-governed system.

melting pot A term referring to the assimilation of diverse ethnic groups into one national mainstream.

mental retardation A condition in which learning proceeds at a significantly slow rate, is limited to concrete experiences, and is accompanied by difficulty functioning in social environments.

metacognition Knowledge about the operations of cognition and how to use them to achieve a learning goal.

microcomputer-based laboratory (MBL) A microcomputer with attached sensors and probes that can quickly represent such data as temperature or speed in multiple ways in order to help students explore concepts, test hypotheses, and repair scientific misconceptions.

microworld Computer scenarios intended to foster cognitive development and overcome misconceptions by allowing students the chance to explore relationships among variables or concepts and build personal models of how things work.

mnemonic device A memory-directed tactic that helps a learner transform or organize information to enhance its retrievability.

morality of constraint Piaget's term for the moral thinking of children up to age ten or so, in which they hold sacred rules that permit no exceptions and make no allowance for intentions. (Also called *moral realism*)

morality of cooperation Piaget's term for the moral thinking of children eleven or older, based on flexible rules and considerations of intent. (Also called *moral relativism*)

moratorium status An adolescent identity status marked by various kinds of identity crises, often involving experimentation and restless searching.

multicultural education An approach to learning and teaching that seeks to foster an understanding of and mutual respect for the values, beliefs, and practices of different cultural groups.

multidisciplinary assessment team A group of people involved in determining the nature of a child's disability, typically consisting of a school psychologist, guidance counselor, classroom teacher, school social worker, school nurse, learning disability specialist, physician, and psychiatrist.

multimedia The combination of several forms of media such as text, graphics, animation, sound, images, and video that can be used by teachers to enrich student understanding and address various student learning styles, preferences, and impairments. (*See* **dual coding theory** *and* **hypermedia**)

negative identity Defiant or destructive behavior engaged in by a young person who is unable to overcome role confusion, often expressed as hostility toward roles offered as desirable by one's family or community.

negative reinforcement A way of strengthening a target behavior by removing an aversive stimulus after a particular behavior is exhibited. (*See* **positive reinforcement**)

negative transfer A situation in which one's prior learning interferes with subsequent learning. (*See* **positive transfer**)

no-lose method A conflict-resolving procedure that involves discussing problems and coming up with a mutually agreeable compromise.

normal curve The bell-shaped distribution of scores that tends to occur when a particular characteristic is measured in thousands of people.

norm group A sample of individuals carefully chosen to reflect the larger population of students for whom a test is intended.

norm-referenced grading A system of grading that assumes classroom achievement will vary among a group of heterogeneous students because of such differences as prior knowledge, learning skills, motivation, and aptitude, and so compares the score of each student to the scores of other students in order to determine grades.

norm-referenced test A test in which individual performance is evaluated with reference to the performance of a norm group.

observational learning A form of learning that deemphasizes the role of reinforcement by attributing initial changes in behavior to the observation and imitation of a model. (*See* **social learning theory**)

operant conditioning   The theory of behavior developed by B. F. Skinner, based on the fact that organisms respond to their environments in particular ways to obtain or avoid particular consequences.

organization   The tendency to systematize and combine processes into coherent general systems.

peer tutoring   An approach to learning that involves the teaching of one student by another, based on evidence that a child's cognitive growth benefits from exposure to alternative cognitive schemes.

percentile rank   A score that indicates the percentage of students who are at or below a given student's achievement level, providing specific information about relative position.

perceptual centration   The tendency to focus attention on only one characteristic of an object or aspect of a problem or event at a time.

performance tests   An assessment system that attempts to gauge how well students can use basic knowledge and skill to perform complex tasks or solve problems under more or less realistic conditions. (Also called *performance-based assessment* and *authentic assessment*)

permissive parents   Parents who make few demands on their children and fail to discourage immature behavior, thus reflecting their own tendency to be disorganized, inconsistent, and lacking in confidence.

play behavior   Kinds of free play observed in preschool children and described by Mildred Parten as consisting of six types: unoccupied, solitary, onlooker, parallel, associative, and cooperative.

positive reinforcement   A way of strengthening a target behavior (increasing and maintaining the probability that a particular behavior will be repeated) by supplying a positive stimulus immediately after a desired response. (*See* **negative reinforcement**)

positive transfer   A situation in which prior learning aids subsequent learning, when for example a new learning task calls for essentially the same response that was made to a similar, earlier-learned task. (*See* **negative transfer**)

Premack principle   A shaping technique that allows students to indulge in a favorite activity after completing a set of instructional objectives. (Also called *Grandma's rule. See* **shaping**)

problem-based learning (PBL)   An instructional method that requires learners to develop solutions to authentic and complex problems through problem analysis, hypothesis generation, collaboration, reflection, and extensive teacher coaching and facilitation.

problem representation/framing   The process of finding ways to express a problem so as to recall the optimal amount of solution-relevant information from long-term memory. (*See* **long-term memory**)

problem solving   The identification and application of knowledge and skills that result in goal attainment.

programmed instruction   A method of instruction developed by B. F. Skinner that presents specially designed written material to students in a predetermined sequence.

project-based learning   An approach to teaching and learning that attempts to motivate students through collaborative investigations of real-world problems that result in tangible products.

psychological androgyny   An acquired sense of gender that combines traditional masculine and feminine traits.

psychomotor domain taxonomy   A classification of instructional outcomes that focuses on physical abilities and skills.

psychosocial moratorium   A period of identity development marked by a delay of commitment, ideally a time of adventure and exploration having a positive, or at least neutral, impact on the individual and society.

punishment   A method of weakening a target behavior by presenting an aversive stimulus after the behavior occurs.

real-time chatting   The sending and receiving of synchronous or real-time messages in a public or private area on a computer network.

recognition   A cognitive process that involves noting key features of a stimulus and relating them to previously stored information in an interactive manner.

reflective   A learning style in which students collect and analyze information before offering an answer to a question or a solution to a problem.

reflective teaching   A way of teaching that blends artistic and scientific elements through thoughtful analysis of classroom activity.

regrouping   A form of ability grouping that brings together students of the same age, ability, and grade but from different classrooms, for instruction in a specific subject, usually reading or mathematics.

rejecting-neglecting parents   Parents who make no demands on their children, provide no structure at home, and do not support their children's goals, activities, and emotional needs.

reliability Consistency in test results, related to the assumption that human characteristics are relatively stable over short periods of time.

response cost The withdrawal of previously earned positive reinforcers as a consequence of undesirable behavior, often used with a token economy. (*See* **token economy**)

ripple effect The extent to which an entire class responds to a reprimand directed at only one student.

role confusion Uncertainty as to what behaviors will elicit a favorable reaction from others.

rubric A scoring guide used in performance assessment that helps define and clarify levels of student performance from poor to exemplary.

scaffolding Supporting learning during its early phases through such techniques as demonstrating how tasks should be accomplished, giving hints to the correct solution to a problem or answer to a question, and providing leading questions. As students become more capable of working independently, these supports are withdrawn.

schema An abstract information structure by which our store of knowledge is organized in long-term memory. (*See* **long-term memory**)

scheme An organized pattern of behavior or thought that children formulate as they interact with their environment, parents, teachers, and agemates.

scholastic aptitude Those cognitive skills that most directly relate to and best predict the ability to cope with academic demands. Often used as a synonym for *intelligence*.

scientific concepts A term coined by Russian psychologist Lev Vygotsky to denote such psychological tools as language, formulas, rules, and symbols that are learned mostly with the aid of formal instruction.

self-actualization The movement toward full development of a person's potential talents and capabilities.

self-concept A self-description of one's physical, social, emotional, and cognitive attributes. (*See* **self-image** and **self-esteem**)

self-efficacy The degree to which people believe they are capable or prepared to handle particular tasks.

self-esteem The evaluative judgments made about self-attributed qualities. (*See* **self-image** and **self-concept**)

self-fulfilling prophecy The tendency of students to achieve the levels expected of them by their teachers. (Also called the *Pygmalion effect*)

self-image A mental self-portrait composed of self-concept and self-esteem elements. (*See* **self-concept** and **self-esteem**)

self-reinforcement A situation in which the individual strives to meet personal standards and does not depend on or care about the reactions of others.

sensory register (SR) The primary memory store that records temporarily (for one to three seconds) an incoming flow of data from the sense receptors.

serial position effect The tendency to learn and remember words at the beginning and end of a list more easily than those in the middle.

sexually transmitted diseases (STDs) Contagious diseases, such as HIV/AIDS, gonorrhea, and herpes, that are spread by sexual contact.

shaping Learning complex behaviors by reinforcing successive approximations to the terminal behavior.

short-term memory (STM) The second temporary memory store, which holds about seven bits of information for about twenty seconds. (Also called *working memory*)

simulations Highly individualized and flexible programs that allow learners to test hypotheses, display knowledge, repair errors in thinking, and solve problems in an artificial environment that imitates the real world.

single-subject achievement test A test designed to assess learning or achievement in a particular basic school subject, such as reading or math.

situated learning The idea that problem-solving skills, cognitive strategies, and knowledge are closely linked to the specific context or environment in which they are acquired; hence, the more authentic, or true to life, the task, the more meaningful the learning. (Also called *situated cognition*. *See* **cognitive apprenticeship**; **inert knowledge**; **teleapprenticeship**)

social class An individual's or a family's relative standing in society, determined by such factors as income, occupation, education, place of residence, types of associations, manner of dress, and material possessions.

social constructivism A form of constructivist learning theory that emphasizes how people use such cultural tools as language, mathematics, and approaches to problem solving in social settings to construct a common or shared understanding of the world in which they live. (*See* **constructivism**)

social learning theory A theory, exemplified in the work of Albert Bandura, that deemphasizes the role of reinforcement in learning by attributing initial changes in behavior to the observation and imitation of a model. (Also called *observational learning*)

socioeconomic status (SES) A quantifiable level of social standing, determined by the federal government on the basis of a person's income, occupation, and education. (*See* **social class**)

special-purpose achievement test A test to determine specific qualifications, such as the College-Level Examination Program or the National Teacher Examination.

specific objectives Objectives that specify the behavior to be learned, the conditions under which it will be exhibited, and the criterion for acceptable performance.

specific transfer A situation in which prior learning aids subsequent learning because of specific similarities between two tasks.

spontaneous concepts A term coined by Russian psychologist Lev Vygotsky to denote the facts, concepts, and rules that young children acquire as a natural consequence of engaging in everyday activities.

spontaneous recovery The reappearance of a seemingly extinguished behavior. (*See* **extinction**)

standard deviation A statistic that indicates the degree to which scores in a group of tests differ from the average or mean.

standardized tests Assessment tools designed by people with specialized knowledge and applied to all students under the same conditions.

stanine score A statistic reflecting a division of a score distribution into nine groups, with each stanine being one-half of a standard deviation unit.

styles of mental self-government theory A theory of learning style formulated by Robert Sternberg that is based on the different functions and forms of civil government. The theory describes thirteen styles that can vary in terms of function, form, level, scope, and learning.

summative evaluation Testing done for the purpose of assigning a letter or numerical grade to sum up a student's performance at a variety of tasks over time.

table of specifications A table used in exam preparation that notes types and numbers of included test items, ensuring systematic coverage of the subject matter.

taxonomy A classification scheme with categories arranged in hierarchical order.

teacher expectancy effect The tendency of students to behave in ways they think the teacher expects them to behave. (Also called *self-fulfilling prophecy* and *Pygmalion effect*)

teaching as an art A way of teaching that involves intangibles such as emotions, values, and flexibility.

teaching as a science A way of teaching based on scientific methods such as sampling, control, objectivity, publication, and replication.

teleapprenticeship The use of networking technologies by experts, mentors, instructors, and peers to demonstrate ideas, pose questions, offer insights, and provide relevant information that can help learners build new knowledge and effectively participate in a learning community. (*See* **cognitive apprenticeship**)

test score pollution Test-related practices that cause scores to fluctuate but which are unrelated to what the test measures.

theoretical learning Learning how to use psychological tools across a range of settings and problem types to acquire new knowledge and skills.

theory of identical elements The theory that a similarity between the stimulus and response elements in two different tasks accounts for transfer of learning from one task to the other. (*See* **transfer of learning**)

theory of multiple intelligences A theory formulated by Howard Gardner that describes intelligence as being composed of seven, and possibly eight, mostly independent capabilities.

time-out A procedure that weakens a target behavior by temporarily removing the opportunity for the behavior to be rewarded.

token economy A behavior strengthening technique that uses items of no inherent value to "purchase" other items perceived to be valuable.

transfer of learning A student's ability to apply knowledge and problem-solving skills learned in school to similar but new situations.

triarchic theory of intelligence A theory formulated by Robert Sternberg that describes intelligence as being composed of practical, creative, and analytical components.

T score A standardized test score that ranges from 0 to 100 and uses a preselected mean of 50 to avoid negative values. (*See* **z score**)

tutorials Programs that attempt to teach facts, definitions, concepts, and other new material to students in either a step-by-step or a more individualized, branching approach.

validity The extent to which a test measures what it claims to measure.

vicarious reinforcement A situation in which the observer anticipates receiving a reward for behaving in a given way because someone else has been so rewarded.

videoconferencing Real-time communications between two or more locations where participants can see and hear each other and share ideas, opinions, and points of view across time zones and geographic distances.

virtual reality A technology to contextualize a student's experience by immersing him or her in a highly interactive, computer-generated, three-dimensional environment that responds in real time to participant movements using special glasses, body suits, headgear, and/or data gloves.

well-structured problems Clearly formulated problems with known solution procedures and known evaluation standards. (*See* **ill-structured problems**)

within-class ability grouping A form of ability grouping that involves the division of a single class of students into two or three groups for reading and math instruction.

withitness An attribute of teachers who prove to their students that they know what is going on in a classroom and as a result have fewer discipline problems than teachers who lack this characteristic.

World Wide Web A global system of interconnected computers that provides access to a wide variety of data in different formats. (Also called *the Internet, the Web,* or *the WWW*)

zero transfer A situation in which prior learning has no effect on new learning.

zone of proximal development (ZPD) Vygotsky's term for the difference between what a child can do on his or her own versus what can be accomplished with some assistance.

z score A standardized test score that tells how far a given raw score differs from the mean in standard deviation units. (*See* **T score**)

References

Achenbach, T. M., & Edelbrock, C. S. (1983). *Manual for the child behavior checklist and revised child behavior profile.* Burlington, VT: University of Vermont.

Adams, G. L., & Engelmann, S. (1996). *Research on direct instruction: 25 years beyond DISTAR.* Seattle, WA: Educational Achievement Systems.

Adelson, J. (1972). The political imagination of the young adolescent. In J. Kagan & R. Coles (Eds.), *Twelve to sixteen: Early adolescence.* New York: Norton.

Adelson, J. (1986). *Inventing adolescence: The political psychology of everyday schooling.* New Brunswick, NJ: Transaction Books.

Adelson, J. (Ed.). (1980). *Handbook of adolescent psychology.* New York: Wiley.

Aedo, I., Miranda, P., Panetsos, F., Torra, N., & Martin, M. (1994). A teaching methodology for the hearing impaired using hypermedia and computer animation. *Journal of Computing in Childhood Education, 5*(3/4), 353–369.

Ainsworth, M. D. S., & Wittig, B. A. (1972). Attachment and exploratory behavior of one-year-olds in a strange situation. In B. M. Foss (Ed.), *Determinants of infant behavior* (Vol. 4). New York: Wiley.

Airasian, P. W. (1997). *Classroom assessment* (3d ed.). New York: McGraw-Hill.

Airasian, P. W., & Walsh, M. E. (1997). Constructivist cautions. *Phi Delta Kappan, 78*(6), 444–449.

Alfassi, M. (1998). Reading for meaning: The efficacy of reciprocal teaching in fostering reading comprehension in high school students in remedial reading classes. *American Educational Research Journal, 35*(2), 309–332.

Allen, D. (1996). Problem-solving strategies. *Teaching PreK-8, 27*(3), 14–16.

Allen, H. A., Splittgerber, F. L., & Manning, M. L. (1993). *Teaching and learning in the middle school.* New York: Merrill.

Almy, M. C., Chittenden, E., & Miller, P. (1966). *Young children's thinking.* New York: Columbia University, Teachers College.

Altschuld, J. W. (1995). Evaluating the use of computers in science assessment: Considerations and recommendations. *Journal of Science Education and Technology, 4*(1), 57–64.

American Psychiatric Association (1994). *Diagnostic and statistical manual of mental disorders* (4th ed.). Washington, DC: Author.

American Psychological Association. (1997). *Learner-centered psychological principles: A framework for school redesign and reform* [On-line], Available: http://www.apa.org/ed/lcp.html.

Ames, C., & Ames, R. (1984). Systems of student and teacher motivation: Toward a qualitative definition. *Journal of Educational Psychology, 76*(4), 535–556.

Ames, N. L., & Miller, E. (1994). *Changing middle schools: How to make schools work for young adolescents.* San Francisco: Jossey-Bass.

Amiram, R., Bar-Tal, D., Alona, R., & Peleg, D. (1990). Perception of epistemic authorities by children and adolescents. *Journal of Youth and Adolescence, 19*(5), 495–510.

Anastasi, A., & Urbina, S. (1997). *Psychological testing* (7th ed.). Upper Saddle River, NJ: Prentice-Hall.

Anderman, E. M., & Maehr, M. L. (1994). Motivation and schooling in the middle grades. *Review of Educational Research, 64*(2), 287–309.

Anderson, J. B., & Freiberg, H. J. (1995). Using self-assessment as a reflective tool to enhance the student teaching experience. *Teacher Education Quarterly, 22*(1), 77–91.

Anderson, J. R., Reder, L. M., & Simon, H. A. (1996). Situated learning and education. *Educational Researcher, 25*(4), 5–11.

Anderson, R. C. (1984). Some reflections on the acquisition of knowledge. *Educational Researcher, 13*(9), 5–10.

Anderson-Inman, L., Knox-Quinn, C., & Horney, M. A. (1996). Computer-based study strategies for students with learning disabilities: Individual differences associated with adoption level. *Journal of Learning Disabilities, 29*(5), 461–484.

André, M. E. D. A., & Anderson, T. H. (1978-1979). The development and evaluation of a self-questioning study technique. *Reading Research Quarterly, 14*(4), 605–623.

Andre, T., & Phye, G. D. (1986). Cognition, learning, and education. In G. D. Phye & T. Andre (Eds.), *Cognitive classroom learning.* Orlando, FL: Academic Press.

Angeli, C., & Cunningham, D. J. (1998). Bubble Dialogue: Tools for supporting literacy and mind. In C. J. Bonk & K. S. King (Eds.), *Electronic collaborators: Learner-centered technologies for literacy, apprenticeship, and discourse.* Mahwah, NJ: Erlbaum.

Appleton, N. (1983). *Cultural pluralism in education.* New York: Longman.

Archer, S. L. (1982). The lower age boundaries of identity development. *Child Development, 53*(6), 1551–1556.

Archer, S. L. (1991). Identity development, gender differences in. In R. M. Lerner, A. C. Peterson, & J. Brooks-Gunn (Eds.), *Encyclopedia of adolescence.* New York: Garland Publishing.

Arias, M. B., & Casanova, U. (Eds.).(1993). *Bilingual education: Politics, practice, and research. Ninety-second yearbook of the National Society for the Study of Education, Part II.* Chicago: National Society for the Study of Education.

Armstrong, T. (1994). *Multiple intelligences in the classroom.* Alexandria, VA: Association for Supervision and Curriculum Development.

Atkinson, J. W. (1964). *An introduction to motivation.* Princeton, NJ: Van Nostrand.

Atkinson, R. C. (1975). Mnemotechnics in second language learning. *American Psychologist, 30*(2), 821–828.

Atkinson, R. C., & Raugh, M. R. (1975). An application of the mnemonic keyword method to the acquisition of a Russian vocabulary. *Journal of Experimental Psychology: Human Learning and Memory, 104*(2), 126–133.

Atkinson, R. C., & Shiffrin, R. M. (1968). Human memory: A proposed system and its control processes. In K. W. Spence & J. T. Spence (Eds.), *The psychology of learning and motivation* (Vol. 2). New York: Academic Press.

Ausubel, D. P., Novak, J. D., & Hanesian, H. (1978). *Educational psychology: A cognitive view* (2d ed.). New York: Holt, Rinehart & Winston.

Ayersman, D. J. (1996). Reviewing the research on hypermedia-based learning. *Journal of Research on Computing Education, 28*(4), 500–525.

Baddeley, A. (1998). *Human memory: Theory and practice* (rev. ed.). Boston: Allyn & Bacon.

Bailey, S. M. (1996). Shortchanging girls and boys. *Educational Leadership, 53*(8), 75–79.

Baines, L., Baines, C., & Masterson, C. (1994). Mainstreaming: One school's reality. *Phi Delta Kappan, 76*(1), 39–40, 57–64.

Baker, E., & O'Neil, Jr., H. F. (1995). Computer technology futures for the improvement of assessment. *Journal of Science Education and Technology, 4*(1), 37–45.

Baker, E., O'Neil, Jr., H. F., & Linn, R. L. (1993). Policy and validity prospects for performance-based assessment. *American Psychologist, 48*(12), 1210–1218.

Baker, E. T., Wang, M. C., & Walberg, H. J. (1994–1995). The effects of inclusion on learning. *Educational Leadership, 52*(4), 33–35.

Balajthy, E. (1998). Voices synthesis for emergent literacy. *The Reading Teacher, 42*(1), 72.

Balk, D. E. (1995). *Adolescent development.* Pacific Grove, CA: Brooks/Cole.

Baloche, L. A. (1998). *The cooperative classroom: Empowering learning.* Upper Saddle River, NJ: Prentice-Hall.

Bandura, A. (1982). Self-efficacy mechanism in human agency. *American Psychologist, 37*(2), 122–147.

Bandura, A. (1986). *Social foundations of thought and action: A social cognitive theory.* Englewood Cliffs, NJ: Prentice-Hall.

Bandura, A. (1989). Human agency in social cognitive theory. *American Psychologist, 44*(9), 1175–1184.

Bandura, A. (1993). Perceived self-efficacy in cognitive development and functioning. *Educational Psychologist, 28*(2), 117–148.

Bandura, A., Ross, D., & Ross, S. (1961). Transmission of aggression through imitation of aggressive models. *Journal of Abnormal and Social Psychology, 63*(3), 575–582.

Bandura, A., Ross, D., & Ross, S. (1963a). Imitation of film mediated aggressive models. *Journal of Abnormal and Social Psychology, 66*(1), 3–11.

Bandura, A., Ross, D., & Ross, S. (1963b). A comparative test of the status envy, social power, and secondary reinforcement theories of identificatory learning. *Journal of Abnormal and Social Psychology, 67*(6), 527–534.

Bangert-Drowns, R. L. (1993). The word processor as an instructional tool: A meta-analysis of word processing in writing instruction. *Review of Educational Research, 63*(1), 69–93.

Bangert-Drowns, R. L., Kulik, C-L. C., Kulik, J. A., & Morgan, M. (1991). The instructional effect of feedback in test-like events. *Review of Educational Research, 61*(2), 213–238.

Bangert-Drowns, R. L., Kulik, J. A., & Kulik, C-L. C. (1985). Effectiveness of computer-based education in secondary schools. *Journal of Computer-Based Instruction, 12*(3), 59–68.

Bangert-Drowns, R. L., Kulik, J. A., & Kulik, C-L., C. (1991). Effects of frequent classroom testing. *Journal of Educational Research, 85*(2), 89–99.

Banks, J. A. (1993). The canon debate, knowledge construction, and multicultural education. *Educational Researcher, 22*(5), 4–14.

Banks, J. A. (1994a). *An introduction to multicultural education.* Boston: Allyn & Bacon.

Banks, J. A. (1994b). *Multiethnic education: Theory and practice* (3d ed.). Boston: Allyn & Bacon.

Banks, J. A. (1994c). Transforming the mainstream curriculum. *Educational Leadership, 51*(8), 4–8.

Banks, J. A. (1997). *Teaching strategies for ethnic studies* (6th ed.). Boston: Allyn & Bacon.

Barab, S. A., Hay, K. E., & Duffy, T. M. (1998). Grounded constructions and how technology can help. *TechTrends, 43*(2), 15–23.

Barowy, B., & Laserna, C. (1997). The role of the Internet in the adoption of computer modeling as legitimate high school science. *Journal of Science Education and Technology, 6*(1), 3–13.

Barr, H.(1994). Social studies by electronic mail. *Social Studies, 85*(6), 281–284.

Barron, B., Vye, N., Zech, L., Schwartz, D., Bransford, J., Goldman, S., Pellegrino, J., Morris, J., Garrison, S., & Kantor, R. (1995). Creating contexts for community-based problem solving: The Jasper challenge series. In C. A. Hedley, P. Antonacci, & M. Rabinowitz (Eds.), *Thinking and literacy: The mind at work.* Hillsdale, NJ: Erlbaum.

Bartlett, F. C. (1932). *Remembering.* London: Cambridge University Press.

Baugh, I. W. (1994). Hypermedia as a performance-based assessment tool. *The Computing Teacher, 21*(6), 14–17.

Baumrind, D. (1971). Current patterns of parental authority. *Developmental Psychology Monographs, 4*(1, Pt.2), 1–103.

Baumrind, D. (1991). Parenting styles and adolescent development. In R. M. Lerner, A. C. Peterson, & J. Brooks-Gunn (Eds.), *Encyclopedia of adolescence.* New York: Garland.

Baumrind, D. (1991). The influence of parenting style on adolescent competence and substance abuse. *Journal of Early Adolescence, 11* (1), 56–95.

Beane, J. A. (1994). Cluttered terrain: The schools' interest in the self. In T. M. Brinthaupt & R. P. Lipka (Eds.), *Changing the self: Philosophies, techniques, and experiences.* Albany, NY: State University of New York Press.

Beane, J. A., & Lipka, R. P. (1986). *Self-concept, self-esteem, and the curriculum.* New York: Teachers College Press.

Beane, J. A., & Lipka, R. P. (1987). *When the kids come first.* Columbus, OH: National Middle Schools Association.

Beck, A. T. (1972). *Depression: Causes and treatment.* Philadelphia: University of Pennsylvania Press.

Becker, D. A., & Dwyer, M. M. (1994). Using hypermedia to provide learner control. *Journal of Educational Multimedia and Hypermedia, 3*(2), 155–172.

Bednar, A. K., Cunningham, D. J., Duffy, T. M., & Perry, J. D. (1991). Theory into practice: How do we link? in G. J. Anglin (Ed.), *Instructional technology: Past, present, and future.* Englewood, CO: Libraries Unlimited.

Bee, H. (1997). *The developing child* (8th ed.). New York: Longman.

Beilin, H., & Pufall, P. B. (Eds.)(1992). *Piaget's theory: Prospects and possibilities.* Hillsdale, NJ: Erlbaum.

Beirne-Smith, M. (1991). Peer tutoring in arithmetic for children with learning disabilities. *Exceptional Children, 57*(4), 330–337.

Beirne-Smith, M., Patton, J. R., & Ittenbach, R. (1994). *Mental retardation* (4th ed.). New York: Merrill.

Bellezza, F S. (1981). Mnemonic devices: Classification, characteristics, and criteria. *Review of Educational Research, 51*(2), 247–275.

Benbow, C. P. (1991). Mathematically talented children: Can acceleration meet their educational needs? In N. Colangelo & G. A. Davis (Eds.), *Handbook of gifted education.* Boston: Allyn & Bacon.

Bender, W. N. (1998). *Learning disabilities: Characteristics, identification, and teaching strategies* (3d ed.). Boston: Allyn & Bacon.

Benjamin, L. J., Jr. (1988). A history of teaching machines. *American Psychologist, 43*(9), 703–712.

Bennett, C. I. (1995). *Comprehensive multicultural education: Theory and practice* (3d ed.). Boston: Allyn & Bacon.

Bennett, N., Desforges, C., Cockburn, A., & Wilkinson, B. (1984). *The quality of pupil learning experiences.* Hillsdale, NJ: Erlbaum.

Bereiter, C., & Scardamalia, M. (1987). *The psychology of written communication.* Hillsdale, NJ: Erlbaum.

Berger, S. L. (Ed.). (1992). *Programs and practices in gifted education.* Reston, VA: Council for Exceptional Children.

Bergin, D. A., Ford, M. E., & Hess, R. D. (1993). Patterns of motivation and social behavior associated with microcomputer use of young children. *Journal of Educational Psychology, 85*(3), 437–445.

Berko, J. (1958). The child's learning of English morphology. *Word, 14*(1-2), 150–177.

Berliner, D. C. (1986). In pursuit of the expert pedagogue. *Educational Researcher, 15*(7), 5–13.

Berliner, D. C. (1992a). Redesigning classroom activities for the future. *Educational Technology, 32*(10), 7–13.

Berliner, D. C. (1992b). Telling the stories of educational psychology. *Educational Psychologist, 27*(2), 143–161.

Berliner, D. C., & Calfee, R. C. (Eds.).(1996). *Handbook of educational psychology.* New York: Simon & Schuster Macmillan.

Berliner, D. C., & Casanova, U. (1993). *Putting research to work in your school.* New York: Scholastic.

Bernhard, J. K., & Siegel, L. S. (1994). Increasing internal locus of controls for a disadvantaged group: A computer intervention. *Computers in the Schools, 11*(1), 59–77.

Biemiller, A. (1993). Lake Woebegon revisited: On diversity and education. *Educational Researcher, 22*(9), 7–12.

Bilsker, D., & Marcia, J. E. (1991). Adaptive regression and ego identity. *Journal of Adolescence, 14*(1), 75–84.

Bjork, R. A. (1979). Information processing analysis of college teaching. *Educational Psychologist, 14*, 15–23.

Blackhurst, A. E. (1997). Perspectives on technology in special education. *Teaching Exceptional Children, 29*(5), 41–48.

Blais, D. M. (1988). Constructivism: A theoretical revolution in teaching. *Journal of Developmental Education, 11*(3), 2–7.

Block, J. H. (1973). Conceptions of sex role: Some cross-cultural and longitudinal perspectives. *American Psychologist, 28*(6), 512–529.

Block, J. H., Efthim, H. E., & Burns, R. B. (1989). *Building effective mastery learning schools.* New York: Longman.

Bloom, B. S. (1968). Learning for mastery. *Evaluation Comment, 1*(2), 1–12.

Bloom, B. S. (1976). *Human characteristics and school learning.* New York: McGraw-Hill.

Bloom, B. S. (1984). The two sigma problem: The search for methods of group instruction as effective as one-to-one tutoring. *Educational Researcher, 13*(6), 4–16.

Bloom, B. S., Englehart, M. B., Furst, E. J., Hill, W. H., & Krathwohl, D. R. (Eds.). (1956). *Taxonomy of educational objectives. The classification of educational goals. Handbook I Cognitive domain.* New York: McKay.

Blustein, D. L., & Palladino, D. E. (1991). Self and identity in late adolescence: A theoretical and empirical investigation. *Journal of Adolescent Research, 6*(4), 437–453.

Blythe, T., & Gardner, H. (1990). A school for all intelligences. *Educational Leadership, 47*(7), 33–37.

Boekarts, M. (1993). Being concerned with well-being and with learning. *Educational Psychologist, 28*(2), 149–167.

Bolin, F. S. (1990). Helping student teachers think about teaching: Another look at Lou. *Journal of Teacher Education, 41*(1), 10–19.

Bond, C. L., Miller, M. J., & Kennon, R. W. (1987). Study skills: Who is taking the responsibility for teaching? *Performance & Instruction, 26*(7), 27–29.

Bonk, C. J., & Cummings, J. A. (1998). A dozen recommendations for placing the student at the center of Web-based instruction. *Educational Media International, 35*(2), 82–89.

Bonk, C. J., & Cunningham, D. J. (1998). Searching for learner-centered, constructivist, and sociocultural components of collaborative educational learning tools. In C. J. Bonk & K. S. King (Eds.), *Electronic collaborators: Learner-centered technologies for literacy, apprenticeship, and discourse.* Mahwah, NJ: Erlbaum.

Bonk, C. J., & Reynolds, T. H. (1992). Early adolescent composing within a generative-evaluative computerized prompting framework. *Computers in Human Behavior, 8*(1), 39–62.

Bonk, C. J., & Sugar, W. A. (1998). Student role play in the World Forum: Analyses of an arctic adventure learning apprenticeship. *Interactive Learning Environments, 6*(1–2), 1–29.

Bonk, C. J., Hay, K. E., & Fischler, R. B. (1996). Five key resources for an electronic community of elementary student weather forecasters. *Journal of Computing in Childhood Education, 7*(1/2), 93–118.

Bonk, C. J., Malikowski, S., Angeli, C., & East, J. (1998). Web-based case conferencing for preservice teacher education: Electronic discourse from the field, *Journal of Educational Computing Research, 19*(3), 267–304.

Boone, R., Higgins, K., Notari, A., & Stump, C. S. (1996). Hypermedia pre-reading lessons: Learner-centered software for kindergarten. *Journal of Computing in Childhood Education, 7*(2), 36–69.

Bower, G. H., Clark, M. C., Lesgold, A. M., & Winzenz, D. (1969). Hierarchical retrieval schemes in recall of categorized word lists. *Journal of Verbal Learning and Verbal Behavior, 8*(3), 323–343.

Bowman, B. T. (1989). Educating language-minority children: Challenges and opportunities. *Phi Delta Kappan, 71*(2), 118–120.

Boyer, C. B., & Hein, K. (1991). Sexually transmitted diseases in adolescence. In R. M. Lerner, A. C. Peterson, & J. Brooks-Gunn (Eds.), *Encyclopedia of adolescence.* New York: Garland Publishing.

Boyer, E. L. (1983). *High school.* New York: Harper & Row.

Bracey, G. W. (1983). On the compelling need to go beyond minimum competency. *Phi Delta Kappan, 64*(10), 717–721.

Bradsher, M. (1996). Making friends in the global village: Tips on international collaborations. *Learning and Leading with Technology, 23*(6), 58–61.

Bransford, J. D., & Stein, B. S. (1993). *The ideal problem solver* (2d ed.). New York: W. H. Freeman.

Bransford, J. D., Sherwood, R., Vye, N., & Rieser, J. (1986). Teaching thinking and problem solving: Research foundations. *American Psychologist, 41*(10), 1078–1089.

Bransford, J., Sharp, D. M., Vye, N. J., Goldman, S. R., Hasselbring, T. S., Goin, L., O'Banion, K., Liverois, J., Saul, E., & The Cognition and Technology Group at Vanderbilt (1996). MOST environments for accelerating literacy development. In S. Vosniadou, E. De Corte, R. Glaser, & H. Mandl (Eds.), *International perspectives on the design of technology-supported learning environments.* Mahwah, NJ: Erlbaum.

Brantlinger, E. A., & Guskin, S. L. (1985). Implications of social and cultural differences for special education with specific recommendations. *Focus on Exceptional Children, 18*(1), 1–12.

Braun, C. (1976). Teacher expectations: Sociopsychological dynamics. *Review of Educational Research, 46*(2), 185–213.

Braun, L. (1993). Educational technology: Help for all the kids. *The Computing Teacher, 20*(8), 11–12, 15.

Brent, G., & DiObilda, N. (1993). Effects of curriculum alignment versus direct instruction of urban children. *Journal of Educational Research, 86*(6), 333–338.

Brewer, D. J., Rees, D. I., & Argys, L. M. (1995). Detracking America's schools: The reform without cost? *Phi Delta Kappan, 77*(3), 210–215.

Brittain, C. V. (1967). An exploration of the bases of peer compliance and parent-compliance in adolescence. *Adolescence, 2*(8), 445–458.

Brody, N. (1992). *Intelligence* (2d ed.). San Diego, CA: Academic Press.

Brooks, H. B., & Brooks, D. W. (1996). The emerging role of CD-ROMs in teaching chemistry. *Journal of Science Education and Technology, 5*(3), 203–215.

Brooks, J. G. (1990). Teachers and students: Constructivists forging new connections. *Educational Leadership, 47*(5), 68–71.

Brooks, J. G., & Brooks, M G. (1993). *In search of understanding: The case for constructivist classrooms*. Alexandria, VA: Association for Supervision and Curriculum Development.

Brooks-Gunn, J., & Furstenberg, F. F., Jr. (1989). Adolescent sexual behavior. *American Psychologist, 44*(2), 249–257.

Brophy, J. E. (1979). Teacher behavior and its effects. *Journal of Educational Psychology, 71*(6), 733–750.

Brophy, J. E. (1981). Teacher praise: A functional analysis. *Review of Educational Research, 51*(1), 5–32.

Brophy, J. E. (1983). Research on the self-fulfilling prophecy and teacher expectations. *Journal of Educational Psychology, 75*(5), 631–661.

Brophy, J. E., & Alleman, J. (1991). Activities as instructional tools: A framework for analysis and evaluation. *Educational Researcher, 20*(4), 9–23.

Brophy, J. E., & Evertson, C. M. (1976). *Learning from teaching*. Boston: Allyn & Bacon.

Brown, A. L., Campione, J. C., & Day, J. D. (1981). Learning to learn: On training students to learn from text. *Educational Researcher, 10*(2), 14–24.

Brown, J. S., Collins, A., & Duguid, P. (1989). Situated cognition and the culture of learning. *Educational Researcher, 18*(1), 32–42.

Brown, R. (1973). *A first language: The early stages*. Cambridge, MA: Harvard University Press.

Brown, S. M., & Walberg, H. J. (1993). Motivational effects on test scores of elementary students. *Journal of Educational Research, 86*(3), 133–136.

Bruce, B., Peyton, J. K., & Batson, T. (Eds.). (1993). *Network-based classrooms: Realities and promises*. New York: Cambridge University Press.

Bruner, J. S. (1960). *The process of education*. New York: Vintage Books.

Bruner, J. S. (1983). *In search of mind: Essays in autobiography*. New York: Harper & Row.

Bryant, P. E. (1984). Piaget, teachers, and psychologists. *Oxford Review of Education, 10*(3), 251–259.

Burch, C. B. (1993). Teachers vs. professors: The university's side. *Educational Leadership, 51*(2), 68–76.

Burden, P. R. (1995). *Classroom management and discipline*. New York: Longman.

Bushrod, G., Williams, R. L., & McLaughlin, T. F. (1995). An evaluation of a simplified daily report system with two kindergarten pupils. *B.C. Journal of Special Education, 19*(1), 35–43.

Bybee, R. W., & Sund, R. B. (1982). *Piaget for educators* (2d ed.). Columbus, OH: Merrill.

Byrd, D. E. (1990). Peer tutoring with the learning disabled: A critical review. *Journal of Educational Research, 84*(2), 115–118.

Cain, K. M., & Dweck, C. S. (1995). The relation between motivational patterns and achievement cognitions through the elementary school years. *Merrill-Palmer Quarterly, 41*(1), 25–52.

Callahan, C. M., & McIntire, J. A. (1994). *Identifying outstanding talent in American Indian and Alaska native students*. Washington, DC: U.S. Department of Education, Office of Educational Research and Improvement.

Callister, T. A., & Dunne, F. (1992). The computer as doorstop: Technology as disempowerment. *Phi Delta Kappan, 74*(4), 324–326.

Cameron, J., & Pierce, W. D. (1994). Reinforcement, reward, and intrinsic motivation: A meta-analysis. *Review of Educational Research, 64*(3), 363–423.

Campbell, L. (1997). How teachers interpret MI theory. *Educational Leadership, 55*(1), 14–19.

Canady, R. L., & Hotchkiss, P. R. (1989). It's a good score! Just a bad grade. *Phi Delta Kappan, 71*(1), 68–71.

Cangelosi, J. S. (1997). *Classroom management strategies: Gaining and maintaining students' cooperation* (3d ed.). White Plains, NY: Longman.

Cardelle-Elawar, M., & Wetzel, K. (1995). Students and computers as partners in developing students' problem-solving skills. *Journal of Research on Computing in Education, 27*(4), 387–401.

Carney, R. N., Levin, J. R., & Levin, M. E. (1994). Enhancing the psychology of memory by enhancing memory of psychology. *Teaching of Psychology, 21*(3), 171–174.

Carrasquillo, A. L. (1991). *Hispanic children and youth in the United States: A resource guide*. New York: Garland Publishing.

Carrasquillo, A. L. (1994). *Teaching English as a second language: A resource guide*. New York: Garland Publishing.

Carroll, J. B. (1963). A model of school learning. *Teachers College Record, 64*(8), 723–733.

Carroll, T., Knight, C., & Hutchinson, E. (1995). Carmen Sandiego: Crime can pay when it comes to learning. *Social Education, 59*(3), 165–169.

Carter, C. J. (1997). Why reciprocal teaching? *Educational Leadership, 54*(6), 64–68.

Carter, D. B. (1987). The role of peers in sex role socialization. In D. B. Carter (Ed.), *Current conceptions of sex roles and sex typing*. New York: Praeger.

Carver, S. M. (1995). Cognitive apprenticeships: Putting theory into practice on a large scale. In C. A. Hedley, P. Antonacci, & M. Rabinowitz (Eds.), *Thinking and literacy: The mind at work*. Hillsdale, NJ: Erlbaum.

Case, R. (1975). Gearing the demands of instruction to the developmental capacities of the learner. *Review of Educational Research, 45*(1), 59–88.

Casey, J., & Martin, L. (1994). Literacy instruction in an integrated curriculum. *The Computing Teacher, 21*(5), 33–34, 36–37.

Cassidy, J., & Johnson, N. (1986). Federal and state definitions of giftedness: Then and now. *Gifted Child Today, 9*(6), 15–21.

Chaillé, C., & Britain, L. (1991). *The young child as scientist: A constructivist approach to early childhood science education*. New York: HarperCollins.

Chance, P. (1992). The rewards of learning. *Phi Delta Kappan, 74*(3), 200–207.

Chance, P. (1993). Sticking up for rewards. *Phi Delta Kappan, 74*(10), 787–790.

Charles, C. M. (1972). *Educational psychology: The instructional endeavor*. St. Louis, MO: Mosby.

Checkley, K. (1997). The first seven . . . . and the eighth: A conversation with Howard Gardner. *Educational Leadership, 55*(1), 8–13.

Chia, J., & Duthie, B. (1993) Primary children and computer-based art work. *Art Education, 46*(6), 23–26, 35–41.

Chinn, P. C., & Plata, M. (1987–1988). Multicultural education: Beyond ethnic studies. *Teacher Education and Practice, 4*(2), 7–10.

Chiou, G. (1994–1995). Learning rationales and virtual reality technology in education. *Journal of Educational Technology Systems, 23*(4), 327–336.

Choate, J. S. (Ed.).(1997). *Successful inclusive teaching: Proven ways to detect and correct special needs* (2d ed.). Boston: Allyn & Bacon.

Christmann, E., Badgett, J., & Lucking, R. (1997). Progressive comparison of the effects of computer-assisted instruction on the academic achievements of secondary students. *Journal of Research on Computing in Education, 29*(4), 325–337.

Christmann, E. P., Lucking, R. A., & Badgett, J. L. (1997). The effectiveness of computer-assisted instruction on the academic achievement of secondary students: A meta-analytic comparison between urban, suburban, and rural educational settings. *Computers in the Schools, 13*(3/4), 31–40.

Cicchetti, D., & Toth, S. L. (1998). The development of depression in children and adolescents. *American Psychologist, 53* (2), 221–241.

Clariana, R. B. (1996). Differential achievement gains for mathematics computation, concepts, and applications with an integrated learning system. *Journal of Computers in Mathematics and Science Teaching, 15*(3), 203–215.

Clariana, R. B. (1997). Considering learning style in computer-assisted learning. *British Journal of Educational Technology, 28*(1), 66–68.

Clark, C. M. (1995). *Thoughtful teaching.* New York: Teachers College Press.

Clark, J. M., & Paivio, A. (1991). Dual coding theory and education. *Educational Psychology Review, 3*(3), 149–210.

Clausen, J. (1975). The social meaning of differential physical and sexual maturation. In S. Dragastin & G. H. Elder, Jr. (Eds.), *Adolescence in the life cycle.* New York: Wiley.

Coates, D. L., & van Widenfeldt, B. (1991). Pregnancy in adolescence. In R. M. Lerner, A. C. Peterson, & J. Brooks-Gunn (Eds.), *Encyclopedia of adolescence.* New York: Garland Publishing.

Cognition and Technology Group at Vanderbilt (1993). Anchored instruction and situated cognition revisited. *Educational Technology, 33*(3), 52–70.

Cognition and Technology Group at Vanderbilt (1994). Multimedia environments for developing literacy for at-risk students. In B. Means (Ed.), *Technology and educational reform: The reality behind the promise.* San Francisco, CA: Jossey-Bass.

Cognition and Technology Group at Vanderbilt. (1991). Some thoughts about constructivism and instructional design. *Educational Technology, 31*(9), 16–18.

Cognition and Technology Group at Vanderbilt. (1992a). The Jasper series: A generative approach to improving mathematical thinking. In K. Sheingold, L. G. Roberts, & S. M. Malcolm (Eds.), *This year in school science 1991: Technology for teaching and learning.* Washington, DC: American Association for the Advancement of Science.

Cognition and Technology Group at Vanderbilt. (1992b). The Jasper series as an example of anchored instruction: Theory, program description, and assessment data. *Educational Psychologist, 27*(3), 291–315.

Cognition and Technology Group at Vanderbilt. (1996). Looking at technology in context: A framework for understanding technology and education research. In D. C. Berliner & R. C. Calfee (Eds.), *Handbook of educational psychology.* New York, NY: Simon & Schuster.

Colangelo, N., & Davis, G. A. (Eds.).(1997). *Handbook of gifted education* (2d ed.). Boston: Allyn & Bacon.

Coleman, J. C. (1980). Friendship and the peer group in adolescence. In J. Adelson (Ed.), *Handbook of adolescent psychology.* New York: Wiley.

Collins, A. (1996). Design issues for learning environments. In S. Vosniadou, E. De Corte, R. Glaser., & H. Mandl (Eds.), *International perspectives on the design of technology-supported learning environments.* Mahwah, NJ: Erlbaum.

Colten, M. E., & Gore, S. (Eds.).(1991). *Adolescent stress.* New York: Aldine de Gruyter.

Comber, C., Colley, A., Hargreaves, D., & Dorn, L. (1997). The effects of age, gender and computer experience upon computer attitudes. *Journal of Educational Research, 39*(2), 123–133.

Combs, A. W. (1965). *The professional education of teachers.* Boston: Allyn & Bacon.

Conger, J. J. (1991). *Adolescence and youth* (4th ed.). New York: HarperCollins.

Connell, J. P., Halpern-Felsher,B. L., Clifford, E. L., Crichlow, W., & Usinger, P. (1995). Hanging in there: Behavioral, psychological, and contextual factors affecting whether African American adolescents stay in school. *Journal of Adolescent Research, 10*(1), 41–63.

Conoley, J. C., & Kramer, J. J. (Eds.). (1989). *Tenth mental measurements yearbook.* Lincoln, NE: Buros Institute of Mental Measurements.

Consortium for Research on Black Adolescence (1990). *Black adolescence: Current issues and annotated bibliography.* Boston: G. K. Hall.

Cooper, H., & Dorr, N. (1995). Race comparisons on need for achievement: A meta-analytic alternative to Graham's narrative review. *Review of Educational Research, 65*(4), 438–508.

Cooper, H. M. (1979). Pygmalion grows up: A model for teacher expectation, communication, and performance influence. *Review of Educational Research, 49*(3), 389–410.

Copen, P. (1995). Connecting classrooms through telecommunications. *Educational Leadership, 53*(2), 44–47.

Cordova, D. I., & Lepper, M. R. (1996). Intrinsic motivation and the process of learning: Beneficial effects of contextualization, personalization, and choice. *Journal of Educational Psychology, 88*(4), 715–730.

Corno, L. (1986). Teaching and self-regulated learning. In D. C. Berliner & B. V. Rosenshine (Eds.), *Talks to teachers.* New York: Random House.

Corston, R., & Colman, A. (1996). Gender and social facilitation effects on computer competence and attitudes toward computers. *Journal of Educational Computing Research, 14*(2), 171–183.

Cosgrove, D. J. (1959). Diagnostic ratings of teacher performance. *Journal of Educational Psychology, 50*(5), 200–204.

Covington, M. V. (1985). Strategic thinking and the fear of failure. In J. W. Segal, S. F. Chipman, & R. Glaser (Eds.), *Thinking and learning skills* (Vol. 1). Hillsdale, NJ: Erlbaum.

Cox, B. D. (1997). The rediscovery of the active learner in adaptive contexts: A developmental-historical analysis of transfer of training. *Educational Psychologist, 32*(1), 41–55.

Crain, W. (1992). *Theories of development: Concepts and applications* (3d ed.). Englewood Cliffs, NJ: Prentice-Hall.

Cronbach, L. J. (1990). *Essentials of psychological testing* (5th ed.). New York: Harper & Row.

Crooks, T. J. (1988). The impact of classroom evaluation practices on students. *Review of Educational Research, 58*(4), 438–481.

Cruickshank, D. R. (1990). *Research that informs teachers and teacher educators.* Bloomington, IN: Phi Delta Kappa Educational Foundation.

Csikszentmihalyi, M., & Larson, R. (1984). *Being adolescent.* New York: Basic Books.

Cuban, L. (1986). *Teachers and machines: The classroom use of technology since 1920.* New York: Teachers College Press.

Cuban, L. (1990). What I learned from what I had forgotten about teaching: Notes from a professor. *Phi Delta Kappan, 71*(6), 479–482.

Cunningham, D. J. (1991). In defense of extremism. *Educational Technology, 31*(9), 26–27.

Daiute, C. (1985). Issues in using computers to socialize the writing process. *Educational Communication & Technology, 33*(1), 41–50.

Damon, W. (1988). *The moral child.* New York: Free Press.

Damon, W., & Hart, D. (1988). *Self-understanding in childhood and adolescence.* New York: Cambridge University Press.

Damon, W., & Phelps, E. (1991). Peer collaboration as a context for cognitive growth. In L. T. Landsmann (Ed.), *Culture, schooling, and psychological development.* Norwood, NJ: Ablex.

Dana, R. H. (1993). *Multicultural assessment perspectives for professional psychology.* Boston: Allyn & Bacon.

Darling-Hammond, L., Ancess, J., & Falk, B. (1995). *Authentic assessment in action.* New York: Teachers College Press.

Darling-Hammond, L., & Falk, B. (1997). Using standards and assessments to support student learning. *Phi Delta Kappan, 79* (3), 190–199.

Dasen, P., & Heron, A. (1981). Cross-cultural tests of Piaget's theory. In H. C. Triandis & A. Heron (Eds.), *Handbook of cross-cultural psychology, developmental psychology* (Vol. 4). Boston: Allyn & Bacon.

Dattilo, D., Stout, C., & Watrous, M. (1991). Super technology time-savers. *Instructor, 101*(1), 74–76.

Davey, T., Godwin, J., & Mittelholtz, D. (1997). Developing and scoring an innovative computerized writing assessment. *Journal of Educational Measurement, 34*(1), 21–41.

Davidson-Shivers, G. V., Rasmussen, K. L., & Bratton-Jeffery, M. F. (1997). Investigating learning strategies generation in a hypermedia environment using qualitative methods. *Journal of Computing in Childhood Education, 8*(2/3), 247–261.

Davies, L. J. (1984). Teaching university students how to learn. *Improving University and College Teaching, 31*(4), 160–165.

Dawe, H. A. (1984). Teaching: A performing art. *Phi Delta Kappan, 65*(8), 548–552.

de Jong, T., & van Joolingen, W. R. (1998). Scientific discovery learning with computer simulations of conceptual domains. *Review of Educational Research, 68*(2), 179–201.

deCharms, R. (1976). *Enhancing motivation: Change in the classroom.* New York: Irvington.

Dede, C. (1996). The evolution of distance education: Emerging technologies and distributed learning. *The American Journal of Distance Education, 10*(2), 4–36.

Dempster, F. N. (1988). The spacing effect: A case study in the failure to apply the results of psychological research. *American Psychologist, 43*(8), 627–634.

Derry, S., & Lesgold, A. (1996). Toward a situated social practice model for instructional design. In D. C. Berliner & R. C. Calfee (Eds.), *Handbook of educational psychology.* New York: Simon & Schuster Macmillan.

DeVillars, R. A., Faltis, C. J., & Cummins, J. P. (Eds.).(1994). *Cultural diversity in schools: From practice to rhetoric.* Albany, NY: State University of New York Press.

DeVries, R. (1997). Piaget's social theory. *Educational Researcher, 26*(2), 4–17.

D'Ignazio, F. (1994). The classroom as knowledge theme park. *The Computing Teacher, 21*(7), 35–37, 50.

di Sibio, M. (1982). Memory for connected discourse: A constructivist view. *Review of Educational Research, 52*(2), 149–174.

Dickinson, K. (1997). Distance learning on the Internet: Testing students using web forms and the computer gateway interface. *TechTrends, 42*(2), 38–42.

Dickson, W. P. (1985). Thought-provoking software: Juxtaposing symbol systems. *Educational Researcher, 14*(5), 30–38.

Doerr, H. M. (1996). Integrating the study of trigonometry, vectors, and force through modeling. *School Science and Mathematics, 96*(8), 407–418.

Doyle, W. (1983). Academic work. *Review of Educational Research, 53*(2), 159–200.

Driscoll, M. P. (1994). *Psychology of learning and instruction.* Boston: Allyn & Bacon.

Duell, O. K. (1986). Metacognitive skills. In G. D. Phye & T. Andre (Eds.), *Cognitive classroom learning.* Orlando, FL: Academic Press.

Duffy, T. M., & Cunningham, D. J. (1996). Constructivism: Implications for the design and delivery of instruction. In D. Jonassen (Ed.), *Handbook of research for educational communications and technology.* New York: Macmillan Library Reference.

Dunn, R., & Dunn, K. (1992). *Teaching elementary students through their individual learning styles.* Boston: Allyn & Bacon.

Dunn, R., & Dunn, K. (1993). *Teaching secondary students through their individual learning styles.* Boston: Allyn & Bacon.

Dusek, J. B. (1991). *Adolescent development and behavior* (2d ed.). Englewood Cliffs, NJ: Prentice-Hall.

Dweck, C. S. (1986). Motivational processes affecting learning. *American Psychologist, 41*(10), 1040–1048.

Eakin, S. S. (1997). Educators on the edge: Spreading the wise use of technology. *Technos, 6*(3), 15–22.

Ebel, R. L., & Frisbie, D. A. (1991). *Essentials of educational measurement* (5th ed.). Englewood Cliffs, NJ: Prentice-Hall.

Ebert, E., & Strudler, N. (1996). Improving science learning using low-cost multimedia. *Learning and Leading with Technology, 24*(1), 23–26.

Eby, J. W. (1994). *Reflective planning, teaching, and evaluation: K–12.* New York: Merrill.

Eccles, J. S., Midgley, C., Wigfield, A., Buchanan, C. M., Reuman, D., Flanagan, C., & Mac Iver, D. (1993). Development during adolescence: The impact of stage-

environment fit on young adolescents' experiences in schools and families. *American Psychologist, 48* (2), 90–101.

Edelson, D. C., Pea, R. D., & Gomez, L. (1996). Constructivism in the collaboratory. In B. G. Wilson (Ed.), *Constructivist learning environments: Case studies in instructional design.* Englewood Cliffs, NJ: Educational Technology Publications.

Edmunds, R. D. (Ed.). (1980). *American Indian leaders: Studies in diversity.* Lincoln, NE: University of Nebraska Press.

Egeland, P. (1996–1997). Pulleys, planes, and student performance. *Educational Leadership, 54*(4), 41–45.

Ehman, L. H., Glenn, A. D., Johnson, V., & White, C. S. (1992). Using computer databases in student problem solving: A study of eight social studies teachers' classrooms. *Theory and Research in Social Education, 20*(2), 179–206.

Eisenberger, R., & Cameron, J. (1996). Detrimental effects of reward: Reality or myth? *American Psychologist, 51*(11), 1153–1166.

Elkind, D. (1968). Cognitive development in adolescence. In J. F. Adams (Ed.), *Understanding adolescence.* Boston: Allyn & Bacon.

Elkind, D. (1989). Developmentally appropriate practice: Philosophical and practical implications. *Phi Delta Kappan, 71*(2), 113–117.

Ellis, H. C. (1965). *The transfer of learning.* New York: Macmillan.

Ellis, H. C. (1978). *Fundamentals of human learning, memory, and cognition* (2d ed.). Dubuque, IA: William C. Brown.

Elrich, M. (1994). The stereotype within. *Educational Leadership, 51*(8), 12–15.

Elwell, C. C., Reeve, K., & Hofmeister, A. (1992). Captioning instructional video. *Educational Technology, 32*(8), 45–50.

Emmer, E. T., Evertson, C. M., Clements, B. S., & Worsham, M. E. (1997). *Classroom management for secondary teachers* (4th ed.). Boston: Allyn & Bacon.

Engebretsen, A. (1997). Visualizing least-square lines of best fit. *The Mathematics Teacher, 90*(5), 405–408.

EPIE Institute. (1993). *The latest and best of TESS: The educational software selector.* Hampton Bays, NY: The EPIE Institute.

Epstein, H. T. (1980). Brain growth and cognitive functioning. In D. R. Steer (Ed.), *The emerging adolescent: Characteristics and educational implications.* Columbus, OH: National Middle School Association.

Erdelyi, M. H., & Goldberg, B. (1979). Let's now sweep repression under the rug: Towards a cognitive psychology of repression. In J. Kihlstrom & F. Evans (Eds.),

Functional disorders of memory. Hillsdale, NJ: Erlbaum.

Erickson, J., & Lehrer, R. (1998). The evolution of critical standards as students design hypermedia documents. *Journal of the Learning Sciences, 7*(3 & 4), 351–386.

Ericsson, K. A., Chase, W. G., & Faloon, S. (1980). Acquisition of a memory skill. *Science, 208*(4448), 1181–1182.

Erikson, E. H. (1963). *Childhood and society* (2d ed.). New York: Norton.

Erikson, E. H. (1968). *Identity: Youth and crisis*. New York: Norton.

Evans, E. D., & Richardson, R. C. (1995). Corporal punishment: What teachers should know. *Teaching Exceptional Children, 27*(2), 33–36.

Evans, R. I. (1967). *Dialogue with Erik Erikson*. New York: Harper & Row.

Evertson, C. M., Emmer, E. T., Clements, B. S., & Worsham, M. E. (1997). *Classroom management for elementary teachers* (4th ed.). Boston: Allyn & Bacon.

Fabris, M. E. (1992–1993). Using multimedia in the multicultural classroom. *Journal of Educational Technology Systems, 21*(2), 163–171.

Fagot, B. I. (1978). The influence of sex of child on parental reactions to toddler children. *Child Development, 49*(2), 459–465.

FairTest. (1990). *Standardized tests and our children: A guide to testing reform*. Cambridge, MA: National Center for Fair and Open Testing.

Fantuzzo, J. W., Polite, K., & Grayson, N. (1990). An evaluation of reciprocal peer tutoring across elementary school settings. *Journal of School Psychology, 28*(4), 309–323.

Fantuzzo, J. W., Riggio, R. E., Connelly, S., & Dimeff, L. A. (1989). Effects of reciprocal peer tutoring on academic achievement and psychological adjustment: A component analysis. *Journal of Educational Psychology, 81*(2), 173–177.

Faw, H. W., & Waller, T. G. (1976). Mathemagenic behaviors and efficiency in learning from prose materials. *Review of Educational Research, 46*(4), 691–720.

Feather, N. T. (1980). Values in adolescence. In J. Adelson (Ed.), *Handbook of adolescent psychology*. New York: Wiley.

Feist, J. (1990). *Theories of personality* (2d ed). Fort Worth, TX: Holt, Rinehart & Winston.

Feldhusen, J. F. (1998). Programs for the gifted few or talent development for the many? *Phi Delta Kappan, 79*(10), 735–738.

Ferguson, P., & Womack, S. T. (1993). The impact of subject matter and education coursework on teaching performance. *Journal of Teacher Education, 44*(1), 55–63.

Ferrini-Mundy, J., & Lauten, D. (1994). Learning about calculus learning. *The Mathematics Teacher, 87*(2), 115–121.

Fetterman, D. M. (1996). Videoconferencing on-line: Enhancing communications over the internet. *Educational Researcher, 25*(4), 23–27.

Feuer, M. J., Fulton, K., & Morison, P. (1993). Better tests and testing practices: Options for policy makers. *Phi Delta Kappan, 74*(7), 530–533.

Feynman, R. P. (1985). *"Surely you're joking, Mr. Feynman."* New York: Norton.

Fischer, M. J. (1996). Integrated learning systems: An application linking technology with human factors and pedagogical principles. *Educational Technology Research and Development, 44*(3), 65–72.

Fitzgerald, G. E., Wilson, B., & Semrau, L. P. (1997). An interactive multimedia program to enhance teacher problem-solving skills based on cognitive flexibility theory: Design and outcomes. *Journal of Educational Multimedia and Hypermedia, 6*(1), 47–76.

Fitzgerald, J. (1995). English-as-a-second-language learners' cognitive reading processes: A review of the research in the United States. *Review of Educational Research, 65*(2), 145–190.

Flanders, N. A. (1970). *Analyzing teacher behavior*. Reading, MA: Addison-Wesley.

Flavell, J. H. (1976). Metacognitive aspects of problem solving. In L. B. Resnick (Ed.), *The nature of intelligence*. Hillsdale, NJ: Erlbaum.

Flavell, J. H. (1987). Speculations about the nature and development of metacognition. In F. E. Weinert & R. H. Kluwe (Eds.), *Metacognition, motivation, and understanding*. Hillsdale, NJ: Erlbaum.

Fletcher-Flinn, C. M., & Gravatt, B. (1995). The efficacy of computer assisted instruction (CAI): A meta-analysis. *Journal of Educational Computing Research, 12*(3), 219–242.

Fletcher-Flinn, C. M., & Suddendorf, T. (1996). Do computers affect "the mind"? *Journal of Educational Computing Research, 15*(2), 97–112.

Flinders, D. J. (1989). Does the "art of teaching" have a future? *Educational leadership, 46*(8), 16–20.

Foot, H. C., Shute, R. H., & Morgan, M. J. (1990). Theoretical issues in peer tutoring. In H. C. Foot, M. J. Morgan, & R. H. Shute (Eds.), *Children helping children*. Chichester, England: John Wiley & Sons.

Fosnot, C. T. (1996). Constructivism: A psychological theory of learning. In C. T. Fos-

not (Ed.), *Constructivism: Theory, perspectives, and practice*. New York: Teachers College Press.

Foster, D. W. (1982). *Sourcebook of Hispanic culture in the United States*. Chicago: American Library Association.

Foyle, H. C., Lyman, L., & Thies, S. A. (1991). *Cooperative learning in the early childhood classroom*. Washington, DC: National Education Association.

Franca, V. M., Kerr, M. M., Reitz, A. L., & Lambert, D. (1990). Peer tutoring among behaviorally disordered students: Academic and social benefits to tutor and tutee. *Education and Treatment of Children, 13*(2), 109–128.

Frank, S. J., Pirsch, L. A., & Wright, V. C. (1990). Late adolescents' perceptions of their relationships with their parents: Relationships among deidealization, autonomy, relatedness, and insecurity and implications for adolescent adjustment and ego identity status. *Journal of Youth and Adolescence, 19*(6), 571–588.

Frasier, M. M. (1987). The identification of gifted black students: Developing new perspectives. *Journal for the Education of the Gifted, 10*(3), 155–180.

Freedman, K., & Liu, M. (1996). The importance of computer experience, learning processes, and communication patterns in multicultural networking. *Educational Technology Research and Development, 44*(1), 43–59.

Friedenberg, E. Z. (1963). *Coming of age in America: Growth and acquiescence*. New York: Vintage Books.

Fuchs, D., Fuchs, L. S., Mathes, P. G., & Simmons, D. C. (1997). Peer-assisted learning strategies: Making classrooms more responsive to diversity. *American Educational Research Journal, 34*(1), 174–206.

Furth, H. G. (1970). *Piaget for teachers*. Englewood Cliffs, NJ: Prentice-Hall.

Gable, R. A., & Warren, S. F. (Ed.).(1993). *Strategies for teaching students with mild to severe mental retardation*. Baltimore, MD: Brookes.

Gaffney, J. S., & Anderson, R. C. (1991). Two-tiered scaffolding: Congruent processes of teaching and learning. In E. H. Hiebert (Ed.), *Literacy in a diverse society: Perspectives, practices, and policies*. New York: Teachers College Press.

Gage, N. L. (1984). What do we know about teaching effectiveness? *Phi Delta Kappan, 66*(2), 87–93.

Gagné, E. D., Yekovich, C. W., & Yekovich, F. R. (1993). *The cognitive psychology of school learning* (2d ed.). New York: HarperCollins.

Gall, M. D. (1970). The use of questions in teaching. *Review of Educational Research*, 40(5), 707–721.

Gall, M. D., Gall, J. P., Jacobsen, D. R., & Bullock, T. L. (1990). *Tools for learning: A guide to teaching study skills*. Alexandria, VA: Association for Supervision and Curriculum Development.

Gallagher, J. J., & Gallagher, S. A. (1994). *Teaching the gifted child*. (4th ed.). Boston: Allyn & Bacon.

Gallagher, P. A. (1995). *Teaching students with behavior disorders: Techniques and activities for classroom instruction*. (2d ed.). Denver: Love.

Gallatin, J. (1980). Political thinking in adolescence. In J. Adelson (Ed.), *Handbook of adolescent psychology*. New York: Wiley.

Gallimore, R., & Tharp, R. (1990). Teaching mind in society: Teaching, schooling, and literate discourse. In L. C. Moll (Ed.), *Vygotsky and education: Instructional implications and applications of sociohistorical psychology*. Cambridge, England: Cambridge University Press.

Gantner, M. W. (1997). Lessons learned from my students in the barrio. *Educational Leadership*, 54(7), 44–45.

García, E. (1994). *Understanding and meeting the challenge of student cultural diversity*. Boston: Houghton Mifflin.

Garcia, J. (1993). The changing image of ethnic groups in textbooks. *Phi Delta Kappan*, 75(1), 29–35.

Gardner, H. (1983). *Frames of mind: The theory of multiple intelligences*. New York: Basic Books.

Gardner, H. (1991). *The unschooled mind: How children think and how schools should teach*. New York: Basic Books.

Gardner, H. (1995). Reflections on multiple intelligences: Myths and messages. *Phi Delta Kappan*, 77(3), 200–209.

Gardner, H., & Hatch, T. (1989). Multiple intelligences go to school. *Educational Researcher*, 18(8), 410.

Garland, A. F., & Zigler, E. (1993). Adolescent suicide prevention: Current research and social policy implications. *American Psychologist*, 48(2), 169–182.

Garner, R. (1987). *Metacognition and reading comprehension*. Norwood, NJ: Ablex Publishing Company.

Garrison, J. W. (1997). *Dewey and Eros: Wisdom and desire in the art of teaching*. New York: Teachers College Press.

Garrod, A. (Ed.).(1993). *Approaches to moral development: New research and emerging themes*. New York: Teachers College Press.

Gelman, R. (1994). Constructivism and supporting environments. In D. Tirosh (Ed.), *Implict and explicit knowledge: An educational approach*. Norwood, NJ: Ablex.

Gelman, R., & Baillargeon, E. E. (1983). A review of some Piagetian concepts. In J. H. Flavell & E. M. Markman (Eds.), *Handbook of child development: Vol. III Cognitive development* (4th ed.). New York: Wiley.

Genesee, F., & Cloud, N. (1998). Multilingualism *is* basic. *Educational Leadership*, 55(6), 62–65.

Gersten, R., & Brengelman, S. U. (1996). The quest to translate research into classroom practice: The emerging knowledge base. *Remedial and Special Education*, 17(2), 67–74.

Gick, M. L. (1986). Problem-solving strategies. *Educational Psychologist*, 21(1,2), 99–120.

Gilligan, C. (1979). Women's place in man's life cycle. *Harvard Educational Review*, 49(4), 431–446.

Gilligan, C. (1982). *In a different voice: Psychological theory and women's development*. Cambridge, MA: Harvard University Press.

Gilligan, C. (1987). Adolescent development reconsidered. In C. E. Irwin, Jr. (Ed.), *Adolescent social behavior and health*. San Francisco: Jossey-Bass.

Gilligan, C. (1988). Exit-voice dilemmas in adolescent development. In C. Gilligan, J. Ward, J. Taylor, & B. Bardige (Eds.), *Mapping the moral domain: A contribution of women's thinking to psychological theory and education*. Cambridge, MA: Harvard University Press.

Ginott, H. (1965). *Between parent and child*. New York: Macmillan.

Ginott, H. (1972). *Teacher and child*. New York: Macmillan.

Ginsburg, H. P., & Opper, S. (1988). *Piaget's theory of intellectual development* (3d ed.). Englewood Cliffs, NJ: Prentice-Hall.

Gipson, J. (1997). Girls and computer technology: Barrier or key? *Educational Technology*, 37(2), 41–43.

Glasgow, N. J. (1997). Keep up the good work! Part II using multimedia to build reading fluency and enjoyment. *Learning and Leading with Technology*, 24(5), 22–25.

Glasser, W. (1986). *Control theory in the classroom*. New York: Harper & Row.

Glasser, W. (1990). *The quality school*. New York: Harper & Row.

Gleason, M. M. (1995). Using direct instruction to integrate reading and writing for students with learning disabilities. *Reading and Writing Quarterly*, 11(1), 91–108.

Gold, M., & Petronio, R. J. (1980). Delinquent behavior in adolescence. In J. Adelson (Ed.), *Handbook of adolescent psychology*. New York: Wiley.

Goldman, S. R., Petrosino, A. J., Sherwood, R. D., Garrison, S., Hickey, D., Bransford, J. D., & Pellegrino, J. W. (1996) Anchoring science instruction in multimedia learning environments. In S. Vosniadou, E. De Corte, R. Glaser, & H. Mandl (Eds.), *International perspectives on the design of technology-supported learning environments*. Mahwah, NJ: Erlbaum.

Goldstein, A. P., Apter, S. J., & Harootunian, B. (1984). *School violence*. Englewood Cliffs, NJ: Prentice-Hall.

Goldstein, A. P., Sprafkin, R. P., Gershaw, N. J., & Nein, P. (1980). *Skillstreaming the adolescent: A structured learning approach to teaching prosocial skills*. Champaign, IL: Research Press.

Gollnick, D. A., & Chinn, P. C. (1994). *Multicultural education in a pluralistic society* (4th ed.). New York: Merrill.

Golub, J. N. (1994). *Activities for the interactive classroom*. Urbana, IL: National Council of Teachers of English.

Gomez, L. M., Fishman, B. J., & Pea, R. D. (1998). The CoVis project: Building a large scale science education testbed. *Interactive Learning Environments*, 6(1–2), 59–92.

Gonzalez, V., Brusca-Vega, R., & Yawkey, T. (1997). *Assessment and instruction of culturally and linguistically diverse students with or at-risk of learning problems: From research to practice*. Boston: Allyn & Bacon.

Good, T. (1982). *Classroom research: What we know and what we need to know* (R&D Report No. 9018). Austin, TX: University of Texas, Research and Development Center for Teacher Education.

Good, T. L., & Brophy, J. (1995). *Contemporary educational psychology* (5th ed.). New York: Longman.

Goodlad, J. I. (1984). *A place called school*. New York: McGraw-Hill.

Goodrich, H. (1996–1997). Understanding rubrics. *Educational Leadership*, 54(4), 14–17.

Gordon, S., & Gilgun, J. F. (1987). Adolescent sexuality. In V B. van Hasselt & M. Hersen (Eds.), *Handbook of adolescent psychology*. New York: Pergamon Press.

Gordon, T. (1974). *TET: Teacher effectiveness training*. New York: McKay.

Gottfredson, G. D., & Gottfredson, D. C. (1985). *Victimization in schools*. New York: Plenum.

Gough, P. B. (1987). The key to improving schools: An interview with William Glasser. *Phi Delta Kappan*, 69(9), 656–662.

Gould, S. J. (1981). *The mismeasure of man*. New York: Norton.

Gouzouasis, P. (1994). Multimedia constructions of children: An exploratory study. *Journal of Computing in Childhood Education, 5*(3/4), 273–284.

Grabe, M., & Grabe, C. (1998). *Integrating technology for meaningful learning* (2d ed.). Boston: Houghton Mifflin.

Graham, S. (1997). Using attribution theory to understand social and academic motivation in African American youth. *Educational Psychologist, 32*(1), 21–34.

Graham, S., & Weiner, B. (1993). Attributional applications in the classroom. In T. M. Tomlinson (Ed.), *Motivating students to learn: Overcoming barriers to high achievement*. Berkeley, CA: McCutchan.

Gray, B. A. (1991). Using instructional technology with at-risk youth: A primer. *Tech Trends, 36*(5), 61–63.

Gredler, G. R. (1997). Intervention programs for young children with learning disabilities. *Psychology in the Schools, 34*(2), 161–169.

Green, K. E., & Stager, S. F (1986-1987). Testing: Coursework, attitudes, and practices. *Educational Research Quarterly, 11*(2), 48–55.

Gresham, F. M., & MacMillan, D. L. (1997). Social competence and affective characteristics of students with mild disabilities. *Review of Educational Research, 67*(4), 377–415.

Groeben, N. (1994). Humanistic models of human development. In T. Husen & T. N. Postlewhaite (Eds.), *International encyclopedia of education* (2d ed., Vol. 5, pp. 2689–2692). New York: Pergamon.

Gronlund, N. E. (1959). *Sociometry in the classroom*. New York: Harper & Row.

Gronlund, N. E. (1995). *How to write and use instructional objectives* (5th ed.). Englewood Cliffs, NJ: Merrill.

Gronlund, N. E. (1998). *Assessment of student achievement* (6th ed.). Boston: Allyn & Bacon.

Gruber, E., & Vonèche, J. J. (Eds.). (1977). *The essential Piaget: An interpretive reference and guide*. New York: Basic Books.

Guild P. (1994). The culture/learning style connection. *Educational Leadership, 51*(8), 16–21.

Guralnick, M. J. (1986). The peer relations of young handicapped and nonhandicapped children. In P. S. Strain, M. J. Guralnick, & H. M. Walker (Eds.), *Children's social behavior: Development, assessment, and modification*. Orlando, FL: Academic Press.

Gutek, G. L. (1992). *Education and schooling in America* (3d ed.). Boston: Allyn & Bacon.

Haberman, M., & Dill, V. (1993). The knowledge base on retention vs. teacher ideology: Implications for teacher preparation. *Journal of Teacher Education, 44*(5), 352–360.

Hakuta, G., & Gould, L. J. (1987). Synthesis of research on bilingual education. *Educational Leadership, 44*(6), 38–45.

Hakuta, K., & Garcia, E. E. (1989). Bilingualism and education. *American Psychologist, 44*(2), 374–379.

Haladyna, T. M., Nolan, S. B., & Haas, N. S. (1991). Raising standardized achievement test scores and the origins of test score pollution. *Educational Researcher, 20*(5), 2–7.

Hall, G. S. (1904). *Adolescence: Its psychology and its relations to physiology, anthropology, sociology, sex, crime, religion, and education* (2 vols.). New York: Appleton.

Halmi, K. A. (1987). Anorexia nervosa and bulimia. In V B. Van Hasselt & M. Hersen (Eds.), *Handbook of adolescent psychology*. New York: Pergamon Press.

Halpern, D. F. (1997). Sex differences in intelligence: Implications for education. *American Psychologist, 52*(10), 1091–1102.

Halpern, D. F. (1998). Teaching critical thinking for transfer across domains. *American Psychologist, 53*(4), 449–455.

Hamilton, R., & Ghatala, E. (1994). *Learning and instruction*. New York: McGraw-Hill.

Han, E. P. (1995). Reflection is essential in teacher education. *Childhood Education, 71*(4), 228–230.

Haney, W. M., Madaus, G. F., & Lyons, R. (1993). *The fractured marketplace for standardized testing*. Boston: Kluwer Academic Publishers.

Hansgen, R. D. (1991). Can education become a science? *Phi Delta Kappan, 72*(9), 689–694.

Harasim, L., Hiltz, S. R., Teles, L., & Turoff, M., (1995). *Learning Networks: A Field Guide to Teaching and Learning Online*. Cambridge, MA: MIT Press.

Harding, C. G., & Snyder, K. (1991). Tom, Huck, and Oliver Stone as advocates in Kohlberg's just community: Theory-based strategies for moral-based education. *Adolescence, 26*(102), 319–330.

Harel, I., & Papert, S. (1990). Software design as a learning environment. *Interactive Learning Environments, 1*(1), 1–32.

Harris, J. (1997). Content and intent shape function: Designs for web-based educational telecomputing activities. *Learning and Leading with Technology, 24*(5), 17–20.

Harter, S. (1988). Developmental processes in the construction of the self. In T. D. Yawkey & J. E. Johnson (Eds.), *Integrative processes and socialization: Early to middle childhood*. Hillsdale, NJ: Erlbaum.

Harter, S. (1990). Self and identity development. In S. S. Feldman & G. R. Elliot (Eds.), *At the threshold: The developing adolescent*. Cambridge, MA: Harvard University Press.

Harter, S., Waters, P. L., & Whitesell, N. R. (1997). Lack of voice as a manifestation of false self-behavior among adolescents: The school setting as a stage upon which the drama of authenticity is enacted. *Educational Psychologist, 32*(3), 153–174.

Hartshorne, H., & May, M. A. (1929). *Studies in service and self-control*. New York: Macmillan.

Hartshorne, H., & May, M. A. (1930a). *Studies in deceit*. New York: Macmillan.

Hartshorne, H., & May, M. A. (1930b). *Studies in the organization of character*. New York: Macmillan.

Hartup, W. W. (1989). Social relationships and their developmental significance. *American Psychologist, 44*(2), 120–126.

Hassett, J. (1984). Computers in the classroom. *Psychology Today, 18*(9), 22–28.

Hatch, T. (1997). Getting specific about multiple intelligences. *Educational Leadership, 54*(6), 26–29.

Hattie, J., Biggs, J., & Purdie, N. (1996). Effects of learning skills interventions on student learning: A meta-analysis. *Review of Educational Research, 66*(2), 99–136.

Hatton, N., & Smith, D. (1995). Reflection in teacher education: Towards definition and implementation. *Teaching and teacher education, 11*(1), 33–49.

Hauser, J., & Malouf, D. B. (1996). A federal perspective on special education technology. *Journal of Learning Disabilities, 29*(5), 504–511.

Hawley, C. L., & Duffy, T. M. (1997, March). Student-teacher interaction in "The Chelsea Bank" simulation. Paper presented at the Annual Meeting of the American Educational Research Association, Chicago, IL.

Heath, I. A. (1996). The social studies video project: A holistic approach for teaching linguistically and culturally diverse students. *The Social Studies, 87*(3), 106–112.

Heaviside, S., Rowand, C., Williams, C., & Farris, E. (1998). *Violence and discipline problems in U.S. public schools: 1996–97* (NCES Publication No. 98-030). Washington, DC: U.S. Department of Education, National Center for Education Statistics.

Hebert, E. A. (1998). Lessons learned about student portfolios. *Phi Delta Kappan, 79*(8), 583–585.

Hedberg, J., & Alexander, S. (1994). Virtual reality in education: Defining researchable issues. *EMI, 31*(4), 214–220.

Hedges, L. V., & Nowell, A. (1995). Sex differences in mental test scores, variability, and numbers of high-scoring individuals. *Science, 269,* 41–45.

Heidemann, S., & Hewitt, D. (1992). *Pathways to play.* St. Paul, MN: Redleaf Press.

Helgeson, S. L., & Kumar, D. D. (1993). A review of education technology in science assessment. *Journal of Computers in Mathematics and Science Teaching, 12*(3/4), 227–243.

Henderson, V. L., & Dweck, C. S. (1990). Motivation and achievement. In S. S. Feldman & G. R. Elliott (Eds.), *At the threshold: The developing adolescent.* Cambridge, MA: Harvard University Press.

Herman, J. L., Gearhart, M., & Baker, E. L. (1993). Assessing writing portfolios: Issues in the validity and meaning of scores. *Educational Assessment, 1*(3), 201–224.

Hersh, R. H., Paolitto, D. P., & Reimer, J. (1979). *Promoting moral growth: From Piaget to Kohlberg.* New York: Longman.

Hetherington, E. M., & Parke, R. D. (1993). *Child psychology: A contemporary viewpoint* (4th ed.). New York: McGraw-Hill.

Hickey, D. T. (1997). Motivation and contemporary socio-constructivist instructional perspectives. *Educational Psychologist, 32*(3), 175–193.

Higbee, K. L. (1979). Recent research on visual mnemonics: Historical roots and educational fruits. *Review of Educational Research, 49*(4), 611–630.

Higgins, K., Boone, R., & Lovitt, T. C. (1996). Hypertext support for remedial students and students with learning disabilities. *Journal of Learning Disabilities, 29*(4), 402–412.

Highet, G. (1957). *The art of teaching.* New York: Vintage Books.

Hill, J. P. (1987). Research on adolescents and their families: Past and prospect. In C. E. Irwin, Jr. (Ed.), *Adolescent social behavior and health.* San Francisco: Jossey-Bass.

Hills, J. R. (1991). Apathy concerning grading and testing. *Phi Delta Kappan, 72*(7), 540–545.

Hirtle, J. S. (1996). Constructing a collaborative classroom (Part 2). *Learning and Leading with Technology, 23*(8), 27–30.

Ho, B. (1995). Using lesson plans as a means of reflection. *ELT Journal, 49*(1), 66–70.

Hoffer, T. B. (1992). Middle school ability grouping and student achievement in science and mathematics. *Educational Evaluation and Policy Analysis, 14*(3), 205–227.

Hoffman, M. L. (1980). Moral development in adolescence. In J. Adelson (Ed.), *Handbook of adolescent psychology.* New York: Wiley.

Hogan, K., & Pressley, M. (Eds.).(1997). *Scaffolding student learning: Instructional approaches and issues.* Cambridge, MA: Brookline Books.

Hoge, R. D., & Renzulli, J. S. (1993). Exploring the link between giftedness and self-concept. *Review of Educational Research, 63*(4), 449–465.

Holder-Brown, L., & Parette, Jr., H. P. (1992). Children with disabilities who use assistive technology: Ethical considerations. *Young Children, 47*(6), 73–77.

Holman, L. J. (1997). Meeting the needs of Hispanic immigrants. *Educational Leadership, 54*(7), 37–38.

Holmes, C. T. (1989). Grade level retention effects: A meta-analysis of research studies. In L. A. Shepard & M. L. Smith (Eds.), *Flunking grades: Research and policies on retention.* London: Falmer Press.

Holzberg, C. S. (1995). Classroom management at your fingertips. *Learning, 23*(4), 57–59.

Horowitz, F., & O'Brien, M. (1986). Gifted and talented children: State of knowledge and directions for research. *American Psychologist, 41*(10), 1147–1152.

Houston, W. R., & Williamson, J. L. (1992-1993). Perceptions of their preparation by 42 Texas elementary school teachers compared with their responses as student teachers. *Teacher Education and Practice, 8*(2), 27–42.

Howard, E. R. (1981). School climate improvement—Rationale and process. *Illinois School Research and Development, 18*(1), 8–12.

Howe, C. K. (1994). Improving the achievement of Hispanic students. *Educational Leadership, 51*(8), 42–44.

Howell, R. (1996). Technological aids for inclusive classrooms. *Theory into Practice, 35*(1), 58–65.

Hoyenga, K. B., & Hoyenga, K. T. (1993). *Gender-related differences: Origins and outcomes.* Boston: Allyn & Bacon.

Huenecke, D. (1992). An artistic criticism of Writing to Read, a computer-based program for beginning readers. *Journal of Curriculum and Supervision, 7*(2), 170–179.

Hughes, F. P. (1991). *Children, play, and development.* Boston: Allyn & Bacon.

Hughes, F. P., & Noppe, L. D. (1991). *Human development across the life span.* New York: Macmillan.

Hunt, N., & Marshall, K. (1994). *Exceptional children and youth.* Boston: Houghton Mifflin.

Huyvaert, S. (1995). *Reports from the classroom: Cases for reflection.* Boston: Allyn & Bacon.

Hyde, J. S. (1986). Gender differences in aggression. In J. S. Hyde & M. C. Linn (Eds.), *The psychology of gender.* Baltimore: Johns Hopkins University Press.

Idstein, P. (1993). Swimming against the mainstream. *Phi Delta Kappan, 75*(4), 336–340.

Irvin, J. L. (1992). Developmentally appropriate instruction: The heart of the middle school. In J. L. Irvin (Ed.), *Transforming middle level education.* Boston: Allyn & Bacon.

Irvin, J. L. (Ed.).(1992). *Transforming middle level education.* Boston: Allyn & Bacon.

Irwin, C. E., Jr., & Millstein, S. G. (1991). Risk-taking behaviors during adolescence. In R. M. Lerner, A. C. Peterson, & J. Brooks-Gunn (Eds.), *Encyclopedia of adolescence.* New York: Garland.

Irwin, M., Moore, M. A., & Stevenson, J. (1994). Enhancing a multicultural program through hypertext links. *Computers in the Schools, 10*(3/4), 255–280.

Jackson, S., & Bosma, H. (1990). Coping and self in adolescence. In H. Bosma & S. Jackson (Eds.), *Coping and self-concept in adolescence.* New York: Springer-Verlag.

Jakobsdottir, S., & Hooper, S. (1995). Computer-assisted foreign language learning: Effects of text, context, and gender on listening comprehension and motivation. *Educational Technology Research and Development, 43*(4), 43–59.

James, W. (1899). *Talks to teachers on psychology: And to students on some of life's ideals.* New York: Holt.

Janzen, R. (1994). Melting pot or mosaic? *Educational Leadership, 51*(8), 9–11.

Jarvela, S. (1995). The cognitive apprenticeship model in a technologically rich learning environment: Interpreting the learning interaction. *Learning and Instruction, 5*(3), 237–259.

Johnson, D. W., & Johnson, R. T. (1995). Cooperative learning and nonacademic outcomes of schooling: The other side of the report card. In J. E. Pederson, & A. D. Digby (Eds.), *Secondary schools and cooperative learning.* New York: Garland

Johnson, D. W., & Johnson, R. T. (1996). Conflict resolution programs and peer mediation programs in elementary and secondary schools: A review of the research. *Review of Educational Research, 66*(4), 459–506.

Johnson, D. W., Johnson, R. T., & Holubec, E. J. (1994). *The new circles of learning: Cooperation in the classroom and school.* Alexandria, VA: Association for Supervision and Curriculum Development.

Johnson, D. W., Johnson, R. T., & Smith, K. A. (1995). Cooperative learning and individual student achievement in secondary schools. In J. E. Peterson, & A. D. Digby (Eds.), *Secondary schools and cooperative learning.* New York: Garland.

Johnson, J. M. (1996–1997). Software for an evaluation workshop. *Learning and Leading with Technology, 24*(4), 96–97.

Johnson, R. E. (1975). Meaning in complex learning. *Review of Educational Research, 45*(3), 425–460.

Jones, A., & Selby, C. (1997). The use of computers for self-expression and communication. *Journal of Computing in Childhood Education, 8*(2/3), 199–214.

Jones, J. A. (1994). Integrated learning systems for diverse learners. *Media & Methods, 31*(1), 14–16.

Jones, M. C. (1957). The later careers of boys who were early- or late-maturing. *Child Development, 28*(1), 113–128.

Jones, M. C. (1965). Psychological correlates of somatic development. *Child Development, 36*(4), 899–911.

Jovanovic, J., & King, S. S. (1998). Boys and girls in the performance-based science classroom: Who's doing the performing? *American Educational Research Journal, 35*(3), 477–496.

Joyce, B., & Weil, M. (1996). *Models of teaching* (5th ed.). Boston: Allyn & Bacon.

Kagan, D. M. (1990). How schools alienate students at risk: A model for examining proximal classroom variables. *Educational Psychologist, 25*(2), 102–125.

Kagan, J. (1964a). *Developmental studies of reflection and analysis.* Cambridge, MA: Harvard University Press.

Kagan, J. (1964b). Impulsive and reflective children. In J. D. Krumbolz (Ed.), *Learning and the educational process.* Chicago: Rand McNally.

Kail, R. (1990). *The development of memory in children* (3d ed.). San Francisco: Freeman.

Kail, R. (1998). *Children and their development.* Upper Saddle River, NJ: Prentice-Hall.

Kalbaugh, P., & Haviland, J. M. (1991). Formal operational thinking and identity. In R. M. Lerner, A. C. Peterson, & J. Brooks-Gunn (Eds.), *Encyclopedia of adolescence.* New York: Garland.

Kameenui, E. J., & Carnine, D. W. (1998). *Effective teaching strategies that accommodate diverse learners.* Upper Saddle River, NJ: Merrill.

Kamii, C. (1984). Autonomy: The aim of education envisioned by Piaget. *Phi Delta Kappan, 65*(6), 410–415.

Kaplan, J. S. (1995). *Beyond behavior modification: A cognitive-behavioral approach to behavior management in the school* (3d ed.). Austin, TX: Pro-Ed.

Karpov, Y. V., & Bransford, J. D. (1995). L. S. Vygotsky and the doctrine of empirical and theoretical learning. *Educational Psychologist, 30*(2), 61–66.

Karpov, Y.V., & Haywood, H. C. (1998). Two ways to elaborate Vygotsky's concept of mediation. *American Psychologist, 53*(1), 27–36.

Katayama, A. D. (1997, November). Getting students involved in note taking: Why partial notes benefit learners more than complete notes. Paper presented at the annual meeting of the Mid-South Educational Research Association, Memphis, TN.

Katz, L. G., & Chard, S. C. (1989). *Engaging children's minds: The project approach.* Norwood, NJ: Ablex.

Kauffman, J. M., Lloyd, J. W., Baker, J., & Reidel, T. M. (1995). Inclusion of all students with emotional or behavioral disorders? Let's think again. *Phi Delta Kappan, 76*(7), 542–546.

Kay, R. (1989). Gender differences in computer attitudes, literacy, locus of control and commitment. *Journal of Research on Computing in Education, 21*(3), 307–317.

Kazdin, A. E. (1993). Adolescent mental health: Prevention and treatment programs. *American Psychologist, 48* (2), 127–141.

Keeler, C. M. (1996). Networked instructional computers in the elementary classroom and their effect on the learning environment: A qualitative evaluation. *Journal of Research on Computing in Education, 28*(3), 329–345.

Kellogg, J. B. (1988). Forces of change. *Phi Delta Kappan, 70*(3), 199–204.

Kellogg, R. T. (1989). Idea processors: Computer aids for planning and composing text. In B. K. Britton & S. M. Glynn (Eds.), *Computer writing environments: Theory, research, and design.* Hillsdale, NJ: Erlbaum.

Kelley, M. L., & Carper, L. B. (1988). Home-based reinforcement procedures. In J. C. Witt, S. N. Elliott, & F. M. Gresham (Eds.), *Handbook of behavior therapy in education.* New York: Plenum Press.

Kerr, M. M., & Nelson, C. M. (1998). *Strategies for managing behavior problems in the classroom* (3d ed.). Upper Saddle River, NJ: Merrill.

Ketterlinus, R. D., & Lamb, M. E. (1994). *Adolescent problem behaviors: Issues and research.* Hillsdale, NJ: Erlbaum.

Keyser, D. J., & Sweetland, R. C. (Eds.). (1984–1991). *Test critiques* (Vols. 1–8). Austin, TX: Pro-Ed.

Khalili, A., & Shashaani, L. (1994). The effectiveness of computer applications: A meta-analysis. *Journal of Research on Computing in Education, 27*(1), 48–61.

Kiewra, K. A., & DuBois, N. F. (1998). *Learning to learn: Making the transition from student to life-long learner.* Boston: Allyn & Bacon.

Kimball, L. (1995). Ten ways to make online learning groups work. *Educational Leadership, 53*(2), 54–56.

Kinard, B., & Bitter, G. G. (1997). Multicultural mathematics and technology: The Hispanic math project. *Using Technology in the Classroom, 13*(2), 77–88.

King, A. (1992a). Comparison of self-questioning, summarizing, and notetaking-review as strategies for learning from lectures. *American Educational Research Journal, 29*(2), 303–323.

King, A. (1992b). Facilitating elaborative learning through guided student-generated questioning. *Educational Psychologist, 27*(1), 111–126.

King, A. (1994). Guiding knowledge construction in the classroom: Effects of teaching children how to question and how to explain. *American Educational Research Journal, 31*(2), 338–368.

King, A. (1998). Transactive peer tutoring: Distributing cognition and metacognition. *Educational Psychology Review, 10*(1), 57–74.

Kirk, S. A., Gallagher, J. J., & Anastasiow, N. J. (1997). *Educating exceptional children* (8th ed.). Boston: Houghton Mifflin.

Kirschenbaum, H., & Simon, S. B. (Eds.). (1973). *Readings in values clarification.* Minneapolis: Winston.

Klauer, K. (1984). Intentional and incidental learning with instructional texts: A meta-analysis for 1970–1980. *American Educational Research Journal, 21*(2), 323–339.

Knapp, M. S., & Shields, P. M. (1990). Reconceiving academic instruction for the children of poverty. *Phi Delta Kappan, 71*(10), 753–758.

Knapp, M. S., Shields, P. M., & Turnbull, B. J. (1995). Academic challenge in high-poverty classrooms. *Phi Delta Kappan, 76*(10), 770–776.

Koch, M. (1994). No girls allowed. *Technos, 3*(3), 14–19.

Kochendorfer, L. (1994). *Becoming a reflective teacher.* Washington, DC: National Education Association.

Koedinger, K. R., & Anderson, J. R. (1993). Reifying implicit planning in geometry: Guidelines for model-based intelligent tutoring system design. In S. Lajoie & S. Derry (Eds.), *Computers as cognitive tools.* Hillsdale, NJ: Erlbaum.

Kohlberg, L. (1963). The development of children's orientations toward a moral order: 1. Sequence in the development of moral thought. *Vita Humana, 6*(1–2), 11–33.

Kohlberg, L. (1969). Stage and sequence: The cognitive-developmental approach to socialization. In D. A. Goslin (Ed.), *Handbook of socialization theory and research.* Chicago: Rand McNally.

Kohlberg, L. (1976). Moral stages and moralization: The cognitive-developmental approach. In T. Lickona (Ed.), *Moral development and behavior: Theory, research, and social issues.* New York: Holt, Rinehart & Winston.

Kohlberg, L. (1978). Revisions in the theory and practice of moral development. In W. Damon (Ed.), *New directions for child development: Moral development* (No.2). San Francisco: Jossey-Bass.

Kohn, A. (1993). Rewards versus learning: A response to Paul Chance. *Phi Delta Kappan, 74*(10), 783–787.

Kohn, A. (1993b). Choices for children: Why and how to let students decide. *Phi Delta Kappan, 75*(1), 8–20.

Kohn, A. (1994). The truth about self-esteem. *Phi Delta Kappan, 76*(4), 272–283.

Kontos, G., & Mizell, A. P. (1997). Global village classroom: The changing roles of teachers and students through technology. *Tech Trends, 42*(5), 17–22.

Kounin, J. S. (1970). *Discipline and group management in classrooms.* New York: Holt, Rinehart & Winston.

Kozma, R. B. (1987). The implications of cognitive psychology for computer-based learning tools. *Educational Technology, 27*(11), 20–25.

Kozma, R. B. (1991). Learning with media. *Review of Educational Research, 61*(2), 179–212.

Kozulin, A., & Presseisen, B. Z. (1995). Mediated learning experience and psychological tools: Vygotsky's and Feuerstein's perspectives in a study of student learning. *Educational Psychologist, 30*(2), 57–75.

Krajcik, J. S., Soloway, E., Blumenfeld, P. C., Marx, R. W., Ladewski, B. L., Bos, N. D., & Hayes, P. J. (1996). The casebook of project practices—An example of an interactive multimedia system for professional development. *Journal of Computers in Mathematics and Science Teaching, 15*(1/2), 119–135.

Kramer, L. R. (1992). Young adolescents' perceptions of school. In J. L. Irvin (Ed.), *Transforming middle level education.* Boston: Allyn & Bacon.

Krathwohl, D. R., Bloom, B. S., & Masia, B. B. (1964). *Taxonomy of educational objectives. Handbook II: Affective domain.* New York: McKay.

Krendl, K., & Broihier, M. (1992). Student responses to computers: A longitudinal study. *Journal of Educational Computing Research, 8*(2), 215–227.

Krulik, S., & Rudnick, J. A. (1993). *Reasoning and problem solving: A handbook for elementary school teachers.* Boston: Allyn & Bacon.

Kubiszyn, T., & Borich, G. (1996). *Educational testing and measurement: Classroom application and practice* (5th ed.). New York: HarperCollins.

Kuhn, D. (1997). Constraints or guideposts? Developmental psychology and science education. *Review of Educational Research, 67*(1), 141–150.

Kulik, C-L., Kulik, J. A., & Bangert-Drowns, R. L. (1990). Effectiveness of mastery learning programs. *Review of Educational Research, 60*(2), 265–299.

Kulik, J. A., & Kulik, C-L. (1984). Effects of accelerated instruction on students. *Review of Educational Research, 54*(3), 409–426.

Kulik, J. A., & Kulik, C.-L. C. (1991). Ability grouping and gifted students. In N. Colangelo & G. A. Davis (Eds.), *Handbook of gifted education.* Boston: Allyn & Bacon.

Kulik, J. A., Kulik, C-L., & Bangert-Drowns, R. L. (1985). Effectiveness of computer-based education in elementary schools. *Computers in Human Behavior, 1*(1), 59–74.

Kumar, D. D., & Helgeson, S. L. (1995). Trends in computer applications in science assessment. *Journal of Science Education and Technology, 4*(1), 29–36.

Kumar, D., & Wilson, C. L. (1997). Computer technology, science education, and students with learning disabilities. *Journal of Science Education and Technology, 6*(2), 155–160.

Kyllonen, P. C. (1996). Is working capacity Spearman's g? In I. Dennis & P. Tapsfield (Eds.), *Human abilities: Their nature and measurement.* Mahway, NJ: Erlbaum.

Labbo, L. D., Murray, B. A., & Phillips, M. (1995–1996). Writing to read: From inheritance to innovation and invitation. *The Reading Teacher, 49*(4), 314–321.

Ladson-Billings, G. (1994). What we can learn from multicultural education research. *Educational Leadership, 51*(8), 22–26.

Lambdin, D. V., Duffy, T. M., & Moore, J. A. (1997). Using an interactive information system to expand preservice teachers' visions of effective mathematics teaching. *Journal of Technology and Teacher Education, 5*(2/3), 171–202.

Lambert, B. G., & Mounce, N. B. (1987). Career planning. In V. B. van Hasselt & M. Hersen (Eds.), *Handbook of adolescent psychology.* New York: Pergamon Press.

Lambrecht, J. (1993). Applications software as cognitive enhancers. *Journal of Research on Computing in Education, 25*(4), 506–520.

Lampert, M. Managing the tensions in connecting students' inquiry with learning mathematics in school. In D. N. Perkins, J. L. Schwartz, M. M. West, & S. Wiske (Eds.), *Software goes to school: Teaching for understanding with new technologies.* New York: Oxford University Press.

Lantieri, L. (1995). Waging peace in our schools: Beginning with the children. *Phi Delta Kappan, 76*(5), 386–388.

Larsen, S. (1995). What is "quality" in the use of technology for children with learning disabilities? *Learning Disability Quarterly, 18*(2), 118–130.

Lavigne, N., & Lajoie, S. (1996). Communicating performance criteria to students through technology. *The Mathematics Teacher, 89*(1), 66–69.

Lazear, D. G. (1992). *Teaching for multiple intelligences.* Bloomington, IN: Phi Delta Kappa Educational Foundation.

Leadbeater, B. (1991). Relativistic thinking in adolescence. In R. M. Lerner, A. C. Peterson, & J. Brooks-Gunn (Eds.), *Encyclopedia of adolescence.* New York: Garland.

Leaver, B. L. (1997). *Teaching the whole class* (4th ed.). Thousand Oaks, CA: Corwin Press.

Lee, W. W. (1987). Microcomputer courseware production and evaluation guidelines for students with learning disabilities. *Journal of Learning Disabilities, 20*(7), 436–438.

LeFrançois, G. (1995). *Of children: An introduction to child development* (8th ed.). Belmont, CA: Wadsworth.

Lehrer, R. (1993). Authors of knowledge: Patterns of hypermedia design. In S. Lajoie & S. Derry (Eds.), *Computers as cognitive tools.* Hillsdale, NJ: Erlbaum.

Lehrer, R., & Littlefield, J. (1991). Misconceptions and errors in LOGO: The role of instruction. *Journal of Educational Psychology, 83*(1), 124–133.

Lehrer, R., Erickson, J., & Connell, T. (1994). Learning by designing hypermedia documents. *Computers in the Schools, 10*(1/2), 227–254.

Lehrer, R., Levin, B. B., DeHart, P., & Comeaux, M. (1987). Voice-feedback as a scaffold for writing: A comparative study. *Journal of Educational Computing Research, 3*(3), 335–353.

Leong, C. K. (1995). Effects of on-line reading and simultaneous DECtalk auding in helping below-average and poor readers comprehend and summarize text. *Learning Disability Quarterly, 18*(2), 101–116.

Lepper, M. R., Keavney, M., & Drake, M. (1996). Intrinsic motivation and extrinsic rewards: A commentary on Cameron and Pierce's meta-analysis. *Review of Educational Research, 66*(1), 5–32.

Lerner, J. (1997). *Learning disabilities: Theories, diagnosis, and teaching strategies* (7th ed.). Boston: Houghton Mifflin.

Lerner, J. W., Lowenthal, B., & Lerner, S. R. (1995). *Attention deficit disorders: Assessment and teaching.* Pacific Groves, CA: Brooks/Cole.

Lessow-Hurley, J. (1991). *A commonsense guide to bilingual education.* Alexandria, VA: Association for Supervision and Curriculum Development.

Levin, J. A., Kim, H., & Riel, M. M. (1990). Analyzing instructional interactions on electronic message networks. In L. M. Harasim (Ed.), *Online education: Perspectives on a new environment.* New York: Praeger.

Levin, J. R. (1982). Pictures as prose-learning devices. In A. Flammer & W. Kintsch (Eds.), *Advances in psychology: Vol. 8. Discourse processing.* Amsterdam: North-Holland.

Levine, D. U., & Havighurst, R. J. (1992). *Society and education* (8th ed.). Boston: Allyn & Bacon.

Leyser, Y., Frankiewicz, L. E., & Vaughn, R. (1992). Problems faced by first-year teachers: A survey of regular and special educators. *Teacher Educator, 28*(1), 36–45.

Liao, Y-K. (1992). Effects of computer-assisted instruction on cognitive outcomes: A meta-analysis. *Journal of Research on Computing in Education, 24*(3), 367–380.

Lickona, T. (1976). Research on Piaget's theory of moral development. In T. Lickona (Ed.), *Moral development and behavior: Theory, research, and social issues.* New York: Holt, Rinehart & Winston.

Lieberman, D. (1985). Research on children and microcomputers: A review of utilization and effects studies. In M. Chen & W. Paisley (Eds.), *Children and microcomputers: Research on the newest medium.* Beverly Hills, CA: Sage.

Lindholm, K. J., & Fairchild, H. H. (1990). Evaluation of an elementary school bilingual immersion program. In A. M. Padilla, H. F. Fairchild, & C. M. Valadez (Eds.), *Bilingual education: Issues and strategies.* Newbury Park, CA: Sage.

Linn, M. C. (1985). The cognitive consequences of programming instruction in classrooms. *Educational Researcher, 14*(5), 14–29.

Linn, M. C. (1992). Science education reform: Building on the research base. *Journal of Research in Science Teaching, 29*(8), 821–840.

Linn, M. C. (1997). The role of the laboratory in science learning. *The Elementary School Journal, 97*(4), 401–417.

Linn, R. L. (1994). Performance assessment: policy promises and technical measurement standards. *Educational Researcher, 23*(9), 4–14.

Linn, R. L., & Gronlund, N. E. (1995). *Measurement and assessment in teaching* (7th ed.). Englewood Cliffs, NJ: Merrill.

Lipka, R. R., Hurford, D. P., & Litten, M. J. (1992). Self in school: Age and school experience effects. In R. P. Lipka & T. M. Brinthaupt (Eds.), *Self-perspectives across the life span.* Albany, NY: State University of New York Press.

Liu, M. (1994). Hypermedia assisted instruction and second language learning: A semantic-network-based approach. *Computers in the Schools, 10*(3/4); 293–312.

Livingston, C., & Borko, H. (1989). Expert-novice differences in teaching: A cognitive analysis and implications for teacher education. *Journal of Teacher Education, 40*(4), 36–42.

Livson, N., & Peskin, H. (1980). Perspectives on adolescence from longitudinal research. In J. Adelson (Ed.), *Handbook of adolescent psychology.* New York: Wiley.

Lockwood, A. (1978). The effects of values clarification and moral development curricula on school age subjects: A critical review of recent research. *Review of Educational Research, 48*(3), 325–364.

Loftus, E. F., & Loftus, G. R. (1980). On the permanence of stored information in the brain. *American Psychologist, 35*(5), 409–420.

Long, J. D., Frye, V. H., & Long, E. W. (1989). *Making it till Friday* (4th ed.). Pennington, NJ: Princeton Book Co.

Lorayne, H., & Lucas, J. (1974). *The memory book.* New York: Ballantine Books.

Losey, K. M. (1995). Mexican American students and classroom interaction: An overview and critique. *Review of Educational Research, 65*(3), 283–318.

Lou, Y., Abrami, P. C., Spence, J. C., Poulsen, C., Chambers, B., & d'Apollonia, S. (1996). Within-class grouping: A meta-analysis. *Review of Educational Research, 66*(4), 423–458.

Lowry, R., Sleet, D., Duncan, C., Powell, K., & Kolbe, L. (1995). Adolescents at risk for violence. *Educational Psychology Review, 7*(1), 7–39.

Lundeberg, M. A., & Fox, P. W. (1991). Do laboratory findings on test expectancy generalize to classroom outcomes? *Review of Educational Research, 61*(1), 94–106.

Luria, A. R. (1968). *The mind of a mnemonist: A little book about a vast memory.* New York: Ballantine Books.

Lyman, L., Foyle, H. C., & Azwell, T. S. (1993). *Cooperative learning in the elementary classroom.* Washington, DC: National Education Association.

MacArthur, C. (1994). Peers + word processing + strategies = a powerful combination for revising student writing. *Teaching Exceptional Children, 27*(1), 24–29.

MacArthur, C. A. (1996). Using technology to enhance the writing processes of students with learning disabilities. *Journal of Learning Disabilities, 29*(4), 344–354.

MacArthur, C. A., & Haynes, J. B. (1995). Student assistant for learning from text (SALT): A hypermedia reading aid. *Journal of Learning Disabilities, 28*(3), 150–159.

Maehr, M. L., & Meyer, H. A. (1997). Understanding motivation and schooling: Where we've been, where we are, and where we need to go. *Educational Psychology Review, 9*(4), 371–409.

Mager, R. F. (1962). *Preparing instructional objectives.* Palo Alto, CA: Fearon.

Mager, R. F. (1997). *Preparing instrumental objectives* (3d ed.), Atlanta, GA: Center for Effective Performance.

Magnusson, S. J. (1996). Complexities of learning with computer-based tools: A case of inquiry about sound and music in elementary school. *Journal of Science Education and Technology, 5*(4), 297–309.

Maker, C. J., & Nielson, A. B. (1996). *Curriculum development and teaching strategies for gifted learners* (2d ed.). Austin, TX: Pro-Ed.

Mantzicopoulos, P., & Morrison, D. (1992). Kindergarten retention: Academic and behavioral outcomes through the end of second grade. *American Educational Research Journal, 29*(1), 182–198.

Marcia, J. E. (1966). Development and validation of ego identity status. *Journal of Personality and Social Psychology, 3*(5), 551–558.

Marcia, J. E. (1967). Ego identity status: Relationship to change in self-esteem, "general adjustment," and authoritarianism. *Journal of Personality, 35*(1), 119–133.

Marcia, J. E. (1980). Identity in adolescence. In J. Adelson (Ed.), *Handbook of adolescent psychology.* New York: Wiley.

Marcia, J. E. (1991). Identity and self-development. In R. M. Lerner, A. C. Peterson, & J. Brooks-Gunn (Eds.), *Encyclopedia of adolescence.* New York: Garland.

Marsh, H. W., Byrne, B. M., & Shavelson, R. J. (1992). A multidimensional, hierarchical self-concept. In T. M. Brinthaupt & R. P. Lipka (Eds.), *The self: Definitional and methodological issues.* Albany, NY: State University of New York Press.

Marsh, H. W., Chessor, D., Craven, R., & Roche, L. (1995). The effects of gifted and talented programs on academic self-concept: The big fish strikes again. *American Educational Research Journal, 32*(2), 285–319.

Marsh, R. S., & Raywid, M. A. (1994). How to make detracking work. *Phi Delta Kappan, 76*(4), 314–317.

Martin, C. D., Heller, R.S., & Mahmoud, E. (1992). American and Soviet children's attitudes toward computers. *Journal of Educational Computing Research, 8*(2), 155–185.

Martinez, M. E. (1998). What is problem solving? *Phi Delta Kappan, 79*(8), 605–609.

Marx, R. W., & Winne, P. H. (1987). The best tool teachers have—their students' thinking. In D. C. Berliner & B. V. Rosenshine (Eds.), *Talks to teachers.* New York: Random House.

Marx, R. W., Blumenfeld, P. C., Krajcik, J. S., & Soloway, E. (1997). Enacting project-based science. *The Elementary School Journal, 97*(4), 341–358.

Maslow, A. H. (1943). A theory of human motivation. *Psychological Review, 50*(4), 370–396.

Maslow, A. H. (1968). *Toward a psychology of being* (2d ed.). Princeton, NJ: Van Nostrand.

Maslow, A. H. (1987). *Motivation and personality* (3d ed.). New York: Harper & Row.

Matthews, C. E., Binkley, W., Crisp, A., & Gregg, K. (1998). Challenging gender bias in fifth grade. *Educational Leadership, 55*(4), 54–57.

Matthews, D. B. (1991). The effects of school environment on intrinsic motivation of middle-class children. *Journal of Humanistic Education and Development, 30*(1), 30–36.

Mayer, R. E. (1987). Learnable aspects of problem solving: Some examples. In D. E. Berger, K. Pezdek, & W. P. Banks (Eds.), *Applications of cognitive psychology: Problem solving, education, and computing.* Hillsdale, NJ: Erlbaum.

Mayer, R. E. (1996). Learners as information processors: Legacies and limitations of educational psychology's second metaphor. *Educational Psychologist, 31*(3/4), 151–161.

McCaslin, M., & Good, T. L. (1992). Compliant cognition: The misalliance of management and instructional goals in current school reform. *Educational Researcher, 21*(3), 4–17.

McConnell, S. R., & Odom, S. L. (1986). Sociometrics: Peer-referenced measures and the assessment of social competence. In P. S. Strain, M. J. Guralnick, & H. M. Walker (Eds.), *Children's social behavior: Development, assessment, and modification.* Orlando, FL: Academic Press.

McLaughlin, T. F., & Williams, R. L. (1988). The token economy. In J. C. Witt, S. N. Elliott, & F. M. Gresham (Eds.), *Handbook of behavior therapy in education.* New York: Plenum Press.

McLellan, H. (1996a). "Being digital": Implications for education. *Educational Technology, 36*(6), 5–20.

McLellan, H. (1996b). Virtual realities. In D. Jonassen (Ed.), *Handbook for research on education communications and technology.* Boston, MA: Kluwer-Nijhoff.

McLeskey, J., & Waldron, N. L. (1996). Responses to questions teachers and administrators frequently ask about inclusive school programs. *Phi Delta Kappan, 78*(2), 150–156.

McLoyd, V. C. (1998). Socioeconomic disadvantage and child development. *American Psychologist, 53*(2), 185–204.

McPartland, J., Jordan, W., Legters, N., & Balfanz, R. (1997). Finding safety in small numbers. *Educational Leadership, 55*(2), 14–17.

McTighe, J. (1996–1997). What happens between assessments? *Educational Leadership, 54*(4), 6–12.

Meagher, M. E. (1995). Learning English on the Internet. *Educational Leadership International, 53*(2), 88–90.

Means, B., & Knapp, M. S. (1991). Introduction: Rethinking teaching for disadvantaged students. In B. Means, C. Chelemer, & M. S. Knapp (Eds.), *Teaching advanced skills to at-risk students.* San Francisco: Jossey-Bass.

Meisels, S. J., & Liaw, F-R. (1993). Failure in grade: Do retained students catch up? *Journal of Educational Research, 87*(2), 69–77.

Melton, R. F. (1978). Resolution of conflicting claims concerning the effect of behavioral objectives on student learning. *Review of Educational Research, 48*(2), 291–302.

Mendoza, J. I. (1994). On being a Mexican American. *Phi Delta Kappan, 76*(4), 293–295.

Mercer, C. D. (1997). *Students with learning disabilities* (5th ed.). Upper Saddle River, NJ: Merrill.

Mergendoller, J. R. (1996). Moving from technological possibility to richer student learning: Revitalized infrastructure and re-

constructed pedagogy. *Educational Researcher, 25*(8), 43–46.

Meskill, C. (1996). Listening skills development through multimedia. *Journal of Educational Multimedia and Hypermedia, 5*(2), 179–201.

Messerer, J. (1997). Adaptive technology. *Learning and Leading with Technology, 24*(5), 50–53.

Messick, S. (1989). Meaning and values in test validation: The science and ethics of assessment. *Educational Researcher, 18*(2), 5–11.

Metcalfe, J., & Shimamura, A. P. (1994). *Metacognition: Knowing about knowing.* Cambridge, MA: MIT Press.

Metz, K. E. (1995). Reassessment of developmental constraints on children's science instruction. *Review of Educational Research, 65*(2), 93–127.

Metzger, M. (1996). Maintaining a life. *Phi Delta Kappan, 77*(5), 346–351.

Mevarech, Z., & Susak, Z. (1993). Effects of learning with cooperative-mastery method on elementary students. *Journal of Educational Research, 86*(4), 197–205.

Meyer, C. A. (1992). What's the difference between authentic and performance assessment? *Educational Leadership, 49*(8), 39–40.

Milgram, J. (1992). A portrait of diversity: The middle level student. In J. L. Irvin (Ed.), *Transforming middle level education.* Boston: Allyn & Bacon.

Miller, D. (1993). Making the connection with language. *Arithmetic Teacher, 40*(6), 311–316.

Miller, L. K. (1989). *Musical savants: Exceptional skill in the mentally retarded.* Hillsdale, NJ: Erlbaum.

Miller, P. H. (1993). *Theories of developmental psychology* (3d ed.). New York: W. H. Freeman.

Miller, P Y., & Simon, W. (1980). The development of sexuality in adolescence. In J. Adelson (Ed.), *Handbook of adolescent psychology.* New York: Wiley.

Milone, Jr., M. N. (1995). Electronic portfolios: Who's doing them and how? *Technology & Learning, 16*(2), 28–29, 32, 34, 36.

Mitchell, J. J. (1990). *Human growth and development: The childhood years.* Calgary, Alberta: Detselig Enterprises Ltd.

Mitchell, J. V., Jr. (Ed.). (1985). *Ninth mental measurements yearbook.* Highland Park, NJ: Gryphon Press.

Mitchell, P.R. (1996). Stop the world—west Georgia is getting on. *Technos, 5*(3), 14–15, 19–20.

Moely, B. E., Hart, S. S., Leal, L., Santulli, K. A., Rao, N., Johnson, T., & Hamilton, L. B. (1992). The teacher's role in facilitating memory and study strategy development in the elementary school classroom. *Child Development*, 63(3), 653–672.

Moersch, C., & Fisher III, L. M. (1995). Electronic portfolios—some pivotal questions. *Learning and Leading with Technology*, 23(2), 10–14.

Mohnsen, B. (1997). Stretching bodies and minds through technology. *Educational Leadership*, 55(3), 46–48.

Moll, L. C. (Ed.).(1990). *Vygotsky and education: Instructional implications and applications of sociohistorical psychology*. New York: Cambridge University Press.

Morgan, H. (1997). *Cognitive styles and classroom learning*. Westport, CT: Praeger.

Morrell, K., Marchionini, G., & Neuman, D. (1993). Sailing Perseus: Instructional strategies for hypermedia in the classics. *Journal of Educational Multimedia and Hypermedia*, 2(4), 337–353.

Morris, P. (1977). Practical strategies for human learning and remembering. In M. J. A. Howe (Ed.), *Adult learning*. New York: Wiley.

Morris, R. B. (Ed.). (1961). *Encyclopedia of American history*. New York: Harper & Row.

Mortimer, J. T. (1991). Employment. In R. M. Lerner, A. C. Peterson, & J. Brooks-Gunn (Eds.), *Encyclopedia of adolescence*. New York: Garland.

Mueller, C. M., & Dweck, C. S. (1998). Praise for intelligence can undermine children's motivation and performance. *Journal of Personality and Social Psychology*, 75(1), 33–52.

Murdick, K. (1996). Short-term sales forecasting. *The Mathematics Teacher*, 89(1), 48–52.

Murphy, D. F. (1988). The just community at Birch Meadow Elementary School. *Phi Delta Kappan*, 69(6), 427–428.

Murphy, J. (1987). Educational influences. In V. B. van Hasselt & M. Hersen (Eds.), *Handbook of adolescent psychology*. New York: Pergamon Press.

Mussen, P. H., & Jones, M. C. (1957). Self-conceptions, motivations, and interpersonal attitudes of late- and early-maturing boys. *Child Development*, 28(2), 243–256.

Nagy, P., & Griffiths, A. K. (1982). Limitations of recent research relating Piaget's theory to adolescent thought. *Review of Educational Research*, 52(4), 513–556.

Nakhleh, M. B. (1994). A review of microcomputer-based labs: How have they affected science learning? *Journal of Computers in Mathematics and Science Teaching*, 13(4), 368–381.

Nastasi, B. K., & Clements, D. H. (1993). Motivational and social outcomes of cooperative computer education environments. *Journal of Computing in Childhood Education*, 4(1), 15–43.

Nastasi, B. K., & Clements, D. H. (1994). Effectance motivation, perceived scholastic competence, and higher-order thinking in two cooperative computer environments. *Journal of Educational Computing Research*, 10(3), 249–275.

National Board for Professional Teaching Standards. (1994). *What teachers should know and be able to do*. Southfield, MI: Author.

Natriello, G., McDill, E. L., & Pallas, A. M. (1990). *Schooling disadvantaged children: Racing against catastrophe*. New York: Teachers College Press.

Naughton, C. C., & McLaughlin, T. F. (1995). The use of a token economy system for students with behaviour disorders. *B.C. Journal of Special Education*, 19(2/3), 29–38.

Neill, S. B., & Neill, G. W. (1993). *Only the best: Annual guide to highest-rated software*. Alexandria, VA: Association for Supervision and Curriculum Development.

Neisser, U. (1976). *Cognition and reality*. San Francisco: Freeman

Neisser, U. (1982). *Memory observed*. San Francisco: Freeman.

Nelson, J. R. (1996). Effects of direct instruction, cooperative learning, and independent learning practices on the classroom behavior of students with behavioral disorders: A comparative analysis. *Journal of Emotional and Behavioral Disorders*, 4(1), 53–62.

Nelson, W., & Palumbo, D. B. (1992). Learning, instruction, and hypermedia. *Journal of Educational Multimedia and Hypermedia*, 1(3), 287–299.

Neuwirth, C. M., & Wojahn, P. G. (1996). Learning to write: Computer support for a cooperative process. In T. Koschmann (Ed.), *CSCL: Theory and practice*. Mahwah, NJ: Erlbaum.

Newman, B. M., & Newman, P. R. (1991). *Development through life: A psychosocial approach* (5th ed.). Pacific Grove, CA: Brooks/Cole.

Newman, F., & Holzman, L. (1993). *Lev Vygotsky: Revolutionary scientist*. London: Routledge.

Newman, J. M. (1991). *Interwoven conversations: Learning and teaching through critical reflection*. Toronto, Canada: Ontario Institute for Studies in Education.

Nicholls, J. G. (1979). Quality and inequality in intellectual development: The role of motivation in education. *American Psychologist*, 34(11), 1071–1084.

Nicholson, J., Gelpi, A., Young, S., & Sulzby, E. (1998). Influences of gender and open-ended software on first graders' collaborative composing activities on computers. *Journal of Computing in Childhood Education*, 9(1), 3–42.

Nickerson, R. S. (1994). The teaching of thinking and problem solving. In R. J. Sternberg (Ed.), *Thinking and problem solving*. San Diego, CA: Academic Press.

Nickerson, R. S. (1995). Can technology help teach for understanding? In D. N. Perkins, J. H. Schwartz, M. M. West, & M. S. Wiske (Eds.), *Software goes to school: Teaching for understanding with new technologies*. New York: Oxford University Press.

Nicol, M. P. (1997). How one physics teacher changed his algebraic thinking. *The Mathematics Teacher*, 90(2), 86–89.

Nieto, S. (1996). *Affirming diversity* (2d ed.). New York: Longman.

Niguidula, D. (1997). Picturing performance with digital portfolios. *Educational Leadership*, 55(3), 26–29.

Norman, D. A., & Rumelhart, D. E. (1970). A system for perception and memory. In D. A. Norman (Ed.), *Models of human memory*. New York: Academic Press.

Novak, J. D., & Gowin, D. B. (1984). *Learning how to learn*. Cambridge, England: Cambridge University Press.

Novak, M. (1971). Rise of unmeltable ethnics. In M. Friedman (Ed.), *Overcoming middle class rage*. Philadelphia: Westminster Press.

Nuttall, E. V. (1987). Survey of current practices in the psychological assessment of limited-English-proficiency handicapped children. *Journal of School Psychology*, 25(l), 53–61.

Nye, R. D. (1979). *What is B. F. Skinner really saying?* Englewood Cliffs, NJ: Prentice-Hall.

O'Lone, D. J. (1997). Student information system software: Are you getting what you expected? *NASSP Bulletin*, 81(585), 86–93.

O'Neil, J. (1992). Putting performance assessment to the test. *Educational Leadership*, 49(8), 14–19.

Oakes, C. (1996). First grade online. *Learning and Leading with Technology*, 24(1), 37–39.

Oakes, J. (1985). *Keeping track: How schools structure inequality*. New Haven: Yale University Press.

Oakes, J., & Lipton, M. (1992). Detracking schools: Early lessons from the field. *Phi Delta Kappan, 73*(6), 448–454.

Oakes, J., & Wells, A. S. (1998). Detracking for high student achievement. *Educational Leadership, 55*(6), 38–41.

Oakes, J., Quartz, K. H., Gong, J., Guiton, G., & Lipton, M. (1993). Creating middle schools: Technical, normative, and political considerations. *The Elementary School Journal, 93*(5), 461–480.

Ochse, R., & Plug, C. (1986). Cross-cultural investigation of the validity of Erikson's theory of personality development. *Journal of Personality and Social Psychology, 50*(6), 1240–1252.

Offer, D., & Offer, J. B. (1975). *From teenage to young manhood: A psychological study.* New York: Basic Books.

Office of the Federal Register. (1994). *Code of Federal Regulations 34. Parts 300 to 399.* Washington, DC: Author.

Ogbu, J. U. (1992). Understanding cultural diversity and learning. *Educational Researcher, 21*(8), 5–14.

Okagaki, L., & Sternberg, R. J. (1990). Teaching thinking skills: We're getting the context wrong. In D. Kuhn (Ed.), *Developmental perspectives on teaching and learning thinking skills.* Basel, Switzerland: S. Karger.

Okagaki, L., & Sternberg, R. J. (Eds.) (1991). *Directors of development: Influences on the development of children's thinking.* Hillsdale, NJ: Erlbaum.

Okey, J. R. (1995). Performance assessment and science learning: Rationale for computers. *Journal of Science Education and Technology, 4*(1), 81–87.

Olson, D. R. (1985). Computers as tools of the intellect. *Educational Researcher, 14*(5), 5–8.

Olson, D. R., & Torrance, N. (Eds.) (1996). *Handbook of education and human development.* Cambridge, MA: Blackwell.

Ormrod, J. E. (1999). *Human learning* (3d ed.). Upper Saddle River, NJ: Merrill.

Ornstein, A. C., & Levine, D. U. (1993). *Foundations of education* (5th ed.). Boston: Houghton Mifflin.

Osgood, C. E. (1949). The similarity paradox in human learning: A resolution. *Psychological Review, 56*(3), 132–143.

Oshima, J., Scardamalia, M., & Bereiter, C. (1996). Collaborative learning processes associated with high and low conceptual progress. *Instructional Science, 24*(1), 125–155.

Overton, W. F., & Byrnes, J. P. (1991). Cognitive development. In R. M. Lerner, A. C.

Peterson, & J. Brooks-Gunn (Eds.), *Encyclopedia of adolescence.* New York: Garland.

Page, E. B. (1994). Computer grading of student prose, using modern concepts and software. *Journal of Experimental Education, 62*(2), 127–142.

Page, E. B., & Petersen, N. S. (1995). The computer moves into essay grading. *Phi Delta Kappan, 76*(7), 561–565.

Pajares, F. (1996). Self-efficacy beliefs in academic settings. *Review of Educational Research, 66*(4), 543–578.

Palincsar, A., & Brown, A. L. (1984). Reciprocal teaching of comprehension-fostering and comprehension-monitoring activities. *Cognition and Instruction, 1*(2), 117–175.

Pallas, A. M., Natriello, G., & McDill, E. L. (1989). The changing nature of the disadvantaged population: Current dimensions and future trends. *Educational Researcher, 18*(5), 16–22.

Pantelidis, V. S. (1993). Virtual reality in the classroom. *Educational Technology, 33*(4), 23–27.

Parette, H. P., Jr., Dunn, N. S., & Hoge, D. R. (1995). Low-cost communication devices for children with disabilities and their family members. *Young Children, 50*(6), 75–81.

Parette, H. P., Jr., Hourcade, J. J. & Van Biervliet, A. (1993). Selection of appropriate technology for children with disabilities. *Teaching Exceptional Children, 25*(3), 18–22.

Paris, S. G., & Ayres, L. R. (1994). *Becoming reflective students and teachers with portfolios and authentic assessment.* Washington, DC: American Psychological Association.

Paris, S. G., Lawton, T. A., Turner, J. C., & Roth, J. L. (1991). A developmental perspective on standardized achievement testing. *Educational Researcher, 20*(5), 12–20.

Parke, C. S., & Lane, S. (1997). Learning from performance assessments in math. *Educational Leadership, 54*(6), 26–29.

Parke, R. D., & Slaby, R. G. (1983). The development of aggression. In E. M. Hetherington (Ed.), *Handbook of child psychology: Socialization, personality, and social development* (Vol. 4). New York: Wiley.

Parten, M. B. (1932). Social participation among preschool children. *Journal of Abnormal and Social Psychology, 27*(3), 243–269.

Pate, P. E., Homestead, E., & McGinnis, K. (1993). Designing rubrics for authentic assessment. *Middle School Journal, 25*(2), 25–27.

Patterson, G. R., DeBaryshe, B. D., & Ramsey, E. (1989). A developmental perspective on

antisocial behavior. *American Psychologist, 44*(2), 329–335.

Pea, R. D. (1985). Beyond amplification: Using the computer to reorganize mental functioning. *Educational Psychologist, 21*(4), 167–182.

Peck, K. L., & Catello, J. P. (1990). Instructional alternatives for at-risk students. *Media & Methods, 26*(5), 12, 54–57.

Pederson, J. E., & Digby, A. D. (Eds.).(1995). *Secondary schools and coopereative learning.* New York: Garland.

Pellegrini, A. D., & Bjorklund, D. F. (1997). The role of recess in children's cognitive performance. *Educational Psychologist, 32*(1), 35–40.

Peltier, G. L. (1991). Why do secondary schools continue to track students? *The Clearing House, 64*(4), 246–247.

Penfield, W. (1969). Consciousness, memory, and man's conditioned reflexes. In K. Pribram (Ed.), *On the biology of learning.* New York: Harcourt Brace Jovanovich.

Perrone, V. (1991). *A letter to teachers: Reflections on schooling and the art of teaching.* San Francisco: Jossey-Bass.

Peskin, H. (1967). Pubertal onset and ego functioning. A psychoanalytic approach. *Journal of Abnormal Psychology, 72*(1), 1–15.

Peskin, H. (1973). Influence of the developmental schedule of puberty on learning and ego functioning. *Journal of Youth and Adolescence, 2*(4), 273–290.

Peterson, A. C. (1988). Adolescent development. In M. R. Rosenzweig & L. W. Porter (Eds.), *Annual review of psychology* (Vol. 39). Palo Alto, CA: Annual Reviews.

Peterson, A. C., & Taylor, B. (1980). The biological approach to adolescence. In J. Adelson (Ed.), *Handbook of adolescent psychology.* New York: Wiley.

Peterson, A. C., Compas, B. E., Brooks-Gunn, J., Stemmler, M., Ey, S., & Grant, K. E. (1993). Depression in adolescence. *American Psychologist, 48* (2), 155–168.

Petti, T. A., & Larson, C. N. (1987). Depression and suicide. In V. B. van Hasselt & M. Hersen (Eds.), *Handbook of adolescent psychology.* New York: Pergamon Press.

Piaget, J. (1952a). *The language and thought of the child.* London: Routledge & Kegan Paul.

Piaget, J. (1952b). *The origins of intelligence in children.* New York: International Universities Press.

Piaget, J. (1965). *The moral judgment of the child* (M. Gabain, Trans.). Glencoe, IL: Free Press. (Original work published 1932.)

Piaget, J., & Inhelder, B. (1956). *The child's conception of space.* London: Routledge & Kegan Paul.

Piaget, J., & Inhelder, B. (1969). *The psychology of the child*. New York: Basic Books.

Piechowski, M. M. (1997). Emotional giftedness: The measure of intrapersonal intelligence. In N. Colangelo & G. A. Davis (Eds.), *Handbook of gifted education* (2d ed.). Boston: Allyn & Bacon.

Pintrich, P. R., & Schunk, D. H. (1996). *Motivation in education: Theory, research, and applications*. Englewood Cliffs, NJ: Merrill.

Pogrow, S. (1990). A Socratic approach to using computers with at-risk students. *Educational Leadership, 47*(5), 61–66.

Pollard, D. S. (1993). Gender, achievement, and African-American students' perceptions of their school experience. *Educational Psychologist, 28*(4), 341–356.

Polya, G. (1957). *How to solve it* (2d ed.). Princeton, NJ: Princeton University Press.

Popham, W. J. (1997). What's wrong—and what's right—with rubrics. *Educational Leadership, 55*(2), 72–75.

Popham, W. J. (1999). *Classroom assessment: What teachers need to know* (2d ed.). Boston: Allyn & Bacon.

Porter, A. C., & Brophy, J. (1988). Synthesis of research on good teaching: Insights from the work of the Institute for Research on Teaching. *Educational Leadership, 45*(8), 74–85.

Premack, D. (1959). Toward empirical behavior laws: 1. Positive reinforcement. *Psychological Review, 66*(4), 219–233.

Pressley, M., Levin, J. R., & Delaney, H. D. (1982). *The mnemonic keyword method. Review of Educational Research, 52*(1), 61–91.

Pressley, M., Woloshyn, V., & Associates. (1995). *Cognitive strategy instruction that really improves children's strategy instruction* (2d ed.). Cambridge, MA: Brookline Books.

Proost, K., Elen, J., & Lowyck, J. (1997). Effects of gender on perception of the preferences for telematic learning environments. *Journal of Research on Computing in Education, 29*(4), 371–385.

Purdie, N., & Hattie, J. (1996). Cultural differences in the use of strategies for self-regulated learning. *American Educational Research Journal, 33*(4), 845–871.

Purkey, W. W., & Novak, J. M. (1996). *Inviting school success: A self-concept approach to teaching, learning, and democratic practice* (3d ed.). Belmont, CA: Wadsworth.

Purkey, W. W., & Strahan, D. B. (1986). *Positive discipline: A pocketful of ideas*. Columbus, OH: National Middle Schools Association.

Putnam, J. W. (Ed.).(1993). *Cooperative learning and strategies for inclusion*. Baltimore, MD: Brookes.

Qin, Z., Johnson, D. W., & Johnson, R. T. (1995). Cooperative versus competitive efforts and problem solving. *Review of Educational Research, 65*(2), 129–143.

Quarles, C. L. (1993). *Staying safe at school*. Thousand Oaks, CA: Corwin Press.

Quay, H. C. (1986). Classification. In H. C. Quay & J. S. Werry (Eds.), *Psychopathological disorders of childhood* (3d ed.). New York: Wiley.

Queen, J. A., & Gretes, J. A. (1982). First year teachers' perceptions of their preservice training. *Phi Delta Kappan, 64*(3), 215–216.

Rabow, J., Charness, M. A., Kipperman, J., & Radcliffe-Vasile, S. (1994). *William Fawcett Hill's learning through discussion* (3d ed.). Thousand Oaks, CA: Sage Publications.

Raison, J., Hanson, L. A., Hall, C., & Reynolds, M. C. (1995). Another school's reality. *Phi Delta Kappan, 76*(6), 480–482.

Rankin, W. (1997). The cyberjournal: Developing writing, researching, and editing skills through e-mail and the world wide web. *Educational Technology, 37*(4), 29–31.

Raskind, M. (1993). Assistive technology and adults with learning disabilities: A blueprint for exploration and advancement. *Learning Disability Quarterly, 16*(3), 185–196.

Ratner, C. (1991). *Vygotsky's sociohistorical psychology and its contemporary applications*. New York: Plenum Press.

Raudenbush, S. W. (1984). Magnitude of teacher expectancy effects on pupil IQ as a function of the credibility of expectancy induction: A synthesis of findings from 18 experiments. *Journal of Educational Psychology, 76*(1), 85–97.

Raudenbush, S. W., Rowan, B., & Cheong, Y. F. (1993). Higher order instructional goals in secondary schools: Class, teacher, and school influences. *American Educational Research Journal, 30*(3), 523–553.

Raugh, M. R., & Atkinson, R. C. (1975). A mnemonic method for learning a second-language vocabulary. *Journal of Educational Psychology, 67*(1), 1–16.

Ravaglia, R., Suppes, P., Stillinger, C., & Alper, T. (1995). *Gifted Child Quarterly, 39*(1), 7–13.

Read, D. A., & Simon, S. B. (1975). *Humanistic education sourcebook*. Englewood Cliffs, NJ: Prentice-Hall.

Redl, F., & Wattenberg, W. W. (1959). *Mental hygiene in teaching* (2d ed.). New York: Harcourt Brace Jovanovich.

Reed, W. M. (1996). Assessing the impact of computer-based writing instruction. *Journal of Research on Computing in Education, 28*(4), 418–437.

Reese, S. (1995). MIDI-assisted composing in your classroom. *Music Educators Journal, 81*(4), 37–40.

Reis, S. M., & Renzulli, J. S. (1985). *The secondary triad model*. Mansfield Center, CT: Creative Learning Press.

Renzulli, J. S., & Reis, S. M. (1985). *The schoolwide enrichment model*. Mansfield Center, CT: Creative Learning Press.

Resnick, L. B. (1987). Learning in school and out. *Educational Researcher, 16*(9), 13–20.

Reynolds, A. J. (1992). Grade retention and school adjustment: An exploratory analysis. *Educational Evaluation and Policy Analysis, 14*(2), 101–122.

Reynolds, T. H., & Bonk, C. J. (1996). Creating computerized writing partner and keystroke recording tools with macro-driven prompts. *Educational Technology Research and Development, 44*(3), 83–97.

Richert, E. S. (1997). Excellence with Equity™ in identification and programming. In N. Colangelo & G. A. Davis (Eds.), *Handbook of gifted education* (2d ed.). Boston: Allyn & Bacon.

Riel, M. (1993). Global education through learning circles. In L. Harasim (Ed.), *Global Networks*. Cambridge, MA: MIT Press.

Riel, M. (1996). Cross-classroom collaboration: Communication and education. In T. Koschmann (Ed.), *CSCL: Theory and practice*. Mahwah, NJ: Erlbaum.

Rivera, D. P., & Smith, D. D. (1997). *Teaching students with learning and behavior problems* (3d ed.). Boston: Allyn & Bacon.

Rocheleau, B. (1995). Computer use by school-age children: Trends, patterns, and predictors. *Journal of Educational Computing Research, 12*(1), 1–17.

Roderick, M. (1995, December). *Grade retention and school dropout: Policy debate and research questions* (Research Bulletin No. 15). Bloomington, IN: Center for Evaluation, Development, and Research.

Roehler, L. R., & Cantlon, D. J. (1997). Scaffolding: A powerful tool in social constructivist classrooms. In K. Hogan & M. Pressley (Eds.), *Scaffolding student learning: Instructional approaches and issues*. Cambridge, MA: Brookline Books.

Rogers, C. R. (1967). Learning to be free. In C. R. Rogers & B. Stevens (Eds.), *The problem of being human*. Lafayette, CA: Real People Press. (Reprinted from S. Farber & R. H. L. Wilson, Eds., 1963, *Conflict and creativity: Control of the mind*, New York: McGraw-Hill.)

Rogers, C. R. (1980). *A way of being*. Boston: Houghton Mifflin.

Rogers, C. R. (1983). *Freedom to learn for the 80's*. Columbus, OH: Merrill.

Rogers, D. (1972). *The psychology of adolescence* (2d ed.). New York: Appleton-Century-Crofts.

Rogers, J. (1993, May). The inclusion revolution. *Phi Delta Kappa Research Bulletin* (No. 11),

Rogoff, B. (1990). *Apprenticeship in thinking: Cognitive development in social context*. New York: Oxford University Press.

Rogoff, B., & Chavajay, P. (1995). What's become of research on the cultural basis of cognitive development? *American Psychologist, 50*(10), 859–877.

Rop, C. (1998). Breaking the gender barrier in the physical sciences. *Educational Leadership, 55*(4), 58-60.

Roschelle, J. (1996). Computer support for knowledge-building communities. In T. Koschmann (Ed.), *CSCL: Theory and practice*. Mahwah, NJ: Erlbaum.

Rosenshine, B. V. (1987). Explicit teaching. In D. C. Berliner & B. V. Rosenshine (Eds.), *Talks to teachers*. New York: Random House.

Rosenshine, B., & Meister, C. (1994a). Reciprocal teaching: A review of the research. *Review of Educational Research, 64*(4), 479–530.

Rosenshine, B. V., & Meister, C. (1994b). Direct instruction. In T. Husen & T. N. Postlewhaite (Eds.), *International encyclopedia of education* (2d ed., Vol. 3, pp. 1524–1530). New York: Pergamon.

Rosenshine, B., Meister, C., & Chapman, S. (1996). Teaching students to generate questions: A review of the intervention studies. *Review of Educational Research, 66*(2), 181–221.

Rosenthal, R. (1985). From unconscious experimenter bias to teacher expectancy effects. In J. B. Dusek (Ed.), *Teacher expectations*. Hillsdale, NJ: Erlbaum.

Rosenthal, R., & Jacobson, L. (1968). *Pygmalion in the classroom*. New York: Holt, Rinehart, & Winston.

Ross, D. D., Bondy, E., & Kyle, D. W. (1993). *Reflective teaching for student empowerment*. New York: Macmillan.

Rotheram-Borus, M. J., & Koopman, C. (1991). AIDS and adolescents. In R. M. Lerner, A. C. Peterson, & J. Brooks-Gunn (Eds.), *Encyclopedia of adolescence*. New York: Garland Publishing.

Rothstein, R. (1998). Bilingual education: The controversy. *Phi Delta Kappan, 79*(9), 672–678.

Rottier, J., & Ogan, B. J. (1991). *Cooperative learning in middle-level schools*. Washington, DC: National Education Association.

Rottier, K. L. (1995). If kids ruled the world: ICONS. *Educational Leadership, 53*(2), 51–53.

Rowan, B. (1994). Comparing teachers' work with work in other occupations: Notes on the professional status of teaching. *Educational Researcher, 23*(6), 4–17.

Rowland, K. L., & Scott, D. (1992). Promoting language and literacy for young children through computers. *Journal of Computing in Childhood Education, 3*, 55–61.

Royer, J. M. (1979). Theories of the transfer of learning. *Educational Psychologist, 14*, 53–72.

Royer, J. M., & Cable, G. W. (1975). Facilitated learning in connected discourse. *Journal of Educational Psychology, 67*(1), 116–123.

Royer, J. M., & Cable, G. W. (1976). Illustrations, analogies, and facilitative transfer in prose learning. *Journal of Educational Psychology, 68*(2), 205–209.

Rubin, K. H., Maioni, T. L., & Hornung, M. (1976). Free play behavior in middle- and lower-class preschoolers: Parten and Piaget revisited. *Child Development, 47*(2), 414–419.

Rubin, L. J. (1985). *Artistry in teaching*. New York: Random House.

Ruggiero, V. R. (1988). *Teaching thinking across the curriculum*. New York: Harper & Row.

Ruggiero, V. R. (1995). *The art of thinking* (4th ed.). New York: HarperCollins.

Runco, M. A. (Ed.). (1994). *Problem finding, problem solving, and creativity*. Norwood, NJ: Ablex.

Ruopp, R., Gal, S., Drayton, B., & Pfister, M. (Eds.). (1993). *LabNet: Toward a community of practice*. Hillsdale, NJ: Erlbaum.

Russell, T., & Munby, H. (Eds.) (1992). *Teachers and teaching: From classroom to reflection*. London: Falmer Press.

Rutledge, M. (1997). Reading the subtext on gender. *Educational Leadership, 54*(7), 71–73.

Rutter, M. (1990). Changing patterns of psychiatric disorders during adolescence. In J. Bancroft & J. M. Reinisch (Eds.), *Adolescence and puberty*. New York: Oxford University Press.

Ryan, R. M., & Deci, E. L. (1996). When paradigms clash: Comments on Cameron and Pierce's claim that rewards do not undermine intrinsic motivation. *Review of Educational Research, 66*(1), 33–38.

Sadker, M. P, & Sadker, D. M. (1991). *Teachers, schools, and society* (2d ed.). New York: Random House.

Sadker, M. P., & Sadker, D. M. (1994). *Failing at fairness: How America's schools cheat girls*. New York: Charles Scribner's Sons.

Salomon, G. (1988). AI in reverse: Computer tools that turn cognitive. *Journal of Educational Computing Research, 4*(2), 123–139.

Salomon, G. (1993). On the nature of pedagogic computer tools. In S. Lajoie & S. Derry (Eds.), *Computers as cognitive tools*. Hillsdale, NJ: Erlbaum.

Salomon, G., & Perkins, D. N. (1989). Rocky roads to transfer: Rethinking mechanisms of a neglected phenomenon. *Educational Psychologist, 24*(2), 113–142.

Salomon, G., Globerson, T., & Guterman, E. (1989). The computer as a zone of proximal development: Internalizing reading-related metacognitions from a reading partner. *Journal of Educational Psychology, 81*(4), 620–627.

Salomon, G., Perkins, D. N., & Globerson, T. (1991). Partners in cognition: Extending human intelligence with intelligent technologies. *Educational Researcher, 20*(3), 2–9.

Sameroff, A., & McDonough, S. C. (1994). Educational implications of developmental transitions: Revisiting the 5- to 7-year shift. *Phi Delta Kappan, 76*(3), 189–193.

Samuda, R. J., Kong, S. L., Cummins, J., Pascual-Leone, J., & Lewis, J. (1991). *Assessment and placement of minority students*. Toronto: C. J. Hofrefe.

Sanders, J.S. (1985). Here's how you can help girls take greater advantage of school computers. *American School Board Journal, 172*(4), 37–38.

Sanders-Phillips, K. (1989). Prenatal and postnatal influences on cognitive development. In G. L. Berry & J. K. Asamen (Eds.), *Black students: Psychosocial issues and academic achievement*. Newbury Park, CA: Sage.

Sandholtz, J. H., Ringstaff, C., & Dwyer, D. C. (1997). *Teaching with technology: Creating student-centered classrooms*. New York: Teachers College Press.

Sarason, S. B. (1993). *The case for change: Rethinking the preparation of educators*. San Francisco: Jossey-Bass.

Sauer, E. (1994). Creative collaboration online. *The Computing Teacher, 21*(7), 38–40.

Savery, J. R., & Duffy, T. M. (1996). Problem-based learning: An instructional model and its constructivist framework. In B. G. Wilson (Ed.), *Constructivist learning environments: Case studies in instructional design*. Englewood Cliffs, NJ: Educational Technology Publications.

Scales, P. (1993). How teachers and education deans rate the quality of teacher preparation for the middle grades. *Journal of Teacher Education, 44*(5), 378–383.

Scardamalia, M., & Bereiter, C. (1991). Higher levels of agency for children in knowledge building: A challenge for the design of new knowledge media. *Journal of the Learning Sciences, 1*(1), 37–68.

Scardamalia, M., & Bereiter, C. (1996). Computer support for knowledge-building communities. In T. Koschmann (Ed.), *CSCL: Theory and practice.* Mahwah, NJ: Erlbaum.

Scardamalia, M., Bereiter, C., McLean, R. S., Swallow, J., & Woodruff, E. (1989). Computer-supported intentional learning environments. *Journal of Educational Computing Research, 5*(1), 51–68.

Scarr, S., Weinberg, R. A., & Levine, A. (1986). *Understanding development.* San Diego, CA: Harcourt Brace Jovanovich.

Schab, F. (1991). Schooling without learning: Thirty years of cheating in high school. *Adolescence, 26*(104), 839–848.

Schery, T., & O'Connor, L. (1997). Language intervention: Computer training for young children with special needs. *British Journal of Educational Technology, 28*(4), 271–279.

Scheurman, G. (1998). From behaviorist to constructivist teaching. *Social Education, 62*(1), 6–9.

Schiever, S. W. (1991). *A comprehensive approach to teaching thinking.* Boston: Allyn & Bacon.

Schifter, D. (1996). A constructivist perspective on teaching and learning mathematics. *Phi Delta Kappan, 77*(7), 492–499.

Schlaefli, A., Rest, J. R., & Thoma, S. J. (1985). Does moral education improve moral judgment? A meta-analysis of intervention studies using the Defining Issues Test. *Review of Educational Research, 55*(3), 319–352.

Scholten, B., & Whitmer, J. (1996). Hypermedia projects. *Learning and Leading with Technology, 24*(3), 59–62.

Schon, D. A. (1987). *Educating the reflective practitioner.* San Francisco: Jossey-Bass.

Schrum, L., & Berenfeld, B. (1997). *Teaching and learning in the information age: A guide to educational telecommunications.* Needham Heights, MA: Allyn & Bacon.

Schultz, T. (1989). Testing and retention of young children: Moving from controversy to reform. *Phi Delta Kappan, 71*(2), 125–129.

Schunk, D. H. (1981). Modeling and attributional effects on children's achievement: A self-efficacy analysis. *Journal of Educational Psychology, 73*(1), 93–105.

Schunk, D. H. (1987). Peer models and children's behavioral change. *Review of Educational Research, 57*(2), 149–174.

Schunk, D. H. (1995). Self-efficacy and education and instruction. In J. E. Maddux (Ed.), *Self-efficacy, adaptation, and adjustment.* New York: Plenum Press.

Schunk, D. H., & Hanson, A. R. (1989). Peer models: Influences on children's self-efficacy and achievement. *Journal of Educational Psychology, 77*(3), 313–322.

Schunk, D. H., & Zimmerman, B. J. (1997). Social origins of self-regulatory competence. *Educational Psychologist, 32*(4), 195–208.

Schwartz, J. (1995). Shuttling between the particular and the general: Reflections on the role of conjecture and hypothesis in the generation of knowledge in science and mathematics. In D. N. Perkins, J. H. Schwartz, M. M. West, & M. S. Wiske (Eds.), *Software goes to school: Teaching for understanding with new technologies.* New York: Oxford University Press.

Scrase, R. (1997). Using scanners linked to talking computers as tools for teaching children to read. *British Journal of Educational Technology, 28*(4), 308–310.

Seagoe, M. V. (1970). *The learning process and school practice.* Scranton, PA: Chandler.

Seagoe, M. V. (1975). *Terman and the gifted.* Los Altos, CA: Kaufmann.

Searleman, A., & Herrmann, D. (1994). *Memory from a broader perspective.* New York: McGraw-Hill.

Secules, T., Cottom, C., Bray, M., & Miller, L. (1997). Creating schools for thought. *Educational Leadership, 54*(6), 56–60.

Seligman, M. E. P. (1975). *Helplessness: On depression, development, and death.* San Francisco: Freeman.

Selman, R. L. (1980). *The growth of interpersonal understanding: Developmental and clinical analyses.* New York: Academic Press.

Selmes, I. (1987). *Improving study skills.* London: Hodder and Stoughton.

Semb, G. B., & Ellis, J. A. (1994). Knowledge taught in school: What is remembered? *Review of Educational Research, 64*(2), 253–286.

Sharan, S. (1995). Group investigation: Theoretical foundations. In J. E. Peterson, & A. D. Digby (Eds.), *Secondary schools and cooperative learning.* New York: Garland.

Sharan, Y., & Sharan, S. (1994). Group investigation in the cooperative classroom. In S. Sharan (Ed.), *Handbook of cooperative learning methods.* Westport, CT: Greenwood Press.

Shashaani, L. (1994). Gender differences in computer experience and its influence on computer attitudes. *Journal of Educational Computing Research, 11*(4), 347–367.

Shavelson, R. J., & Baxter, G. P. (1992). What we've learned about assessing hands-on science. *Educational Leadership, 49*(8), 20–25.

Shepard, L. A., & Bliem, C. L. (1995). Parents' thinking about standardized tests and performance assessments. *Educational Researcher, 24*(8), 25–32.

Shepard, R. N. (1978). Externalization of mental images and the act of creation. In B. S. Randhawa & W. E. Coffman (Eds.), *Visual learning, thinking, and communication.* New York: Academic Press.

Shepardson, D. P., & Britsch, S. J. (1996). When dinosaurs roamed: Hypermedia and the learning of mathematics and science. *Journal of Computers in Mathematics and Science Teaching, 15*(1/2), 7–18.

Shook, S. C., LaBrie, M., Vallies, J., McLaughlin, T. F., & Williams, R. L. (1990). The effects of a token economy on first grade students' inappropriate social behavior. *Reading Improvement, 27*(2), 96–101.

Shrader, G., Lento, E., Gomez, L., & Pea, R. (1997). Inventing interventions: Cases from CoVis: An analysis by SES. Paper presented at the Annual Meeting of the American Educational Research Association, Chicago, IL. (ERIC Document Reproduction Service No. ED 412 115)

Shulman, L. S. (1986). Those who understand: Knowledge growth in teaching. *Educational Researcher, 15*(2), 4–21.

Siegel, M. A., & Kirkley, S. E. (1998). Adventure learning as a vision of the digital learning environment. In C. J. Bonk & K. S. King (Eds.), *Electronic collaborators: Learner-centered technologies for literacy, apprenticeship, and discourse.* Mahwah, NJ: Erlbaum.

Siegler, R. S. (1994). Cognitive variability: A key to understanding cognitive development. *Current Directions in Psychological Science, 3*(1), 1–5.

Sigelman, C. K., & Shaffer, D. R. (1991). *Life-span human development.* Pacific Grove, CA: Brooks Cole.

Sikula, J. (Ed.).(1996). *Handbook of research on teacher education* (2d ed.). New York: Simon & Schuster Macmillan.

Simon, A., & Boyer, E. G. (Eds.). (1974). *Mirrors for behavior III: An anthology of observation instruments.* Wyncote, PA: Communication Materials Center.

Simpson, E. J. (1972). *The classification of educational objectives: Psychomotor domain.* Urbana, IL: University of Illinois Press.

Simpson, M. L. (1984). The status of study strategy instruction: Implications for classroom teachers. *Journal of Reading, 29*(2), 136–143.

Singer, A. (1994). Reflections on multiculturalism. *Phi Delta Kappan, 76*(4), 284–288.

Singletary, T. J., & Jordan, J. R. (1996). Exploring the globe. *The Science Teacher, 63*(3), 36–39.

Singley, M. K., & Taft, H. L. (1995). Open-ended approaches to science assessment using computers. *Journal of Science Education and Technology, 4*(1), 7–20.

Skinner, B. F. (1948). *Walden two.* New York: Macmillan.

Skinner, B. F. (1968). *The technology of teaching.* New York: Appleton-Century-Crofts.

Skinner, B. F. (1976). *Particulars of my life.* New York: Knopf.

Skinner, B. F. (1979). *The shaping of a behaviorist.* New York: Knopf.

Skinner, B. F. (1983). *A matter of consequences.* New York: Knopf.

Skinner, B. F. (1984). The shame of American education. *American Psychologist, 39*(9), 947–954.

Skinner, B. F. (1986). Programmed instruction revisited. *Phi Delta Kappan, 68*(2), 103–110.

Skinner, L., Gillespie, P., & Balkam, L. (1997). Waysiders in America's classrooms. *Technos, 6*(1), 29–31.

Slavin, R. E. (1989). PET and the pendulum: Faddism in education and how to stop it. *Phi Delta Kappan, 79*(10), 752–758.

Slavin, R. E. (1990a). IBM's Writing to Read: Is it right for reading? *Phi Delta Kappan, 72*(3), 214–216.

Slavin, R. E. (1990b). Achievement effects of ability grouping in secondary schools: A best-evidence synthesis. *Review of Educational Research, 60*(3), 471–500.

Slavin, R. E. (1994). Student teams-achievement divisions. In S. Sharan (Ed.), *Handbook of cooperative learning methods.* Westport, CT: Greenwood Press.

Slavin, R. E. (1995). *Cooperative learning: Theory, research, and practice* (2d ed.). Boston: Allyn & Bacon.

Sleeter, C. E., & Grant, C. A. (1994). *Making choices for multicultural education* (2d ed.). New York: Merrill.

Small, R. V., & Ferreira, S. M. (1994). Information location and use, motivation, and learning patterns when using print or multimedia information resources. *Journal of Educational Multimedia and Hypermedia, 3*(3/4), 251–273.

Smelter, R. W., Rasch, B. W., & Yudewitz, G. J. (1994). *Phi Delta Kappan, 76*(1), 35–38.

Smilansky, S. (1968). *The effects of sociodramatic play on disadvantaged preschool children.* New York: Wiley.

Smith, D. D. (1998). *Introduction to special education* (3d ed.). Boston: Allyn & Bacon.

Smith, K., Johnson, D. W., & Johnson, R. T. (1981). Can conflict be constructive? Controversy versus concurrence seeking in learning groups. *Journal of Educational Psychology, 73*(5), 651–663.

Smith, M. L. (1991). Put to the test: The effects of external testing on teachers. *Educational Researcher, 20*(5), 8–11.

Snider, S. L, & Badgett, T. L. (1995). "I have this computer, what do I do now?" Using technology to enhance every child's learning. *Early Childhood Education Journal, 23*(2), 101–105.

Snir, J., Smith, C., & Grosslight, L. (1993). Conceptually enhanced simulations: A computer tool for science teaching. *Journal of Science Education and Technology, 2*(2), 373–388.

Snow, R. E. (1986). Individual differences and the design of educational programs. *American Psychologist, 41*(10), 1029–1039.

Snow, R. E. (1992). Aptitude testing: Yesterday, today, and tomorrow. *Educational Psychologist, 27*(1), 5–32.

Snowman, J. (1986). Learning tactics and strategies. In G. D. Phye & T. Andre (Eds.), *Cognitive classroom learning: Understanding, thinking, and problem solving.* New York: Academic Press.

Snowman, J. (1987, October). The keys to strategic learning. Paper presented at the annual meeting of the Mid-Western Educational Research Association, Chicago, IL.

Soldier, L. L. (1989). Cooperative learning and the Native American student. *Phi Delta Kappan, 71*(2), 161–163.

Soldier, L. L. (1997). Is there an "Indian" in your classroom? Working successfully with urban Native American students. *Phi Delta Kappan, 78*(8), 650–653.

Songer, N.B. (1998). Can technology bring students closer to science? In K. Tobin & B. Fraser (Eds.), *The international handbook of science education.* The Netherlands: Kluwer.

Spear, N. E., & Riccio, D. C. (1994). *Memory: Phenomena and principles.* Boston: Allyn & Bacon.

Spear, R. C. (1992). Appropriate grouping practices for middle level students. In J. L. Irvin (Ed.), *Transforming middle level education.* Boston: Allyn & Bacon.

Spear-Swerling, L., & Sternberg, R. J. (1998). Curing our "epidemic" of learning disabilities. *Phi Delta Kappan, 79*(5), 397–401.

Spector, J. E. (1995) Phonemic awareness training: Application of principles of direct instruction. *Reading and Writing Quarterly, 11*(1), 37–51.

Spiro, R. J., Feltovich, P. J., Jacobson, M. J., & Coulson, R. L. (1991). Knowledge representation, content specification, and the development of skill in situation-specific knowledge assembly: Some constructivist issues as they relate to cognitive flexibility theory and hypertext. *Educational Technology, 31*(9), 22–25.

Sprinthall, N. A., & Sprinthall, R. C. (1987). *Educational psychology; A developmental approach* (4th ed.). New York: Random House.

Sprinthall, N. A., Sprinthall, R. C., & Oja, S. N. (1994). *Educational psychology: A developmental approach* (6th ed.). New York: McGraw-Hill.

Standing, L. (1973). Learning 10,000 pictures. *Quarterly Journal of Experimental Psychology, 25*(2), 207–222.

Standing, L., Conezio, J., & Haber, R. (1970). Perception and memory for pictures: Single trial learning of 2500 visual stimuli. *Psychonomic Science, 19*(2), 73–74.

Staub, D., & Peck, C. A. (1994–1995). What are the outcomes for nondisabled students? *Educational Leadership, 52*(4), 36–40.

Steffe, L. P., & Gale, J. (Eds.).(1995). *Constructivism in education.* Hillsdale, NJ: Erlbaum.

Stephen, J., Fraser, E., & Marcia, J. E. (1992). Moratorium-achievement (mama) cycles in lifespan identity development: Value orientations and reasoning system correlates. *Journal of Adolescence, 15*(3), 283–300.

Sternberg, R. J. (1985). *Beyond IQ: A triarchic theory of human intelligence.* New York: Cambridge University Press.

Sternberg, R. J. (1994). Allowing for thinking styles. *Educational Leadership, 52*(3), 36–40.

Sternberg, R. J. (1996a). Myths, countermyths, and truths about intelligence. *Educational Researcher, 25*(2), 11–16.

Sternberg, R. J. (1996b). Matching abilities, instruction, and assessment: Reawakening the sleeping giant of ATI. In I. Dennis & P. Tapsfield (Eds.), *Human abilities: Their nature and measurement.* Mahwah, NJ: Erlbaum.

Sternberg, R. J. (1997a). What does it mean to be smart? *Educational Leadership, 54*(6), 20–24.

Sternberg, R. J. (1997b). *Thinking styles.* New York: Cambridge University Press.

Sternberg, R. J. (1997c). Technology changes intelligence: Societal implications and soaring IQ's. *Technos, 6*(2), 12–14.

Sternberg, R. J. (1998). Abilities are forms of developing expertise. *Educational Researcher, 27*(3), 11–20.

Sternberg, R. J., & Horvath, J. A. (1995). A prototype view of expert teaching. *Educational Researcher, 24*(6), 9–17.

Sternberg, R. J., & Spear-Swerling, L. (1996). *Teaching for thinking.* Washington, DC: American Psychological Association.

Sternberg, R. J., Ferrari, M., Clinkenbeard, P., & Grigorenko, E. L. (1996). Identification, instruction, and assessment of gifted children: A construct validation of a triarchic model. *Gifted Child Quarterly, 40*(3), 129–137.

Sternberg, R. J., Torff, B., & Grigorenko, E. (1998). Teaching for successful intelligence raises school achievement. *Phi Delta Kappan, 79*(9), 667–671.

Stevens, R. J., & Slavin, R. E. (1995), The cooperative elementary school: Effects on students' achievement, attitudes, and social relations. *American Educational Research Journal, 32*(2), 321–351.

Stiffman, A. R., Earls, F., Robins, L. N., Jung, K. G., & Kulbok, P. (1987). Adolescent sexual activity and pregnancy: Socioenvironmental problems, physical health, and mental health. *Journal of Youth and Adolescence, 16*(5), 497–509.

Stiggins, R. J. (1997). *Student-centered classroom assessment* (2d ed.). Upper Saddle River, NJ: Merrill.

Stipek, D. J. (1998). *Motivation to learn: From theory to practice* (3d ed.). Boston: Allyn & Bacon.

Stitt, B. A. (1988). *Building gender fairness in schools.* Carbondale, IL: Southern Illinois University Press.

Streib, L. Y. (1993). Visiting and revisiting the trees. In M. Cochran-Smith & S. L. Lytle (Eds.), *Inside/outside: Teacher research and knowledge.* New York: Teachers College Press.

Stronge, J. H., Lynch, C. D., & Smith, C. R. (1987). Educating the culturally disadvantaged gifted student. *The School Counselor, 34*(5), 336–344.

Strother, D. B. (1986). Suicide among the young. *Phi Delta Kappan, 67*(10), 756–759.

Sulzer-Azaroff, B., & Mayer, G. R. (1986). *Achieving educational excellence: Using behavioral strategies.* New York: Holt, Rinehart & Winston.

Susman, E. J. (1991). Stress and the adolescent. In R. M. Lerner, A. C. Peterson, & J. Brooks-Gunn (Eds.), *Encyclopedia of adolescence.* New York: Garland.

Sutton, R. (1991). Equity and computers in the schools: A decade of research. *Review of Educational Research, 61*(4), 465–503.

Swisher, J. F., Vickery, J. R., & Nadenichek, P (1983). Humanistic education: A review of research. *Journal of Humanistic Education and Development, 22*(1), 8–15.

Tanner, J. M. (1972). Sequence, tempo, and individual variation in growth and development of boys and girls aged twelve to sixteen. In J. Kagan & R. Coles (Eds.), *Twelve to sixteen: Early adolescence.* New York: Norton.

Taylor, C. A. (1989). *Guidebook to multicultural resources 1989–1990 edition.* Madison, WI: Praxis Publications.

Taylor, R. P. (Ed.). (1980). *The computer in the school: Tutor, tool, tutee.* New York: Teachers College Press.

Teles, L. (1993). Cognitive apprenticeship on global networks. In L. M. Harasim (Ed.), *Global networks: Computers and international communications.* Cambridge, MA: MIT Press.

Templeton, S. (1995). *Children's literacy: Contexts for meaningful learning.* Boston: Houghton Mifflin.

Terwilliger, J. (1997). Semantics, psychometrics, and assessment reforms: A close look at "authentic" assessment. *Educational Researcher, 26*(8), 24–27.

Thoma, S. J. (1986). Estimating gender differences in the comprehension and preference of moral issues. *Developmental Review, 6*(2), 165–180.

Thomas, W. P., & Collier, V. P. (1997–1998). Two languages are better than one. *Educational Leadership, 55*(4), 23–26.

Thompson, A. M. (1996). Attention deficit hyperactivity disorder: A parent's perspective. *Phi Delta Kappan, 77*(6), 433–436.

Thompson, C. P., Cowan, T. M., & Frieman, J. (1993). *Memory search by a memorist.* Hillsdale, NJ: Erlbaum.

Thorndike, E. L., & Woodworth, R. S. (1901). The influence of improvement in one mental function upon the efficiency of other functions. *Psychological Review, 8,* 247–261.

Thurston, C. O., Secaras, E. D., & Levin, J. A. (1997). Teaching telapprenticeships: An innovative model for integrating technology into teacher education. *Journal of Research on Computing in Education, 29*(4), 385–391.

Tidwell, R. (1989). Academic success and the school dropout: A minority perspective. In G. L. Berry & J. K. Asamen (Eds.), *Black students: Psychosocial issues and academic achievement.* Newbury Park, CA: Sage Publications.

Tinker, R., & Haavind, S. (1996). Netcourses and netseminars: Current practice and new designs. *Journal of Science Education and Technology, 5*(3), 217–223.

Tomchin, E. M., & Impara, J. C. (1992). Unraveling teachers' beliefs about grade retention. *American Educational Research Journal, 29*(1), 199–223.

Tomlinson, T. M. (Ed.).(1993). *Motivating students to learn: Overcoming barriers to high achievement.* Berkeley, CA: McCutchan.

Toomey, R., & Ketterer, K. (1995). Using multimedia as a cognitive tool. *Journal of Research on Computing in Education, 27*(4), 472–482.

Torgesen, J. K., & Barker, T. A. (1995). Computers as aids in the prevention and remediation of reading disabilities. *Learning Disability Quarterly, 18*(2), 76–87.

Trentin, G. (1997). Computerized adaptive tests and formative assessment. *Journal of Educational Multimedia and Hypermedia, 6*(2), 201–220.

Triandis, H. C. (1986). Toward pluralism in education. In S. Modgil, G. K. Verma, K. Mallick, & C. Modgil (Eds.), *Multicultural education: The interminable debate.* London: Falmer.

Tsangaridou, N., & O'Sullivan, M. (1994). Using pedagogical reflective strategies to enhance reflection among preservice physical education teachers. *Journal of Teaching in Physical Education, 14*(1), 13–33.

Tudge, J. R. H., & Rogoff, B. (1989). Peer influences on cognitive development: Piagetian and Vygotskian perspectives. In M. H. Bornstein & J. S. Bruner (Eds.), *Interaction in human development.* Hillsdale, NJ: Erlbaum.

Tudge, J. R. H., & Winterhoff, P. A. (1993). Vygotsky, Piaget, and Bandura: Perspectives on the relations between the social world and cognitive development. *Human Development, 36*(2), 61–81.

Tulving, E., & Pearlstone, Z. (1966). Availability vs. accessibility of information in memory for words. *Journal of Verbal Learning and Verbal Behavior, 5*(4), 381–391.

Tuttle, H. G. (1997). Electronic portfolios tell a personal story. *MultiMedia Schools, 4*(1), 32–37.

Tyler, D. K., & Vasu, E. S. (1995). Locus of control, self-esteem, achievement motivation, and problem-solving ability: LogoWriter and simulations in the fifth-grade classroom. *Journal of Research on Computing in Education, 28*(1), 98–121.

Udrey, J. R. (1990). Hormonal and social determinants of adolescent sexual initiation. In J. Bancroft & J. M. Reinisch (Eds.), *Adolescence and puberty.* New York: Oxford University Press.

Urdan, T. Midgley, C., & Anderman, E. M. (1998). The role of classroom goal structure in students' use of self-handicapping strategies. *American Educational Research Journal, 35*(1), 101–122.

U.S. Bureau of the Census. (1996). *Poverty in the United States: 1995*. Washington, DC: Author.

U.S. Department of Education (1998). *To Assure the Free Appropriate Public Education of All Children with Disabilities, Nineteenth Annual Report to Congress on the Implementation of the Individuals with Disabilities Education Act*. Washington, DC: Author.

U.S. Department of Justice (1996). *1996 statistical yearbook of the Immigration and Naturalization Service*. Washington, DC: Author.

Valli, L. (1993). Teaching before and after professional preparation: The story of a high school mathematics teacher. *Journal of Teacher Education, 44*(2), 107–118.

van der Voort, T. H. A. (1986). *Television violence: A child's-eye view*. Amsterdam: North-Holland.

Van Dusen, L. M., & Worthen, B. R. (1995). Can integrated instructional technology transform the classroom? *Educational Leadership, 53*(2), 28–33.

van Hasselt, V. B., & Hersen, M. (Eds.). (1987). *Handbook of adolescent psychology*. New York: Pergamon Press.

Van Wagenen, L., & Hibbard, K. M. (1998). Building teacher portfolios. *Educational Leadership, 55*(5), 26–29.

Vargas, J. (1986). Instructional design flaws in computer-assisted instruction. *Phi Delta Kappan, 67*(10), 738 744.

Vasquez, J. A. (1990). Teaching to the distinctive traits of minority students. *The Clearing House, 63*(7), 299–304.

Vitz, P. C. (1990). The use of stories in moral development: New psychological reasons for an old educational method. *American Psychologist, 45*(6), 709–720.

Vockell, E. L., & Fiore, D. J. (1993). Electronic gradebooks: What current programs can do for teachers. *The Clearing House, 66*(3), 141–145.

Vondracek, F. W., Schulenberg, J., Skorikov, V., Gillespie, L. K., & Wahlheim, C. (1995). The relationship of identity status to career indecision during adolescence. *Journal of Adolescence, 18*(1), 17–30.

Vygotsky, L. S. (1986). *Thought and language* (A. Kozulin, Trans.). Cambridge, MA: MIT Press. (Original work published 1934.)

Wadsworth, B. J. (1989). *Piaget's theory of cognitive and affective development* (4th ed.). New York: Longman.

Wainryb, C., & Turiel, E. (1993). Conceptual and informational features in moral deci-

sion making. *Educational Psychologist, 28* (3), 205–218.

Walberg, H. J. (1990). Productive teaching and instruction: Assessing the knowledge base. *Phi Delta Kappan, 71*(6), 470–478.

Walker, H. M., Colvin, G., & Ramsey, E. (1995). *Antisocial behavior in school: Strategies and best practices*. Pacific Groves, CA: Brooks/Cole.

Walker, J. E., & Shea, T. M. (1999). *Behavior management A practical approach for educators* (7th ed.). Upper Saddle River, NJ: Merrill.

Walsh, W. B., & Betz, N. E. (1995). *Tests and assessment* (3d ed.). Englewood Cliffs, NJ: Prentice-Hall.

Wang, M. C., Haertel, G. D., & Walberg, H. J. (1993). Toward a knowledge base for school learning. *Review of Educational Research, 63*(3), 249–294.

Waterman, A. S. (1988). Identity status theory and Erikson's theory: Communalities and differences. *Developmental Review, 8*(2), 185–208.

Waterman, A. S., & Archer, S. L. (1990). A life-span perspective on identity formation: Developments in form, function, and process. In P. B. Baltes, D. L. Featherman, & R. M. Lerner (Eds.), *Life-span development and behavior* (Vol. 10). Hillsdale, NJ: Erlbaum.

Watson, J. B. (1913). Psychology as the behaviorist views it. *Psychological Review, 20*, 158–177.

Watson, M. F., & Protinsky, H. (1991). Identity status of black adolescents: An empirical investigation. *Adolescence, 26*(104), 963–966.

Wechsler, D. (1975). Intelligence defined and undefined: A relativistic appraisal. *American Psychologist, 30*(2), 135–139.

Wechsler, D. (1981). *Wechsler adult intelligence scale—revised*. New York: Psychological Corporation.

Wechsler, D. (1991). *Wechsler intelligence scale for children-III*. New York: Psychological Corporation.

Weiner, I. B. (1975). Depression in adolescence. In F. F Flach & S. C. Draghi (Eds.), *The nature and treatment of depression*. New York: Wiley.

Weinstein, C. S., & Mignano, A. J., Jr. (1997). *Elementary classroom management: Lessons from research and practice* (2d ed.). New York: McGraw-Hill.

Wellesley College Center for Research on Women. (1992). *How schools shortchange girls*. Washington, DC: American Association of University Women Educational Foundation, National Education Association.

Wellman, H. M., & Gelman, S. A. (1992). Cognitive development: Foundational theories of core domains. In M. R. Rosenzweig & L. W. Porter (Eds.), *Annual review of psychology* (Vol. 43). Palo Alto, CA: Annual Reviews.

Westerman, D. A. (1991). Expert and novice teacher decision making. *Journal of Teacher Education, 42*(4), 292–305.

Wheatley, G. H. (1991). Constructivist perspectives on science and mathematics learning. *Science Education, 75*(1), 9–21.

Wheelock, A. (1992). *Crossing the tracks: How "untracking" can save America's schools*. New York: The New Press.

Wheelock, A. (1994). *Alternatives to tracking and ability grouping*. Arlington, VA: American Association of School Administrators.

Whimbey, A., & Lochhead, J. (1991). *Problem solving and comprehension* (5th ed.). Hillsdale, NJ: Erlbaum.

White, B. L., & Watts, J. C. (1973). *Experience and environment: Major influences on the development of the young child*. Englewood Cliffs, NJ: Prentice-Hall.

White, C. (1995). Two CD-ROM products for social studies classrooms. *Social Education, 59*(4), 203–207.

White, C. S. (1987). Developing information-processing skills through structured activities with a computerized filemanagement program. *Journal of Educational Computing Research, 3*(3), 355–375.

Whitmore, J. (1987). Conceptualizing the issue of underserved populations of gifted students. *Journal for the Education of the Gifted, 10*(3), 141–153.

Wicks-Nelson, R., & Israel, A. C. (1991). *Behavior disorders of childhood* (2d ed.). Englewood Cliffs, NJ: Prentice-Hall.

Wiedmer, T. L. (1998). Digital portfolios: Capturing and demonstrating skills and levels of performance. *Phi Delta Kappan, 79*(8), 586–589.

Wiggins, G. (1993). Assessment: Authenticity, context, and validity. *Phi Delta Kappan, 75*(3), 200–214.

Wilen, D. K., & Sweeting, C. (1986). Assessment of limited English proficiency Hispanic students. *School Psychology Review, 15*(1), 59–75.

Wiles, J., & Bondi, J. (1993). *The essential middle school* (2d ed.). New York: Macmillan.

Willig, A. C. (1985). A meta-analysis of selected studies on the effectiveness of bilingual education. *Review of Educational Research, 55*(3), 269–318.

Winner, E. (1997). Exceptionally high intelligence and schooling. *American Psychologist, 52* (10), 1070–1081.

Witkin, H. A., Moore, C. A., Goodenough, D. R., & Cox, P. W. (1977). Field-dependent and field-independent cognitive styles and their educational implications. *Review of Educational Research, 47*(1), 1–64.

Wittrock, M. W. (Ed.).(1986). *Handbook of research on teaching* (3d ed.). New York: Macmillan.

Wlodkowski, R. J. (1978). *Motivation and teaching: A practical guide.* Washington, DC: National Education Association.

Wlodkowski, R. J., & Ginsberg, M. B. (1995a). A framework for culturally responsive teaching. *Educational Leadership, 53*(1), 17–21.

Wlodkowski, R. J., & Ginsberg, M. B. (1995b). *Diversity and motivation: Culturally responsive teaching.* San Francisco: Jossey-Bass.

Wlodkowski, R. J., & Jaynes, J. H. (1990). *Eager to learn.* San Francisco: Jossey-Bass.

Woditsch, G. A. (1991). *The thoughtful teacher's guide to thinking skills.* Hillsdale, NJ: Erlbaum.

Wong, B. Y. L. (1985). Self-questioning instructional research: A review. *Review of Educational Research, 55*(2), 227–268.

Wood, F. W., & Zabel, R. H. (1978). Making sense of reports on the incidence of behavior disorders/emotional disturbance in school-aged populations. *Psychology in the Schools, 15*(1), 45–51.

Woodring, P. (1957). *A fourth of a nation.* New York: McGraw-Hill.

Woods, P. (1996). *Researching the art of teaching: Ethnography for educational use.* New York: Routledge.

Woolsey, K., & Bellamy, R. (1997). Science education and technology: Opportunities to enhance student learning. *The Elementary School Journal, 97*(4), 385–399.

Worthen, B. R. (1993). Critical issues that will determine the future of alternative assessment. *Phi Delta Kappan, 74*(6), 444–454.

Wuthrick, M. A. (1990). Blue jays win! Crows go down in defeat! *Phi Delta Kappan, 71*(7), 553–556.

Wynn, R. L., & Fletcher, C. (1987). Sex role development and early educational experiences. In D. B. Carter (Ed.), *Current conceptions of sex roles and sex typing.* New York: Praeger.

Xin, F., Glaser, C. W., & Rieth, H. (1996). Multimedia reading: Using anchored instruction and video technology in vocabulary lessons. *Teaching Exceptional Children, 29*(2), 45–49.

Yates, F. A. (1966). *The art of memory.* London: Routledge & Kegan Paul.

Ysseldyke, J. E., & Algozzine, B. (1995). *Special education: A practical approach for teachers.* (3d ed.). Boston: Houghton Mifflin.

Zehavi, N. (1997). Diagnostic learning activities using DERIVE. *Journal of Computers in Mathematics and Science Teaching, 16*(1), 37–59.

Zeichner, K. M. (1996). *Reflective teaching: An introduction.* Mahwah, NJ: Erlbaum.

Zellermayer, M., Salomon, G., Globerson, T., & Givon, H. (1991). Enhancing writing-related metacognitions through a computerized writing partner. *American Educational Research Journal, 28*(2), 373–391.

Zigmond, N., Jenkins, J., Fuchs, L. S., Deno, S., Fuchs, D., Baker, J. N., Jenkins, L., & Couthino, M. (1995). Special education in restructured schools: Findings from three multi-year studies. *Phi Delta Kappan, 76*(7), 531–540.

Zwier, G., & Vaughan, G. M. (1984). Three ideological orientations in school vandalism research. *Review of Educational Research, 54*(2), 263–292.

Author/Source Index

Subject Index

553

Credits

Text Credits

p. 13 *Case in Print:* Special Young Teacher Wins a $1,500 Apple by Carolyn Bower, *St. Louis Post-Dispatch*, September 7, 1996. Reprinted with permission of the *St. Louis Post-Dispatch*, Copyright 1996; **p. 117** *Table 4.2:* Sternberg, R. J., "What Does It Mean to be Smart?" *Educational Leadership*, 54, 6:22, Figure 1. Used by permission of the Association for Supervision and Curriculum Development. Copyright © 1997 by ASCD. All rights reserved; **p. 126** *Case in Print:* Micky Baca, *Merrimack Valley Sunday*, Amesbury, MA 8/7/94. Reprinted by permission; **p. 158** *Case in Print:* Dine, Philip. Reprinted with permission of the *St. Louis Post-Dispatch*, copyright 1995; **p. 183** *Case in Print:* Armstrong, Kiley. Reprinted by permission of Associated Press; **p. 229** *Case in Print:* Pfeiffer, Sacha, Reprinted with permission of the author; **p. 246** *Table 7.3:* Vargas, From "Instructional Design Flaws in Computer-Assisted Instruction" by J. S. Vargas, 1986 *Phi Delta Kappan*, 67, p. 744. Copyright 1986 by Phi Delta Kappa. Adapted by permission; **p. 262** *Case in Print:* "You Must Remember This" by Sharon Begley with Martha Brant. From *Newsweek*, September 26, 1994 © 1994 Newsweek, Inc. All rights reserved. Reprinted by permission; **p. 257** *Figure 8.2:* From G. H. Bower, M. C. Clark, A. M. Lesgold, and D. Winzenz, "Hierarchical Retrieval Schemes in Recall of Categorized Word Lists." *Journal of Verbal Learning and Verbal Behavior*, 1969, 8, 323–343. Copyright 1969 by Academic Press. Reproduced by permission of the publisher and the authors; **p. 271** *Table 8.2:* From King A. (1992), "Facilitating elaborative learning through guided student-generated questioning." *Educational Psychologist*, 27 (1), 111–126. Reprinted by permission of Lawrence Erlbaum Associates, Inc; **p. 298** *Case in Print:* Spin Doctors by William Allen, *St. Louis Post-Dispatch*, May 20, 1996. Reprinted with permission of the *St. Louis Post-Dispatch*, Copyright 1996; **p. 313** *Venn Diagram:* "Solution Using Venn Diagram," adapted from A. Whimbey and J. Lochead, *Problem Solving and Comprehension*, Fifth Edition, © 1991, p. 272. (Hillsdale, NJ: Lawrence Erlbaum Associates, Inc. Publishers). Reprinted by permission; **p. 314** *Flow Diagram* "Solution Using Flow Diagram," adapted from A. Whimbey and J. Lochead, *Problem Solving and Comprehension*, Fifth Edition, © 1991, p. 126. (Hillsdale, NJ: Lawrence Erlbaum Associates, Inc. Publishers). Reprinted by permission; **p. 344** *Figure 10.1:* Source: Novak, J.D. & Gowin, D.B. (1984). *Learning How to Learn*. Cambridge, England: Cambridge University Press. Reprinted by permission; **p. 350** *Case in Print:* Copyright 1998, *USA Today*. Reprinted with permission; **p. 386** *Case in Print:* Shein, Esther, Reprinted with permission of the author; **p. 396** *Table 11.2:* Jere Brophy. "Teacher Praise: A Functional Analysis," *Review of Educational Research*, 51, No. 1 (1981), 5-32. Copyright © 1981. American Educational Research Association, Washington, D.C. Used with permission; **p. 430** *Case in Print:* Mickey Baca, *Merrimack Valley Sunday*, Amesbury, MA 3/5/95; **p. 444** *Figure 13.1:* Parke, C. S. and Lane, S., "Learning from Performance Assessments in Math." *Educational Leadership*, 54, 4:28, Figure 3. Used by permission of the Association for Supervision and Curriculum Development. Copyright © 1997 by ASCD. All rights reserved; **p. 446** *Table 13.1:* Goodrich, Heidi (1996/1997). "Understanding Rubrics," *Educational Leadership*, 54(4), 14–17. Reprinted by permission of Heidi Goodrich Andrade, who would like to acknowledge the contributions of Patricia Crosby and Pamela Heinz in the development of this rubric; **p. 448** *Case in Print:* Teachers Look for New Ways to Measure Learning by Dale Singer, *St. Louis Post-Dispatch*, January 26, 1998. Reprinted with permission of the *St. Louis Post-Dispatch*, Copyright 1998; **p. 475** *Case in Print:* Test Scores Show: What do They Tell? by Dale Singer, *St. Louis Post-Dispatch*, April 28, 1997. Reprinted with permission of the *St. Louis Post-Dispatch*, Copyright 1997; **p. 489** *Figure 14.4:* Shepard, L. A. & Bliem, C. L. (1995). Parents' Thinking about Standardized Tests and Performance Assessments, *Educational Researcher*, 24(8), 25-32. Copyright (1995) American Educational Research Association. Reprinted with permission; **p. 508** *Case in Print:* Portfolios Give Prospective Teachers an Edge When They Interview for Jobs by Valerie Schremp, *St. Louis Post-Dispatch*, December 14, 1997. Reprinted with permission of the *St. Louis Post-Dispatch*, Copyright 1997.

Photo Credits

p. 5 D. Dengan/H. Armstrong Roberts; *p. 10* Bob Daemmrich; *p. 12* Elizabeth Crews; *p. 15* Frank Siteman/The Picture Cube; *p. 17* C. Bachmann/The Image Works; *p. 30* Bob Daemmrich; *p. 39* Martha Cooper; *p. 43* Robert Finken/The Picture Cube; *p. 52* David Young Wolff/Photo Edit; *p. 56* Bob Daemmrich; *p. 63* Kindra Cineff/The Picture Cube; *p. 72* Elizabeth Crews; *p. 74* K.B. Kaplan/The Picture Cube;

Suggestions for Teaching

Over 30 percent of the text is devoted to extensive SUGGESTIONS FOR TEACHING IN YOUR CLASSROOM—concrete examples and discussion of how to apply psychological research to the classroom.

Index to Suggestions for Teaching in Your Classroom